BEST OF THE PERL JOURNAL

Computer Science and Perl Programming

BEST OF THE PERL JOURNAL

Computer Science and Perl Programming

Edited by Jon Orwant

O'REILLY®

Beijing · Cambridge · Farnham · Köln · Paris · Sebastopol · Taipei · Tokyo

Computer Science and Perl Programming: Best of the Perl Journal
compiled and edited by Jon Orwant

Published by O'Reilly & Associates, Inc., 1005 Gravenstein Highway North, Sebastopol, CA 95472.

O'Reilly & Associates books may be purchased for educational, business, or sales promotional use. Online editions are also available for most titles (*safari.oreilly.com*). For more information contact our corporate/institutional sales department: (800) 998-9938 or *corporate@oreilly.com*.

Editor:	Jon Orwant
Production Editor:	Colleen Gorman
Cover Designers:	Hanna Dyer and Ellie Volckhausen
Interior Designer:	David Futato

Printing History:

November 2002:   First Edition.

ISBN: 0-596-00310-2
[C]

Table of Contents

Part II. Regular Expressions

Part III. Computer Science

Part IV. Programming Techniques

Part V. Software Development

Part VI. Networking

Part VII. Databases

Part VIII. Internals

Foreword

Mark Jason Dominus

It's flattering that Jon Orwant invited me to write the foreword for this book. After all, the title is "Computer Science and Perl Programming," and that pretty much covers it all: "Programming" is anything with any practical relevance, and "Computer Science" neatly includes everything else. You folks haven't seen the Table of Contents for the second and third Best of TPJ books yet, but I have. Take my word for it, they're concerned with "Computer Science and Programming" also.

Why did I get this job? Partly because I've written more articles for TPJ than anyone else, unless you count Chris Nandor's "Perl News" columns. But I think it's also because I got a reputation for writing articles about "Computer Science and Programming," at least as much as anyone except perhaps Damian Conway. And Damian's too busy to write forewords, whereas I'm unemployed.

Perhaps I should say something about what you'll find in this book. The theory is that the casual browser standing in the bookstore might flip to the foreword to find out what the book is about. It's a rotten theory, because hardly anyone reads the foreword even after they've bought the book. More likely, you are a reviewer, hoping for some guidance about what to say in the review. Hello, reviewer! I am happy to assist.

This book is indeed the "Best of the Perl Journal," biased though my opinion might be by the inclusion of ten of my own articles. It does not suffer from the usual flaw of the anthology, which is that the best you can hope for is that more than half of the articles are above average. On the contrary, it is by turns brilliant, witty, and profound. (Please be sure to say so in the review, and be sure that nothing could ever induce me to exaggerate the merits of this volume. No, not even the hope of an increased royalty.)

The book begins, aptly enough, with a selection of articles for beginners. (Jon used to complain that not enough people wanted to write these: "All the clueful writers want to write about stuff that displays their cluefulness," he once told me.) The following section is about regexes, and the notable feature is the series of articles by Jeffrey Friedl on understanding regular expressions. These came along very early in the magazine's history, and were a major contributor to its success, since they were important articles by a Famous Person.

The third section is the "Computer Science" section. Most of the articles in that section turn out to be more practical than you would think—Perl programmers have a wonderful way of making everything useful and of cannibalizing the most abstruse theory. I suppose cannibalization becomes a habit after a while.

Section 4 is titled "Perl Programming Techniques," a mixed bag of subsystems (source filters and operator overloading), alternative approaches to OOP (using arrays or closures instead of hashes), and miscellany (my attempt to summarize Perl's grotesque namespace semantics, which migrated here from the "Beginners" section, and the article I wrote as a followup when the tech editors complained about my advice in the first article.) Section 5 is another mixed bag, this one loosely about tools that support development: benchmarking and configuration utilities, for example.

Sections 6, 7, and 8, on networking, databases and internals, respectively, are more homogeneous. Note that the "Networking" section covers almost every important network application *except* the Web; those articles will be in the second Best of the Perl Journal book, title *Web, Graphics & Perl/Tk*. The section on databases includes an early article on Perl's ubiquitous DBI. The "Internals" section collects the excellent *Guts* series by Chip Salzenberg.

All together, there are 71 of the best articles I can remember from the magazine. The only important omission is that there's no article by Larry Wall; for that you'll have to wait until the third book.

Now a personal note: In revising my articles for this book, I built a little tool to compute the word-by-word differences between my own master copies and the versions Jon Orwant provided that were to go into the book. I didn't expect many changes, because Jon had told me in the past that my articles required very little editing. I always believed that my articles went into the magazine almost exactly as I had written them. But when I saw the results of the automatic comparison, I was rather dismayed. I understood at last how often Jon had tightened my phrasing, cleaned up my rhetoric, and eradicated my verbal tics. (The original draft of this foreword began with the words "It's pretty flattering;" if it begins with anything else now, you will know that Jon has picked up after me again.) Not only did he do this with such a light touch that I was unaware of it until now, but he was willing to spare my vanity and let me take the credit for his work. So there you have it: Jon Orwant is not only a fine writer and an acute editor, but also a kind, kind man. He is the author of only one of the articles here, but it's nevertheless his book more than anyone else's.

Please enjoy the fruits of Jon's work as much as I have.

Preface

Jon Orwant

This is the first of three "Best of the Perl Journal" O'Reilly books, containing the crème de la crème of the 247 articles published during the Perl Journal's five-year existence as a standalone magazine. This particular book covers computer science topics, advanced Perl programming techniques, and other subjects: together, the 70 articles in this book constitute a compendium of Perl lore. Little of what you'll find here is covered in any other book.

This book is divided into eight sections:

Part I, *Beginner Concepts*

> The book starts with articles about some of the corners of Perl that flummox beginners—and often experienced Perl programmers as well. You'll find information here that many tutorials lack.

Part II, *Regular Expressions*

> The articles in this section look under the hood of Perl's regular expression engine, showing you how to create perfect patterns the first time you write them. If you don't know why it's important that Perl's regex engine implements a non-deterministic finite automaton, you don't know everything you should about Perl's regular expressions.

Part III, *Computer Science*

> In this section, Perl is used to demonstrate key computer science topics, ranging from practical implementations of complex data structures to information retrieval and pseudorandom number generation.

Part IV, *Programming Techniques*

> Perl's motto is There's More Than One Way To Do It. This section shows you how to turn this flexibility to your advantage, demonstrating how to create your own data structures, change the behavior of Perl's operators, extend Perl's object-oriented mechanisms, and more.

Part V, *Software Development*

> The articles in this section discuss systems and techniques for creating, testing, and debugging Perl programs.

Part VI, *Networking*

This section shows you why Perl has a reputation as a "glue" language, demonstrating its use for creating client-server applications, sending mail, streaming audio, ferrying files around the Internet, and making Microsoft Office applications scriptable from your programs.

Part VII, *Databases*

Perl's database support makes it possible for your Perl programs to stay the same no matter what database you're using. You can migrate from MySQL to Oracle (or back!) seamlessly using the DBI module. This section covers the DBI, LDAP, ODBC, Access, Excel, and a customized web database created for the Human Genome Project.

Part VIII, *Internals*

This section dives into Perl's guts, showing you how Perl works under the hood and explaining the components of the Perl distribution.

Be aware that this book has 41 different authors. The articles within each section are loosely ordered from general to specific, and also from simplest to most complex, but since these spectra are not one and the same, the progression is not always uniform. The book may be read straight through, or sampled at random. (In deference to the Perl motto, There's More Than One Way To Read It.)

Normally, O'Reilly likes their books to be written by one author, or just a few. Books that are collections of many independently-written chapters may get to press more quickly, but discordant tones, styles, and levels of exposition can be jarring; worse, authors writing in parallel and under deadline rarely know what other contributors have covered, and therefore can't provide the appropriate context to the reader.

That would indeed be a problem for this book had it been written in 2 months by 41 authors writing simultaneously. But in a sense, this book was written very carefully and methodically over six years. As editor, I had a difficult decision to make with every issue. TPJ was a grass-roots publication with no professional publishing experience behind it; I couldn't afford to take out full color ads or launch huge direct-mail campaigns. So word of the magazine spread slowly, and instead of a steady circulation, it started tiny (400 subscribers for issue #1) and grew by several hundred each issue, peaking at 12,000 when EarthWeb began producing the magazine with issue #13.

Every issue, there were a lot of new subscribers, many of whom were new to Perl. Common sense dictated that I should include beginner articles in every issue, but I didn't like where that line of reasoning led. If I catered to the novices in every issue, far too many articles would be about beginner topics, crowding out the advanced material. And I'd have to find a way to cover the important material over and over, imparting a fresh spin every time. Steve Lidie's Perl/Tk column was a good example: it started with the basics and delved deeper with every article. Readers new to Perl/Tk who began with TPJ #15 didn't need to know about the intricacies of Perl/Tk menus covered in that issue; they wanted to know how to create a basic Perl/Tk application—a topic covered way back in TPJ #1. But if I periodically "reset" topics and ran material already covered in past issues, I'd alienate long-time subscribers.

So I did something very unusual for a magazine: I made it easy (and cheap) for subscribers to get all of the back issues when they subscribed, so they'd be able to enjoy the introductory material. Unfortunately, that meant I had to keep reprinting back issues as I ran out. This is called a Supply Chain Management problem in the business world. (The solution: my basement.)

A side effect of this approach was that the articles hang together well: they tell a consistent "story" in a steady progression from TPJ #1 through TPJ #20, with little redundancy. TPJ was always a book—it just happened to be published in 20 quarterly installments.

There is another advantage to having a book with programs by 41 Perl experts: collectively, the articles constitute a good sampling of Perl "in the wild." Every author has his own preferences—whether it's use of the English pragma, prototyping subroutines, embracing or eschewing object-oriented programming, or any of the other myriad ways in which Perl's expressivity is enjoyed. When you read a book by one author, you experience a single coherent (and hopefully good) style; when you read a book by dozens of experienced authors, you benefit from the diversity.

Naturally, there's some TPJ material that doesn't hold up well over time: modules become obsolete, features change, and news becomes history. Those articles didn't make the cut; the rest are in this book and the two companion books, *Web, Graphics and Perl/Tk: Best of The Perl Journal* and *Games, Diversions and Perl Culture: Best of The Perl Journal*.

Enjoy!

Finding Perl Resources

Beginning with TPJ #10, I placed boxes at the top of most articles telling readers where they could find any resources mentioned in the article. Often, it ended up looking like this, because nearly everything in Perl is available on CPAN:

```
Perl 5.004 or later..................CPAN
Class::ISA...........................CPAN
Memoize..............................CPAN
Class::Multimethods..................CPAN
```

The CPAN (Comprehensive Perl Archive Network) is a worldwide distributed repository of Perl modules, scripts, documentation, and Perl itself. You can find the CPAN site nearest you at *http://cpan.org*, and you can search CPAN at *http://search.cpan.org*. To find, say, the Class::Multimethods module, you could search for "Multimethods" at *http://search.cpan.org*, or you could visit *http://cpan.org* and click on "Modules" and then "All Modules." Either way, you'll find a link for a *Class-Multimethods.tar.gz* file (which will include a version number in the filename). Download, unpack, build, and install the module as I describe in *http://cpan.org/modules/INSTALL.html*.

For information and code that isn't available on CPAN, there are Reference sections at the ends of articles.

Conventions Used in This Book

The following conventions are used in this book:

Italic
> Used for filenames, directory names, URLs, emphasis, and for the first use of a technical term.

`Constant width`
> Used for code, command output, program names, and email addresses.

`Constant width bold`
> Used for user input and code emphasis.

`Constant width italic`
> Used for code placeholders, e.g., open(*ARGUMENTS*).

Comments and Questions

Please address comments and questions concerning this book to the publisher:

> O'Reilly & Associates, Inc.
> 1005 Gravenstein Highway North
> Sebastopol, CA 95472
> (800) 998-9938 (in the United States or Canada)
> (707) 829-0515 (international/local)
> (707) 829-0104 (fax)

There is a web page for this book containing all of the major code listings as well as any auxiliary files, errata, or additional information. You can access this page at:

> *http://www.oreilly.com/catalog/tpj1*

To comment or ask technical questions about this book, send email to:

> *bookquestions@oreilly.com*

For information about books, conferences, Resource Centers, and the O'Reilly Network, see the O'Reilly web site at:

> *http://www.oreilly.com*

Acknowledgments

First, an obvious thanks to the 120 TPJ contributors, and a special shout-out to the most prolific: Lincoln D. Stein, Mark Jason Dominus, Felix Gallo, Steve Lidie, Chris Nandor, Nathan Torkington, Sean M. Burke, and Jeffrey Friedl.

Next up are the people who helped with particular aspects of TPJ production. TPJ was mostly a one-man show, but I couldn't have done it without the help of Nathan Torkington, Alan Blount, David Blank-Edelman, Lisa Traffie, Ellen Klempner-Beguin, Mike Stok, Sara Ontiveros, and Eri Izawa.

Sitting in the third row are people whose actions at particular junctures in TPJ's existence helped increase the quality of the magazine and further its reach: Tim O'Reilly, Linda Walsh, Mark Brokering, Tom Christiansen, Jeff Dearth, the staff of Quantum Books in Cambridge, Lisa Sloan, Neil Bauman, Monica Lee, Cammie Hufnagel, and Sandy Aronson. Best wishes to the folks at CMP: Amber Ankerholz, Edwin Rothrock, Jon Erickson, and Peter Westerman.

Next, the folks at O'Reilly who helped this book happen: Hanna Dyer, Paula Ferguson, David Futato, Colleen Gorman, Sarmonica Jones, Linda Mui, Erik Ray, Mike Sierra, Betsy Waliszewski, Johnna VanHoose Dinse, Ellie Volckhausen, Neil Walls, Sue Willing, and the late Frank Willison.

People who helped out in small but crucial ways: David H. Adler, Tim Allwine, Elaine Ashton, Sheryl Avruch, Walter Bender, Pascal Chesnais, Damian Conway, Eamon Daly, Liza Daly, Chris DiBona, Diego Garcia, Carolyn Grantham, Jarkko Hietaniemi, Doug Koen, Uri Guttman, Dick Hardt, Phil Hughes, Mark Jacobsen, Lorrie LeJeune, Kevin Lenzo, LUCA, Tuomas J. Lukka, Paul Lussier, John Macdonald, Kate McDonnell, Chris Metcalfe, Andy Oram, Curtis Pew, Madeline Schnapp, Alex Shah, Adam Turoff, Sunil Vemuri, and Larry Wall.

Finally, a very special thanks to my wife, Robin, and my parents, Jack and Carol.

## CHAPTER 1

Introduction

Jon Orwant

"Perl is a language for getting your job done," begins *Programming Perl*. As programming languages go, Perl is something of a grab bag, and so is this book.

In this introduction I'll tell you how the book came to be, first by talking about the history of TPJ, and then about why computer science and Perl programming are a natural combination.

History of TPJ

In 1995, I was angry. Perl had broken away from being stereotyped as a system administration langauge or text processing language, and had managed to claw itself up to merely being stereotyped as a web programming language. I had seen Perl used for AI, astronomy, biology, graphics, natural language processing, and other areas—but Perl's generality wasn't being communicated to the programming world. Perl wasn't getting the reputation it deserved.

So when Tom Christiansen floated the notion of a Perl newsletter on the perl5-porters mailing list, it seemed like a natural idea. I'd just seen my first Perl book printed with my ampersands translated into eights, my vertical bars translated into ones, and my bullet marks depicted as planets complete with rings. (As you might guess, the publisher wasn't O'Reilly.) I wanted to do Perl publishing right, and at the same time show the world that Perl wasn't just for system administration any more. And so I set to work with my NeXT workstation and a copy of Framemaker. I found a Boston-area printer via the Yellow Pages, and hit up the Perl gurus for articles. I announced the magazine on Usenet, and that was the extent of my marketing.

The reception was mostly enthusiastic, although there was some initial skepticism: people said I was crazy to attempt print rather than web publication. But print has a portability and resolution unrivalled by computer displays, and professional printing provides a sense of permanence that web sites can't match. Paper affords a control over the graphical layout that is hard to achieve in a browser (even with Cascading Style Sheets). For instance, in my TPJ article on Data Hiding, I hid a message in the spacing between letters, and screened in a faint watermark on the page. And I had a hidden message perpetrated on me in the cover of TPJ #3, where photographer Alan Blount hid "perl sux" in his cover photograph.

I also knew that it would be too easy to let quality slip with a web magazine. The high cost of printing gives each issue a stamp of finality; in contrast, a mistake on a web page could always be fixed later. Masochistic as it sounds, I wanted the dead-lines that ink-on-dead-trees printing imposed. And print has more prestige: I wanted Perl to get the respect it deserved, and that meant people finding the magazine in their local bookstore.

Content was the easy part—there's never been a shortage of people creating interesting applications with Perl, and there are enough nooks and crannies to the language that I was never low on article ideas. By 1999, I had between 50 and 70 article proposals pending at any time, and space for only 15 in each issue. It was the design and visual appearance I was worried about: making it look like a magazine. For the first issue, I bought a stuffed camel at FAO Schwarz and had it photographed for the cover. I couldn't afford full color printing; I had only enough money for one spot color, and I chose brown for the first issue so that the camel would look natural.

I established the company with $20 and a trip to City Hall in Cambridge, and on a blustery day in February 1996 I printed TPJ's first issue: five articles and 32 pages. With no idea how popular the magazine would be, and aware of how much it costs to reprint an issue, I decided to aim high: 5,000 copies.

The volume of 5,000 copies of a 32-page magazine, each page slightly thicker than newsprint, was not a calculation that crossed my mind until an eighteen-wheeler pulled up and unloaded 22 boxes of magazines into my tiny two-room apartment. The boxes were stacked from floor to ceiling; I was eating off them, and by the time the deadline for TPJ #2 arrived I was sleeping on them as well.

Over the next year I learned all about United States Postal Service regulations, courtesy of the nice folks at Boston's South Station 24-hour post office and a scary tattooed bulk-mail freak at Cambridge's Central Square post office. I learned about presorting mail with rubber bands into dirty sacks with "U.S. MAIL" stenciled on them. I bought Glu-Stik by the case for attaching address labels. I got a swollen tongue from licking too many stamps back in the days before I splurged on a postage meter.

And I hacked. I wrote Perl programs to generate PostScript UPC bar codes, print address labels, convert author drafts from HTML, LaTeX, pod, and plain text into typeset pages. I wrote code to verify the accuracy of the programs in the magazine, correct grammar and spelling mistakes, and maintain subscriber, author, and advertiser databases. I created an entire subscription management system that answered many of the common subscriber requests, from address changes to questions about when the next issue would arrive and when subscriptions would expire. I probably wrote hundreds of quick one-off programs to do things like generate an ASCII copy of the magazine for TPJ's sole blind subscriber, and to compute circulation demographics (the top Perl countries are, in order, the U.S., the U.K., Germany, Canada, Australia, France, Japan, Switzerland, Sweden, Holland, Norway, Denmark, Finland, and Italy). I wrote the Business::CreditCard module to verify credit card numbers once I became able to accept VISA and MasterCard later in 1996.

To accept credit card numbers, I had to visit my bank and convince a loan officer that they should give a student with a few thousand dollars to his name, living in a rent-controlled apartment with only his 21-inch computer monitor as collateral, the ability to withdraw arbitrarily large sums of money from VISA and MasterCard accounts. That was the one day in TPJ's history when I wore a suit, and it paid off; they approved my application, and six weeks later I was accepting credit cards. (My application was delayed because I lived on Pearl Street and wanted an account in the name of the Perl Journal, which they assumed was a typo.)

I toddled into my favorite bookstore with a box of TPJ #2 and naively asked if they wanted to stock the magazine. There I learned about magazine distribution and consignment sales (if a bookstore doesn't sell a book or magazine, they can send it back to the publisher for a full refund).

With TPJ #4, I decided to go glossy—just the cover at first. This was a big decision; after my initial $3,000 investment, I had only grown the magazine as much as revenue permitted, and a glossy cover meant dipping into my savings again. I realized this was the right choice at the 1997 Usenix technical convention, when an attendee uttered these telling words: "Cool! So it's a magazine now. I'll subscribe."

Sales took off from there, the the next few years saw the magazine taking an increasingly large amount of my time. I would typically stay up all night before my scheduled press date, tweaking fonts, doing last-minute proofreading, and shifting ads around. Since I hated reading magazines with jumps (e.g., "Continued on page 53"), I vowed never to do that, no matter how difficult it made layout.

The magazine grew, and I had offers to translate it into other languages and sell posters of some of the covers. I received moral support, good advice, and marketing agreements with O'Reilly (and to a lesser extent, the Linux Journal). I endured shipping problems in Canada and credit card fraud in the Ukraine, but in spite of the occasional bad apple I enjoyed making personal connections with subscribers, many of whom were surprised to be corresponding directly with the editor-in-chief. I considered branching out into other magazine areas, or even novelties—I sold Magnetic Perl Poetry Kits briefly in 1998. But the all-nighters got old after a while; producing a magazine solo was getting to be too much work, and it was taking time away from my day job as a graduate student. The magazine was growing too fast for me to keep up, and so in 1999 I sold it to EarthWeb, staying on as editor. They [TEXT DELETED ON ADVICE OF COUNSEL]. In December 2000, they suspended TPJ #20 one day before it was to be printed.

In March 2001, I took them to arbitration and got the magazine back, which I lateralled to CMP, publisher of Dr. Dobb's, Sys Admin, and C/C++ Users Journal. (My day job here at O'Reilly prevents me from returning to that frenzied pace again.) It's now in good hands, and Perl's future is looking brighter than ever with the advent of Perl 6.

Computer Science and Perl Programming

When you pursue a computer science degree, you learn about not just computers but *computability*; not just how to program, but strategies for solving problems and expressing those solutions as algorithms. But what you don't often learn is "computer science in the wild"—how the lofty abstractions, generalizations, and precepts are implemented in the real world.

Perl is very much a real world language. It's been taught in middle schools all the way up through graduate programs, but it's not the best first language for computer science students, partly because it does so much for you, and partly because it's so expressive that it allows you to program badly. This is exactly what you want if you need to dash off a one-liner to generate a report from the company database in the next minute, but it's not desirable in a computer science curriculum where purity is valued over expedience.

If you were taking a class on compilers, you'd learn about how programs are turned from source code into binaries. Typically, this is expressed in several phases: lexical analysis, syntax analysis, semantic analysis, code generation, and optimization. And in that class, you'd write a simple compiler for a toy language, perhaps taking a couple of weeks to implement each of these phases. Very clean.

Now consider how Perl parses programs, as described in the article *Lexical Analysis*. Perl's semantic analysis affects its lexical analysis, so they occur at the same time. Unclean.

The programming component of my undergraduate computer science education primarily used Scheme, a dialect of LISP. It's as clean as a language can be, with a mathematical simplicity and elegance. I believe that every freshman should study LISP, and I recommend my undergraduate text: *Structure and Interpretation of Computer Programs* (MIT Press). Scheme is the perfect instructional language because its syntax is minimal.

Perl, it might be said, has maximal syntax. A few keystrokes can do a lot. One of the notions of Huffman coding (discussed in *Compression*) is that frequently occurring things should be represented more concisely than infrequently occuring things; that's why an E in Morse code is a single dot while a Z is dash dash dot dot, and that's why the function to search and replace strings in Perl is an s while the operator to translate a network protocol number to its corresponding name is getprotobynumber. (Neither of these situations occurred from explicit design, since each operator got its name from already existing libraries. Sometimes good design just evolves naturally out of common usage.) Scalars begin with $, arrays begin with @, and hashes begin with %. Perl's punctuation holds a great deal of meaning, enabling you to express a lot with a little.

Minimal syntax languages such as Scheme are the best for learning about computer science, and maximal syntax languages such as Perl are the best for getting your job done. This book illuminates some selected corners of computer science with Perl—certainly no substitute for a real computer science book, but a helpful complement, showing you how to apply some of those concepts to get your job done. You'll learn about high-concept data structures like infinite lists and B-trees, and how to create your own data structures like the Schmidt Hash. You'll see how generic concepts like a memoizing cache can be implemented, and learn to write your own parsers—not the clean parsers you'd create in the aforementioned class on compilers, but potentially messy parsers that end up being a whole lot more useful.

Most of the articles in this book will teach you some principle that you can apply beyond Perl programming. For some articles, the application is obvious: *Client-Server Applications* shows how to create your own network service on the Internet; *Information Retrieval* teaches the basics of information retrieval using Perl; *Making Life and Death Decisions with Perl* demonstrates the basics of conditional probability. For others, the relationship to computer science is a bit more subtle. *Building Software with Cons*, for instance, is ostensibly about a replacement for make, but even this pragmatic topic takes an academic twist. How can a build system determine whether a file has been modified since the last build? make looks at the file's modification date; seemingly sensible, until you realize that clock skew dooms this approach. So Cons computes an MD5 cryptographic signature of each file. Reading the article makes it obvious that this is the right solution, and yet no one ever integrated it into make.

You'll learn about different programming paradigms. In a computer science curriculum, you'd learn about the advantages of object-oriented programming. You probably wouldn't learn about the *disadvantages* of OO, since that's messy real world stuff, having to do with speed and program maintainability. Here, you'll see ways to fiddle with Perl's OO to make it messier or cleaner, whatever suits the application at hand. You'll see how to insert a "source filter" into your program immediately before Perl begins lexical analysis—again, not something you'll learn in a compiler class, but interesting if only for the fact that it's necessary in the real world. In *Using Other Languages from Perl*, you'll see how to have your program trigger the compilation of programs in other languages, enabling you to use C or Java or assembly language from Perl. Unclean, but incredibly useful.

As another example of the occasional divergence between clean computer science and the messy real world, you'll learn about variable scope in *Scoping*; how it was done imperfectly in Perl 4, and how Perl 5 and 5.6 were able to improve Perl's scoping behavior while maintaining backward compatibility.

One final example: A class on theoretical computer science will teach you the difference between deterministic and nondeterministic finite automata, two abstractions used to explore computability. In *Understanding Regular Expressions, Part I*, you'll learn why that difference directly impacts the speed of regular expressions in different languages—an understanding that enables you to see why a particular Perl regex takes hours to run, while a slight variant takes only a few seconds. That's why understanding the underlying computer science can help Perl programmers function even better in the real world.

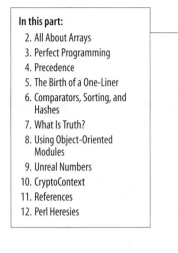

PART I

Beginner Concepts

In this first section, eleven articles teach you some of the corners of Perl that you won't find in beginner books or tutorials, but are nevertheless critical bits of knowledge.

We start with two articles by Nathan Torkington. One of the first things novices learn is that Perl has three basic data structures: scalars, arrays, and hashes. Scalars are single chunks of data, such as strings or numbers. Arrays are an ordered sequence of scalars, and Nathan's article, *All About Arrays*, teaches you how to manipulate them. His second article, *Perfect Programming*, shows you how to program defensively, demonstrating techniques for identifying mistakes and preventing them from occurring in the first place.

Next, Mark Jason Dominus's *Precedence* shows how Perl's operators "grab" the operands around them—some tightly, some loosely, and some in ways that you were never taught in grade school. After reading his article, you'll understand exactly when you need parentheses in your expressions. Art Ramos's *The Birth of a One-Liner* then shows you why Perl programs sometimes look inscrutable to the untrained eye.

Frossie Economou's *Comparators, Sorting, and Hashes* shows how to use hashes (which map strings to values), demonstrating comparators and Perl's sorting techniques along the way. Nathan Torkington continues his explanation of Perl's syntax with *What Is Truth?*

Sean Burke explains how to use others' object-oriented code in *Using Object-Oriented Modules*, and Tom Phoenix explores the sometimes obscure ramifications of arithmetic on a binary computer in *Unreal Numbers*.

Nathan returns with his fourth article in this section, *CryptoContext*. The notion of *context* is unusual in computer languages, and confuses a lot of novices who haven't yet embraced the notion that what you get from an operator (or subroutine) depends on how you ask for it. Ask for a number and you'll get a number; ask for a string and you'll get a string; ask for a list and you'll get a list. Perl programmers call these situations *numeric context*, *string context*, and *list context*, respectively. Nathan focuses on the difference between scalar context and list context when calling subroutines, explaining Perl's prototypes as an added bonus.

You can't call yourself an experienced Perl programmer until you understand *references*. Mark Jason's article, *References*, explains the 10% of what you need to know to get 90% of the benefit. Finally, Jon Drukman follows with an article about a few pieces of advice that are prescribed more often than followed in *Perl Heresies*.

## CHAPTER 2

All About Arrays

Nathan Torkington

Arrays are one of Perl's three primary data types (the other two are scalars and hashes). This article will help you understand everything that can be done with them.

Basics

All array variables begin with an @ sign. They hold a list of scalar values (such as a string or number) whose positions are numbered beginning from 0. So in this code, blue is in position number 2 of the @colors array, and 42 is in position 3 of the @data array:

```
@colors = ("red", "green", "blue");
@data   = ("Perl", 2_000_000, "Wall", 42);
```

At this early point it's good to start distinguishing lists from arrays. Perl gurus try to be precise about this distinction when they talk about their code: both are sequences of scalars, but while arrays are true stored variables, lists are merely temporary sequences of values. Subroutines accept lists, and can return them; as you pass an array into a subroutine, it becomes a list of values. Likewise, when a subroutine returns a list, you can store it in an array.

You store a list inside an array variable if you want to access the list's values later. Subroutines and functions don't, strictly speaking, accept arrays, except for a few special functions that we'll see later. Where Perl expects a bunch of values to work on, those values can come from a list, whether it's hardcoded in the program, returned by a function, or extracted from an array.

Inside double-quoted strings, arrays interpolate (expand) into their values, separated by spaces:

```
print "Primary colors are: @colors\n";
red green blue
```

Spaces are the default separator, but you can change this with the $" variable:

```
$" = ' and ';
print "Primary colors are: @colors\n";
red and green and blue
```

Positions

To access a single value from an array, use square brackets:

```
$colors[2]
```

The name of the array is "colors", the $ in front indicates a scalar value, and the position of that value, called a *subscript*, is in the square brackets. This notation works for both storing and fetching values.

```
$colors[0] = "pink";
print $colors[0];
```

Array subscripts also interpolate inside double-quoted strings:

```
print "The 0th color is $colors[0]\n";
```

To make life easy for programmers, who often need to refer to both ends of the array conveniently, a negative subscript counts back from the end of the array:

```
print $colors[-1];
blue
```

```
print $colors[-3];
pink
```

An attempt to fetch a nonexistent negative position returns undef, but an attempt to store in such a position is a fatal error:

```
print $colors[-4];
Use of uninitialized value ...
```

```
$colors[-4] = "ultraviolent";
Modification of non-creatable array value attempted,
  subscript -4 at ...
```

Perl has dynamic data structures that grow as needed. They only grow when assigned to, though, and never simply by reading. So if you attempt to access an element beyond the end of the array, you'll get undef—and the array's size won't change as a result.

To determine the size of an array, you can evaluate it in scalar context by assigning it to a scalar:

```
$size_before = @colors;
print $colors[5];
$size_after  = @colors;
print "$size_before $size_after\n";
Use of uninitialized value at ...
3 3
```

```
$size_before = @colors;
$colors[5] = "burgundy";
$size_after  = @colors;
print "$size_before $size_after\n";
Use of uninitialized value at ...
3 6
```

When you assigned to position five, Perl created values in positions three and four as well. Now you have six elements in the array, in positions zero through five.

Position Versus Count

Welcome to the torture of counting array positions. Because positions start at zero, the size and last position always differ by one. If the only value in the array is at position zero, then there is one element. If there are two elements, they must be in positions zero and one.

Each array has an accompanying scalar variable containing the last position of the array. That variable is $#, followed by the array name (no @ sign, since it's a scalar we're after):

```
print $#colors;              # last position
5

print scalar(@colors);       # number of elements
6
```

This often confuses beginners when they use loops to count over the positions of an array. There are two right ways to do it:

```
for ($i=0; $i <   @colors; $i++) { ... }      # A
for ($i=0; $i <= $#colors; $i++) { ... }      # B
```

And two wrong ways:

```
for ($i=0; $i <= @colors; $i++) { ... }       # C
for ($i=0; $i <  $#colors; $i++) { ... }       # D
```

Option C executes the loop body for one too many positions (if there are six things in @colors, the loop executes when $i is six, even though that's not a valid position). Likewise, option D executes the body one too few times (if the last position is five, the loop stops after executing the loop with $i set to four). I prefer option A because it takes fewer keystrokes than option B.

The $#array variable has another use: you can set it, which pre-extends the array. If you know your array will eventually have a thousand elements in it, you can tell Perl to allocate all the elements at once rather than making Perl allocate the thousand items incrementally as you grow the array.

```
$#numbers = 999;
for ($i=0; $i < 1000; $i++) {
    $numbers[$i] = 5 * $i + 1;
}
```

Foreach Loops

Many times, you won't need the position of the current element; you'll only need its value. Rather than use a C-style for loop as above, use a Perl-style foreach loop:

```
@colors = ("red", "green", "blue");
foreach $c (@colors) {
```

```
    print "$c\n";
}
red
green
blue
```

You may choose any loop variable (the $c above) that you wish. If you follow tight programming discipline and used the strict pragma to prevent accidental use of global variables, you can mix my or local with the foreach:

```
#!/usr/bin/perl -w

use strict;

my @colors = ("red", "green", "blue");
foreach my $c (@colors) {
    print "$c\n";
}
red
green
blue
```

Inside foreach loops, the loop variable is actually an alias for the value in the list. So if you change the loop variable, you change the element in the list:

```
@colors = ("red", "brown");
foreach $c (@colors) {
    $c = "hot $c";
}
print "@colors\n";
```

```
hot red hot brown
```

If you omit the variable, Perl will use $_ as the default variable:

```
foreach (@colors) {
    print "Current item is $_\n";
}
```

This is useful when you combine it with the string functions that use $_ as their default values:

```
foreach (@colors) {
    tr/A-Z/a-z/;
    s/pink|burgundy/red/i;
    print length, "\n";
}
```

The Reverse and Sort Functions

What else can you do with arrays? You can reverse the order of the elements:

```
@inverted = reverse @colors;
print "@inverted\n";
blue green red
```

You can sort the elements in ASCIIbetical order:

```
@colors = ("pink", "purple", "mauve");
@ordered = sort @colors;
print "@ordered\n";
mauve pink purple
```

What if you prefer reverse alphabetical order? You might write this:

```
@ordered  = sort @colors;
@inverted = reverse @ordered;
print "@inverted\n";
purple pink mauve
```

This works, but you can be even more concise. Like many functions, reverse and sort take any list of values as arguments:

```
@inverted = reverse sort @colors;
```

Can you see why the following won't work?

```
@inverted = sort reverse @colors;   # WRONG
```

The answer is at the end of the chapter.

Even when you combine sort and reverse in the right order, it's rather inefficient. sort returns a temporary list of values, which is then reversed. It'd be more efficient to tell sort to sort in the order you want. You can do that!

sort accepts a code block before the list of values to sort. The code block tells sort how to order any two values. Those values are put into the global variables $a and $b before the code block is executed. (Most code blocks use Perl's <=> or cmp operators to compare things numerically or ASCIIbetically.)

The default comparison routine is:

```
$a cmp $b
```

cmp compares values as strings, and by putting $a before $b, you get an ascending sort. If you wanted to sort from highest to lowest, it's as simple as flipping the order of $a and $b in the comparison: instead of telling sort that "green" should come after "blue", it'll now say that "green" should come *before* "blue":

```
@colors = ("pink", "purple", "mauve");
@inverted_ordered = sort { $b cmp $a } @colors;
print "@inverted_ordered\n";
purple pink mauve
```

There are many more complicated sorts, up to and including the Schwartzian Transform. But I digress. If you want more information on sorting, consult a good Perl book like *The Perl Cookbook* by Tom Christiansen and yours truly (O'Reilly & Associates), or *Effective Perl Programming* by Joseph Hall (Addison-Wesley).

Slices

You now know how to talk about the array as a whole, and how to talk about single values from the array, but what about subsets of the array? For that you need to know about *array slices*:

```
@subset = @colors[0,2];
print "@subset\n";
pink mauve
```

The @ sign at the beginning indicates that you want multiple values back. Inside the square brackets is a list of values. In this case, it's just positions zero and two you want, but you can have any list you like:

```
($x, $y, $z) = @big_array[5, 2, 100];
```

That's like saying this, except that your fingers don't get worn out:

```
$x = $big_array[5];
$y = $big_array[2];
$z = $big_array[100];
```

When you want a range of values (e.g., from positions two through eight) you can use the range (..) operator:

```
@subset = @big_array[2..8];
```

Which, again, is like typing this, but without fingerprint damage:

```
@subset = @big_array[2, 3, 4, 5, 6, 7, 8];
```

Adding and Deleting Values

Perl has five functions for inserting and removing values from an array. Four of those functions are quite specialized, working with only the start or end of the array. The last, splice, is far more general. Let's cover the specialized functions first.

push and pop act on the end of the array. push adds values to the end of the array; pop removes the last value and returns it:

```
@characters = ("Buffy", "Willow", "Xander");
push(@characters, "Giles", "Anya");
print "@characters\n";
$ex_demon = pop @characters;
print "popped $ex_demon\n";
print "@characters\n";
Buffy Willow Xander Giles Anya
popped Anya
Buffy Willow Xander Giles
```

The corresponding functions that work on the start of the array are shift and unshift:

```
@baddies = ("Spike", "Mayor", "Adam");
$in_wuv = shift @baddies;
```

```
print "removed $in_wuv\n";
print "left: @baddies\n";
unshift @baddies, "Dracula";
print "@baddies\n";
removed: Spike
left: Mayor Adam
Dracula Mayor Adam
```

If you shift or pop but don't give an array name, Perl assumes you mean the current arguments. If you're in a subroutine definition, the array that's operated on is @_, containing the subroutine arguments. If you're not in a subroutine definition, @ARGV is shifted or popped.

The uber-function for arrays is splice, which lets you perform any combination of inserting, deleting, or replacing. You give it an array to work on, the position at which to begin deleting elements, the number of elements to delete, and any elements to insert in place of those deleted. splice returns the deleted elements, if any:

```
@gals = ("Buffy", "Willow", "Anya", "Faith");
@cut = splice @gals, 1, 2, "Tara";
print "@gals\n";
print "@cut\n";
Buffy Tara Faith
Willow Anya
```

The two things starting at position one were "Willow" and "Anya". In their place was put "Tara".

You can delete zero elements, and use splice only for its ability to insert:

```
@gals = ("Buffy", "Willow", "Anya");
splice @gals, 2, 0, "Tara";
print "@gals\n";
Buffy Willow Tara Anya
```

You can insert no elements, and only use splice for its ability to delete:

```
@gals = ("Buffy", "Cordelia", "Faith", "Willow", "Anya");
@cut = splice @gals, 1, 2;
print "@gals\n";
print "@cut\n";
Buffy Willow Anya
Cordelia Faith
```

And of course, by giving positions at the start or end of the array, you can insert or delete there:

```
splice @gals, @gals, 0, "Tara";    # push @gals, "Tara";
splice @gals, $#gals, 1;           # pop @gals;

splice @gals, 0, 0, "Tara";        # unshift @gals, "Tara";
splice @gals, 0, 1;                # shift @gals;
```

These five functions are the only functions in Perl where you need to provide an array and not merely a list. You cannot push onto a list, because a list is simply a fleeting gathering of values, and you need a persistent collection if you want to modify it. Your program won't compile if you try to use one of these functions with a first argument that lacks an @ sign.

Lists to Strings and Back Again

How do you create a list? You can hardcode it in your program or accumulate it element by element with push or unshift. Often you just read the list from a file.

Imagine a list of words on one line:

```
Buffy The Vampire Slayer
```

You would like an array with each element as a single word. You could do this with repeated matches:

```
while ($string =~ m/(\S+)/g) {
    push @words, $1;
}
```

But the easiest way is to use the split function, which takes up to three arguments. The first is a regular expression matching the stuff *between* the values you want. Here, you'll need a regular expression matching spaces. The second argument to split is the string to be split up. The third and final argument is the number of fields you want back, but if you omit it you'll get all the fields.

```
@words = split /\s+/, $string;
```

If you omit the second argument, split looks in $_ for the string. This makes it perfect for these kinds of loops:

```
while (<SOMEFILE>) {
    @words = split /\s+/;
    #...
}
```

In fact, if you have your string in $_ and you want it split on whitespace, you don't even need the regular expression—the default regular expression *is* whitespace!

```
while (<SOMEFILE>) {
  @words = split;
  # ...
}
```

Of course, your strings don't always have fields separated by spaces. The Unix password file, for instance, separates fields with colons:

```
while (<PASSWDFILE>) {
    @fields = split /:/;
    # ...
}
```

split has some quirks: it ignores any trailing empty fields, so if your colon-separated record was big:deal:::, you'd get two fields back: big and deal. This is sometimes what you want, but not always.

The opposite of split is join. split extracts fields that have been separated. join produces a string of separated fields. The first argument is the separator (an exact string, not a regular expression), and the rest of the arguments are values to join together with the separator in between each pair. For instance:

```
@adjectives = ("hot", "damp", "sticky");
$line = join(" and ", @adjectives);
print $line;
hot and damp and sticky
```

Putting It All Together

So here's how you reverse the order of words for each line in a file:

```
while (<INFILE>) {
    @fields = split;
    @new    = reverse @fields;
    $line   = join " ", @new;
    print OUTFILE "$line\n";
}
```

More concisely:

```
while (<INFILE>) {
    print OUTLINE join(" ", reverse split), "\n";
}
```

Answer to the earlier question. The code said to reverse the list, then sort it. The call to reverse is useless, because sort sorts the list into ascending order.

In the next article, I'll take a step back and examine some of the common mistakes beginners make, and how you can avoid them.

CHAPTER 3
Perfect Programming

Nathan Torkington

Imagine a world ten years from now. Programmers know everything there is to know about their language, algorithms, and requirements. They apply this knowledge to produce flawless programs, which work correctly the first and every time. Users read the manuals, never provide false or misleading input, and always know what to do next. Clients never change their minds and maintenance is unnecessary.

You can wake up now. We both know this won't happen so long as boneheads like us keep programming, morons like our customers keep giving us incomplete and perpetually changing requirements, and the prerequisite for being a user is that you demonstrate zero ability to read, think, or act without tech support or a programmer holding your hand. Everyone in the programmer-client-user world is a weak link, and programmers must be prepared for mistakes. There are three major classes of mistakes: user mistakes, client mistakes, and programmer mistakes.

User mistakes
> When users are to blame, it's typically because they do something like providing incorrect input to your program, or calling your program in an unexpected way. Paranoid programmers check everything provided by the users (and use the taint mechanism to help them). This has the side benefit of making their programs more secure against exploitation by The Bad Guys. The Bad Guys like to mess with a program's environment, input, and configuration files, in the hope they can trick it into displaying */etc/master.passwd*, or changing the permissions of /bin/sh to 4755, making it setuid.

Client mistakes
> Customers are fickle. Sometimes they request minor changes ("We want to sort the addresses by zipcode"); sometimes the changes are major ("The CEO just bought an Oracle database. Use it."). Changes run the risk of breaking software that worked previously. The programmer must write code in such a way that substantial changes in behavior can be implemented with minimum risk.

Programmer mistakes
> Finally, as unwilling as we all are to accept it, programmers make mistakes. They're typically things like using variables that don't yet have a value, giving

incorrect values to a function, and creating language misunderstandings like $#array versus @array. Programmers who believe in their own fallibility (does the Pope program in Perl?) write code that checks its values, checks return values from system calls, and uses tools like -w and use `strict`. These humble programmers also know how to debug when all else goes wrong.

What follows is a list of techniques that I've found useful in real programs. The larger the program you want to write, the more desirable these techniques become. One-liners, or even five-pagers, are short and uncomplicated enough that debugging them is easy. That can't be said for some of the 10,000 line multimodule nightmares that I've given birth to. Consider these techniques your armory for the fight.

Warnings with -w

This is the programmer's most useful debugging aid. As Larry says, Perl's biggest bug is that -w is optional. Some of the things that a hashbang line of #!/usr/bin/perl -w will catch are: use of undefined values (typically a sign that you're expecting a variable to have a value when it doesn't), nonnumeric arguments (a string was given instead of a number, which probably means it would be interpreted as 0 instead of being flagged as an error), = instead of ==, and much more.

Sometimes you want -w checks in some places but not others. If there's a chunk of code you just *know* will work even though -w complains about it, you can disable warnings as follows:

```
{

    local($^W) = 0;        # disable warnings...
    your code here

}                          # warnings back on now
```

This traps only runtime warnings. Disabling compile-time warnings is also possible; see the perllexwarn documentation for details.

There has been a vigorous debate on the subject of -w in production programs. New versions of Perl have created new warnings, which show up as "errors" (broken web pages, strange cron mailings, STDERR sent to users' screens) in programs that worked previously. Tracking these down can be a nontrivial task. I like to keep my code -w clean for all versions, because it makes future changes easier to test with -w. Your mileage may vary.

The strict Pragma

If you're using references or trying to write maintainable or reusable code, you probably want to use `strict`. This is a shorthand for use `strict 'refs', 'subs', 'vars',` which catches the following things:

use strict 'refs'

Prevents suspicious dereferences. If a subroutine expects a hard reference to a value (the kind of reference you get with \), but you supply it the wrong arguments or the right arguments in the wrong order, you can cause a string or a number to be inadvertently dereferenced. Consider this code:

```perl
sub setref {
    my $string_ref = shift;
    my $string = shift;
    $$string_ref = $string;
}

setref("Googol", $plexref);   # wrong argument order
```

Here, the setref subroutine is passed "Googol" where it expects a reference to a string. Without use strict 'refs', Perl assumes you meant $Googol. This is called a *soft*, or *symbolic*, reference. When you use that pragma, however, Perl whines and dies. Because soft references are almost never needed, use strict "refs" catches a lot of errors that would otherwise silently cause bizarre behavior.

use strict 'vars'

Catches stray variables. It expects you to either qualify every variable completely ($Package::Var) or to declare them with my. In almost every case, you really want to use my to scope your variable so that code outside the file or block can't perturb its value. Using my to predeclare all variables (or using cumbersome fully-qualified variable names) will predispose you to document your variables for the hapless fool who must modify your program in a year's time. Don't laugh. It might be you.

```perl
if ($core->active) {
    my $rems;              # active radiation in rems
    my $rod_volume;        # volume of carbon rod remaining
    your code here
}
```

use strict 'subs'

Forbids stray barewords. When it's in effect, you can't use the bareword style of calling subroutines with no arguments (e.g., $result = mysub;) unless the subroutine was declared before its use, either with a prototype or with the subroutine definition itself. If you don't want to predeclare, you must preface the subroutine call with & or append ( ) so that it looks like a subroutine call. This doesn't affect the use of barewords in hashes in curly braces (e.g., $hash{key}) or on the left side of the => symbol (e.g., %hash = (key => value)).

```perl
use strict 'subs';

print count;         # an error with use strict 'subs'

sub count;           # prototyping count( ) is sufficient

print count;         # Not an error because Perl now knows about count( )
```

Note that simply saying sub mysub; before using the bareword mysub is enough to keep use strict 'subs' quiet.

Tainting and Safe

When Perl encounters a variable with a value that hasn't been hardcoded into the program, it marks the variable as *tainted* if the program is running under the -T flag, or if the program's permissions are setuid (meaning that it assumes the identity of its owner rather than whoever is running the program). Use of a tainted value in exec or similar calls, or opening a filename for writing, causes a fatal error. To untaint data, you should extract the safe portion (for a filename, that might be /^([\w.\@-]+)$/) with a regular expression and use $1, $2, and similar variables to access the part of the tainted variable guaranteed to be safe. Full details can be found in the perlsec manual page.

Running with -T is almost always a good idea when you're programming defensively. It forces you to validate every piece of user-supplied data with regular expressions before you use them. Not only does this guard against potentially security-compromising errors, it also lets you catch situations where the user gives the wrong type of data (a string instead of a number, for instance).

A different approach is to use the Safe module, which traps certain operations. You can run code that uses untrustworthy data inside a Safe "compartment," knowing that it can't unlink files, fork processes, or do other nasty things.

Checking Return Values

Not every fork will succeed, not every file can be opened, not every child process terminates without error. The return values from system calls contain valuable information on the success or failure of those calls—check them!

The most important things to check are return values of open, fork, exec, and the contents of $? (or $CHILD_ERROR if you use English).

The same wisdom applies to CPAN or library modules, and to your own modules. Your modules should perform sanity checks and return 0 or undef if something went wrong.

Planning for Failure

Part of catching errors is deciding what to do when they occur. Even before I begin programming, I enumerate the various ways my code can fail, and then decide what to do for each possibility. With some errors it's okay to tell the user exactly what went wrong ("You gave me the name of a user who isn't in the database"), but others shouldn't be made so public ("The database doesn't exist," or "I couldn't fork"). User errors typically warrant a message that pats their hand and gives them a chance to try again. System errors should be logged to a file, the administrators notified, and the user told that "The system is down," and they should try again later.

The Perl Debugger

There is only so much that stack traces and strategically placed print statements can do. When you've located the problem, it can still be difficult to infer the cause. The next step is to write a small program that exhibits the bug and then steps through it with Perl's symbolic debugger (perl -d mysmallprogram). Of course, you can always invoke the debugger directly with perl -de 0 to initiate an interactive session.

Debugging will be most comfortable if you've installed the Term::ReadLine module, or if you use the Ilya Zakharevich's nice Emacs interface, *cperl-mode.el*. Even without these whizzy utilities, the debugger is still useful. You can step through your code and set breakpoints: locations in your program at which execution stops, giving you a chance to inspect or change variables, thus letting you discover the particular states that trigger the bug you're trying to fix. Consult the perldebug documentation for more information.

The Perl Profiler

When your program works, but runs as slow as a dog, Dean Roehrich's Devel::DProf module (available on the CPAN) will help you determine why. perl -d:DProf myprogram runs your program and creates a file called *tmon.out* in your current working directory. You then run the dprofpp program to analyze that file and display the fifteen subroutines occupying the most time.

There are other features of the profiler (see the dprofpp documentation for more information) but this list of the most time-consuming subroutines is probably the most important. It pinpoints the parts of your program that use the most time, and hence are most suited for optimizing, rewriting, inlining, or avoiding.

Stack Traces

The terse little warnings and die messages that you're provided are often not sufficient when it comes to working out where things went wrong. For that you need the awesome power of Jack Shirazi's Devel::DumpStack. When I'm debugging a CGI script that refuses to play ball, I'll use this code, which traps warnings and fatal errors, displaying them in an HTML document instead of burying them in a web server error log:

```
#!/usr/bin/perl -w

use Devel::DumpStack qw(stack_as_string);
use HTML::Entities;
```

```perl
sub my_die {
    select(STDOUT); $|=1;
    printf(<<"EOF", $?, $!, stack_as_string());
Content-Type: text/html

<HTML><HEAD><TITLE>System Error</TITLE></HEAD>

<BODY>
<H1>System Error</H1>
A seriously bad system error happened:<P>

<B>Exit Status</B>: %d<BR>
<B>Error String</B>: %s<P>

<B>Stack Dump</B>:
<PRE>
%s
</PRE>

</BODY></HTML>
EOF

    exit;
}

BEGIN {
  $SIG{__WARN__} = $SIG{__DIE__} = \&my_die;
}

$a = undef + 4;

exit;
```

I wouldn't recommend leaving this code in your final product, however. The sight of a stack dump can mentally scar a user for life.

CHAPTER 4

Precedence

Mark Jason Dominus

What Is Precedence?

What's $2 + 3 \times 4$?

We learned about this in grade school; it was fourth-grade material in the New York City public school I attended. If not, that's okay too; I'll explain everything.

It's well-known that $2 + 3 \times 4$ is 14, because we are supposed to do the multiplication before the addition. 3×4 is 12, and then we add the 2 and get 14. What we do *not* do is perform the operations in left-to-right order; if we did that we would add 2 and 3 to get 5, then multiply by 4 and get 20.

This is just a convention about what an expression like $2 + 3 \times 4$ means. It's not an important mathematical fact; it's just a rule about how to interpret certain ambiguous arithmetic expressions. It could have gone the other way, or we could have the rule that the operations are always done left-to-right. But we don't have those rules; we have the rule that says that you do the multiplication first and then the addition. We say that multiplication takes *precedence* over addition.

What if we really do want to say: "Add 2 and 3, and multiply the result by 4"? Then we use parentheses, like this: $(2 + 3) \times 4$. The rule about parentheses is that expressions in parentheses must always be fully evaluated before anything else.

If we always used the parentheses, we wouldn't need rules about precedence. There wouldn't be any ambiguous expressions. We have precedence rules because we're lazy and we like to leave out the parentheses when we can. The fully-parenthesized form is always unambiguous. The precedence rule tells us how to interpret a version with fewer parentheses to decide what it would look like if we wrote the equivalent fully-parenthesized version. In the example above:

- $2 + (3 \times 4)$
- $(2 + 3) \times 4$

Is $2 + 3 \times 4$ like the first or like the second? The precedence rule just tells us that it is like the first.

Rules and More Rules

In grade school we learned a few more rules:

$$4 \times 5^2$$

Which of these interpretations is correct?

$$(4 \times 5)^2 = 400$$

or

$$4 \times (5^2) = 100$$

The rule is that exponentiation takes precedence over multiplication, so it's 100 and not 400.

What about $8 - 3 + 4$? Is this like $(8 - 3) + 4 = 9$ or $8 - (3 + 4) = 1$? Here the rule is a little different. Neither + nor − has precedence over the other. Instead, the − and + are just done left-to-right. This rule handles the case of $8 - 4 - 3$ also. Is it $(8 - 4) - 3 = 1$ or is it $8 - (4 - 3) = 7$? Subtractions are done left-to-right, so it's 1 and not 7. A similar left-to-right rule handles ties between × and /.

Our rules are getting complicated now:

1. Exponentiation first.
2. Next multiplication and division, left to right.
3. Then addition and subtraction, left to right.

Can we leave out the "left-to-right" part and just say that all ties will be broken left-to right? No, because for exponentiation that isn't true.

$$2^{2^3}$$

means

$$2^{(2^3)} = 256, \quad \text{not} \quad (2^2)^3 = 64.$$

So exponentiations are resolved from upper-right to lower-left. Perl uses the token ** to represent exponentiation, using x**y instead of x^y. In this case x**y**z means x**(y**z), not (x**y)**z, so ** is resolved right-to-left.

Programming languages have the same notational problem, except it's even worse than in mathematics, partly because programmer's languages have so many different operator symbols. For example, Perl has at least 70 different operator symbols. This is a problem, because communication with the compiler and with other programmers must be unambiguous. We don't want to write something like $2 + 3 \times 4$ and have Perl compute 20 when we wanted 14, or vice versa.

Nobody knows a really good solution to this problem, and different languages solve it in different ways. For example, the language APL, which has a whole lot of unfamiliar operators like ρ and ∆, dispenses with precedence entirely and resolves them all from right-to-left. The advantage of this is that we don't have to remember any rules, and the disadvantage is that many expressions are confusing: if we write 2 × 3 + 4, you get 14, not 10. In LISP the issue never comes up, because in LISP the parentheses are required, and so there are no ambiguous expressions. (Now you know why LISP looks the way it does.)

Perl, with its 70 operators, has to solve this problem somehow. The strategy Perl takes (and most other programming languages as well) is to take the fourth-grade system and extend it to deal with the new operators. The operators are divided into many *precedence levels*, and certain operations, like multiplication, have higher precedence than other operations, like addition. The levels are essentially arbitrary, and are chosen without any deep plan, but with the hope that you will be able to omit most of the parentheses most of the time and still get what you want. So, for example, Perl gives * a higher precedence than +, and ** a higher precedence than *, just like in grade school.

An Explosion of Rules

Let's see some examples of the reasons for which the precedence levels are set the way they are. Suppose we wrote something like this:

```
$v = $x + 3;
```

This is actually ambiguous. It might mean:

```
($v = $x) + 3;
```

or it might mean:

```
$v = ($x + 3);
```

The first of these is silly, because it stores the value $x into $v, and then computes the value of $x + 3 and throws the result of the addition away. In this case, the addition was useless. The second one, however, makes sense, because it does the addition first and stores the result into $v. Since people write things like:

```
$v = $x + 3;
```

all the time, and expect to get the second behavior and not the first, Perl's = operator has low precedence, lower than the precedence of +, so that Perl uses the second interpretation.

Here's another example:

```
$result =  $x =~ /foo/;
```

means this:

```
$result = ($x =~ /foo/);
```

which looks to see if $x contains the string foo, and stores a true or false result into $result. It doesn't mean this:

```
($result = $x) =~ /foo/;
```

which copies the value of $x into $result and then looks to see if $result contains foo. In this case it's likely that the programmer wanted the first meaning, not the second. But sometimes we do want it to go the other way. Consider this expression:

```
$p = $q =~ s/w//g;
```

Again, this expression is interpreted this way:

```
$p = ($q =~ s/w//g);
```

All the w's are removed from $q, and the number of successful substitutions is stored into $p. However, sometimes we really do want the other meaning:

```
($p = $q) =~ s/w//g;
```

This copies the value of $q into $p, and then removes all the w's from $p, leaving $q alone. If we want this, we have to include the parentheses explicitly, because = has lower precedence than =~.

Often, the rules do what we want them to. Consider this:

```
$worked = 1 + $s =~ /pattern/;
```

There are five ways to interpret this:

1. ($worked = 1) + ($s =~ /pattern/);
2. (($worked = 1) + $s) =~ /pattern/;
3. ($worked = (1 + $s)) =~ /pattern/;
4. $worked = ((1 + $s) =~ /pattern/);
5. $worked = (1 + ($s =~ /pattern/));

We already know that + has higher precedence than =, so it happens before =, and that rules out (1) and (2).

We also know that =~ has higher precedence than =, so that rules out (3).

To choose between (4) and (5), we need to know whether = takes precedence over =~ or vice versa. (4) will convert $s to a number, add 1 to it, convert the resulting number to a string, and do the pattern match. That is a pretty silly thing to do. (5) will match $s against the pattern, return a boolean result, add 1 to that result to yield the number 1 or 2, and store the number into $worked. That makes a lot more sense; perhaps $worked will be used later to index an array. We should hope that Perl chooses interpretation (5) rather than (4). And in fact, that is what it does, because =~ has higher precedence than +. =~ behaves similarly with respect to multiplication.

Our table of precedence is shaping up:

1. ** (right to left)
2. =~
3. * /, (left to right)
4. + -, (left to right)
5. =

How are multiple symbols resolved? Left-to-right, or right-to-left? The question is whether this:

```
$a = $b = $c;
```

will mean this:

```
($a = $b) = $c;
```

or this:

```
$a = ($b = $c);
```

The first one means to store the value of $b into $a, and then to store the value of $c into $a; this is obviously not useful. But the second one means to store the value of $c into $b, and then to store that value into $a also, and that obviously is useful. So, = is resolved right-to-left.

Why does =~ have lower precedence than **? No good reason. It's just a side effect of the low precedence of =~ and the high precedence of **. It's probably very rare to have =~ and ** in the same expression anyway. Perl tries to get the common cases right. Here's another common case:

```
if ($x == 3 && $y == 4) { ... }
```

Is this interpreted as:

1. (($x == 3) && $y) == 4
2. ($x == 3) && ($y == 4)
3. ($x == (3 && $y)) == 4
4. $x == ((3 && $y) == 4)
5. $x == (3 && ($y == 4))

We really hope that it will be (2). To make (2) occur, && must have lower precedence than ==; if the precedence is higher we'll get (3) or (4), which would be awful. So && has lower precedence than ==. If this seems like an obvious decision, consider that Pascal got it wrong.

|| has about the same precedence as &&, but slightly lower, in accordance with the usual convention of mathematicians, and by analogy with * and +. ! has high precedence, because when people write:

```
!$x .....some long complicated expression....
```

they almost always mean that the ! applies to the $x, not to the entire long complicated expression. In fact, almost the only time they don't mean this is in cases like this one:

```
if (! $x->{annoying}) { ... }
```

It would be very annoying if this were interpreted to mean:

```
if ((! $x)->{annoying}) { ... }
```

The same argument we used to explain why ! has high precedence works even better and explains why -> has even higher precedence. In fact, -> has the highest precedence of all. If ## and @@ are any two operators at all, then:

```
$a ## $x->$y
```

and

```
$x->$y @@ $b
```

always mean

```
$a ## ($x->$y)
```

and

```
($x->$y) @@ $b
```

and not

```
($a ## $x)->$y
```

or

```
$x->($y @@ $b)
```

For a long time, the operator with lowest precedence was the , operator. The , operator is for evaluating two expressions in sequence. For example:

```
$a*=2 , $c*=3
```

doubles $a and triples $c. It would be a shame if we wrote something like this:

```
$a*=2 , $c*=3 if $change_the_variables;
```

and Perl interpreted it to mean this:

```
$a*= (2, $c) *= 3 if $change_the_variables;
```

That would certainly be bizarre. The very low precedence of , ensures that we can write:

```
EXPR1, EXPR2
```

for any two expressions at all, and be sure that they are not going to get mashed together to make some nonsense expression like $a *= (2, $c) *= 3.

The comma is also the list constructor operator. If we want to make a list of three things, we have to write:

```
@list = ('Gold', 'Frankincense', 'Myrrh');
```

because if we left off the parentheses, like this:

```
@list = 'Gold', 'Frankincense', 'Myrrh';
```

what we would get would be the same as this:

```
(@list = 'Gold'), 'Frankincense', 'Myrrh';
```

This assigns @list to have one element (Gold) and then executes the two following expressions in sequence, which is pointless. So this is a prime example of a case where the default precedence rules don't do what we want. But people are already in the habit of putting parentheses around their list elements, so nobody minds this very much, and the problem isn't really a problem at all.

Precedence Traps and Surprises

This very low precedence for commas causes some other problems, however. Consider the common idiom:

```
open(F, "< $file") || die "Couldn't open $file: $!";
```

This tries to open a filehandle, and if it can't, it aborts the program with an error message. Now watch what happens if we leave the parentheses off the open call:

```
open F, "< $file" || die "Couldn't open $file: $!";
```

The comma has very low precedence, so the || takes precedence here, and Perl interprets the expression as if we had written this:

```
open F, ("< $file" || die "Couldn't open $file: $!");
```

This is totally bizarre, because the die will only be executed when the string "< $file" is false, which never happens. Since the die is controlled by the string and not by the open call, the program will not abort on errors the way we wanted. Here we wish that || had lower precedence, so that we could write:

```
try to perform big long hairy complicated action     || die ;
```

and be sure that the || was not going to gobble up part of the action the way it did in our open example. Perl 5 introduced a new version of || that has low precedence, for exactly this purpose. It's spelled or, and in fact it has the lowest precedence of all Perl's operators. We can write:

```
try to perform big long hairy complicated action     or die ;
```

and be quite sure that or will not gobble up part of the action the way it did in our open example, whether or not we leave off the parentheses. To summarize:

```
open(F, "< $file") or die "Couldn't open $file: $!";   # OK
open F, "< $file"  or die "Couldn't open $file: $!";   # OK
open(F, "< $file") || die "Couldn't open $file: $!";   # OK
open F, "< $file"  || die "Couldn't open $file: $!";   # Whoops!
```

If we use or, we're safe from this error, and if we always put in the parentheses, we're safe. Pick a strategy and stick with it.

The other major use for || is to select a value from the first source that provides it. For example:

```
$directory = $opt_D || $ENV{DIRECTORY} || $DEFAULT_DIRECTORY;
```

This looks to see if there was a -D command-line option specifying the directory first; if not, it looks to see if the user set the DIRECTORY environment variable; if neither of these is set, it uses a hard-wired default directory. It gets the first value that it can; for example, if we have the environment variable set and supply an explicit -D option when we run the program, the option overrides the environment variable. The precedence of || is higher than =, so this means what we wanted:

```
$directory = ($opt_D || $ENV{DIRECTORY} || $DEFAULT_DIRECTORY);
```

But some people might end up sabotaging themselves by writing something like this:

```
$directory = $opt_D or $ENV{DIRECTORY} or $DEFAULT_DIRECTORY;
```

or has extremely low precedence, even lower than =, so Perl interprets this as:

```
($directory = $opt_D) or $ENV{DIRECTORY} or $DEFAULT_DIRECTORY;
```

$directory is *always* assigned from the command-line option, even if none was set. Then the values of the expressions $ENV{DIRECTORY} and $DEFAULT_DIRECTORY are thrown away. Perl's -w option will warn us about this mistake if we make it. To avoid it, remember this rule of thumb: use || for selecting values, and or for controlling the flow of statements.

List Operators and Unary Operators

A related problem is that all of Perl's list operators have high precedence, and tend to gobble up everything to their right. (A *list operator* is a Perl function that accepts a list of arguments, like open or print.) We already saw this problem with open. Here's a similar problem:

```
@successes = (unlink $new, symlink $old, $new, open N, $new);
```

This isn't even clear to humans. What we really meant was:

```
@successes = (unlink($new), symlink($old, $new), open(N, $new));
```

which performs the three operations in sequence and stores the three success-or-failure codes into @successes. But what Perl thought we meant here was something totally different:

```
@successes = (unlink($new, symlink($old, $new, open(N, $new))));
```

It thinks that the result of the open call should be used as the third argument to symlink, and that the result of symlink should be passed to unlink, which will try to remove a file with that name. This won't even compile, because symlink wants two arguments, not three. We saw one way to disambiguate this; another is to write it like this:

```
@successes = ((unlink $new), (symlink $old, $new), (open N, $new));
```

Again, pick a style and stick with it.

Why do Perl list operators gobble up everything to the right? Often, it's very handy. For example:

```
@textfiles = grep -T, map "$DIRNAME/$_", readdir DIR;
```

Here Perl behaves as if we had written this:

```
@textfiles = grep(-T, (map("$DIRNAME/$_", (readdir(DIR)))));
```

Some filenames are read from the directory handle with `readdir`, and the resulting list is passed to `map`, which turns each filename into a full pathname and returns a list of paths. Then `grep` filters the list of paths, extracts all the paths that refer to text files, and returns a list of just the text files from the directory.

One possibly fine point is that the parentheses might not always mean what we want. For example, suppose we had this:

```
print $a, $b, $c;
```

Then we discover that we need to print out double the value of $a. If we do this, we're safe:

```
print 2*$a, $b, $c;
```

but if we do this, we might get a surprise:

```
print (2*$a), $b, $c;
```

If a list operator is followed by parentheses, Perl assumes that the parentheses enclose *all* the arguments, so it interprets this as:

```
(print (2*$a)), $b, $c;
```

It prints out twice $a, but doesn't print out $b or $c at all. (Perl warns us about this if we have -w on.) To fix this, add more parentheses:

```
print ((2*$a), $b, $c);
```

Some people will suggest that we do this instead:

```
print +(2*$a), $b, $c;
```

Perl does what we want here, but I think it's bad advice because it looks bizarre.

Here's a similar example:

```
print @items, @more_items;
```

Say we want to join up the @items with some separator, so we use `join`:

```
print join '---', @items, @more_items;
```

Oops; this is wrong; we only want to join @items, not @more_items also. One way we might try to fix this is:

```
print (join '---', @items), @more_items;
```

This falls afoul of the problem we just saw: Perl sees the parentheses, assumes that they contain the arguments of `print`, and never prints @more_items at all. To fix this, use either of these constructs:

```
print ((join '---', @items), @more_items);
print join('---', @items), @more_items;
```

Sometimes we won't have this problem. Some of Perl's built-in functions are *unary operators*, which means that they always get exactly one argument. `defined` and `uc` are examples. They don't have the problem that the list operators have of gobbling everything to the right; they only gobble one argument. Here's an example similar to the one just shown:

```
print $a, $b;
```

Now we decide we want to print $a in all lowercase letters:

```
print lc $a, $b;
```

Don't we have the same problem as in the print join example? If we did, it would print $b in all lowercase also. But it doesn't, because lc is a unary operator and only gets one argument. This doesn't need any fixing.

Complete Rules of Precedence

Perl's complete precedence table is shown in Table 4-1.

Table 4-1. Perl's operator precedences

Operator	Associativity
Terms and list operators (leftward)	left
->	left
++ --	nonassoc
**	right
! ~ \ and unary + and −	right
=~ !~	left
* / % x	left
+ - .	left
<<>>	left
Named unary operators	nonassoc
< > <= >= lt gt le ge	nonassoc
== != <=> eq ne cmp	nonassoc
&	left
| ^	left
&&	left
||	left
.. ...	nonassoc
?:	right
= += -= *= etc.	right
, =>	left
List operators (rightward)	nonassoc
not	right
and	left
or xor	left

This is straight out of the *perlop* documentation that comes with Perl. *left* and *right* mean that the operators associate to the left or the right, respectively; *nonassoc* means that the operators don't associate at all. For example, if we try to write:

```
$a < $b < $c
```

Perl 5 will deliver a syntax error message. Perhaps what we really meant was:

```
$a < $b && $b < $c
```

The precedence table is much too big and complicated to remember; that's a problem with Perl's approach. We have to trust it to handle to common cases correctly, and be prepared to deal with bizarre, hard-to-find bugs when it doesn't do what we wanted. The alternatives have their own disadvantages.

How to Remember All the Rules

Probably the best strategy for dealing with Perl's complicated precedence hierarchy is to cluster the operators mentally:

Arithmetic: +, -, *, /, %, **
Bitwise: &, |, ~, <<, >>
Logical: &&, ||, !
Comparison: ==, !=, >=, <=, >, <
Assignment: =, +=, -=, *=, /=, etc.

Try to remember how the operators behave within each group. Mostly the answer will be "They behave as expected." For example, the operators in the "arithmetic" group all behave the according to the rules from fourth grade. The "comparison" group all have about the same precedence, and we aren't allowed to mix them anyway, except to say something like:

```
$a<$b == $c<$d
```

which compares the *truth values* of $a<$b and $c<$d.

Then, once we're familiar with the rather unsurprising behavior of the most common groups, we can just use parentheses liberally everywhere else.

Starting in Perl 5.005_03, we can use the B::Deparse module to print out what the expression would look like if it had all the implied parentheses inserted. We can use this to make sure Perl is interpreting an expression in the way we think it is. For example, let's check to make sure we gave the right interpretation of `$worked = 1 + $s =~ /pattern/` earlier:

```
perl -MO=Deparse,-p -e '$worked = 1 + $s =~ /pattern/'
```

Perl prints out:

```
($worked = (1 + ($s =~ /pattern/)));
```

as we expected. The p option here stands for "print precedence-preserving parentheses."

Quiz

Try to guess how Perl interprets the following expressions: (or use B::Deparse.)

1. $x = $x | $y << 3;
2. $y % 4 == 0 && $y % 100 != 0 || $y % 400 == 0
3. $V = 4/3*$PI*$r**3;
4. $x >= 1 || $x <= 10

Answers

1. $x = ($x | ($y << 3));
2. ((($y % 4) == 0) && (($y % 100) != 0)) || (($y % 400) == 0) (This computes whether or not the year $y is a leap year.)
3. $V = ((4/3)*$PI*($r**3)); (This is the volume of a sphere with radius $r.)
4. ($x >= 1) || ($x <= 10)

CHAPTER 5

The Birth of a One-Liner

Art Ramos

In the old days, if you wrote a program to perform data manipulation on some file, there were standard operations that had to be implemented to access the file's data. Your program would have to open the file, read each record and process it, decide what to do with the newly manipulated data, and close the file. Perl doesn't let you avoid any of these steps, but by employing some of Perl's unique features, you can express your programs much more concisely—and they'll be faster, too.

In this article, we'll take a simple task and show how familiarity with Perl idioms can reduce the size and complexity of the solution. Our task is to display the lines of a file that are neither comments nor blank. Here's our first attempt:

```perl
#!/usr/bin/perl -w

# Obtain filename from the first argument.

$file = $ARGV[0];

# Open the file -- if it can't be opened, terminate
# and print an error message.

open INFILE, $file or die "Cannot open $file: $!";

# For each record in the file, read it in and process it.

while (defined($line = <INFILE>)) {

    # Grab the first one and two characters of each line.
    $firstchar = substr($line,0,1);
    $firsttwo  = substr($line,0,2);

    # If the line does NOT begin with a #! (we want to see
    # any bang operators) but the first character does begin
    # with a # (we don't want to see any # comments), skip it.

    if ($firsttwo ne "#!" && $firstchar eq "#") { next }
```

```
    # Or, if the line consists of only a newline (i.e. it's
    # a blank line), skip it.

    elsif ($firstchar eq "\n") { next }

    # Otherwise display the line to standard output (i.e.
    # your terminal).

    else { print $line }

    # Proceed to next record.
}

# Close the input file.

close INFILE;
```

This script works just fine, but it's pretty large—we have to look at a lot of lines to figure out what it does. Let's streamline this code step-by-step until we're left with the bare essentials.

First, while (<>) opens the files provided on the command line and reads input lines without us having to explicitly assign them to a variable. Let's remove the comments and change the Perl script to use this feature.

```
#!/usr/bin/perl -w

while (<>) {
    $firstchar = substr($_,0,1);
    $firsttwo  = substr($_,0,2);
    if ($firsttwo ne "#!" && $firstchar eq "#") {
        next;
    } elsif ($firstchar eq "\n") {
        next;
    } else {
        print $_;
    }
}
```

As each line is read, it is stored in the scalar $_. We changed our call to substr (which extracts or replaces individual characters from a string) and the print statement to use this internal variable.

We can even make the while loop implicit as well. The -n switch wraps our program inside a loop: LINE: while (<>) { our_code }.

So we can shorten our little program even more:

```
#!/usr/bin/perl -wn

$firstchar = substr($_,0,1);
$firsttwo  = substr($_,0,2);
if ($firsttwo ne "#!" && $firstchar eq "#") { next }
elsif ($firstchar eq "\n") { next }
else { print $_ }
```

In Perl, there's more than one way to do nearly anything, even good old conditionals. We can use an alternate form—and the fact that our loop is now implicitly named LINE—to rewrite our program with even less punctuation:

```
#!/usr/bin/perl -wn

$firstchar = substr($_,0,1);
$firsttwo  = substr($_,0,2);
next LINE if $firsttwo ne "#!" && $firstchar eq "#";
next LINE if $firstchar eq "\n";
print $_;
```

The next LINE commands aren't executed unless their if statements are true.

The intermediate variables $firstchar and $firsttwo make sense if they're going to be used repeatedly, but for our program they aren't. They require unnecessary amounts of time and memory, so let's eliminate them by using the substr function on the left side of the comparisons:

```
#!/usr/bin/perl -wn
next LINE if substr($_,0,2) ne "#!" && substr($_,0,1) eq "#";
next LINE if substr($_,0,1) eq "\n";
print $_;
```

Our Perl program is now down to three lines of code (not counting the #! line). By combining the two ifs into one compound if, we can reduce the program to two lines:

```
#!/usr/bin/perl -wn
next LINE if (substr($_,0,2) ne "#!" && substr($_,0,1) eq "#") || substr($_,0,1) eq "\n";
print $_;
```

That next LINE statement won't fit in one column, but as usual There's Always More Than One Way To Shorten It. Using the match operator (m//), we can construct regular expressions, which determine whether a string matches a pattern. Some simple regular expressions relevant to our task are shown in Table 5-1.

Table 5-1. Some simple regular expressions

Regular expression	Meaning
m/^#!/	Check whether the string begins (^) with #!
m/^#/	Check whether the string begins (^) with #
m/^\n$/	Check whether the string begins (^) with a newline (\n) and end ($) with it too

The =~ and !~ operators are used to test whether the pattern on the right applies to the string on the left. $string =~ /^#/ is true if $string begins with a #, and $string !~ /^#/ is true if it doesn't. The program can now be shortened even further:

```
#!/usr/bin/perl -wn
next LINE if ($_ !~ m/^#!/ && $_ =~ m/^#/) || $_ =~ m/^\n$/;
print $_;
```

What if there are blank lines with whitespace preceding the newline? Then `m/^\n$/` won't be true, and the line will be displayed, which isn't what we want to happen. Inside a pattern, Perl can test for a whitespace character with `\s`, which matches not only spaces but tabs and carriage returns as well.

Inside a pattern, we can specify how much we want of something with a *quantifier*. The quantifiers are shown in Table 5-2.

Table 5-2. Regex quantifiers

Quantifier	Meaning
*	0 or more times
+	1 or more times
?	0 or 1 time
{x,y}	At least *x* but not more than *y* times

Since we might have any amount of extraneous whitespace, even none, * fits the bill. `\s*` means zero or more whitespace characters. When we add this to our match, our program now reads:

```
#!/usr/bin/perl -wn
next LINE if ($_ !~ m/^#!/ && $_ =~ m/^#/) || $_ =~ m/^\s*\n$/;
print $_;
```

Perl often uses `$_` as a default variable for its operators. It does this both with pattern matches and print:

```
#!/usr/bin/perl -wn
next LINE if (!m/^#!/ && m/^#/) || m/^\s*\n$/;
print;
```

If we're applying a pattern match to `$_`, we can leave off the m in `m//` matches:

```
#!/usr/bin/perl -wn
next LINE if (!/^#!/ && /^#/) || /^\s*\n$/;
print;
```

We can combine these two lines into one by using `unless`, and since `&&` binds more tightly than `||`, we can remove the parentheses:

```
#!/usr/bin/perl -wn
print unless !/^#!/ && /^#/ || /^\s*\n$/;
```

We can execute this program directly from the command line with the -e flag. We can even trim the semicolon, because it's the last statement of a block:

```
% perl -wne "print unless !/^#!/ && /^#/ || /^\s*\n$/"
```

(We may need to escape the exclamation points if our shell tries to interpret them as history characters.)

Finally, we can use Perl's negative lookahead operator ((?!)) to combine the two patterns into a single pattern that matches lines beginning with a # and is not followed by a !.

```
% perl -wne "print unless /^\s*$/ || /^#(?!!)/"
```

Note that we've swapped the order of the two patterns. Since we expect to find blank lines more often than # lines, this provides a slight optimization. We can allow for indented comments by placing a \s* in front of the #:

```
% perl -wne "print unless /^\s*$/ || /^\s*#(?!!)/"
```

Our two patterns now look similar, and indeed we can combine them with |:

```
% perl -wne "print unless /^\s*($|#(?!!))/"
```

If we wanted to pile on, we could use the short-circuiting effect of || to make the code even more obfuscated:

```
% perl -wne "/^\s*($|#(?!!))/||print"
```

We've now taken a program from the verbose to the concise to the insane. Once you get used to these idioms, you'll be able to spill out code with whatever mix of brevity and clarity you like. Have fun!

## CHAPTER 6

Comparators, Sorting, and Hashes

Frossie Economou

> *Shall I compare thee to a summer's day?*
> *Thou art more lovely and more temperate...*
> —William Shakespeare, Sonnet XVIII
> *"I'd like to know if I could compare you to a summer's*
> *day. Because well, June 12th was quite nice, and..."*
> —Terry Pratchett, *Wyrd Sisters*

Perl has two types of *comparators*, so called because they compare something to something else. Half of them compare one number to another, and the other half compare strings. Don't mix them! The comparators are shown in Table 6-1.

Table 6-1. Perl's comparators

Number	String	Meaning
==	eq	Equal
!=	ne	Not equal
<	lt	Less than
>	gt	Greater than
<=	le	Less or equal
>=	ge	Greater or equal
<=>	cmp	Compare

You've probably seen them all before, with the possible exception of <=> and cmp.

To see where these comparators come in handy, consider a series of questions posed to a politician:

```
Q. Will you raise taxes?  ($newtax > $oldtax)
A. No.

Q. So you will lower taxes? ($newtax < $oldtax)
A. No.

Q. Ah, you'll keep them the same? ($newtax == $oldtax)
```

You could have combined all three questions into one, presuming your politician understands the <=> comparator:

```
Q. Will you raise/lower/maintain taxes? ($newtax <=> $oldtax)
```

The expression $foo <=> $bar returns −1, 0, or 1 depending on whether $foo is smaller, equal to, or greater than $bar.

cmp behaves the same way as <=>, but it operates on strings instead of numbers.

Sorting

Comparators are often used to help sort a list of numbers or strings. Perl's sort function expects its first parameter to be something that behaves just like <=> and cmp:

```
sort SUBROUTINE_OR_BLOCK LIST
```

sort calls the subroutine (or invokes the block) repeatedly with two values that are always stored in the special variables $a and $b. The subroutine's job is to answer the question, "Which is higher, or are they the same?" and expects an answer of 1 if $a is higher, −1 if $b is higher, or 0 if they're equal.

The Simplest Way to Sort

The simplest possible sort is ascending numerical order:

```
sort {$a <=> $b} 4,2,5
```

This returns the list 2,4,5. Descending order is achieved by swapping $a and $b:

```
sort {$b <=> $a} 4,2,5
```

This evaluates to the list 5,4,2. It's the same with strings. Suppose you want to sort a list of 1996 Formula One drivers alphabetically:

```
@unsorted = qw/Schumacher Hill Alesi Villeneuve Coulthard/;
@sorted = sort {$a cmp $b} @unsorted;
```

Unless you've forgotten your ABCs, the result shouldn't surprise you: "Alesi", "Coulthard", "Hill", "Schumacher", "Villeneuve". Without a subroutine, sort defaults to string comparison, so we could have written this even more succinctly:

```
@sorted = sort @unsorted;
```

One common pitfall is forgetting that cmp uses ASCII order, which ranks lowercase letters higher than uppercase letters. If you want true alphabetical order, use {lc($a) cmp lc($b)} as your sort block.

Tinkering with the Sort

Let's rewrite the above example using a named subroutine:

```
@sorted = sort honestly @unsorted;

sub honestly {
  $a cmp $b;
}
```

If you can't be honest, be creative. Suppose you want to sort the list in cmp's ASCII order, but want Damon Hill to always come first, because he, um, used to be good. Now, sort doesn't care what the subroutine does, so long as it returns –1, 0, or 1. So what you'll do is replace honestly with a subroutine that checks if "Hill" is one of its arguments, and fudges the result if so.

```
@sorted = sort fraudulently @unsorted;

sub fraudulently {
  return -1 if $a eq 'Hill';
  return  1 if $b eq 'Hill';
  return $a cmp $b;
}
```

This produces "Hill", "Alesi", "Coulthard", "Schumacher", "Villeneuve".

One common pitfall is thinking that all you need is the if $a case. Try the above without the if $b line and see what happens!

Sorting Hashes

You can't. Go home.

Hashes simply map a set of scalars (the *keys*) to another set of scalars (the *values*); they have no beginning and no end, so they can't be sorted. So you can't sort a hash—but you can certainly sort its keys and values.

In keeping with this theme, let's make a hash of some Formula One teams (keys) and the companies that provide their car engines (values). In Formula One parlance, these combinations of racing team and engine are called *constructors*, and every season there is a constructor championship in parallel with the driver championship. For example, the 1996 season was won by Williams-Renault because the most points were won by cars built by the Williams team using the Renault engine.

```
%constructors = (
  "Williams" => "Renault",
  "McLaren"  => "Mercedes",
  "Benetton" => "Renault",
  "Ferrari"  => "Ferrari",
  "Arrows"   => "Yamaha",
);
```

If you haven't used hashes much, you might be wondering whether it makes any difference which elements are keys and which are values. Keys must be unique; that's why it would have been silly to use the engines as the keys and the teams as the values. You can't have two racing teams of the same name any more than you can have two NFL teams called "Dallas Cowboys." But two football teams could play in the same stadium, just as two racing teams can and do buy engines from the same manufacturer. As you can see, both the Williams and the Benetton teams buy their engines from Renault.

Sorting by Key

Every Perl hash has its own internal ordering; that's what makes them so efficient to manipulate. You can't change that ordering, but you can sort the order in which you retrieve keys with Perl's builtin keys operator. keys returns a list of the hash keys, which can then be sorted with the techniques discussed above.

Here's how you could produce a listing of constructors in team order:

```
@teams = sort {$a cmp $b} keys %constructors;

foreach $team (@teams) {
  print $team, "-", $constructors{$team}, "\n";
}
```

This displays:

```
Arrows-Yamaha
Benetton-Renault
Ferrari-Ferrari
McLaren-Mercedes
Williams-Renault
```

Don't be afraid to take advantage of the shortcuts Perl offers. You already know that sort defaults to a string comparison and keys returns a list, so you can fold the above sort statement into the foreach loop:

```
foreach $team (sort keys %constructors) {
  print $team, "-", $constructors{$team}, "\n";
}
```

It's not complicated; in fact, it's much easier to verbalize ("For each $team in the list of sorted constructor keys") than the first, more verbose, example ("Let @teams be the list sorted by string comparison of constructor keys; for each $team in @teams").

Sorting a Hash by Value

keys has a brother, values, that returns a list of all the hash values. Now of course you can sort the values just as you sorted the keys, but will that help you at all in sorting your hash? No, because the hash is indexed by key, not by value, so you still need to arrange the keys first. But you can organize those any way you want: by value, by size, or by phase of the moon if that's your pleasure.

Before, you sorted the keys by key (that is, the teams by team name) with this snippet:

```
@teams = sort {$a cmp $b} keys %constructors;
```

Now, you want to sort the keys by their corresponding values (that is, the teams by engine):

```
@teams = sort { $constructors{$a} cmp $constructors{$b} } keys %constructors;
```

which, followed again with:

```
foreach $team (@teams) {
  print $team,"-",$constructors{$team},"\n";
}
```

prints:

```
Ferrari-Ferrari
McLaren-Mercedes
Williams-Renault
Benetton-Renault
Arrows-Yamaha
```

This is exactly what you wanted: a list of constructors sorted by engine.

Sorting a Hash by Key and Value

If you made it to this point, you probably know enough to fulfill all your sorting needs. To demonstrate, here's a more sophisticated example that can be easily solved using what you know so far.

Suppose you wanted to sort the hash (constructors) by value (engine) as above but, knowing that the value may not always be unique, want to sort by key (team) in the case of identical engines. In other words, you want a primary sort by engine and a secondary sort by team name. Here are the four steps:

1. First, get the keys (teams) sorted in the order you want:

    ```
    @teams = sort myway keys %constructors;
    ```

2. You can sort them using any subroutine you like:

    ```
    sub myway {
      # are the engines different?
      if ($constructors{$a} ne $constructors{$b}) {
        # engines different - compare engines
        $constructors{$a} cmp $constructors{$b};
      } else {
        # engines same - compare teams
        $a cmp $b;
      }
    }
    ```

3. Display the teams using the using the sorted keys:

    ```
    foreach $team (@teams) {
        print $team, "-", $constructors{$team}, "\n";
    }
    ```

4. Glow with satisfaction when the output arrives as desired:

    ```
    Ferrari-Ferrari
    McLaren-Mercedes
    Benetton-Renault
    Williams-Renault
    Arrows-Yamaha
    ```

Efficient Sorting

Once you've figured out how to do something, the next step is often figuring out how to do it fast. If you have a complicated sorting operation, consider doing as much work as possible before the sort, rather than embedding the work in the sort subroutine (which is likely to be called over and over). This occasionally requires some lateral thinking, but that's where all the fun is anyway, right?

In the first example you had these drivers:

```
@unsorted = qw/Schumacher Hill Alesi Villeneuve Coulthard/;
```

You were trying to fudge the order so that Hill came first:

```
sub fraudulently {
  return -1 if $a eq 'Hill';
  return  1 if $b eq 'Hill';
  $a cmp $b;
}
```

This puts the computational burden of cheating on the sort subroutine. But is there a more efficient way to make sure Hill stays on top? Well, since the null string ("") is always going to be first alphabetically, you could create another array that contains every driver's name–except for Hill, who'll have a null string in his place.

```
# copy the array
@idx = @unsorted;

# replace Hill with the null string in the array
foreach (@idx) { $_ = "" if $_ eq "Hill" }
```

Now you've created the array @idx with five elements with the values "Schumacher", "", "Alesi", "Villeneuve", and "Coulthard". What you want is to sort @idx and then the order the original array, @sorted, in the same order.

You can do this all in one statement:

```
@sorted = @unsorted[ sort { $idx[$a] cmp $idx[$b] } 0 .. $#idx ];
```

Done! Missed it? Here's the slow motion replay.

0..$#idx is 0,1,2,3,4 because that's how many elements you have. But remember

```
$idx[0] is "Schumacher"
$idx[1] is ""
$idx[2] is "Alesi"
$idx[3] is "Villeneuve"
$idx[4] is "Coulthard"
```

Let's focus on the sort expression:

```
sort { $idx[$a] cmp $idx[$b] } 0 .. $#idx
```

This takes 0,1,2,3,4 and returns whatever order is specified by an alphabetical sorting of "Schumacher", "", "Alesi", "Villeneuve", "Coulthard": which makes "" end on top.

Now, this isn't quite what you want—who's this "" bloke? You want the original unsorted list in the same order, which you can obtain via an array slice:

```
@unsorted[1,2,4,0,3].
```

Got it?

```
@sorted = @unsorted[1,2,4,0,3];
```

which came from this:

```
@sorted = @unsorted[ sort { $idx[$a] cmp $idx[$b] } 0,1,2,3,4 ];
```

which came from this:

```
@sorted = @unsorted[ sort { $idx[$a] cmp $idx[$b] } 0..$#idx ];
```

End of replay.

This one-liner might look complicated on first inspection, but all it says is, "Give me the elements of @unsorted in the order specified by comparing their indexed counterparts." A similar example can be found, not coincidentally, in the Perl FAQ.

Further Reading

The description for sort in O'Reilly's *Programming Perl*, or the online *perlfunc* documentation.

"How do I sort an array by (anything)" entry of the Perl FAQ.

The "Advanced Sorting" section in O'Reilly's *Learning Perl*.

For information on the current Formula One season, you should check out *http://www.galeforcef1.com*.

## CHAPTER 7

What Is Truth?

Nathan Torkington

Some programming languages give you a single TRUE and a single FALSE. Others make us represent each with integers (typically 1 and 0). But not Perl. Truth plays a larger role in Perl than most other languages, and its subtleties often confuse beginners.

In Perl, truthfulness is determined from a few simple rules. To understand one of those rules, though, we need to first learn about good programming practice, warnings, laziness, and undef. Then we can learn the nature of truth and see how to apply it in our own programs.

The undef Function

Perl was designed for system administrators who want to automate the automatable tasks of their jobs. Such people typically produce small programs, and don't need to worry about formally verifiable correctness, corporate coding standards, and other such things. They just want to get the job done.

For this reason, Perl's default behavior allows the programmer to be lazy and leave off parentheses around function arguments, use subroutines before they're defined, and use variables without initializations or even definitions.

However, the same practices that enable small programs to be written quickly can bog down larger programs by permitting subtle errors. Because Perl assumes that the programmer is all-knowing and perfect, it fails to notice things that smart and lazy programmers do deliberately but are mistakes for the rest of us. That's what Perl's -w flag is for.

The -w flag turns on warnings for ambiguous or possibly erroneous practices. One of the things it catches is the use of a variable before it has a value. Here's the simplest possible demonstration of that:

```
#!/usr/bin/perl -w
print $x;
```

This actually generates two warnings: `$main::x only used once` and `Use of uninitialized value`. The first warning comes after Perl has finished compiling our program and realizes "Hey, I only saw that variable once. That's probably a mistake." The second warning comes at runtime, when we attempt to print out `$x` without giving it a value. In cases like these, `$x` contains "the undefined value" or "the uninitialized value" and is written as undef. This value is completely separate from any other Perl value: it isn't the empty string, nor is it zero. It's almost like NULL in C. undef is a special value used whenever a variable hasn't yet been assigned a value. We can test for undef with the defined function:

```
if (defined $x) {
  print "x has value $x\n";
} else {
  print "x is undefined\n";
}
```

Any attempt to use `$x` as though it were a real value (by treating it like a string or a number, for instance) generates a warning at runtime if you're using -w. This means we can't use == or eq with `$x`, since those are number and string comparison operators and we'll get a warning for trying to use undef as a number or string.

If we *do* try, Perl will emit its warning if we used -w, but keep on going whether or not we used -w. This is how the lazy programmers were able to leave warnings off and have their code still work: Perl treats undef as either zero or the empty string. That's why we don't see anything when we try to print an undefined variable. Similarly:

```
#!/usr/bin/perl -w
$y = $x + 3;           # $y = 3, warning emitted
$y = length $x;        # $y = 0, warning emitted
```

We can return a scalar variable to its initial pristine undefined state by using undef as either a function or a value:

```
undef $x;
$x = undef;
```

defined and undef are good for testing and setting scalars. Don't try them with arrays, though. Presently, defined(@array) returns true if Perl has allocated storage for @array, something that is weird and not useful to the average programmer. To return an array to its initial state, we say:

```
@array = ();
```

To say `@array = undef` is to make @array contain a one-element list, with the single element being the scalar value undef. This is hardly ever what we want.

Back to Truth

So how does this fit into truth in Perl? Perl has some simple rules for determining whether something is true or false. One of those rules involves undef.

Here are the rules:

1. True/false are scalar concepts
2. undef is false
3. "" is false
4. 0 is false
5. 0.0 is false
6. "0" is false
7. Everything else is true

Rule 1 is important: only scalars can be tested for true and false. We'll see why this is important after examining the rest of the rules.

Rule 2 says that any uninitialized value is false. Because undef behaves as 0 when evaluated as a number and "" when evaluated as a string, it's easy to see why rules 3 and 4 are there. Rule 5 is a weird one: internally, Perl can store numbers either as integers or as floating point numbers (that is, numbers with a decimal point), and will convert between the two as needed. Because 0 (an integer) is false, it would be inconsistent to have the floating point version of 0 (0.0) be anything other than false.

Rule 6 is similar to Rule 5: since Perl converts between strings and numbers on demand, the string "0" must be false as well. Not "0.0", though, nor "0.00".

Rule 7 simply says that if it's not one of those five false values, it's true. This means that references are true, positive numbers are true, negative numbers are true (this surprised one of my students, and immediately identified the bug he'd been working for hours to fix), and every string is true with the exception of the empty string and "0".

Truth in Perl is really used to test for *interesting* values: if we've got a variable $name that might hold someone's name, it'll either be true (if we have a valid name) or it'll be false (if it's undefined, an empty string, or a form of 0). Either way, true means we want to work on it and false means we don't:

```
if ($name) {
  print "Hello, $name!\n";
} else {
  print "You didn't enter your name.  What do you have to hide?\n";
}
```

Similarly, if we've asked for someone's age:

```
if ($age) {
  $average = $total / $age;
} else {
  print "You didn't give me an age value.\n";
}
```

The 0 age is almost always wrong. For cases when we do want to permit an age of 0, we have to drop back and test with defined:

```
if (defined $age) {
  if ($age) {
    $average = $total / $age;
  } else {
    print "Can't average a 0 age.\n";
    $average = 0;
  }
} else {
  print "You really didn't give me an age value.\n";
}
```

It's worth emphasizing: truth and definedness are different. There are four false values that are defined: 0, "0", 0.0, and "". If you're in doubt, you can write a small program to test this:

```
#!/usr/bin/perl -w
$x = 0;
print "$x is defined\n" if defined $x;
$x = 0.0;
print "$x is defined\n" if defined $x;
# ...
```

Truth in Context

Every Perl expression is used in a particular *context*. At its most basic level, context is the answer to the question, "Am I producing a single value, or am I producing many values?" If the expression is meant to produce a single value, it's in scalar context. If the expression is to produce many values, it's in list context.

Scalar context is most often seen in assignments to scalar variables, boolean testing, and scalar subscripts:

```
$x = EXPR;              # EXPR in scalar context

if (EXPR)               # EXPR in scalar context

$foo[EXPR]              # EXPR in scalar context
```

List context is most often seen in assignments to array variables, arguments to an unprototyped function (or a function prototyped to take a list), and slices:

```
@x = EXPR;              # EXPR in list context

foo(EXPR);              # EXPR in list context

@foo[EXPR]              # EXPR in list context
```

When we say this, we're forcing @array into scalar context:

```
$count = @array;        # number of elements in @array
```

Perl has rules for evaluating lists, arrays, and hashes in scalar context. An array in scalar context behaves like the number of things in the array, so $count gets set to the number of elements in @array.

Because boolean tests also provide scalar context, we can say:

```perl
if (@array) {
  print "There are values in @array\n";
}
```

@array in scalar context is 0 (false) if the array is empty, and some non-zero number (true) if the array has values in it.

However, it's not just if that provides scalar context. Any boolean operator forces its arguments into scalar context:

```perl
if ($must_process_array && @array) {
  # process the array
}
```

Applications

Here's the meaty part. Perl programmers use true and false all the time. If you've used Perl for any length of time, you'll have seen something like this:

```perl
open(FH, "< $filename") || die "Couldn't open $filename: $!\n";
```

The open function returns true if it succeeds, false if it doesn't. If it returns false, the || operator runs its right-hand side and calls die. This relies on the short-circuit property of Perl's boolean operators: if we're testing a logical OR expression like the one above, and the left-hand side of the || or or is true, we know that the OR expression will be true; as a result, we don't have to test the right-hand side. Similarly, AND can immediately return false if the left-hand side returns false because the right-hand side no longer matters.

Perl programmers also use logical OR to supply variables with default values. Here's an excerpt from one of my programs:

```perl
$Data_File = $opt_t || "/tmp/web.data";
```

If $opt_t was given a value (say, from the command-line option parsing module Getopt::Std), that value will be assigned to $Data_File. If $opt_t wasn't given a value (because the user didn't supply a -t command-line option) then $Data_File gets set to "/tmp/web.data".

This single expression replaces a more verbose if statement:

```perl
if ($opt_t) {
  $Data_File = $opt_t;
} else {
  $Data_File = "/tmp/web.data";
}
```

Finally, let's end with a more involved example: sorting on two criteria. We already know that the sort function sorts a list of values in ASCII order:

```perl
@sorted = sort @unsorted;
```

If we want to sort by some other means, for instance numerically, we have to give sort a code block (or a subroutine name) that compares two elements and returns a negative, zero, or positive value to indicate how they should be sorted. This example uses the Perl operator <=> to sort an array of numbers from smallest to largest:

```
@sorted = sort { $a <=> $b } @unsorted;        # sort numerically
```

Because 0 is used to tell sort "These two elements should sort to the same position," we can use the || operator to connect two sorts:

```
@sorted = sort { (-s $a <=> -s $b) || ($a cmp $b) } @filenames;
```

Here we're sorting filenames, so the block of code gets called with $a and $b as the two filenames to compare. We first use the -s operator to fetch the size of the files and compare those file sizes numerically. If they're the same size, <=> will return 0, and the || will instead use the value of the right-hand side, a string comparison of the filenames.

We can write that more prettily as follows:

```
@sorted = sort { -s $a <=> -s $b
                        ||
                 $a cmp $b } @filenames;
```

Conclusion

And on that elegant note I leave you. We've explored Perl's notions of true and false, and found some common applications. Hopefully now when you see an || or an if (@array), you'll know what's going on.

Here are some things I didn't discuss; you might try reading the online documentation or Programming Perl to learn about them:

- How lists and hashes behave in scalar context
- The *important* difference between "or" and "||"
- How subroutines can learn their context with wantarray
- How context propagates through subroutine calls to the return statement

CHAPTER 8

Using Object-Oriented Modules

Sean M. Burke

The first time most Perl programmers run into object-oriented programming is when they need to use a module with an object-oriented interface. This is often a mystifying experience, since talk of "methods" and "constructors" is unintelligible to programmers who thought that functions and variables were all there was to worry about.

Articles and books that explain object-oriented programming (OOP) do so from the perspective of the programmer. That's understandable, and if you learn to write object-oriented code of your own, you'd find it easy to use object-oriented code that others write. But this approach is the long way around for people whose immediate goal is just to use existing object-oriented modules, but don't yet want to know all the gory details of writing such modules for themselves.

This article is for those programmers—programmers who want to know about objects from the perspective of using object-oriented modules.

Modules and Their Functional Interfaces

Modules are the primary mechanism for bundling up Perl code for later use by yourself or others. As I'm sure you can't help noticing from reading *The Perl Journal*, CPAN (the Comprehensive Perl Archive Network) is the repository for modules that others have written, for anything from composing music to downloading web pages. Many modules are bundled with every installation of Perl.

Text::Wrap is one module you may have used that has a fairly typical interface. It comes with Perl, so you don't even need to install it from CPAN. You use it in a program by having your program say:

```
use Text::Wrap;
```

After that, you can access a function called `wrap`, which inserts linebreaks in text that you feed it, so that the text will be wrapped to 72 (or however many) columns.

The way this use `Text::Wrap` business works is that the module Text::Wrap exists as the file *Text/Wrap.pm* somewhere in one of your library directories. That file contains

Perl code* that, among other things, defines a function called `Text::Wrap::wrap`, and then *exports* that function. That means when you say `wrap` after having said use `Text::Wrap`, you'll actually be calling the `Text::Wrap::wrap` function. (Some modules don't export their functions, so you have to call them by their fully qualified name: `Text::Wrap::wrap` instead of simply `wrap`.)

Regardless of whether a module exports the functions it provides, it's basically just a container for chunks of code that do useful things. The module allows you to interact with it through its *interface*. And when, as with Text::Wrap, its interface consists of functions, the module is said to have a *functional interface*.†

Using modules with functional interfaces is straightforward—instead of defining your own `wrap` function with `sub wrap { ... }`, you entrust use `Text::Wrap` to do that for you, along with whatever other functions it defines and exports according to the module's documentation. Without too much bother, you can even write your own modules to contain your frequently used functions; I suggest having a look at the *perlmod* documentation for leads on how to do this.

Modules with Object-Oriented Interfaces

Suppose you want to write a program that automates the process of downloading a bunch of files from a server to your local machine, and then uploading them to another server, all with FTP.

A quick browse through search.cpan.org turns up the module Net::FTP, which you can download and install using normal installation instructions (unless your systems administrator has already installed it, as many have).

Like Text::Wrap or any other module with a familiar functional interface, you start using Net::FTP in your program by saying:

```
use Net::FTP;
```

However, that's where the similarity ends. The first hint of difference is that the documentation for Net::FTP refers to classes, which you find only in object-oriented modules.

Whereas modules like Text::Wrap provide bits of useful code as functions to be called as `function(PARAMETERS)` or `PackageName::function(PARAMETERS)`, Net::FTP and other modules with object-oriented interfaces provide methods. *Methods* are like functions in that they have a name and parameters, but methods look different, and

---

* And mixed in with the Perl code is documentation, which is what you read with `perldoc Text::Wrap`. The `perldoc` program simply ignores the code and formats the documentation, whereas use `Text::Wrap` loads and runs the code while ignoring the documentation.

† The term "function" (and therefore "functional") has various meanings. I use the term here to mean *subroutine*: a chunk of code called by some name that takes some parameters and returns a value.

are different, because you have to call them with a class name or an object as an argument. First I'll explain the syntax for method calls, and then I'll explain what everything means.

Class Methods

Some methods are meant to be called as *class methods*, with the class name (which is usually just the module name) as a special argument. Class methods look like this:

```
ClassName->methodname(parameter1, parameter2, ...)
ClassName->methodname()    # if no parameters
ClassName->methodname      # same as above
```

You'll sometimes see this written as follows:

```
methodname ClassName (parameter1, parameter2, ...)
methodname ClassName    # if no parameters
```

Most class methods are for making new objects. The methods that make objects are called *constructors*, and the process of making them is called "constructing" or "instantiating" an object. Constructor methods typically have the name new, or something including "new" (for instance, new_from_file), but they can be named however the programmer likes. DBI's constructor is named connect, for example.

The object returned by a constructor is typically captured in a scalar variable:

```
$object = ClassName->new(param1, param2...);
```

Object Methods

Once you have an object (more later on exactly what that is), you can use the other kind of method call syntax, the syntax for *object method* calls. You call object methods just like class methods, except that instead of the ClassName as the special argument, you use an expression that yields an object. Usually this is just a scalar variable that captures the output of the constructor. Object method calls look like this:

```
$object->methodname(parameter1, parameter2, ...);
$object->methodname()    # if no parameters
$object->methodname      # same as above
```

They are sometimes written like this as well:

```
methodname $object (parameter1, parameter2, ...)
methodname $object    # if no parameters
```

Some examples of method calls:

```
my $session1 = Net::FTP->new("ftp.myhost.com");
# Calls a class method "new", from class Net::FTP,
#  with the single parameter "ftp.myhost.com",
#  and saves the return value (which is, as usual,
#  an object), in $session1.
# Could also be written new Net::FTP('ftp.myhost.com')
```

```
$session1->login("sburke", "aoeuaoeu")  # call the 'login' object method
  || die "failed to login!\n";

print "Dir:\n", $session1->dir(), "\n";

$session1->quit;        # same as $session1->quit()
print "Done\n";
exit;
```

Incidentally, I recommend always using the parentheses and -> and avoiding the forms that begin methodname $object or methodname ModuleName. When everything's going right, they all mean the same thing as the -> variants, but the -> is visually more distinct from function calls, as well as immune to some rare but puzzling ambiguities that can arise when you're trying to call methods that have the same name as subroutines you've defined.

Syntax aside, all this talk of constructing objects and object methods begs the question—what *is* an object? There are several angles to this question that the rest of the article will answer in turn: what can you do with objects? What's in an object? What's an object value? And why do some modules use objects at all?

What Can You Do with Objects?

You've seen that you can make objects, and call object methods with them. But what are object methods for? The answer depends on the class. For Net::FTP, an object represents a session between your computer and an FTP server. So the methods you call on a Net::FTP object are for doing whatever you'd need to do across an FTP connection. You make the session and log in:

```
my $session = Net::FTP->new('ftp.aol.com');

die "Couldn't connect!" unless defined $session;
  # The class method call to "new" will return
  # the new object if it goes OK.  Otherwise it
  # will return undef.

$session->login('sburke', 'p@ssw3rD')
  || die "Did I change my password again?";
  # The object method "login" will give a true
  # return value if actually logs in, otherwise
  # it'll return false.
```

You can use the session object to change the directory on that session:

```
$session->cwd("/home/sburke/public_html") || die "That was REALLY supposed to work!";
# if the cwd fails, it'll return false
```

And then get files from the machine at the other end of the session:

```
foreach my $f ('log_report_ua.txt', 'log_report_dom.txt',
               'log_report_browsers.txt') {
    $session->get($f) || warn "Getting $f failed!"
};
```

And plenty more, culminating with closing the connection:

```
$session->quit( );
```

In short, object methods are for doing things related to whatever the object represents. For FTP sessions, they're for sending commands to the server at the other end of the connection, and that's about it—the methods are for doing something to the world outside the object, and the object is just something that specifies what bit of the world (that is, the FTP session) to act upon.

With most other classes, however, the object itself stores some kind of information, and it typically makes no sense to do things with an object without considering the data inside.

What's in an Object?

An object is (with rare exceptions) a data structure containing a bunch of attributes, each of which has a value. Some of the object's attributes are private, meaning you'll never see them documented because they're not for you to read or write. But most of the object's documented attributes are at least readable, and usually writable, by you. Net::FTP objects are a bit thin on attributes, so we'll use objects from the class Business::US_Amort for this example. Business::US_Amort is a very simple class (available from CPAN) that I wrote for making loan calculations (specifically amortization, using U.S.-style algorithms).

An object of the class Business::US_Amort represents a loan with particular attributes. The most basic attributes of a "loan object" are the interest rate, the principal (how much money it's for), and the term (how long it'll take to repay). You need to set these attributes before anything else can be done with the object, and you set them with accessors. An *accessor* is simply a method that accesses an attribute, either retrieving (reading, getting, fetching) or storing (writing, setting, putting). Moreover, accessors are typically the *only* way you can change an object's attributes.

Usually, for simplicity's sake, an accessor is named after the attribute it reads or writes. With Business::US_Amort objects, the accessors you need to use first are principal, interest_rate, and term. With at least those attributes set, you can call the run method to figure out several things about the loan. Then you can call various accessors, like total_paid_toward_interest, to read the results:

```
use Business::US_Amort;
my $loan = Business::US_Amort->new;
# Set the necessary attributes:
$loan->principal(123654);
$loan->interest_rate(9.25);
$loan->term(20); # twenty years

# NOW we know enough to calculate the interest to be paid:
$loan->run;
```

```
print "Total paid toward interest: A WHOPPING ",
    $loan->total_paid_toward_interest, "!!\n";
```

This illustrates a convention common to accessors: reading the value of an attribute by calling an accessor with no arguments (as with $loan->total_paid_interest), and setting the value by providing a value (as with $loan->term(20)). This stands to reason—why would you be providing a value if not to store it?

Although a loan's term, principal, and interest rates are all single numeric values, an object's values can be any kind of scalar, array, or hash. Moreover, an attribute's values can itself be an object. For example, consider the MIDI files I wrote about in TPJ #13. A MIDI file usually consists of several musical tracks, and is complex enough to be an object of its own with attributes like tempo, file-format, and a list of instrument tracks. But tracks themselves are complex enough to be objects too, with attributes like their type, and either a list of MIDI commands or raw data.

I ended up writing the MIDI modules so that the tracks attribute of a MIDI::Opus object is an array of objects from another class: MIDI::Track. This may seem like a runaround—you ask what's in one object, and get *another* object, or several! But in this case, it reflects exactly what the module is for: MIDI files contain MIDI tracks, which themselves contain data.

What Is an Object Value?

When you call a constructor like Net::FTP->new(*hostname*), you store the result in a variable, like $session or $loan. We've been pretending that those *are* the objects you're dealing with. This idea is innocuous up to a point, but it's a misconception.* The reality is that the variables $session and $loan are not objects. It's a little more indirect—they *hold* values that symbolize objects. The kind of value that $session or $loan contains is what I'm calling an *object value*.

To understand what kind of value this is, first think about the other kinds of scalar values you know about: the first two scalar values you encountered in Perl were probably numbers and strings, which you learned (or just assumed) will turn into each other on demand; that is, the three-character string "2.5" can become the quantity two and a half, and vice versa. Then, especially if you started using the -w switch early on, you learned about the *undefined value*, which can turn into 0 if you treat it as a number, or an empty string if you treat it as a string.†

---

* It depends, very presidentially, on what our definitions of "are" are.

† You may *also* have learned about references, in which case you're ready to hear that object values are just a kind of reference, except that they reflect the class that created them in addition to being an array reference, hash reference, or something else. If this makes sense to you, and you want to know more about how objects are implemented in Perl, have a look at the *perltoot* documentation or the sidebar.

The Gory Details

For the sake of clarity, I had to oversimplify some of the facts about objects. Here are a few of the gorier details:

- Every example I gave of a constructor was a class method. But object methods can be constructors, too, if the class was written to work that way: `$new = $old->copy`, `$node_y = $node_x->new_subnode`, or the like.

- I've given the impression that there's two kinds of methods: object methods and class methods. In fact, the same method can be both, because the distinction has to do only with how it parses parameters.

- The term "object value" isn't something you'll find used much anywhere else. It's just my shorthand for what would properly be called an "object reference" or "reference to a blessed item." In fact, people usually say "object" when they properly mean a reference to that object.

- I mentioned creating objects with *con*structors, but I didn't mention destroying them with *de*structors—a destructor is a kind of method that you call to tidy up the object once you're done with it, and want it to neatly go away (close connections, delete temporary files, free up memory, and so on). But because of the way Perl handles memory, most modules don't require destructors.

- I said that class method syntax has to have the class name, as in `$session = `**Net::FTP**`->new($host)`. Actually, you can use any expression that returns a class name: `$ftp_class = 'Net::FTP'; $session = `**$ftp_class**`->new($host)`. Moreover, instead of the method name for object- or class-method calls, you can use a scalar holding the method name: `$foo->`**$method**`($host)`. In practice, these formulations are rarely useful.

Finally, to learn about objects from the perspective of writing your own classes, see the *perltoot* documentation, or Damian Conway's exhaustive, clearly explained book *Object Oriented Perl* (Manning Publications).

And now you're learning about object values. An *object value* is a value that points to a data structure somewhere in memory, where all the attributes for this object are stored. That data structure as a whole belongs to a class (probably the one you named in the constructor method, like `ClassName->new`), so that the object value can be used as part of object method calls.

If you want to actually *see* what an object value is, you might try just saying `print $object`. That'll get you something like this:

```
Net::FTP=GLOB(0x20154240)
```

or

```
Business::US_Amort=HASH(0x15424020)
```

That's not very helpful if you wanted to get at the object's innards, but it happens because the object value is only a symbol for the object. This may all sound very abstruse and metaphysical, so a real-world allegory might be useful.

You get an advertisement in the mail saying that you have been (im)personally selected to have the rare privilege of applying for a credit card. For whatever reason, this offer sounds good to you, so you fill out the form and mail it back to the credit card company. They gleefully approve the application and create your account, and send you a card with a number on it.

Now, you can do things with the number on that card: clerks at stores can ring up things you want to buy, and charge your account by keying in the number on the card. You can pay for things you order online by punching in the card number as part of your online order. You can pay off part of the account by sending the credit card people a check and their pre-printed slip with the card number for the account. And you should be able to call the credit card company's computer and ask it things about the card, like its balance, its credit limit, its APR, and maybe an itemization of recent purchases and payments.

What you're *really* doing is manipulating a credit card *account*, a completely abstract entity with some data attached to it (balance, APR, and so on). But for ease of access, you have a credit card *number*—a symbol representing that account. That symbol is just a bunch of digits, and the number is effectively meaningless and useless in and of itself. But in the appropriate context, it's understood to *mean* your account.

This is exactly the relationship between objects and object values, and from this analogy, several facts about object values are a bit more explicable:

- An object value does nothing in and of itself, but it's useful when you place it in the context of an `$object->method` call, the same way that a card number is useful in the context of some operation dealing with a card account.

  Moreover, several copies of the same object value all refer to the same object, the same way that making several copies of your card number won't change the fact that they all still refer to the same single account (this is true whether you're "copying" the number by just writing it down on different slips of paper, or whether you go to the trouble of forging exact replicas of your own plastic credit card). That's why this:

  ```
  $x = Net::FTP->new("ftp.aol.com");
  $x->login("sburke", "aoeuaoeu");
  ```

  does the same thing as this:

  ```
  $x = Net::FTP->new("ftp.aol.com");
  $y = $x;
  $z = $y;
  $z->login("sburke", "aoeuaoeu");
  ```

  That is, $x and $y and $z are three different *slots* for values, but what's in those slots are all object values pointing to the same object. You don't have three different FTP connections, just three variables with values pointing to the some single FTP connection.

- You can't tell much of anything about the object just by looking at the object value, any more than you can see your credit account balance by holding the plastic card up to the light, or by adding up the digits in your credit card number.

- You can't just make up your own object values and have them work: they can come only from constructor methods of the appropriate class. Similarly, you get a credit card number *only* when a bank approves your application for a credit card account—at which point *they* let *you* know the number of your new card.

There's more to the fact that you can't just make up your own object value. Although you can print an object value and get a string like Net::FTP=GLOB(0x20154240), that string is just a *representation* of an object value.

Internally, an object value has a different type from a string, or a number, or the undefined value: if $x holds a real string, then that value's slot in memory says "This is a string value, and its characters are...". But if it's an object value, the slot in memory says, "This is a reference value, and the location in memory that it points to is...". By looking at what's at that location, Perl can tell what class the object belongs to.

Perl programmers don't have to think about all these details. Many other languages force you to be conscious of the differences between types (and even between types of numbers, which are stored differently depending on their size and whether they have fractional parts). But Perl does its best to hide the different types of scalars from you; it turns numbers into strings and back as needed, and takes the string or number representation of undef or of object values as needed. However, you can't go from a string representation of an object back to the object value. And that's why this doesn't work:

```
$x = Net::FTP->new('ftp.aol.com');
$y = Net::FTP->new('ftp.netcom.com');
$z = Net::FTP->new('ftp.qualcomm.com');

$all = join(' ', $x, $y, $z);

...later...

($aol, $netcom, $qualcomm) = split(' ', $all);

$aol->login("sburke", "aoeuaoeu");
$netcom->login("sburke", "qjkxqjkx");
$qualcomm->login("smb", "dhtndhtn");
```

This fails because $aol ends up holding merely the *string representation* of the object value from $x, not the object value itself. When join tried to join the characters of the "strings" $x, $y, and $z, Perl saw that they weren't strings at all, so it gave join their string representations.

Unfortunately, the distinction between object values and their string representations doesn't really fit into the credit card analogy, because credit card numbers really *are* numbers; even though they don't express any meaningful quantity, if you stored one in a database as a quantity (as opposed to an ASCII string), that wouldn't stop them from being valid as credit card numbers.

This may seem rather academic, but there are two common mistakes programmers new to objects often make, both having to do with the distinction between object values and their string representations.

The first common error involves forgetting (or never having known in the first place) that when you go to use a value as a hash key, Perl uses the string representation of that value. When you want to use the numeric value two and a half as a key, Perl turns it into the three-character string "2.5". But if you then want to use that string as a number, Perl will treat it as meaning two and a half, so you're usually none the wiser that Perl converted the number to a string and back. But recall that Perl can't turn strings back into objects—so if you tried to use a Net::FTP object value as a hash key, Perl would actually use its string representation, like Net::FTP=GLOB(0x20154240). That string is unusable as an object value. (Incidentally, there's a module—Tie::RefHash—supplying hashes that *do* let you use real object-values as keys.)

The second common error programmers make while working with object values is in trying to save an object value to disk (whether printing it to a file, or storing it in a conventional database file). All you'll get is the string, which will be useless.

When you want to save an object and restore it later, you may find that the object's class already provides a method specifically for this situation. For example, MIDI:: Opus provides methods for writing an object to disk as a standard MIDI file. The file can later be read back into memory by a MIDI::Opus constructor method, which returns a new MIDI::Opus object representing whatever file you tell it to read into memory. Similar methods are available with, for example, classes that manipulate graphic images and can save them to files that can be read back later.

But some classes, like Business::US_Amort, don't give you a way to store an object in a file. In that case, you can try using any of the Data::Dumper, Storable, or FreezeThaw modules. These will be worry-free for objects of most classes, but they may run into limitations with others. For example, a Business::US_Amort object can be turned into a string with Data::Dumper, and that string written to a file. When it's restored later, its attributes will be accessible as normal. But in the unlikely case that the loan object was saved in mid-calculation, the calculation may not be resumable. This is because of the way that *particular* class does its calculations, but similar limitations may occur with objects from other classes.

Often, even *wanting* to save an object is basically wrong: what would saving an FTP session mean? Saving the hostname, username, and password? The current directory on both machines? The local TCP/IP port number? In the case of "saving" a Net::FTP object, you're better off just saving whatever details you actually need for your own purposes, so that you can make a new object later and just set those values for it.

So Why Do Some Modules Use Objects?

All these details of using objects are definitely enough to make you wonder—is it worth the bother? If you're a module author, writing your module with an object-oriented interface restricts the audience of potential users to those who understand the basic concepts of objects and object values, as well as Perl's syntax for calling methods. Why complicate things by having an object-oriented interface?

Basically, a module will have an object-oriented interface because its innards are written in an object-oriented style. This article is about the basics of object-oriented *interfaces*, and it's beyond our scope to talk about object-oriented *design*. But the short story is that object-oriented design is just one way of attacking messy problems. It's a way that many programmers find very helpful (and others find to be far more hassle than it's worth), and it just happens to show up for the user as the style of interface.

## CHAPTER 9

Unreal Numbers

Tom Phoenix

God created the integers, all else is the work of man.
—Leopold Kronecker, 1823–1891

Out of a possible 99 points on a professor's final exam, one student, the worst in the class, scored only 47. She marked the student's test 47.4747..., since that's 47/99. Another student got 83 correct, so she wrote 83.8383... at the top. But when she found that one student had gotten all 99 correct, she wrote 99.9999... on the exam. After a moment's reflection, she added, "Although I can find nothing at fault with your answers, somehow you seem to have fallen a little short of perfection!"

A Surprising Program

Consider another scenario. Your manager brings this program to you:

```
#!/usr/bin/perl -w
# See whether Perl can add?

use strict;
my $total = 19.08 + 2.01;
my $expected_total = 21.09;

print "The total is \$$total\n";
print "The expected total is \$$expected_total\n";

if ($total == $expected_total) {
    print "They are equal.\n";
} else {
    print "They aren't equal.\n";
}
```

Because when he ran it, this is what he saw:

```
The total is $21.09
The expected total is $21.09
They aren't equal.
```

Even if you don't see this result on your computer, there is a similar program that demonstrates the same bizarre behavior.

Your manager wants you to stop using Perl, since you're developing a financial application and it looks like Perl has serious bugs in its ability to handle basic arithmetic.

One of your co-workers pops in to say that he can fix that program. In a moment, he's re-coded the comparison to look like the following. "Now it works!" he says. "I use this trick all the time in my scripts." What do you think?

```
# A better way?
if ($total =~ /$expected_total/) {
    print "They are equal.\n";
} else {
    print "They aren't equal.\n";
}
```

This prints:

```
The total is $21.09
The expected total is $21.09
They are equal.
```

What went wrong in the first example? The professor, manager, and co-worker all made the mistake of confusing a *numeral*—a number's representation—with the number itself. In the professor's case, she assumed that the number she was writing as 99.9999... was somehow different than 100. (If you don't believe that 99.9999... is exactly equal to 100, consider that 0.3333... times 3 is 0.9999.... But 0.3333... is one-third, and three times one-third is one. So 0.9999... is the same thing as 1.0 and therefore 99.9999... is 100.)

Unfortunately, your manager *can't* count on Perl to know how to add a few numbers. It's not Perl's fault; this problem affects every computer and every programming language in one way or another. The truth is, whenever you add, subtract, multiply, or divide in Perl, you're not using numbers. You're using numerals, and therein lies the difference.

Remember the number line from grammar school math class? It's infinitely long, and every real number is found somewhere along this line. Stand at the zero position, with one, two, three falling neatly in order on one side, negative one, two, and three on the other. If you look closely, you can see non-integers like 1.5 and two-thirds. π is in there, so is *e*, and one trillion. If you squint, you can see a googol (10^{100}) in the distance, and beyond that a googolplex (10^{googol}). Somewhere near here, still in sight, is the point that represents your age, slipping away so slowly that it takes a whole year to crawl from one integer to the next. For most of us nonmathematicians, these are all the numbers we'll ever need or want. These are the numbers that most people mean when they think of arithmetic. But what we actually use for arithmetic on a computer is a numeral, which isn't always the same.

A numeral is merely a representation of a number. Hardly anybody makes this distinction between "number" and "numeral" in casual usage, or even in documentation. I certainly don't, and I don't expect anyone else to do so.

Of course, we all work with common numbers like 29, 19.95, and –40, and even less common ones like 5.004, 6.022 × 10²³, and 98.6. But few of us work with π itself, for example. Instead, we call upon one of its close friends, like 3.14159, knowing (or forgetting) that we are missing the mark by a tiny bit. (Not that it usually matters in everyday life. If you used that value in place of π to calculate how long a string you'd need to encircle the moon's equator, you'd be off by just a few meters—and your error would likely be dwarfed by the fact that the moon isn't perfectly round.) Similarly, when we work with the number two-thirds, we are usually satisfied with 0.66667 or so; with many numbers like the 6.022 × 10²³ I mentioned earlier, we intentionally retain only a few significant digits because that's all we need or know.

These numerals don't behave the same as the numbers they represent. For instance, if you triple 0.66667, you get 2.00001. That's not two, even though the professor's students might disagree.

Computers work with different numerals, but in a similar way. If we want to store the number 7 exactly in a computer's memory, that's not hard to do. But most real numbers need to be stored as an approximation, and this affects the accuracy of our results.

How accurate is Perl? That depends upon your machine, and how your C compiler implements double precision numbers. But that should be enough accuracy for all everyday applications. If you need more accuracy than Perl provides by default, check out the Math::BigFloat module.

Although your computer may store numerals differently than mine, virtually all modern computers use the same technique. They convert the number to an internal binary form that is more easily manipulated than our familiar decimal notation. And, in the same way that we round off two-thirds to 0.66667 or so, the computer has to round off numbers like three-tenths.

At first glance, this may seem surprising. A simple number like 0.3 shouldn't need to be rounded, should it? But even though 0.3 seems simple in our familiar decimal notation, it's not so simple in binary. In binary, the first digit after the decimal point (the phrase "binary point" is more accurate, but we'll let it slide) is not the "tenths place," but the "halves place." The next bit is the "fourths," and the third is the "eighths." The binary form of 0.3 is 0.010011001100110011...—an infinitely repeating sequence. And in much the same way that the decimal 0.66666... is normally rounded off for convenience, the value for 0.3 is rounded off inside the computer. Can a program be made to work with endlessly-repeating numbers without rounding them off? Yes, but it would be slower, take more memory, or both. (Note that you can use the `bigrat.pl` library file bundled with Perl to perform arithmetic with fractions.)

The problem isn't that our computers use binary, but that they use only a small number of bits to represent numbers. That means that some numbers have to be represented imprecisely—and some of those numbers surprise us because they happen to have concise representations in base 10.

So, what are you going to tell your manager? Now that you've seen that this sort of thing affects all of the ways in which you do arithmetic, you can point out that this isn't the fault of Perl; a similar program can be written in C or Fortran or Pascal, or any other language for that matter. And a similar confusion even happens to human beings, as the professor's class learned. It's a fundamental consequence of performing arithmetic with numerals.

But Perl uses another kind of numeral as well, and that's what your co-worker was using with his regex test. In most computer languages, there is a strong distinction between numbers (actually, numerals) and strings. But they're used interchangeably in Perl, with conversions triggered automatically as needed. That is, Perl will convert the string "10" to the number ten (or, at least, its numeral) and back again as needed. (Worried about efficiency? Don't be. When Perl performs the conversion, it saves the result, so the computation is only performed once.) So, with Perl, you now have numbers, computer numerals (used internally), and numbers-as-strings. Converting from a number-as-string to Perl's internal format (and back) isn't always precise.

For the co-worker's regular expression, Perl implicitly converted both numbers to their string forms.

```
$total =~ /$expected_total/
# Both are used as strings
```

Then, Perl interpreted $expected_total as a regular expression. Eek!

```
$total =~ /21.09/
```

If you know regular expressions, you'll see why this matches the string form of $total, which is 21.09. Unfortunately, it will also match some erroneous values, like 121.093, 21309, and 21a09. This solution is the scariest kind of programming: completely superficial, and implemented without understanding of where it will go wrong.

But your co-worker's flawed approach could lead to one possible solution. When Perl converts a numeral to a string, it naturally rounds the value a little. (If you wish to control exactly how your numbers are converted to strings, use the builtin sprintf function.) You could use this to our advantage, and create something like this:

```
# string comparison
if ($total eq $expected_total) { ... }
```

This way, Perl converts both numbers to strings, then checks whether they're identical. Unfortunately, this is a relatively slow computation. Worse, it assumes that you want to call two numbers the same if they both turn into the same string on the current machine, which may use a different numeral-to-string conversion than other machines. Not very portable, and therefore not very reliable.

If you need to compare two numbers in a "fuzzy" way, in which small differences are allowed, here is one way to do that.

```
if ( $total > $expected_total - 0.0000001 and
     $total < $expected_total + 0.0000001 ) {
    ...
}
```

This makes it clear just how fuzzy the comparison can be. But you can use a little math to simplify this.

```
if (abs($total - $expected_total) < 0.0000001) { ... }
```

In this case, you're seeing just how different these numbers are, and requiring that the absolute difference be less than a certain amount. This allowed difference traditionally goes by the name *epsilon*, so you might see that name used in snippets like the following:

```
# Defined once at top of script
use constant EPSILON => 1e-7;

if (abs($total - $expected_total) < EPSILON) { ... }
```

If the use constant pragma doesn't work, you're using a version of Perl prior to 5.004, and should upgrade.

To be sure, it's more acceptable to define epsilon in a way that takes into account the scale of the numbers being compared. And you may want to put the comparison into a subroutine, like this:

```
sub close_enough ($$) {
    my ($expected, $actual) = @_;
    if ($expected) { # allow for 0
        abs( ($actual-$expected) / $expected ) < EPSILON;
    } else {
        abs($actual) < EPSILON;
    }
}

if (close_enough($expected_total, $total)) { ... }
```

Note that the order of parameters is important, since now epsilon is used as a fraction of the expected value; this is actually a different comparison rule than the one used before. (The ($$) in the first line of close_enough is a *prototype*. This one means that the subroutine expects two arguments, both scalars. More information about prototypes is available in the perlsub documentation and the next article, *CryptoContext*.)

The Right Way

But there's actually a better way to implement financial applications like the one shown at the beginning of this article. Don't be misled by the decimal point: an amount of money like $21.09 is actually an integral number of pennies. If you do the calculations with exact integers, putting in the decimal point only at output, you'll win, because integers are more accurately represented than real numbers.

In the program below, the line $num = sprintf "%03d", $num makes the integer $num into a string with at least three digits. Leading zeroes are added as needed, so 2001 becomes 2001, 20 becomes 020, and 2 becomes 002. That way, we can add a decimal point to get 0.02.

```
#!/usr/bin/perl -w
# A better way to work with financial values

use strict;
sub money ($) {

    # Given a non-negative integer number of pennies,
    # returns that figure as a dollars-and-cents
    # amount, like '$12345.67'.

    # Assign the first (and only) argument to $num
    my $num = shift;
    warn "Bad amount of money: $num" if $num < 0;

    # Make $num into a string
    $num = sprintf "%03d", $num;
    substr($num, -2, 0) = "."; # add the decimal point
    return '$' . $num;
}

my $total = 1908 + 201; # integers now
my $expected_total = 2109;

print "The total is ", money($total), "\n";
print "The expected total is ", money($expected_total), "\n";

# Comparing numbers of pennies
if ($total == $expected_total) {
    print "They are equal.\n";
} else {
    print "They aren't equal.\n";
}
```

Armed with this knowledge, you should find it easier to get the answers that you expect from your Perl programs.

## CHAPTER 10

CryptoContext

Nathan Torkington

Perl is a language of acceptable subsets. Larry Wall has said many times that it's okay not to know everything. If you know enough to get the job done, then obviously you know all you need.

The more you know about Perl, though, and the more of its features you use, the more you must understand how they work. When you put features together, they can often interact in surprising ways. This article explores the interaction between context, prototyping, and subroutine calls.

Tom Christiansen has long been in favor of reducing these interactions, namely by dropping context. In fact, he goes so far as to call it *cryptocontext*, and he came up with the challenge that prompted this article. Given these initial statements:

```
sub f($$);

@a = (5, 9);
```

Explain what each of these does, and why:

```
&f;
&f();
f();
f;
f(@a);
f(@a[0,1]);
f(@a, @a);
&f(@a);
&f(@a,@a);
f(`ls /bin`, `ls /tmp`);
&f(`ls /bin`, `ls /tmp`);
```

Frightened that these may not do the obvious? Read on, and I'll explain what happens.

Context

Context is one of the gnarlier parts of Perl. While Tom is obviously anti-context, Larry Wall is a proponent of it (as he should be, since he put it into Perl in the first place). Larry is a linguist, and he tried to incorporate some of the features of success-ful natural languages in the hopes of making Perl a successful unnatural language. Context was one of those features.

When compiling and running your program, the Perl interpreter associates a context with every expression. There are two main contexts: scalar and list, and this article focuses on the difference between them.

You've probably already seen the effects of context in Perl operators like backticks (e.g. `ls`) and in angle brackets (e.g., <STDIN>).

```
@list_context   = `ls`;

$scalar_context = `ls`;
```

@list_context now holds the output of ls, one line per list element. $scalar_context has the output of ls as one big string, with embedded newlines. The backticks know what to return (one big string of many lines, or many one-line strings) because of their context.

You also see context in other situations:

```
if (@array) {
    # the array is not empty
}
```

The if statement needs to test the truth of @array, and so evaluates it in a scalar con-text. It just so happens that an array in scalar context evaluates to the number of ele-ments in the array. That's why the following two lines set $count to 4:

```
@array = ('a', 'b', 'c');
$count = @array + 1;
```

This is where the distinction between arrays and lists becomes important. Lists don't behave the same way:

```
$count = (5, 7, 9) + 1;
```

This sets $count to 10. A list in scalar context evaluates to the value of the last ele-ment (9, in this case).

You see why context is confusing. Let's stop talking context and look at prototypes.

Prototypes

Version 5.003 of Perl added support for prototypes. They let you tell Perl what type of arguments your subroutines expect; Perl can then do some elementary type-check-ing and optimizations with that information.

A prototyped subroutine looks like this:

```
sub add_two ($$) {
    return $_[0] + $_[1];
}
```

The ($$) is the prototype. It's a shorthand to identify the types of the arguments that will be passed to your subroutine. In this case, Perl is told to expect two scalars.

You can also prototype your subroutines without defining them:

```
sub add_two ($$);          # add_two will be fully declared later
```

If you then try to call your subroutine without two arguments that can be evaluated as scalars, the compiler will complain. (However, almost everything can be coerced to a scalar. Scalar prototypes accept @arrays and %hashes without warning!)

All prototype checking is performed during compilation—before your program is run. This means that the prototype-checking stage of the compiler is necessarily limited in what it can deduce. In particular, you can't build up an array of arguments and pass the array to a subroutine prototyped to take many scalars:

```
sub complain_about ($$$$);

@args = ( 0, 1, 2, 3 );

complain_about(@args);          # WRONG
```

The compiler can't know how big @args is when complain_about is called, since that can only be known once your program is running. (Sure, @args was just assigned to, but the compiler only built the internal instructions to make that assignment—it hasn't actually created the array in memory.) That won't happen until your program runs, so the compiler sees an array where it was expecting four scalars, and complains.

This behavior can sometimes be annoying, so Perl provides a way to bypass prototype checking in the syntax for subroutine calls.

Subroutine Calls

You can turn off the prototype checking by using an &:

```
&complain_about(@args);     # ALLOWED
```

& is also used for another shortcut. If you call a subroutine with & and give it no argument list, Perl will use the current @_ as the subroutine's argument list.

```
@_ = ( 4, 6, 8 );

sub count_args {
    return scalar(@_);
}

$two   = count_args(3,5);
$two   = &count_args(3,5);
$zero  = &count_args();
$three = &count_args;
```

The first two calls to count_args below are identical. If count_args had been prototyped, they'd be different, but since they aren't, the & is redundant.

The third example, $zero = &count_args( ), also bypasses the nonexistent prototype and calls count_args with no arguments. The fourth example shows how the @_ of the caller (that is, (4, 6, 8)) becomes the @_ (the argument list) of the subroutine. It's the same @_, not a copy.

Putting Them All Together

Here's the crux of the interaction: when a subroutine is prototyped (and isn't being bypassed with &), the prototype specifies the context for evaluating arguments.

Let's revisit the examples at the beginning of the article. First, the prelude:

```
sub f($$);

@a = (5, 9);
```

Now let's consider Tom's subroutine calls one by one and see what happens to each of them.

```
&f;
```

The & bypasses subroutine prototypes, so the compiler won't complain about the subroutine call not matching its prototype. The call also has no argument list, so f is called with its caller's @_.

```
&f( );
```

f is called with an empty argument list. The compiler won't complain because, again, the & causes the subroutine prototypes to be bypassed.

```
f( );
```

No & means that the compiler will check subroutine calls against its prototype, and when it sees that f is being called with an empty argument list but was prototyped to take two scalars, it will complain. In short, it won't compile.

```
f;
```

This is the same as above. The only difference between f( ) and f is that use strict prevents f from compiling.

```
f(@a);
```

No & means subroutine prototypes are being checked. The single array argument doesn't match the two scalar arguments in the prototype, so the compiler will complain and stop the program.

```
f(@a[0,1]);
```

This also won't compile. Although we're taking a two-element slice from the array, the compiler sees the array slice and not two scalars. If this seems a little odd, consider that we could have had @a[$b..$c], the size of which can't be known until runtime.

```
f(@a, @a);
```

Alarmingly, this does compile. The compiler knows from the prototype that f takes two scalars. An array can be evaluated in scalar context, so this call is equivalent to f(2, 2) because @a in scalar context evaluates to 2. Surprised?

```
&f(@a);
```

This also compiles. The & disables prototype checking, so @a becomes the @_ of the subroutine. This is equivalent to f(5,9).

```
&f(@a,@a);
```

This is equivalent to f(5,9,5,9). The & turns off prototype checking, and so the list (@a,@a) is flattened to (5,9,5,9).

```
f(`ls /bin`, `ls /tmp`);
```

This compiles, and calls f with two long strings. Each string is the complete output of an ls command, embedded newlines and all. The prototype tells the compiler to evaluate the arguments in scalar context, so each pair of backticks results in one long string.

```
&f(`ls /bin`, `ls /tmp`);
```

By turning off prototype checking with &, we prevent f's arguments being evaluated in scalar context. The subroutine call provides a list context to its arguments, which means the backticks yield many strings. Right now, on my system, this is equivalent to calling f with about seventy arguments.

Conclusion

There are two lessons to learn from this (besides "anything can be made hard if you think about it long enough").

Context Is Subtle

If you're having trouble with subroutine calls, and you're using prototypes, look at how the compiler is behaving as a result of the prototypes. Perhaps context is causing your problems.

Prototypes Are a Mixed Blessing

In some relatively straightforward situations, prototypes are a useful way to catch incorrect subroutine calls. In other situations, though, they may cause problems. You should probably use them only to mimic the behavior of built-in functions like push and splice.

CHAPTER 11

References

Mark Jason Dominus

One of the most important new features in Perl 5 was the capability to manage complicated data structures like multidimensional arrays and nested hashes. To enable these, Perl 5 introduced a feature called *references*, and using references is the key to managing complicated, structured data in Perl. Unfortunately, there's a lot of funny syntax to learn, and the manual is not as clear in this area as it usually is. The manual is quite complete, and a lot of people find that a problem, because it can be hard to tell what is important and what isn't.

Fortunately, you only need to know 10% of what's in the manual to get 90% of the benefit. This article is going to show you that 10%.

Who Needs Complicated Data Structures?

One problem that came up all the time in Perl 4 was how to represent a hash with values that were lists. Perl 4 had hashes, of course, but the values had to be scalars; they couldn't be lists.

Why would you want a hash of lists? As a simple example, suppose you have a file of city and state names, like this:

```
Chicago, Illinois
New York, New York
Albany, New York
Springfield, Illinois
Trenton, New Jersey
Evanston, Illinois
```

You want to produce an output like this, with each state mentioned once, and then an alphabetical list of the cities in that state:

```
Illinois:  Chicago, Evanston, Springfield.
New Jersey: Trenton
New York: Albany, New York.
```

The natural way to do this is using a hash with keys that are state names. Associated with each state name is a list of the cities in that state. Whenever you read a line of input, you split it into a state and a city, look up the list of cities already known to be in that state, and append the new city to the list. When you're done reading the input, you can iterate over the hash with keys or each, sorting each list of cities before you print it out.

If hash values can't be lists, you lose. In Perl 4, hash values can't be lists; they can only be numbers or strings. You lose. You'd probably have to combine all the cities into a single string somehow, and when the time came to write the output, you'd have to break the string into a list, sort the list, and turn it back into a string. This is messy and error-prone. And it's frustrating, because Perl already has perfectly good lists that would solve the problem—if only you could use them.

The Solution

Unfortunately, by the time Perl 5 rolled around, you were already stuck with this design: hash values must be scalars. The solution is references.

A reference is a scalar value that *refers to* an entire array or an entire hash (or just about anything else). You're already familiar with English names, which are a kind of reference. Think of the President: a messy, inconvenient bag of blood and bones. But to talk about him, or to represent him in a computer program, all you need is the easy, convenient scalar string "Bill Clinton".

References in Perl are like names for arrays and hashes. They're Perl's private, internal names, so you can be sure they're unambiguous. Unlike common names such as "Bill Clinton", a reference always refers to only one thing, and you always know what it refers to. If you have a reference to an array, you can recover the entire array from it. If you have a reference to a hash, you can recover the entire hash. But the reference is still an easy, compact scalar value.

You can't have a hash with values that are arrays; hash values can only be scalars. You're stuck with that. But a single reference can refer to an entire array, and references are scalars; so you can have a hash of references to arrays, and it'll act a lot like a hash of arrays; and, it'll be just as useful as a hash of arrays.

I'll come back to this city-state problem later, after you've seen some syntax for managing references. There are only two ways to make a reference, and only two ways to use it once you do.

Making References

Make Rule 1. If you put a \ in front of a variable, you get a reference to that variable.

```
$aref = \@array;        # $aref now holds a reference to @array
$href = \%hash;         # $href now holds a reference to %hash
```

Once the reference is stored in a variable such as $aref or $href, you can copy it or store it like any other scalar value:

```
$xy = $aref;          # $xy now holds a reference to @array
$p[3] = $href;        # $p[3] now holds a reference to %hash
$z = $p[3];           # $z now holds a reference to %hash
```

These examples show how to make references to variables with names. Sometimes you want to make an array or a hash that doesn't have a name. This is analogous to the way you like to be able to print the string "\n" or the number 80 without having to store it in a variable first.

Make Rule 2. [*ITEMS*] makes a new, anonymous array, and returns a reference to that array. { *ITEMS* } makes a new, anonymous hash, and returns a reference to that hash. Remember: square brackets are for arrays, curly brackets for hashes. The kind of bracket you use is the same as you'd use if you were subscripting the object.

```
$aref = [ 1, "foo", undef, 13 ];
# $aref now holds a reference to an array

$href = { APR => 4, AUG => 8 };
# $href now holds a reference to a hash
```

The references you get from Rule 2 are the same kind of references that you get from Rule 1:

```
$aref = [ 1, 2, 3 ];

@array = (1, 2, 3);
$aref = \@array;
```

The first line is an abbreviation for the following two lines, except that it doesn't create the superfluous array variable @array.

Using References

What can you do with a reference once you have it? It's a scalar value, and you've seen that you can store it as a scalar and get it back again just like any scalar. There are just two more ways to use it.

Use Rule 1. If $aref contains a reference to an array, then you can put {$aref} anywhere you would normally put the name of an array. For example, you can use @{$aref} instead of @array.

Some examples are shown in Table 11-1. Two expressions that do the same thing are on each line. The left-hand versions operate on the array @a, and the right-hand versions operate on the array that is referred to by $aref, but once they find the array they're operating on, they do the same things to the arrays.

Table 11-1. Using array references

	Array	Array reference
An array	@a	@{$aref}
Reverse the array	reverse @a	reverse @{$aref}
An element of the array	$a[3]	${$aref}[3]
Assigning an element	$a[3] = 17	${$aref}[3] = 17

Using a hash reference is *exactly* the same, as shown in Table 11-2.

Table 11-2. Using hash references

	Hash	Hash reference
A hash	%h	%{$href}
Get the keys from the hash	keys %h	keys %{$href}
An element of the hash	$h{'red'}	${$href}{'red'}
Assigning an element	$h{'red'} = 17	${$href}{'red'} = 17

Most often when you have an array or a hash, you want to set or get a single element from it. ${$aref}[3] and ${$href}{'red'} have too much punctuation, so Perl lets you abbreviate.

Use Rule 2. ${$aref}[3] is too hard to read, so you can write $aref->[3] instead. ${$href}{red} is also too hard to read, so you can write $href->{red} instead.

If $aref holds a reference to an array, then $aref->[3] is the fourth element of the array. Don't confuse this with $aref[3], which is the fourth element of a totally different array, deceptively named @aref. $aref and @aref are unrelated.

Similarly, $href->{red} is part of the hash referred to by the scalar variable $href, perhaps even one with no name. $href{red} is part of the deceptively named %href hash. It's easy to forget to put in the ->, and if you do forget, you'll get bizarre results when your program gets array and hash elements from arrays and hashes that weren't the ones you wanted to use. The -w switch and strict pragma find these errors for you.

An Example

Let's see a quick example of how all this is useful.

First, remember that [1, 2, 3] makes an anonymous array containing (1, 2, 3), and gives you a reference to that array.

Now think about this array:

```
@a = ( [1, 2, 3],
       [4, 5, 6],
       [7, 8, 9] );
```

@a is an array with three elements, and each one is a reference to another array.

$a[1] is one of these references. It refers to an array, the array containing (4, 5, 6), and because it is a reference to an array, Use Rule 2 says that you can write $a[1]->[2] to get the third element from that array. $a[1]->[2] is 6. Similarly, $a[0]->[1] is 2. What you have here is like a two-dimensional array; you can write $a[*ROW*]->[*COLUMN*] to set or get the element in any row and column of the array.

The notation still looks a little cumbersome, so there's one more abbreviation.

The Arrow Rule. Between two subscripts, the arrow is optional.

Instead of $a[1]->[2], you can write $a[1][2]; it means the same thing. Instead of $a[0]->[1], you can write $a[0][1]; it means the same thing.

Now it really looks like a two-dimensional array!

You can see why the arrows are important. Without them, you would have had to write ${$a[1]}[2] instead of $a[1][2]. For three-dimensional arrays, they let you write $x[2][3][5] instead of the unreadable ${${$x[2]}[3]}[5].

Solution

Here's the answer to the problem posed at the beginning of the article:

```
1       while (<>) {
2           chomp;
3           my ($city, $state) = split /, /;
4           push @{$table{$state}}, $city;
5       }
6
7       foreach $state (sort keys %table) {
8           print "$state: ";
9           my @cities = @{$table{$state}};
10          print join ', ', sort @cities;
11          print ".\n";
12      }
```

The program has two pieces: lines 1–5 read the input and build a data structure, and lines 7–12 analyze the data and print out the report.

In the first piece, line 4 is the important one. You're going to have a hash, %table, with keys that are state names, and with values that are (references to) arrays of city names. After acquiring a city and state name, the program looks up $table{$state}, which holds (a reference to) the list of cities seen in that state so far. Line 4 is totally analogous to:

```
    push @array, $city;
```

except that array has been replaced by {$table{$state}}. The push adds a city name to the end of the array that is referred to.

In the second part, line 9 is the important one. Again, `$table{$state}` is (a reference to) the list of cities in the state, so you can recover the original list and copy it into the array `@cities` using `@{$table{$state}}`. Line 9 is analogous to:

```
@cities = @array;
```

except that the name `array` has been replaced by `{$table{$state}}`. The `@` tells Perl to get the entire array.

The rest of the program is just familiar uses of `chomp`, `split`, `sort`, and `print`, and doesn't involve references at all.

There's one fine point I skipped. Suppose the program has just read the first line in its input that mentions the state of Ohio. It's on line 4: `$state` is `Ohio`, and `$city` is `Cleveland`. Since this is the first city in Ohio, `$table{$state}` is undefined—in fact, there isn't an `Ohio` key in `%table` at all. What does line 4 do here?

```
4        push @{$table{$state}}, $city;
```

This is Perl, so it does exactly the right thing. It sees that you want to push `Cleveland` onto an array that doesn't exist, so it helpfully makes a new, empty, anonymous array for you, installs it in the table, and then pushes `Cleveland` onto it.

The Rest

I promised to give you 90% of the benefit with 10% of the details, and that means I left out 90% of the details. Now that you have an overview of the important parts, it should be easier to read the *perlref* documentation bundled with Perl, which discusses 100% of the details.

Some highlights of *perlref*:

- You can make references to anything, including scalars, functions, and other references.

- In Use Rule 1, you may omit the curly braces if the reference expression is a simple scalar variable. For example, `@$aref` is the same as `@{$aref}`, and `$$aref[1]` is the same as `${$aref}[1]` (and the same as `$aref->[1]`).

- To see if a variable contains a reference, use the `ref` function. It returns true if its argument is a reference. Actually, it's a little better than that: It returns `HASH` for hash references and `ARRAY` for array references.

- If you try to use a reference like a string, you get strings like `ARRAY(0x80f5dec)` or `HASH(0x826afc0)`. If you ever see a string that looks like this, you'll know you printed a reference by mistake.

  A side effect of this representation is that you can use `eq` to see if two references refer to the same thing. (You can also do that with `==`, which is faster.)

- You can use a string as a kind of reference. If you use the string `foo` as an array reference, it's taken to be a reference to `@foo`. This is called a *soft reference* or *symbolic reference*.

You might prefer to go on to the *perllol* documentation instead of *perlref*; *perllol* discusses lists of lists and multidimensional arrays in detail. After that, you should move on to *perldsc*, which is a Data Structure Cookbook that shows recipes for using and printing out arrays of hashes, hashes of arrays, and other kinds of data.

In Summary

Everyone needs compound data structures, and the way you get them in Perl is with references. There are four important rules for managing references, two for making references, and two for using them. Once you know these rules, you can do most of the important things you need to do with references.

## CHAPTER 12

Perl Heresies

Jon Drukman

Perl has a lot of slogans. Probably the most popular is "There's More than One Way To Do It" (TMTOWTDI). However, some ways of doing things are frowned upon in the Perl community. In this article, I present four heresies for those pariahs who dare to go against the establishment.

I have two reasons for disliking the Perl Orthodoxy. First, it discourages the idea that if you know enough Perl to get your job done, then you know enough Perl. Second, programming is an artistic as well as a technical discipline, so just as "wrong notes" can make a good piece of music better, programmers should be free to use these forbidden constructs if it makes their programs more aesthetically pleasing. However, this comes with a caveat: as with music, if you don't know *why* you're breaking the rules, you probably shouldn't be.

Don't Use -w

According to my reading of the 5.004 source, Perl has around sixty optional warnings. If you are a moderately skilled Perl programmer, you will see only one or two of them on a regular basis.

I rarely use -w. For whatever reason, the kind of mistakes I make are not ones that it catches. The most frequent appearance of -w warnings in my programs is due to DBI queries that return rows with empty columns. Since there's no way to predict in advance which columns will be empty, I get a slew of Use of uninitialized value at line ... messages.

Because -w generates its warnings based on conditions that change at runtime, it makes the behavior of your programs unpredictable. If your program is sending data to something that merges STDOUT and STDERR (such as a web server), this unpredictability could spell death. If you're doing something interactively, a user unfamiliar with Perl might be unnecessarily alarmed by its warning messages. In these situations, I recommend developing with -w and then removing it for production use. Sometimes it's nice to have Perl hold your hand, but sometimes it's impractical.

Don't forget that warnings can be turned on and off within a program:

```
with no -w, code here will run without warnings ...
{
  local $^W=1;

  ... code here will run with warnings ...
}
```

After the curly-brace-delimited block, $^W reverts to its previous value, and warnings are no longer on.

Don't Use Regular Expressions Just Because They're Cool

Regular expressions are an extremely powerful tool. They can also quickly become difficult to decipher and maintain. Perl has a rich palette of string-handling functions, many of which don't involve regular expressions. One of my favorite techniques is using substr as an lvalue. To change the first three characters on a line, you could do this:

```
$string =~ s/^.../abc/;
```

or you could say:

```
substr($string,0,3) = 'abc';
```

The second one is a few characters longer, but to me the meaning leaps off the screen. Unfortunately, clarity sometimes comes at the cost of speed. I benchmarked this script:

```
use Benchmark;

$string = 'mary had a little lamb.';

timethese (800000, {
  regex  => sub { $string =~ s/^.../abc/;        },
  substr => sub { substr($string,0,3) = 'abc'; }
});
```

However, the results were inconclusive. On my FreeBSD box, substr had the slight edge. On a Sun Ultra Enterprise 450, the regex was a tad faster. Try it yourself and see.

Don't Always Use Modules

Modules are great—they save time and prevent you from making common mistakes. However, they also create dependencies, add to loading time, and sometimes keep you from exploring a subject on your own. One of the first medium-size programs I ever wrote (in BASIC/PLUS on a PDP-11) was a mail program. Of course, I didn't write the world's best mailer right out of the gate, but it did work and I learned a lot in the process. I sometimes feel that Perl's module-oriented culture prevents people from exploring for the sake of knowledge. True, if you're programming on someone else's dime you owe it to them to do the job efficiently, but if you're just messing around, "reinventing the wheel" can be rewarding.

For instance, the sixth field of localtime contains the current day of the week. If you know this basic fact, you can do a number of useful calculations with simple arithmetic. What day of the week was yesterday? The answer is:

```
$yesterday_day = (localtime(time-86400))[6];
```

This returns a number in the range 0–6, with 0 denoting Sunday. One line of code, using one built-in Perl function.

Compare that to the Date::Manip module, weighing in at 5,790 lines as of this writing. Even the author admits there are many situations in which Date::Manip is not practical. On the other hand, if you are trying to handle dates in the form "1st Thursday in June 1992", you're better off using Date::Manip rather than writing your own parser from scratch.

You might want to avoid modules just to get a little practice. HTML::Parser can handle a wide range of possibilities, but if your HTML is machine-generated, you may not need all of its power. At work, if I want to build up concordance of title tags, I can rely on the regular expression <TITLE>(.*?)</TITLE> to get the job done. Most of the time, I prefer to handle our files by creating regular expressions—since regexes are such a powerful tool, I like to get as much practice with them as possible.

This leads us to a mini-heresy.

Partial Solutions Are Okay

You don't always have to create a generic solution that will solve every possible case. This is more about software design than Perl, but as Perl lends itself to rapid application development so well, there's no reason to fear the *rapid* part. For one thing, you'll undoubtedly discover new and better ways to solve the problem as you gain experience, and trying to rewrite a huge program that has a fundamental design flaw is harder than expanding a simple program that only requires a few tweaks.

Also, partial solutions can sometimes help you avoid difficult tasks. Consider the ever-popular task of validating an email address. While it's impossible to make sure the sender is an honest-to-goodness human, it's often easy to determine if a given address is syntactically invalid. For example, the address jsd@.bud.com (note the extraneous period) is obviously undeliverable, and this is easy to verify with a specific regular expression. We can avoid the need for a complete solution with an instantaneous partial solution that catches a lot of simple typing errors.

PART II

Regular Expressions

Perl lets you search huge collections of data with its built-in support for pattern-matching. To match a pattern, you create a *regular expression*, and test whether a string contains the pattern with the =~ and !~ operators, like so:

```
print "Match!" if $greeting =~ /Hello/;
```

If $greeting contains the five-character sequence Hello, this code snippet prints Match!.

Regular expressions constitute a little language inside Perl, with their own peculiar syntax inherited from history. From a computer scientist's point of view, Perl's regular expressions aren't even regular; features like \1 and \2, which allow you to refer to portions of already-matched text inside a pattern, aren't permitted in "traditional" regular expressions.

This section won't give you a tour of all of Perl's regular expression metacharacters and assertions. For that, consult the perlre online documentation, or another Perl book. Instead, the five chapters here help you understand how Perl's regular expressions work under the hood.

Four of the five articles are written by the world's foremost regex guru: Jeffrey Friedl, author of O'Reilly's *Mastering Regular Expressions*. His often-cited article *Understanding Regular Expressions, Part I* explains *backtracking*, one of the key concepts in regular expressions that cleanly separates the beginners from experts. In *Understanding Regular Expressions, Part II*, Jeffrey takes a simple problem—matching two substrings without regard to ordering—and shows you ten different solutions, explaining which is best and why, so that you can apply the reasoning to other problems. *Understanding Regular Expressions, Part III* dives more deeply into backtracking and the behavior of greedy quantifiers. ("Greediness" refers to the behavior of * and +, which match as much text as they can; for instance, a+ means "match one or more as, as many as possible.) In *Nibbling Strings*, he demonstrates a powerful technique for speeding up huge regular expression matches that he's put into practice at Yahoo!. Every time you see a Yahoo! article mentioning a publicly traded company, you see a link to the company's stock information; that link is provided by the code Jeffrey shows you in the article.

The fifth article, *How Regexes Work*, is a more theoretical piece by Mark Jason Dominus showing you how to build your own regular expression engine. There's little reason to do that when you have Perl, of course, but his explanation of the processes involve will help you to understand why Perl's regular expression engine behaves the way it does. The theoretically-minded may wish to read Mark Jason's chapter immediately after *Understanding Regular Expressions, Part I*. The practically-minded should read them in the order presented.

## CHAPTER 13

Understanding Regular Expressions, Part I

Jeffrey Friedl

I'd like to tell you a story about a friend of mine, Fred. Because of the nature of the story, I talk a lot about Perl regular expressions and how they work behind the scenes. I assume you know Perl at least as well as Fred. That's not saying a great deal, since he doesn't know it all that well, although he thinks he does.

Regular expressions need not be difficult, and need not be a mystery. Frankly, if you put aside all the theoretical mumbo-jumbo and look from a practical point of view *how* the Perl regular-expression engine works, then you too can think along those lines and *know* how an expression will act in any given situation.

So, I believe that with a bit of explanation and a healthy dose of experience, you'll become an undaunted expert. This story covers the whole range, from the Fred level all the way up to the expert level.

Note that the approach I take for explaining regular expressions is perhaps quite different than what you or Fred have seen before. The story approaches Perl regular expressions "from the back." Documentation tends to provide a raw "these metacharacters do such-and-such" table along with a few examples. Rather than rehashing that old story, I'll present the regular-expression engine's point of view, showing what it actually *does* when attempting a match. Eventually, we will work our way "to the front" to see what relation these workings have to the metacharacters you feed it. It's a longer path to get there, but the added understanding will usually make the difference between hoping an expression will work, and knowing it will.

This is a long story, and because of the "from the back" approach, you might not always see where I'm heading or the relevance of what I discuss. But as I said, eventually we will indeed work our way to the front, and things should suddenly become much clearer when you start to compare what I've written with the experience and knowledge you already have.

So, if you feel daunted at all—anything less than utmost confidence around even the most hairy regular expression—it is my hope you will get something real, tangible, and useful out of this story. Hey, even Fred did!

Before starting with the story, I'd like to comment on a few of the ways "regular expression" is abbreviated. I use "regex." An alternate spelling, "regexp," also seems somewhat popular although I can't quite comprehend why; it's difficult to pronounce and to pluralize. "Regex" just rolls right off the tongue.

The Story of Fred

Fred was a happy programmer. Like with so many projects before, Fred needed to verify some data, but this time the data was pretty simple—just numbers and colons. The (small) catch was that the colons must come in pairs, with no singletons allowed.

Sounds like a regular-expression match is just the hammer for this nail, and that's exactly what Fred used.

Fred wants to match the line exactly (/^...$/), allowing a bunch of digits (/[0-9]+/) or pairs of colons (/::/) as many times as happen to be there (/(...)*/). Putting it all together, Fred gets /^([0-9]+|::)*$/.

That was pretty easy, even for Fred. Testing it quickly, he dumps some sample data:

```
::1234::5678901234567890::::1234567890::888
```

into a file named *data* and tests it:

```
% perl -ne 'die "bad data" unless m/^([0-9]+|::)*$/' data
```

Fred realizes that with this test, no news is good news.

Heck, as an aside, Fred even noticed that this task is so simple that he can use the exact same regex to test it with egrep or awk (two tools, he knows, whose regex flavor is similar to Perl's):

```
% egrep -v '^([0-9]+|::)*$' data
```

```
% awk '! /^([0-9]+|::)*$/ { print "bad data" }' data
```

So anyway, Fred's Perl script is happily using this test to verify the data until one day the program just locks up dead. Debugging, Fred tracks it down to the regex match. The match starts, but never returns a result. It seems that there's an infinite loop during the match.

Fred looks at the particular data that was being checked at the time:

```
::1234::5678901234567890::::1234567890::888:
```

and notices that it is not valid (this is the valid data from above, but with a singleton ":" tacked onto the end, making it invalid).

Dumbfounded, Fred returns to the egrep and awk tests and finds that they still work, even on this data. Fred even tries the same tests on various other machines, all with the same result: the Perl program locks up when it hits this data. So why does the regex match seem to run forever? Fred thinks it's a bug in Perl.

Reality Check

It's not a bug in Perl at all—it's simply doing exactly what Fred asked it to do. "Well," Fred replies, "I didn't ask it to lock up. And anyway, the egrep and awk tests work fine, so it must be a bug in Perl!" The bug, I'm afraid, is Fred's understanding of Perl and regular expressions (or lack thereof).

The problem is *backtracking*, something the Perl regex engine has to do, but the egrep and awk engines do not. I'll go into the details a bit later, but the result is that the Perl regex engine needs to perform about 140 billion tests before it can report for sure that the data in question doesn't match m/^([0-9]+|::)*$/. Yes, folks, 140 *billion*. Even on Fred's fastest machine, that's likely to take a few hours, thus exhibiting what appears to be an infinite loop.

The awk and egrep regex engines, however, are able to find the answer (match, or in this case, no match) immediately. Fred is confused.

Regular Expression Background

The regular expressions that we know and love started out as a formal algebra in the early 1950s, but believe me, I don't want to get into a discussion of the theory (mostly because I don't know it). What is relevant here is that there are two basic methods to implement a regular expression engine: *NFA engines* and *DFA engines*.

For those who want to impress their mothers, NFA and DFA stand for *Nondeterministic Finite Automata* and *Deterministic Finite Automata*, but this is the only time in this article you'll see them spelled out. From a theoretical point of view, there's a lot packed into those terms. But who can figure out all that mumbo-jumbo? For practical purposes, just consider "NFA engine" and "DFA engine" as names, like "Moe" or "Shemp."

Perl has always used an NFA engine, as does vi, sed, GNU emacs, Python, Tcl, expect, and most versions of grep. On the other hand, most versions of egrep, awk, and lex are built with DFA engines. The two types are different in important ways, but practically speaking, you don't need to care about one to study the other. So while this article looks at Perl's NFA engine in depth, a few comments about how NFA and DFA engines differ might be useful to whet the appetites of the curious.

DFA Versus NFA

When a DFA engine first encounters a regular expression, it spends some time analyzing the expression, creating an understanding of every type of string it could possibly match. As a particular string is checked, the DFA engine always knows the status (no match, partial match, or full match) of the text checked so far. Once the text has been scanned to the end, the engine can simply report the final verdict.

An NFA, on the other hand, goes about things quite differently. It is what I call "regex directed," and approaches a match in a way that humans can relate to. For example, if something in the regex is optional, it might try the optional match, and come back later to retry an alternative it if the first try didn't work out. This is called *backtracking*.

Each of the two styles has its own pluses and minuses, which is why both are still around. A DFA engine tends to need more time and memory for the initial check of any particular regular expression, but because it is deterministic and never needs to backtrack, it will tend to do individual matches faster. Sometimes much, much faster. But because of how it works internally, a pure DFA can't provide backreferences or the $1, $2, and friends that Perl's NFA so importantly provides. Chapter 3 of Aho, Sethi, and Ullman's *Compilers* (a.k.a. The Dragon Book, Addison Wesley) provides an extremely rigorous presentation of the theory behind these engines.

NFA Versus NFA, DFA Versus DFA

Each program that implements regular expressions has its own special features and problems. There are "Perl 5.6 regular expressions," "GNU awk 2.15 regular expressions," and so on. While there are obvious similarities among them, there is little meaning to taking "regular expressions" out of context of their intended use. This story is about Perl 5.002 regular expressions, which are the same as Perl's current regular expressions, but without a few of the obscure nooks and crannies.

So what does all this mean?

Fred has a superficial understanding of regular expressions. He knows more or less what the metacharacters do, but doesn't really *understand* how a regex match is attempted, and so is never really sure what will happen with anything nontrivial until he actually tries it. He doesn't really understand the differences among regex flavors, so certainly doesn't know about the backtracking that Perl is forced to do. Fred is often confused when regexes that have /.*/ in them don't work as he expects, and he often wonders why he always seems to be getting the wrong results. When it comes down to it, Fred is never really comfortable around regular expressions. Fred is confused all the time.

But you don't have to be like Fred. One nice characteristic of an NFA engine is that it is pretty easy to understand. Understanding how it works will take the magic and the wonder out of Perl regular expressions. You'll be in the know. You'll be confident. You won't be a Fred.

Perl Regex Engine Basics

The first thing the regex engine does when it sees a regular expression is to *compile* it. The regex is analyzed, checked for errors, and reduced to an internal form that can be used later to quickly check a particular string for a match. Since the compilation itself is unrelated to an actual match attempt, it needs to be done just once, usually when the whole Perl script is first loaded. The internal form will then be used repeatedly to do the actual matches during the script's execution.

This article focuses on how the engine actually applies a regex to a string to see if there is a match. This is definitely a case where what goes on behind the scenes is not out-of-sight, out-of-mind; as Fred learned, some matches take much longer than others. We can use our (perhaps newfound) knowledge of what goes on behind the scenes to rewrite the regex that Fred used in such a way that it works quickly in every situation. Fred would be very grateful.

A Sample Regex

Let's look at the simple regex /".*"/, ostensibly used to match a double-quoted string. From a superficial point of view, this means: "Match a double quote, then any amount of anything (except newlines), and finally another double quote."

With the example text:

```
And then "Right," said Fred, "at 12:00" and he was gone.
```

we can easily see that there will certainly be a match, so the question becomes *which text* will actually be matched. Looking at the English description above, there are four ways it might possibly apply:

```
And then "Right," said Fred, "at 12:00" and he was gone.
         |<---->|<---------->|<------>|
         |<---------------->|
                 |<------------------>|
         |<------------------------->|
```

So which will it be? And more importantly, *why?*

"The Longest Match Wins" and Other Myths

If you've been using Perl for more than a day or three, you probably already know that /.*/ is "greedy" and will "match as much as it can," so you probably know which of the above is the result you can expect from Perl. Heck, even Fred knows. Fred knows about "greedy," and has heard various other rules such as "the longest match wins" or maybe "the first match wins" or even "the first longest match wins." Fred can't quite keep them all straight, but feels these rules make him a Power User.

The problem is that *none* of these rules apply to Perl. As we will see, some are close, but rather than remember a bunch of rules that aren't even correct, I think it is better to Know What Happens. When it comes to complex situations where the rules start to fail, your knowledge will put you light years ahead of Fred.

The First Real Rule of Regexes

Matches that start earlier *always* take precedence over matches that start later. Why?

The first real rule of regexes is that the regex engine first tries to find a match *starting at the first position in the text*, and only if a match is not found will it then bump along and attempt the match from the next position, and the next, and so on until some individual attempt succeeds.

Looking at our sample text, we know we can eliminate half of the possibilities because they start later than the three that start at the first quote. We are then left with three possibilities:

```
And then "Right," said Fred, "at 12:00" and he was gone.
          |<---->|
          |<--------------->|
          |<------------------------->|
```

This doesn't explain one way or the other which of the remaining three will be chosen, as they all start at the same equally-leftmost position. But we know that in attempting this match, the engine will make nine failed attempts on matches starting with the A, n, d, and so on.

There's one particularly interesting effect of this "earlier-starting matches take precedence" rule. Let's look at /-?[0-9]*\\.?[0-9]*/, which is ostensibly meant to match a floating-point number.[*] We have an optional minus sign, some digits, perhaps a decimal point, and then perhaps some more digits. Indeed, it will match a wide range of examples such as 1, 3.1415, -.007, -1223.3838, 19., and so on.

But will it? Breaking this regex into its component parts, we can view it as

/-?/ and then /[0-9]*/ and then /\\.?/ and then /[0-9]*/

The "-" is allowed, but not required. Digits are allowed as well, but also not required. In fact, looking at all the components we realize that *nothing is required* for a match!

Applying it to Fred's example, the engine will first attempt a match beginning from the start of the string. Were it to fail, and continue failing until the start of the 12, it would get a chance to match. But since nothing is required to match, we're *guaranteed* to be successful here with the first try. There is only one plausible match starting at And then, and that's the match of nothingness at the start.

Now, had our text been, say, 4.0, patchlevel 36, there would have been a number of plausible matches right at the start—the nothingness that we know is always allowed with this regex, or perhaps the full 4.0. Or perhaps just 4.. All in all, there are five plausible matches. We still don't know anything about *which* match it will be, but whichever it is, we know the match will begin at the start of the text.

A regex that doesn't require anything for a successful match will *always* succeed with a match beginning at the start of the target.

So, knowing how the Perl regex engine approaches a string overall, let's look at how any one particular attempt behaves. Knowing this tells us which of the plausible matches will actually be returned, and why. This is where things really get interesting.

---

[*] This regex actually appeared in a book written by a friend of mine for a famous publisher. In the unforgettable words of Dave Barry, "I'm not making this up."

A Single Match Attempt

The top half of Figure 13-1 shows, from a practical point of view, how the regular expression engine views /".*"/. The bottom half shows the metacharacters relating to the top half.

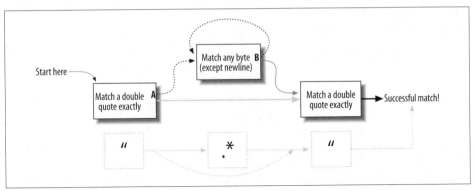

Figure 13-1. How perl views /"."/*

It helps to consider the regex engine as an entity moving from square to square along the black and gray connecting lines. If it moves into a square and can make the match noted there, it is then free to move along. If not, it must do something else (that "something else" is backtracking, but I'm getting a bit ahead of myself).

Multiple Paths

Sometimes there is more than one path the engine can take at any one point. In Figure 13-1, these are marked A and B. It is useful to note that the gray paths represent the skipping of something that is allowed but not required (i.e., optional). The dashed black path from A represents an attempt at /.*/, while the gray path represents its omission. The omission reflects that /.*/ can match nothing, yet still be successful.

The dashed black path from B represents the attempt at another /./ by the /.*/ construct, while the gray path represents breaking out of the /.*/ to continue on. This reflects that no matter how much has already been matched by /.*/, further matches are still optional.

Perl's NFA regex engine can take only one path at a time, so at these places where there is more than one option, what should it do? This is an extremely important point. It may well be that one path will lead to a match, while others will not. The point is, the NFA regex engine doesn't know which path will lead to a match until it actually tries.

Looking at Figure 13-1 and starting at the marked position in:

```
And then "Right," said Fred, "at 12:00" and he was gone.
      ^
```

The first "match a double quote" box is successful. This moves us to just before Right, in the text, but the engine still has to move to another box. At A it has the choice between the gray and black arrows. If it happens to choose the black path over to the second "match a double quote" box, we can see it will fail, since a double quote won't match the R we're currently at. We can see it will fail, but the regex engine can't. Remember, it doesn't know until it actually tries.

Which path will it choose? What will it do if it chooses wrong? These are the key issues for understanding the NFA regex engine. Once you understand them, you are 90% of the way to becoming an expert. Fortunately, these issues are quite easy to understand.

"Byte" Versus "Character"

Most people don't differentiate between the terms "byte" and "character," although they can be quite different. With normal 7-bit ASCII, for example, there are characters for only the first 128 values that a byte could have. A byte with value of decimal 212 simply has no meaning in normal ASCII, yet is M in EBCDIC, ô in the ISO-8859-1 ("Latin-1") encoding, and ヤ in the Japanese JIS-Roman encoding.

The difference becomes a very real concern when working with multibyte encodings such as Unicode, EUC, and Big Five, among others. In the EUC Japanese encoding, for example, two bytes with decimal value 212 together encode the single Japanese character for Austria.

Text is simply a lump of bytes, and a character encoding tells how to interpret it. Perl regular expressions don't know what encoding the data was *intended* to be interpreted as—for the most part, it treats everything in a pseudo-ASCIIish way. This method is fine when working with straight English text or ASCII, and so in this article, I use "byte" and "character" interchangeably. Perl 5.8 has new bytes and utf8 pragmas that give you finer-grained control over how your lumps of bytes are interpreted.

You can still use Perl to work with other encodings (I use it often to process text encoded via several different Japanese encodings), but it takes extra work and care. Knowing that /./ matches a *byte* and not a *character* becomes extremely important, for example. The definitive reference on Asian encodings (which tend to be multibyte) is Ken Lunde's *CJKV Information Processing*, published by O'Reilly.

Backtracking

When the regex engine is faced with multiple paths, it chooses one (exactly which path it chooses and why is quite important, and discussed later), and marks the other paths as untried. Later during the match, if the regex engine finds it has taken a path that has lead to failure, it can return to the situation where it began and try another one of the marked paths. This is known as *backtracking*.

Returning to our example, we found ourselves in the text just before `"Right,"` and in the regex at A. For the purposes of discussion, let's say that the regex chooses the gray path first. In doing so, it will remember that, should the need ever arise, it can retry from that position via the black path.

Indeed, the need arises quickly. As mentioned above, the second "match quote" box certainly fails to match the `R`. Normally, this local failure would mean overall match failure, but because we have a *remembered state*, we know that there are options that were allowed but have not yet been tried. *Backtracking is nothing more than returning to yet-to-be-tried options when the current path fails.*

So, we return to A and take the black path. This time, the "match any byte" successfully matches the `R`. Now what to do? At B now, we again have a choice. For the purposes of the current discussion, let's say that the black path is chosen. In doing so, the engine will remember:

> `can take the gray path from B while at R`

So, taking that black path we wind up at the same box. This time, the any-byte matched is the `i`. As before, we have a choice. Let's say that the black path is chosen again. In doing so, we're bypassing *another* opportunity to take the gray path, so we add:

> `can take the gray path from B while at Ri`

to our list of remembered states. In fact, we add a state each time we go through this loop. Assuming we take the black path the next time as well, we also add:

> `can take the gray path from B while at Rig`

during the next loop, leaving us just after `Righ` in the text.

Let's say, for the purposes of the discussion, that at this point the regex engine decides to take the gray path. Now we're bypassing a chance to take the black path at this juncture, so we add:

> `can take the black path from B while at Righ`

Unfortunately, the gray path from B at this point immediately leads to failure, as the text's `t` can't match the required double quote. A local failure? No problem! We have plenty of saved states to retry from, and one or more might eventually lead to a match.

When the regex engine is forced to backtrack, it will always backtrack to the most recently saved state that is available (the others will be used, in turn, when and if needed).

So we backtrack to:

> `can take the black path from B while at Righ`

and take the black path. We match the `t` and find ourself at B for about the half-dozenth time, and as with each time before, we have two fresh choices.

This description is getting a bit long-winded, and I think by now even Fred is getting the picture. We still haven't gotten to the whole issue of how the engine decides which of its possible paths to choose at any particular point (remember, all the decisions reported above are for the purposes of discussion and don't necessarily reflect what any known regex engine will actually do in the same situation).

To make this go a bit more quickly, let's assume that from now on the regex engine will always chose the black path when it reaches B. This would result in a lot of looping, with the "any byte" matching each byte of the target text in succession. And, of course, each time we choose the black path, the gray is remembered in yet another saved state.

By the time the engine has neared the end of the string, we've accumulated quite a few saved states. Listing them in reverse order, we have:

```
can take the gray path from B while at was gon
can take the gray path from B while at was go
can take the gray path from B while at was g
...
can take the gray path from B while at Rig
can take the gray path from B while at Ri
can take the gray path from B while at R
```

Anyway, that's the current status, but we still haven't reached an overall match yet. As we've been doing, we take the black path, this time adding:

```
can take the gray path from B while at was gone
```

We can match the ., and so follow with another black path, adding:

```
can take the gray path from B while at was gone.
```

But this time, the "any byte" box can't match because we're at the end of the string. Had it been a "match the end of the text" box, we'd be fine, but it's not, so we have a local failure and need to backtrack. We go back to this most-recently saved state, but fail there as well (this time because "double quote" can't match the nothingness at the end of the string). Still no worries—we have plenty of saved states. The most recent is now:

```
can take the gray path from B while at was gone
```

but this also fails: a double quote and a period don't mesh. In fact, the next dozen or so backtracks fail in the same way. It's only when we finally backtrack to:

```
can take the gray path from B while at 12:00
```

that the double quote can match. After this is done, there is only one path from that box, so no decision needs to be made nor any new state saved. And as it turns out, we have an overall match!

```
And then "Right," said Fred, "at 12:00" and he was gone.
                       |<------------------------->|
```

Now that we've reached an overall match, we can consider ourselves done. Sure, there are some other saved states that may well also lead to overall matches (actually, there are two others still in there), but since we have a match already, who cares? (Answer: a POSIX engine might, but not Perl.) Thus, we come to another rule: the first match reached wins.

Note that this is not "the shortest match" or "the first match I see" or "the match I, as a programmer, am hoping for," but the first match that the regex engine actually reaches. The decisions about which path to take at any particular point has a direct influence as to the specific match the regex engine will find first.

Now remember—and I can't stress this enough—the decisions about which path to take have thus far in this article been randomly chosen off the top of my head and have no relation to reality. I wanted to explain the mechanics of how backtracking works, and do so without muddying the waters with the (equally important) issue of path selection. Had I happened to write the story such that the regex engine made different decisions, the results could have been different.

For example, had I decided that during the "any byte" loop, as the regex matched everything just before the a in Fred, at the engine suddenly decided to take the gray path, we would have immediately matched the double quote and then reached the overall match:

```
And then "Right," said Fred, "at 12:00" and he was gone.
         |<----------------->|
```

Or had I written that the gray path was suddenly chosen as the engine reached the space in 12:00 and, we would have reached the same match as in the story, but in quite a more efficient way. In the original story, we'd matched all the characters of and he was gone., only to undo that by backtracking to the final double quote. This illustrates two different avenues to the same match, one with a lot of what turns out to be extra work, and one without.

Options, Options, Options

Before getting into the details about *which* path is chosen, let's look at the various regex constructs that yield multiple choices in the first place. The quick summary is that when something is *optional*, the regex engine needs to decide if it should attempt to match the optional part first, or if it should try the overall match skipping this optional part first. Each choice represents a path, and in either case the choice not taken is remembered for later use if backtracking so dictates. Remember: *every option means multiple paths*.

The most basic "optional" item is anything governed by ?, like the /(blah)/ in /(blah)?/. We know that Perl's ?? means optional as well, and that it is "non-greedy," but what does that really mean? It is directly related to path selection (you'll be able to cast aside any shroud of mystery you might have about this in just a moment), but first I'd like to continue summarizing items that are considered optional.

Items governed by * (and *?) are optional not only once, but repeatedly, forever. Similarly, items governed by + and +? are optional only after their first match (the first match is required). Items governed by {*min,max*} and {*min,max*}? are optional once their required *min* matches have been made, and are only optional until the *max* has been reached. With {*num*}, nothing is optional (which, as you might realize, is why {*num*}? is always exactly the same as *num*).

Alternation

Let's not forget about alternation. With something like /moe|fred|shemp/, if /moe/ is attempted first, it is optional because its failure does not mean the entire regex necessarily fails; /fred/ and /shemp/ are still available. If /moe/ fails and, say, /shemp/ is tried next, it too can be considered optional because there's still /fred/ left to try. But if /shemp/ also fails, then /fred/ suddenly becomes required. Thus, alternates are optional only as long as other alternates are available.

When alternation is surrounded by parentheses, this "failure" becomes failure of the component, not of the entire regex. For example, failure to match any of the alternates in /(moe|fred|shemp)?/ doesn't mean overall failure, since matching any of the alternates was optional via the ? in the first place.

Character Classes

One quick note about character classes. A character class alone does *not* represent anything optional. /[xyz]/, for example, does *not* mean: "Try to match x, or match y, or match z." (That would be /x|y|z/.) Rather, /[xyz]/ means: "Let's check out one byte, and if it is an x, y, or z, we match." It is a subtle distinction in English, but a huge distinction to the regex engine. It should be apparent that the character class is much more efficient than the /x|y|z/, which might perform up to three separate matches rather than the one check required by /[xyz]/.

A negated character class (such as /[^xyz]/) is no more or no less efficient than a normal one. The meaning of the list of characters is simply toggled from "these allowed" to "something except these allowed."

All the other regex constructs, from /^/ to /\b/ to /(?!)/ to /\3/, do not represent anything optional. They might become optional when governed by other metacharacters, but there is nothing intrinsically optional about them.

How the Path Is Chosen

Finally, the last piece of the puzzle! We know about saving states for untried paths, and we know about using those states to backtrack if needed. Only one question remains: when faced with multiple paths, which one will the Perl regular expression engine actually attempt first?

Rephrasing the above in a more human point of view, when faced with an optional item (or with alternation items), will the Perl regular expression engine attempt to match the optional item first, or will it attempt to skip the optional item first? (Or in the case of alternation, in which order will the items be tried?)

The so-called "greedy" or "maximal matching" metacharacters ?, *, +, and {*min,max*}, will always *attempt an optional item first*. They will skip an optional item only if forced via backtracking.

The so-called "ungreedy" or "minimal matching" metacharacters ??, *?, +?, and {*min,max*}?, will always *skip an optional item first*. They will return to try matching the item only if forced via backtracking.

With alternation, Perl always *attempts the alternates in order* (counting from left to right). The first alternate will always be attempted first. The second and subsequent alternates will be attempted (in turn) only if forced via backtracking.

That's Pretty Much It

If I were writing about Japanese instead of regular expressions, the point we've reached would be comparable to my having told you 90% of the grammar rules and vocabulary of the Japanese language. Were that the case, I certainly wouldn't expect you to start having conversations in Japanese—it takes time and experience to internalize the information and to draw out the relevance to what you already know about human communications or, as the case may be, Perl regular expressions.

So far I've given you motions, but no directions. Words, but no acting. Fred has this funny look on his face, not really sure if he understands why he's been listening for the last hour. Depending on your previous exposure to Perl regular expressions, you might well be thinking, "Wow, so *that's* why such-and-such turns out that way!" But for most, I think the lessons of this story require a fair amount of real-world context before they sink in completely.

As I noted early on, even Fred knew that /".*"/ would match:

```
And then "Right," said Fred, "at 12:00" and he was gone.
         |<------------------------->|
```

But rather than "because /.*/ is greedy," it is instructive to carefully run through the match sequence yourself, counting tests, saved states, and backtracks. This will explain in a very tangible way why /".*"/ does not match:

```
And then "Right," said Fred, "at 12:00" and he was gone.
         |<----->|
```

as many new Perl hackers expect. Furthermore, applying the same rigorous step-through for /".*?"/ shows why it *does* match Right,.

Please try working through these examples on your own. In Chapter 14, I'll focus much more on how to put these mechanics to practical use, but to use them effectively you must understand them completely. Working through these two simple examples is a good start.

As you work through them, keep a tally of how many individual tests are performed (such as "does 'match a double quote' succeed?"), noting how many are successful and how many fail. Keep a count of how many times you have to backtrack, and also note exactly how many states are discarded as no longer needed once the overall match is found. For the purposes of all these counts, start counting with the first successful match of the leading /"/ as test (and match) number 1. Once you feel comfortable that you understand how the matching proceeds, compare your answers to Table 13-1.

As a bonus, it's quite instructive to do the same work-through with /"[^"]*"/. The associated statistics are shown in Table 13-1.

Match Statistics

Against the text:

    And then "Right," said Fred, "at 12:00" and he was gone.>

with the count starting at the marked position, the match statistics are shown in Table 13-1.

Don't let the 67 tests of the first example intimidate you—it's not as complicated as it might seem. Starting from the first successful match of the leading /"/, we follow with 46 successful matches of /./. The test finally fails attempting to match the nothingness at the end of the text. We backtrack to try skipping the most recently attempted /./, leading us to attempt the final /"/. This also fails to match the nothingness at the end of the text. So far: 47 successful tests, 2 failures.

Backtracking again (which effectively "unmatches" the /./ that matched the text-ending period), we have another failure, as /"/ can't match it. This backtrack-and-fail cycle continues for a total of 17 times (once for each character in .enog saw eh dna) until we finally backtrack to unmatch the final quote, allowing a successful match of /"/.

This leaves us with 1 + 46 + 1 = 48 matches, and 2 + 17 = 19 failures.

Table 13-1. Match efficiency

Regex	Tests (pass/fail)	Backtracks	Abandoned states
/".*"/	67 (48/19)	19	28
/".*?"/	14 (8/6)	6	1
/"[^"]*"/	9 (8/1)	1	6

In *Understanding Regular Expressions, Part II*, I'll start to develop some working rules and conclusions from all this, but hopefully you'll be able to make some of your own as you re-examine what you already know.

Perl sometimes optimizes regular expression processing. Sometimes it might actually perform fewer tests than I've described. Or it may do some tests more efficiently than others. For example, /x*/ is internally optimized such that it is more efficient than /(x)*/ or /(?:x)*/. Sometimes Perl can even decide that a regex can *never* match the particular string in question, so it bypasses the test altogether.

These optimizations are interesting, but the basic operation is much more important. Once you've got that down pat, you can start to delve into the nitty-gritty details and incorporate an understanding of them into your regular expressions.

Now, one final item before I close the article. Fred is still asking why on earth his /^([0-9]+|::)*$/ was taking so long. Work through how Perl applies this regex to the text 12:. We know it will fail, but the regex engine doesn't until it tries all the matching and backtracking that this article has described. Then try the text 123:, and if you still don't get the picture, try 1234:. I hope the reason becomes clear and you can explain it *to* Fred instead of being *a* Fred.

## CHAPTER 14

Understanding Regular Expressions, Part II

Jeffrey Friedl

Maybe I'm somewhat of a kook, but I get a lot of pleasure (and instruction) from taking some simple task and really investigating all the ways to go about solving it, comparing and contrasting the various solutions.

Usually, the end result is only a better understanding of Perl (and often, Perl's regular expressions), but sometimes there is a tangible benefit. For example, the Perl FAQ about removing whitespace from strings is the result of a long day of benchmarking.

Not long ago in comp.lang.perl.misc, someone asked if there was an "and" for regular expressions comparable to the "or" in /this|that/. That is, he wanted to find lines that matched two otherwise unrelated expressions. The quick answer provided by many was an && between *two* regular expressions: /this/ && /that/, although some offered solutions such as /this.*that|that.*this/.

Randal Schwartz came up with the silly but ingenious /^(?=.*one)(?=.*two)/, and when Tom Christiansen asked why the ^ was included, I got the itch to delve a bit deeper.

Knowing Versus Knowing on Paper

Japanese has an expression that translates to English as "paper driver." These people have driver's licenses (hard to get in Japan) but don't have a car and hardly ever drive —they're drivers only on paper. I tend to think twice before getting in the car when they're behind the wheel. Textbook knowledge without experience to back it up doesn't mean much.

In *Understanding Regular Expressions, Part I*, I told the story of Fred (Full Regular Expression Description) that hopefully helped remove the shroud of mystery around regexes. But knowing how the regex engine works is only the first step: it takes experience to turn that into *knowing* the wider-perspective effects. The aforementioned question about /this/ && /that/ is basically a simple one, so without the details of the problem getting in the way, I'd like to look at a series of alternate solutions. We'll use our knowledge of how regexes actually work to derive points for comparison.

The basic goal is this: given some text, determine whether it can match two unrelated expressions. I've assembled a list of various ways we might go about this, using both my own ideas and those from members of the studio audience (such as Randal's offering). Here they are:

1. `/one/ && /two/`

2. `/one.*two|two.*one/`

3. `/one.*?two|two.*?one/`

4. `/one.*two/ || /two.*one/`

5. `/one.*?two/ || /two.*?one/`

6. `/^(?=.*one)(?=.*two)/`

7. `/^(?=.*?one)(?=.*?two)/`

8. `/(?=.*one)(?=.*two)/`

9. `/(?=.*?one)(?=.*?two)/`

The first thing to do is understand *if* and *why* they work, and what practical differences they have with respect to exactly what, where, and when they will match. Once those things are understood, we can move on to looking at their relative efficiency.

Will They Work at All?

Contestant 1 is pretty simple to understand, and is the most direct rendition of what was asked. Contestants 2 and 3 take quite a different approach, noting that either /one/ follows /two/ (that is, /two.*one/), or the other way around. They differ only in that one uses the greedy .* while the other the non-greedy .*?. They're different, but will always succeed and fail on the same texts.

Contestants 4 and 5 are comparable to contestants 2 and 3, but 4 and 5 use the non-regex "or" instead of the regex one. The basic premise of "they're either in this order or that" still holds.

Finally, contestants 6 through 9 are variations on a theme. Because parts of each regex are enclosed in "nonconsuming" (?=...) parentheses, Perl will insist that they match, but won't consider them part of the match results ($&). The regexes will simply return true if /one/ matches somewhere (i.e., after /.*/), and /two/ matches somewhere as well. The differing /^/ merely indicates the logical conclusion that if the rest of the expression can't match right away, it won't match later on either (since the /.*/ or /.*?/ run off to the end of the line).

Of course, there are plenty of other regexes, including hybrids like /one(?=.*two)/ || /two(?=.*?one)/ but I'll try to contain my excitement to the nine shown above.

How Do They Differ?

Obviously, there's a large difference between the solutions as to how they affect $& and other side effects. It seemed that the comp.lang.perl.misc fellow merely wanted a true/false answer, so these differences aren't important to us. But the fact that /one/ && /two/ leaves $& in quite a different state than /one.*two/ || /two.*one/ could prove very important, so it's good to at least mention the issue before dismissing it (as I intend to do for the rest of the article).

More to the point, there *are* differences in which solution will match what, and two examples should make it clear: one is the text "one\\ntwo" and the other "twone".

The first issue (which might never matter unless you work with multiline text) has to do with the dot not normally matching a newline. This allows /one/ && /two/ to match text that the others can't. The /s modifier removes the issue, as it causes the dot to match any byte *including* newline. The issue is even more touchy among the solutions in Group 4. Text such as "blah blah blah\\n one and two" could be matched by contestants 8 and 9, but not 6 and 7 (unless, of course, the /s or /m modifiers were used). Think about it for a moment if it's not clear. Tom made a very valid point when he brought up /^/, although for the common case of processing lines, the dot-doesn't-match-newline issue is irrelevant.

The second issue is much more important. Contestants 1 and 6 through 9 will match if each regex "can match the target text, period." With the rest, the serial ordering within the regex requires that the two matches *not overlap*. It might be a very important distinction.

Which set of semantics is correct? It depends entirely on the particular needs of the situation. If, for example, you are trying to match English words, your regexes should probably include a generous supply of /\\b/'s, one result of which is that the differing semantics would become irrelevant (consider that /\\bone\\b/ && /\\btwo\\b/ would never be able to match the previous bone of contention, "twone"). In any case, you can make the appropriate decisions on a case-by-case basis as long as you're cognizant of the issues involved.

Which Is Best?

So, which contestant is best? What exactly *is* behind door #2? Beauty is in the eye of the beholder, and which is "best" depends on your criteria. The differing semantics aside, /one/ && /two/ definitely wins the "simplistic beauty" award, while Randal's / ^(?=.*one)(?=.*two)/ might go well toward impressing your friends (and, perhaps, judges of TPJ's Obfuscated Perl Contest).

Depending on the need, efficiency may well be important too, and this is where our detailed knowledge of how the regex engine works can really pay off.

Efficiency

In some cases, efficiency is a black and white issue that's easy to analyze. For instance, /[abc]/ is always more efficient than /(a|b|c)/. But in many cases efficiency is not so clear, and involves more than just the regex engine. The rest of this article considers the efficiencies of our nine expressions. Often, because of the many variables involved (particularly, the differing kinds of target text), the discussion becomes necessarily vague. At the end I'll tie things together with some benchmarking, at which point a re-read might help the subtler points sink in.

Greediness

First, let's compare and contrast the .* versus .*? aspect. If you remember from the previous column, the difference between * and *? is *greediness*: * matches as much as it can, while *? matches as little as it can. Keeping this in mind while considering the regexes /one.*two/ and /one.*?two/. Here's a quick quiz: given this text, which would find the match more quickly, and why?

one two blah blah blah blah blah blah blah

Simply following in your mind what you know the engine must do will quickly reveal the answer. After matching /one/, the first option's /.*/ will blindly zip to the end of the string, at which point it will try to apply /two/ and fail. It will then backtrack once to retry and fail again. In the end, it will have to backtrack almost all the way before /two/ can match.

Now consider /one.*?two/. Before the *? even attempts the first /./, it will try the /two/ at tw. It will fail, backtrack and immediately apply dot to match the space after one, at which point /two/ is attempted again and matches. Thus, the *? version matches this data much more quickly than the * version.

What does this tell us about /one.*two/ and /one.*?two/? Frankly, nothing, because the tables are completely turned with the data:

one blah blah blah blah blah blah blah **two**

where the * version outshines the *? version almost exactly as much as *? outshined * with the first example text. And, of course, I hope Fred's woes in the previous column reminds you to consider a line such as:

one blah blah blah blah blah blah blah

that won't match. Which of our two samples will have to backtrack less before it is able to fail? Again, an understanding of the engine helps. Both versions attempt to look at exactly the same matches—the difference is simply in the order checked, so both will have to exhaustively work exactly the same amount before admitting failure.

Of course, this is all in theory. In practice, .* seems to be optimized quite a bit more than .*?, as some benchmarks will soon reveal.

Logical "or" Versus Regex "or"

Let's leave * versus *? for a moment and look at how /one.*two|two.*one/ compares to /one.*two/ || /two.*one/.

They might well appear similar, but they are *extremely* different. Although in this article we're not concentrating on what text is actually matched, it may be instructive to note that with this text, one of these expressions will match one way, the other another.

A ne**two**rk's number **one** priority is accuracy, **two** is throughput.

Because /one.*two|two.*one/ is one expression, it is attempted as a whole at each successive character position, while the other applies /one.*two/ completely as two separate regex matches before even bothering to apply /two.*one/ (and will only do so if necessary). It might be a good exercise to consider how the other expressions compare.

As for these two expressions' efficiency, we get into the fuzzy area of extra-expression optimizations. Usually, if the engine can decide that some fixed text (particularly leading fixed text) is required for a match, it can use a faster fixed-string search to quickly rule out quickly sections of text that couldn't possibly match. With each part of /one.*two/ || /two.*one/, it's relatively simple for the regex engine to realize that matches must start with one and two respectively, and so it can use these optimizations to speed things up. Furthermore, in these "fixed text known" cases, study can help speed things up even more.

Now consider the expression /one.*two|two.*one/. As the expression is being compiled, the engine can derive the "fixed text required" for each alternative, but it requires more work combining the results to realize that any matching line must have one and two in them somewhere. It's conceivable that Perl could eventually do this job, but right now it doesn't, so the result is that none of the extra-expression optimizations are done. Perhaps the amount of time needed to analyze these complicated situations is more than they might eventually save.

Understanding exactly when these optimizations will kick in involves some magic, but if your Perl was compiled with DEBUGGING, you can have it tell you what it's derived about your expression with the -Dr option:

```
% perl5.6.1 -Dr -c -e '/one.*two/'
Compiling REx `one.*two'
size 7 first at 1
rarest char w at 1
rarest char o at 0
   1: EXACT <one>(3)
   3: STAR(5)
   4:   REG_ANY(0)
   5: EXACT <two>(7)
   7: END(0)
```

Benchmarking

When it comes down to it, theory only goes so far—benchmarking representative data is where you get the answers straight from the horse's mouth. Figure 14-1 shows some benchmarks of our regexes with Perl 5.6.1.

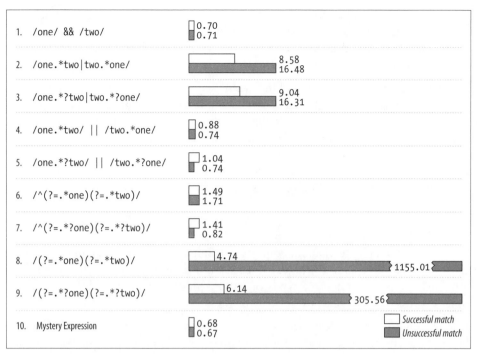

Figure 14-1. Regex performance on successful and unsuccessful matches (lower is faster)

We can draw these conclusions:

- Contestants 4 and 5 did very well, and contestants 2 and 3 did poorly. With 4 and 5, the extra-regex optimizations probably short-circuit the regular expressions entirely.

- Not shown in Figure 14-1 (but verified in my benchmark): since contestants 4 and 5 must exhaust the first expression completely before the second expression can match, they take longer when the input has a two followed by a one.

- Also not shown in Figure 14-1 (but verified in my benchmark) is that the relative speed of the matches is directly proportional to how early the first match can be found.

- Sometimes greedy expressions are faster than their nongreedy equivalents, and sometimes they aren't.

To sum up: we can conclude that /one.*two|two.*one/ is not as good as /one.*two/ || /two.*one/ for a variety of reasons, even if we can find specific data for which the first works faster. (Quiz: can you think of test data that would take *substantially* longer, say an order of magnitude, with contestants 4 and 5 than with 2 and 3?)

Now I'd like to look at Randal's /^(?=.*one)(?=.*two)/. By itself, /.*one/ would have some chance at the fixed-string optimizations, but -Dr shows that in this case none are done for the entire expression. In a string where both /one/ and /two/ can match, the overall expression must simply .* to the end of the string and backtrack to /one/, then do the same for /two/. If the /one/ and /two/ are near the end of the string, they'll be found in short order. If they're near the beginning, the *? version will be the one that finds them quickly.

It's interesting to note that by looking at the graph, the lack of change from contestants 6 to 8 and 7 to 9 might make one conclude that /^/ makes no difference *presuming the match succeeds*. This is the Fred syndrome. With a string that doesn't match (and even worse, one that has many ones but no twos), the non-/^/ versions can take orders of magnitude longer, since they have to fail all over again when restarting the match from the second character, third character, etc., through the whole length of the string. The spikes in Figure 14-1 demonstrate this.

Conclusion

I haven't mentioned much about contestant 1, but as you might imagine, it performs quite well. It's amenable to the extra-regex optimizations, and doesn't suffer from any backtracking. With some types of data, it might be slower than some of the other expressions, but generally it performs well even in the wild cases.

Contestants 1, 6, and 10 are fairly resilient to inputs. Contestants 4 and 5 look good, but their performance degrades for a test that I proposed in the quiz—a test that shows contestants 2 and 3 outperforming 4 and 5. Here it is:

```
two one one one one one one one one one
```

With this string, the first expression has to try many times before failing and then matching with the second.

So who is our Mystery Expression? I did these benchmarks using /one/ and /two/ as the sample expressions, but in general they could be any regular expression. However, if they really are fixed strings, then we could just use:

```
index($_, "one") >= 0 and index($_, "two") >= 0
```

for the test, so I decided to include it for comparison. As you can see, it's the fastest of all.

My goal was not to show one particular fact, technique, or answer, but to expose you to some of the thought processes that I go through when evaluating an expression, and the regex theory and Perl practice behind the evaluations. As anyone with a degree from the School of Hard Knocks will tell you, experience is a great teacher, so I aspired to share some of mine with you. One of the most important points I hope you'll take away with you is that when evaluating, make sure to include a wide variety of test data, including various kinds of nonmatching data. As Fred will tell you, failing efficiency can sometimes be more important than matching efficiency.

## CHAPTER 15

Understanding Regular Expressions, Part III

Jeffrey Friedl

In *Understanding Regular Expressions, Part II*, I used our knowledge of how Perl's regex engine goes about a match to analyze and evaluate a few different solutions to a problem. I'd like to continue to look at the effects of greediness, backtracking, and other important aspects of Perl's regex engine, this time to demonstrate some gotchas that await the unwary. A basic understanding of backtracking is a prerequisite; I recommend *Understanding Regular Expressions, Part I*.

Let's start with a simple but illustrative example taken from daily life: continuation lines. Let's say you've got the text of a csh-style configuration file in $_, and want to pluck alias definitions. You might use:

```
while (m{^ \s* alias \s+ (\S+) \s+ (.*) }xmg) {
    ($alias, $cmd) = ($1, $2);
    ...work with $alias and $cmd as you like...
}
```

This works fine if your string is from a tcsh shell's startup script and has a line such as the following, put there as some jerk's idea of a practical joke:

```
alias ls 'echo Ha, got you, sucker! ; rm *'
```

However, if the jerk tried to be smart and cover his tracks a bit, the line might look like this:

```
alias ls 'echo Ha, got you, sucker! ; rm * ;\
        alias ls echo Ha, got you, sucker!'
```

In this version, the rm action of the alias happens just once, so by the time you know to look for an alias, you won't see the rm. Anyway, this kind of "line" would break our approach, since it's two physical lines.

Well, we know regular expressions, so no problem! A continuation line is a backslash followed by a newline followed by the next line. We can express that directly with /\\ \n .*/x.

In adding this to our match, we'll want to wrap it with (?:...)? because it's optional. Actually, we can use (?:...)* to allow any number of lines.

Adding this to our match, we get:

```
m{^ \s* alias \s+ (\S+) \s+ (.* (?:\\ \n.*)*) }xm
```

It won't work.

If this surprises you, review the basics of how Perl's NFA regex engine goes about a match attempt: by the time the first /.*/ stops and control moves to /\\ \n .*/x, the backslash that was ostensibly supposed to be matched by \\ has *already* been matched by /.*/, and so the whole /\\ \n .*/x fails. That's okay, since it's wrapped by (...)*, but the result is that the match stops at the end of the line—not what we intend.

It's interesting to note that this is yet another example of why the common "Perl regexes are greedy" myth is wrong. Were they truly greedy, the longest possible match would be found (in this case, one comprising both lines). The saying *should* be "Perl quantifiers are greedy."

Ah, but not *all* Perl's quantifiers are greedy. Our regex uses seven quantifiers: three pluses and four stars. What if we made some of them non-greedy? Which ones? Well, it doesn't matter for the first three, since with any given text there is no choice about what they match. As a result, the order of checking doesn't matter except for efficiency. (This was a main topic of *Understanding Regular Expressions, Part II*—on a local level, /\s*/ is much more efficient than /\s*?/.)*

Our problem cropped up because /.*/ was too greedy, so what about "degreedying" that one? If we use /.*?/, it checks what follows, /(?:\\\n.*)*/, before each attempt at its own dot. This means that the backslash will be matched by /\\ \n .*/x if possible, pulling it out from under the initial /.*/.

Along the same lines, we'd want the second /.*/ to be /.*?/ as well. What about the quantifier governing (:...)? Making that non-greedy tells the regex engine that it's okay to not even bother checking for continuation lines before ending the match, so we definitely want to keep it greedy.

This leaves us with:

```
m{^ \s* alias \s+ (\S+) \s+ ( .*? (?:\\ \n .*? )* ) }xm
```

Does all this make sense?

I sure hope not, because this regex won't work either!

Think about what happens when we reach /.*? (?:\\\n.*?)*/x. The initial /.*?/ knows that it can match any (non-newline) character, but because it is non-greedy, it will first defer to what follows, returning to actually try /./ if and only if what fol-

---

* This /^ \s* alias \s+ (\S+)/x is a situation where it would be nice to have quantifiers that are *possessive* (never give up what they match). In this case, such quantifiers would provide a measure of efficiency. Because they're used in the overall regex, we can see that any backtracking they might do is irrelevant, so telling the regex engine that they should backtrack would save time. As of Perl 5.6, you can now do this.

lows isn't successful. What follows is governed by star, *so it's always successful*. It might not match anything, but being successful even when not matching is what star is all about! If the alias begins with a continuation backslash, it and its newline will match (and match as many empty continuation lines as are in a row), but otherwise, /.*? (?: \\ \n .*?)*/x at the end of a regex like this is *guaranteed* never to match any text.

It might have been surprising because my description was meant to lead you into thinking it would work, but there's no magic here—it all makes perfect sense in the scheme of how backtracking works. If a cup of coffee and a second reading doesn't clear it up, go directly to *Understanding Regular Expressions, Part I*. Do not pass Go and do not collect $200.

So, how could we match continuation lines in this case? Well, we want a bunch of "escaped newlines or other stuff," so how about using this instead of /.*/ in the original regex?

```
m/(?: \\ \n | . )* /x
```

We know that Perl tries each alternative in turn, so if a backslash is followed by a newline, it will be matched before /./ can get to the backslash, thereby vaulting us past the newline:

```
m{^ \s* alias \s+ (\S+) \s+ (?: \\ \n | . )* }xm
```

There is one problem with this, however. A line ending with \\ before the newline is *not* a continuation line, but will be treated as one by our regex. The first backslash is not part of an escape-newline sequence, so is not matched by /\\ \n/x. This is good. However, the next backslash can match it, which is bad. /\\ \n/x vaults us past escaped newlines, but we really want it to vault us past any escaped sequences.

We'd like to be able to replace the /\n/ by /./, but dot doesn't normally match a newline. That's a key feature of dot's other use in the regex, so using the /s modifier to have dot match newline would cause a problem. It can be taken care of easily, and the result creates a cleaner regex, I think:

```
m{^ \s* alias \s+ (\S+) \s+ (?: \\. | [^\\\n] )* }xms
```

Notice that I used both the /m and the /s modifiers. That creates what I call a *clean multiline* matching mode: the anchors will match at embedded newlines (the influence of /m), and dot will match any byte (the influence of /s).

This regex now works as desired, but the alternation at each character is not efficient. One thing that might come to mind to speed it up is to quantify /[^\n]/ with a plus. There are two concerns. First, considering only [^\n], the change makes it an effective /([^\n]+)*/x, which is the quintessential neverending match that caused Fred so many problems before. Ah, but nested quantifiers alone do not a neverending match make. A neverending match "never ends" because it is checking a bazillion permutations in search of a match. That's not a concern here because (...)* *can never fail*. If there were something after it that could fail, then our regex /(?: \\. | [^\n]+)*/x would indeed be very dangerous. But it's okay in this case.

Secondly, we'd relied on the position of /\\./ in the alternation to have it match a backslash when possible (rather than /[^\n]/). But now, there's nothing stopping /[^\n]+/ from matching a backslash—until we change it to /[^\n\\]+/.

So, making these changes and benchmarking, I find that this:

    /(?: \\. | [^\n\\]+)*/x

is about 30 times faster than this:

    /(?: \\. | [^\n])*/x.

Wow!

This part of the regex can also be written as:

    /[^\n\\]* (\\. [^\n\\]*)*/x

This is derived using a technique I call *unrolling the loop*, and has a number of benefits. It's about 15% faster than the fast regex in the previous paragraph, and it doesn't suffer the neverending-match fate if inserted before something that could fail. It's a powerful technique that I use often.

The next article features a case study, illustrating an aspect of how I use regular expressions at Yahoo!.

## CHAPTER 16

Nibbling Strings

Jeffrey Friedl

Several months ago I began working at Yahoo!, where I apply my text-processing enthusiasm to financial information and news feeds. You can see the result at *http://quote.yahoo.com*.

It's fertile ground for Perl to flex its muscle, but I recently came across a problem that had me stumped until the oft-ignored pos came to the rescue. In this article, we'll take a look at the problem and at a few different tactics I used trying to solve it. I hope it'll provide some interesting techniques to help you with similar problems.

The Problem

Because Yahoo! receives articles from various news services, we'd like to link them to the news page for each company mentioned in the article. Sometimes the news services encode information about which companies are referenced, and sometimes not. For these articles, I proposed that we scan the articles for company names.

Easier said than done. Considering that Yahoo! maintains news on over 15,000 companies, think how you might go about identifying the companies mentioned in any particular article. Cycling through each company name to see if it's present is simple, but would take forever. And one huge /Yahoo|Intel|Adaptec|General Motors|.../ regex to match all company names would also take way too long to run.

Those who are familiar with the different styles of regex engines will recognize that a huge /this|that|other|.../ set of alternates will generally run slowly in Perl, but faster with a tool like lex or flex (which use a potentially time-consuming preprocessing stage that ends up reaping huge runtime wins with regexes like this). Unfortunately, it turned out that the enormous regular expression required was too large even for flex. I needed a different approach.

The main obstacle so far is that the size of the problem—the set of all company names—is so huge that we can't use any of the normal tools off the shelf. If we can reduce this set, we can return to using those powerful and familiar approaches.

One way to reduce the size of the problem is to consider only those company names that begin with a particular word. Once we have the word "Yahoo", we then have to consider only "Yahoo Inc", which is a simple task. On the other hand, if we have a more common word like "America" we'll have to consider names such as "America Online", "America West Airlines", and "America First Participating Preferred Equity Mortgage Fund", among many others. Still, it's manageable.

To prepare, I created two databases using tied hashes. One maps all of the first words in company names to a list of possible stock tickers (symbols used to trade the stock, such as YHOO for Yahoo) designating companies whose name begins with the word. The other database maps stock tickers to the full company name. Then, when I come across a word that might start a company name, I use the list of stock tickers to match the full name, reporting the stock tickers of the matching companies. We link news via stock ticker, so ultimately I need to generate a list of stock tickers.

Now, how to go about the processing? I first tried a "nibble" approach that I've had luck with before. I put the entire article into a string and nibbled off items from the front, processing each as I liked:

```
$_ = $entire_article;

while (length $_) {

    ## try to grab a leading capitalized word...
    if (s/^([A-Z]\w*)//) {
        my $word = $1;
        ## do something with word ...
    }
    ## get rid of any leading "else" ...
    s{^\w*    # a non-capitalized word, if any
      \W+     # non-word stuff
     }{}x;
}
```

The "do something with word" code involves checking to see if there's a company beginning with $word, and if so, seeing whether the full name matches at that point. Since $word is stripped from the beginning of $_, we want to see if the *rest* of the company name can be found there. Omitting the first word of the company name (rather than keeping the full name) keeps the database a bit smaller. *

How can we search for the company name? We can't use a simple string comparison with eq because the word might be broken by some amount of whitespace—we'd have to search for /Yahoo\s+Inc\b/ instead of the fixed string "Yahoo Inc". The trailing /\b/, a word boundary, is important since it ensures that the "Inc" is not embed-

---

* The second substitution in the snippet uses the s/.../.../x form of Perl's substitution operator, which allows comments and free whitespace (outside of character classes). That substitution is equivalent to s/^\w*\W+/. Readers unfamiliar with the /x modifiers and selectable delimiters should see Chapter 5 of *Programming Perl* or my *Mastering Regular Expressions* (both published by O'Reilly).

ded within some other word. This allows "Yahoo Inc" to match, but prohibits "Yahoo Incubators".

One approach could be to preprocess $entire_article to normalize all spans of whitespace to a single space. This saves having to convert the name to a regular expression (and the overhead of then applying it), but it requires an extra overall search and replace on $entire_article, and removes some of the flexibility of using regular expressions (such as the convenience of /\b/, or recognizing "Inc" and "Incorporated" with a regex that matches both, like /Inc(?:\b|Incorporated)/).

Unfortunately, both methods ended up taking several seconds per article—too slow for Yahoo!. I tried a number of tricks to gain some speed. I changed the ticker-to-name database to a ticker-to-regex database, where the regex matched the rest of the name. It's not always a straightforward task to turn a fixed string into a regex when you want to use a trailing /\b/, since something like /Yahoo!\b/ would not produce the expected results (it could match "Yahoo!oohaY" but not "Yahoo! Inc"), so some caution is required.

Accomplishing this in a preprocessing stage, before any articles are processed, allows me to compute without worrying about saving cycles. Some of the data I ended up with is shown below in a sampling of %word2ticker database entries:

```
Acme           ACE|AMI|ACU
International ...|IBM|...|IGT|...
Adaptec        ADPT
```

Here's a sampling of %ticker2restofname database entries:

```
ADPT Inc(?:\b|orporated\b)
ACE  Electric\s+Corp(?:\b|oration\b)
ACU  United\s+Corp(?:\b|oration\b)
AMI  Metals\s+Inc(?:\b|orporated\b)
IBM  Business\s+Machines\s+Corp(?:\b|oration\b)
IGT  Game\s+Technology\s+Inc(?:\b|orporated\b)
```

When the script finds the word "Adaptec", it looks in %word2ticker to see if it might be the start of the company name for ADPT. The other database, %ticker2restofname, then tells us that if we can match /Inc(?:\b|orporated\b)/ we'll have found the company "Adaptec Incorporated".

You'll notice that each regex of %ticker2restofname begins directly with a word. This means that as our script nibbles off words to be checked, it'll also have to remove any trailing whitespace. This allows the %ticker2restofname regexes to be applied directly.

Putting this all together, the main body of the routine then looked like:

```
MAIN:
  while (length) {
      if (s{ ^ ([A-Z]\w*) \s* }{}x ) { # capitalized word
          if ($tickers = $word2ticker{$1}) {
```

```
            # for each company beginning with this word...
            while ($tickers =~ m/([^|]+)/g) {

                $regex = $ticker2restofname{$ticker = $1};
                if (s/^$regex//g) {
                    ## mark the ticker as seen
                    $found{$ticker} = 1;
                    next MAIN;
                }
            }
        }
    }
    s/^\w*\W+//; # get rid of anything else
}
```

This works well enough, but was still slower than I wanted. One problem is the incessant modification of the string as it's nibbled away. I used the nibbling approach because it was convenient, not because of an inherent need to modify the article. I thought that it might be faster if I could dispense with all the substitutions.

Going on a Diet

Since the nibbling occurs at the beginning of the string, I had to try matching the full name only at the beginning—I could use /^/, which can speed up matching considerably. It's a useful technique, but in this case it's overkill. It was time to stop nibbling.

Remember the difference between list and scalar contexts when matching globally (m/.../g). In a list context (for example, @matches = m/.../g), the regex is applied over and over, and the results are returned as a list (a list of matches, or, if the regex contains capturing parentheses, a list of captured elements for each overall match) that is then assigned to @matches.

In a scalar context, such as while (m/.../g), the "next" occurrence in the target string is matched. Rather than all matches happening at once, one match attempt takes place each time the program executes the regex. The first time through, the first possible match is selected; subsequent iterations (until the target string is modified, or until there are no more matches) select the next match. Consider this loop:

```
while ( m/ ([A-Z]\w*) \s* /gx ) {
    my $word = $1;
    printf "found [$word] ending at %d\n", pos($_);
}
```

After a scalar context m/.../g is executed (and only then), Perl's built-in pos function returns the position at which the match ended. Looking at it another way, it's the offset at which the next match will be attempted. (These two viewpoints are almost always the same, but in certain cases where the regex can successfully match nothingness, the regex engine will actually start a match from one character beyond pos to avoid an infinite loop.)

This pos behavior applies to the string, not to the regex. So we can use *additional* scalar-context m/.../g matches on the same string to match something else where the first match (our word-grabber) left off. Consider the not-quite-correct code:

```
while ( m{ ([A-Z]\w*) \s* }gx ) {
    my $word = $1;
    if (m{ \G Inc\b }gx) {
        print "Found ''$word Inc''.\n";
    }
}
```

We can use this approach to solve the company-matching problem more efficiently, but some caution is called for. First, all matches to be done "down the string" *must* be applied via scalar-context m/.../g operators, and it's easy to forget the /g in a scalar context.

Secondly, if we want a regex to match only at the position where the previous one left off, we have to take care to use /\G/ at the beginning. This prohibits the normal "bump along" down the string in search of a match.

Finally, the remembered position in the string is reset upon a failing match, so we need to save and restore it manually, via a variable that I'll call $offset.

```
while ( m{ ([A-Z]\w*) \s* }gx ) {
    my $word = $1;
    my $offset = pos($_); # where next match starts
    if (m{ \G Inc\b }gx) {
        print "Found ''$word Inc''.\n";
    } else {
        pos($_) = $offset; # we failed, restore pos
    }
}
```

Note that we don't restore $offset when the attempt to match the rest of the name (just "Inc" in this example) succeeds. When it does succeed, the position is moved beyond the end of the name—right where we want it so that we can start afresh to search for another name.

When I implemented the full match algorithm using this method, the result looked something like this:

```
MAIN:
while ( m{ ([A-Z]\w*) \s* }gx ) {
    my $word = $1;
    if ($tickers = $word2ticker{$word})          {
        my $pos = pos; # next match start position

        # for each company beginning with this word
        while ($tickers =~ m/([^|]+)/g) {
            $regex = $ticker2restofname{$ticker = $1};
            if (m/\G$regex/g) {
                $found{$ticker} = 1;
                next MAIN;
```

```
        }
        pos = $pos; # we failed, so restore the match
      }
    }
  }
```

The speedup over the previous implementation was substantial. However, there are still other ways to speed things up. For example, it's a simple test to see if the character at pos($_) matches the first character of the rest-of-name regex (which, we know, always starts with literal text). This could be as simple as the following example after we know there are company names that begin with $word:

```
$char = ord(substr($_, pos, 1));
```

and this just inside the check-each-company loop:

```
next if ord($regex) != $char;
```

This is a quick check that short-circuits the application of most regexes, which saves both regex compile time and execution time.

Another way to speed things up is to help lead the main first-word regex to a quicker match. We know it will fail at each character position until an uppercase letter is found. Since we care only that we isolate a capitalized word, we can add a leading /\W*/ and it won't hurt a thing. It explicitly tells the regex engine that it can continue past any /\W/ characters on the way to matching /[A-Z]\w*/ and the rest.

If we add /[a-z0-9_]\w*/, we can bypass noncapitalized words as well. Thus, a leading /\W* (?: [a-z0-9_]\w*\W*)*/ allows the regex itself (rather than the bump-along-on-failure mechanics of the regex engine) to skip over uninteresting parts of the text. Since we take care of this ourselves, we can use a leading \G to have the regex fail a bit more quickly when no words are left.

Putting this all together, we get

```
while (m{\G\W*
          (?:
                # At this point we have either
                # nothing or a "word." If not an
                # uppercase word, skip and try again.
                [a-z0-9_]\w*\W*
          )*
          (\w+)\s*
      }gx) {
  my $word = $1;
  if ($tickers = $word2ticker{$word}) {
      my $pos = pos; # save next match start position
      my $char = ord(substr($_, $pos, 1));

      # for each company that begins with this word...
      while ($tickers =~ m/([^|]+)/g) {
          $regex = $ticker2restofname{$ticker = $1};
          next if ord($regex) != $char;
```

```
            if (m/\G$regex/g) {
                $found{$ticker} = 1;
                next MAIN;
            }
            pos = $pos; # we failed, so must restore match
        }
    }
}
```

Depending on how the routine is used, there are a few other possible enhancements. For example, if it's to be applied to a lot of text, it might make sense to cache the compiled rest-of-name regexes (as it is, they are recompiled each time they're used, which might be many times per article). Even without that optimization, however, we have a much improved solution at hand.

CHAPTER 17

How Regexes Work

Mark Jason Dominus

This isn't an article about how to use regexes; you've seen plenty of those already. It's about how you would write a regex package from scratch, in a language like C that didn't already have one. I demonstrate a new module, Regex.pm, which implements regexes from nothing, in Perl. This will give you an idea of how regex matching is possible, although the details differ rather substantially from what Perl actually does.

Here's the basic strategy. We'll see a kind of "machine" that reads some input, one character at a time, and then, depending on what's in the input and on the various wheels and gears in the machine, says either "yes" or "no". The machines are simple, and it turns out that if we have a regex, it's not hard to construct a machine that says "yes" for exactly those strings that match the regex, and "no" for all the other strings.

When our program wants to see if S matched /R/, it'll do something like this:

- Look at R.
- Construct the machine that corresponds to R.
- Feed S into the machine.
- If the machine says "yes", then S matched /R/. (Otherwise, it didn't.)

Maybe this sounds bizarre, but it's what Perl does. If you can follow what happens in this article, you'll know what Perl is really up to when it performs a regex match.

Machines

We're on a tight budget here, so our machines will be made of circles and arrows instead of wheels and gears. This diagram shows a machine.

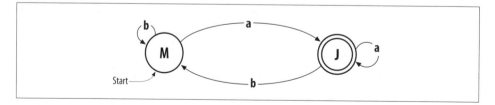

Let's see if this machine says "yes" to the string "abaa". How do we do that?

We start by putting a penny down on the **M** circle, because the **M** circle is the *start circle*. We can tell that **M** is the start circle because it has that arrow pointing to it that says "start". The letter **M** could have been anything; it's not actually part of the machine. I just put it on so you would know which circle I meant.

Now the machine will read the first character in the string: "a". There's an arrow leading out of the **M** circle that's labeled "a", so we move the penny along the arrow from **M** to **J**.

Next, the machine will read the "b". The penny moves back to **M**. Then the machine reads another "a", and the penny moves back once more to **J**. Finally, the machine reads the last "a", and the penny follows the "a" arrow that leads from **J** back to **J**.

The penny is finally on **J**. We're done. So, how do we tell if the machine said "yes"? The rule is this: some circles, like **J**, are double circles. These are called *final circles*. At the end of the input, if there are any pennies on final circles, the machine says "yes". If no pennies are on final circles, the machine says "no". In this case, there's a penny on **J**, so the machine says "yes".

Now, that's not so hard to do, and it's easy to see that this machine will say "yes" to some strings and "no" to others. It so happens that it says "yes" to any string that is matched by the regex /^(a|b)*a$/, and "no" to all the strings not matched. We say that the machine is *equivalent* to the regex.

Soon we'll see how to make machines that are equivalent to any regex we like. First, though, we'll add a couple of features to the machines that will make this easier.

Blank Arrows

So far every arrow we've seen has been labeled with a letter. But some machines have unlabeled arrows, like in this diagram.

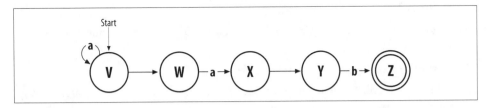

The instant a penny arrives in any circle with a blank arrow leading out of it, we place *another* penny on the circle at the far end of the blank arrow.

Let's look at the machine above and see what it says about "ab". The start circle is **V**, so we start by putting a penny there. And then, because there's a blank arrow from **V** to **W**, we immediately put a second penny on **W**. Now the machine is ready to read input. It reads the "a". The penny on **V** moves along the arrow to **V**, and the penny on **W** moves along the arrow to **X**, so we now have pennies on **V** and **X**. Next, because there's a blank arrow leading from **X** to **Y**, we place a third penny on **Y**, and because there's a blank arrow from **V** to **W**, we place a fourth penny on **W**.

Next, the machine reads "b". The penny on **Y** moves to **Z**. But what happens to the pennies on **V**, **W**, and **X**? There's a special rule for this: pennies that have nowhere to go must leave. We take away the pennies on **V**, **W**, and **X**. Only the penny on **Z** remains. Now the machine is done reading the input. There's a penny on **Z**, which is a final circle, so the machine says "yes".

Sometimes a machine will have two arrows from the same circle that also have the same label, as shown in this diagram.

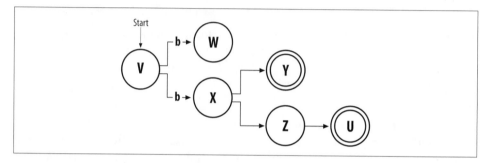

The penny here starts on **V**. What happens when this machine reads the string "b"? There's a "b" arrow from **V** to **W** and also from **V** to **X**. The rule here is simple: the penny clones itself. One clone goes one way and the other goes the other way, and we end up with pennies on both **W** *and* **X**.

You'll notice blank arrows from **X** to **Y** and from **X** to **Z**; as soon as the penny arrives at **X**, we put new pennies on **Y** and **Z** also. Then, because a penny just arrived at **Z**, we put one on **U** as well.

Rules Again

Before we see how to turn a regex into a machine, let's recap the rules for moving pennies:

1. To start, put a penny on the circle labeled "start".

2. If there is a blank arrow leading from **X** to **Y**, then whenever a penny arrives at **X**, put another penny at **Y** also.

3. Whenever the machine reads an input character c, move all the pennies. If a penny is on a circle that has an outgoing arrow labeled "c", move the penny along the arrow, and then follow rule 2 if appropriate. If there is more than one such arrow, the penny clones itself and one clone follows each arrow. If a penny is on a circle with no arrow labeled "c", remove that penny.

4. When all input is read, the machine says "yes" if any penny is on a final circle, and "no" otherwise.

Perhaps you can imagine that it might not be hard to write a program to carry out these four simple rules, to keep track of where the pennies are, and to yield the final "yes" or "no".

In fact, that's exactly how regexes work. Perl turns the regex into a machine, simulates the positions of the pennies, and at the end of the input reports whether any pennies are on final circles. The only question left is: how can we turn a regex into a machine?

How to Turn a Regex into a Penny Machine

First, we're going to assume that all our regexes are anchored at the front and the back. That is, we're only going to deal with regexes that look like /^P$/, where P might be complicated. It turns out that this doesn't give anything away, because if /Q/ is a regex that isn't anchored, then /^.*Q.*$/ is a completely equivalent anchored regex that matches the same strings. If someone wanted us to make a machine for /Q/, we could make one for /^.*Q.*$/ instead, and they'd never be the wiser. From now on I'm going to leave out the ^ and the $, because it makes the examples easier to read.

There are two kinds of regexes. They're either very simple things like /x/, or they're more complex things, built out of simpler regexes. For example, if P is a regex, then P* is also a regex. That means we're going to have to do two things: we'll have to see how to build simple machines for the simple regexes, and we'll have to see how to combine those simple machines into more complicated machines.

Here's the machine for the regex /a/.

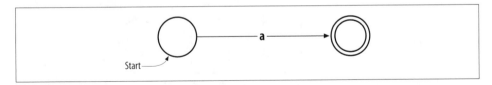

Stare at this a while to convince yourself that it really says "yes" only for the string "a" and not for any other string. What does it say about the empty string? What about "b"? "aa"?

And here's an even simpler machine. It's equivalent to //.

Remember that I left out ^ and $, so // really matches only the empty string, and the equivalent machine will say "yes" only for the empty string.

Now let's suppose we already have machines for /P/ and /Q/, and let's try to figure out how to make a machine for /P|Q/. That's pretty easy.

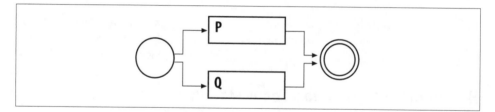

The penny starts on the left. Clones are immediately created and move to the circles that used to be the start circles for P and for Q. For the machine to say "yes", the P penny must make its way to what used to be P's final circle, or the Q penny must make its way to what used to be Q's final circle; if either of those things happen, that penny will clone itself to the real final circle on the far right. If neither of those things happens, no penny will escape from either machine P or machine Q. Any string that P would have matched will get a penny through P to the final circle, and any string that Q would have matched will get a penny through Q to the final circle. So this machine says "yes" for any string that either P or Q would have said "yes" to, and not to any other strings. That's exactly what we wanted.

How about if we have machines for /P/ and /Q/, and we want to make a machine for /PQ/? We can do it as shown here.

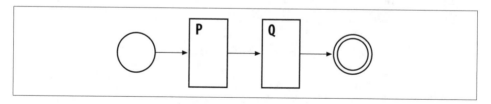

It's easy to see that we can chain together as many machines as we want this way. For example, here is a machine that is equivalent to the regex /perl/.

Now let's tackle /P+/, which turns out to be a little easier than /P*/.

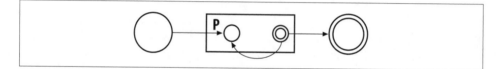

Once the penny passes through **P**, it clones itself. One clone immediately moves to the final circle, and one moves back to the beginning of **P** to try again, in case there are more **P**s coming up.

Now that we've seen this process, /P*/ is easy too; we just short-circuit the beginning to the end, so that the penny doesn't have to go through **P** even once.

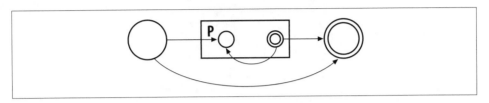

Oh, now we're done.

What Do You Mean, Done?

Well, we left out character classes. But [abc] is the same as (a|b|c), so we can handle that by pretending the user wrote it that way.

We left out \d, \s, and all those things. But those are just character classes; . is also a character class if we don't mind writing it as (\000|\001|...|\255). That makes the machine big and inefficient, but it works. We'll see later on how to make it better.

We left out ?. But /P?/ is just the same as /(P|)/, so it's really there too. And we left out {*n*}. But /P{3}/ is just the same as /PPP/, so we really don't need {*n*}. Similar arguments work for {*m*,} and {*m*,*n*}.

We left out the nongreedy quantifiers. But those don't change *whether* the regexes will match, only *how* the regexes match, so they don't affect our program. We can ignore them.

We left out ^ and $, but they're in there by default; if you want to take them away you can attach .* at the beginning or the end, or both.

We left out zero-width assertions like \b and (?:...) and (?!...). But this is an introductory article, so I made a command decision to leave them out.

We also left out backreferences, but I'll show how to put them in later, just to prove I'm not a slacker.

By the way, this construction for turning regexes into machines was invented in 1968 by a fellow named Ken Thompson. You may have heard of Thompson; he and Dennis Ritchie invented Unix around the same time.

The Regex Module

The module has three parts. It has a part for turning strings into regexes, a part for turning regexes into machines, and a part for shuffling the pennies around. Here's a program that looks to see whether the string "abbbbb" matches the pattern /^ab+$/.

```
use Regex;

$regex   = Regex->parse('ab+');  # Parse the string
$machine = NFA->compile($regex); # Build the machine

# Does "abbbbb" match /ab+/ ?
$result  = NFA_Exec->match($machine, 'abbbbb');

print "It ", ($result ? "did ": "did not "), "match.\n";
```

The output, as we would hope, is:

```
It did match.
```

Try it yourself. Regex.pm is available at *http://perl.plover.com/Regex/*. You'll find a sample grep program in the directory.

Implications for Perl

Is this really what Perl does? Pretty much, except Perl's regexes are written in C, while Regex.pm is written in Perl. Perl parses the regex string into an internal format, and then turns the internal format into a machine. Perl's machine works a little differently from the ones I showed, but the principle is the same.

Constructing the machine for a certain regex can take a relatively long time, but once it's constructed, running an input through it is very fast, and you can run lots of different inputs through it without reconstructing it. That is just what Perl does; when you first run your program, Perl turns all your regexes into machines and saves the machines for later. Then it can do fast pattern-matching with any of them because the machines are already on the shelf waiting to be used.

Actually, I lied. Perl can't always build the machines as soon as you run your program. Consider this program, which reads an input, and prints out each line if it happens to contain its own line number ($. is the line number of the current line of input):

```
while (<>) {
    print if /$./;
}
```

Perl can't possibly build the machine for /$./ as soon as your program is run, because /$./ changes from line to line. Perl has to build a new machine every time through the loop. That makes this a slow program.

Let's consider a slightly different program. This one is like the Unix grep command: you give it a pattern as the command-line argument, and it prints all the lines from its input that match that pattern:

```
my $pat = shift;

while (<>) {
    print if /$pat/;
}
```

Again, Perl rebuilds the machine every time through the loop. It does this because it is afraid that $pat might have changed since last time, and it is too dumb to see that $pat never actually changes. If only there were a way to tell Perl that $pat never changes!

There *is* a way to tell Perl that $pat never changes: the /o modifier.

```
my $pat = shift;

while (<>) {
    print if /$pat/o;
}
```

Normally, Perl likes to build its machine when it compiles the rest of your program. For regexes with variables in them, it rebuilds the machine every time it uses the regex—unless you put in /o. If you do that, Perl builds the machine for the regex exactly once (o is for "once"), the first time it uses the regex, and puts it on the shelf for later. After the first time, it assumes that the variables are always the same, and uses the machine from the shelf instead of making a new one every time.

Beginners are always writing slow programs like this:

```
my @pats = ('fo*', 'ba.', 'w+3');

while (<>) {
    foreach $pat (@pats) {
        print if /$pat/;
    }
}
```

Perl has to build a new machine every time $pat changes. If there are a million lines in the input, Perl builds the same three machines a million times each. You can make this program much faster by writing it like this:

```
my @pats = ('fo*', 'ba.', 'w+3');

my $pat = join('|', @pats);

while (<>) {
    print if /$pat/o;
}
```

By arranging to have only one pattern that never changes, instead of three patterns that are used alternately, we can tell Perl to build a regex machine exactly once instead of three million times.

What About Backreferences?

I promised to show you how to do this to prove I wasn't a slacker. You can skip this section if you don't care how to do backreferences, as long as you agree first that I'm not a slacker.

Just to make things a little easier to discuss, we'll pretend that you can have only one backreference in each regex. \1 will work, but \2 and \3 won't. After you see how to make \1 work, it'll be easy to see how to make the rest work too.

To do backreferences, we need to add a tape recorder to each penny. If the tape recorder is on, it records the input that the machine is receiving.

We also add three new kinds of circles: a "record" circle, a "stop" circle, and a "replay" circle. When the penny enters a "record" circle, its tape recorder starts recording. When the penny enters a "stop" circle, it stops recording.

The "replay" circle is a little different. It has exactly one outgoing arrow. When the penny enters the "replay" circle, it stops and rewinds the tape. Then it waits on the replay circle while the machine reads more input, and it compares the input to what's on the tape. If the input doesn't match what's on the tape, or if the input runs out before the tape does, the penny dies. But if the input does match the tape, the penny immediately moves off the "replay" circle along the outgoing arrow, and then continues moving normally.

If P is a regex, here's how we build the machine for /(P)/; it's just like /P/ except it also records the input that matched P.

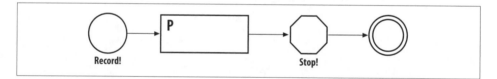

Here's the machine for /\1/.

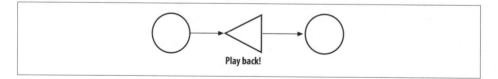

Here's the machine for /(a+)\1/.

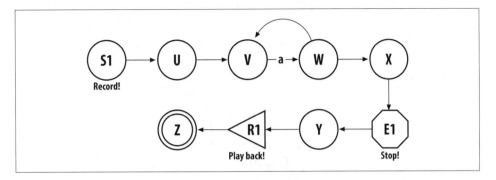

Let's see what happens when this machine reads the string "aaaa". We put a penny on **S1**, the start circle, and the penny immediately begins recording on its tape recorder. The penny clones itself and its tape recorder, and the clones move to **U** and to **V**.

Now, every time the machine reads an "a", a penny gets through to **W** with an additional "a" written on its tape. This penny moves through to **E1**, which shuts off the tape recorder. The first such penny has just "a" on is tape. It arrives at **R1**; when the machine reads the second "a" it moves to **Z**, and then on the third "a" it dies. But the second penny to come out at **X** has two "a"s on its tape; it gets out of **R1** just after the machine reads the third and fourth "a"s, and it gets to **Z** just in time for the end of the input. The penny on **Z** at the end of the input signals a "yes", and the "aa" on its tape means that $1 is "aa".

There were two other pennies that came out at **X**, one with "aaa" on its tape and one with "aaaa". But those pennies stayed stuck in **R1** waiting for the machine to read more "a"s.

If you want more backreferences, just add more tape recorders to each penny. And you have one kind of "record", "stop", and "replay" circle for every backreference. /\3/ becomes a circle that says "replay tape 3", and the fifth (in a regex becomes a circle that says "start recording on tape 5".

Internals of Regex.pm

The module's NFA->compile method transforms a regex into a machine, following pretty much the same steps that we did in the article. It starts with the subexpressions, and then combines smaller machines into one large machine. The structure for a machine is so simple that I'll just give an example.

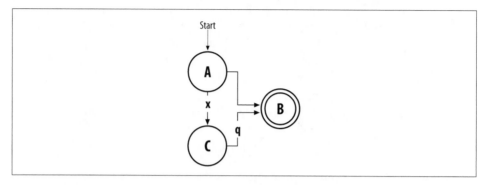

This has the following representation:

```
{
  A => { ''  => B,      # Unlabeled arrow from A to B
         'x' => C,      # Arrow labeled 'x' from A to C
       },
  B => { },             # No arrows from B
  C => { 'q' => B },    # Arrow labeled 'q' from C to B
  Symbols => [ A, B ],  # Start and final circles.
}
```

This is convenient because it's easy to look up where a given penny should move to when the machine reads a certain character in the input.

The best way to see what the module is really doing is to run the test program under the debugger and ask it to print out the data structures. Once you know about the machines and the pennies, the whole thing should be almost transparent. (Warning: the circle names are generated automatically, so they all have names like "Saa01".)

The module performs a very ordinary simulation of where the pennies are after each character in the input. Here's a simple example: When the input has run out, the simulator just looks to see if there is a penny on the final circle, something like this:

```
foreach $s ($self->circles_with_pennies) {
    if ($self->{machine}->is_final_circle($s)) {
        # Aha! We win!
        return 1;
    }
}
# No penny on a final circle; pattern match fails.
return 0;
```

The real code uses technical jargon, but this code is identical except for the jargon. You can find the code in the function NFA_Exec->final_state.

Lies

Perl doesn't really do it exactly the way I showed you. It's close, and the principle is the same, but there's one big difference. The difference is that Perl never moves more than one penny at a time.

Whenever a penny clones itself, Perl makes a choice about which one to move, and saves the locations of the others. If the penny that Perl is moving dies, Perl *backtracks* to one of the other pennies, and picks up where it left off. This has a number of benefits. If the penny Perl happens to be moving ends on the final circle at the end of the input, then Perl knows that the input matched, even though it didn't move the other pennies, so it is able to save time.

Alternately, if the programmer asks for a second match, Perl merely has to go back and try some more pennies until it finds a second one that wins; the path that the second penny took is the second match. When you move all the pennies at once, you get all the matches at once too, and there's no good way to make use of all the information you get.

When a penny clones itself, Perl has to make a choice about which penny to follow and which to save for later. By making the decision one way, it gets the greedy operators *, +, and ?; by choosing the other penny in each case, the operators become the nongreedy versions, *?, +?, and ??.

The one-penny-at-a-time system that Perl uses is also more convenient for handling backreferences. Instead of having to associate a set of tape recordings with each penny, Perl only needs to have one set of tape recordings for the single current penny, and some saved tape recordings for the pennies it might have to backtrack to.

However, the one-penny-at-a-time system also has a terrible drawback: for some patterns, the number of saved pennies can become huge, and Perl can spend literally hours returning to one saved penny after another. For example, consider the pattern /^(\d+)*$/. For a complete discussion of a similarly rotten expression, see *Understanding Regular Expressions, Part I*. Here's the short summary: any idiot can see that a string like "1234567890:" won't match because of the : on the end. But Perl wastes a lot of time pointlessly backtracking.

Perl sees the *, and it needs to decide how many times to repeat the preceding expression, the (\d+). This means it gets to use as many \d+s as it wants to. First it lets \d+ match 1234567890, using only one \d+; but that doesn't work, because of the :, so Perl backs off and lets \d+ match just 123456789, and it uses a second \d+ to match the 0; but that doesn't work either. So it retreats and lets the first \d+ match 012345678, and the second match 90. That fails, so it tries making the second \d+ match only the 9, and uses a third instance of \d+ for the 0. That fails too, so it shortens the first \d+ again to match only the 01234567. And so on. What a disaster.

The many-pennies-at-once approach scores a huge win here. The machine doesn't have very many circles, at most two for every symbol in the regular expression, and so there need never be very many pennies. Suppose two pennies happen to move onto the same circle. The one-at-a-time approach would have dealt with them separately, at different times. But the many-pennies-at-once approach can replace these two pennies with one penny.* The result: fewer pennies get moved, there's no backtracking, and the regular expression finishes quickly instead of slowly.

The program at *http://perl.plover.com/Regex/demo.pl* demonstrates this approach. It builds and runs the equivalent Regex.pm penny machine first, and that takes less

---

* Only if we're ignoring backreferences. We can't join pennies if we're saving backreferences, because the two pennies probably have different recordings on their tapes.

than two seconds, even on a 75 MHz Pentium. Then it tries using Perl's built-in regular expressions, and that takes hours, even on a speedy workstation. (Improvements were made to the regex system in Perl 5.6 that solved this particular problem in a different way, so you will want to run the demo with Perl 5.005 or earlier.)

Other Directions

For an easy project, try adding the . symbol. You'll have to modify the parser a little, and machines will need to have a new kind of arrow that indicates a transition on any input at all. From there it's only a small step to adding general character classes. (A solution is available at *http://perl.plover.com/Regex/dot-diffs*.)

OMAR (Our Most Assiduous Reader) might enjoy adding backreferences to the Regex module. Probably the most difficult part will be fixing the string-to-regex parser, which is a terrible hack; the rest of the code is much more flexible.

If you're interested in the details of how Perl's internal machines work, you might enjoy running this to see what happens:

```
perl -Dr -ne 'print if /SOMETHING/';
```

On a Perl compiled with the -DDEBUGGING flag, -Dr displays the details of the regular expression machinery, both at the time that the machines are constructed and when they're used. Be prepared for surprises! For example, the * in /x*/ is different from the * in /(xy)*/. The former is a real *, but the latter is treated as if you had written /(xy){0,32767}/ instead.

Bibliography

Introduction to Compiler Construction, Thomas W. Parsons, pp. 20-46 and especially 40-46. Computer Science Press, New York, 1992.

"Regular Expression Search Algorithm," Ken Thompson. *Communications of the ACM*, vol. 11, no. 6, pp. 419-422, 1968.

PART III

Computer Science

From my point of view, there are two kinds of articles in this section: the half that are by me, and the half that are by other people. Among the articles by other people, there are two articles about random number generation. *Randomness*, by Jon Orwant, is one of those magical articles that somehow starts with a technical topic and expands like a 1950s horror movie monster to cover everything in its path, such as cryptanalytic attacks and Vegas mafia thugs. Along the way, he discusses the use and internals of random number generators in general, and Perl's in particular. *Random Number Generators and XS*, by Otmar Lendl, picks up where Jon's article leaves off, discussing many of those topics in more detail, covering the entropy source devices available in the Linux kernel, and finishing with an introduction to XS, the glue system for installing new built-in functions into Perl.

The two large articles in this section are by Sean Burke and Damian Conway. Damian's article *Parsing* is a long and detailed discussion of his brilliant and extremely useful Parse::RecDescent module. Sean's article *Trees and Game Trees* is another one of those wonderful monster-movie creatures: he starts by discussing tree structures in general, and works around to trees that contain data, and then to tree structures as the result of an HTML parsing process, the HTML::TreeBuilder module and how you might use it to transform HTML documents, trees as representations of a game, and then tree search as a technique for computing game strategies.

Ulrich Pfeifer's article on *Information Retrieval* discusses weighting systems for selecting documents that are most relevant to a user's query. Richard Dice's *Making Life and Death Decisions with Perl* is a discussion of conditional probability and presents code to analyze the results of medical experiments.

I ultimately owe my own small fame in the Perl world to the other half of the articles in this chapter. The articles on *B-Trees* and *Compression* discuss fundamental technologies of advanced computer applications. Data compression is familiar to everyone who's ever run out of disk space. B-trees are the complex data structures used to implement fast keyed database indices (including Perl's familiar "DBM" files, for example.)

The other two articles, on *Memoization* and *Infinite Lists*, are my favorites. They're both attempts to speed up computation by skipping some of the work. *Infinite Lists* was my first article, and discusses the technique of *lazy computation*, which is essentially computerized procrastination. Instead of computing the results the user asks for, you give the user back an IOU. But it's a trick IOU, and when the user looks at it to see what the results were, you distract them and replace the IOU with the result they originally wanted. The benefit to you is that if the user asks for more data than they actually need, you can save a lot of time because most of the IOU's are never cashed; the benefit to the user is that they can ask for tons of data even if they don't plan to use all of it. Memoization is an elaboration of *caching*, which is the art of saving results secretly after you compute them; then if someone asks for them again, you don't have to recompute the same things. Many programmers know how to fix up functions to do caching, but the amazing thing about Perl is that Perl can add caching behavior to any function automatically; you don't have to do a thing. This is memoization.

Now the plug. (Jon said I could put this in.) Both articles give a glimpse of a much deeper and more general topic, called *functional programming*, which is the use of dynamically generated functions as data. The original *Infinite Lists* article was the beginning of what turned out to be a several-year investigation into functional programming techniques in Perl; my conclusion was that since most Perl programmers come from a C and Unix background, or were trained by books written by people who did, they were writing C-like programs in Perl without meaning to, when in fact Perl was a much better language than C, with all sorts of wonderful features that most people in the Perl community weren't using effectively. Memoization is one of the useful techniques that's enabled by these features; it is completely impossible in C. If you find these articles interesting, please investigate my upcoming book, which will be published in 2003 by Morgan Kaufmann. The title is still undetermined, but you can find out about it at *http://perl.plover.com/book/*, and the entire text will be on-line at that address once it is published.

—Mark Jason Dominus

## CHAPTER 18

Infinite Lists

Mark Jason Dominus

Many of the objects in programming are at least conceptually infinite—the text of the Associated Press newswire, the log output from a web server, or the digits of π. There's a general principle in programming that we should model things as simply and straightforwardly as possible, so that if an object is infinite, we should model it as infinite. That means an infinite data structure.

Of course, we can't have an infinite data structure, can we? After all, the computer only has a finite amount of memory. But that doesn't matter. We're all mortal and so we, and our programs, wouldn't really know an infinite data structure if we saw one. All that's really necessary is a data structure that behaves *as if* it were infinite.

A Unix pipe is a great example of such an object—think of a pipe that happens to be connected to the standard output of the yes program. From its manual page:

> **yes** prints the command line arguments, separated by spaces and followed by a newline, forever until it is killed.

The output of yes might not be infinite, but it's a credible imitation. So is the output of `tail -f` when applied to our web access log.

In this article I'll demonstrate how to implement a data structure called a *stream* that behaves as if it were infinite. We can keep pulling data out of this data structure, and it never runs out. Streams can be filtered, just like Unix data streams can be filtered with grep, and they can be transformed and merged, just like Unix streams. Programming with streams is a lot like programming with pipelines in the shell—we can construct a simple stream, then transform and filter it to get the stream we really want. To those used to programming with pipelines, programming with streams will feel very familiar.

As an example of a problem that's easy to solve with streams, we'll look at a classic algorithms problem.

Hamming's Problem

Hamming wanted an efficient algorithm that generates the list of all numbers of the form $2^i3^j5^k$ for i, j, k at least 0, in ascending order. This list is called the *Hamming sequence*, and begins like this:

    1 2 3 4 5 6 8 9 10 12 15 16 18 ...

Let's say we want compute the first three thousand of these. This problem was popularized by Edsger Dijkstra.

There's an obvious brute force technique: take the first number we haven't checked yet, divide it by 2s, 3s, and 5s until we can't do that any more. If we're left with 1, then the number should go on the list. Otherwise, throw it away and try the next number. So:

- Is 19 on the list? No, because it's not divisible by 2, 3, or 5.
- Is 20 on the list? Yes, because after we divide it by 2, 2, and 5, we're left with 1.
- Is 21 on the list? No, because after we divide it by 3, we're left with 7, which isn't divisible by 2, 3, or 5.

This obvious technique has one problem: it's mind-bogglingly slow. The problem is that most numbers aren't on the list, and we waste an immense amount of time discovering that. Although the numbers at the beginning of the list are pretty close together, the 2,999th number in the list is 278,628,139,008. Even if we had time to wait for the brute-force algorithm to check all the numbers up to 278,628,139,008, think how much longer we'd have to wait for it to find the next number in the sequence, which is 278,942,752,080.

It can be surprisingly difficult to solve this problem efficiently with conventional programming techniques. But it turns out to be easy with the techniques we'll explore in this article.

Streams

A *stream* is like the stream that comes out of a garden hose, except that what emerges isn't water but data. Whenever we need another data item, we pull one out of the stream, which produces data on demand forever. The key point is that, unlike a regular array that has all the data items stored away somewhere, the stream computes the data just as they're needed, at the moment our program asks for them. The data never takes any more space or time than necessary. We can't have an array of all the odd integers, because it would have to be infinitely long and consume an infinite amount of memory. But we can have a stream of all the odd integers, and pull as many odd integers out of it as we need, because it only computes the odd numbers one at a time as we ask for them.

We'll return to Hamming's problem later, after we've seen streams in more detail.

Unlike a regular Perl list, a stream is represented internally with a linked list made of *nodes*. Each node has two parts: the *head*, which contains a data item, and the *tail*, which points to the next node in the stream. In Perl, we'll implement this as a hash with two members. If %node is such a hash, then $node{h} will be the head, and $node{t} the tail. The tail will usually be a reference to another such node. A stream will be a linked list of the nodes, shown in Figure 18-1.

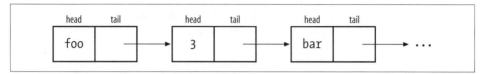

Figure 18-1. The stream ('foo', 3, 'bar', ...)

We'll be able to assign values to our stream as follows:

```
$stream->{h} = 'foo';
$stream->{t}{h} = 3;
$stream->{t}{t}{h} = 'bar';
$stream->{t}{t}{t}{h} = ... ;
```

We still have the problem of how to create an infinite stream, because clearly we can't construct an infinite number of these nodes. But here's the secret: a stream node might not have a tail—that is, it might not have been computed yet. If a stream doesn't have a tail, it has a *promise* instead. Our stream promises to compute the next node if you ever need the data item that would be in its head, as shown in Figure 18-2.

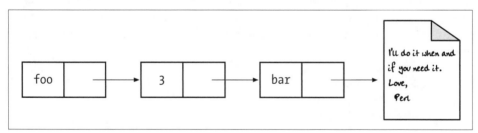

Figure 18-2. The "complete" stream ('foo', 3, 'bar', ...)

How can we program a promise? Perl doesn't have promises, does it? But it does! Here's what a promise to compute an expression looks like:

```
$promise = sub { EXPRESSION };
```

Perl doesn't compute the value of the expression right away; instead, it constructs an anonymous function that computes the expression and returns the value when you call it:

```
$value = $promise->( ); # Evaluate expression
```

That's just what we want. When we want to promise something without actually computing it, we'll just wrap it up in an anonymous function, and when we want to collect on the promise, we'll call the function.

How can we tell when a value is a promise? In our simple examples, we'll just look to see if it's a reference to a function:

```
if (ref $something eq CODE) { # It's a promise... }
```

In a real project, we might do something a little more elaborate, like inventing a Promise package with Promise objects, but in this article, we'll just stick with plain vanilla CODE refs.

Here's a simple function that constructs a stream node. It expects two arguments, a head and a tail. The tail should be either another stream or a promise to compute one. The function then takes the head and the tail, puts them into an anonymous hash with h and t members, and blesses the hash into the Stream package.

```
package Stream;

sub new {
    my ($package, $head, $tail) = @_;
    bless { h => $head, t => $tail } => $package;
}
```

The head method, which returns the head of a stream, is now easy to implement. We simply return the h member of the hash:

```
sub head { $_[0]{h} }
```

The tail method is a little more complicated because it must cope with two possibilities: if the tail of the stream is another node, tail can return it right away. But if the tail is a promise, then tail must collect on the promise and compute the real tail to return.

```
sub tail {
    my $tail = $_[0]{t};
    if (ref $tail eq CODE) {
        # Collect on the promise
        $_[0]{t} = $tail->();
    }
    $_[0]{t};
}
```

We also want a notation for an empty stream, or for a stream that has run out of data, in case we want finite streams as well as infinite ones. If a stream is empty, we'll represent it with a node that is missing the usual h and t members, and instead has an e member to show that it's empty. Here's a function to construct an empty stream:

```
sub empty {
    my $pack = shift;
    $pack = ref($pack) || $pack || Stream;
    bless {e => 'I am empty.'} => $pack;
}
```

And here's a function that tells us whether a stream is empty:

```
sub is_empty { exists $_[0]{e} }
```

These and all the other functions in this article are available at *http://perl.plover.com/Stream/Stream.pm*.

Let's see an example of how to use this. Here is a function that constructs an interesting stream: we give it a reference to a function $f, and a number $n, and it constructs the stream of all numbers of the form $f(n)$, $f(n+1)$, $f(n+2)$ etc.:

```
sub tabulate {
    my $f = shift;
    my $n = shift;
    Stream->new($f->($n), sub { &tabulate($f, $n+1) })
}
```

How does it work? The first element of the stream is just $f(n)$, which in Perl notation is $f->($n)$.

Rather than computing all the rest of the elements of the table (there are an infinite number of them, after all) this function promises to compute more if we want them. The promise is:

```
sub { &tabulate($f, $n+1) }
```

When invoked, this calls tabulate again, to compute all the values from $n+1 on up. Of course, it won't really compute *all* the values from $n+1 on up; it'll just compute $f(n+1)$, and give back a promise to compute $f(n+2)$ and the rest if they're needed.

Here's an example:

```
sub square { $_[0] * $_[0] }
$squares = &tabulate( \&square, 1);
```

The show utility, supplied in Stream.pm, prints out the first few elements of a stream—the first 10, if you don't say otherwise. $squares->show prints 1 4 9 16 25 36 49 64 81 100.

Let's add a little debugging to tabulate so we can see what's going on better. This version of tabulate is the same as the one above, except that it prints an extra line of output just before it calls the function f:

```
sub tabulate {
    my $f = shift;
    my $n = shift;
    print STDERR "-- Computing f($n)\n"; # For debugging
    Stream->new($f->($n), sub { &tabulate($f, $n+1) } )
}

$squares = &tabulate( \&square, 1);
        -- Computing f(1)
$squares->show(5);
        1 -- Computing f(2)
        4 -- Computing f(3)
```

```
       9 -- Computing f(4)
      16 -- Computing f(5)
      25 -- Computing f(6)
$squares->show(6);
      1 4 9 16 25 36 -- Computing f(7)
$squares->show(5);
      1 4 9 16 25
```

Something interesting happened with show(6) up there—the stream object called the tabulate function only once, to compute the square of 7. The other six elements had already been computed and saved, so it didn't need to compute them again. Similarly, the second time we executed show(5), the program didn't need to call tabulate at all; it had already computed and saved the first five squares, so it just printed them out. I discuss how to save computed function values using this technique in the article *Memoization*.

Someday, we could come along and try:

```
$squares->show(1_000_000_000);
```

and the stream would compute 999,999,993 squares for us, but until we ask for them, it won't. That saves space and time, and is called *lazy evaluation*.

To solve Hamming's problem, we need only one more tool, called merge, a function that takes two streams of numbers in ascending order and merges them together into one stream of numbers in ascending order, eliminating duplicates. For example, merging:

```
1 3 5 7 9 11 13 15 17 ...
```

with:

```
1 4 9 16 25 36 ...
```

yields:

```
1 3 4 5 7 9 11 13 15 16 17 19 ...

sub merge {
    my $s1 = shift;
    my $s2 = shift;
    return $s2 if $s1->is_empty;
    return $s1 if $s2->is_empty;
    my $h1 = $s1->head;
    my $h2 = $s2->head;
    if ($h1 < $h2) {
        Stream->new($h1, sub { &merge($s1->tail, $s2      ) })
    } elsif ($h2 < $h1) {
        Stream->new($h2, sub { &merge($s1,       $s2->tail) })
    } else { # heads are equal
        Stream->new($h1, sub { &merge($s1->tail, $s2->tail) })
    }
}
```

Hamming's Problem Revisited

Now we have enough tools to solve Hamming's problem. We know that the first element of the Hamming sequence is 1. That's easy. The rest of the sequence is made up of multiples of 2, multiples of 3, and multiples of 5.

Let's think about the multiples of 2 for a minute. Here's the Hamming sequence, with multiples of 2 in bold:

> 1 **2** 3 **4** 5 **6** **8** 9 **10** **12** 15 **16** **18** ...

Now here's the Hamming sequence again, with every element multiplied by 2:

> 2 4 6 8 10 12 16 18 20 24 30 32 36 ...

Notice how the second row of numbers contains all of the bold numbers from the first row—if a number is even, and it's a Hamming number, then it's two times some other Hamming number. That means that if we had the Hamming sequence hanging around, we could multiply every number in it by 2, and that would give us all the even Hamming numbers. We could do the same thing with 3 and 5 instead of 2. By multiplying the Hamming sequence by 2, 3, and 5, and merging those three sequences together, we'd get a sequence that contained all the Hamming numbers that were multiples of 2, 3, and 5. That's all of them, except for 1, which we could just tack on the front. This is how we'll solve our problem.

Let's build a function that takes a stream and multiplies every element in it by a constant:

```
# Multiply every number in a stream $self
# by a constant factor $n

sub scale {
    my $self = shift;
    my $n = shift;
    return Stream->empty if $self->is_empty;
    Stream->new($self->head * $n, sub { $self->tail->scale($n) });
}
```

Here's the solution to the Hamming sequence problem: We use scale to scale the Hamming sequence by 2, 3, and 5, merge those three streams together, and finally tack a 1 on the front.

```
# Construct the stream of Hamming's numbers.
 sub hamming {
    my $hamming;
    $hamming = Stream->new(
        1,
        sub { &merge($hamming->scale(2),
            &merge($hamming->scale(3),
                $hamming->scale(5))) });
    $hamming;
}
```

The only tricky thing here is that we must assign $hamming on the line *after* we declare it. This is because the $hamming variable comes into scope only on the line *after* it's declared.

hamming works, and it's efficient:

```
&hamming( )->show(20);
1 2 3 4 5 6 8 9 10 12 15 16 18 20 24 25 27 30 32 36 40
```

It only takes about 20 seconds to compute 3,000 Hamming numbers, even on my dinky 75 MHz Pentium.

We could make this more efficient by fixing up merge to merge three streams instead of two, but that's left as an exercise for Our Most Assiduous Reader. (Or see *http:// perl.plover.com/Stream/* for a sample solution.)

Dataflow Programming

The great thing about streams is that we can treat them as sources of data, and we can compute with these sources by merging and filtering data streams. This is called a *dataflow* paradigm. Unix programmers are probably already familiar with dataflow, because programming with pipelines in the shell is similar.

Here's an example of a function, filter, that accepts one stream as an argument, filters out all the elements from it that we don't want, and returns a stream of the elements we do want—it does for streams what the Unix grep program does for pipes, or what the Perl grep function does for lists.

filter's second argument is a predicate function that is applied to each element of the stream, returning true if the element should be left in the stream, false if it is discarded.

```
# Return a stream on only the interesting elements of $arg.
sub filter {
    my $stream = shift;

    # Second argument is a predicate function that returns
    # true only when passed an interesting element of $stream.
    my $predicate = shift;

    # Look for next interesting element
    until ($stream->is_empty || $predicate->($stream->head)) {
        $stream = $stream->tail;
    }

    # If we ran out of stream, return the empty stream.
    return Stream->empty if $stream->is_empty;

    # Construct new stream with the interesting element at
    # its head and the rest of the stream, appropriately
    # filtered, at its tail.
    Stream->new($stream->head, sub { $stream->tail->filter($predicate) } );
}
```

Let's find perfect squares that are the same printed forwards and backwards:

```
sub is_palindrome { $_[0] eq reverse $_[0] }
$squares->filter(\&is_palindrome)->show(10);
1 4 9 121 484 676 10201 12321 14641 40804
```

You could do all sorts of clever things with this:

- If $input were a stream with elements that were the lines of our input, we could construct:

  ```
  $input->filter(sub {$_[0] =~ /PATTERN/})
  ```

  to return the stream of input lines that matched a certain pattern.

- If $queens were a stream that produced arrangements of eight queens on a chessboard, we could build a filter that checked each arrangement to see if any queens attacked one another, and then we'd have a stream of solutions to the famous eight-queens problem. If we wanted only one solution, we could ask for -> show(1), and our program would stop as soon as it found a single solution; if we wanted all the solutions, we could ask for ->show(ALL).

Here's a particularly clever application: using filtering to compute a stream of prime numbers.

```
sub prime_filter {
    my $s = shift;
    my $h = $s->head;
    Stream->new($h, sub {
                    $s->tail->filter(sub { $_[0] % $h })->prime_filter()
                });
}
```

To use this, we apply it to the stream of integers starting at 2:

```
2 3 4 5 6 7 8 9 ...
```

The first thing it does is to pull the 2 off the front and return it. It then filters the tail of the stream and throws away all the elements that are divisible by 2. It gets the next available element, 3, and returns that, filtering the rest of the stream (which was already missing the even numbers) to throw away the elements that are divisible by 3. Then it pulls the next element, 5, off the front, and so on.

If we're going to have fun with this, we need to start it off with the integers beginning at 2:

```
$iota2 = &tabulate(sub {$_[0]}, 2);
$iota2->show;
        2 3 4 5 6 7 8 9 10 11
$primes = $iota2->prime_filter
$primes->show;
        2 3 5 7 11 13 17 19 23 29
```

This is the Sieve of Eratosthenes. It's not the best algorithm for computing primes, but at 2,300 years old, it's the oldest.

There are a very few basic tools that we need to make good use of streams. filter was one; it filters uninteresting elements out of a stream. Similarly, transform takes one stream and turns it into another. Think of filter as a stream version of Perl's grep function, and think of transform as the stream version of Perl's map function:

```
sub transform {
    my $self = shift;
    return Stream->empty if $self->is_empty;
    my $map_function = shift;
    Stream->new($map_function->($self->head),
            sub { $self->tail->transform($map_function) }
            );
}
```

If we had known about transform when we wrote hamming above, we would never have built a separate scale function; instead of $s->scale(2), we might have written $s->transform(sub { $_[0] * 2 }). We'll see a better use of this a little later.

$squares->transform(sub { $_[0] * 2 })->show(5)
        2 8 18 32 50

Here are a couple of very Perlish streams:

```
# Stream of key-value pairs in a hash
sub eachpair {
    my $hr = shift;
    my @pair = each %$hr;
    if (@pair) {
        Stream->new([@pair], sub {&eachpair($hr)});
    } else { # There aren't any more
        Stream->empty;
    }
}
```

```
# Stream of input lines from a filehandle
sub input {
    my $fh = shift;
    my $line = <$fh>;
    if ($line eq '') {
        Stream->empty;
    } else {
        Stream->new($line, sub {&input($fh)});
    }
}
```

```
# Get first 3 lines of standard input that contain 'hello'
@hellos = &input(STDIN)->filter(sub {$_[0] =~ /hello/i})->take(3);
```

iterate takes a function and applies it to an argument, then applies the function to the result, then the new result, and so on:

```
# compute n, f(n), f(f(n)), f(f(f(n))), ...
sub iterate {
    my $f = shift;
    my $n = shift;
    Stream->new($n, sub { &iterate($f, $f->($n)) });
}
```

One use for `iterate` is to build a stream of pseudorandom numbers:

```
# This is the RNG from the ANSI C standard

sub next_rand {
    int(($_[0] * 1103515245 + 12345) / 65536) % 32768
}

sub rand {
    my $seed = shift;
    &iterate(\&next_rand, &next_rand($seed));
}
```

```
&rand(1)->show
    16838 14666 10953 11665 7451 26316 27974 27550 31532 5572
&rand(1)->show
    16838 14666 10953 11665 7451 26316 27974 27550 31532 5572
&rand(time)->show
    28034 22040 18672 28664 13341 15205 10064 17387 18320 32588
&rand(time)->show
    13922 629 7230 7835 4162 23047 1022 5549 14194 25896
```

Some people in comp.lang.perl.misc have pointed out that Perl's built-in random number generator doesn't have a good interface—it's supposed to be seeded only once, but there's no way for two modules written by different authors to agree on which one should provide the seed. Also, two or more independent modules drawing random numbers from the same source may reduce the randomness of the numbers that each of them gets. But with random numbers from streams, we can manufacture as many independent random number generators as we want, and each part of our program can have its own supply, and use it without interfering with the random numbers generated by other parts of our program. Suppose we want random numbers between 1 and 10 only. Just use `transform`:

```
$rand = &rand(time)->transform(sub {$_[0] % 10 + 1});
```

```
$rand->show(20);
        1 5 8 2 8 10 4 7 3 10 3 6 3 8 8 9 7 7 8 8
```

If we `$rand->show(20)` again, we get exactly the same numbers. There are an infinite number of random numbers in `$rand`, but the first 20 are always the same. We can get to some fresh elements by invoking the `drop` subroutine: `$rand = $rand->drop(10);`. This is such a common operation that we have a shorthand for it: `$rand->discard(10)`.

We can also use `iterate` to investigate the *hailstone numbers*, which star in a famous unsolved mathematical problem called the Collatz conjecture. Start with any integer. If it's odd, multiply it by 3 and add 1; if it's even, divide it by 2. Repeat forever. Depending on where we start, one of three things will happen:

1. We will eventually fall into the loop 4, 2, 1, 4, 2, 1, ...
2. We will eventually fall into some other loop.
3. The numbers will never loop; they will increase without bound forever.

The unsolved question is: are there any numbers that *don't* fall into the 4-2-1 loop?

```
# Next number in hailstone sequence
sub next_hail {
    my $n = shift;
    ($n % 2 == 0) ? $n/2 : 3*$n + 1;
}

# Hailstone sequence starting with $n
sub hailstones {
    my $n = shift;
    &iterate(\&next_hail, $n);
}
```

```
&hailstones(15)->show(23)
15 46 23 70 35 106 53 160 80 40 20 10 5 16 8 4 2 1 4 2 1 4 2
```

iterate_chop takes the infinite stream produced by iterate and chops off the tail before the sequence starts to repeat.

```
&hailstones(15)->iterate_chop->show(ALL)
15 46 23 70 35 106 53 160 80 40 20 10 5 16 8 4 2
```

By counting the length of the resulting stream, we can see how long it took the hailstone sequence to start repeating:

```
print &hailstones(15)->iterate_chop->length
17
```

Of course, we need to be careful not to ask for the length of an infinite stream!

Other Directions

We could have solved all of the problems in this article without streams, but it was simpler to express them in terms of filtering and merging. Streams provide a convenient notation for powerful dataflow ideas, and we can apply our experience to programming Unix shell pipelines.

These techniques of memoization and lazy evaluation can be applied to almost any problem or data structure. For example, if we were writing a chess program, we could build a lazy move tree structure (the first row contains all of our possible moves, the second row contains all of our opponent's responses to each of those moves, the third row contains our counterresponses, and so on) analogous to the lazy lists in this article, and expand the tree only when necessary.

The implementation of streams in Stream.pm is wasteful of space and time because it uses an entire two-element hash to store each element of the stream, and because finding the nth element of a stream requires following a chain of n references. A better implementation might cache all the memoized stream elements in a single array where they could be accessed conveniently. Our Most Assiduous Reader might like to construct such an implementation.

A better programming interface for streams might be to tie the Stream package to an array so that the stream would seem like a normal Perl array. Unfortunately, back when I wrote this article for TPJ, Perl didn't have a complete implementation of tied arrays. Now it does.

References

ML for the Working Programmer, L.C. Paulson. Cambridge University Press, 1991, pp. 166-185.

Structure and Interpretation of Computer Programs, Harold Abelson and Gerald Jay Sussman. MIT Press, 1985, pp. 242-286.

CHAPTER 19

Compression

Mark Jason Dominus

You are probably familiar with Unix `compress`, `gzip`, or `bzip2` utilities, or the DOS `pkzip` utility. These programs all make files smaller; such files are *compressed*. Compressed files take less disk space and less network bandwidth when you move them around. The downside of compressed files is that it they are full of unreadable gibberish; you usually have to run another program to uncompress them before you can use them again. In this article we'll see how file compression works, and I'll demonstrate a simple module that includes functions for compressing and uncompressing files.

Morse Code

The idea behind data compression is very simple. In a typical text file, every character takes up the same amount of space: eight bits. The letter "e" is represented by the bits 01100101; the letter "Z" is represented by the bits 010110010. But in a text file, "e" occurs much more frequently than "Z"—about 75 times as frequently. If you could give the common symbols short codes, you'd save space.

This isn't a new idea. It was exploited by Samuel Morse in the Morse code, a very early digital data transmission protocol. Morse code was designed to send text files over telegraph wires. A telegraph is very simple; it has a switch at one end, and when you close the switch, an electric current travels through a wire to the other end, where there is a relay that makes a click. By tapping the switch at one end, you make the relay at the other end click. Letters and digits are encoded as sequences of short and long clicks. A short click is called a *dot*, and a long click is called a *dash*.

The two most common letters in English text are "E" and "T;" in Morse code these are represented by a single dot and a single dash, respectively. The codes for "I," "A," "N," and "M," all common letters, are ••, •–, –•, and ––. In contrast, the codes for the uncommon letters "Q" and "Z" are ––•– and ––••.

Computer file compression does a similar thing. It analyzes the contents of the data, figuring out which symbols are frequent and which are infrequent. Then you assign short codes to the frequent symbols and long codes to the infrequent symbols. You write out the coded version of the file, and that usually makes it smaller.

Ambiguous Codes

There's a problem with Morse code: you need a third symbol, typically a long pause, to separate the dots and dashes that make up one letter from the dots and dashes that make up the next. Otherwise, if you get •-, you don't know whether it's the single letter "A" or the two letters "ET"—or it might be the first bit of the letter "R" or "L." In a long message, all the dots and dashes run together and you get a big mess that can't be turned back into text. In Morse code, it can be hard to tell "Eugenia" from "Sofia," because without the interletter pauses, they're identical:

•••---••-••••-

Those interletter spaces take up a lot of transmission time, and it would be nice if you didn't need them. It turns out that if you arrange the code properly, you don't. The ambiguity problem with Morse code occurs because some codes are *prefixes* of others: there are some letters where the code for the first part of one letter is just the same as the code for the other letter, but with something extra tacked on. When you see the shorter code, you don't know if it's complete or if it should be combined with the following symbols.

Suppose for simplicity that you only need to send the letters A, C, E, and S over the telegraph. Instead of Morse code, you could use the following code table:

```
A        –
C        ••
E        •–•
S        •--
```

Suppose you receive the message -••••••-••--•---•-••-- What was the message? Well, the first symbol is –, so the first letter in the message must be A, because that's the only letter with a code that starts with a –. Then the next two symbols are ••, so the second letter must be a C, because all the other codes that start with •. have a – after the • instead of another •. Similar reasoning shows that the third letter is also C. After that, the code is •–•; it must be an E. You continue through the message, reading one letter at a time, and eventually you get the whole thing this way.

It's so simple that a computer can decode it, if the computer is equipped with a decision tree like the one shown in Figure 19-1.

Start at "Start", and look at the symbols in the message one by one. At each stage, follow the appropriate labelled branch to the next node. If there's a letter at that node, output the letter and go back to the start node. If there's no letter at the node, look at the next symbol in the input and continue down the tree towards the leaves.

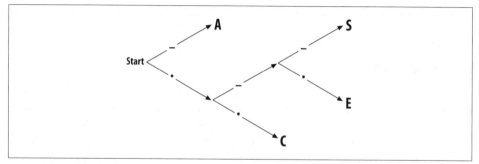

Figure 19-1. A decision tree for our simple encoding

Huffman Coding

Obviously, it's important to choose the right code. If Morse had made • the code for Z and ••–• the code for E, he wouldn't be famous.

Choosing the right code can be tricky. Consider the example of the previous section, where you assumed your messages contained nothing but A, C, E, and S. The code I showed is good when you expect your messages to contain more As than Es or Ss. If S were very common, you clearly could have done better; less clearly, if all four letters were about equally common, then you could still have done better, by assigning each letter a code of the same length, as shown in Figure 19-2.

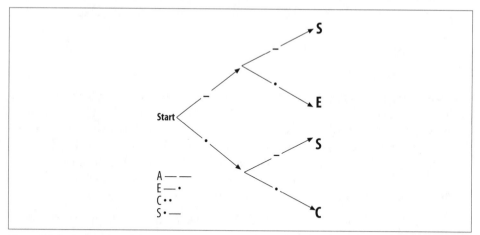

Figure 19-2. Assigning each letter a code of the same length

Suppose your message happened to contain 200 of each of the four letters. Then the first code would use 1,800 symbols, and the second code would use only 1,600.

In 1952, David A. Huffman discovered a method for producing the *optimal* unambiguous code. For a given set of symbols, if you know the probability of each symbol occurring in the input, you can use Huffman's method to construct an unambiguous code that encodes the typical message with fewer symbols than any other code.

The method is very simple and ingenious. For concreteness, let's suppose that the (rather silly) message is:

THE_THIRSTIEST_SISTERS_TEETH_RESIST_THIS_STRESS

(I used _ instead of space so that it'll be easier to see.)

Start with the table of relative probabilities; you can get this by counting the number of occurrences of every symbol in the message. This is called *histogramming*. (A histogram is a bar chart; *histos* is Greek for a beam or a mast.) The histogram for the symbols in our sample message is shown in Table 19-1.

Table 19-1. A sample histogram

S	11
T	10
E	7
_	6
I	5
H	4
R	4

Now take the two least common entries in the table: H and R. They'll get the longest codes, because they're least common. Simplify this by pretending that H and R are the same, and lumping them together into one category, called HR. Then assign codes to all the other letters and to HR. When you're done, you still have to distinguish between H and R. Now, HR has some code. You don't know what it is yet, so let's symbolize it with <HR>. You don't really need to use <HR> in our message, because the is no such thing as the letter HR, so split it in two, and let the code for H be <HR>• and the code for R be <HR>–. As a result, the codes for H and R will be longer than the codes for the other letters, but if that has to happen, it's best for it to happen for H and R, because they are the least common letters in the message.

Lump H and R together and pretend temporarily that they are only one letter. Your table then looks like this:

S	11	R = <HR>–
T	10	H = <HR>•
HR	8	
E	7	
_	6	
I	5	

Repeat the process. The two least common symbols are now I and _. Lump them together into a new "symbol" called I_, and finish assigning the codes to S, T, HR, E, and I_. When you're done, I will get the code <I_>• and _ will get the code <I_>–.

S	11	R = <HR>–
I_	11	H = <HR>•
T	10	_ = <I_>–
HR	8	I = <I_>•
E	7	

Lump HR and E together:

HRE	15	R	= \<HR\>–
S	11	H	= \<HR\>•
I_	11	_	= \<I_\>–
T	10	I	= \<I_\>•
		HR	= \<HRE\>–
		E	= \<HRE\>•

Next lump T and I_ together:

I_T	21	R	= \<HR\>–
HRE	15	H	= \<HR\>•
S	11	_	= \<I_\>–
		I	= \<I_\>•
		HR	= \<HRE\>–
		E	= \<HRE\>•
		I_	= \<I_T\>–
		T	= \<I_T\>•

Then lump S and HRE together:

SHRE	25	R	= \<HR\>–
I_T	21	H	= \<HR\>•
		I	= \<I_\>–
		_	= \<I_\>•
		HR	= \<HRE\>–
		E	= \<HRE\>•
		I_	= \<I_T\>–
		T	= \<I_T\>•
		S	= \<SHRE\>–
		HRE	= \<SHRE\>•

Now you only have two symbols left. There's only one way to assign a code to two symbols; one of them gets • and the other gets –. It doesn't matter which one gets which symbol, so let's say that SHRE gets • and I_T gets –.

Now the codes fall out of the table you've built up in the right-hand column:

```
SHRE = •
           S = •–
         HRE = ••
               HR = ••–
                         R = ••––
                         H = ••–•
               E = •••

   I_T = –
         I_ = ––
                   _ = –––
                   I = ––•
         T = –•
```

Throw away the codes for the fictitious compound symbols, and you're left with the real code:

```
S = •–
T = –•
```

```
E = •••
_ = ---
I = --•
H = ••-•
R = ••--
```

As promised, the code is unambiguous, because no code is a prefix of any other code. Your original message encodes like this:

```
-•••-••••----•••-•--••--•--•--••••--•---
•---••--••••••--•-----••••••••-•••-•---
••--••••---••--•----•••-•--•••----
•--•••--••••-•-
```

This version has a total of 128 dots and dashes, an average of 2.72 symbols per character, and a 9.3% improvement over the 141 symbols you would have had to use if you had given every letter a three-symbol code.

The Code

For this article, I implemented a demonstration module that compresses files. You can retrieve the module from my Perl Paraphernalia web site at *http://perl.plover.com/ Huffman/*. The program htest.pl compresses an input and saves it to the file /tmp/ htest.out; then it opens this file, reads in the compressed data, decompresses it, and prints the result to standard output.

Most of the real work is in the Huffman module that htest.pl uses. I'll now discuss the important functions that htest.pl calls.

```
my $hist = Huffman::histogram(\@symbols);
```

This function generates the histogram of the input text. The histogram is the tally of the number of occurrences of each symbol. The argument to histogram is an array of symbols, passed by reference for efficiency, because it is likely to be very large. It might have been simpler to pass the input as a single string, but this way you can assign codes per-word instead of per-character if you want to, just by splitting the input into an array in a different way.

```
my $codes = Huffman::tabulate($hist);
```

The tabulate function generates the code table from the histogram using Huffman's method. (This has the side effect of destroying the histogram.) The code table is just a hash that maps symbols to codes; the codes themselves are strings like 0010011.

```
Huffman::save_code_table(*FILE, $codes);
```

This function writes the code table to the file.

```
Huffman::encode(*FILE, $codes, \@symbols);
```

This encodes the input text and writes the result to the file.

```
my $codes = Huffman::load_code_table(*FILE);
my $coded_data = <FILE>;
my $text = Huffman::decode($codes, $coded_data);
```

This is the decompression process. The return value from load_code_table is a code table in a rather interesting form. It's a decision tree, just like the ones earlier in the article. Each node of the tree is either a single string (which is the symbol that the decoder should output) or it's an array with two elements: the 0th element is the part of the tree on the branch labeled 0, and the 1st element is the part of the tree on the branch labeled 1. For example, treating • as 0 and – as 1, the first decision tree in this article would be represented like this:

```
[[C,        # ••
    [E,     # •–•
     S      # •––
    ]
  ],
  A         # –
]
```

The Rub

You can compress the file, but unless you include the code table in the compressed file, you won't be able to uncompress it again, and files that can't be uncompressed are not very useful. But sometimes the code table is bigger than the savings that you got from compressing the file, especially if the original file is small. On a sample file of comp.lang.perl.misc articles, the compressor reduced the file size by 32%, from 42,733 bytes to 29,114. But when I ran it on its own source code, the file size increased from 987 bytes to 1,321. The compressed data was only 631 bytes long, but the code table and other overhead took up 690 bytes.

Another Rub

Huffman coding is optimal for compressing a given set of symbols into the smallest space possible. But if you readjust your idea of a symbol, you get better compression.

Suppose you're compressing English text. If you histogram the characters and use Huffman's method, you'll get the optimal way to encode the characters. Because each character has its own code, your result could also encode random gibberish. It should be clear that this expressiveness has a price. For English text, you don't need so much expressiveness; it's clearly more efficient to assign a code to each *word* instead of to each character. In doing so, you lose the ability to encode random gibberish, but your compressed data becomes much smaller. Suppose there are about 2^{17} words in English; if you assign each one a different 17-bit code, you can then encode your original seven-word message:

THE THIRSTIEST SISTERS TEETH RESIST THIS STRESS

into 7 times 17 = 119 bits, already an improvement on the 128 from before. And if you use Huffman's method to assign long codes to rare words and short codes to common words, you can do even better.

Using this method, I compressed the comp.lang.perl.misc articles by 63%. Unfortunately, the code table blew up as a result, and took up 43,739 bytes, which was larger than the original uncompressed data.

Other Methods

Most modern data compression doesn't use Huffman coding directly. A better method was proposed in 1977 and 1978 by Jakob Ziv and Abraham Lempel. The Lempel-Ziv methods scan the input data, and when they find a substring that occurs twice, they replace the second occurrence with a reference back to the first. The references can then be Huffman-compressed.

These methods have several advantages over the basic scheme implemented previously. One important benefit of Lempel-Ziv compression methods is that they don't have to analyze the entire input in advance; they can construct a code table as they go along, basing it on only the portion of the input seen so far. This is important for practical applications. The data compression in your modem wouldn't be very useful if the modem had to gather and histogram a week's worth of traffic before it could send or receive anything.

An extra payoff of building the code table on the fly is that if the algorithm notices that the code table it's using isn't performing well, it can start over with a new code table in the middle. If the data is in several pieces that have very different personalities—say a graphic image embedded in a text file—this method will be a win over straight Huffman coding because it'll be able to apply an appropriate code table to each part of the data. LZW (Lempel-Ziv-Welch), the compression algorithm used by the DOS lha program, doesn't do this, but the variation of it employed by the Unix compress program does. The algorithm used by GNU gzip and zlib is different but also periodically throws away the code tables and starts over.

The best thing about Lempel-Ziv and related methods is that they don't need to decide in advance how to break up the input into symbols. LZW, for example, puts any string that it hasn't seen before into the code table, under the assumption that if it appeared once, it'll probably appear again. As the input comes in, longer and longer substrings of the input go into the code table; long substrings go in only when their shorter prefixes have appeared multiple times. If the file is best broken up into words, the algorithm will eventually detect that; if it is best broken up into single characters, the algorithm will detect that too.

Other Directions

If you want an easy but possibly amusing project, try altering the module so that the code tables are smaller. At present, the module does not assume that the coding is done per-character, so you shouldn't break that. Actually, assigning the codes per-word seems to blow up the code table more than it saves. I haven't yet found a case where it's worthwhile.

Finally, the decision-tree data structure in the decoder is probably over-clever. It would be simpler to represent the same information with a *state table* as shown here.

	0	1
0	1	A
1	C	2
2	E	S

The leftmost column lists the three states of our table: 0, 1, and 2. Each internal node in the decision tree is assigned a state; the root node gets the number 0. To decode, the decoder keeps track of the state number, which says the internal node it's currently at. Each time it reads a 0 or 1, it looks in the table to decide where to go next. If it sees a symbol, that means it reached a leaf, and should output that symbol and start over at state 0; if it sees a number, that means it's now at a different internal node and should read more bits. I'm not sure whether this would be more efficient than the original way, but it would probably be easier to understand.

Bibliography

Symbols, Signals, and Noise, J.R. Pierce, pp. 94–97. Harper, New York, 1961.

The comp.compression FAQ is an excellent starting source of information, especially part 2. It is available from *ftp://rtfm.mit.edu/pub/usenet/news.answers/compression-faq/*.

## CHAPTER 20

Memoization

Mark Jason Dominus

Caching is a useful general technique that sometimes makes programs run faster. It does this by exchanging space for time: caching tries to save previously computed results in an attempt to reuse them later rather than recomputing them.

Caching is useful in all kinds of situations, including almost any kind of searching (cache the results of the search so that we can skip it next time), HTML generation (cache the results of the generation process so that you never have to regenerate the page), and numeric computation (cache the results of the computation). As a specific example, consider a function for preparing graphic images to be printed on an industrial offset printer. Four-color printing processes, commonly used in magazines and color printers, use four colors of ink: cyan, magenta, yellow, and black, collectively referred to as CMYK. Graphics files, however, usually record colors by indicating the desired intensities of red, green, and blue light (RGB). The RGB format has to be converted to CMYK values prior to printing.

Each pixel needs to have its color converted; this typically requires a fairly expensive calculation. But in many graphics formats, such as GIF, there are few colors relative to the number of pixels. A naïve approach would compute the CMYK values for each color repeatedly.

To speed up the caculation of CMYK values, we save each CMYK set in a data structure, called a *cache*. Later, if we use the function to compute the CMYK values for the same color, the function looks in the data structure to see if it already knows the right values. If it finds them there, it returns them immediately, avoiding the lengthy calculation. If not, it computes them, installs them in the data structure, and returns them to the caller.

Caching therefore trades space for time. A function that uses caching may run faster than one without, but it uses up more memory. The basic strategy looks like this:

```
sub fake_function {
    if (@_ looks familiar) {
        return cached value from the cache;
    } else {
```

```
            $val = real_function(@_);
            store $val in the cache;
            return $val;
        }
    }
```

Then when we call fake_function instead of real_function, it takes care of managing the cache and returning the values that real_function would have returned had we called it directly. If real_function takes a long time to run, this process can yield a substantial savings.

Obviously, this technique is inappropriate for many functions. For example, we wouldn't like it if the time or rand function used caching, because then they would return the same time or the same random number every time we called them. But for many functions, the result depends only on the arguments, and not on anything in the outside world like the time of day. Some of these functions are candidates for caching strategies.

Here's a common example: the factorial function. (The factorial of n is the number of different orders for a list of n items.) This function accepts an argument that is a non-negative integer. The factorial can be computed as follows:

```
sub factorial {
    my $n = shift;
    if ($n == 0) { return 1 }
    else        { return $n * factorial($n-1) }
}
```

factorial is suitable for caching because it is a *pure* function. A pure function is one with no side effects, with a return value that depends only on the values of its arguments. It's easy to see that no matter how many times we compute factorial(7), the result will always be the same. This is exactly the property that makes it suitable for caching: since it'll always be the same, we'll remember the result from the first time we call it, and return that same result on the subsequent calls.

It's easy to take the factorial function above and turn it into a version with caching. Since the argument to factorial is always a non-negative integer, we'll just use an ordinary Perl array as the cache. When we compute factorial($n), we'll store the result in $cache[$n]. Then when we need to see if we've computed factorial($n) previously, we'll just look to see if $cache[$n] is defined. The code is simple:

```
1       { my @cache;
2         sub factorial {
3             my $n = shift;
4             return $cache[$n] if defined $cache[$n];
5
6             my $result;
7             if ($n == 0) { $result = 1 }
8             else         { $result $n * factorial($n-1) }
9
10            $cache[$n] = $result;
```

```
11                return $result;
12          }
13      }
```

Line 1 sets up the cache array; the my confines it to the block that ends on line 13, so it's only visible to the factorial function. After the function gets the argument on line 3, it checks line 4 to see if it already knows the factorial. If so, it returns the result immediately.

Something interesting and subtle is going on here. The caching is a bigger win than it might appear. Suppose we've used factorial(12) to compute the factorial of 12, and we need to compute factorial(13). $cache[13] isn't defined yet, so control passes to line 8, which wants to compute 13 * factorial(12), so it makes a recursive call. But the recursive call for factorial(12) returns immediately, because $cache[12] *is already defined*. We got factorial(13) almost immediately, even though the value wasn't in the cache yet, because we did have the result of a *partial* computation in the cache.

Similarly, let's ask for factorial(11). Even though we never explicitly asked for this before, the result is already in the cache, because it was computed and recorded in the process of computing factorial(12).

Caching not only speeds up calls for arguments that we've used before, it sometimes also speeds up the computations for arguments that we haven't used before.

Here's an example where caching turns into a huge win for this reason: The *Fibonacci* function. In 1202 the Italian mathematician Leonardo of Pisa, also called "Fibonacci," asked how quickly a colony of immortal rabbits would increase if every month each pair of adult rabbits spawned a new baby pair that took another month to grow up to be adults themselves.

It's not hard to discover that if $f(n)$ is the number of pairs of rabbits in month n, then:

```
f(n) = n              # (if n < 2)
f(n) = f(n-1) + f(n-2)  # (otherwise)
```

The outputs of this function, 1, 1, 2, 3, 5, 8, 13, 21, and so on, are the famous *Fibonacci numbers*. The code for the function to compute them is simple:

```
# Compute nth Fibonacci number
sub fib {
    my $n = shift;
    if ($n < 2) { return $n }
    else        { return fib($n-1) + fib($n-2) }
}
```

However, this simple function is very slow. It takes a long time to compute fib(20), because it first wants to compute fib(19) and fib(18), and add the results. But to compute fib(19), it first has to compute fib(18) and fib(17), and when it is done it comes back and computes fib(18) all over again even though the answer is the same as it was before. Both of the times that it wants to compute fib(18), it has to compute fib(17) from scratch, and then it has to do that again each time it wants to compute `fib(19)`. This function does so much recomputing of old results that it takes a really long time to run. `fib(20)` makes about 22,000 recursive calls to compute and recompute things that it already computed.

Here's a version with caching:

```
{ my @cache;
  sub fib {
      my $n = shift;
      return $cache[$n] if defined $cache[$n];

      my $result;
      if ($n < 2) { $result = $n }
      else { $result = fib($n-1) + fib($n-2) }

      $cache[$n] = $result;
      return $result;
  }
}
```

Caching here is a big win; we reduce those 22,000 function calls to about 40. Even if we never ask for `fib(20)` again, we get a huge benefit.

We can write the caching version a bit more tidily this way:

```
1 { my @cache;
2   BEGIN { @cache = (0, 1) }
3     sub fib {
4         my $n = shift;
5         return $cache[$n] if defined $cache[$n];
6
7         return $cache[$n] = fib($n-1) + fib($n-2);
8     }
9 }
```

There are two tricks here. One is that by initializing the cache to contain the two special cases $n=0$ and $n=1$, we can eliminate the code that deals with those special cases. The other trick is that we can eliminate the $result variable: we compute the result, stick it right into the cache, and return it, all on line 7.

Recursive Functions

Lots of people advise avoiding recursion, because recursive functions are often so much less efficient than iterative ones. But for some problems, recursion leads to much simpler and more natural code, and it can be hard to decide whether to trade off efficiency for simplicity.

Caching often improves the performance of recursive functions to the point that we don't care about the small additional gain we might get by rewriting the function iteratively. So before rewriting, try memoizing. Recursion's reputation for bad performance is partly undeserved; often the poor performance is the result of careless algorithms similar to the first version of fib above, and could be eliminated immediately with a bit of caching.

The Memoize Module

In the words of Alfred North Whitehead, "Civilization advances by extending the number of important operations which we can perform without thinking." Like all tools, caching is better when we don't have to think about it. I like caching, so I wrote a module that adds caching behavior to functions automatically. This process of rewriting functions automatically to have caching behavior is called *memoization*. (The word "memoize" was coined by Donald Michie in 1968.) If we have the Memoize module, we can say:

```
use Memoize;
memoize 'fib';
```

and it'll automatically memoize the fib function. We can try memoizing a function to see if we get a performance increase, and if not we can turn it off again without wasting any time actually modifying the code or thinking about how to organize the cache. Very handy, and available from CPAN.

Module Internals

Usually when I write a module for TPJ, I try to make it readable, even if that means leaving out features or sacrificing efficiency. But I wrote Memoize.pm a long time ago, and it's a three-hundred-line monster full of all sorts of bells and whistles. So for this article, I wrote a tiny version of Memoize.pm. It leaves out the fancy features and weighs in at a mere 31 lines of significant code (51 altogether).

```
1       package MiniMemoize;
2       use Exporter;
3       @ISA = qw(Exporter);
4       @EXPORT = qw(memoize);
5       use Carp;
6       use strict;
7
8       my %memotable;
9
10       sub memoize {
11         my $function = shift;
12         my $funcname;
13         if (ref $function eq '') {
14           my $caller = caller;
15           # Convert to code reference
16           $function = $caller . "::$function" unless $function =~ /::/;
17           $funcname = $function;
18           no strict 'refs';
19           $function = \&$function;
20         }
21
```

```
22        my $stub = eval qq{sub { _check_cache("$function", \@_) }};
23        $memotable{$function} =
24          { original => $function,
25            cache => { },
26          };
27
28
29        { no strict 'refs';
30          *{$funcname} = $stub if defined $funcname;
31        }
32        $stub;
33    }
34
35
36    sub _check_cache {
37      my $what_func = shift;
38      unless (exists $memotable{$what_func}) {  # should never happen
39        croak("Tried to check cache of non-memoized function
40                                    `$what_func'; aborting");
41      }
42
43      my $cache  = $memotable{$what_func}{cache};
44      my $argstr = join $;, @_;
45      if (exists $cache->{$argstr}) { return $cache->{$argstr} }
46
47      my $real_function = $memotable{$what_func}{original};
48      $cache->{$argstr} = $real_function->(@_);
49    }
50
51    1;
```

There are two functions here. _check_cache is private, and is responsible for maintaining the cached function values and returning them when appropriate. memoize is called directly by the user of the package, whom we'll call "you," and sets things up so when you think you're calling your own function, you're really calling _check_cache instead.

We'll see memoize first, because it's called first. It's reponsible for memoizing a function and setting up the cache. Suppose you call memoize 'fib' in the main package. What does memoize do to set up the cache and arrange to have the cache checked at the right time?

The first thing it needs to do is find the actual function and get a reference to it. This occurs on lines 14–19. If the argument you passed to memoize was already a reference to a function, you find that out on line 13 and skip this part. Supposing that what you got is a function name; you first find out the name of the calling package with caller (line 14). Then you put the function name together with the package name to get the full name of the function, something like main::fib. If the name contained ::, you assume that it already has its package name attached and skip that part. You save the complete name in $funcname (you'll need it again later) and replace the name of the function in $function with a reference to the function itself on line 19. Turning a name into a reference this way is usually something people do by accident, so use strict will abort the program if you do it. But here it's really on purpose, so you shut off strict 'refs' for just that one line.

Now $function has a reference to the function you wanted to memoize, and $funcname has the full name of that function, if it was available.

Now let's jump ahead a little. You might like to memoize more than one function at a time, so you need some way of keeping the caches for separate functions separate. It would be terrible if you memoized fib and fact and then fib(7) returned 5,040 instead of 13.

Each cache will be an anonymous hash. The keys will look like function arguments, and the values will be function return values. The cache hashes will be stored in another hash, keyed by function name. Given the name of a function, you can look in the main hash to find the cache hash for that function. This main hash is %memotable, declared on line 8. %memotable is the most important data structure in the module.

Actually I fibbed a little. The keys of %memotable aren't function names, because memoize might not know the function name. You can ask memoize to memoize a reference to a function, like this:

```
memoize \&fib;
```

in which case the name won't be available to memoize. You can also memoize an anonymous function:

```
memoize sub { gethostbyname(@_) || 'Sorry.' };
```

Here, there's no name at all. But how can memoize identify a function if it doesn't have a name? You'll play a sly trick. If you have a reference to a function, you can convert it to a string, and get something that looks like CODE(0x811f744). Two references to the same function always yield the same string, and references to different functions always yield different strings. This means that the "stringified" references serve to identify the functions. You'll use these stringified references as the keys into %memotable.

You're ready to create a new function that will replace fib when fib becomes memoized. This happens on line 22. The new function won't have a name, but it's very simple:

```
sub { _check_cache("CODE(0x811f744)", @_) }
```

Call this a *stub*, because it's so small. CODE(0x811f744) here is the stringified version of $function, which as you'll recall is a reference to fib. Every time you memoize a new function, you'll create a new stub, each one slightly different from the others. Each will call _check_cache with a slightly different $_[0] that uniquely identifies the memoized function it was called for.

All the stub does is pass along the memoized function's arguments to _check_cache, with an extra argument slapped on the front to say which function was originally called. _check_cache can use the first argument to know which cache to consult and which real function to call to populate the cache. When it sees CODE(0x811f744), it'll remember that was the string that corresponded to `fib`, and it'll consult `fib`'s private cache and call the real `fib` function if necessary.

Lines 23–26 fill in `%memotable`. In addition to the cache, which is initially empty, `%memotable` records the location of the original, unmemoized function so `_check_cache` can call it if it needs to.

Line 30 is the real magic. If you know the name of the function you are memoizing, you reach into the Perl symbol table and replace that function with the stub that calls `_check_cache`. Afterwards, when you try to call `fib`, you'll really be calling the stub, which will hand off control to `_check_cache`. You saved a reference to the original function in `%memotable` so that `_check_cache` will be able to find it again when it needs to. Tampering with the symbol table is another thing that `use strict` wants to protect you from, so you turn it off again.

Finally, you return the stub, which is your entry to the memoized version of the original function. You will need this if you weren't able to install it into the symbol table, which would happen if you didn't tell `memoize` the name of the memoized function. For example, just saying this:

```
memoize sub { gethostbyname(@_) || 'Sorry.' };
```

is useless, because the memoized version of the function is lost. You need to be able to say this:

```
$fast_gethostbyname = memoize sub { gethostbyname(@_) || 'Sorry.' };
$name = $fast_gethostbyname->('tpj.com');
```

This would be impossible if `memoize` didn't return the stub.

Compared with all the tricky things we've been doing so far, the code to actually *call* a memoized function is very simple. There's only one strange trick, and because it isn't really very strange, I'm going to explain it up front so we can run right over it when we meet it on the road.

Cached function return values are stored in the cache hash, and we need some way to turn the function's arguments into a hash key so that we can look up the cached return value associated with a particular argument list. But the arguments are a list, and hash keys can only be strings, not lists. The method we use to turn a list into a string has some problems, but in practice the problems don't come up very often. We turn an argument list into a hash key on line 44:

```
44          my $argstr = join $;, @_;
```

`$;` is a special Perl variable with a value that is normally a string containing the single unlikely and unprintable character "control-backslash."

Joining the arguments into a single string with `join` is a little risky, because it *doesn't* always turn different lists into different strings. For example, the two argument lists (`"x$;"`, `"y"`) and (`"x"`, `"$;y"`) both turn into the string `"x$;$;y"` under this transformation. But it works properly *almost* all the time. It always works when there's only a single argument, and it always works when none of the arguments contain control-backslash, so for real applications it's almost good enough, and for a demonstration it is good enough.

With that out of the way, let's suppose that fib has been memoized, and the user asks for fib(7). The name fib is no longer attached to the real fib function, but instead it's attached to the stub. The stub, as we saw, looks something like this:

```
sub { _check_cache("CODE(0x811f744)", @_) }
```

The stub calls _check_cache with two arguments: first, the stringified version of the reference to the real fib; second, the number 7. The first thing _check_cache does is grab the stringified reference (line 37), which is its key into %memotable. If there *isn't* any entry in %memotable for that key, it aborts the program (lines 38–41), but that should never happen, because we installed the entry back on line 23.

Presuming the entry exists, _check_cache retrieves the cache hash on line 43. On line 44, it turns the argument list into a hash key. _check_cache then checks the cache. If there is a cached return value available, _check_cache returns it immediately (line 45). Otherwise, it retrieves a reference to the original, unmemoized version of the function (line 47), invokes it, stores the result in the cache, and returns the result (line 48).

That was a lot of magic, but the end result is that it's totally transparent. My web site has a sample demonstration program that looks like this:

```
print "fib(20) = ", fib(20), "\n";
memoize 'fib';                          # Make fib go faster
print "fib(20) = ", fib(20), "\n";
```

memoize 'fib' is supposed to magically make fib go faster, and that's exactly what it does. The goal was to advance civilization by extending the number of important operations that could be performed without thinking, and we certainly did meet the goal.

Some Other Applications of Memoization

There are a number of ways to use memoization beyond simply minimizing the number of function calls during one program execution.

Persistent Cache

Storing the cache in memory is handy and can speed up a function. But when our process exits, the cache is lost. Since the function is pure, its values will be the same the next time we run the program, and it's a shame to have the later invocation recompute the values that were already computed by earlier invocations.

If the cache is in a file instead of in memory, our program will never have to compute the function twice for the same arguments. After the first time, it'll just retrieve the value that it saved on the disk.

We can even populate the cache in advance, with a throwaway program that runs over the weekend and does nothing but call the memoized function with different arguments. When we come back on Monday we'll find that *any* program that calls our slow function is faster, because the formerly slow function now returns almost instantaneously.

We could write the code to do this and stick it into all our programs. But the real Memoize module on CPAN already has an option to record the cache results on disk, and using it is simple. Just tie a hash to a disk file as usual, and then use the HASH option to tell Memoize to use that hash as the cache hash, instead of making up a new, empty hash as usual:

```
use DB_File;
tie my %cache, 'DB_File', $filename, O_RDWR | O_CREAT, 0666;
Memoize 'fib', SCALAR_CACHE => [ HASH => \%hash ];
```

or:

```
use Memoize::Storable;
# Memoize::Storable is a front-end on Storable that makes it
# suitable for use with Memoize.
tie my %cache, 'Memoize::Storable', $filename;
Memoize 'fib', SCALAR_CACHE => [ HASH => \%cache ];
```

This is a very powerful and useful feature, and the programming required to support it couldn't be simpler: the memoize function just uses the supplied hash in place of the new empty one at line 25.

Profiling Execution Speed

If our program is too slow, we will need to speed it up by making the slow functions faster. But it is notoriously difficult to decide which functions are slowing a program down! If we guess wrong, we might waste effort trying to speed up a function that only contributes to 1% of the program's entire run time; at best this will make the program 1% faster.

The first thing to do in this situation is to *profile* the program to find out which parts are really taking the most time, and then concentrate our efforts on just those parts. Profiling can be a pain, and the Perl profiler, Devel::DProf, isn't as well-developed as we might like.

We can use memoizing as an alternative, and it's sometimes preferable. Suppose we have a function f that we think is a possible candidate to be optimized. Run the program three times: once with no memoizing, once with f memoized (this will populate the cache), and once with f memoized and the cache already populated. This last run will simulate the speed of the program with f's contributions removed. If the runtime with the cache populated is 98% of the runtime with no memoizing, then no possible rewriting of f can speed up the program more than about 2%—so we'll know to look elsewhere.

The Orcish Maneuver

Memoizing is very useful for sort comparison functions, which tend to get called over and over again with the same arguments, and are almost always pure.

Suppose we have a bunch of strings in the form Jan 14, 2002 and we want to sort them into chronological order. Here's the obvious way:

```
%m2n =
  ( jan => 0, feb =>  1,  mar =>  2,
    apr => 3, may =>  4,  jun =>  5,
    jul => 6, aug =>  7,  sep =>  8,
    oct => 9, nov => 10,  dec => 11, );

sub compare_dates {
  my ($am, $ad, $ay) = ($a =~ /(\w{3}) (\d+), (\d+)/);
  my ($bm, $bd, $by) = ($b =~ /(\w{3}) (\d+), (\d+)/);

            $ay  <=>         $by
  || $m2n{lc $am} <=> $m2n{lc $bm}
  ||          $ad  <=>        $bd;
}

  sort compare_dates @datestrings;
```

Now, suppose @datestrings contains 1,000 of these strings. We're going to make about 8,700 calls to compare_dates, so about 17,500 pattern matches, and that means that each date string was parsed and split an average of 17.5 times, the last 16.5 of which were a complete waste of time.

One way out of this is to use the Schwartzian Transform, which builds a list of data structures that contain both the numeric and printable versions of the dates, sorts this list by the numeric versions, and then throws away the numeric version, leaving only the printable ones in the result. Another way is to define an auxiliary function that turns a date into a number, and then memoizes it:

```
use Memoize;

sub compare_dates {
  to_number($a) <=> to_number($b);
}

# Convert "Nov 5, 1605" to "16051105"
sub to_number {
  my ($m, $d, $y) = ($_[0] =~ /(\w{3}) (\d+), (\d+)/);

  sprintf("%04d%02d%02d", $y, $m2n{$m}, $d);
}

memoize 'to_number';
```

Now we only do 1,000 pattern matches, which is a big improvement. The other 16,500 times, the result is already in the cache.

In sort comparators, we often need more speed, and the slow part of this comparator is the two calls to to_number. We've replaced 17,500 pattern matches with 17,500 calls to to_number, which is an improvement, but not as much of an improvement as we'd like. So instead of using the Memoize module, we can just inline the memoization, like this:

```
{ my %cache;

  sub compare_dates {
    ($cache{$a} ||= to_number($a)) <=>
    ($cache{$b} ||= to_number($b))
  }
}
```

||= is a Perl operator that suits this application perfectly. It gets the value of the expression on the left and returns it, unless it's a false value, in which case it evaluates the thing on the right, assigns it to the thing on the left, and returns it. If the numeric version is already in the cache, we get it immediately; otherwise we compute it and put it in the cache. Result: exactly 1,000 calls to to_number.

Joseph Hall, author of *Effective Perl Programming* (Addison Wesley), dubbed this the *Orcish Maneuver*, because the notable features of this approach are the || and the cache.

Dynamic Programming

Dynamic programming is a technique in which a problem is broken down into smaller subproblems, solved separately, and then built up into a solution to the big problem. The merge sort is a good example. For a more interesting example, we'll look at the *partition problem*.

In the partition problem, we have a list of numbers. We want to divide the list into two groups so that the sum of the numbers in each group is the same.

If you learned about dynamic programming in school (assuming you went to school) you probably spent a lot of time working out the details of how to represent and locate the solutions to the subproblems. But we can think of memoization as an automatic dynamic programming technique.

We're going to solve the partition problem by writing a recursive function. Suppose the list has five elements, with a sum of 30. Then what we really need to do is find some subset of those elements with a sum of 15. If we can do that, or prove there is no such subset, we've solved the partition problem.

Suppose the first element is an 8. This 8 might be part of the subset we want to find, or it might not. If it is part of the subset, then the remaining elements of the subset must add up to 7; if it isn't, then they add up to 15. So throw away the 8, and recursively inquire if some subset of the remaining elements can be made to add up to 7 or 15.

We repeat this until we've thrown away all but one of the elements, at which point the solution is trivial; it's either equal to the target sum, or it isn't.

Our recursive function T will take a list of numbers and a target sum, and it'll try to see whether there's a subset of the numbers that adds up to the target sum. If it can find such a subset, it returns a list of them, and otherwise it returns undef. Here's the code:

```
# Take a list of numbers and a target sum.  return a sublist that
# add up to the target, if possible, or undef otherwise.

sub T {
  my ($list, $target) = @_;
  my $answer;
  return undef if $target < 0;

  if (@$list == 0) {
    return ($target == 0) ? [] : undef
  }

  my ($first, @rest) = @$list;

  # Does the rest of the list contain a solution?
  $solution = T(\@rest, $target);
  return $solution if defined $solution;

  # Try the other way
  $solution = T(\@rest, $target - $first);
  return [$first, @$solution] if defined $solution;

  # Nope.
  return undef;
}
```

Now let's ask it if it can find a way to split the elements of (8,2,7,3,10) into two lists, each of which adds up to 15. The call looks like this:

```
T([8,2,7,3,10], 15)
```

And sure enough, the function returns (2,3,10).

Actually, this function is too slow to use for large problems; it takes exponential time just like the Fibonacci number function did. And again, we can solve the problem by memoizing. A sample run of the program on a list of 21 numbers took 90 seconds and called T 4,194,303 times; the memoized version took 0.42 seconds and called T only 1,521 times.

There's a slight problem here: the caching strategy showed earlier doesn't work. It stores the cached value in a hash, keyed by join $;, @_;. In this case, the two arguments to T are a reference to a list of numbers, and a target sum. When we use the reference in the join statement, we get something like ARRAY(0xae050). These strings are always different for different arrays, even if the contents of the arrays are the same. This means that _check_cache can't tell that the arguments are the same even when they are.

The Memoize module has a feature that solves this problem: it lets us override the function that converts argument lists to hash keys, so we can tell the memoizer explicitly what parts of the arguments aren't important. This lets us say that in a call like T([1,2,3], 7), the 1, 2, and 3 are important, but the identity of the array that happens to contain them is not important. Here's what the call to memoize looks like:

```
memoize 'T', NORMALIZER => sub { my ($arr, $t) = @_;
                                 join ' ', @$arr, $t;
                               };
```

The NORMALIZER is the function that converts argument lists to hash keys. In this case, it extracts the numbers from the array and joins them together into a string. The results of the call T([1,2,3], 7) will be stored in the hash under the key "1 2 3 7".

When Memoizing Doesn't Work

Disaster will ensue unless the function that we memoize is pure. Its return value must depend only on its arguments, and it must not have any side effects.

To see what happens when the function depends on something other than its arguments, consider this:

```
# Return the current time of day as "5:24:32"
sub time { my ($s, $m, $h) = localtime;
    sprintf "%d:$02d:%02d", $s, $m, $h;
}
```

If we memoize this, it'll return the correct time the first time we call it, but after that the time will be in the cache and whenever we call it we'll get the cached value.

To see what happens when the function has side effects, consider this:

```
sub squawk {
  my $a = shift;
  print STDERR "There were only $a fields in the record!\n";
}
```

Suppose that the main program is reading a file with records that have 15 fields each. It uses this function to deliver an error message each time it encounters a record with the wrong number of fields. The first time we see a record with only 14 fields, it works properly. The second time, the memoizer sees that the argument is the same and returns the cached return value (which is 1, not that you cared) without actually calling the function—so no message comes out.

There's one other kind of function to avoid memoizing, and the problem is a little more subtle. If the function returns a reference to a structure that will be modified by its callers, it cannot be memoized. To see why not, consider this function:

```
sub iota {
  my $n = shift;
  return [ 1 .. $n ];
}
```

iota returns a reference to a list of the numbers from 1 to *n*, where *n* is its argument. If iota is memoized, the cached value will be a reference to the list.

Suppose that iota( ) is memoized, and the caller does something like this:

```
$i10 = iota(10);
$j10 = iota(10);
```

$i10 and $j10 look like they're both arrays containing the numbers from 1 to 10. But they're not really; they're both references to the same array! If iota hadn't been memoized, they would be references to different arrays. Now the punchline:

```
pop @$i10;
```

This modifies $j10 also, because it's the same array. If iota weren't memoized, $j10 would have been unaffected.

Sometimes there are exceptions to these perils. For example, the gethostbyname function often takes a long time, because Perl has to open a network socket, send data to the name server, and wait for the reply to come back. Memoizing gethostbyname is technically incorrect, because the address data *might* change between calls. But in practice, address data doesn't usually change very quickly, and memoizing gethostbyname doesn't lead to any real problems except in long-running programs.

Bibliography

Improving the Performance of AI Software: Payoffs and Pitfalls in Using Automatic Memoization. Hall, Marty and James Mayfield. *Proceedings of the Sixth International Symposium on Artificial Intelligence*, Monterrey, Mexico, September 1993.

Memo Functions and Machine Learning. Michie, Donald. *Nature*, 218, #1, April 1968, pp. 19-22.

Structure and Interpretation of Computer Programs. Abelson, Hal, and Gerald Jay Sussman. MIT Press, Cambridge, 1985. pp. 218-219.

The Memoize module is standard with Perl 5.6.1, and is available from CPAN and from *http://perl.plover.com/Memoize/*. The source code for the MiniMemoize module, and the other programs described in this article, is available from *http://perl.plover.com/MiniMemoize/*.

CHAPTER 21

Parsing

Damian Conway

So who cares about parsing anyway?

Er, well, humans do. Our brains seem to be hard-wired for a syntactic view of the world, and we strive (often unreasonably) to find or impose grammatical structures in our lives. Homo Sapiens is a species evolved for language (or possibly, by it). We are compulsive and incessant parsers: of written text, spoken words, our children's faces, dogs' tails, politicians' body language,* the simple grammar of traffic lights, and the complex syntax of our own internal aches and pains. You're parsing right now: shapes into letters, letters into words, words into sentences, sentences into messages, messages into (dis)belief!

It's not surprising that programmers (many of whom were once human) should be concerned with parsing, too. If you use any of the modules in the Pod::, Date::, HTML::, CGI::, LWP::, or Getopt:: hierarchies, the Expect module, TeX::Hyphen, Text::Refer, ConfigReader, PGP, Term::ReadLine, CPAN, Mail::Tools, or one of the database interface modules, or even if you just read in a line at a time and match it against some regular expressions, then you're parsing. Sometimes in the privacy and comfort of your own home.

Each of those modules contains a chunk of custom-made, carefully tuned, walnut-veneered code, which takes ugly raw data and sculpts it into finely chiseled information you can actually use.

Of course, if the CPAN doesn't supply a parsing system for the particular ugly raw data you need to process, then you're going to have to roll your own. That's what parser generators like Parse::RecDescent are for.

---

* It is said that touching of the nose is an infallible nonverbal cue that a politician is lying. Also, covering the mouth, adjusting shirt cuffs, or smiling without showing any teeth. Or looking down. Or pointing. Or fidgeting. Or breathing.

A Sample Parse

To use tools like Parse::RecDescent, you first need to know something about formal grammars. Now just relax! This next bit won't hurt. Suppose, for example, you want to "reverse" the output of a Unix diff (i.e., as if the two files had been compared in the opposite order). Here's a typical diff output:

```
17,18d16
< (who writes under the
<  pseudonym "Omniscient Trash")
45,46c43,44
< soon every Tom, Dick or Harry
< will be writing his own Perl book
---
> soon every Tom, Randal and Larry
> will be writing their own Perl book
69a68,69
> Copyright (c) 1998 The Perl Journal.
> All Rights Reserved.
```

Each chunk encodes a single transformation of the original file. For example, the first three lines mean "at lines 17 to 18 of the original file perform a Delete operation, leaving us at line 16 in the second file." It then shows the two lines to be removed, each prefixed by a less-than sign.

The next six lines mean "at lines 45 to 46 of the first file do a Change operation, producing lines 43 to 44 in the second file." It then shows the lines to be replaced (prefixed by less-than signs) and the replacement lines (with greater-than signs). The last three lines mean "at line 69 in the first file do an Append operation to produce lines 68 to 69 in the second file." The lines to be added are then listed, prefixed by greater-than signs.

So a diff output consists of a series of operations, each of which in turn consists of a command followed by context information. Commands consist of a single letter sandwiched between numbers that represent line ranges in each file. Context information consists of one or more lines of left context, right context, or both, where each context line consists of a line of text preceded by a less-than or greater-than sign.

Formal Grammars

Phew! That's a lot of structure for such a small piece of text. But it's useful structure. Let's take this English and turn it into a *formal grammar* that conveys the same information more precisely (and in a more compact and readable format):

```
DiffOutput    -> Command(s) EOF

Command       -> LineNum A_CHAR LineRange
                     RightLine(s)
               | LineRange D_CHAR LineNum
                     LeftLine(s)
               | LineRange C_CHAR LineRange
                     LeftLine(s)
                     SEPARATOR
                     RightLine(s)
```

```
LineNum      ->  DIGITS

LineRange    ->  LineNum COMMA LineNum
             |   LineNum

LeftLine     ->  LEFT_BRACKET TEXTLINE

RightLine    ->  RIGHT_BRACKET TEXTLINE
```

The way to read a formal grammar is to replace each -> with the words "consists of" and each | with "or possibly." The parenthesized (s) means the same as in English, namely, "one or more times." For example, the above grammar says that a LineRange consists of either a LineNum subrule, then a COMMA, and finally another LineNum, or possibly just a single LineNum. Each of the six chunks of this grammar specifies a separate *rule*. Each identifier on the left of an -> is the rule's name, and each list of items to the right of an -> (or |) specifies the sequence of things that together comprise the rule. Such sequences are called *productions*. The vertical bars separate alternatives, any one of which is an acceptable set of components for the rule as a whole.

Items in a production may be either the name of some other rule (such items are called *nonterminals* or *subrules*), or the name of something that represents actual text (such items are called *terminals*). In the above grammar, the nonterminals are in mixed-case and the terminals in uppercase.

The use of named terminals implies that something else—usually a specially written subroutine called a *lexer*—is going to preprocess the original input text and transform it into a sequence of labelled strings (called *tokens*). It is the labels on those tokens which will (hopefully) match the terminals. More on lexers and lexing later.

If you gave the full grammar to a parser generator, you'd get back a piece of code that is able to recognize any text conforming to the grammar's rules and, more importantly, can identify each part of the text (17,18 is a LineRange, d is a D_CHAR, 16 is a LineNum, and so on). Of course, recognizing the text is only half the battle. The real goal is to reverse it. Fortunately, reversing a diff output is easy. You just change every Append command to a Delete, and vice versa, and then swap the order of line numbers and the contexts associated with every command (including those belonging to Change commands). The contexts also have their leading less-than and greater-than signs reversed. Making those changes to the example text above you get:

```
16a17,18
> (who writes under the
>  pseudonym "Omniscient Trash")
43,44c45,46
< soon every Tom, Randal and Larry
< will be writing their own Perl book
...
> soon every Tom, Dick or Harry
> will be writing his own Perl book
68,69d69
< Copyright (c) 1998 The Perl Journal.
< All Rights Reserved.
```

O'REILLY BOOK REGISTRATION

Register your book with O'Reilly by completing this card and receive a **FREE** copy of our latest catalog. Or register online at **register.oreilly.com** and, in addition to our catalog, we'll send you email notification of new editions of this book, information about new titles, and special offers available only to registered O'Reilly customers.

Which book(s) are you registering? Please include title and ISBN # (above bar code on back cover)

_____

Title   ISBN #

_____

Title   ISBN #

_____

Title   ISBN #

_____

Name   Company/Organization

_____

Address

_____

City   State   Zip/Postal Code   Country

_____

Telephone   Email address

Part #10326

www.oreilly.com

BUSINESS REPLY MAIL

FIRST CLASS MAIL   PERMIT NO. 80   SEBASTOPOL, CA

Postage will be paid by addressee

O'Reilly & Associates, Inc.

BOOK REGISTRATION

1005 GRAVENSTEIN HIGHWAY NORTH

SEBASTOPOL, CA 95472-9910

For the grammar shown earlier to automatically reverse diff output, it needs to know what to do whenever it recognizes something reversible (i.e., a complete command). You tell it what to do by embedding blocks of code (Perl in this example), which the parser then automatically calls whenever it successfully recognizes the corresponding production. Adding the equivalent Perl actions into the above grammar:

```
DiffOutput    -> Command(s) EOF

Command       -> LineNum A_CHAR LineRange
                     RightLine(s)
                         { print "$item3 d $item1\n";
                           $item4 =~ s/^>/</gm;
                           print $item[4];
                         }
                 | LineRange D_CHAR LineNum
                     LeftLine(s)
                         { print "$item3 a $item1\n";
                           $item4 =~ s/^</>/gm;
                           print $item[4];
                         }
                 | LineRange C_CHAR LineRange
                     LeftLine(s) SEPARATOR RightLine(s)
                         { print "$item3 c $item1\n";
                           $item4 =~ s/^</>/gm;
                           $item6 =~ s/^>/</gm;
                           print $item6, $item5, $item4;
                         }
LineNum       -> DIGITS

LineRange     -> LineNum COMMA LineNum
                 | LineNum

LeftLine      -> LEFT_BRACKET TEXTLINE

RightLine     -> RIGHT_BRACKET TEXTLINE
```

Note that the actions need access to the various bits of data that have been recognized, in order to reprint them. In this example, they access the data by referring to the lexically scoped variables $item1, $item2, $item3, and so on. These variables are automagically assigned the substrings of the original text that were matched by each item in the current production (just as $1, $2, and $3 automagically receive the values of the last matched parentheses of a regular expression). So the production:

```
Command   -> LineNum A_CHAR LineRange
                 RightLine(s)
                 { print "$item3 d $item1\n";
                   $item4 =~ s/^>/</gm;
                   print $item[4];
                 }
```

has now been told that if a Command rule matches an Append command, it should print out the text matching the LineRange (item 3 of the production), then a d, then the original text that matched the LineNum (item 1). Then it should reverse the less-than and greater-than signs on the context lines (item 4) and print those out, too.

The Different Types of Parsers

Having specified the grammar and its behavior when various productions are recognized, all you need to do is build an actual parser that implements the grammar. Of course, building the parser is the tedious and difficult bit. That's why there are automated parser construction tools like Parse::RecDescent, and its distant cousins yacc, perl-byacc, PCCTS, libparse, and the Perl Parse::Yapp module.

When it comes to such tools, the lazy programmer is spoiled with choices. There are dozens of freely-available packages for generating parsers in a variety of languages (but mostly in C, C++, Java, and Perl). Almost all of the parser generators belong to one of two families: *top-down* or *bottom-up*. The names describe the way the parsers they create compare a text to a grammar.

Bottom-Up Parsers

Bottom-up parsers (sometimes called LR parsers: "scan Left, expanding Rightmost subrule in reverse") are usually implemented as a series of states, encoded in a lookup table. The parser moves from state to state by examining the next available token in the text and then consulting the table to see what to do next. The choices are: perform an action, change to a new state, or give up in disgust.

A bottom-up parse succeeds if all the text is processed and the parser is left in a predefined "successful" state. Parsing can fail at any time if the parser sees a token for which there is no suitable next state, and is therefore forced to give up.

In effect, a bottom-up parser converts the original grammar into a maze, which the text must thread its way through, state-to-state, one token at a time. If the trail of tokens leads to a dead end, then the text didn't conform to the rules of the original grammar and is rejected. In this metaphor, any actions embedded in the grammar are scattered throughout the maze and are executed when they are encountered. The bottom-up "maze" for the diff-reversing grammar looks like Figure 21-1.

Top-Down Parsers

Top-down parsers (sometimes called LL parsers: "scan Left, expanding Leftmost subrule") work quite differently. Instead of working token-to-token through a flattened-out version of the grammar rules, top-down parsers start at the highest level and attempt to match the most general rule first.

Thus, a top-down parser starts by attempting to match the entire DiffOutput rule, and immediately realizes that to do so it must match one or more instances of the Command rule. It attempts to match a Command rule, and immediately realizes that to do so it must match one of the three productions in the Command rule. So it tries to match the first production, and realizes that it must first match a LineNum, and so on.

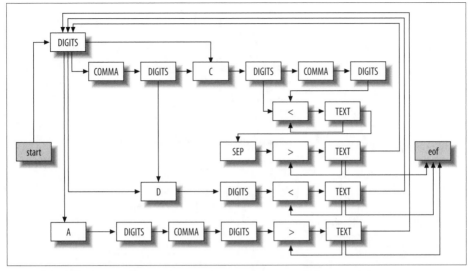

Figure 21-1. A bottom-up maze

It keeps moving further down the hierarchy of rules until it actually reaches a point where it can try and match a terminal (against the first available token). If the terminal and token match, the parser moves back up the hierarchy looking for the next bit of the enclosing production, and following that down until the next token is matched. If all the parts of the production are matched, the parser moves back up, matching higher and higher rules, until it succeeds in matching the topmost rule completely.

If at some point a token fails to match, then the parser works back up the tree, looking for an alternative way of matching the original rule (i.e. via a different production of the same rule). If all alternatives eventually fail, then the parse as a whole fails.

In other words, a top-down parser converts the grammar into a tree (or more generally, a graph), which it traverses in a top-to-bottom, left-to-right order. If a particular branch of the tree fails to match, then the parser backs up and tries the next possible branch. If all branches fail, then the parse itself fails. In this approach, embedded actions represent leaves on the tree, and are executed if the traversal ever reaches them.

The top-down "tree" for the `diff`-reversing grammar looks like Figure 21-2.

The Descent of RecDescent

Tools for building bottom-up parsers have a long and glorious history, dominated by the yacc program developed by Stephen Johnson at Bell Labs in the mid 1970s. yacc accepts a grammar very similar to those shown above and generates C code, which can be compiled into a function that acts as parser for the language the grammar describes. Rick Ohnenus adapted a modern variant of yacc to create `perl-byacc`, which generates Perl code directly. Later, Jake Donham developed a set of patches allowing `perl-byacc` to generate parser objects (rather than parsing functions). Perl's parsing is discussed in

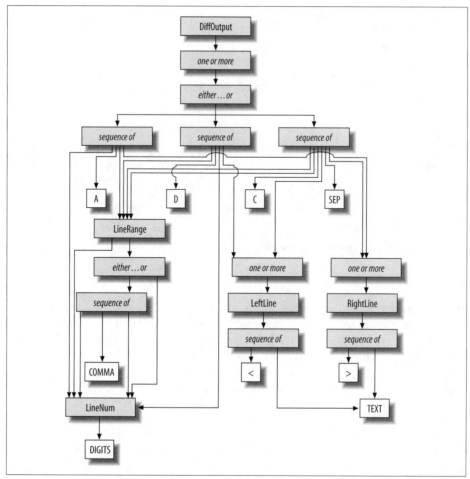

Figure 21-2. A top-down tree

this book in the article *Lexical Analysis*. Recently, François Desarmenien went one better and implemented a complete object-oriented yacc-like parser generator called Parse::Yapp directly in Perl (it also generates its parsers as Perl code).

Top-down parsing has been less popular, but one prominent tool that uses this approach is PCCTS, developed as a Ph.D. research project by Terence Parr. PCCTS provides much more power and flexibility than the yacc family, but generates C++ and not Perl. John Wiegley's libparse bundle is an extremely comprehensive and ambitious parsing system that does generate Perl code. It is still in alpha release, but can already generate top-down parsers, at least on NT machines. Finally, my own Parse::RecDescent module—the topic of the rest of this article—creates very flexible top-down parsers in Perl. For a comparison of some of these tools, see the sidebar "A Comparison of Parser Generators."

A Comparison of Parser Generators

In Table 21-1, the yacc column covers all yacc derivatives, including perl-byacc, Parse:: Yapp, and the currently available components of libparse. The column entitled "hand-made" refers to special purpose parsers, such as those are found inside many CPAN modules, which are usually coded directly, without recourse to automated tools.

Table 21-1. Features of parser generators

Feature	RecDescent	yacc	PCCTS	Handmade
Regular expressions as terminals	Y	Y	Y	Sometimes
Parse-time interpolated literal terminals	Y	N	N	N
Context-sensitive lexing	Y	Hard	Hard	Sometimes
Tunable token separators	Y	Hard	Hard	N
Requires separate tokenizer	N	Y	Y	Sometimes
Noncontiguous productions	Y	N	N	N/A
Subrule quantifiers (repetitions, optionals)	Y	N	Y	N/A
Nongreedy quantifiers	Coming	N	N	N/A
Inlined subproductions	Y	N	N	N/A
Subrule arguments	Y	N	Y	Rarely
User-defined lexical variables in subrules	Y	N	Y	Often
Stubbing of missing subrules	Y	N	N	N/A
Positive and negative lookahead rules	Y	N	N	Rarely
Data driven subrule selection (matchrule)	Y	N	N	Rarely
Subrule templates	Y	N	N	N
Embedded actions	Y	Y	Y	Y
Deferred embedded actions	Y	N	N	Rarely
Tunable default embedded actions	Y	N	N	N
Line and position information in actions	Y	Poor	Y	Some
Automated error messages	Y	Poor	Some	N
Conditional error messages	Y	N	N	N
Tree pruning and unpruning (commit/ uncommit)	Y	N	N	Sometimes
Runtime modification of parser	Y	N	N	Rarely
Regex-based resync after fail	Y	N	N	N
Object-oriented parser	Y	Some	Y	Sometimes
Parsing directly from an input stream	N	Y	Y	Sometimes
Multiple start rules	Y	N	N	Rarely

—continued—

Table 21-1. Features of parser generators (continued)

Feature	RecDescent	yacc	PCCTS	Handmade
Implementation language	Perl	C	C++	Various
Parsing model	LL(k)-(recursive)	LALR(1)-(table)	LL(k)-(table)	Various
Generates runtime parsers	Y	N	N	N/A
Generates compile-time parser code	Option	Y	Y	N/A
Fast	Coming	Y	Y	Y
Handles left recursion	N	Y	Y	Sometimes

Building a Parser with Parse::RecDescent

Most parser generators involve an unpleasantly complicated ritual. First, you create a lexer to split up your text into labelled tokens. That process usually involves hand-crafting some code or using a lexer-generator tool (such as lex, flex, or DLG). Next, you create your grammar and feed it to a parser generator. The parser generator spits out some more code: your parser. Then you write your program, importing both the lexer and parser code you built previously. You hook the three bits together and voilá! Typically, that looks something like Figure 21-3.

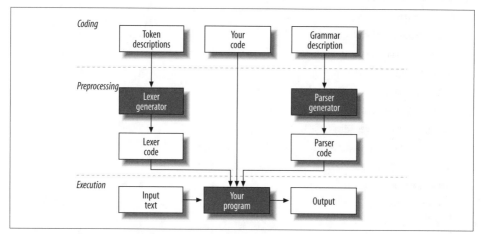

Figure 21-3. Steps involved in creating your own parser

Of course, this multi-stage, multi-task, multi-file, multi-tool approach quickly becomes a multi-lobe headache. Which is one reason Parse::RecDescent was created. The steps of building a parser with Parse::RecDescent are shown in Figure 21-4.

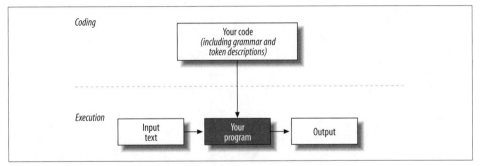

Figure 21-4. *Steps involved in using Parse::RecDescent*

The entire parsing program is specified in a single file of Perl code. To build a parser, you create a new Parse::RecDescent object, passing it the required grammar. The new object provides methods you can then use to parse a string. For example, here is the complete diff reverser implemented using Parse::RecDescent:

```perl
#!/usr/bin/perl -w

use Parse::RecDescent;

my $grammar = q{
    DiffOutput: Command(s) /\Z/

    Command:
        LineNum 'a' LineRange RightLine(s)
            { print "$item[3]d$item[1]\n";
              print map {s/>/</; $_} @{$item[4]};
            }
        | LineRange 'd' LineNum LeftLine(s)
            { print "$item[3]a$item[1]\n";
              print map {s/</>/; $_} @{$item[4]};
            }
        | LineRange 'c' LineRange
          LeftLine(s) "---\n" RightLine(s)
            { print "$item[3]c$item[1]\n";
              print map {s/>/</; $_} @{$item[6]};
              print $item[5];
              print map {s/</>/; $_} @{$item[4]};
            }
        | <error: Invalid diff(1) command!>

    LineRange:
        LineNum ',' LineNum
            { join '',@item[1..3] }
        | LineNum

    LineNum:    /\d+/

    LeftLine:   /<.*\n/
```

```
        RightLine:    />.*\n/
};

my $parser = new Parse::RecDescent($grammar);

undef $/;
my $text = <STDIN>;

$parser->DiffOutput($text);
```

The structure of the program is quite straightforward. First, specify the grammar as a string ($grammar). Next, create a new Parse::RecDescent object, passing $grammar as an argument to new. Assuming the grammar was okay (and in this case it was), new returns an object (a blessed reference). This object has a method corresponding to each rule in the grammar it was given.

You then read the entire STDIN into another string ($text) and pass that text to the parser object's DiffOutput method, causing the parser to attempt to match the string against that rule.

As the match proceeds, the various actions specified for each rule will be executed. If the text is successfully parsed, the actions that get fired off along the way will cause the program to print a "diff-reversed" version of its input.

How Parse::RecDescent Works

Let's dissect the program. Notice the grammar passed to Parse::RecDescent::new is very much like the one in the examples above, except that it uses a colon to define new rules, instead of an arrow.

Note, too, that the grammar constitutes the vast bulk of the program. In fact, the rest of the code could be reduced to a single line:

```
    Parse::RecDescent->new($grammar)->DiffOutput(join '', <>);
```

Handling Items

Parse::RecDescent uses an array (@item) to represent matched items, instead of individual scalars ($item1, $item2, and so on). The automagical behavior of this @item array merits a little more explanation. When a subrule in a production matches during a parse, that match returns the scalar value of the *last* item (terminal, nonterminal, or action) matched by the subrule. The returned value is assigned to the corresponding element of @item in the production that requested the subrule match.

Consequently, if a rule consists of a single item (for example, LineNum: /\d+/), the substring matched by that regular expression is returned up the parse tree when the rule succeeds. On the other hand, if a production consists of several items in sequence (e.g., LineRange: LineNum ',' LineNum), then only the value of the second LineNum subrule is returned.

It's a reasonable default, but if it's not the behavior you want, you need to add an action as the last item (e.g., {join '', @item[1..3]}), to ensure the appropriate value is returned for use higher up in the grammar.

Handling Repeated Items

Another special case to keep in mind: if you specify a repeated subrule in a production (like Command(s) or LeftLine(s)), the scalar value that comes back to @item is a *reference* to an array of values, one for each match. That's why the print statement for the c command prints @{$item[4]} (i.e., the actual array of values matched by LeftLine(s)), instead of just $item[4].

By the way, the various map operations applied to these arrays simply reverse the less-than and greater-than signs (as diff requires).

No Lexer

The other major difference between the Parse::RecDescent version of the grammar and those shown earlier is that, where the previous grammars had token names like DIGITS, SEPARATOR, A_CHAR, EOF, and so on as its terminals, this version has quoted strings ('a' instead of A_CHAR, "---\n" instead of SEPARATOR), or regular expressions (/\d+/ instead of DIGITS, /\Z/ instead of EOF). This is because, unlike nearly all other parser generators, Parse::RecDescent creates a parser that doesn't require a separate lexer subroutine to chew its input into predigested pieces.

Instead, when a Parse::RecDescent parser reaches a quoted string or regular expression in one of its productions, it simply matches the specified text or pattern against its original input string. This is known as *on-the-fly* or *context-sensitive* tokenization, and is a more flexible strategy than the usual pretokenization, because it allows different productions to interpret the same input differently. *

Error Handling

A final addition to the Parse::RecDescent version of the grammar is the fourth production of the Command rule:

```
<error: Invalid diff(1) command!>
```

This is not a specification of what to match, but rather a *directive* that tells the parser what to do if it reaches that point without having matched anything else. This particular directive tells the parser to generate the error message Invalid diff(1) command, and then fail. That failure will be fatal, because it will stop the repeated Command subrule from matching any further, and will cause the following /\Z/ terminal to *not* find the end of the input.

---

* A well known case that cries out for such context-sensitive lexing is in the grammar for C++, where nested templates (such as List<List<int>>) routinely generate syntax errors because the pretokenizing lexer classifies the trailing >> as a single "right shift" token. A Parse::RecDescent parser would have no such difficulties.

An In-Depth Example

Grammar-based parsing certainly isn't restricted to processing rigidly defined data formats such as what `diff` produces. Here's another example that's about as far away as you can get. It's the classic "Who's On First?" routine, as performed by a pair of Parse::RecDescent parsers named $abbott and $costello.

```perl
#!/usr/bin/perl -w

use vars qw( %base %man @try_again );
use Parse::RecDescent;
sub Parse::RecDescent::choose { $_[int rand @_]; }

$abbott = new Parse::RecDescent <<'EOABBOTT';
    Interpretation: ConfirmationRequest | NameRequest | BaseRequest
    ConfirmationRequest:
                Preface(s?)  Name  /[i']s on/ Base
                { (lc $::man{$item[4]} eq lc $item[2])
                  ? "Yes"
                  : "No, $::man{$item[4]}\'s on $item[4]"
                }

            |   Preface(s?)  Name  /[i']s the (name of the)?/
                Man /('s name )?on/  Base
                { (lc $::man{$item[6]} eq lc $item[2])
                  ? "Certainly"
                  : "No. \u$item[2] is on " . $::base{lc $item[2]}
                }

    BaseRequest: Preface(s?)  Name  /(is)?/
                { "He's on " . $::base{lc $item[2]} }

    NameRequest: /(What's the name of )?the/i  Base  "baseman"
                { $::man{$item[2]} }

    Preface:    ...!Name /\S*/

    Name:       Name12  | /I Don't Know/i

    Name12:     /Who/i  | /What/i

    Base:       'first' | 'second' | 'third'

    Man:        'man'   | 'guy'    | 'fellow'
EOABBOTT

$costello = new Parse::RecDescent <<'EOCOSTELLO';
    Interpretation:
        Meaning <reject:$item[1] eq $thisparser->{prev}>
                { $thisparser->{prev} = $item[1] }
        | { choose(@::try_again) }

    Meaning: Question | UnclearReferent | NonSequitur
```

```
        Question: Preface  Interrogative  /[i']s on/  Base
                        { choose ("Yes, what is the name of the guy on $item[4]?",
                          "The $item[4] baseman?",
                          "I'm asking you! $item[2]?",
                          "I don't know!") }

             | Interrogative
                        { choose ("That's right, $item[1]?",
                          "What?",
                          "I don't know!") }

        UnclearReferent: "He's on"  Base
                        { choose ("Who's on $item[2]?",
                          "Who is?",
                          "So, what is the name of the guy on $item[2]?"
                          ) }

        NonSequitur: ( "Yes" | 'Certainly' | /that's correct/i )
                { choose("$item[1], who?",
                   "What?",
                   @::try_again) }

        Interrogative: /who/i | /what/i

        Base:    'first' | 'second' | 'third'

        Preface: ...!Interrogative /\S*/

EOCOSTELLO

%man = ( first => "Who", second => "What", third => "I Don't Know" );
%base = map { lc } reverse %man;

@try_again = ( "So, who's on first?",
                 "I want to know who's on first!",
                 "What's the name of the first baseman?",
                 "Let's start again. What's the name of the guy on first?",
                 "Okay, then, who's on second?",
                 "Well then, who's on third?",
                 "What's the name of the fellow on third?" );

$costello->{prev} = $line = "Who's on first?";

while (1) {
    print "<costello>  ", $line, "\n" and sleep 1;
    $line = $abbott->Interpretation($line);
    print "<abbott>    ", $line, "\n" and sleep 1;
    $line = $costello->Interpretation($line);
}
```

Each of the parsers encodes a particular world view, which is a combination of a set of interpretations of the sentences it is parsing, together with some text generation logic that allows it to respond appropriately to those interpretations.

The Abbott grammar treats each line to be parsed as either a statement that requires confirmation (a ConfirmationRequest), or as a name or position enquiry (a BaseRequest or NameRequest), for which the appropriate fielding position or player name should be supplied.

In contrast, the Costello grammar treats each parsed line as either a rephrasing of a previous question (a Question), which it tries to confirm, or as an ambiguous statement (UnclearReferent), which it tries to clarify, or as an inexplicable utterance (a NonSequitur), which derails the entire dialogue and forces it to start the conversation from scratch. The humor resides in the fact that, although the responses provided by each parser are entirely consistent (within each grammar's world view), they mesh seamlessly into inescapable mutual incomprehension.

This example illustrates some additional features of the RecDescent package: free-form grammars, parser return values, object-oriented parsing, explicit rejection, "inlined" subrules, optional and specified-repetition subrules, and rule lookaheads.

Freeform Grammar

Notice that the rules in the above grammars are formatted in a variety of ways. The Parse::RecDescent module places very few restrictions on the formatting of a grammar. So a rule like:

```
Base:    'first' | 'second' | 'third'
```

could also be written:

```
Base:    'first'
       | 'second'
       | 'third'
```

or:

```
Base :    'first'
        | 'second'
        | 'third'
```

In fact, just about the only restriction on a Parse::RecDescent grammar is that a colon must appear on the same line as the preceding rule name.

Parser return values. Just as each subrule in a Parse::RecDescent parser evaluates to a single scalar value, the parse invocation (e.g., $costello->Interpretation) returns a scalar value. Specifically, it returns the value assigned to the Interpretation rule within the grammar.

The program uses this feature to extract responses from both grammars. Each response is generated within some lower-level subrule of each grammar by embedded actions that either analyze whether the recognized statement is true (ConfirmationRequest) look up the information requested (NameRequest) or, in desperation, choose a random (but relevant) response (UnclearReferent).

The generated response bubbles back up the parse tree, to be returned by the topmost rule. The `while` loop then feeds that response into the other parser, where a similar "parse-interpret-generate-respond" process is repeated, with a response that is in turn fed back to the first parser. The ensuing alternation generates the dialogue.

Although it can't happen in either of these parsers, the parser returns `undef` if the initial rule fails to match. Hence a common idiom with Parse::RecDescent parsers is this:

```
$result = $parser->InitialRule($text) or die "Bad input!\n";
```

Object-oriented parsing. Parsers generated with Parse::RecDescent are Perl objects (specifically, blessed hash references), and the Costello grammar takes advantage of that fact in two ways.

First, it makes use of the `Parse::RecDescent::choose` function (which is not part of Parse::RecDescent, but was added by the main program) to randomly select from a range of possible responses.

Second, the Costello grammar adds an extra member to the `$costello` parser object: `$thisparser->{prev}`. It uses that to cache information between parses (more on that in a moment).

The `$thisparser` variable is automatically generated by Parse::RecDescent, and it is the way actions in a grammar can refer to the parser that is executing them. It's much like the variable `$self`, used when writing method subroutines for Perl classes.

Explicit rejection. You can explicitly cause a production to reject itself under specified conditions by using the `<reject:...` directive. This directive takes a Perl expression and evaluates it. If the expression is true, the directive immediately causes the current production to fail. If the expression is false, the directive is ignored and matching continues in the same production.

The Costello grammar uses this facility in order to avoid repeating its responses. Its top-level rule:

```
Interpretation:
    Meaning <reject:$item[1] eq $thisparser->{prev}>
        { $thisparser->{prev} = $item[1] }
    | { choose(@::try_again) }
```

first tries to match a `Meaning`, but rejects the match if the returned response is the same as the previously cached value (in `$thisparser->{prev}`). If the returned response isn't rejected, the following action caches it for next time. And since the action is the last item of the production, it returns that value as the value of the entire `Interpretation` rule.

On the other hand, if the response *was* rejected, then the first production immediately fails, and the second production is tried. That production immediately chooses a random response from the list in `@try_again` and returns it as the value of the entire `Interpretation` rule.

Rejection can even take factors outside the grammar into account. For instance, a rule like this:

```
Filename: /\w+/ <reject: !-r $item[1]>
```

allows your grammar to recognize an identifier as a filename, but only if the string is the name of a readable file.

"Inlined" subrules. Alternative subproductions can be specified in parentheses within a single production. For example, the subproduction:

```
NonSequitur:
        ( "Yes" | 'Certainly' | /that's correct/i )
            { choose("$item[1], who?", "What?", @::try_again) }
```

performs the same action for Yes, Certainly, or anything matching /that's correct/i.

Optional and specified-repetition subrules. Just as subrules in a production can be made repeatable with a trailing (s), they can also be made optional with a trailing (?), or optional *and* repeatable with a trailing (s?), or even made to repeat an exact number of times if a numeric range is specified in the trailing parentheses.

For example, the rule:

```
BaseRequest: Preface(s?) Name /(is)?/
```

specifies that a name may be preceded by zero or more prefaces. Alternatively, you could set a limit with an explicit range:

```
BaseRequest: Preface(0..10) Name /(is)?/
```

Rule lookaheads. Parse::RecDescent also provides a mechanism similar to zero-length lookaheads in regular expressions (i.e., (?=) and (?!)). Parse::RecDescent lookaheads act just like other production items when matching, except that they do not "consume" the substrings they match. That means the next item encountered after a lookahead item will attempt to match at the same starting point as that lookahead.

Negative lookaheads are specified as with a ...! prefix and are typically used as guards to prevent repeated subrules from eating more than they should. The Abbott grammar, for example, uses a negative lookahead to make sure that the Preface subrule doesn't consume a significant name:

```
Preface: ...!Name /\S*/
```

The ...! preceding Name means that in order to match a Preface, the string being parsed must first *not* match a Name before the specified pattern.

Positive lookaheads are specified with a ... prefix, and are also useful for ensuring that repetitions don't get too greedy. They aren't used in the Abbott or Costello grammars, but they're handy in situations like this:

```
Move:
    'mv' File ExtraFile(s) Destination
  | 'mv' File File
```

```
ExtraFile:
    File ...File

Destination:
    File
```

Here, an ExtraFile only matches a File followed by another File; exactly one file will always be left after the ExtraFile subrule has matched repeatedly, ensuring that the trailing Destination item will match. Without the trailing lookahead, the ExtraFile subrule would match all the files, leaving nothing for Destination.

Advanced Features of Parse::RecDescent

Parse::RecDescent has features and abilities far beyond those described so far. Some of its more interesting abilities follow.

Automated Error Reporting

The < error: *message* > directive used in the diff-reverser prints a fixed message when triggered. Parse::RecDescent provides a related directive, <error>, which automatically generates an error message, based on the specific context in which it's triggered. Consider this rule:

```
Command:
        LineNum 'a' LineRange RightLine(s)
      | LineRange 'd' LineNum LeftLine(s)
      | LineRange 'c' LineRange
        LeftLine(s) "---\n" RightLine(s)
      | <error>
```

If none of the preceding productions had matched anything, it would automatically generate the message:

```
ERROR (line 10): Invalid Command: was expecting LineNum or LineRange
```

when fed invalid diff output at line 10.

Integrated Tracing Facilities

Tracking down glitches when a large grammar is applied to a long string can be tricky. Parse::RecDescent makes it easier with extensive error checking, and a tracing mode that provides copious information on parser construction and execution.

As the parser is constructed from a grammar, Parse::RecDescent automatically diagnoses common problems such as invalid regular expressions used as terminals, invalid Perl code in actions, incorrect use of lookaheads, unrecognizable elements in the grammar, unreachable rule components, the use of undefined rules as production items, and cases where greedy repetition behavior will almost certainly cause the failure of a production.

Other, less critical problems are reported if the directive <warn> appears at the start of the grammar. Extra information and hints for remedying problems can also be supplied by including the directive <hint>.

Two more directives, <trace_build> and <trace_parse>, can be used to trace the parser's construction and execution. Parse::RecDescent reports on the construction progress (via STDERR), indicating how each element of the grammar was interpreted. This feature can be especially useful for tracing down mismatched quotes or parentheses, and other subtle bugs in the grammar specification. The debugging facilities are designed for unobtrusiveness and ease of use. They can be invoked without making any other changes to the original grammar, reducing the incedence of heisenbugs.

Position Information Within Actions

You can refer to $thisline, $thiscolumn, and $thisoffset in any action or directive. These store the current line number, column number, and offset from the start of the input data. For example:

```
Sequence: BaseSequence(s)

BaseSequence: /[ACGT]+/
            | <error: alien DNA detected at byte $thisoffset!>
```

Parse Tree Pruning

Sometimes you know more about the structure of the input than can easily be expressed in a grammar. Such knowledge can be used to "prune" unpromising productions out of the parse tree.

On certain inputs, a production may be able to *commit* itself at some point, effectively saying: "At this point, we know enough that if the current production fails, all the rest must also fail." For example, in this rule:

```
Command: 'find' <commit> Filename
       | 'delete' <commit> Filename
       | 'move' Filename 'to' Filename
```

the first production can commit itself after matching find, since the other two productions have no hope of matching in that case.

Argument passing and generic rules. Any nonterminal in a production can be passed arguments in a pair of square brackets immediately after the subrule name. Such arguments are then available (in the array @arg) within the corresponding subrule.

Better still, since double-quoted literal terminals and regular expression terminals are both interpolated during a parse (in the normal Perl manner), a rule can be parameterized according to the data being processed. For example, the rules:

```
Command: Keyword Statement(s) End[$item[1]]

Keyword: 'if' | 'while' | 'for'

End:    "end $arg[0]"
```

ensure that command keywords are always matched by a corresponding end *keyword* delimiter, because the Command rule passes the matched keyword ($item[1]) to the End subrule, which then interpolates it into a string terminal ("end $arg[0]") to be matched.

It's even possible to interpolate a *subrule* within a production by using the
<matchrule:...> directive:

```
Command:   Keyword Statement(s) <matchrule:"End_$item[1]">

Keyword:   'if' | 'while' | 'for'

End_if:    'end if'

End_while: 'end while'

End_for:   'end for'
```

In this version, the <matchrule:"End_$item[1]"> directive interpolates the text
matched by Keyword into a new subrule (either End_if, End_while, or End_for) and
then attempts to match it.

Deferred Actions

One of the limitations of embedding actions in rules is that they are executed as the
rule is matched, even if some higher level rule eventually fails. At best, that means
wasted effort; at worst, it leads to incorrect behavior, especially if the actions have
side effects such as printing.

For example, if the diff-reversing grammar were to encounter incorrect input half-
way through its parse, it would have already printed some of the reversed commands when it finds the error, reports it, and stops. That's just plain messy.
Fortunately, parser actions in Parse::RecDescent can be deferred until the entire
parse has succeeded. Such deferred actions are specified using the <defer:...> directive around curly braces.

Here's the diff-reversing grammar from the first example, with deferred actions instead:

```
DiffOutput: Command(s) /\Z/

Command: LineNum 'a' LineRange RightLine(s)
            <defer:
              { print "$item[3]d$item[1]\n";
                print map {s/>/</; $_} @{$item[4]};
              }>

        | LineRange 'd' LineNum LeftLine(s)
            <defer:
              { print "$item[3]a$item[1]\n";
                print map {s/</>/; $_} @{$item[4]};
              }>

        | LineRange 'c' LineRange
            LeftLine(s) "---\n" RightLine(s)
            <defer:
              { print "$item[3]c$item[1]\n";
                print map {s/>/</; $_} @{$item[6]};
                print $item[5];
```

```
        print map {s/</>/; $_} @{$item[4]};
        }>

    | <error: Invalid diff(1) command!>

LineNum: /\d+/

LineRange: LineNum ',' LineNum
        { join '',@item[1..3] }
        | LineNum

LeftLine: /<.*\n/

RightLine: />.*\n/
```

Now the various calls to print are only executed after the entire input string is correctly parsed. The grammar either reverses the entire diff or prints a single error message.

As each deferred action is encountered during the parse, it is squirreled away and only executed when the entire grammar succeeds. More importantly, deferred actions are only executed if they are part of a subrule that succeeded during the parse. That means you can defer actions in many alternative productions, and Parse:: RecDescent will only invoke those that belonged to subrules contributing to the final successful parse.

Extensible Grammars

This is probably the weirdest science in Parse::RecDescent. Unlike other parser generators, you can extend or replace entire rules in a parser at runtime. The bit that usually freaks out yacc devotees is that you can even change the grammar *while the parser is actually parsing with it!*

For example, suppose you are parsing a programming language that allows you to define new type names, and those new type names are subsequently invalid as normal identifiers. In Parse::RecDescent, you could do it like this:

```
TypeName:   'number' | 'text' | 'boolean'

TypeDefn:   'type' Identifier 'is' TypeName
            { $thisparser->Extend("TypeName: '$item[2]'") }

Identifier: ...!TypeName /[a-z]\w*/i
```

Traditional parsers for languages like this require you to send *semantic feedback* to the lexer, informing it that certain identifiers are now to be treated as type names instead. Parse::RecDescent allows you to do the same job using the much simpler notion of *lexical feedback*, by making the parser update itself when a type definition effectively modifies the language's syntax.

Practical Applications of Parsing

Here's a list of typical applications of Parse::RecDescent:

- Building natural language parsers for user interfaces, text summarization, or searching

- Extracting data from structured reports (like those generated by the system monitors, execution profilers, or traffic analyzers)

- Implementing command languages, query languages, configuration file processors, or even full programming language emulators in Perl

- Creating parsers for special purpose data specification languages (scene description languages for computer graphics, for example)

- Constructing analyzers for large structured data sets (such as genetics and bioinformatics databases)

- Building decommenters, syntax checkers, or pretty-printers for various languages (sorry, there are no Parse::RecDescent grammars available for Perl, C, or C++—yet!)

- Building data translators (Pod to XML, XML to RTF, RTF to /dev/null)

- Processing complex comma-separated values (i.e, multiple mixed formats, handling unquoted commas, and so on)

Anywhere that you can specify the structure of some data in a grammar, you can build a recognizer for that data using Parse::RecDescent.

Limitations of Parse::Recdescent

Parse::RecDescent is powerful, but far from perfect. Some of its limitations stem from the type of parsers it builds—others from its own ragged evolution.

No Left-Recursion

Unfortunately, the most significant limitation is inherent to Parse::RecDescent's nature: like all top-down parsers, it doesn't do left recursion. That means it can't build parsers for certain perfectly reasonable grammars. For instance, a fairly typical way of specifying the left-associativity of addition is to write a rule like this:

```
Addition: Addition '+' Term
        | Term
```

ensuring that terms are eventually grouped to the left.

Bottom-up parsers like yacc have no trouble unravelling left-recursive rules, but top-down parsers can't handle them, because the first thing it tells them to do when matching an Addition is to match an Addition, which in turn requires them to first match an Addition, and so on.

Parse::RecDescent can at least diagnose these cases for you (they can be much more subtle than the example above), but it will probably never be able to build parsers for them. Fortunately, it isn't a big problem, since you can achieve the same effect with this:

```
Addition: (Term '+')(s?) Term
```

Coming Attractions

Features slated for future releases of Parse::RecDescent include:

Tokenized input
> You'll be able to use a preliminary lexer if you choose to (which may significantly speed up some parsing tasks where context-sensitivity isn't an issue).

Automatic backtracking
> Within productions with repetitions, automatic backtracking will eliminate the problems of overly greedy matches "starving" later items.

Nongreedy repetitions
> These will match a minimal number of times, rather than a maximal number (just like nongreedy qualifiers in regular expressions).

Autocommiting
> You'll be able to tell the parser to analyze a grammar and automatically insert commit and uncommit directives wherever they will do some good.

More Information

The canonical reference is the dragon book, *Compilers: Principles, Techniques, and Tools* by Aho, Sethi & Ullman (Addison-Wesley). For a less rigorous but more readable approach, try *The Art of Compiler Design* by Pittman and Peters (Prentice Hall).

A few online resources are also worth looking into. Two places to start are the catalog of parsing tools at *http://www.first.gmd.de/cogent/catalog* and the even larger parsing-related repository at *http://www.km-cd.com.dragon_fodder/html/ToolBuildingBNF.html*. If you're searching for other such sites, try the keywords: parse, compiler, generator, BNF, or grammar.

If you're specifically interested in using yacc and lex, the Mothers of All Parser Generators, O'Reilly publishes the excellent *lex & yacc*.

Parse::RecDescent, Parse::Yapp, and libparse are each available from CPAN, while PCCTS is available from its homepage at *http://dynamo.ecn.purdue.edu/~hankd/PCCTS/*.

Finally, if you want to know more about the facilities of Parse::RecDescent, there's 40 pages of pod documentation that comes with the distribution. You can also point your fevered browser at *http://theory.uwinnipeg.ca/CPAN/data/Parse-RecDescent/Parse/RecDescent.html*.

Acknowledgments

My deepest gratitude to Nathan Torkington for suggesting this article, and for his heroic efforts cleaning up the Augean stables of my prolixity. No good deed ever goes unpunished. Thanks also to the (foreign) legion of Parse::RecDescent testers, users, and other guinea-pigs for their feedback, complaints, and wild-and-crazy suggestions. In particular, Helmut Jarausch, Theo Petersen, and Mark Holloman have a lot to answer for.

Grammars and Metagrammars

It's possible to summarize the various components that make up a grammar as follows:

- A *grammar* is a collection of rules that describe how a language is structured.
- A *rule* is a collection of productions that list the alternative ways parts of language can appear.
- A *production* is a list of nonterminals and/or terminals that must appear in the text being parsed if the surrounding rule is to match.
- A *nonterminal* is a reference to some other rule that must be matched as part of the patching of the surrounding rule.
- A *terminal* is something that can literally appear in a text (a word in the grammar's vocabulary).

What's interesting about that summary is how similar it is to a grammar. Just as each grammar rule is defined as a series of references to other rules (nonterminals) and token names (terminals), so the terms *grammar*, *rule*, *production*, *nonterminal*, and *terminal* are defined by reference to other terms (non-terminals) or by self-contained explanations (terminals). That leads to the somewhat recursive conclusion that you could define a grammar using a grammar. *Or maybe even using the same grammar!*

Now you're asking yourself "does Parse::RecDescent itself use a Parse::RecDescent grammar to convert grammars into parsers?" The answer is no. If Parse::RecDescent had to call Parse::RecDescent to build a parser for the Parse::RecDescent grammar, then that second version of Parse::RecDescent would itself have to call Parse::RecDescent to build a parser for the "Parse::RecDescent grammar" grammar, and that version would in turn have to call Parse::RecDescent to build a parser for the "'Parse::RecDescent grammar' grammar" grammar, and so on right down to Little Cat Z.

Hence, although it can automatically build parsers for just about any other purpose, for the moment Parse::RecDescent must content itself with a hand-built parser.

But plans are afoot.

## CHAPTER 22

Trees and Game Trees

Sean M. Burke

Perl's facility with references, combined with its automatic management of memory allocation, makes it straightforward to write programs that store data in structures of arbitrary form and complexity.

But I've noticed that many programmers, especially those who started out with more restrictive languages, seem at home with complex but uniform data structures—multidimensional arrays, or more struct-like things like hashes-of-arrays (-of-hashes[-of-hashes]), and so on—but they're often uneasy buliding more freeform, less tabular structures, like trees.

Trees are easy to build and manage in Perl, as I'll demonstrate by showing how the HTML::Element class manages elements in an HTML document tree, and by walking you through a from-scratch implementation of game trees. First, I need to nail down what I mean by a "tree."

What Is a Tree?

My first brush with tree-shaped structures was in linguistics classes, where tree diagrams were used to describe the syntax underlying natural language sentences. After learning my way around *those* trees, I started to wonder—are what I'm used to calling "trees" the same as what programmers call "trees?" I asked lots of helpful and patient programmers how they would define a tree. Many replied with a answer in jargon that they could not really explain (understandable, since explaining things, especially defining things, is harder than people think):

Q: *So what* is *a "tree?" A tree-shaped data structure?*

A: A tree is a special case of an acyclic directed graph!

Q: *What's a "graph"?*

A: Um, lines, and... you draw it... with... arcs! nodes! Um...

The most helpful were folks who couldn't explain it directly, but with whom I could get into a rather Socratic dialog (where I asked the half-dim, half-earnest questions), often with a lot of doodling.

Q: *So what's a tree?*

A: A tree is a collection of nodes that are linked together in a tree-like way! Like this (drawing on a napkin):

```
    A
   / \
  B   C
     / | \
    D  E  F
```

Q: *So what do these letters represent?*

A: Each is a different node, a chunk of data. Maybe C is a bunch of data that stores a number, maybe a hash table, maybe nothing at all besides the fact that it links to D, E, and F, which are other nodes.

Q: *So what are the lines between the nodes?*

A: Links. Also called "arcs." They just symbolize the fact that each node holds a list of nodes it links to.

Q: *So what if I draw nodes and links, like this? Is this still a tree?*

```
     B -- E
    / \  / \
   A   C
    \ /
     E
```

A: No, not at all. There are a lot of un-treelike things about that. First, E has a link coming off of it going into nowhere. You can't have a link to nothing—you can only link to another node. Second, I don't know what that sideways link between B and E means.

Q: *Okay, let's work our way up from something simpler. Is this a tree?*

```
   A
```

A: Yes, I suppose. It's a tree with just one node.

Q: *So how about this?*

```
   A

   B
```

A: No, you can't just have nodes floating there, unattached.

Q: *Okay, I'll link A and B. How's this?*

```
   A
   |
   B
```

A: Yup, that's a tree. There's a node A, and a node B, and they're linked.

Q: *How is that tree any different from this one?*

```
   B
   |
   A
```

A: In both cases A and B are linked. But in a different direction.

Q: *Direction? What does the direction mean?*

A: It depends what the tree represents. If it represents a categorization, like this:

```
          citrus
         /   |   \
        /    |    \
   orange  lemon  kumquat
```

then you mean to say that oranges, lemons, and kumquats are all kinds of citrus fruit. But if you drew it upside down, you'd be saying, falsely, that citrus is a kind of kumquat, a kind of lemon, and a kind of orange. If the tree represented cause-and-effect (or at least what situations could follow others), or represented what is a part of what, you wouldn't want to get those backwards, either. So with the nodes you draw together on paper, one has to be over the other, so can tell which way the relationship in the tree works.

Q: *So are these two trees the same?*

```
    A            A
   / \          / \
  B   C        B   \
                    C
```

A: Yes, although by convention we often try to line up things in the same generation, like your first tree.

Q: *"Generation?" This is a family tree?*

A: Not unless it's a family tree for yeast cells or something else that reproduces asexually.

But for the sake of having lots of terms to use, we just pretend that links in the tree represent the "is a child of" relationship, instead of "is a kind of" or "is a part of," or "could result from," or whatever the real relationship is. So we get to borrow a lot of kinship words for describing trees: B and C are "children" (or "daughters") of A; A is the "parent" of B and C. Node C is a "sibling" (or "sister") of node C; and so on, with terms like "descendants" and "generation" (all the nodes at the same "level" in the tree are either all grandchildren of the top node, or all great-grandchildren, etc.), and "lineage" or "ancestors."

So then we get to express rules in terms like "a node cannot have more than one parent," which means that this is not a valid tree:

```
    A
   / \
  B   C
   \ /
    E
```

Another rule is, "A node can't be its own parent," which excludes this looped-up connection:

```
    /\
  A  |
    \/
```

Or, put more generally, "a node can't be its own ancestor," which excludes the above loop, as well as the one here:

That tree is excluded because A is a child of Z, and Z is a child of C, and C is a child of A, which means A is its own great-grandparent. This whole network can't be a tree, because it breaks the meta-rule: once any node in the supposed tree breaks the rules for trees, you don't have a tree anymore.

Q: *Okay. So are these two trees the same?*

```
    A          A
  / | \      / | \
  B C D      D C B
```

A: It depends whether you think of the nodes as having an unordered list of children, or an ordered list of children. It's a question of whether ordering is important for what you're doing. With my diagram of citrus types, ordering isn't important, so these tree diagrams express the same relationships:

```
            citrus
        /     |    \
    orange  lemon  kumquat
```

```
            citrus
        /      |      \
    kumquat  orange  lemon
```

It doesn't make sense to say that oranges are "before" or "after" kumquats in the whole botanical scheme of things. (Unless, of course, you *are* using ordering to mean something, like a degree of genetic similarity.)

But consider a tree that's a diagram of what steps constitute an activity, to some degree of specificity:

```
            make tea
          /    |    \
        /      |      \
    pour     infuse   serve
  hot water   / \
  in cup/pot /   \
            /     \
          add     let
          tea     sit
        leaves
```

This means that making tea consists of putting hot water in a cup or pot, infusing it (adding tea leaves and letting it sit), and then serving it—in that order. If you serve an empty dry pot, let it sit, add tea leaves, and pour in hot water, then what you're doing is performance art, not tea preparation:

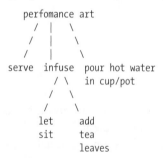

```
perfomance art
  /  |   \
 /   |    \
/    |     \
serve infuse pour hot water
        / \   in cup/pot
       /   \
      /     \
    let      add
    sit      tea
             leaves
```

Except for the renamed root, this tree is the same as the tea-making tree as far as what's under what, but it differs in order, and what the tree means makes the order important.

Q: *"Root?" What's a root?*

A: Besides kinship terms like "sister" and "daughter," the jargon for tree parts also has terms from real-life tree parts: the part that everything else grows from is called the root; and nodes that don't have children are called "leaves."

Q: *But you've been drawing all your trees with the root at the top and leaves at the bottom!*

A: For some reason, that's the way everyone seems to think of trees. They can draw trees as above; or they can draw them sort of sideways with indentation representing what nodes are children of what:

```
* make tea
  * pour hot water in cup/pot
  * infuse
    * add tea leaves
    * let sit
  * serve
```

But folks almost never seem to draw trees with the root at the bottom. So imagine it's a spider plant in a hanging pot. Unfortunately, spider plants *aren't* botanically trees, they're plants; but "spider plant diagram" is a mouthful, so let's call them trees.

Formal Definition

In time, I digested these assorted facts about programmers' ideas of trees (which turned out to be just a more general case of linguistic ideas of trees) into a single rule:

> A node is an item that contains (or "is over," or "is parent of") zero or more other nodes.

From this you can build up formal definitions for useful terms:

- A node's *descendants* are defined as all its children, and all their children, and so on. Or, stated recursively: a node's descendants are all its children, and all its children's descendants. (And if it has no children, it has no descendants.)

- A node's *ancestors* consist of its parent, and its parent's parent, and so on up to the root. Or, recursively: a node's ancestors consist of its parent and its parent's ancestors. (If it has no parent, it has no ancestors.)

- A *tree* is a root node and all the root's descendants.

And you can add a proviso or two to clarify exactly what I mean by the word "other" in "other nodes":

- A node cannot contain itself, or contain any node that contains it. Looking at it the other way: a node cannot be its own parent or ancestor.

- A node can be the root (that is, no other node contains it) or it can be contained by only one parent; no node can have more than one parent.

Add to this the idea that children are sometimes ordered, and sometimes not, and that's about all you need to know about defining a tree. From here, it's a matter of using them.

Markup Language Trees

Not *all* markup languages are inherently tree-like, but the best known ones (HTML, SGML, and XML) are about as tree-like as you can get. In these languages, a document consists of elements and character data in a tree structure in which there is one root element, and elements can contain either other elements, or character data.*

For example, consider this HTML document:

```
<html lang="en-US">
  <head>
    <title>
      Blank Document!
    </title>
  </head>
  <body bgcolor="#d010ff">
    I've got
    <em>
      something to saaaaay
    </em>
    !
  </body>
</html>
```

---

* For the sake of simplicity, I'm glossing over comments (<!-- ... -->), processing instructions (<?xml version='1.0'?>), and declarations (<!ELEMENT ...>, <!DOCTYPE ...>). And I'm not bothering to distinguish entity references (<, @) or CDATA sections (<![CDATA[...]]>) from normal text.

I've indented this to point out which nodes (elements or text items) are children of which, with each node on a line of its own.

The HTML::TreeBuilder module (in the HTML-Tree bundle on CPAN) takes some HTML text and constructs a tree that the document source represents. It requires the HTML::Parser module (described in the O'Reilly books *Perl and LWP* and *Web, Graphics & Perl/Tk: Best of the Perl Journal*), which tokenizes the source, identifying tags, bits of text, comments, and so on.

The tree structure that it builds represents bits of text with normal Perl scalar string values, but elements are represented with objects—that is, chunks of data belonging to a class (in this case, HTML::Element). HTML::Element provides methods for accessing the pieces of data in each element, and otherwise doing things with elements. (See *Using Object-Oriented Modules* for a quick explanation of objects, the perltoot documentation bundled with Perl for a longer explanation, or Damian Conway's excellent book *Object-Oriented Perl* from Manning Publications for the full story.)

Each HTML::Element object contains a number of pieces of data:

- The element name ("html", "h1", and so on, accessed as $element->tag)
- A list of elements (or text segments) that it contains, if any (accessed as $element->content_list or $element->content, depending on whether you want a list, or an array reference)
- What element, if any, contains it (accessed as $element->parent)
- Any SGML attributes the element has such as lang="en-US" or align="center", which would be accessed as $element->attr('lang') and $element->attr('center')

For example, when HTML::TreeBuilder builds the tree for the above HTML document source, the object for the "body" element has these pieces of data:

```
element name: "body"

nodes it contains:
  the string "I've got "
  the object for the "em" element
  the string "!"

its parent:
  the object for the "html" element

bgcolor: "#d010ff"
```

Once you have this tree of objects, almost anything you do with it starts by searching the tree for some bit of information in some element.

Accessing a piece of information in a hash of hashes of hashes, for example, is straightforward:

```
$password{sean}{sburke1}{hpux}
```

because you know that all data points in that structure are accessible with that syntax, just with different keys. Now, the "em" element in the above HTML tree does happen to be accessible as the root's first child's first child:

```
$root->content->[1]->content->[1]
```

But with trees, you typically don't know the exact location (via indexes) of the data you're looking for. Instead, finding what you want typically involves searching through the tree, and seeing if every node is the kind you want. Searching the whole tree is simple enough—look at a given node, and if it's not what you want, look at its children, and so on. HTML-Tree provides several methods that do this for you, such as find_by_tag_name, which returns the elements (or the first element, if called in scalar context) under a given node (typically the root).

For example, that em node can be found as:

```
my $that_em = $root->find_by_tag_name('em');
```

or as:

```
@ems = $root->find_by_tag_name('em');
  # will only have one element for this particular tree
```

Now, given an HTML document of whatever structure and complexity, let's suppose you wanted to do something like change every:

```
<em>stuff</em>
```

to:

```
<em class="funky"><b>[-</b>stuff<b>-]</b></em>
```

The first step is to frame this operation in terms of what you're doing to the tree. You're changing this:

```
em
|
|
...
```

to this:

```
      em
    / | \
   /  |  \
  b  ...  b
  |       |
 "[-"    "-]"
```

In other words, you're finding all elements with the tag name em, setting its class attribute to funky, and adding one child to the start of its content list—a new b element with the content of the text string [-, and one to the end of its content list—a new b element with the content of the text string -].

Once you've got it in these terms, it's just a matter of reading the HTML::Element documentation, and coding this up with calls to the appropriate methods, like so:

```
use HTML::Element 1.53;
use HTML::TreeBuilder 2.96;
# Build the tree by parsing the document
my $root = HTML::TreeBuilder->new;
$root->parse_file('whatever.html'); # source file

# Now make new nodes where needed
foreach my $em ($root->find_by_tag_name('em')) {
    $em->attr('class', 'funky'); # Set that attribute

    # Make the two new B nodes
    my $new1 = HTML::Element->new('b');
    my $new2 = HTML::Element->new('b');
    # Give them content (they have none at first)
    $new1->push_content('[-');
    $new2->push_content('-]');

    # And put 'em in place!
    $em->unshift_content($new1);
    $em->push_content($new2);
}
print "<!-- Looky see what I did! -->\n", $root->as_HTML( ), "\n";
```

The class HTML::Element provides just about every method I can imagine you needing for manipulating trees made of HTML::Element objects. (And what it doesn't directly provide, it gives you the components to create.)

Building Your Own Trees

Theoretically, any tree is pretty much like any other tree, so you could use the HTML::Element module for anything you'd ever want to do with tree-arranged objects. However, as its name suggest, HTML::Element is designed for HTML elements; it has lots of features that only make sense for HTML elements—like the idea that every element must have a tag name. And it lacks some features that might be useful for general applications, such as any sort of checking to make sure that you're not trying to arrange objects in a non-treelike way. For a general-purpose tree class that does have such features, you can use the Tree::DAG_Node module, also available from CPAN.

However, if your task is simple enough, it might be overkill to use Tree::DAG_Node. In any case, I find that the best way to learn how something works is to implement it (or something like it, but simpler) yourself. So I'll discuss how you'd implement a tree structure from scratch, without using any of the existing classes for tree nodes.

An Implementation: Game Trees for Alak

Suppose the task at hand is to write a program that can play against a human opponent at a board game. For most such games, a "game tree" is an essential part of the
program (as I will argue below), and this will be our test case for implementing a tree
structure from stratch. To choose moves, we'll develop a subroutine that examines
the tree by evaluating moves, responses to those moves, and responses to those
responses; such algorithms are called *minimax algorithms*.

For sake of simplicity, our game is not chess or backgammon, but a much simpler
game called Alak, invented by the mathematician A. K. Dewdney and described in
his 1984 book *Planiverse*. The rules of Alak are simple: [*]

- Alak is a two-player game played on a one-dimensional board with eleven slots
  on it. Each slot can hold at most one piece at a time. There's two kinds of pieces,
  which I represent here as x and o. x's belong to a player called X, and o's to a
  player called O.

- The initial configuration of the board is:

  xxxx___oooo

  For sake of the article, the slots are numbered from 1 (on the left) to 11 (on the
  right), and X always has the first move.

- The players take turns moving. At each turn, each player can move only one
  piece, once. (Unlike checkers, in which you move one piece at a time, but get to
  keep moving if you jump over your opponent's piece.) A player cannot give up
  his turn. A player can move any one of his pieces to the next unoccupied slot to
  its right or left, which may involve jumping over occupied slots. A player cannot
  move a piece off the side of the board.

- If a move creates a pattern where the opponent's pieces are surrounded on both
  sides by two pieces of the mover's color (with no intervening unoccupied blank
  slot), those surrounded pieces are removed from the board.

- The goal of the game is to remove all of your opponent's pieces, at which point the
  game ends. Removing all pieces but one ends the game as well, since the opponent can't surround you with one piece and will always lose within a few moves.

Consider, then, this rather short game where X starts:

    xxxx___oooo
      ^

Move 1: X moves from 3 (shown with a caret) to 5, yielding the board below. (Note
that any of X's pieces could move, but that the only place they could move to is 5.)

    xx_xx__oooo
       ^

---

[*] Actually, I'm describing only one interpretation of the rules Dewdney describes in *Planiverse*. Many other
interpretations are possible.

Move 2: O moves from 9 to 7.

```
xx_xx_oo_oo
       ^
```

Move 3: X moves from 4 to 6.

```
xx__xxoo_oo
      ^
```

Move 4: O (stupidly) moves from 10 to 9.

```
xx__xxooo_o
        ^
```

Move 5: X moves from 5 to 10, making the board xx___xoooxo. The three o's that X just surrounded are removed:

```
xx___x___xo
      ^
```

O has only one piece, and therefore loses. Now, move 4 could have gone the other way, with O moving from 8 to 4 and making the board xx_oxxo__oo. The surrounded x's are removed:

```
xx_o__o__oo
    ^
```

Move 5: X moves from 1 to 2.

```
_xxo__o__oo
  ^
```

Move 6: O moves from 7 to 6.

```
_xxo_o___oo
     ^
```

Move 7: X moves from 2 to 5, removing the o at 4.

```
__x_xo___oo
    ^
```

And so on.

To teach a computer program to play Alak (as player X, for instance), the program needs to be able to look at the configuration of the board, figure out what moves it can make, and weigh the benefits and costs, immediate or eventual, of those moves.

Consider the board from just before move 3, and figure all the possible moves X could make. X has pieces in slots 1, 2, 4, and 5. The leftmost two x's (at 1 and 2) are up against the end of the board, so they can move only right. The other two x's (at 4 and 5) can move either right or left:

```
Starting board: xx_xx_oo_oo
  moving 1 to 3 gives _xxxx_oo_oo
  moving 2 to 3 gives x_xxx_oo_oo
  moving 4 to 3 gives xxx_x_oo_oo
```

```
moving 5 to 3 gives xxxx__oo_oo
moving 4 to 6 gives xx__xxoo_oo
moving 5 to 6 gives xx_x_xoo_oo
```

For the computer to decide which of these is the best move to make, it needs to quantify the benefit of these moves as a number, which I'll call the *payoff*. The payoff of a move can be figured as the number of x pieces removed by the most recent move, minus the number of o pieces removed by the most recent move. (It so happens that the rules of the game mean no move can delete both o's and x's, but the formula still applies.) Since none of these moves removed any pieces, all these moves have the same immediate payoff: 0.

Now, you could race ahead and write an Alak-playing program that used the immediate payoff to decide the best move to make. When there's more than one best move (as here, where all the moves are equally good), it could choose randomly between the good alternatives. This strategy is simple to implement, but it makes for a very dumb program. Consider what O's response to each of the potential moves (above) could be. Nothing immediately suggests itself for the first four possibilities (X having moved something to position 3), but either of the last two (illustrated below) are pretty perilous, because in either case O has the obvious option (that he would be foolish to pass up) of removing x's from the board:

```
xx_xx_oo_oo
   ^
```

X moves 4 to 6, yielding this board:

```
xx__xxoo_oo
     ^
```

O moves 8 to 4, giving xx_oxxo__oo. The two surrounded x's are removed:

```
xx_o__o__oo
   ^
```

or X could have moved 5 to 6 instead of 4 to 6, yielding:

```
xx_x_xoo_oo
     ^
```

O moves 8 to 5, giving xx_xoxo__oo. The sole surrounded x is removed.

```
xx_xo_o__oo
     ^
```

Both contingencies are quite bad for X. What's needed is for X to think more than one step ahead—to consider not merely what it can do in this move, and what the payoff is, but to consider what O might do in response, and the payoff of those potential moves, and so on, calculating X's possible responses to those cases. All these possibilities form a *game tree:* a tree in which each node is a board, and its children are successors of that node—that is, boards that could result from every move possible, given the parent's board.

But how to represent the tree, and how to represent the nodes?

Consider that a node holds several pieces of data.

1. The configuration of the board, which, since it is nice and simple and one-dimensional, can be stored as just a string, like xx_xx_oo_oo.

2. Whose turn it is, X or O. (Or, who moved last, from which we can deduce whose turn it is).

3. The successors (child nodes).

4. The immediate payoff of having moved to this board position from its predecessor (parent node).

5. What move got us from our predecessor node to here. (Granted, knowing the board configuration before and after the move, it's easy to figure out the move; but it's easier still to store it as the node's successors are being computed.)

6. Whatever we might want to add later.

These could be stored equally well in an array or in a hash, but it's my experience that hashes are best for cases in which you have more than two or three bits of data, especially when you might need to add new bits of data. Moreover, hash key names are mnemonic: $node->{'last_move_payoff'} is plain as day, whereas it's not so easy with an array to remember that $node->[3] is where you're storing the payoff.

Of course, there are ways around that problem: just swear you'll never use a real numeric index to access data in the array, and instead use constants with mnemonic names:

```
use strict;
use constant idx_PAYOFF => 3;
...
$n->[idx_PAYOFF]
```

But I prefer to keep it simple and use a hash.

These are, incidentally, the same arguments that people weigh when trying to decide whether their object-oriented modules should be based on blessed hashes, blessed arrays, or something else. The only difference here is that you're not blessing your nodes or talking in terms of classes and methods.

Anyway, you might as well represent nodes like so:

```
$node = { # hashref
    'board'            => ...board string, like "xx_x_xoo_oo"

    'last_move_payoff' => ...payoff of the move
                             that got us here.

    'last_move_from'   => ...the start...
    'last_move_to'     => ...and end point of the move
                             that got us here.  Say, 5 and 6,
                             representing a move from 5 to 6.
```

```
  'whose_turn'         => ...whose move it then becomes,
                            just an 'x' or 'o'.

  'successors'         => ...the successors
};
```

Note that you could have a field called something like last_move_who to denote who moved last, but since turns in Alak always alternate (and no one can pass), storing whose move it is now *and* who moved last is redundant—if X moved last, it's O's turn now, and vice versa. I chose to have a whose_turn field instead of a last_move_who, but it doesn't really matter. Either way, you'll end up inferring one from the other at several points in the program.

When you want to store the successors of a node, should you use an array or a hash? On the one hand, the successors to $node aren't ordered, so there's no reason to use an array per se; on the other hand, if you use a hash, with successor nodes as values, you don't have anything particularly meaningful to use as keys. (And you can't use the successors themselves as keys, since the nodes are referred to by hash references, and you can't use a reference as a hash key.) I chose to just use an array to store all a node's successors, although the order is never actually used for anything:

```
$node = {
  ...
  'successors' => [ ...nodes... ],
  ...
};
```

In any case, now that you've settled on what should be in a node, let's make a little sample tree out of a few nodes and see what you can do with it:

```
# Board just before move 3 in above game
my $n0 = {
  'board' => 'xx_xx_oo_oo',
  'last_move_payoff' => 0,
  'last_move_from'   => 9,
  'last_move_to'     => 7,
  'whose_turn'       => 'x',
  'successors'       => [],
};

# And, for now, just two of the successors:

# X moves 4 to 6, giving xx__xxoo_oo
my $n1 = {
  'board' => 'xx__xxoo_oo',
  'last_move_payoff' => 0,
  'last_move_from'   => 4,
  'last_move_to'     => 6,
  'whose_turn'       => 'o',
  'successors'       => [],
};
```

```
# or X moves 5 to 6, giving xx_x_xoo_oo
my $n2 = {
  'board' => 'xx_x_xoo_oo',
  'last_move_payoff' =>  0,
  'last_move_from'   =>  5,
  'last_move_to'     =>  6,
  'whose_turn'       => 'o',
  'successors'       => [],
};

# Now connect them...
push @{$n0->{'successors'}}, $n1, $n2;
```

Digression: Links to Parents

In comparing what is stored in an Alak game tree node to what HTML::Element stores in HTML element nodes, you'll note one big difference: every HTML::Element node contains a link to its parent, whereas the Alak nodes don't keep a link to theirs.

This is an important difference because it can affect how Perl knows when you're not using pieces of memory anymore. Consider the tree you just built above:

```
        node 0
       /    \
      /      \
  node 1   node 2
```

Perl knows there are two ways you could be using memory. The memory might belong directly to a variable or it might be used by a reference. In the above code, Perl knows that the hash for node 0 (for board xx_xx_oo_oo) is in use because something (namely, the variable $n0) holds a reference to it. Now, even if you followed the above code with this:

```
$n1 = $n2 = 'whatever';
```

to make your variables $n1 and $n2 stop holding references to the hashes for the two successors of node 0, Perl would still know that those hashes are in use, because node 0's array of successors holds a reference to those hashes. And Perl knows that node 0 is in use because something still holds a reference to it. Now, if you added this, it would change nothing:

```
my $root = $n0;
```

There are just *two* things holding a reference to the node 0 hash, which in turn holds a reference to the node 1 and node 2 hashes. And if you added:

```
$n0 = 'stuff';
```

Again, nothing would change, because something ($root) still holds a reference to the node 0 hash. But once *nothing* holds a reference to the node 0 hash, Perl knows it can destroy that hash (and reclaim the memory for later use, for example), and once it does that, nothing will hold a reference to the node 1 or the node 2 hashes, and those will be destroyed, too.

But consider if the node 1 and node 2 hashes each had an attribute "parent" (or "pre-decessor") that held a reference to node 0. If your program stopped holding a reference to the node 0 hash, Perl couldn't say that *nothing* holds a reference to node 0—because node 1 and node 2 still would. So, the memory for nodes 0, 1, and 2 would never get reclaimed (until your program ends, at which point Perl destroys everything). If your program grew and discarded lots of nodes in the game tree, but didn't let Perl know it could reclaim their memory, your program could grow to use immense amounts of memory—never a good thing. There are three ways around this problem.

First, when you finish with a node, delete the reference each of its children have to it (in this case, deleting $n1->{'parent'}, for instance). When you finish with a whole tree, just go through the whole tree erasing links that children have to their children.

Second, reconsider whether you really need to have each node hold a reference to its parent. Getting rid of those links will avoid the whole problem.

Third, use the WeakRef module if you have Perl 5.6 or later. This module allows you to "weaken" some references (like the references that node 1 and 2 could hold to their parent) so that they don't count when Perl asks whether anything holds a reference to a given piece of memory. This wonderful new module eliminates the headaches that can often crop up with either of the two previous methods.

It so happens that Alak is simple enough that you don't need nodes to have links to their parents, so the second solution is fine. But in a more advanced program, the first or third solutions might be unavoidable.

Recursively Printing the Tree

I don't like working blind—if I have any kind of a complex data structure in memory for a program I'm working on, the first thing I do is write something that can print the structure. Now, I could just use the x pretty-printer command in Perl's interactive debugger, or I could have the program use the Data::Dumper module. But in this case, I think the output from those options is too verbose. Once you have trees with dozens of nodes in them, you'll want a dump of the tree to be as concise as possible, hopefully just one line per node. What I'd like is something that can print $n0 and its successors (see above) as something like:

```
xx_xx_oo_oo  (O moved 9 to 7, O payoff)
xx__xxoo_oo  (X moved 4 to 6, O payoff)
xx_x_xoo_oo  (X moved 5 to 6, O payoff)
```

A subroutine to print a line for a given node, and then do it again for each successor, would look something like:

```
sub dump_tree {
    my $n = $_[0]; # "n" is for node
    print
        ...something expressing $n's content...
    foreach my $s (@{$n->{'successors'}}) {
        dump($s);
    }
}
```

You could just start that out with a call to dump_tree($n0).

Since this routine does its work (dumping the subtree at and under the given node) by calling itself, it's *recursive*. However, there's a special term for this kind of recursion across a tree: traversal. To *traverse* a tree means to do something to a node, and to traverse its children. This can happen in two ways: *pre-order* and *post-order*. With pre-order, you do something to X and then traverse its children; with post-order, you traverse X's children before operating on X.

Dumping the tree to the screen the way you want it happens to be a matter of pre-order traversal, since the thing you do (print a description of the node) happens before you recurse into the successors.

When you write the print statement for your above dump_tree, you might get something like this:

```
sub dump_tree {
    my $n = $_[0];

    # "xx_xx_oo_oo  (O moved 9 to 7, 0 payoff)"
    print $n->{'board'}, "  (",
        ($n->{'whose_turn'} eq 'o' ? 'X' : 'O'),
        # Infer who last moved from whose turn it is now.
        " moved ", $n->{'last_move_from'},
        " to ",    $n->{'last_move_to'},
        ", ",      $n->{'last_move_payoff'},
        " payoff)\n";

    foreach my $s (@{$n->{'successors'}}) {
        dump_tree($s);
    }
}
```

If you run this on $n0 from above, you get this:

```
xx_xx_oo_oo  (O moved 9 to 7, 0 payoff)
xx__xxoo_oo  (X moved 4 to 6, 0 payoff)
xx_x_xoo_oo  (X moved 5 to 6, 0 payoff)
```

Each line on its own is fine, but you forgot to allow for indenting, and without that you can't tell what's a child of what. (Imagine if the first successor had successors of its own—you wouldn't be able to tell if it were a child, or a sibling.) To get indenting, you'll need to have the instances of the dump_tree routine know how far down in the tree they're being called, by passing a depth parameter between them:

```
sub dump_tree {
    my $n = $_[0];
    my $depth = $_[1];
    $depth = 0 unless defined $depth;
    print "  " x $depth,
        ...more stuff to print...
    foreach my $s (@{$n->{'successors'}}) {
        dump_tree($s, $depth + 1);
    }
}
```

When you call dump_tree($n0), $depth (from $_[1]) is undefined, so it gets set to 0, which translates into an indenting of no spaces. But when dump_tree invokes itself on $n0's children, those instances see $depth + 1 as their $_[1], providing appropriate indenting.

Growing the Tree

Your dump_tree routine works fine for the sample tree you've got, so now you should get the program working on making its own trees, starting from a given board.

In Games::Alak (the CPAN-released version of Alak that uses essentially the same code as discussed in this article), there's a routine called figure_successors that, given one childless node, figures out all its possible successors. That is, it looks at the current board, looks at every piece belonging to the player whose turn it is, and considers the effect of moving each piece every possible way—notably, it figures out the immediate payoff, and if the move would end the game, it notes that fact by setting an endgame entry in that node's hash. (That way, you know it's a node that *can't* have successors.)

In the code for Games::Alak, figure_successors does all these things, in a rather straightforward way. I won't walk you through the details of the figure_successors code I've written, since the code has nothing much to do with trees, and is all just implementation of the Alak rules for what can move where, with what result. Especially interested readers can puzzle over that part of code in the source listing in the archive from CPAN, but others can just assume that it works as described above.

But consider that figure_successors, regardless of its inner workings, does not grow the tree; it only makes one set of successors for one node at a time. It has to be up to a different routine to call figure_successors, and to keep applying it as needed, in order to make a nice big tree that the game-playing program can base its decisions on.

Now, you could do this by just starting from one node, applying figure_successors to it, then applying figure_successors on all the resulting children, and so on:

```
sub grow {  # Just a first attempt at this!
    my $n = $_[0];
    figure_successors($n) unless @{$n->{'successors'}} or $n->{'endgame'};
    foreach my $s (@{$n->{'successors'}}) {
        grow($s); # Recurse
    }
}
```

If you have a game tree for tic-tac-toe, and you grow it without limitation (as above), you will soon enough have a fully "solved" tree, where every node that can have successors does, and all the leaves of the tree are all the possible endgames (where, in each case, the board is filled). But a game of Alak is different from tic-tac-toe, because it can, in theory, go on forever. For example, the following sequence of moves is quite possible:

```
xxxx___oooo
xxx_x__oooo
```

```
xxx_x_o_ooo
xxxx__o_ooo (x moved back)
xxxx___oooo (o moved back)
...repeat forever...
```

If you tried using our above attempt at a grow routine, Perl would happily start trying to construct an infinitely deep tree, containing an infinite number of nodes, consuming an infinite amount of memory, and requiring an infinite amount of time. As the old saying goes: "You can't have everything—where would you put it?" We have to place limits on how much we'll grow the tree.

There's more than one way to do this:

1. You could grow the tree until you hit some limit on the number of nodes you'll allow in the tree.

2. You could grow the tree until you hit some limit on the amount of time you're willing to spend.

3. You could grow the tree until it is fully fleshed out to a certain depth.

Since you already know to track depth (as you did in writing dump_tree), do it that way (the third way). The implementation for that third approach is pretty straightforward:

```
$Max_depth = 3;
sub grow {
    my $n = $_[0];
    my $depth = $_[1] || 0;
    figure_successors($n)
        unless $depth >= $Max_depth
            or @{$n->{'successors'}}
            or $n->{'endgame'};
    }
    foreach my $s (@{$n->{'successors'}}) {
        grow($s, $depth + 1);
    }
    # If we're at $Max_depth, then figure_successors
    #  didn't get called, so there are no successors
    #  to recurse under -- that's what stops recursion.
}
```

If you start from a single node (whether it's a node for the starting board xxxx___oooo, or for whatever board the computer is considering), set $Max_depth to 4, and apply grow to it, the tree will grow to include several hundred nodes. [*]

---

[*] If at each move there are four pieces that can move, and they can each move right or left, the "branching factor" of the tree is eight, giving a tree with 1 (depth 0) + 8 (depth 1) + 8^2 + 8^3 + 8^4 = 4681 nodes in it. But, in practice, not all pieces can move in both directions (none of the x pieces in xxxx___oooo can move left, for example), and there may be fewer than four pieces, if some were lost. For example, there are 801 nodes in a tree of depth four starting from xxxx___oooo, suggesting an average branching factor of about five ($801^{1/4}$ is about 5.3), not eight.

What you need to derive from that tree is the information about the best moves for X. The simplest way to consider the payoffs of different successors is to just average them—but what you average aren't always the immediate payoffs (because that'd leave you using only one generation of information), but the average payoff of *their* successors, if any. Formalize this as:

```
To figure a node's average payoff:
  If the node has successors:
    Figure each successor's average payoff.
    My average payoff is the average of theirs.

  Otherwise:
    My average payoff is my immediate payoff.
```

Since this algorithm involves recursing into the successors *before* doing anything with the current node, it will traverse the tree in post-order.

You could work that up as a routine of its own, and apply that to the tree after you've applied grow to it. But since you'd never grow the tree without also figuring the average benefit, you might as well make that figuring part of the grow routine itself:

```perl
$Max_depth = 3;
sub grow {
    my $n = $_[0];
    my $depth = $_[1] || 0;
    figure_successors($n)
      unless $depth >= $Max_depth
            or @{$n->{'successors'}}
            or $n->{'endgame'};

    if (@{$n->{'successors'}}) {
        my $a_payoff_sum = 0;
        foreach my $s (@{$n->{'successors'}}) {
            grow($s, $depth + 1);  # RECURSE
            $a_payoff_sum += $s->{'average_payoff'};
        }

        $n->{'average_payoff'} =
            $a_payoff_sum / @{$n->{'successors'}};
    } else {
        $n->{'average_payoff'} = $n->{'last_move_payoff'};
    }
}
```

By the time grow has applied to a node (wherever it is in the tree), it will have figured successors if possible (which, in turn, sets last_move_payoff for each node it creates), and will have set average_benefit.

Beyond this, all that's needed is to start the board out with a root node of xxxx___oooo, and have the computer (X) take turns with the user (O) until someone wins. Whenever it is O's turn, Games::Alak presents a prompt to the user, letting her know the state of the current board, and asking what move she selects. When it is X's turn, the computer grows the game tree as necessary (using the grow routine from above), then selects the move with the highest average payoff (or one of the highest, in case of a tie).

In either case, "selecting" a move means setting that move's node as the new root of the program's game tree. The sibling nodes and their descendants (the boards that didn't get selected) and the parent node will be erased from memory, since they will no longer be in use (as Perl can tell by the fact that nothing holds references to them anymore).

The interface code in Games::Alak (the code that prompts the user for her move) actually supports quite a few options besides just moving, including dumping the game tree to a specified depth (using a slightly fancier version of dump_tree above), resetting the game, changing $Max_depth in the middle of the game, and quitting the game. Like figure_successors, it's a bit too long to print here, but interested users are welcome to peruse (and freely modify) the code, as well as to enjoy playing the game.

In practice, there's more to game trees than this: for games that have a larger branching factor than Alak (most of them do!), game trees of depth four or larger would contain too many nodes to be manageable, and most of those nodes would be strategically quite uninteresting for either player. Dealing with game trees specifically is therefore a matter of recognizing uninteresting contingencies and not bothering to grow the tree under them. For example, if O has a choice between moves that put him in immediate danger of X winning and moves that don't, then O won't ever choose the dangerous moves, so there's no point in growing the tree any further beneath those nodes.

This sample implementation illustrates the basics of how to build and manipulate a simple tree structure in memory. And once you understand the basics of tree storage here, you should be ready to better understand the complexities and peculiarities of other systems for creating, accessing, and changing trees, including Tree::DAG_Node, HTML::Element, XML::DOM, or related formalisms like XPath and XSL.

References

Dewdney, Alexander Keewatin. *Planiverse: Computer Contact with a Two-Dimensional World.* Poseidon Press, New York. 1984.

Knuth, Donald Ervin. *Art of Computer Programming, Volume 1, Third Edition: Fundamental Algorithms.* Addison-Wesley, Reading, MA. 1997.

Wirth, Niklaus. *Algorithms + Data Structures = Programs* Prentice-Hall, Englewood Cliffs, NJ. 1976.

Wirth's classic, currently lamentably out of print, has a good section on trees. I find it clearer than Knuth's (if not quite as encyclopedic), probably because Wirth's example code is in a block-structured high-level language (basically Pascal), instead of in assembler (MIX).

## CHAPTER 23

B-Trees

Mark Jason Dominus

B-trees are often described as a good way to store and retrieve data, especially to and from disk. They're efficient to use and easy to program—they're often mentioned, but not so often discussed. They show up all over the place, such as in the Berkeley DB_ File package, large high-performance databases, and in IBM's well-known VSAM files.

In this article we'll see how they work. First, we'll review how ordinary binary trees store data, and we'll see the potential disadvantages of that. We'll look over the B-tree algorithm in the abstract, and see how it corrects the flaws of binary trees. Then we'll look at the code of a Perl module that implements the B-tree algorithms and see how B-trees can be implemented in Perl.

Both binary trees and B-trees are structures for storing and retrieving data, just like hashes. In fact, to the user, they look exactly like hashes. Each contains a collection of keys, and each key is associated with a particular datum. In order to be efficient, data structures should allow us to look up the datum associated with a particular key very quickly. Hashes, binary trees, and B-trees all do that.

You're supposed to learn about binary trees early in your programming career, so the next part of this article should be a review. If you don't know about binary trees yet, you might want to read a book on data structures first, such as the one in this article's bibliography or O'Reilly's *Mastering Algorithms with Perl*. Otherwise, this article might not make much sense.

A Review of Binary Trees

A binary tree is made of *tree nodes*. Each node has a key and some associated data. Each node also has between zero and two *children*, which are also tree nodes. See Figure 23-1.

Children can have other children in turn, so the entire tree might be very big. Until we actually see the implementation later in this article, we're going to forget about the data; just imagine it's stored in the nodes along with the keys. The searching

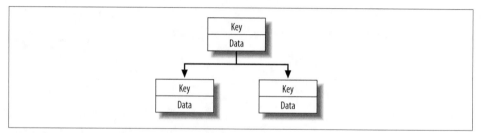

Figure 23-1. Binary tree node, with children

algorithms we'll see only look at the keys, never at the data, until it comes time to actually do the implementation. Figure 23-2 shows a little tree.

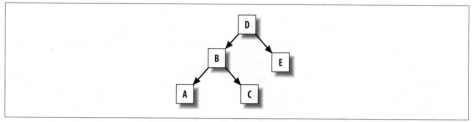

Figure 23-2. A little tree

In the little tree of Figure 23-2, A and C are children of B. We also say that B is the *parent* of A and C. Nodes with no children, such as A, C, and E, are called *leaves*. The topmost node, which has no parent, is called the *root*: node D is the root here. Notice that if we ignore D and E, B is the root of its own little tree of just A, B, and C. This mini-tree is called the *left subtree* of D. The right subtree of D is the even smaller tree that contains just E and nothing else.

Keys must be orderable, so that we can say for sure when one is "less than" another. The exact ordering method doesn't matter much; for this discussion we'll suppose that the keys are strings and that the ordering is the usual string ordering defined by Perl's string comparison operators such as lt. From now on when we say that one key is less than another, we mean the "less than" implied by lt.

The essential property of the binary tree is this: if a certain node contains a key, say K, then the left subtree of that node contains only keys that are less than K, and the right subtree contains only keys that are greater than K.

This means we can quickly search the tree for a particular key. Here's how: suppose we're looking for K. Start at the root; if the key in the root is K, we've found it. If K is less than the key in the root, move down to the root of the left subtree and repeat the process; otherwise, move down to the right. Typically, each time we move down to a subtree, the number of nodes left below where we are decreases by about half (hence the "binary" in the name), so we'll quickly find the node we want.

Normally, if we search for a key and don't find it, we've ended at a leaf. If the reason we were searching was that we wanted to add a key, we build a new node with our new key and data and attach it as a subtree of this leaf. Let's see an example, where the keys are B, D, C, A, E, delivered in that order. Figure 23-3 shows each stage of the construction.

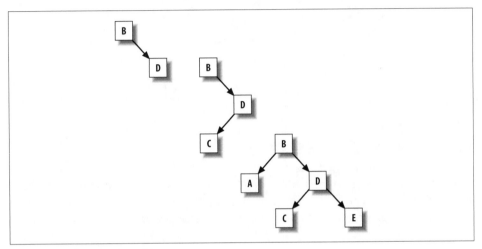

Figure 23-3. Constructing a binary tree

First, we build a B node as the root. We attach D as the right subtree of B, because D is greater than B. Next, we attach C as the left subtree of D. (C comes after B but before D.) Then we attach A as the left subtree of B. (A comes before B.) Finally, we attach E as the right subtree of D. (E comes after B and after D.)

The average depth of a key here is 2.2, which means that to look up a key to see if it is in this tree, we expect to perform about 2.2 comparisons with the keys in the tree.

The Problem with Binary Trees

The problem with binary trees is that sometimes, if we're not careful, we can build them wrong—and then they're unbalanced. What does this mean? We'd like the tree to be pretty shallow, because that means we'll never have to perform many comparisons to find out if a key is there or not. When the tree is shallow and bushy, no node's right subtree is much deeper than its left subtree. When this is true, the tree is said to be *balanced*.

Let's see what happens when the tree isn't balanced. If, in the example above, we had encountered the keys A, B, C, D, E in alphabetical order, then instead of growing the tree we saw before of maximum depth 3 and average depth 2.2, we would have the tree in Figure 23-4, of maximum depth 5 and average depth 3. It's more like a vine than a tree.

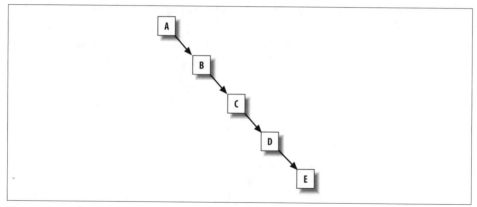

Figure 23-4. When binary trees go wrong

The average depth here is 3, which is 36% worse than the example tree we saw earlier. If we get unlucky when we build the tree, and get a vine or a tall spindly thing that didn't have enough light, we pay a stiff performance penalty. In this case, whenever we search, we make 36% more comparisons than we would if the tree were nice and bushy. For larger trees, the costs of vininess are even worse.

B-Trees Are Always Balanced

B-trees avoid this vine problem by incorporating two improvements over ordinary binary trees.

First, the nodes contain many keys instead of only one, so the trees are not binary. Instead of nodes like the one in Figure 23-5, we use nodes like the one in Figure 23-6.

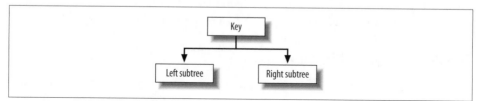

Figure 23-5. A typical binary tree node

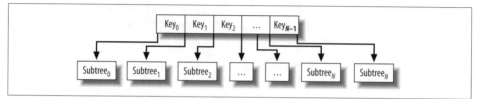

Figure 23-6. A typical B-tree node

The nodes are analogous to the nodes in a binary tree. The keys in a node obey the ordering:

$$Key_0 < Key_1 < Key_2 < \ldots < Key_{N-1}$$

so the keys in a node are always in sorted order. Furthermore,

All the keys in Subtree$_0$ are less than Key$_0$.
All the keys in Subtree$_1$ are greater   than Key$_0$ and less than Key$_1$.
All the keys in Subtree$_2$ are greater   than Key$_1$ and less than Key$_2$.

...

All the keys in Subtree$_{N-1}$ are greater   than Key$_{N-2}$ and less than Key$_{N-1}$.
All the keys in Subtree$_N$ are greater   than Key$_{N-1}$.

To search the tree, start at the root node, and perform a binary search on the keys in the node. This is the kind of search we use when we look something up in the encyclopedia or the telephone book; we can do this because the keys in the node are in sorted order. Look at a clump of names, determine whether the name we're looking for appears earlier or later, turn elsewhere in the book, and repeat.

If the key we want is in the node, we're done. If the key isn't in the node, then we have found a key that is larger than the one we want and a key that is smaller, so we move down to the appropriate subtree in between and continue. Because the fan-out is greater, a B-tree is not as deep as a binary tree. This is the "moving down" portion of the B-tree algorithm.

The real improvement, however, comes when we want to insert a new key into a tree. When we insert, we have a trick that prevents the tree from getting too deep too quickly, and from turning into a vine. This is the "moving up" portion of the algorithm. Here's how it works.

Every B-tree has a constant B, and each node in the tree is allowed to have as many as B keys, but no fewer than $B/2$. (B is always even.) For concreteness, let's suppose that B is four. Then nodes are allowed to have as few as two keys and no more than four.

Now suppose we searched for a key and didn't find it. That means that we've moved all the way down to a leaf of the tree, and now we want to insert the new key. If the leaf has fewer than four keys already, there is no problem; we just put the new key into one of the empty slots in the node, and the tree is no deeper than before.

If the leaf node is full—that is, it already has $B=4$ keys—we do something interesting. We insert the key into the node anyway. But now it's too big; it has five keys and it's only allowed four. The overstuffed node looks like Figure 23-7.

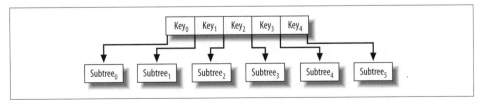

Figure 23-7. An overstuffed B-tree node

Then we break it in half, so that it looks like Figure 23-8.

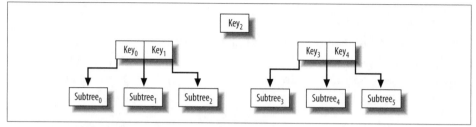

Figure 23-8. An overstuffed B-tree node, broken in half

There are now two nodes, one with Key_0 and Key_1, and one with Key_3 and Key_4, and there's a leftover key, Key_2.

And now the trick: if the leaf node's *parent* has room for a new key, we promote Key_2 there. We attach the two new half-full nodes as subnodes of the parent, one just to the left of Key_2 and one just to the right. Everything remains in the correct order.

If we can do this, we've added a key into a full node without making the tree any deeper, by splitting the overfull node into two half-full nodes at the same level, and promoting the extra key up into the parent node, where there was room.

What if there wasn't room for Key_2 in the parent node? We repeat the process. We promote Key_2 into the full parent anyway, and we split the parent node in two and promote the middle key from the parent node into the grandparent node. This splitting and promoting continues until either there's a node somewhere up in one of the ancestors of the leaf that does have room, or until we get to the root.

If the root is full, we split it, and since there's nowhere to promote the middle key, it gets promoted into a new root node all by itself. This is the exception to the rule that says there can't be fewer than $B/2$ keys in a node; in this case, the root node has only one key. It's also the only time the tree gets any deeper. Since the tree grows from the root up instead of from the leaves down, the leaves are all always at the same depth, which means that the tree is always balanced and never gets all viney.

Let's see that A-B-C-D-E example again, the one that gave us a horrible spindly vine. Only this time let's insert these keys into a B-tree, with $B=2$. This means nodes are allowed to have no more than two keys, and no fewer than one key each.

First we make a new root node for A, shown in Figure 23-9.

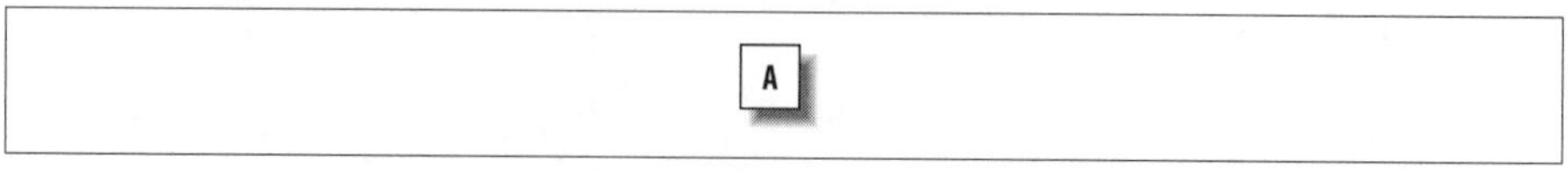

A

Figure 23-9. New root node for A

Since there's room in the root node for B, we add it (Figure 23-10).

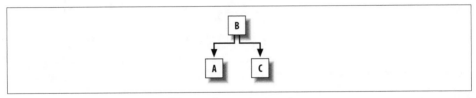

Figure 23-10. Add B to the root node

(We use the double box to show that A and B are sharing living quarters in the same node.)

Then we need to insert C into the (only) node. But there's no room, so we split the node into two and try to promote the middle key of the three (which is B). But there's nowhere to promote to, so B gets its own new root node, as shown in Figure 23-11.

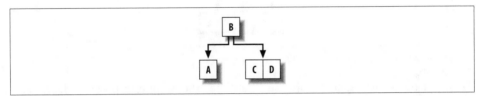

Figure 23-11. B gets its own root node

Now we need to insert D; it's greater than B, so we move down to C's node. We can insert it because there's room (Figure 23-12).

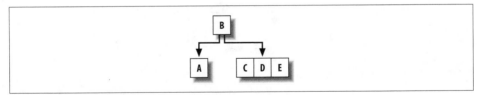

Figure 23-12. Insert D in C's node

Now we want to insert E. We would have liked to put it into the C-D node as shown in Figure 23-13.

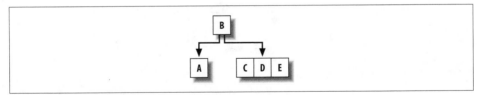

Figure 23-13. Add E to the C-D node

But we're out of room, so we split the C-D-E node, and promote D, the middle key, into the parent node (B). There is room for D there, so we're left with Figure 23-14.

Just for kicks, let's see what happens if we get the keys in the order B, D, C, A, E, as in the very first binary tree example. First B goes into a new root node, and D joins it.

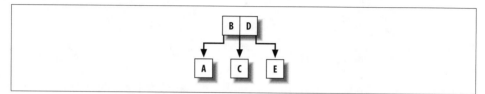

Figure 23-14. Promote D into the parent node

Then C wants to join also, but now the (only) node is full, so it splits, and C is promoted to a new root node (Figure 23-15).

Figure 23-15. C becomes a new root node

Figure 23-16 shows A going into B's node and E going into D's node.

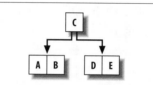

Figure 23-16. A in B's node and E in D's

This isn't the same tree as before, but it still has the minimum possible depth. Just for fun, let's add F. F wants to go in with D and E, but there isn't room. So D-E-F splits, and E is promoted one level up, with C, as shown in Figure 23-17.

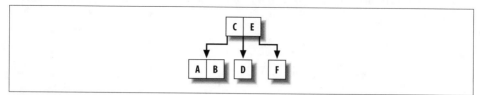

Figure 23-17. E is promoted one level

You might have heard of *2-3 trees* and *red-black trees*. When *B* is two, as in the examples, the B-tree is called a 2-3 tree because nodes always have either two or three subtrees. Red-black trees are 2-3 trees disguised as binary trees.

A Guided Tour of the Program

Now the implementation. To see it all at once, the source code can be found at *http://www.plover.com/~mjd/perl/BTree/BTree.pm*. There's also a sample test program on the web site for this book and at *http://www.plover.com/~mjd/perl/BTree/testbt.pl*. The main part of the program, which we'll see in detail, is only about forty lines.

BTree.pm defines two classes. The important one is BTree, whose objects represent entire trees. BTree objects support methods for searching trees for keys and inserting new data into trees.

The file also defines a class that's used internally by BTree, called BTree::Node, whose objects are single tree nodes. This package includes methods for getting and setting the keys and data in a particular node. We'll look at the important BTree class first, and at the subsidiary BTree::Node class only as it becomes necessary.

A BTree has only two properties: it has a root node, and it has a constant *B*. We represent a B-tree as a hash with two keys, named B and Root. If $self is a BTree object, then $self->B returns the *B* constant and $self->root returns the root node, which is a BTree::Node object.

Moving Down

The most important method in BTree is called B_search, which searches a B-tree for a specified key, returns the associated datum if there is one, and possibly adds new data to the tree.

There are several different behaviors that are useful here, and it is simpler to wrap them up into one function than to write four nearly-identical functions. For example, suppose that the search process fails to find our key. We might want to add that key with a new datum, or we might not. Similarly, if the search succeeds and our key is in the tree, we might have been looking for it because we wanted to know what data was associated with it, or we might have wanted to throw away the data and replace it with a new one.

B_search accepts arguments in "named parameter" format, like so:

```
$btree->B_search(Key => $your_key,      # Required
            Data => $your_new_data, # Sometimes required
          Insert => 1,              # Optional
         Replace => 1,              # Optional
             );
```

The Key is always required, and tells B_search what key to search for. Whether Data is required depends on the presence of Insert or Replace.

If the key is not in the tree, B_search might do one of two things. It might simply return a failure code, or it might insert the new key. We can select the latter behavior by including the Insert => 1 flag in the arguments. In this case, the Data parameter is required; it is inserted into the tree along with the Key.

If the key is in the tree, B_search might simply return its associated data, or it might replace that value with new data. We select the latter behavior by including the -Replace => 1 flag in the arguments. In this case, the Data parameter is again required, and is used to replace the data that is already there.

If neither insert nor update mode is in effect, we say that B_search is in *search mode*. In search mode we cannot supply a Data parameter—what would it be used for?

Let's look at B_search in detail. The central idea is that the method keeps track of a "current node" with a variable called $cur_node. The current node starts at the root of the tree and moves downward until the key is found or until the search terminates at a leaf. In either case, what happens next depends on the flags: the method returns or modifies the associated data, or returns undef, or inserts the new key and its associated data into the tree.

```
1 sub B_search {
2     my $self = shift;
3     my %args = @_;
4     my $cur_node = $self->root;
5     my $k = $args{Key};
6     my $d = $args{Data};
7     my @path;
```

Here we just initialize some important variables. $self is the tree we're searching; line 4 initializes the current node to be the root of that tree. Line 3 loads the parameters into a hash so that we can access them by name, as for example on lines 5–6.

```
9     if ($cur_node->is_empty) { # Empty root
10        if ($args{'Insert'}) {
11            $cur_node->insert_kdp($k => $d);
12            return $d;
13        } else {
14            return undef;
15        }
16    }
```

Lines 9–16 handle the special case of a B-tree that doesn't have any keys yet. Line 9 checks to see if the root node is empty by calling $cur_node->is_empty. If the root node *is* entirely empty, the subroutine doesn't have much work to do: there are no keys in the tree at all, and the search fails immediately. If the subroutine is not in insert mode, it just returns undef on line 14 to indicate failure. In insert mode, the subroutine calls $cur_node->insert_kdp (on line 11) to insert the new key and its associated data into the root. (kdp stands for "key-data pair.") Normally, it would have to worry that it might be overfilling the node, but in this case it can be sure that there's room, because the node is entirely empty.

```
18    # Descend tree to leaf
19    for (;;) {
20
```

With this trivial special case out of the way, the rest of B_search is a big endless loop, lines 19–51, in which $cur_node (the current node) moves down the tree one step for each pass through the loop. We can see $cur_node starting at the root node on line 4. The subroutine leaves the loop by returning when the search succeeds (line 28) or fails (line 40).

```
21          # Didn't hit bottom yet.
22
23          my($there, $where) = $cur_node->locate_key($k);
```

On each pass through the loop, the subroutine checks to see if the desired key is in the current node. It does this on line 23 by calling $cur_node->locate_key.

locate_key returns two values, called $there and $where. They are the answers to two questions:

1. "Is this key in this node?" ($there)
2. "Where, exactly, is the key?" ($where)

$there is a boolean value that says whether the key is in the node or not. It answers the question, "Is it there?" We put the results in the variable $there and write if ($there) ... to mean "if the key was there in the current node..." Line 24 checks to see if the key was in the current node in exactly this way. (In hindsight, it would have been simpler to return only $where, to let $where be undefined when the key was not in the node, and to replace if ($there) with if (defined $where). For some reason, I didn't think of this in 1997.)

```
24          if ($there) { # Found it!
25              if ($args{'Replace'}) {
26                  $cur_node->kdp($where, $k => $d);
27              }
28              return $cur_node->data($where);
29          }
```

If $there is true, the key is in the current node. The search is done because the subroutine found the key that it was looking for.

The key is in the node, but it is one of many such keys, and $where is an index that identifies which one it is. Later, we can use this index in calls to $node->kdp($where) to get or replace the key and its associated data. Line 25 checks to see if the subroutine is in replace mode. If not, line 28 just uses $cur_node->data($where) to fetch the $whereth data item from $cur_node, which happens to be the one associated with the key, and the subroutine returns the data item. In replace mode (line 26), the subroutine uses $cur_node->kdp($where, $k => $d), which replaces the $whereth key in $cur_node with $k and $d. The subroutine then returns the new data.

```
31          # Not here---must be in a subtree.
32
33          if ($cur_node->is_leaf) { # But no subtrees
34              return undef unless $args{Flags} & $BTREE_INSERT;
35              # Search failed, so stuff it in
```

```
36          $cur_node->insert_kdp($k => $d);
37          if ($self->node_overfull($cur_node)) { # No room!
38              $self->split_and_promote($cur_node, @path);
39          }
40          return $d;
41      }
```

If the key was not in the node, $where identifies which of $cur_node's several subtrees contains the key. But if $cur_node is a leaf, it has no subtrees, and the search
is finished, since we know that the key isn't anywhere to be found. Line 33 uses
$cur_node->is_leaf to check whether the current node is a leaf.

If the current node is a leaf, then the search has failed, and the key is not in the tree.
This part of the program is complicated, because it's where we might have to insert
new keys, split nodes, move up the tree, promote keys to parent nodes, or possibly
make a new root. We'll come back to it later.

```
43          # There are subtrees, and the key is in one of them.
44
45          push @path, [$cur_node, $where]; # Record path from root.
```

If the current node is *not* a leaf, control passes to line 45. Line 45 is responsible for
making a record of the path that the search has taken, starting from the root, and
making its way downwards. It does this so that if we get to the "moving up" part of
the algorithm, we can remember where we came from and where keys should be promoted. The record is maintained in a variable called @path, which is a list of the
nodes that the subroutine visited on the way down from the root, and also of the
$where values that the subroutine used to get from one node to the next.

```
47          # Move down to search the subtree
48          $cur_node = $cur_node->subnode($where);
49
50          # and start over.
51      }                                   # for (;;) ...
```

Line 48 then uses $cur_node->subnode($where) to get the identity of the $whereth sub-
node of the current node. The new node is the one that locate_key claimed would
contain the search key. B_search sets $cur_node to be this new node, and then begins
the loop over again.

What if the search fails? That's checked on line 33. In that case, $there was false, so
the key wasn't in the current node, and we'd like to search in a subnode of the current node. But we know that $cur_node->is_leaf was true, which means the current
node has no subnodes.

```
34      return unless $args{'Insert'}; # Search failed
35      # Stuff it in
36      $cur_node->insert_kdp($k => $d);
37      if ($self->node_overfull($cur_node)) { # Oops--no room.
38          $self->split_and_promote($cur_node, @path);
39      }
40      return $d;
```

If the subroutine is not in insert mode, it returns undef on line 34 to indicate failure.

In insert mode, the subroutine first inserts the new key and data into the appropriate place in the current node on line 36 with $cur_node->insert_kdp($k => $d). Then it checks to see whether the current node is too full with a call to the node_overfull method on line 37: $self->node_overfull($cur_node).

If the node isn't overfull, the subroutine's work is done, because insert_kdp already put the key and data into the right place in the current node, so it just returns the data associated with the key.

If the node is overfull, however, control moves into the "moving up" part of the algorithm; we have to split the current node, promote the middle key, and possibly repeat. For convenience and readability, this all happens in a separate subroutine, called split_and_promote.

Moving Up

```
1 sub split_and_promote {
2     my $self = shift;
3     my ($cur_node, @path) = @_;
```

split_and_promote takes two arguments. The first is the current node, where it starts. The other is @path, which you'll recall contains a complete record of how we got to $cur_node in the first place. The last item in @path mentions the last node we visited, and that's where split_and_promote will promote the middle key of $cur_node. The next-to-last item in @path mentions the next-to-last node we visited, and if split_and_promote has to promote a key up another level, the next-to-last node is the one it goes into.

```
5     for (;;) {
```

split_and_promote is an infinite loop (lines 5–21) like B_search, interrupted by a return when it is done. It too has a notion of the current node ($cur_node), which starts out at the leaf node passed from B_search and moves up, one step per pass through the loop.

```
6         my ($newleft, $newright, $kdp) = $cur_node->halves($self->B / 2);
```

The first thing split_and_promote does on each pass is to split the current node in two; it does this with the halves method. $cur_node->halves breaks the node anywhere we tell it to; by passing it $B/2$, we break the node in the middle, so that key number $B/2$ is left over. halves returns three things: $newleft and $newright, which contain the left and right halves of the old node, and $kdp, which contains the leftover key and data that will be promoted. In Figure 23-8, $newleft is the node on the left, with Key_0, Key_1, $Subtree_0$, $Subtree_1$, and $Subtree_2$. $newright is the node on the right, with Key_3, Key_4, $Subtree_3$, $Subtree_4$, and $Subtree_5$. $kdp is the leftover key and its associated data, which is Key_2 in the picture.

After splitting the overfull node, `split_and_promote` determines where to promote the leftover key and where to reattach $newright and $newleft. This information is in the @path list. Line 7 extracts the last element from @path; this element mentions $up, the node above the current one, and $where, which says that $cur_node is the $whereth subnode of $up.

```
7       my ($up, $where) = @{pop @path};
8       if ($up) {
```

If the @path array was exhausted on line 7, we know that $cur_node is the root of the tree, that the root was overfull, and that line 6 actually split the root node. We test for this possibility on line 8, which checks to see if the $up node we thought we got from @path was actually defined.

If so, $up looks like Figure 23-18.

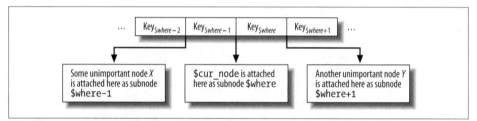

Figure 23-18. $up before the promotion of $kdp

`split_and_promote`'s job then is to make $up look like Figure 23-19 instead.

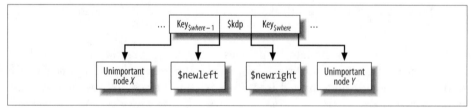

Figure 23-19. $up after the promotion of $kdp

`split_and_promote` calls $up->insert_kdp(@$kdp) to insert the leftover key into the appropriate place in $up (at line 9 in the program). insert_kdp takes care of moving around the subnodes that are already there so that they stay in the right places. In lines 10–11, `split_and_promote` attaches $newleft and $newright as subnodes of $up, adjacent to $kdp, by calling $up->subnode.

If we were paranoid, we could ensure that $kdp went into $up where we expected by calling $up->locate_key($kdp->[0]) and seeing if $there was true, and if the $where we got back matched the one that we got from @path. (The BTree.pm module actually does include these checks, but I left them out of the article for clarity.)

```
12          return unless $self->node_overfull($up);
13          $cur_node = $up;
```

After attaching the new subnodes, split_and_promote checks to see if $up is overfull, on line 12. If it isn't, then split_and_promote is finished, and returns. Otherwise, it sets $cur_node to $up (line 13) to move one step up the tree, and it starts the infinite loop over again to split $up and promote its middle key another step up.

If the promotion goes all the way to the root, and even the root is overfull, then we have to split the root. When line 7 tries to get the parent of the root from the @path, it gets nothing, and control passes to line 14:

```
14        } else { # We're at the top; make a new root.
15            my $newroot = new BTree::Node ([$kdp->[0]],
16                                           [$kdp->[1]],
17                                  [$newleft, $newright]);
18            $self->root($newroot);
19            return;
20        }
```

Lines 15–17 call new BTree::Node to manufacture a new root node with the leftover key and associated data, and with $newleft and $newright as its only subnodes. Then line 18 sets the root of the tree to be the new root node, and line 19 returns because the whole process is done.

Details

It's been a long rough journey, but we have covered the important methods and how they work; everything else is just details. The most important detail is the internal structure of a BTree::Node.

A node needs three things: keys, data associated with those keys, and subnodes. In this program, we store these as three lists, so that each node will be a reference to a list of three lists: the list of keys, the list of data, and the list of subnodes. If there are *N* keys, there are also *N* data, and *N+1* subnodes. Figure 23-20 depicts this.

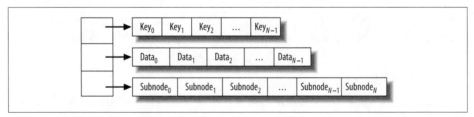

Figure 23-20. Keys, data, and subnodes

Empty nodes are represented by a completely empty list []. They only occur as the root nodes of completely empty trees.

The node constructor, BTree::Node::new, accepts three parameters, which it installs as the three lists of the new node. If we omit the three lists, it installs nothing, and we get an empty node:

```
sub new {
    my $self = shift;
    my $package = ref $self || $self;
    bless [@_] => $package;
}
```

split_and_promote uses the new method when it constructs a new root.

The package contains a lot of simple methods for getting and setting keys and sub-nodes and the like; for example, there's a subnode method, that returns the $nth subnode of the node if we invoke it like this:

```
$node->subnode($n)
```

It sets and returns the $nth subnode if we invoke it like this:

```
$node->subnode($n, $new_subnode);
```

Here's the subroutine:

```
sub subnode {
    my ($self, $n, $newnode) = @_;
    $self->[$SUBNODES][$n] = $newnode if defined $newnode;
    $self->[$SUBNODES][$n];
}
```

$SUBNODES is a constant. If $self is a BTree::Node, it has three lists, and the third of these is the list of subnodes of $self. $SUBNODES is just 2, so that we can write $self->[$SUBNODES] instead of $self->[2] when we want to get the list of subnodes. Similarly, we can write $self->[$SUBNODES][$n] instead of $self->[2][$n] to get the $nth subnode. In the same vein, $KEYS and $DATA, not shown here, are constants equal to 0 and 1.

The BTree::Node::locate_key method might be instructive if you've never seen a binary search before. I won't show it, but I will point out a useful software engineering tactic: binary search is notoriously hard to write correctly (it has a lot of funny boundary cases), so for the early versions of the module, I didn't bother writing it correctly. I used an easy-to-program linear search instead, and replaced slow linear search with quick binary search once everything else was already working.

Other Directions

The most important point about B-trees is that it's easy to implement a version that saves the tree on disk. The tree nodes never need to grow or shrink, so we never have the problem of moving one to a different place in the file when we insert a key. For this reason, they are frequently used for disk databases where the data have to be accessed by key. I didn't show this because the basic algorithm is already complicated enough; Our Most Assiduous Reader might like to modify BTree.pm so that it stores and maintains its tree structure in a file instead of memory, using tie.

By now you should be thinking of DBM files. A DBM file is a database on disk. The data in the file are available to your Perl program through a special hash variable, called a "tied" variable. The tied variable looks just like a regular hash variable, except that when you read from it the data come from the disk, and when you store something in it the data are written back to the disk. They persist beyond the lifetime of your program.

One DBM package commonly used with Perl is the Berkeley DB_File package, which can use a B-tree structure to store and retrieve data by key. Our Most Assiduous Reader might like to add a "tied hash" interface to the BTree package presented here. The fetching and storing methods are quite simple; fetching is just a call to B_search in search mode, and storing is just a call in insert-and-replace mode. Only nextkey, which is used by the keys, values, and each functions, presents any real difficulty.

When used in DBM files, B-trees have another big advantage over binary trees, even balanced binary trees. The binary search that occurs in a B-tree node takes about the same amount of CPU time as the binary search on the nodes of a binary tree with the sane number of keys. But when the tree lives on disk, each node must be loaded into memory before it can be examined. In a B-tree, you can adjust B so that each entire node can be loaded with exactly one disk operation, and then searched quickly in memory. In a binary tree, each key resides in its own node, which must be loaded from disk separately. Therefore, a binary tree typically requires between $B/2$ and B times as many disk accesses as a B-tree of similar size, because it has fewer keys per node. When the tree lives on the disk, the time to search the tree is dominated by the disk access time. As a result, B-trees are much faster than even balanced binary trees.

DBM files are almost invariably implemented with either B-trees or hash tables. (Hash tables are the method that Perl uses for regular in-memory hash variables.) However, B-trees present one enormous advantage over hash tables: the keys are stored in sorted order. Why is this important? Suppose you have a range, and you want to retrieve all the data for all the keys in that range. You can do this efficiently if your database is stored using B-trees: locate the two keys corresponding to the upper and lower bounds of the range, and then take all the keys in between. (If you did the previous exercise, you can use your nextkey function to get the keys in between.) With hash tables, the keys are not stored in any particular order, so there is no "in between," and to retrieve a range of them you must retrieve *all* the keys, extract the ones you want, sort them into order, and then query the hash once for each key. That's vastly less efficient.

Bibliography

Fundamentals of Data Structures in Pascal, Ellis Horowitz and Sartaj Sahni. Computer Science Press, pages 491–512, 1984.

CHAPTER 24

Making Life and Death Decisions with Perl

Richard Dice

Imagine a community in Canada's far north, 1,000 people with not so much as a caribou between themselves and the North Pole. It's suspected that this community might be experiencing an outbreak of a nasty disease called backslashitis, so the public health department has organized a general test of the population.

Backslashitis is fatal, but it can be successfully treated if caught in its earliest stage. However, the treatment is almost as bad as the disease. It's painful, lengthy, expensive, and would require relocating the patient to the nearest major urban center— Edmonton, over two thousand kilometers away. Long-term studies have shown that contaminated regions tend to have one infected individual per thousand.

The test for backslashitis isn't perfect, however. An infected individual will be correctly diagnosed 99 times out of 100, while a healthy individual will incorrectly register a positive test result 1 time in 1,000.

Now, we have to make a tough decision: based on the results of this test throughout the population of the community, what course of action will we recommend to people who test positive? Are we willing to advise them to leave their families for months and endure a great deal of hardship for the sake of curing a disease they might not even have?

We'll examine this situation in two ways. First, with probability theory, and then with Perl. In this article, we work through the simple but often misunderstood notion of *conditional probability*—a misunderstanding that applies to a lot more than just diseases.

Probability Theory

The methodology is fairly straightforward. First, we will identify the relevant events in our scenario. Then, we'll determine what probabilities we know about these events. From there, we will apply a little probability theory to arrive at a guideline for making our tough decisions. Then we'll back up the math with some empirical data generated by a Perl program.

The basic events involved are easy to pick out from the scenario given above. The first of these is that a person has backslashitis. We'll call this event A. The other event is that the person yields a positive test result, which we'll call B. Rather than making wholly new labels for the complementary events of "not being infected with backslashitis" and "not yielding a positive test result," We'll just give our previously defined labels stylish flat-top hats: $\overline{A}$ and B.

The probability that a random person in the community has the disease can be read directly out of the scenario: $P(A) = 1/1000$. Therefore $P(A) = 999/1000$.

We don't care about $P(B)$. The test only matters to the extent that it helps us determine whether an individual has backslashitis. What we want to find out is $P(A|B)$, which is the probability that an individual is infected given that they have tested positive; this is called the *conditional probability*. The scenario doesn't tell us this, though. It tells us that $P(B|A) = 99/100$, which is the probability that a test yields a positive result given that the person is infected. So, $P(B|A) = 1/100$. Also, $P(B|A)$, the probability that the test yields a false negative, is $1/1000$, and the probability that the test correctly yields a negative result is $P(B|A) = 999/1000$.

Really, what we want to know is $P(A|B)$, the probability that a person has backslashitis given that their test result is positive. That's what will help us decide whether to recommend that they pack up their things and head to Edmonton. If $P(A|B)$ is very nearly 1, then it is almost certain that the person has the disease and should be sent to Edmonton for treatment. Since our test is so good, what with $P(B|A) = 99/100$ and all, we would expect $P(A|B)$ to be equally good—wouldn't we?

Well, let's do the math to find out.

Our primary challenge is to find a way to obtain $P(A|B)$ given the information at our disposal above. The very definition of conditional probability is:

$$P(A|B) = \frac{P(A \cap B)}{P(B)}$$

In English, this equation states that given that B has occurred, the probability of A occurring is the probability of both A and B (that's the $\cap$) occurring, divided by the probability of just B occurring. That's great, but how can we use this to determine $P(A|B)$? We currently know neither $P(A \cap B)$ nor $P(B)$.

Lucky for us, determining $P(B)$ is pretty easy. The probability of a positive test result is the weighted average of all possible situations that might lead to such a result. In our situation, positive test results can be either a "true positive" or a "false positive."

$$P(B) = P(B|A)P(A) + P(B|\overline{A})P(\overline{A})$$

$$= \left(\frac{99}{100}\right)\left(\frac{1}{1000}\right) + \left(\frac{1}{1000}\right)\left(\frac{999}{1000}\right)$$

$$= \left(\frac{1989}{1000000}\right)$$

Now, we need to peg down P($A \cap B$). We can compute this with the Multiplicative Law of Probability:

$$P(A \cap B) = P(A)P(B|A) = P(B)P(A|B)$$

The middle form will be helpful to us, since we already know P(*A*) and P(*B*|*A*):

$$P(A \cap B) = \left(\frac{1}{1000}\right)\left(\frac{99}{100}\right) = \frac{99}{100000}$$

With all this, P(*A*|*B*) comes out of the mix:

$$P(A|B) = \frac{P(A \cap B)}{P(B)} = \frac{99/100000}{1989/1000000} \approx 0.4977$$

Whoa!

This result is something of a surprise—even though our test is "99% accurate," the odds that someone with a positive result actually has the disease is only about fifty-fifty.

With this kind of uncertainty, it's difficult to make the clear-cut policy decisions we want. But without our analysis, we might have sent everyone to Edmonton without a second thought.

Perl

A quick Perl program can be useful in analyzing these concepts. First, it's convenient—I don't have a small northern community in my office, but I do have Linux. This step will help me compare my analytic results to my simulated experiment as a sort of sanity check. Beyond that, a Perl program can allow me to tweak the parameters, to see if small changes in the numbers make for qualitatively different scenarios.

The program I wrote to test these ideas, shown at the end of the article, is essentially a small town medical test simulator. Howver, it's a bit more complicated, because I have it loop through multiple experiments and multiple towns.

The outermost loop, while (<IN>), parses lines in the external data file *prob.data*, shown below.

```
# Column 0 -- number of trials to be performed and averaged over with
#             the following information
# Column 1 -- the population of the community
```

```
# Column 2 -- prob. that a given member in the community is infected, P(A)
# Column 3 -- prob. that test yields positive given infected, P(B|A)
#               (a "true positive")
# Column 4 -- prob. that test yields positive given not infected, P(B|not-A)
#               (a "false positive")
#
# The variable names of these columns as used in prob.pl are:
#         $trials, $pop, $inf_prob, $tpos_prob, $fpos_prob
#
# Notes:
#   * Lines beginning with # are treated as comment lines by prob.pl
#     and are ignored.
#   * Lines consisting solely of whitespace are ignored.
#   * Column values in this file can be expressed either as real numbers
#     or as fractions.
#   * Any amount or type of whitespace (not including newlines) can be used
#     to delimit between columns.
#   * No whitespace may preceed the 0-th column.
#   * No error trapping regarding whitespace, # of columns, contents of
#     columns, etc. is performed by prob.pl, so don't mess this file up!
#

10      1000     1/1000     .99     1/1000
100     1000     1/1000     .99     1/1000
1000    1000     1/1000     .99     1/1000
100     10000    1/100      .9      .1
```

Each line is an independent experiment, with opportunities to change the various parameters: the number of people in the community, $P(A)$, $P(B)$, and $P(B|A)$.

The next level of looping, for ($j = 0; $j < $trials; $j++), is tied to the first field in *prob.data*. This is a somewhat artificial "trial smoothing" value. Basically, this variable tells the program to visit *N* different (yet identical) computer-generated small towns. The program averages the results collected in these *N* trials in the hopes that this procedure will make the numerically generated data less subject to randomness and more convergent on a true value.

The third and final level of looping, for ($i = 0; $i < $pop; $i++), is simply the number of people tested in a town, as given by the second field in *prob.data*. The procedure for testing a person is an amazingly straightforward random number test that I managed to make unduly complicated by cramming lots of code all in one place. First, a random number is generated to see if the person is "really" infected with the disease. If so, another is generated to see whether the test yields a true positive or a false negative result. If not, then a random number is still generated but used to see if the test yields a false positive or a true negative.

Just shy of the halfway mark through the program, I use a somewhat rare form of the ?: ternary operator to determine which of two variables is incremented:

```
( expression ? variable1 : variable2 )++;
```

After finishing the two innermost loops, the program evaluates a handful of probability statistics and displays the values using a Perl format. I have a top-of-page format containing the title and column headings of my report, and the format proper at the end of the program. The write_form_line subroutine is called at the end of the outermost loop; the write statement triggers the format, which is displayed to STDOUT. The output follows.

```
                 Analytic and Experimental Results
                  from our Population Testing Scenario
============================================================================
                 P(A)    P(not-A)    P(B|A)    P(B|not-A)    P(A|B)
============================================================================
Experiment #:        1
Trials Run  :       10
Pop. Size   :     1000
Analytic Results     :  0.00100   0.99900   0.99000     0.00100   0.49774
Experimental Results :  0.00130   0.99870   1.00000     0.00060   0.68421
============================================================================
Experiment #:        2
Trials Run  :      100
Pop. Size   :     1000
Analytic Results     :  0.00100   0.99900   0.99000     0.00100   0.49774
Experimental Results :  0.00106   0.99894   1.00000     0.00118   0.47321
============================================================================
Experiment #:        3
Trials Run  :     1000
Pop. Size   :     1000
Analytic Results     :  0.00100   0.99900   0.99000     0.00100   0.49774
Experimental Results :  0.00097   0.99903   0.98871     0.00095   0.50472
============================================================================
Experiment #:        4
Trials Run  :      100
Pop. Size   :    10000
Analytic Results     :  0.01000   0.99000   0.90000     0.10000   0.08333
Experimental Results :  0.01016   0.98984   0.90116     0.09956   0.08500
============================================================================
```

Last Words

Just as the theoretical analysis yielded a somewhat counterintuitive result, the numerical trials present a few noteworthy points as well. I ran quite a number of these numerical experiments to get a feel for how things would work out. Some observations follow.

The numerically calculated probability statistics come very close to the theoretically determined ones, but only when the number of trials performed is very large. After running 50 different trials of our scenario, I found a great deal of variation in the numeric P(A) between trials, ranging from 0 to 0.003. I'm sure that the average converges on the expected 0.001, but that won't be much comfort to the poor schmoe I sent to Edmonton to be poked and prodded. Example 24-1 shows the whole program.

Example 24-1. prob.pl

```perl
#!/usr/bin/perl

use FileHandle;
STDOUT->format_top_name("TOP");
STDOUT->format_name("LINE");
srand;                    # Seed the random number generator

open(IN, ($datafile = "prob.data"))
  or die('Can\'t open datafile "' . $datafile . "\":\n$!");

while (<IN>) {
  chomp;
  next if /^#/; # skips "commented" lines
  next if !/\S/g; # skips lines consisting only of whitespace

  # Keeps track of which experiment we are currently working on.
  $exp_num++;

  # Clears out variables from the previous trial.
  $total_inf_count = $total_tpos_count = $total_tneg_count =
                     $total_fpos_count = $total_fneg_count = 0;

  foreach $item (($trials,$pop,$inf_prob,$tpos_prob,$fpos_prob) = split) {
    $item = eval $item;
  }

  for ($j = 0; $j < $trials; $j++) {

    # Clear out variables from values of their previous population trial.
    $inf_count = $tpos_count = $tneg_count = $fpos_count = $fneg_count = 0;

    for ($i = 0; $i < $pop; $i++) {
      if ( $inf_prob > rand ) {
        $inf_count++;
        (($tpos_prob > rand) ? $tpos_count : $fneg_count) += 1;
      } else {
        (($fpos_prob > rand) ? $fpos_count : $tneg_count) += 1;
      }
    }

    # Keep running total of trial-derived information across all trials
    $total_inf_count  += $inf_count;  $total_tpos_count += $tpos_count;
    $total_tneg_count += $tneg_count; $total_fpos_count += $fpos_count;
    $total_fneg_count += $fneg_count;
  }

  # Normalize the total counts based on the number of trials that were run
  $total_inf_count  /= $trials;
  $total_tpos_count /= $trials;
  $total_tneg_count /= $trials;
  $total_fpos_count /= $trials;
  $total_fneg_count /= $trials;
```

Example 24-1. prob.pl (continued)

```perl
    # Compute probabilities from the data in the numerical experiment.
    $prob_a            = $total_inf_count / $pop;
    $prob_not_a        = 1 - $prob_a;
    $prob_b_given_a    = $total_tpos_count / $total_inf_count;
    $prob_b_given_not_a = $total_fpos_count / ($pop - $total_inf_count);
    $prob_a_given_b    = ($prob_a * $prob_b_given_a) /
                         ($prob_a * $prob_b_given_a +
                          $prob_not_a * $prob_b_given_not_a);


    # Output the results of this experiment to our formatted report.

    write_form_line($exp_num, $trials, $pop,
      $inf_prob, 1 - $inf_prob, $tpos_prob, $fpos_prob,
        ($inf_prob * $tpos_prob) /
          ($inf_prob * $tpos_prob + (1-$inf_prob) * $fpos_prob),
            $prob_a, $prob_not_a, $prob_b_given_a,
              $prob_b_given_not_a, $prob_a_given_b);
} # End of while loop
close(IN);

sub write_form_line {
  my ($experiment, $trial_runs, $population,
      $apA, $apnA, $apBA, $apBnA, $apAB,
      $epA, $epnA, $epBA, $epBnA, $epAB) = @_;
  write;
}

format TOP =
                    Analytic and Experimental Results
                    from our Population Testing Scenario
=============================================================================
                        P(A)    P(not-A)   P(B|A)   P(B|not-A)   P(A|B)
=============================================================================
.

format LINE =
Experiment #:@>>>>>>>>
$experiment
Trials Run  :@>>>>>>>>
$trial_runs
Pop. Size   :@>>>>>>>>
$population
Analytic Results:       @.#####    @.##### @.#####      @.##### @.#####
                        $apA,      $apnA,  $apBA,       $apBnA, $apAB
Experimental Results:   @.#####    @.##### @.#####      @.##### @.#####
                        $epA,      $epnA,  $epBA,       $epBnA, $epAB
=============================================================================
.
```

## CHAPTER 25

Information Retrieval

Ulrich Pfeifer

 The code presented here is derived from the `perlindex` script (available on CPAN), rewritten to emphasize clarity over speed. The scripts here are self-contained and are useful for simple applications; I reused them myself a couple of times when the full power of the WAIT wasn't required. (WAIT is a Perl implementation of the WAIS information retrieval system, available on CPAN.)

Information retrieval—the science of matching documents to users—depends heavily on *relevance*: identifying when a document matches a user's needs. Relevance is something that only users can assess; there's no surefire way to compute it. IR researchers detest SQL-style document retrieval, because true IR systems take the users into account; they're rated by their ability to fulfill users' needs, not by the speed at which they process SQL statements. Good IR systems are like Perl—designed with the human being in mind.

In this article, we'll develop a simple IR application: retrieving appropriate documents from a set of online manuals. Since our knowledge about the user's need is inevitably incomplete, and the collection of documents is limited, the retrieval is doomed to some fuzziness.*

Figure 25-1 depicts a generic IR system. On the left, knowledge in the real world is incorporated into a document, which in turn is transformed into some representation usable by the system. On the right, a user's need is expressed in a query language that is also transformed into an internal representation. How the representations are compared is defined by the *retrieval model*, typically implemented as a function that computes the likelihood that the document matches the query. The system cannot

---

* IR people tend to avoid the term *database* in favor of the term *collections*, and the objects in the collections are usually referred to as *documents* even if they're not text.

determine the relevance itself; at best, it only guess the *probability* that a user will consider the document an acceptable response to his query.

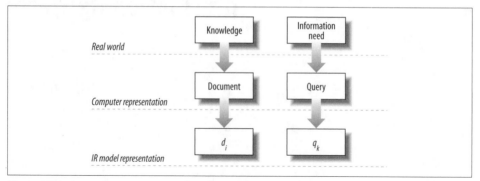

Figure 25-1. A generic IR system matching knowledge to information needs

The arrows in Figure 25-1 represent transformations that are always imperfect. This unavoidable loss is called *uncertainty* when applied to documents, and *vagueness* when applied to queries.

There are three categories of document attributes that can be expressed with queries:

Logical attributes
> These are the familiar attributes that we might find in a conventional database-backed retrieval system, for instance, title and author. Good information retrieval systems provide some means of dealing with uncertainty in the input, such as typographic errors.

Syntactic attributes
> These attributes contain information about the layout of the document. ("Find me that business letter with this blue logo on the top right corner.")

Semantic attributes
> These attributes encapsulate the system's understanding of the document content. For instance, if the IR system classifies a document as pertaining to the "baseball" concept, that would be a semantic attribute.

Text Searches on Manual Pages

Now that we've got the big picture, let's consider a simple application. Most questions lobbed at system administrators can be answered with two words. The first is man and the second regrettably varies. Wouldn't it be nice if the user could enter his query as "How do I..." to our application and be referred automatically to the set of relevant manual pages?

This application will let us focus on the semantic attributes of manual pages. Manuals mostly look alike, so the syntactic layout information is of little use. We'll also ignore the logical attributes, although some of them (for instance, the size and date of the files) could be helpful.

We have to decide what retrieval model to use. We resort to a simple yet powerful approach: Salton's Vector Space model, which represents queries and documents as vectors of real numbers, each dimension representing a term in the dictionary. The value of the nth entry of the vector is called the "weight" of word n with respect to the document. Comparing the query and a document vector (say, by computing the scalar product) yields the probability of relevance of the document with respect to the query.[*] This value is often called the *retrieval status value* (RSV) to stress that it is not an estimate of the probability, but rather some transformation of it.

For the query vector, we simply set the corresponding vector element to 1 if the word is present in the query and 0 otherwise. For the document vectors, we do something slightly more elaborate. Let's assume that the query word under consideration occurs in n of all N documents. It occurs *tf* times in the current document, and the most frequent word in the document occurs *maxtf* times. Given that, we define the weight for a word i as:

$$w_i = \frac{tf_i}{maxtf_i} \log\left(\frac{N}{n}\right)$$

We see that the more frequent the word, the higher its weight. Since longer documents tend to have more occurrences of any given word, the *maxtf* term compensates by decreasing the weight accordingly. The logarithm ensures that words occurring in many documents (e.g., "print") yield a lower weight than others.

The Implementation

Let's recall what we need. For each document, we need to know how often the most frequent word occurs. We also need a *headline*: some information to display describing the document. For each word in the query, we need the list of documents containing the word along with the frequency of the word in the documents. To save disk space, we won't store the filenames, but will number the documents instead. If we want to be able to incrementally update our index, we also need the reverse mapping to check if a manual is already indexed.

To make our code usable by both the indexer and the query interface, we encapsulate it in a module called Man::Index. The module's constructor, new, takes two named arguments: a directory where the index files are stored and a flag indicating whether the index files should be opened for updating or just for reading.

---

[*] Salton used several other similarity functions such as *cosine* and *dice* that require normalizing the vector lengths.

```perl
sub new {
    my $type = shift;
    my %parm = @_;
    my $self = {};
    my $index = $parm{'index'} || croak "No 'index' argument given\n";
    my $rw = $parm{rw};
    my $flags = ($rw) ? O_RDWR : O_RDONLY;
    unless (-d $index) {
        if ($rw) {
            mkpath($index,1,0755) || croak "Could not mkpath '$index': $!\n";
            $flags |= O_CREAT;
        } else {
            croak "No index directory '$index': $!\n";
        }
    }

    tie %{$self->{documents}}, 'AnyDBM_File',
        "$index/documents", $flags, 0644
        or die "Could not tie '$index/documents': $!\n";

    tie %{$self->{doc_entry}}, 'AnyDBM_File',
        "$index/doc_entry", $flags, 0644
        or die "Could not tie '$index/doc_entry': $!\n";

    tie %{$self->{doc_no}}, 'AnyDBM_File',
        "$index/doc_no", $flags, 0644
        or die "Could not tie '$index/doc_no': $!\n";

    bless $self, $type;
}
```

The first hash, %{self->{documents}}, maps the dictionary words to a list of document numbers and frequencies. This index is often called an *inverted file* because it represents the "inverse" of the documents that can themselves be thought of as mapping document numbers to words. For convenience, we implement a documents method that, depending on the number of arguments, either returns the list of documents for a word, or appends to that list:

```perl
sub documents {
    my $self = shift;
    my $word = shift;
    if (@_) {      # @_ = ($document_number, $frequency)
        $self->{documents}->{$word} .= pack 'ww', @_; }
    else {
        unpack 'w*', $self->{documents}->{$word};
    }
}
```

We use pack 'w' instead of pack 'I' or pack 'S' to store our word frequencies as *compressed integers*, saving space.

If we were looking for documents about cars, we might use this as a simple query:

```perl
%frequency = $self->documents('cars');
@document_numbers = keys %frequency;
```

The second hash, %{self->{doc_entry}}, maps document numbers to the document related data: maximum frequency, path, and headline. We use the special entry __maximum_document_number__ to store the number of documents in the index. The %{$self->{doc_no}} hash is used for the inverse mapping (path to document number).

```
sub make_document_entry {
    my ($self, $path, $maxtf, $headline) = @_;
    my $docno = ++$self->{doc_entry}->{__maximum_document_number__};
    $self->{doc_entry}->{$docno} = pack('S',$maxtf) . join($;, $path, $headline);
    $self->{doc_no}->{$path} = $docno;
    return $docno;
}
```

The methods maxtf, path, and headline (not shown here) look up the values for a given document number.

Using these methods, we can implement another method for adding a document to our index. It takes a filename as its argument after the obligatory first argument containing the object itself:

```
sub add_document {
    my ($self, $file) = @_;

    # Check for symbolic links or already indexed files
    return unless $self->is_reasonable($file);

    # Handle compression
    my $fh = $self->open_file($file) || return;

    my ($headline, $maxtf, %frequency, $line);
    while (defined($line = <$fh>)) {
        if (!$headline and $line =~ /\.S[Hh] NAME/) {
            $headline = $self->get_headline($fh);
        }
        for my $term ($self->words($line)) {
            $frequency{$term}++;
            $maxtf = $frequency{$term} if $frequency{$term} > $maxtf;
        }
    }

    $headline ||= $path;
    my $doc_number = $self->make_document_entry($path, $maxtf, $headline);
    while (my($term, $freq) = each %frequency) {
        $self->documents($term, $doc_number, $freq);
    }
    return ($doc_number, $headline);
}
```

The first while loop iterates over the lines of the file. After checking for the headline, the words method splits each line into words, counts the occurrences, and computes the maximum frequency. Then a new document entry is generated and the second while loop appends the ($doc_number, $freq) pair to the appropriate inverted lists. (This is often called *posting*.) The method returns the document number and its headline so that the caller can print something meaningful while we wait for it to finish.

Although the three helper functions is_reasonable, open_file, and get_headline are conceptually simple, the method words is more exciting since it will greatly influence the retrieval quality and the index size. A minimal implementation might look like this:

```
sub words {
    my ($self, $text) = @_;
    for ($text) {
        s/\f.//g; # \fB and the like
        tr/A-Za-z0-9/ /cs;
    }
    split ' ', $text;
}
```

Here the \f macros (which control font selection in *troff*-encoded manpages) are removed, all nonalphanumeric characters are replaced by spaces, and the result is split on spaces. Unfortunately, this simple implementation treats the words "computer" and "computers" as different words. Searching for one of them will miss the other. Since manpages are generally in English, we can use the Text::English module from CPAN to map the words to their stems. This solves the problem and reduces the index size at the same time. Furthermore, since roughly half of normal text consists of two hundred so-called *stopwords* like "the" and "an", we could save about the same fraction of index space by removing them. This can be done simply by checking all the words for existence in a hash of stopwords.

We're ready to write a make_index script. Error handling and option parsing have been removed for clarity:

```
my $index = new Man::Index index => '/tmp/man', rw => 1;

for my $dir (@mandir) {
    opendir BASE, $dir;
    for my $sub (grep -d "$dir/$_", grep /^man/,readdir BASE) {
        my $path = "$dir/$sub";
        opendir SUBDIR, $path;
        for my $page (grep -f "$path/$_", readdir SUBDIR) {
            if (my ($number, $headline) = $index->add_document("$path/$page")) {
                printf("%4d %s\n", $number, $headline);
            }
        }
    }
    closedir BASE;
}
```

This indexer takes a long time when given a large collection of manpages. While we're waiting for it to finish, we can implement the search method:

```
sub search {
    my $self = shift;
    $self->search_raw($self->words(shift));
}
```

```
sub search_raw { # Assumes query words are normalized
    my $self = shift;
    my (%score);
 WORD:
    for my $term (@_) {
        if (my %post = $self->documents($term)) {
            # document frequency
            my $n = scalar keys %post;
            my $idf = log($self->num_documents / $n);

            # Term occurs in every document
            next WORD if $idf == 0;
            for my $doc_no (keys %post) {
                my $maxtf = $self->maxtf($doc_no);
                $score{$doc_no} += $post{$doc_no} / $maxtf * $idf;
            }
        }
    }
    \%score;
}
```

search just splits the query string into words and calls upon search_raw to do the real
work. In search_raw, we loop over the words and look up the posting list for each of
them. The total number of documents (stored in __maximum_document_number__ and
assessed via the num_documents method) is divided by the number of documents in
the list—our *n* above. The logarithm of the result is the second part of our formula
for the document weight. The *for* loop computes the first part for each document;
the frequency of each word is divided by the maximum word frequency. The product of both parts is then added to the current score for the document, which implements the dot product of the document vector and the query vector. The method
returns a reference to a hash where the keys are the document numbers and the values are their scores.

A minimal search script using our system might look like this:

```
my $x = new Man::Index index => '/tmp/man';
my $score = $x->search(join ' ', @ARGV);
my $display = 10;

for my $doc_no (sort {$score->{$b} <=> $score=>{$a}} keys %$score) {
    printf "%5.3f %s\n\t%s", $score->{$doc_no},
    $x->headline($doc_no),
    $x->path($doc_no);
    last unless --$display;
}
```

Before we can sell this system, we need an interface that lets users enter queries and
inspect the results, and my system contains a simple shell-based interface (not shown
here). In addition to its retrieval capabilities, it collects relevance judgments from the
users. They can mark individual answers as relevant or irrelevant to their current
query, and we can make use of this data with the *Binary Independence Retrieval*

Model, or BIR, discussed in Robertson's *Relevance Weighting of Search Terms,* cited at the end of this article.

Relevance Feedback

The BIR uses two pieces of information to determine the relevance of a document: whether a query word is present in the document (frequency is ignored; hence the "Binary"), and the relevance feedback from the user. We assume that the user has judged r documents relevant and i documents irrelevant. For a given word, we compute P_k, the probability that it occurs in a relevant document, and Q_k, the probability that it occurs in an irrelevant document:

$$p_k = \frac{r_k + 0.5}{r + 1.0}$$

$$q_k = \frac{i_k + 0.5}{i + 1.0}$$

(The 0.5 and 1.0 ensure that we never divide by zero.) We then compute the weight for a document as the sum over all query words:

$$score = \sum_{k=0} \log\frac{p_k(1 - q_k)}{q_k(1 - p_k)}$$

The mathematics is explained in Robertson's article. Our implementation assumes that %all indexes the document numbers of judged documents and %good indexes the document numbers of relevant documents.

```perl
my $good = scalar keys %good;
my $all = scalar keys %all;
my %score;

for my $word ($self->words($QUERY)) {
    my ($f, $r);
    my %document = $INDEX->documents($word);
    for my $docno (keys %all) {
        # document contains the word
        if ($document{$docno}) {
            $f++;
            $r++ if $good{$docno};
        }
    }
    my $p = ($r+0.5) / ($good+1);
    my $q = ($f-$r+0.5) / ($all-$good+1);
    for my $docno (keys %document) {
        $score{$docno} += log( $p * (1-$q) / $q / (1-$p) );
    }
}
```

The iman script I wrote contains this code; experiment! As a rule of thumb, the more words our query contains, the better our results will be. We are doing IR here—not mega-grep implementations like most Internet search engines. We will never be confronted with 20,000 hits in no particular or justifiable order. After providing feedback to the system, we can expect the relevant documents among the top ranked ones.

"Advanced" Search Operators

Wish this system had boolean operators or regular expressions? Don't! We built the system for novice users who might not be familiar with Boolean logic or regular expression metacharacters. With our system, they'll get an answer even if only one query word is present in only one man page in the entire collection. With Boolean expressions, even if a user succeeds in entering syntactically correct queries, he'll often get no result at all. Some studies (such as *Extended Boolean Information Retrieval*, cited at the end of this article) have shown that Boolean logic doesn't buy the casual user much.

Conclusion

In this article, I've presented a conceptual framework for information retrieval as well as a simple but useful implementation. Feel free to extend the system by adding other retrieval models or by modifying the current ones; for instance, consider the advantages of splitting the manual into sections and paragraphs—what would the representation then look like? Or consider the possibilities for enhancing the user interface by replacing man -1 with a pager that highlights the query terms. If you get nothing else from this article, don't forget that information retrieval is not about applying SQL to databases of documents, but providing humans with whatever information they need.

References

Robertson, S. and Sparck Jones, K. *Relevance Weighting of Search Terms*. Journal of the American Society for Information Science 27, pp. 129–146, 1976.

Salton, G., E. Fox, and H. Wu. *Extended Boolean Information Retrieval*. Communications of the ACM 26, pp. 1022–1036, 1983.

Salton, G. and McGill, M. J. *Introduction to Modern Information Retrieval*. McGraw-Hill, New York, 1983.

## CHAPTER 26

Randomness

Jon Orwant

One of the common questions on comp.lang.perl.misc is "How come my random numbers aren't random?" Usually, a simple prescription to use srand is sufficient. But the simplicity of these answers belies just how hard it is to have a computer generate good random numbers. In fact, it's downright *impossible*.

While no source provides completely random numbers, some sources are more random than others. The PGP encryption package, for instance, has you type aimlessly at your keyboard, using the intervals between keystrokes as a source of random numbers. It measures tiny time differences, making it a good source of random numbers unless you possess a truly robotic sense of rhythm, in which case you probably have career options that don't involve the use of contraband cryptosystems.

The measurement of keystrokes is slow and intrusive, so some computers rely on rapidly changing areas of computer memory for their random numbers, or network packet arrival times. Others amplify ambient noise collected from disconnected audio or video inputs. Still others calculate disk seek times; minute variations in speed are caused by air turbulence, which is pretty hard to predict.

Computers that take their randomness seriously have physical hardware dedicated to random number generation: unstable free-running oscillators, a source of radioactive decay, or thermal noise from an amplified diode. That's about as random as it gets.

But the vast majority of computers generate random numbers the same way. They're more properly called *pseudorandom* numbers, because if you know what number the computer just picked, you can predict the next number.

This is why Las Vegas Mafia thugs break your kneecaps if you try to pry open a slot machine. All modern slot machines first determine what your payoff will be using a pseudorandom number generator, and *then* spin the wheels so that the appropriate fruits appear. That way, wear and tear on the moving parts of a slot machine won't affect the payoffs. (Vegas slot machines are networked in a WAN of sorts; that's how multimillion-dollar progressive jackpots are possible.)

Congruential Generators

Many computers use *linear congruential generators* to create random numbers. It's a lousy method. There are plenty of better ones, but they're slower, which accounts for the near-universality of this lame scheme, which works as follows:

- Take the last random number.
- Multiply it by something.
- Add something else.
- Take the remainder when you divide by something else.

That's all there is to it. Expressed as an equation:

$$n_{j+1} = an_j + b(\text{mod } c)$$

where n_{j+1} is the new random number, n_j is the last random number, and a, b, and c are all positive integers specific to a particular generator.

Every random number is determined by the previous random number except for the first, which comes from you. That first number is called the *seed* of the random number generator, and you provide it to Perl (and C) with the srand function. This is why we see all those questions on comp.lang.perl.misc: people don't realize that without seeding their generators, they'll get the same sequence of random numbers each time. Less often, you see people who know they're supposed to use srand, but they aren't quite sure what it does, so they use it as often as possible, with disastrous (but predictable!) results.

Choosing the Seed

Astute readers will notice that linear congruential generators produce only integers. And sure enough, if you use rand in a C program, you'll get integers. But Perl's rand, like Perl itself, is a little quirky and a little more useful: it divides the integer by the system constant RAND_MAX, yielding a fraction between 0 and 1. On systems that use these generators, the c in the above equation will be RAND_MAX + 1.

Linear congruential generators can be cracked, yielding the values of a, b, and c, with only moderate difficulty. There's a complete scheme in *How to Predict Congruential Generators*, cited at the end of this article; to give you a taste, I've created an imaginary generator by choosing an a, b, and c. Your task is to deduce their values. Table 26-1 gives you four pairs of numbers, each containing a seed fed to srand and the result from rand.

Table 26-1. Behavior of a simple pseudorandom number generator

Seed	Result of rand
1	26
2	3

Seed	Result of rand
3	12
4	21

I picked this generator out of thin air. Real computers wouldn't use such simple generators, of course, but I got a little lucky: my generator happens to be *maximal-length*, which means that it will only repeat itself after *c* calls to rand. Had I picked bad values for *a*, *b*, and *c*, the result would have been a generator that repeats much more quickly. This is a recurring problem.

The ANSI C committee hasn't been much help, either. They published a mediocre generator ($a = 1,103,515,245$, $b = 12,345$, and $c = 32,768$) that was meant to demonstrate how pseudorandom number generation might be implemented. As *Numerical Recipes in C* (cited at the end of this article) points out, the ANSI generator was meant *only as an example*. But sure enough, many major operating systems even today use it as their rand. Run this program to see if your computer falls victim to the ANSI plague.

```perl
#!/usr/bin/perl -w

use Config;

print "Your random number generator repeats itself after\n";
print "no more than ", 2 ** $Config{randbits}, "numbers.\n";

srand(1);

if (int(rand( ) * (2 ** $Config{randbits})) == 16838) {
    print "Uh oh!  Looks like your computer uses the ANSI example.\n";
    print "I bet the next three rands are 5758, 10113, and 17515.\n";

    foreach (1,2,3) {
        print rand( ) * (2 ** $Config}{randbits}), "\n";
    }
}
```

The $c = 32,768$ is especially troubling, since it means that your computer will repeat itself after 32,768 calls to rand. Many years ago, when writing an image processing program, I noticed that my 512×512 image had a discernible repeating pattern in the supposedly random white noise that I added to it. The reason was that I was using a computer with the weak ANSI generator; since my image had more than 32,768 pixels, the generator had run through all its numbers and cycled back to the beginning over and over.

In its discussion of pseudorandom number generators, *Numerical Recipes in C* notes that the only thing worse than the ANSI generator is a system that tries to fix it:

> ...one popular 32-bit PC-compatible computer provides a long generator that uses the above congruence, but swaps the high-order and low-order 16 bits of the returned value. Somebody probably thought that this extra flourish added randomness; in fact it ruins the generator.

Tampering with the result of a generator is like shuffling a deck of cards again to make them more random. Sometimes it does; sometimes it doesn't. (If you can shuffle a 52-card deck *perfectly* 8 times in a row, you'll return the deck to its original order.)

Linear congruential generators are pretty fast: one multiply, one add, one modulus, and bang, you're done. But for the speed freaks among us, it turns out that a *mulplicative congruential generator*:

$$n_{j+1} = an_j (\text{mod } c)$$

(that is, a linear congruential generator with $b = 0$) can do just as well if you choose your a and c wisely.

LFSRs

Linear Feedback Shift Registers, or LFSRs, are another popular way of producing random numbers. Like congruential generators, LFSRs are completely deterministic, but they can be embedded in electronic devices with less hardware.

An LFSR provides an endless procession of pseudorandom bits, as opposed to full-fledged pseudorandom integers. Don't fret about the fact that LFSRs only produce a bit at a time: by combining multiple bits, you can create a pseudorandom number as large as you want.

As an aside, cryptographers often talk about a coin flip as if it were the ideal generator of random bits. Skilled prestidigitators, however, can manipulate coin flips. And because of the way coins are struck by dies at the mint, the edges are often not quite perpendicular to the sides. If you don't believe me, balance a penny on its edge and then bump the table. It'll fall heads more than half the time.

You can think of every LFSR as containing a "window" of bits. In a 4-bit LFSR, the system sees four bits at a time; when a user wants a random bit, the system extracts the rightmost bit, shifts the other three bits one place to the right, and calculates a new leftmost bit by XORing some of those four bits together.

For instance, a very simple LFSR might operate on four bits at a time, XORing the first and third bits. Let's say you seed this generator with 15, which is 1111 in binary. Then the first nine pseudorandom bits will be 1, 1, 1, 1, 0, 1, 0, 0, and 1, because they're the rightmost bits of this sequence:

```
1111
0111
1011
0101
0010
1001
1100
1110
0111
```

Consider the fourth state: 0101. We arrive at the fifth state by XORing the first and third bits, 0 and 0, yielding 0. That's our new leftmost bit; the other bits are the underlined leftover bits from the fourth state, shifted right.

As with congruential generators, you need to be very careful when choosing the parameters; you can't just XOR any bits you like. The four bit generator above is a "real" LFSR. It's maximal length; no matter what seed you provide, it will repeat after no less than seven iterations. Here's a nine bit generator; can you crack the generator by deducing which bits are XORed?

```
1 0 1 1 0 1 0 0 1
1 1 0 1 1 0 1 0 0
0 1 1 0 1 1 0 1 0
0 0 1 1 0 1 1 0 1
1 0 0 1 1 0 1 1 0
0 1 0 0 1 1 0 1 1
1 0 1 0 0 1 1 0 1
0 1 0 1 0 0 1 1 0
1 0 1 0 1 0 0 1 1
0 1 0 1 0 1 0 0 1
1 0 1 0 1 0 1 0 0
1 1 0 1 0 1 0 1 0
0 1 1 0 1 0 1 0 1
0 0 1 1 0 1 0 1 0
0 0 0 1 1 0 1 0 1
1 0 0 0 1 1 0 1 0
0 1 0 0 0 1 1 0 1
0 0 1 0 0 0 1 1 0
0 0 0 1 0 0 0 1 1
0 0 0 0 1 0 0 0 1
0 0 0 0 0 1 0 0 0
1 0 0 0 0 0 1 0 0
0 1 0 0 0 0 0 1 0
```

Unfortunately, I wasn't as lucky as when I made up my congruential generator; this LFSR repeats itself after 127 iterations, which I learned from the program below.

```perl
#!/usr/bin/perl -w

# LFSR - Implement arbitrary-sized linear feedback shift registers

# Convert the seed from decimal to binary
$seed = dec2bin(shift);

@array = split('', $seed);

@xor_bits = @ARGV;

# Assumes integers are 32 bits.
splice(@array, 0, 31-$ARGV[0]);

# Let the user bang on <ENTER> until he's had his fill of random bits
while (1) {
```

```
getc();
$new_bit = 0 + $array[0];   # The "0 +" forces numeric context
foreach (@xor_bits[1..$#xor_bits]) {
    $new_bit ^= $array[$#array - $_];
}
print pop @array;
unshift (@array, $new_bit);
}

sub dec2bin { unpack("B*", pack("N", shift)) }
```

If you don't think any of this stuff matters, consider a great cryptosystem. A *superb* cryptosystem, one that uses, say, hundred-thousand-bit keys. To generate those keys, it needs random numbers. Now suppose your computer uses an eight-bit random number generator. Guess how many attempts you need to crack the cryptosystem through exhaustive search. Not 2^{65536}, but $2^8 = 256$.

And yes, my computer (a DEC Alpha running Digital Unix) still uses that primitive ANSI generator.

In the sequel to this article, Otmar Lendl goes into the state of pseudorandom number generation in more detail, delivering a brief XS tutorial in the process.

References

D. Eastlake 3rd, S. Crocker, and J. Schiller. *Randomness Recommendations for Security*. RFC 1750.

Krawczyk, H. *How to Predict Congruential Generators*. Journal of Algorithms, 13(4), December 1992.

Press, W., S. Teukolsky, W. Vetterling, and B. Flannery. *Numerical Recipes in C: The Art of Scientific Computing, Second Edition*. Cambridge University Press, 1992.

Schneier, B. *Applied Cryptography: Protocols, Algorithms, and Source Code in C, 2nd edition*. John Wiley & Sons, 1995.

## CHAPTER 27

Random Number Generators and XS

Otmar Lendl

This article is a follow-up to John Orwant's article, *Randomness*. I'd like to give some more background, provide another code snippet for serious pseudorandom number generation, and give a tour of XS, the bridge between Perl and C.

Random Versus Pseudorandom Numbers

Cryptography is the classic example of a domain that requires a good source of *truly* random numbers. Random numbers are used as session keys, initialization vectors, seeds for RSA prime number generation, and myriad other applications.

The security of a cryptographic algorithm usually depends on the futility of guessing the random numbers chosen by the computer. The key concept is *entropy*, a measure of the uncertainty contained in a set of values. For example, a user asked to type some random characters is much more likely to type asdf than 9m]g; the entropy is thus not as high as it would be if all strings were equally likely. Thus, even though we type in seven-bit ASCII, we can't generate 35 random bits from just five keystrokes; a common rule of thumb is that the entropy per keystroke is in the range of 1.0 to 1.5 bits.[*] So to generate 35 truly random bits, we need to use at least 35 keystrokes.

We can use this rule to build a random number generator that combines the entropy inherent in various computer components. They'll be deterministic, but unpredictable from the outside—people who don't have physical access to the computer haven't a prayer of guessing the seed.

We have to be very careful to acquire enough entropy per bit. Netscape learned this the hard way when Ian Goldberg and David Wagner broke the SSL (Secure Socket Layer) implementation in Netscape Navigator 1.2 because it only used the PID (process ID), PPID (parent process ID), and the current time as the seed for the random number generator.

---

[*] Schneier, p.190.

Collecting entropy is a task best left to the operating system kernel, since that's where all the entropy-producing events occur. Theodore Ts'o implemented such a generator for the Linux kernel (see the sidebar "The Linux /dev/random Device"). Here's how the *dev/random* device can be used to seed Perl's pseudorandom number generator:

```perl
#!/usr/bin/perl

open(RAND, "/dev/random") or die "No /dev/random?\n";
read(RAND, $seed, 4);
close(RAND);

print "Seed = ", unpack("H*", $seed) , "\n";
srand(unpack("L", $seed));

foreach (1..10) {
    print rand( ), "\n";
}
```

If our operating system doesn't support such a convenient device, we can use the Math::TrulyRandom module (C code by Matt Blaze and Don Mitchell, Perl wrapper by Systemics Ltd., available from CPAN), which uses interrupt timing discrepancies as its source of entropy.

The Linux /dev/random Device

Most Linux kernels include the *dev/random* and *dev/urandom* devices created by Theodore Ts'o. If these devices are not under */dev*, create them using these commands:

```
mknod /dev/random c 1 8
mknod /dev/urandom c 1 9
```

The device driver mixes data and timings from the keyboard, mouse, and disks into a 512-byte *entropy pool*. Random numbers are generated by calculating a secure hash (SHA or MD5) of these bytes. In order to guarantee the quality of the output, the driver keeps an estimate of the amount of entropy currently in the pool. As new input is mixed in, this count increases according to the uncertainty in the input, whereas each byte read from the device reduces the counter by eight bits.

dev/random and *dev/urandom* differ in how they react to an empty entropy pool: */dev/random* simply blocks and waits until enough entropy has accumulated to fulfill the request, while */dev/urandom* keeps on generating numbers.

Many applications need random numbers, but not necessarily numbers unpredictable from the "inside." In fact, they often require a source of random numbers that generates the same sequence whenever the program is run. This repeatability is essential for debugging some programs, since if our numbers aren't predictable, we can't replicate bugs.

Pseudorandom number generators (PRNGs) are deterministic algorithms that produce such streams of repeatable (and thus predictable) numbers. A good PRNG a) behaves in all important respects like a random variable, and b) is fast. What a) means and how one can test for it is the subject of endless scientific discussions.

Linear Congruential Generators Revisited

Jon wrote about linear congruential generators (LCGs), one of which was proposed by the ANSI C committee. LCGs are defined with a simple recursion formula that calculates the new random number from the last one:

$$n_{j+1} = an_j + b(\bmod\ c)$$

It's Not That Bad

The ANSI C generator uses parameters designed for a simple and fast implementation on 32-bit computers ($a = 1,103,515,245$, $b = 12,345$, $c = 2^{31}$). With such a c, the modulus operation translates to just ignoring the overflow. As usual, an advantage in one area is balanced by a disadvantage in another. In this case, our price is an unfortunate regularity in the lower bits of the numbers. Returning these numbers is dangerous, since the user might just extract bit 0 (calculating, say, $n_j \bmod 2$) to arrive at a sequence of bits that aren't random at all. With this generator, they'd be 01010101010101.

To avoid such pitfalls, Digital Unix shifts n_j by 16 bits to the right before returning. The constant RAND_MAX is thus set to 2^{15}, and consequently Perl's Config module sets $Config{randbits} to 15. This doesn't imply that the period length of rand( ) is 2^{15}, but only that we shouldn't use more than the first 15 bits from any random number. The period length of this generator is the same as that of the ANSI C generator, namely 2^{31}.

As LCGs go, the ANSI C generator is... okay. Consecutive numbers are largely uncorrelated, as shown in Figure 27-1.

For this plot, I used the first 5,000 pairs of the form (n_j, n_{j+1}), scaled to [0,1].

It's Not Good, Either

This looks fine and dandy; no patterns are visible. But what happened to Jon's image? In his article he wrote about strange things happening when he used the ANSI C generator to add white noise to a 512×512 image. That calls for 262,144 random numbers. The first and second random numbers affect pixels next to one another, of course, but there's a twist: the first and 513th numbers *also* affect adjacent pixels, since the 513th pixel is directly below the first. We can again use a plot of pairs to visualize correlations, but this time we use (n_{16384j}, $n_{16384(j+1)}$) to get Figure 27-2.

Figure 27-1. Pseudorandom white noise

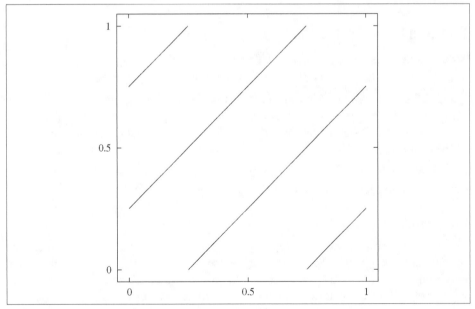

Figure 27-2. Correlations from an LCG

Oops. No wonder patterns appeared in the image. We stumbled on an intrinsic feature of every LCG: they exhibit long-range correlations of the worst kind. If we take subsequences from an LCG or otherwise combine numbers from different parts of the period, we can expect nasty surprises. Images are especially prone to these dangers because of their two-dimensional nature.

A large set of alternatives to LCGs has been published; for a good survey on the current menagerie of PRNGs see the papers by Nieder and L'Ecuyer (cited at the end of this chapter). It can be proved that certain generators, such as the EICG (Explicit Inversive Congruential Generator), are not prone to such deficiencies.

A Better Generator for Perl

A close relative to the Linear Feedback Shift Register generators (see Jon's article) is the Twisted Generalized Feedback Shift Register (tGFSR). It's extremely fast and can achieve high period lengths.

I created a Perl implementation of the TT800 generator proposed by Matsumoto and Kurita in their paper "Twisted GFSR Generators II." With a period length of 2^{800}, the generator has a long enough cycle for even the most demanding applications, and it has performed very well in all empirical tests done by the pLab group at Salzburg University.

The Perl implementation is almost a 1:1 translation of the original C code. I only had to work around the sign-preserving nature of the right shift operator (>>) in Perl. Furthermore, I added support for multiple independent streams of pseudorandom numbers.

Bridging C and Perl with XS

Although the Perl implementation of TT800 is pretty fast, the speed freaks among us might want to make it even faster by implementing it as an XS module.

XS modules are Perl extensions written in C that can be loaded dynamically when our Perl program runs. They can be used to make low-level system features available to Perl (as seen in the POSIX and Fcntl modules), or to link in external C libraries such as Tk, GDBM, and NDBM. We use XS primarily for the speed boost it provides.

I'll report on what I had to do for this simple case; full documentation on this topic can be found in the *perlxstut* and *perlxs* online documentation.

XS Overview

The glue between Perl and C is provided by the XS language. XS lets us create *.xs* files containing XSUBs, stub subroutines that we use to enable Perl to supply data to, and understand the return values of, a C function. We can embed C code directly in the *.xs* file, but typically the XSUB calls functions declared in previously existing *.c* files.

Using the interface definitions and code fragments in the *.xs* file, the *xsubpp* program bundled with Perl generates C code that does all the bridging for us. The whole process of writing an extension module is closely guided by various programs in our Perl distribution. (Editor's note: the SWIG utility, which wasn't available when

Otmar wrote this article, can further automate the creation of some XS code; and Perl 6 is likely to do away with XS altogether. See the article *SWIG*, later in this book, for more details.)

One of these programs is *h2xs*, which helps generate a framework for the XS module. In our case, invoking h2xs -A -n Math::TT800 creates six files: *TT800.pm*, *TT800.xs*, *Changes*, *MANIFEST*, *Makefile.PL*, and *test.pl*.

Types and the Typemap

The next step is deciding how to map the data types between Perl and C. In this case we can equate the C struct tt800_state with the Math:TT800 object in Perl. On the C side we create a *tt800.h* include file containing the type declarations, as shown in Example 27-1.

Example 27-1. tt800.h

```
#define TT800_N 25
#define TT800_M 7
#define TT800_INV_MOD 2.3283064370807974e-10 /* 1.0 / (2^32-1) */

struct tt800_state {
  U32 x[TT800_N]; /* Uses the Perl type U32 */
  int k;
};

typedef struct tt800_state *TT800;

extern struct tt800_state tt800_initial_state;
U32 tt800_get_next_int(TT800 g);
```

Next, we create the *typemap* file containing the mapping instructions. We could map TT800, to the predefined Perl type T_PTROBJ; that would automatically bless all C TT800 structs to a Perl object of the same name. But since we want the Perl object to be named Math::TT800, we simply adapt the definition of T_PTROBJ and create the typemap file shown in Example 27-2.

Example 27-2. typemap

```
TYPEMAP
TT800 T_TT800

INPUT
T_TT800
  if (sv_isa($arg, \"Math::TT800\")) {
    IV tmp = SvIV((SV*)SvRV($arg));
    $var = ($type) tmp;
  }
  else croak(\"$var not of type Math::TT800\")
```

Example 27-2. typemap (continued)

```
OUTPUT
T_TT800
  sv_setref_pv($arg, \"Math::TT800\", (void*) $var);
```

(On my system, the predefined type mappings are in */usr/lib/perl5/ExtUtils/*typemap.)
We place the C implementation of the main generation function of TT800 in the file
tt800.c, shown in cs_random_xs_tt800. See Example 27-3.

Example 27-3. tt800.c

```c
#include "EXTERN.h"
#include "perl.h"
#include "tt800.h"

struct tt800_state tt800_initial_state = {
    { /* initial 25 seeds */
        0x95f24dab, 0x0b685215, 0xe76ccae7, 0xaf3ec239, 0x715fad23, 0x24a590ad,
        0x69e4b5ef, 0xbf456141, 0x96bc1b7b, 0xa7bdf825, 0xc1de75b7, 0x8858a9c9,
        0x2da87693, 0xb657f9dd, 0xffdc8a9f, 0x8121da71, 0x8b823ecb, 0x885d05f5,
        0x4e20cd47, 0x5a9ad5d9, 0x512c0c03, 0xea857ccd, 0x4cc1d30f, 0x8891a8a1,
        0xa6b7aadb
    },
    0 /* initial k */
};

static unsigned int mag01[2] = { 0x0, 0x8ebfd028 };

U32 tt800_get_next_int(TT800 g) {
  U32 y;

  if (g->k == TT800_N) { /* generate TT800_N words at once */
    int kk;

    for (kk=0; kk < TT800_N - TT800_M; kk++) {
      g->x[kk] = g->x[kk+TT800_M] ^ (g->x[kk]>> 1) ^ mag01[g->x[kk]&1];
    }

    for (; kk<TT800_N; kk++) {
      g->x[kk] = g->x[kk+(TT800_M-TT800_N)]^(g->x[kk]>>1)^mag01[g->x[kk]&1];
    }

    g->k=0;
  }

  y = g->x[g->k];
  y ^= (y << 7) & 0x2b5b2500;
  y ^= (y << 15) & 0xdb8b0000;
  g->k++;
  y ^= (y>> 16); /* added in the 1996 version of the tt800 */
  return(y);
}
```

This completes the C part of the extension module. We now write the XS functions implementing the Perl module by augmenting the skeleton *TT800.xs* generated by h2xs. The result is the XS file shown in Example 27-4.

Example 27-4. TT800.xs

```
#ifdef __cplusplus
extern "C" {
#endif
#include "EXTERN.h"
#include "perl.h"
#include "XSUB.h"
#include <string.h>
#ifdef __cplusplus
}
#endif

#include "tt800.h"

MODULE = Math::TT800      PACKAGE = Math::TT800

TT800 new(class = "Math::TT800", ...)
  char * class
  CODE:
    {
      int i;
      RETVAL = (TT800) safemalloc(sizeof(struct tt800_state));
      memcpy(RETVAL, (char * ) &tt800_initial_state,
             sizeof(struct tt800_state));

      if ( items > (TT800_N + 1))
        items = TT800_N + 1;
        for (i = 1; i < items; i++)
          RETVAL->x[i-1] = (U32) SvIV(ST(i));
    }

  OUTPUT:
    RETVAL

void DESTROY(tt)
  TT800 tt
  CODE:
    safefree((char *) tt);

U32 next_int(tt)
  TT800 tt
  CODE:
    RETVAL = tt800_get_next_int(tt);
  OUTPUT:
    RETVAL

double next(tt)
  TT800 tt
```

Example 27-4. TT800.xs (continued)

```
CODE:
  RETVAL = tt800_get_next_int(tt) * TT800_INV_MOD;
OUTPUT:
  RETVAL
```

The new is of particular interest. First, it allocates memory for the C structure tt800_state (and therefore for the the Math::TT800 object as well) in RETVAL, which will eventually be returned by the XSUB. Then we initialize the generator by copying the default state with memcpy. If there were additional parameters (indicated by the items variable predefined by XS), we extract the integer value (SvIV) from the ith parameter (ST(i)) and store it in the state vector RETVAL. We don't need to manually bless the return value here; that's taken care of by the *typemap* file.

In order to compile the extension module, we need to adjust *Makefile.PL*, shown in Example 27-5.

Example 27-5. Makefile.PL

```
use ExtUtils::MakeMaker;

# See lib/ExtUtils/MakeMaker.pm for details
# of how to change the Makefile created by
# MakeMaker.

WriteMakefile(
  'NAME'         => 'Math::TT800',
  'DISTNAME'     => 'Math-TT800',
  'VERSION_FROM' => 'TT800.pm',
  'OBJECT'       => 'TT800.o tt800.o',
  'LIBS'         => [''], # e.g. '-lm'
  'DEFINE'       => '',    # e.g. '-DHAVE_SOMETHING'
  'INC'          => '', # e.g. '-I/usr/include/foo'
);
```

We're now pretty much done. The only thing left to do is to polish *TT800.pm* by modifying the @EXPORT array, adding documentation, updating the list of files in *MANIFEST*, and including some testing code in *test.pl*. Then we can build the new extension module as follows:

```
% perl Makefile.PL
% make
```

and test it with make test.

The *Makefile* supports two other interesting targets: make dist generates an archive of this extension suitable for uploading to CPAN, and make install adds the module to our computer's Perl library.

From the user's point of view, there is no difference between a module written in pure Perl and an XS module. Using the newly installed Math::TT800 pseudorandom number generator is this simple:

```
#!/usr/bin/perl

use Math::TT800;
$tt = new Math::TT800;

for ($i=0; $i<100; $i++) {
    printf "%.8f\n", $tt->next();
}
```

Writing such Perl extensions may look like black magic at first, but once you begin to understand the basic principles, the implementation is quite simple.

Acknowledgments

Peter Hellekalek leads the pLab group at Salzburg University, and supervised the thesis on which this article is based. The research was supported by the Austrian Science Foundation (FWF), project P11143-MAT.

References

L'Ecuyer, P. Random Number Generation. In *Handbook on Simulation*, Jerry Banks, ed. Wiley, New York, 1997.

Matsumoto, M. and Y. Kurita. Twisted GFSR Generators II. *ACM Trans. Model. Comput. Simul.*, 4:254-266, 1994.

Netscape Communications Corporation. *Potential Vulnerability in Netscape Products.* (*http://www.netscape.com/newsref/std/random_seed_security.html*).

Niederreiter, H. New developments in uniform pseudorandom number and vector generation. In H. Niederreiter and P.J.-S. Shiue, eds., *Monte Carlo and Quasi-Monte Carlo Methods in Scientific Computing*, vol. 106 of *Lecture Notes in Statistics*. Springer-Verlag, New York, 1995.

Schneier, B. *Applied Cryptography First editon.* John Wiley & Sons, Inc., 1993.

PART IV

Programming Techniques

The ten articles in Part III, *Computer Science* covered topics that can be applied to all modern programming languages; in this section, ten articles explore some Perl-specific programming techniques. Mark Jason Dominus begins with *Suffering from Buffering*. In his own words:

> I got tired of hearing people ask in newsgroups and on IRC why their web page output was in the wrong order, so I wrote this article explaining the buffering behavior of the standard I/O library. Those questions still come up, and when someone on IRC asks, "Why is my output coming out in the wrong order?" I get a big charge out of giving them the URL for this article and saying, "Look in the section titled 'Why is my output coming out in the wrong order?'"

Mark Jason follows with two articles on scoping. *Scoping* explains the difference between my and local, and why you should prefer my; *Seven Useful Uses of local* explores the unusual situations in which you really do want to use local.

Next, Johan Vromans demonstrates a few techniques for creating programs that provide command-line switches for their users, and Dan Schmidt follows with a lucid article on how he came to realize that he needed a data type that Perl didn't offer, and how he created it.

Perl lets you declare actions to be taken as your program is being compiled (and before it is run). For instance, when you say use lib '/home/my_perl_modules', Perl will search in that directory for modules. This enables you to create *source filters* that process your program in some way—for instance, decrypting it before execution. Paul Marquess, the designer of source filters, shows you how to use them.

Hildo Biersma follows with an article about how to give familiar Perl operators new behaviors in *Overloading*. This process is frequently used in object-oriented programming (for instance, to define what it means to "add" two objects), and the final three articles in this section continue the object-orientation theme.

Perl's style of object-orientation is elegant precisely because it doesn't put OO on a pedestal. As *Programming Perl* puts it, an object is simply a reference, a class is simply a package, and a method is simply a subroutine. These are simple words about a particular implementation, but they reveal a truth lost on some programmers who try to force everything they write into the OO mold, asking themselves "What classes do I need?" rather than "What problem am I trying to solve?"

But I digress. Enclosed please find three articles showing you some techniques for manipulating the references, packages, and subroutines of Perl's OO. Most Perl programmers create their objects as references to hashes, but Greg Bacon shows you why you might prefer to create them as references to arrays instead in *Building Objects Out of Arrays*. Nigel Chapman follows with a subtle technique for enforcing data privacy by using anonymous subroutines in *Hiding Objects with Closures*. Finally, Damian Conway returns with a more flexible way to control which methods are invoked on your objects in *Multiple Dispatch in Perl*.

## CHAPTER 28

Suffering from Buffering

Mark Jason Dominus

"My log file has nothing in it!"
"My output is coming out in the wrong order!"
"When my program terminates abnormally, the output is incomplete!"
"My web server says I didn't send the right headers, but I'm sure I did!"
"I'm trying to send data over the network, but nothing is sent!"

I'm afraid you're probably a victim of buffering.

What Is Buffering?

All input and output in your programs is performed by your operating system. When Perl wants to read data from the disk, or to write it to the network, or to read or write data anywhere, Perl has to make a request to the operating system and ask that the data be read or written. This is an example of "making a system call." (Don't confuse this with Perl's system function, which is totally unrelated.)

Making a system call is a relatively slow operation. On top of that, if the data is coming from the disk, you might have to wait for the disk to spin to the right position (the *latency time*) and you might have to wait for the disk heads to move over to the right track (the *seek time*). As computer operations go, that wait is unbearably long—typically, several milliseconds. For comparison, a typical computer operation, such as assigning to a variable or adding two numbers, takes a fraction of a microsecond.

Suppose you're reading a 10,000 line file line-by-line:

```
while (<FILE>) { print if /treasure/; }
```

If Perl made a system call for every read operation, that would be 10,001 system calls in all (one extra to detect end-of-file), and if the file was on disk, it would have to wait for the disk at least 10,000 times. That would be very slow.

For efficiency, Perl uses a trick called *buffering*. The first time you ask to read from the file, Perl has to make a system call. Since system calls are expensive, it plans ahead on the assumption that if you read a little bit of text, you'll probably want to read the rest later. The blocks on your disk are probably about 8 kilobytes, and your computer hardware is probably designed to transfer an entire block of data from the disk at once. So instead of asking the system for a little bit of text, Perl actually asks the system for an entire blockful, which takes only a little longer to get than a little bit would have. Then it stores this block of data in a region of memory called a *buffer*, and gives you back the one line you asked for. The next time you ask for a line, Perl already has the line you want in memory in the 8K buffer. It doesn't have to make another system call; it just gives you the next line out of the buffer. Eventually you read up to the end of the buffer, and then Perl makes another system call to get another bufferful of data.

If lines typically have about 60 characters each plus a newline, then the 10,000-line file has about 610,000 characters in it. Reading the file line-by-line with buffering only requires 75 system calls and 75 waits for the disk, instead of 10,001. On my system, a simple program with buffered reading ran about 40% faster than the corresponding program that made a system call for every line.

For writing, Perl uses the same trick. When you write data to a file with `print`, the data doesn't normally go into the file right away. Instead, it goes into a buffer. When the buffer is full, Perl writes all the data in the buffer at once. This is called *flushing the buffer*. Here the performance gain is even bigger than for reading, about 60%.

But the buffering can sometimes surprise you.

Surprise!

Imagine you have a program like this:

```
foreach $item (@items) {
    think_for_a_long_time($item);
    print LOG "Finished thinking about $item.\n";
}
```

Suppose there are 1,000 items, and the program has to think about each one for two minutes. The program will take about 35 hours to complete, and you'd like to be able to peek at the log file to see how it is doing. You start up the program, wait ten minutes, and peek at the log file—but there's nothing there. Disaster! What happened? Is the program stuck? Is it taking five times as long to think about the items as you thought it would?

No, the program is not stuck, or even slow. The problem is that the prints to the log file are being buffered. The program has thought about the first five items, and it wrote the log messages for them, but the writes went into the buffer, and Perl isn't going to make a system call to send the buffer to the disk until the buffer is full. The buffer is probably 8K bytes, and the log messages are about 28 bytes each, so what's going to happen is that you won't see anything in the log file for about 10 hours, when the first 292 messages will appear all at once. After that, you won't get any more messages for another 10 hours.

That's a problem, because it's not what you wanted. Here you don't really care about the efficiency gain of buffered writes. On the plus side, you're saving about 4 seconds over the 35-hour lifetime of the program. On the minus side, it's making your log facility useless. You think having the log is worth waiting an extra four seconds, so you'd like to turn off the buffering.

Disabling Inappropriate Buffering

In Perl, you can't turn the buffering off, but you can get the same benefits by making the filehandle *hot*. Whenever you print to a hot filehandle, Perl flushes the buffer immediately. In the log file example, Perl will flush the buffer every time you write another line to the log file, so the log file will always be up-to-date.

Here's how to make the filehandle hot:

```
{
  my $ofh = select LOG;
  $| = 1;
  select $ofh;
}
```

The key item here is the $| variable. If you set it to a true value, it makes the current filehandle hot. What's the current filehandle? It's the one last selected with the select operator. So to make LOG hot, you select it, set $| to a true value, and then you re-select whatever filehandle was selected before we selected LOG.

Now that LOG is hot, Perl will flush the buffer every time you print to LOG, so messages will appear in the log file as soon as you print them.

Sometimes you might see code like this:

```
select((select(LOG), $|=1)[0]);
```

That's a compressed way of writing the code above that makes LOG hot.

If you happen to be using the FileHandle or IO modules, there's a nicer way to write this:

```
use FileHandle; # Or "IO::Handle" or "IO::"-anything-else
...
LOG->autoflush(1); # Make LOG hot.
...
```

Hot and Not Hot

If Perl is really buffering output, how is it you didn't notice it before? For example, run this program, called favorite:

```
print "What is your favorite number? ";
$num = <STDIN>;
$mine = $num + 1;
print "Well, my favorite is $mine, which is a much better number.\n";
```

```
% ./favorite
What is your favorite number? 119
Well, my favorite is 120, which is a much better number.
```

If you run this, you find that it works the way you expect: the prompt appears on the screen right away. Where's the buffering? Why didn't Perl save up the output until it had a full buffer? Because that's almost never what you want when you're writing to a terminal, the standard I/O library that Perl uses takes care of it for you. When a filehandle is attached to the terminal, as STDOUT is here, it is in "line buffered mode" by default. A filehandle in line buffered mode has two special properties: it's flushed automatically whenever you print a newline character to it, and it's flushed automatically whenever you read from the terminal. The second property is at work here: STDOUT is flushed automatically when you read from STDIN.

But now let's try it with STDOUT attached to a file instead of to the terminal:

```
% ./favorite > OUTPUT
```

Here the STDOUT filehandle has been attached to the file OUTPUT. The program has printed the prompt to the file, and is waiting for you to enter your favorite number. But if you open another window and look into OUTPUT, you'll see that the prompt that favorite printed isn't in the file yet; it's still in the buffer. STDOUT is attached to a file, rather than to a terminal, so it isn't line buffered; only filehandles attached to the terminal are line buffered by default.

When the program finishes, it flushes all its buffers, so after you enter your favorite number all the output, including the prompt, appears in the file at the same time.

There's one other exception to the rule that says that filehandles are cold unless they're attached to the terminal: the filehandle STDERR, which is normally used for error logging, is never buffered. If the original example had used STDERR instead of LOG, you wouldn't have had the buffering problem.

Other Perils of Buffering

We've covered the first complaint at the beginning of this article. In this section, we'll cover the remaining four.

"My Output Is Coming Out in the Wrong Order!"

Here's a typical program that exhibits this common problem:

```
print "FILE LISTING OF DIRECTORY $dir:\n";
print "--------------------------------\n";
system("ls -l $dir");
print "--------------------------------\n";
```

On a terminal, this comes out okay. But if you run it with STDOUT redirected to a file, it doesn't work: the header appears after the file listing, instead of at the top.

Why didn't it work? Standard output is buffered, so the header lines are saved in the buffer and don't get to the file just yet. Then you run ls, which has its own buffer;

that buffer is flushed when ls exits, and the ls output is appended to the file. Then you print the footer line and it goes into your program's buffer. Finally, your program finishes and flushes its buffer, and all three lines go into the output file, after the output from ls. To fix this, make STDOUT hot.

Now that you know why the data got into the file in the wrong order, that raises another question: if you have it print to the terminal, why does the output come out in the right order instead of the wrong order? Because when STDOUT is attached to the terminal, it is in line buffered mode, and is flushed automatically whenever you print a newline character to it. The two header lines are flushed immediately, because they end with newlines; then comes the output of ls, and finally the footer line.

"My Web Server Says I Didn't Send the Right Headers, but I'm Sure I Did!"

Here's a typical program that exhibits this common problem:

```
print "Content-type: text/html\n\n";
print "<title>What Time Is It?</title>\n";
print "<h1>The Current Time in Philadelphia is</h1>\n\n";
print "<pre>\n";
system("date");
print "</pre>\n\n";
```

You might think that the output is going to come out in the order you put it in the program: the Content-type header, then the title, with the date in between the pre tags. But it isn't. The print statements execute, but the output goes into your program's buffer. Then you run date, which generates some output, this time into the date command's buffer. When date exits (almost immediately), this buffer is flushed, and the server (which is listening to your standard output) gets the date before it gets the output from your prints; your print data is still in the buffer. Later, when your program exits, its own buffer is flushed and the server gets the output from the prints.

The server was expecting to see that Content-type line first, but it got the date first. It can't proceed without knowing the content-type of the output, so it gives up and sends a message to the browser that says something like 500 Internal Server Error.

Solution 1: make STDOUT hot.

Solution 2: collect the output from date yourself and insert it into your buffer in the appropriate place:

```
...
$the_date = `date`;
print $the_date;
...
```

Here's a similar sort of problem that stems from a program aborting prematurely:

```
print "Content-type: text/html\n\n";

print "<title>Division Table</title>\n";
print "<h1>Division Table</h1>\n\n";
```

```
for (i=0; $i<10; $i++) {
    for (j=0; $j<10; $j++) {
        print $i/$j, "\t"; # Ooops
    }
    print "\n";
}
```

This program will abort when it divides by zero, and it's going to print the message:

```
Illegal division by zero at division.cgi line 8.
```

What you actually see on your web browser depends on the details of the web server, but here's one possible scenario: the server will collect all the output from your program, and send it back to the browser. You might think that the Content-type line will come first, followed by the title, and then the division by zero message, but you'd be wrong. The content-type and the title are printed to STDOUT, which is buffered, but the division by zero message is printed to STDERR, which isn't buffered. The result is that the content-type and title are buffered. The error message arrives, and when the program exits, the STDOUT buffer is flushed and the content-type and title arrive at last. The server expects to see the content-type right away, gets confused because it appears to be missing, and reports an error.

As usual, you can fix this by making STDOUT hot. Another way to fix it is to redirect error messages to a separate file, like this:

```
open STDERR, "> /tmp/division.err";
```

Here's a third way:

```
use CGI::Carp 'fatalsToBrowser';
```

The CGI::Carp module arranges for fatal error messages to be delivered to the browser with a simple prefabricated HTTP header, so that the browser displays the error message properly.

"I'm Trying to Send Data over the Network, but Nothing Is Sent!"

This problem is the plague of novice network applications programmers; it bites almost everyone the first time they write a network application.

For concreteness, suppose you're writing a mail client that opens a connection to the mail server and tries to send a mail message to it. Your client needs to use SMTP (Simple Mail Transfer Protocol) to talk to the server. In SMTP, the client opens a connection and then engages the server in a conversation that goes something like this:

```
Server says: 220 gradin.cis.upenn.edu ESMTP
Client says: HELO plover.com
Server: 250 gradin.cis.upenn.edu Hello mailuser@plover.com
Client: MAIL From: <mjd@plover.com>
Server: 250 <mjd@plover.com>... Sender ok
```

And so on.

The usual complaint is: "I opened the connection all right, and I got the greeting from the server, but it isn't responding to my client's commands!" By now you know the reason why: the client's output to the network socket is being buffered, and Perl is waiting to send the data over the network until there's a whole bufferful. The server hasn't responded because it hasn't received anything to respond to.

The solution is to make the socket filehandle hot. Another solution involves using the IO::Socket module; recent versions (since Version 1.18) make sockets hot by default.

"When My Program Terminates Abnormally, the Output Is Incomplete!"

When the program exits normally, by executing die or exit or by reaching the end of the program, it flushes all the buffers. But if the program is killed suddenly, it might exit without flushing the buffers, and then the output files will be incomplete. The Unix kill command destroys a process in this way and can leave behind incomplete files.

Even worse, a file that exits in this way can leave behind *corrupt* data. For example, imagine a program that writes out a database file. The database file is supposed to contain records of exactly 57 characters each.

Suppose the program has printed out 1,000 records, and then someone kills it and it doesn't have a chance to flush its buffer. It turns out that only 862 complete records made it into the file, but that's not the worst part. The buffer is flushed every 8,192 bytes, and 57 does not divide 8,192 evenly, so the last record that was flushed to the file is incomplete; only its first 18 bytes appear in the file. The other 39 bytes were still in the buffer, and they're lost. The file is now corrupted, and any program that reads it assuming that each record is exactly 57 bytes long is going to get garbled data and produce the wrong results.

One possible solution to this is to simply make the filehandle hot. Another is to do the buffering yourself: accumulate 57-byte records into a scalar variable until you have a lot of them, and then write them all at once. A third solution is to use a method called setvbuf, provided by the FileHandle and IO:: modules, to make the buffer size an exact multiple of 57 bytes; then it'll never contain any partial records when it's flushed. That looks like this:

```
use IO::Handle '_IOFBF'; # FBF means Fully Buffered

FH->setvbuf($buffer_var, _IOFBF, 8151);
```

(I picked 8,151 because it's the largest number less than 8K that is a multiple of 57.) A fourth solution is to manually flush the buffer before it is completely full. The next section explains how to do this.

Flushing on Command

Sometimes you'd like to have buffering, but you want to control when the buffer is flushed. For example, suppose you're writing a lot of data over the network to a logging service. For efficiency, you'd like buffering, but you don't want the log to get too far out of date. You want to let data accumulate in the buffer for up to ten seconds, and then flush it out, at least six times per minute.

Here's a typical strategy for doing that:

```
if (time > $last_flush_time + 10) {
    my $ofh = select LOG;
    $| = 1;                 # Make LOG socket hot
    print LOG "";           # print nothing
    $| = 0;                 # LOG socket is no longer hot
    select $ofh;
    $last_flush_time = time;
}
... Do something else ...
```

You select the LOG filehandle and make it temporarily hot. Then you print an empty string to the filehandle. Because the handle is hot, this flushes the buffer—printing to a hot filehandle always flushes the buffer. Finally, you return the filehandle to its unhot state so that future writes to LOG will be buffered.

If you're using the FileHandle or IO modules, there's a simpler interface:

```
$filehandle->flush( ); # Flush the buffer
```

It does exactly the same as the code above.

Other Directions

If for some reason you want to avoid buffering entirely, you can use Perl's sysread and syswrite operators. These don't use buffering at all. That makes them slow, but they are often appropriate for tasks such as network communications, in which you don't want buffering, anyway. All Perl's other I/O functions, including write, print, read, <FILEHANDLE>, and getc, are buffered. If you do both buffered and unbuffered I/O on the same filehandle, you're likely to confuse yourself, so beware.

Summary

For efficiency, Perl does not read or write the disk or the network when you ask it to. Instead, it reads and writes large chunks of data to a buffer in memory, and performs I/O on the buffer; this sequence is much faster than making a request to the operating system for every read or write. Usually this is what you want, but sometimes the buffering causes problems. Typical problems include communicating with conversational network services and writing up-to-date log files. In such circumstances, you would like to disable the buffering. You can do that in Perl by setting $|=1. This special variable makes the currently selected filehandle hot, so that the buffer is flushed after every write.

## CHAPTER 29

Scoping

Mark Jason Dominus

In the Beginning, some time around 1960, every part of a program had access to all the variables in every other part of the program. This caused a lot of bugs when people forgot where their variables were used, so language designers invented local variables, which were visible in only a small part of the program. That way, programmers who used a variable x could be sure nobody tampered with the contents of x behind their back. They could also be sure that by using x, they weren't tampering with someone else's variable by mistake.

Every programming language has a philosophy, and these days most of these philosophies have to do with the way the names of variables are managed. Details of which variables are visible to which parts of the program, and what names mean what, and when, are of prime importance. The details vary from somewhat baroque, in languages like Lisp, to extremely baroque, in languages like C++. Unfortunately, Perl is on the rococo end of this scale.

The problem with Perl isn't that it has no clearly defined system of name management, but rather that it two systems, both working at once. Here's the Big Secret about Perl variables that most people learn too late: Perl has *two* completely separate, independent sets of variables. One is left over from Perl 4 (the way your vermiform appendix and midbrain are left over from a previous geologic era), and the other set is new. The two sets of variables are called *package variables* and *lexical variables*, and they have nothing to do with each other.

Package variables came first, so I'll talk about them first. Then I'll demonstrate some problems with package variables, and how lexical variables were introduced in Perl 5 to avoid these problems. Finally, I'll show you how to get Perl to automatically diagnose places where you might not be getting the variable you meant to get, and find mistakes before they turn into bugs.

Package Variables

If you have a simple line like this in your program:

```
$x = 1
```

then $x is a package variable. There are two important things to know about package variables:

1. Package variables are what you get if you don't say otherwise.
2. Package variables are *always* global.

"Global" means that package variables are always visible everywhere in every program. After you do $x = 1, any other part of the program—even some other subroutine defined in another file—can inspect and modify the value of $x. There's no exception to this; package variables are always global. Don't say "But...." There are no buts.

Package variables are divided into families, called *packages*. Every package variable has a name with two parts. The two parts are like the variable's given name and family name. You can call our ex-Vice-President of the United States "Al," if you want, but that's really short for his full name, which is "Al Gore." Similarly, $x has a full name, which is something like $main::x. The main part is the *package qualifier*, analogous to the "Gore" part of "Al Gore." Al Gore and Al Capone are different people even though they're both named "Al." In the same way, $Gore::Al and $Capone::Al are different variables, and $main::x and $DBI::x are different variables.

You're always allowed to include the package part of the variable's name, and if you do, Perl will know exactly which variable you mean. But for brevity, you usually like to leave the package qualifier off. What happens if you do?

The Current Package

If you just say $x, Perl assumes that you mean the variable $x in the current package. What's the current package? It's normally main, but you can change the current package by writing:

```
package Mypackage;
```

in your program; from that point on, the current package is Mypackage. The only thing the current package does is affect the interpretation of package variables that you wrote without package names. If the current package is Mypackage, then $x really means $Mypackage::x. If the current package is main, then $x really means $main::x.

If you were writing a module, let's say the MyModule module, you would probably put a line like this at the top of the module file:

```
package MyModule;
```

Thereafter, all the package variables you used in the module file would be in package MyModule, and you could be pretty sure that those variables wouldn't conflict with the variables in the rest of the program. It wouldn't matter if both you and the author of DBI were to use a variable named $x, because one of those would be $MyModule::x and the other would be $DBI::x.

Remember that package variables are always global. Even if you're not in package DBI, even if you've never *heard* of package DBI, nothing can stop you from reading from or writing to $DBI::errstr. You don't have to do anything special. $DBI::errstr, like all package variables, is a global variable, and it's available globally; all you have to do is mention its full name to get it. You could even say:

```
package DBI;
$errstr = 'Ha ha Tim!';
```

in your own file, and that would modify $DBI::errstr.

Package Variable Trivia

There are only three other things to know about package variables, and you might want to skip them on the first reading:

1. The package with the empty name is the same as main. So $::x is the same as $main::x for any x.

2. Some variables are always forced to be in package main. For example, if you mention %ENV, Perl assumes that you mean %main::ENV, even if the current package isn't main. If you want %Fred::ENV, you have to say so explicitly, even if the current package is Fred. Other names that are special this way include INC, all the one-punctuation-character names like $_ and $$, @ARGV, and STDIN, STDOUT, and STDERR.

3. Package names can contain ::, but not variable names. You can have a variable named $DBD::Oracle::x. This means the variable x in the package DBD::Oracle; it has nothing at all to do with the package DBD, which is unrelated. Isaac Newton is not related to Olivia Newton-John, and $Newton::Isaac is not related to $Newton::John::Olivia. Even though it appears that they both begin with Newton, the appearance is deceptive. $Newton::John::Olivia is in package Newton::John, not package Newton. The slogan is: "Packages do not nest."

That's all there is to know about package variables.

Package variables are global, which is dangerous, because you can never be sure that someone isn't tampering with them behind your back. Up through Perl 4, all variables were package variables, which was worrisome. So Perl 5 added new variables that aren't global.

Lexical Variables

Perl's other set of variables are called *lexical variables* (I'll explain why later) or *private variables* because they're private. They're also sometimes called "my variables" because they're always declared with my. It's tempting to call them "local variables," because their effect is confined to a small part of the program, but don't do that, because people might think you're talking about Perl's local operator, which I'll discuss later. When you want a "local variable," think my, not local.

The declaration:

```
my $x;
```

creates a new variable, named x, which is totally inaccessible to most parts of the program—the whole program, except for the block in which the variable was declared. This block is called the *scope* of the variable. If the variable wasn't declared in any block, its scope is the entire file, beginning at the place it was declared.

You can also declare and initialize a my variable by writing something like this:

```
my $x = 119;
```

You can even declare and initialize several at once:

```
my ($x, $y, $z, @args) = (5, 23, @_);
```

Let's see an example in which some private variables are useful. Consider this subroutine:

```
sub print_report {
    @employee_list = @_;
    foreach $employee (@employee_list) {
        $salary = lookup_salary($employee);
        print_partial_report($employee, $salary);
    }
}
```

If lookup_salary happens to also use a variable named $employee, that's going to be the same variable as the one used in print_report, and the works might get gummed up. lookup_salary might modify $employee in a way that takes print_report by surprise, and then print_report might do the wrong thing. The two programmers responsible for print_report and lookup_salary will have to coordinate to make sure they don't use the same variables. That's a pain. In fact, even for a medium-sized project, it's an intolerable pain.

The solution is to use my variables:

```
sub print_report {
    my @employee_list = @_;
    foreach my $employee (@employee_list) {
        my $salary = lookup_salary($employee);
        print_partial_report($employee, $salary);
    }
}
```

my @employee_list creates a new array variable that is totally inaccessible outside the print_report function. foreach my $employee creates a new scalar variable that is totally inaccessible outside the foreach loop, as does my $salary. You don't have to worry that the other functions in the program are tampering with these variables, because they can't; they don't know where to find them since the names have different meanings outside the scope of the my declarations.

These my variables are sometimes called *lexical* because their scope depends only on the program text itself, and not on details of execution, such as what is executed in what order. You can determine the scope by inspecting the source code without knowing what it does. Whenever you see a variable, look for a my declaration higher up in the same block. If you find one, you can be sure that the variable is inaccessible outside that block. If you don't find a declaration in the smallest block, look at the next larger block that contains it, and so on, until you find one. If there is no my declaration anywhere, the variable is a package variable.

my variables are not package variables. They're not part of a package, and they don't have package qualifiers. The current package has no effect on the way they're interpreted. Here's an example:

```
my $x = 17;

package A;
$x = 12;

package B;
$x = 20;

# $x is now 20.
# $A::x and $B::x remain undefined
```

The declaration my $x = 17 at the top creates a new lexical variable named x with a scope that continues to the end of the file. This new meaning of $x overrides the default meaning, which was that $x meant the package variable $x in the current package.

package A changes the current package, but because $x refers to the lexical variable, not to the package variable, $x = 12 has no effect on $A::x. Similarly, after package B the expression $x = 20 modifies the lexical variable, and none of the package variables.

At the end of the file, the lexical variable $x holds 20, and the package variables $main::x, $A::x, and $B::x are still undefined. If you had wanted them, you could have accessed them explicitly by using their full names.

The rules you must remember are: package variables are global variables; and for private variables, you must use my.

local and my

Almost everyone already knows that there's a local function that has something to do with local variables. What is it, and how does it related to my? The answer is simple, but bizarre: my creates a local variable, but local doesn't.

First, here's what local $x really does: it saves the current value of the package variable $x in a safe place, and replaces it with a new value or with undef if no new value is specified. It also arranges for the old value to be restored when control leaves the current block. The variables that it affects are package variables. But package variables are always global, and a local package variable is no exception. To see the difference, try this:

```perl
$lo = 'global';
$m  = 'global';
A();

sub A {
    local $lo = 'string';
    my    $m  = 'string';
    B();
}

sub B {
    print "B ", ($lo eq 'string' ? 'can' : 'cannot'),
                " see the value of lo set by A.\n";
    print "B ", ($m eq 'string' ? 'can' : 'cannot'),
                " see the value of m set by A.\n";
}
```

This prints:

```
B can see the value of lo set by A.
B cannot see the value of m set by A.
```

What happened here? The local declaration in A saved a new temporary value, string, in the package variable $lo. The old value, global, will be restored when A returns, but before that happens, A calls B. B has no problem accessing the contents of $lo, because $lo is a package variable and package variables are always available everywhere. So it can detect the local value, string, that was set in A.

In contrast, the my declaration created a new, lexically scoped variable named $m, which is only visible inside of function A. Outside of A, $m retains its old meaning: it refers to the package variable $m; still set to global. This is the variable that B sees. It can't see the value string, because the variable with the value string is a lexical variable, and only exists inside of A.

What Good Is local?

Because local does not actually create local variables, it is not of very much use. If B happened to modify the value of $1 in the example above, then the value set by A would be overwritten. That is exactly what you don't want to happen. You want each function to have its own variables, untouchable by the others. This is what my does.

Why have local at all? The answer is 90% history. Early versions of Perl had only global variables. local was very easy to implement, and was added to Perl 4 as a partial solution to the local variable problem. Later, in Perl 5, more work was done, and real local variables were put into the language. But the name "local" was already taken, so the new feature was invoked with the word "my." my was chosen because it suggests privacy, and also because it's very short; the shortness is supposed to encourage you to use it instead of local. my is also faster than local.

When to Use my and When to Use local

Always use my; never use local.

Wasn't that easy?

Other Properties of my Variables

Whenever Perl reaches a my declaration, it creates a new, fresh variable. For example, this code prints x=1 50 times:

```
for (1 .. 50) {
    my $x;
    $x++;
    print "x=$x\n";
}
```

You get a new $x, initialized to undef, every time through the loop.

If the my were outside the loop, control would only pass it once, so there would only be one variable:

```
{ my $x;
  for (1 .. 50) {
      $x++;
      print "x=$x\n";
  }
}
```

This prints x=1, x=2, ..., x=50.

You can use this to play a useful trick. Suppose you have a function that needs to remember a value from one call to the next. For example, consider a random number generator. A typical random number generator (like Perl's rand function) has a *seed* in it. The seed is just a number. When you ask the random number generator for a random number, the function performs an arithmetic operation that scrambles the seed, returning the result. It also saves the result and uses it as the seed for the next call.

Here's typical code (I stole it from the ANSI C standard, but it behaves poorly, so don't use it for anything important):

```
$seed = 1;
sub my_rand {
    $seed = int(($seed * 1103515245 + 12345) / 65536) % 32768;
    return $seed;
}
```

And typical output:

```
16838
14666
10953
11665
```

```
7451
26316
27974
27550
```

There's a problem. $seed is a global variable, and that means you have to worry that someone might inadvertently tamper with it. Or they might tamper with it on purpose, which could affect the rest of the program. What if the function were used in a gambling program, and someone tampered with the random number generator?

But you can't declare $seed as a my variable in the function:

```
sub my_rand {
    my $seed;
    $seed = int(($seed * 1103515245 + 12345) / 65536) % 32768;
    return $seed;
}
```

If you did, it would be initialized to undef every time you called my_rand. You need it to retain its value between calls. Here's the solution:

```
BEGIN {
  { my $seed = 1;
    sub my_rand {
        $seed = int(($seed * 1103515245 + 12345) / 65536) % 32768;
        return $seed;
    }
  }
}
```

The declaration is outside the function. As a result, it only happens once, at the time the program is compiled, not every time the function is called. But it's a my variable, and it's in a block, so it's only accessible to code inside the block. my_rand is the only other thing in the block, so $seed is only accessible to the my_rand function. The whole thing is wrapped in a BEGIN block to make sure $seed is properly initialized during compilation.

$seed is sometimes called a *static* variable, because it stays the same in between calls to the function. (And because there's a similar feature in the C language that is activated by the static keyword.)

my Variable Trivia

Here are three bits of trivia about my you may find useful:

1. You can't declare a variable my if its name is a punctuation character such as $_, @_, or $$. You can't declare the backreference variables $1, $2, etc., as my. The authors of my thought that that would be too confusing.

2. Obviously, you can't say my $DBI::errstr, because it's contradictory—it says that the package variable $DBI::errstr is now a lexical variable. But you *can* say local $DBI::errstr; it saves the current value of $DBI::errstr and arranges for it to be restored at the end of the block.

3. Starting in Perl 5.004, you can write:

```
foreach my $i (@list) {
```

instead, to confine $i to the scope of the loop. Similarly,

```
for (my $i=0; $i<100; $i++) {
```

confines the scope of $i to the for loop.

Declarations

If you're writing a function, and you want it to have private variables, you need to declare the variables with my. What happens if you forget?

```
sub function {
    $x = 42;          # Oops, should have meen "my $x = 42".
}
```

In that case, your function modifies the global package variable $x. If you were using that variable for something else, it could be a disaster.

There is protection available that you can enable if you want. If you put:

```
use strict 'vars';
```

at the top of your program, Perl insists that all package variables have an explicit package qualifier. The $x in $x = 42 has no such qualifier, so the program won't even compile; instead, the compiler will abort and deliver this error message:

```
Global symbol "$x" requires explicit package name at ...
```

If you want $x to be a private variable, you can go back and add the my. If you really want to use the global package variable, you can go back and change it to $main::x = 42 or whatever is appropriate.

The package variables named $a and $b are always exempt from strict vars checking, because they're commonly used with the sort function and it would be inconvenient to have to declare them whenever you wanted to use sort.

Just saying use strict turns on strict vars, and several other checks besides. Type perldoc strict for more details.

use vars and our

Now suppose you're writing the Algorithm::KnuthBendix module, and you want the protections of strict vars. But you're afraid that you won't be able to finish the module because your fingers are starting to fall off from typing $Algorithm::KnuthBendix::Error all the time.

Save your fingers and tell strict vars to make an exception:

```
package Algorithm::KnuthBendix;
use vars '$Error';
```

This exempts $Algorithm::KnuthBendix::Error from triggering a strict vars failure if you refer to it by its short name, $Error.

Starting in Perl 5.6, there is another solution: the our declaration. The use of our is similar to use vars; the example above would become:

```
package Algorithm::KnuthBendix;
our $Error;
```

One benefit of the our declaration is that its syntax is less bizarre than that of use vars. The syntax of our is exactly the same as the syntax of my, so you may write our $Error = 1 or our($x, $y);, for example. Another benefit of our is that its effect is confined to the block in which it appears:

```
use strict 'vars';
{ our $Error;
  $Error = 1; # I meant to do this
}
$Error = 2;    # This was a mistake
```

The $Error = 2 line will cause Perl to report a fatal compile-time error, because it is outside the scope of the our declaration. This is probably what you wanted. If you had used use vars '$Error' intead of our $Error, Perl would not have reported any errors, because the use vars declaration is globally effective.

One thing use vars does that our doesn't is disable Perl's Name used only once: possible typo warning. Perl suppresses this warning for variables that are declared with use vars, but not those declared with our.

What's our really doing? It's actually a variation on my. It declares a lexical variable with the specified name, just as my does, and that's why the variable is exempt from strict vars failures. But where my creates a new, fresh variable, the variable created by our is just another way to get to the package variable with the same name. (You say that the variable declared by our is an *alias* for the package variable.)

Often the simplest thing to do when you want to get around strict vars is to turn it off. You can also turn strict vars off for the scope of one block by writing

```
{ no strict 'vars';
  # strict vars is off for the rest of the block.
}
```

This leaves the strict vars protections in place for the entire file, except for the one block in which it's off.

Summary

Package variables are always global. They have a name and a package qualifier. You can omit the package qualifier, in which case Perl uses a default that is set with the package declaration. For private variables, use my. Don't use local; it's obsolete. Avoid using global variables because it can be hard to be sure that no two parts of the program are using the same global variables by mistake.

To avoid using global variables by accident, add use strict 'vars' to your program. It checks to make sure that all variables are either declared private, explicitly qualified with package qualifiers, or explicitly declared with use vars or our.

## CHAPTER 30

Seven Useful Uses of local

Mark Jason Dominus

In *Scoping*, I offered the advice "Always use my; never use local." The most common use for both is to provide subroutines with private variables, and for this application you should always use my, and never local. But many readers (and TPJ's tech editors) noted that local isn't entirely useless; there are cases in which my doesn't work, or doesn't do what you want. I promised a followup article on useful uses for local; here they are.

1. Special Variables

my makes most uses of local obsolete. So it's not surprising that the most common useful uses of local arise because of peculiar cases where my happens to be illegal.

The most important examples are the punctuation variables such as $", $/, $^W, and $_. Long ago, Larry Wall decided it would be too confusing if you could my them; they're exempt from the normal package scheme for the same reason. If you want to change them, but have the change apply to only part of the program, you'll have to use local.

As an example of where this might be useful, let's consider a function whose job is to read in an entire file and return its contents as a single string:

```perl
sub getfile {
    my $filename = shift;
    open F, "< $filename" or die "Couldn't open `$filename': $!";
    my $contents = '';
    while (<F>) {
        $contents .= $_;
    }
    close F;
    return $contents;
}
```

This is inefficient, because the <F> operator makes Perl go to all the trouble of breaking the file into lines and returning them one at a time, and then all you do is put them back together again. It's cheaper to read the file all at once, without the splitting and reassembling. (Some people call this *slurping* the file.) Perl has a special feature to support this. If the $/ variable is undefined, the <> operator will read the entire file all at once.

```
sub getfile {
    my $filename = shift;
    open F, "< $filename" or die "Couldn't open `$filename': $!";
    $/ = undef;                 # Read entire file at once
    $contents = <F>;            # Return file as one single "line"
    close F;
    return $contents;
}
```

There's a serious problem here, which is that $/ is a global variable that affects the semantics of every <> in the entire program. If getfile doesn't put it back the way it was, some other part of the program is probably going to fail disastrously when it tries to read a line of input and gets the rest of the file instead. Normally, you'd use my to make the change local to the functions. But you can't here, because my doesn't work on punctuation variables; you would get this error if you tried:

```
Can't use global $/ in "my" ...
```

Also, more to the point, Perl itself knows that it should look in the global variable $/ to find the input record separator; even if you could create a new private variable with the same name, Perl wouldn't know to look there. Instead, you need to set a temporary value for the global variable $/, and that is exactly what local does:

```
sub getfile {
    my $filename = shift;
    open F, "< $filename" or die "Couldn't open `$filename': $!";
    local $/ = undef;           # Read entire file at once
    $contents = <F>;            # Return file as one single "line"
    close F;
    return $contents;
}
```

The old value of $/ is restored when the function returns. In this example, that's enough for safety. In a more complicated function that might call some other functions in a library somewhere, you'd still have to worry that you might be sabotaging the library functions with your strange $/. It's probably best to confine changes to punctuation variables to the smallest possible part of the program:

```
sub getfile {
    my $filename = shift;
    open F, "< $filename" or die "Couldn't open `$filename': $!";
    my $contents;
    { local $/ = undef;         # Read entire file at once
      $contents = <F>;          # Return file as one single "line"
    }                           # $/ regains its old value
    close F;
    return $contents;
}
```

This is a good practice, even for simple functions like this that don't call any other subroutines. By confining the changes to $/ to just the one line you want to affect, you've prevented the possibility that someone in the future will insert calls to other functions that will break because of the change. This is called *defensive programming*.

Although you may not think about it much, localizing $_ this way can be very important. Here's a slightly different version of getfile, one which throws away comments and blank lines from the file that it gets:

```
sub getfile {
    my $filename = shift;
    local *F;
    open F, "< $filename" or die "Couldn't open `$filename': $!";
    my $contents;
    while (<F>) {
        s/#.*//;                # Remove comments
        next unless /\S/;       # Skip blank lines
        $contents .= $_;        # Save current (nonblank) line
    }
    return $contents;
}
```

This function has a terrible problem: if you call it like this, it clobbers the elements of @array.

```
foreach (@array) {
    ...
    $f = getfile($filename);
    ...
}
```

Why? Because inside a foreach loop, $_ is aliased to the elements of the array; if you change $_, it changes the array. And getfile does change $_. To prevent getfile from sabotaging the $_ of anyone who calls it, getfile should have local $_ at the top.

Other special variables present similar problems. For example, it's sometimes convenient to change $", $,, or $\ to alter the way print works, but if you don't put them back the way they were before you call any other functions, you might get a disaster:

```
# Good style:
{ local $" = ')(';
  print "Array a: (@a)\n";
}
# Program continues safely...
```

Another common situation in which you localize a special variable is when you want to temporarily suppress warning messages. Warnings are enabled by the -w command-line option, which in turn sets the variable $^W to a true value. Resetting $^W to a false value turns the warnings off. An example: my Memoize module (described in the article *Memoization*) creates a frontend to the user's function and then installs it into the symbol table, replacing the original function. That's what it's for, and it would be awfully annoying to get this warning every time someone tries to use that module:

```
Subroutine factorial redefined at Memoize.pm line 113
```

So I have this, which turns off the warning for just the one line:

```
{
  local $^W = 0;                    # Shut UP!
  *{$name} = $tabent->{UNMEMOIZED};
}
```

The old value of $^W is automatically restored after the chance of getting the warning is over.

2. Localized Filehandles

Let's look back at that getfile function. To read the file, it opened the filehandle F. That's fine, unless some other part of the program already opened a filehandle named F, in which case the old file is closed, and when control returns from the function, that other part of the program is going to become very confused and upset. This is the "filehandle clobbering problem."

This is exactly the sort of problem that local variables were supposed to solve. Unfortunately, there's no way to localize a filehandle directly in Perl.

Well, that's not exactly true. There are three ways to do it. First, you can cast a magic spell in which you create an anonymous glob, extract the filehandle from it, and discard the rest of the glob. Second, you can use the Filehandle or IO::Handle modules, which cast the spell I just described, and present you with the results, so that you don't have to perform any sorcery yourself.

The third way to solve the filehandle clobbering problem, the simplest and cheapest, is a little bit obscure. You can't localize the filehandle itself, but you can localize the entry in Perl's symbol table that associates the filehandle's name with the filehandle. This entry is called a *glob*. In Perl, variables don't have names directly; instead the glob has a name, and the glob gathers together the scalar, array, hash, subroutine, and filehandle with that name. In Perl, the glob named F is denoted with *F. To localize the filehandle, you actually localize the entire glob, which is a little hamfisted:

```
sub getfile {
    my $filename = shift;
    local *F;
    open F, "< $filename" or die "Couldn't open `$filename': $!";
    local $/ = undef;          # Read entire file at once
    $contents = <F>;           # Return file as one single "line"
    close F;
    return $contents;
}
```

local on a glob does the same as any other local: it saves the current value somewhere, creates a new value, and arranges for the old value to be restored at the end of the current block. In this case, this sequence means that any filehandle formerly attached to the old *F glob is saved, and the open applies to the filehandle in the new, local glob. At the end of the block, filehandle F regains its old meaning.

This technique works most of the time, except you still have the usual local worries about called subroutines changing the localized values. You can't use my here because globs are all about the Perl symbol table; the lexical variable mechanism is totally different, and there is no such thing as a lexical glob.

With this technique, you have the new problem that getfile can't access $F, @F, or %F either, because you localized them along with the filehandle. But you probably weren't using any global variables anyway. Were you? getfile won't be able to call &F, for the same reason. There are a few ways around this, but the easiest one is that if getfile needs to access @F or to call &F, it should name the local filehandle something other than F.

use FileHandle does have fewer strange problems than using a glob. Unfortunately, it also sucks a few thousand lines of code into your program. Now someone will probably complain that I'm exaggerating, because it isn't really 3,000 lines, some of those are white space, blah, blah, blah. Okay, let's say it's only 300 lines to use FileHandle, probably a gross underestimate. It's still only *one* line to localize the glob. For many programs, localizing the glob is a cheap, simple way to solve the problem.

Localized Filehandles Revisited

When a localized glob goes out of scope, its open filehandle is automatically closed. So the close F in getfile is unnecessary:

```perl
sub getfile {
    my $filename = shift;
    local *F;
    open F, "< $filename" or die "Couldn't open `$filename': $!";
    local $/ = undef;          # Read entire file at once
    return <F>;                # Return file as one single `line'
}   # F is automatically closed here
```

That's such a convenient feature that it's worth using even when you're not worried that you might be clobbering someone else's filehandle. The filehandles that you get from FileHandle and IO::Handle do this also.

Marginal Uses of Localized Filehandles

As I was researching this article, I kept finding common uses for local that turned out not to be useful, because there were simpler and more straightforward ways to do the same thing without using local.

Here is one that turns up far too often. People sometimes want to pass a filehandle to a subroutine, and they know that they can pass a filehandle by passing the entire glob, like this:

```perl
$rec = read_record(*INPUT_FILE);

sub read_record {
    local *FH = shift;
    my $record;
    read FH, $record, 1024;
    return $record;
}
```

Here you pass in the entire glob INPUT_FILE, which includes the filehandle of that name. Inside read_record, you temporarily alias FH to INPUT_FILE, so that the filehandle FH inside the function is the same as whatever filehandle was passed in from outside. When you read from FH, you're actually reading from the filehandle that the caller wanted. But there's a more straightforward way to do the same thing:

```
$rec = read_record(*INPUT_FILE);

sub read_record {
    my $fh = shift;
    my $record;
    read $fh, $record, 1024;
    return $record;
}
```

You can store a glob into a scalar variable, and you can use such a variable in any of Perl's I/O functions wherever you might have used a filehandle name. The local was unnecessary here.

Dirhandles

Filehandles and dirhandles are stored in the same place in Perl, so everything this article says about filehandles applies to dirhandles.

3. The First Class Filehandle Trick

Often you want to put filehandles into an array, or treat them like regular scalars, or pass them to a function, and you can't, because filehandles aren't really first class objects in Perl. As noted above, you can use the FileHandle or IO::Handle packages to construct a scalar that acts something like a filehandle, but there are some definite disadvantages to that approach.

Another approach is to use a glob as a filehandle; it turns out that a glob will fit into a scalar variable, so you can put it into an array or pass it to a function. The only problem with globs is that they are apt to have strange and magical effects on the Perl symbol table. What you really want is a glob that has been disconnected from the symbol table, so that you can use it like a filehandle and forget that it might once have had an effect on the symbol table. It turns out that there is a simple way to do that:

```
my $filehandle = do { local *FH };
```

do introduces a block that will be evaluated and returns the value of the last expression that it contains, which in this case is local *FH. The value of local *FH is a glob. But what glob?

local takes the existing FH glob and temporarily replaces it with a new glob. Then it immediately goes out of scope and puts the old glob back, leaving the new glob without a name. But then it *returns the new, nameless glob*, which is stored into $filehandle. This is just what you wanted: a glob that has been disconnected from the symbol table. You can make a whole bunch of these, if you want:

```
for $i (0 .. 99) {
    $fharray[$i] = do { local *FH };
}
```

You can pass them to subroutines, return them from subroutines, put them in data structures, and give them to Perl's I/O functions like open, close, read, print, and <>, and they'll work just fine.

4. Aliases

Globs are very useful. You can assign an entire glob, as you saw above, and alias an entire symbol in the symbol table. But you don't have to do it all at once. If you say:

```
*GLOB = $reference;
```

then Perl only changes the meaning of part of the glob. If the reference is a scalar reference, it changes the meaning of $GLOB, which now means the same as whatever scalar the reference referred to; @GLOB, %GLOB, and the other parts don't change at all. If the reference is a hash reference, Perl makes %GLOB mean the same as whatever hash the reference referred to, but the other parts stay the same. It is similar for other kinds of references.

You can use this for all sorts of wonderful tricks. For example, suppose you have a function that is going to do a lot of operations on $_[0]{Time}[2] for some reason. You can say:

```
*arg = \$_[0]{Time}[2];
```

and from then on, $arg is synonymous with $_[0]{Time}[2], which might make your code simpler, and probably more efficient, because Perl won't have to go digging through three levels of indirection every time. But you'd better use local, or you'll permanently clobber any $arg variable that already exists. (Gurusamy Sarathy's Alias module does this.)

You can create locally scoped subroutines that are invisible outside a block by saying:

```
*mysub = sub { ... } ;
```

and then call them with mysub(...). But you must use local, or else you'll permanently clobber any mysub subroutine that already exists.

5. Dynamic Scope

local introduces *dynamic scope*, which means that the "local" variable that it declares is inherited by other functions called from the one with the declaration. Usually this isn't what you want, and it's rather a strange feature, unavailable in many programming languages. To see the difference, consider this example:

```
first();

sub first {
    local $x = 1;
```

```
    my    $y = 1;
    second();
}

sub second {
    print "x=", $x, "\n";
    print "y=", $y, "\n";
}
```

The variable $y is a true local variable. It's available only from the place that it's declared up to the end of the enclosing block. In particular, it's unavailable inside of second, which prints "y=", not "y=1". This is is called *lexical scope*.

local, in contrast, does not actually make a local variable. It creates a new "local" value for a *global* variable, which persists until the end of the enclosing block. When control exits the block, the old *value* is restored. But the variable and its new "local" value are still global, and hence accessible to other subroutines called before the old value is restored. second above prints "x=1", because $x is a global variable that temporarily happens to have the value 1. Once first returns, the old value will be restored. *Dynamic scope* is a misnomer, because it's not really a scope at all.

For "local" variables, you almost always want lexical scope, because it ensures that variables you declare in one subroutine can't be tampered with by other subroutines. But every once in a strange while, you actually do want dynamic scope, and that's the time to get local out of your bag of tricks.

Here's the most useful example I could find, and one that really does bear careful study. I'll make my own iteration syntax, in the same family as Perl's grep and map. I'll call it listjoin; it'll combine two lists into one:

```
@list1 = (1,2,3,4,5);
@list2 = (2,3,5,7,11);
@result = listjoin { $a + $b } @list1, @list2;
```

Now the @result is (3,5,8,11,16). Each element of the result is the sum of the corresponding terms from @list1 and @list2. If I wanted differences instead of sums, I could have used { $a - $b }. In general, I can supply any code fragment that does something with $a and $b, and listjoin will use my code fragment to construct the elements in the result list. Here's a first cut at listjoin:

```
sub listjoin (&\@\@) {
```

Oops! The first line already has a lot of magic. I'll stop here and sightsee a while before I go on. The (&\@\@) is a *prototype*. In Perl, a prototype changes the way the function is parsed and the way its arguments are passed.

In (&\@\@), the & warns the Perl compiler to expect to see a brace-delimited block of code as the first argument to this function, and tells Perl that it should pass listjoin a reference to that block. The block behaves just like an anonymous function. The \@\@ says that listjoin should get two other arguments, which *must* be arrays; Perl will pass

---

listjoin references to these two arrays. If any of the arguments are missing, or have the wrong type (a hash instead of an array, for example), Perl signals a compile-time error.

The result of this little wad of punctuation is that I can write:

```
listjoin { $a + $b } @list1, @list2;
```

and Perl will behave as if I had written:

```
listjoin(sub { $a + $b }, \@list1, \@list2);
```

With the prototype, Perl knows enough to let me leave out the parentheses, the sub, the first comma, and the slashes. Perl has too much punctuation already, so take advantage of every opportunity to use less.

Now that that's out of the way, the rest of listjoin is straightforward:

```
sub listjoin (&\@\@) {
    my $code = shift;          # Get the code block
    my $arr1 = shift;          # Get reference to first array
    my $arr2 = shift;          # Get reference to second array
    my @result;

    # Get the length of the shorter array
    my $len = @$arr1 < @$arr2 ? @$arr1 : @$arr2;
    for my $i (0 .. $len-1) {
        my $a = $arr1->[$i];       # Element from array 1 into $a
        my $b = $arr2->[$i];       # Element from array 2 into $b
        push @result, &$code();  # Execute code block and get result
    }
    return @result;
}
```

listjoin simply runs a loop over the elements in the two arrays, putting elements from each into $a and $b, respectively, and then executing the code and pushing the result into @result. All very simple and nice, except that it doesn't work: by declaring $a and $b with my, I've made them lexical, and they're unavailable to $code.

Removing the mys from $a and $b makes it work:

```
$a = $arr1->[$i];
$b = $arr2->[$i];
```

But this solution is boobytrapped. Without the my declaration, $a and $b are *global* variables, and whatever values they had before I ran listjoin are lost.

The correct solution is to use local. This preserves the old values of the $a and $b variables, if there were any, and restores them when listjoin is finished. But because of dynamic scoping, the values set by listjoin are inherited by the code fragment. Here's the correct solution:

```
sub listjoin (&\@\@) {
    my $code = shift;
    my $arr1 = shift;
    my $arr2 = shift;
    my @result;
```

```
        # Get the length of the shorter array
        my $len = @$arr1 < @$arr2 ? @$arr1 : @$arr2;
        for my $i (0 .. $len-1) {
            local $a = $arr1->[$i];
            local $b = $arr2->[$i];
            push @result, &$code();
        }
        return @result;
    }
```

You might worry about another problem: suppose you had strict 'vars' in force. Shouldn't listjoin { $a + $b } be illegal? It should be, because $a and $b are global variables, and the purpose of strict 'vars' is to forbid the use of unqualified global variables.

But actually, there's no problem, because strict 'vars' makes a special exception for $a and $b. These two names, and no others, are exempt from strict 'vars', because if they weren't, sort wouldn't work either, for exactly the same reason. I'm taking advantage of that here by giving listjoin the same kind of syntax that sort has. It's a peculiar and arbitrary exception, but one that I'm happy to use.

Here's another example in the same vein:

```
    sub printhash (&\%) {
        my $code = shift;
        my $hash = shift;
        local ($k, $v);
        while (($k, $v) = each %$hash) {
            print &$code();
        }
    }
```

Now I can say:

```
    printhash { "$k => $v\n" } %capitals;
```

and I'll get something like:

```
    Athens => Greece
    Moscow => Russia
    Helsinki => Finland
```

Or I can say:

```
    printhash { "$k," } %capitals;
```

and I'll get:

```
    Athens,Moscow,Helsinki,
```

Note that because I used $k and $v here, I might get into trouble with strict 'vars'. I'll either have to change the definition of printhash to use $a and $b instead, or I'll have to declare $k and $v with use vars qw($k $v) or our($k,$v).

6. Dynamic Scope Revisited

Here's another possible use for dynamic scope: you have a subroutine whose behavior depends on the setting of a global variable. This is usually a result of bad design, and should be avoided unless the variable is large and widely used. Suppose that this is the case, and that the variable is called %CONFIG.

You want to call the subroutine, but you want to change its behavior. Perhaps you want to trick it about what the configuration really is, or you want to see what it would do *if* the configuration were different, or you want to try out a fake configuration to see if it works. But you don't want to change the real global configuration, because you don't know what bizarre effects that will have on the rest of the program. Do this:

```
local %CONFIG = (new configuration here);
the_subroutine( );
```

The changed %CONFIG is inherited by the subroutine, and the original configuration is restored automatically when the declaration goes out of scope. Actually in this circumstance you can sometimes do better. Here's how: imagine that the %CONFIG hash has lots and lots of members, but you only want to change $CONFIG{VERBOSITY}. The obvious thing to do is something like this:

```
my %new_config = %CONFIG;           # Copy configuration
$new_config{VERBOSITY} = 1000;      # Change one member
local %CONFIG = %new_config;        # Copy changed back, temporarily
the_subroutine( );                  # Subroutine inherits change
```

But there's a better way:

```
local $CONFIG{VERBOSITY} = 1000; # Temporary change to one member!
the_subroutine( );
```

You can actually localize a single element of an array or a hash. It works just like localizing any other scalar: the old value is saved, and restored at the end of the enclosing scope.

Marginal Uses of Dynamic Scoping

Like local filehandles, I kept finding examples of dynamic scoping that seemed to require local, but on further reflection didn't. Lest you be tempted to make one of these mistakes, here they are.

One application people sometimes have for dynamic scoping is like this: suppose you have a complicated subroutine that does a search of some sort, locates a bunch of items, and returns a list of them. If the search function is complicated enough, you might like to have it simply deposit each item into a global array variable when it's found, rather than returning the complete list from the subroutine, especially if the search subroutine is recursive in a complicated way:

```
sub search {
    # do something very complicated here
```

```
    if ($found) {
        push @solutions, $solution;
    }
    # do more complicated things
}
```

This is dangerous, because @solutions is a global variable, and you don't know who else might be using it. In some languages, the best answer is to add a frontend to search that localizes the global @solutions variable:

```
sub search {
    local @solutions;
    realsearch(@_);
    return @solutions;
}

sub realsearch {
    # ... as before ...
}
```

Now the real work is done in realsearch, which still gets to store its solutions in the global variable. But since the user of realsearch is calling the frontend search function, any old value that @solutions might have had is saved beforehand and restored again afterwards.

There are two other ways to accomplish the same thing, and both of them are better. Here's one:

```
{ my @solutions;  # This is private, but available to both functions
  sub search {
      realsearch(@_);
      return @solutions;
  }

  sub realsearch {
      # ... just as before ...
      # but now it modifies a private variable instead of a global one.
  }
}
```

Here's the other:

```
sub search {
    my @solutions;
    realsearch(\@solutions, @_);
    return @solutions;
}

sub realsearch {
    my $solutions_ref = shift;
    # do something very complicated here
    if ($found) {
        push @$solutions_ref, $solution;
    }
    # do more complicated things
}
```

One or the other of these strategies will solve most problems in which you might want to use a dynamic variable. They're both safer than the solution with `local` because you don't have to worry that the global variable will leak out into the subroutines called by `realsearch`.

One final example of a marginal use of `local`: I can imagine an error-handling routine that examines the value of some global error message variable such as `$!` or `$DBI::errstr` to decide what to do. If this routine seems to have a more general utility, you might want to call it even when there wasn't an error, because you want to invoke its cleanup behavor, or you like the way it issues the error message, or whatever. It *should* accept the message as an argument instead of examining some fixed global variable, but it was badly designed and now you can't change it. If you're in this kind of situation, the best solution might turn out to be something like this:

```
local $DBI::errstr = "Your shoelace is untied!";
handle_error();
```

Probably a better solution is to find the person responsible for the routine and sternly remind them that functions are more flexible and easier to reuse if they don't depend on hardwired global variables. But sometimes time is short and you have to do what you can.

7. Perl 4 and Other Relics

A lot of the useful uses for `local` became obsolete with Perl 5; `local` was much more useful in Perl 4. The most important of these was that `my` wasn't available, so you needed `local` for private variables.

If you find yourself programming in Perl 4, expect to use a lot of `local`. `my` hadn't been invented yet.

Summary

Useful uses for `local` fall into two classes: first, places where you would like to use `my`, but can't because of some restriction; second, rare, peculiar, or contrived situations.

For the vast majority of cases, you should use `my`, and avoid `local` whenever possible. In particular, use `my` when you want private variables because local variables aren't private. Even the useful uses for `local` are mostly not very useful.

Revised rule of when to use `my` and when to use `local`:

1. Beginners and intermediate programmers: always use `my`; never use `local` unless you get an error when you try to use `my`.

2. Experts only: experts don't need me to tell them what the real rules are.

## CHAPTER 31

Parsing Command-Line Options

Johan Vromans

Controlling a computer by typing commands into a shell is still the preferred way of working for most programmers. Despite the capabilities of modern window systems, working from a shell is faster and simpler than sequences of mouse movements and button clicks—once you know the names of the commands and how they work.

The expressiveness of a command-line program depends on what *options* it supports, and how they're parsed, converted into a form that your program can understand. When you execute `ls -l /tmp` on Unix, or `dir /w c:\windows` on MS-DOS, or `your_program -height=80`, the `-l`, `/w`, and `-height=80` are options. Sometimes the shell handles the parsing; that's what happens with the `/w` in DOS. More often, the program named by the command (`ls` and `your_program`) must handle the parsing itself. In this article, I'll show you how your Perl programs can parse their own options.

Option Parsing Conventions

Under modern command shells, including those on Unix and Windows, options can be either letters or words. Programs that accept single letters might be invoked as `program -a -b -c`. Or, they might be invoked as `program -abc`, meaning the same thing. If the options take values, you can bundle them together: `-aw80L24x` is equivalent to `-a -w 80 -L 24 -x`. With option words, you sacrifice brevity for clarity: `program --all --width=80 --length 24 --extend`.

In either case, options precede other program arguments (the `/tmp` in `ls -l /tmp`) and the parsing stops as soon as a non-option argument is encountered. A double dash by itself immediately terminates option parsing.

These conventions are not universal. Some programs accept option words with a single dash (e.g., `-h` for height); some let you mix option letters and option words. Some programs let you mix options and regular program arguments. Options can be mandatory or optional, case-sensitive or case-insensitive, and can expect an argument afterward—or not.

Parsing options in Perl isn't very hard, but after writing eight subroutines for eight programs, you might wonder if there's a better way. There is. In fact, there are several ways.

The Simplest Way

Perl directly supports the single-character style of options with the -s switch. If you invoke Perl as follows:

```
perl -s script.pl -foo -bar=blech myfile.dat
```

Perl will remove -foo and -bar=blech from @ARGV and set $foo to true and $bar to blech. Note that the options are words preceded with a single dash. When Perl encounters an argument without the dash, it stops looking for options. It also stops looking when it sees a double dash (--), removing the double dash from @ARGV as well.

The Easy Way

Perl comes with two modules that handle command-line options: Getopt::Std and Getopt::Long.

Getopt::Std provides two subroutines, getopt and getopts. Each expects a single dash before option letters and stops processing options when the first non-option is detected. As with -s, it stops option processing whenever it encounters a double dash.

getopt takes one argument, a string containing all the option letters that expect values. For example, getopt ('lw') lets your program be invoked as program -l24 -w 80 (or program -l 24 -w80), and it will set $opt_l to 24 and $opt_w to 80. Other option letters are also accepted; for example, program -w80 -ab will also set both $opt_a and $opt_b to 1. Don't try something like -w=80 unless you want $opt_w to contain "=80", and if you use a double dash to introduce the w, (e.g., --w=80), that will set $opt_w but will also set $opt_- to 1.

When you don't want global variables defined in this way, you can pass a hash reference to getopt. The hash maps the option letters to their values (or 1 if the option doesn't take a value).

getopts allows a little more control. Its argument is a string containing the option letters of *all* recognized options. Options that take values are followed by colons. For example, getopts ('abl:w:') makes your program accept -a and -b without a value, and -l and -w with a value. Any other arguments beginning with a dash result in an error. As with getopt, a hash reference can be passed as an optional second argument.

The Advanced Way

Getopt::Long provides the GetOptions function, which gives you ultimate control over command-line options. Version 2.25 is bundled with Perl and provides support for:

- Single-letter options, with bundling (-abc)
- Option words, using a single dash, double dash, or plus sign (a standard briefly adopted by GNU)
- A mix of the above, in which case the long options *must* start with a double dash.

Other features include:

- Option values that can be designated mandatory or optional
- option values that can be strings or numbers
- Full control over where the option value will be delivered
- Full checking of options and values

Option Words

In its standard configuration, GetOptions handles option words, ignoring case. Options may be abbreviated, as long as the abbreviations are unambiguous. Options and other command-line arguments can be mixed; options will be processed first, and the other arguments will remain in @ARGV.

This call to GetOptions allows a single option, -foo.

```
GetOptions ('foo' => \$doit);
```

When the user provides -foo on the command line, $doit is set to 1. In this call, -foo is called the *option control string*, and \$doit is called the *option destination*. Multiple pairs of control strings and destinations can be provided. GetOptions will return true if processing was successful, and false otherwise, displaying an error message with warn.

The option word may have *aliases*, alternative option words that refer to the same option:

```
GetOptions ('foo|bar|quux' => \$doit);
```

If you want to specify that an option takes a string, append =s to the option control string:

```
GetOptions ('foo=s' => \$thevalue);
```

When you use a colon instead of an equal sign, the option takes a value only when one is present:

```
GetOptions ('foo:s' => \$thevalue, 'bar' => \$doit);
```

Calling this program with arguments -foo bar blech places the string "bar" in $thevalue, but when called with -foo -bar blech, something different happens: $thevalue is set to an empty string, and $doit is set to 1.

These options can also take numeric values; you can use =i or :i for integer values, and =f or :f for floating point values.

Using and Bundling Single-Letter Options

Using single-letter options is trivial; bundling them is a little trickier. Getopt::Long has a Configure subroutine that you can use to fine-tune your option parsing. For

bundling single-letter options, you would use `Getopt::Long::Configure` ('bundling').
Now `GetOptions` will happily accept bundled single-letter options:

```
Getopt::Long::Configure ('bundling');
GetOptions ( 'a' => \$all,
             'l=i' => \$length,
             'w=i' => \$width);
```

This allows options of the form -a -l 24 -w 80 as well as bundled forms, e.g., -al24w80.
You can mix these with option words:

```
GetOptions (     'a|all' => \$all,
             'l|length=i' => \$length,
              'w|width=i' => \$width);
```

However, the option words require a double dash. For example, --width 24 is acceptable, but -width 24 is not. (That causes the leading w to be interpreted as -w, and results in an error because idth isn't a valid integer value.)

`Getopt::Long::Configure('bundling_override')` allows option words with a single dash, where the words take precedence over bundled single-letter options. For example:

```
Getopt::Long::Configure ('bundling_override');
GetOptions ('a' => \$a, 'v' => \$v, 'x' => \$x, 'vax' => \$vax);
```

This treats -axv as -a -x -v, but treats -vax as a single option word.

Advanced Destinations

You don't need to specify the option destination. If you don't, `GetOptions` defines variables $opt_*OPTION* (where *OPTION* is the name of the option), just like getopt and getopts. Similarly, `GetOptions` also accepts a reference to a hash (as its first argument) and places the option values in it.

If you do specify the option destination, it needn't be a scalar. If you specify an array reference, option values are pushed into this array:

```
GetOptions ('foo=i' => \@values);
```

Calling this program with arguments -foo 1 -foo 2 -foo 3 sets @values to (1,2,3).

The option destination can also be a hash reference:

```
my %values;
GetOptions ('define=s' => \%values);
```

If you call this program as `program-define EOF=-1 -define bool=int`, the %values hash will have the keys EOF and bool, set to -1 and 'int' respectively.

Finally, the destination can be a reference to a subroutine. This subroutine will be called when the option is handled. It expects two arguments: the name of the option and the value.

The special option control string <> can be used in this case to have a subroutine process arguments that *aren't* options. This subroutine is then called with the name of the non-option argument. Consider:

```perl
GetOptions ('x=i' => \$x, '<>' => \&doit);
```

When you execute this program with -x 1 foo -x 2 bar this invokes doit with argument 'foo' and $x equal to 1, and then calls doit with argument 'bar' and $x equal to 2.

Other Configurations

GetOptions supports several other configuration characteristics. For a complete list, see the Getopt::Long documentation.

Getopt::Long::Configure ('no_ignore_case') matches option words without regard to case.

Getopt::Long::Configure ('no_auto_abbrev') prevents abbreviations for option words.

Getopt::Long::Configure ('require_order') stops detecting options after the first non-option command-line argument.

Help Messages

People often ask me why GetOptions doesn't provide facilities for help messages. There are two reasons. The first reason is that while command-line options adhere to conventions, help messages don't. Any style of message would necessarily please some people and annoy others, and would make calls to GetOptions much lengthier and more confusing.

The second reason is that Perl allows a program to contain its own documentation in pod (Plain Old Documentation) format, and there are already modules that extract this information to supply help messages. The following subroutine uses Pod::Usage for this purpose (and demonstrates how Pod::Usage can be loaded on demand):

```perl
sub options () {
    my $help = 0;   # handled locally
    my $ident = 0;  # handled locally
    my $man = 0;    # handled locally

    # Process options.
    if ( @ARGV > 0 ) {
        GetOptions('verbose' => \$verbose, 'trace' => \$trace,
                   'help|?' => \$help,   'manual' => \$man,
                   'debug' => \$debug) or pod2usage(2);
    }
    if ( $man or $help ) {
        # Load Pod::Usage only if needed.
        require "Pod/Usage.pm";
        import Pod::Usage;
        pod2usage(1) if $help;
        pod2usage(VERBOSE => 2) if $man;
    }
}
```

Pod::Usage is bundled with modern versions of Perl. The latest version of Getopt::Long can be found on CPAN in *authors/Johan_Vromans*. This kit also contains a script template that uses both Getopt::Long and Pod::Usage.

Other Option Handling Modules

Other option handling modules can be found on CPAN:

Getopt::Attribute

Provides an attribute wrapper around Getopt::Long. Instead of declaring the options in a hash with references to the variables and subroutines affected by the options, you can use the "Getopt" attribute on the variables and subroutines directly.

Getopt::Declare

Yet another command-line argument parser, specifically designed to be powerful but exceptionally easy to use.

Getopt::Mixed

Provides handling for option words and option letters. It was developed a couple of years ago, when Getopt::Std only handled option letters and Getopt::Long only handled option words. It's obsolete now.

Getopt::Regex

An option handler that uses regular expressions to identify the options, and closures to deliver the option values.

Getopt::EvaP

Uses a table-driven option handler that provides help messages in addition to most Getopt::Long features.

Getopt::Tabular

Another table-driven option handler loosely inspired by Tcl/Tk. Powerful, but very complex to set up.

Getopt::ArgvFile

Allows command-line options to be read from files and passed to Getopt::Long.

Getopt::AutoConf

Provides command-line parameter parsing similar to that provided by GNU autoconf. Getopt::AutoConf simplifies parsing of arguments in the form --with, --without, --enable, and --disable.

Getopt::constant

Parses command-line options into constants instead of variables.

Getopt::Function

Provides a more sophisticated interface to Getopt::Mixed.

Getopt::GetArgs

Actually for parsing subroutine arguments; not a command-line processor at all.

Getopt::Casual

Yet another simple command-line processor.

Getopt::Simple

Yet another simple command line-processor, written in 1997.

Getopt::Tiny

Yet another simple command-line processor, written in 1998.

## CHAPTER 32

Building a Better Hash with tie

Dan Schmidt

Introduction

One of the nice things about Perl is its support for reuse. I can solve a problem once, and generalize it so everyone with the same problem can use my solution. In this article, I'll examine a simple problem and take it through the steps required to turn the solution into a reusable module. Along the way, I'll visit the topics of data structures, ties, optimization, and testing.

The Problem

Someone on the Boston Perl Mongers mailing list asked how to efficiently manage a collection of items such that it is possible to insert and delete values quickly, but also choose random values quickly.

In a hash, it's easy to insert and delete values:

```
$hash{$key} = $value;
delete $hash{$key};
```

But accessing random values is inefficient:

```
my @k = keys %hash;
$rand = $k[rand @k];
```

You can access random values quickly in an array, but you can't insert and delete values quickly.

I might run into this problem if I were a soft-hearted person running an ongoing raffle. I'd keep track of the tickets people buy, and choose one randomly whenever it's time to select a winner. Because I'm a nice guy, I'd let people drop out of the raffle whenever they want and get their money back. If someone wanted to drop out of the raffle like that, I'd need a way to find his or her ticket quickly.

Discussion

To restate the problem a little more formally, I want some sort of lookup table in which *insertion*, *lookup*, *deletion*, and *random selection* are all fast.

Do any of Perl's built-in data types do the trick? Table 32-1 compares the various naive data structures I could use for this problem.

Table 32-1. A comparison of arrays and hashes for common operations

	Array	Hash
Insertion	O(1)	O(1)
Lookup	O(n)	O(1)
Deletion	O(n)	O(1)
Random key	O(1)	O(n)

O(n) (pronounced "order n") time is *linear time*: when there are *n* elements in the data structure, the operation takes time proportional to *n*. If an operation is O(1), it takes time proportional to 1; that is, it runs in constant time.

Arrays are great for selecting a random key, since it's easy to choose a random index, and then my random key is just the element at that index. But arrays are lousy for looking up keys, since I have to look through all the elements until I find the key I'm looking for. When Bartholomew asks for his ticket back, I'll have to look through all of the tickets one at a time until I find the one with his name on it.

Hashes were invented specifically to perform fast lookup, but there's no quick way of indexing all the entries of a hash. I can easily obtain a list of the keys with keys %hash, but that requires a pass through the whole hash to find all the keys, which takes too much time for this problem. When it's time to choose a raffle winner, I don't want to have to take time out and count through every single ticket.

It's important to note that if I don't have to select a random key very often, hashes are fine. If I only have to select a raffle winner once, it's not a big deal to spend a long time doing it. Similarly, if I never need to lookup or delete elements, arrays work great. (Hash behavior is a little more complicated than I'm pretending here, but element access is effectively O(1).)

Attempted Solutions

So how am I going to construct a new column in that table in which every operation is O(1)?

It seems clear that I need a hash of some sort; it's just too hard to get fast lookup otherwise. How can I add a fast random key selection operation to a hash?

Check for Built-In Support

The first thing to do is to see if the solution is already built into Perl. Maybe the internal representation of a hash includes an array of keys, and keys %hash simply returns an alias to it. Perl does enough smart things under the hood that it's worth checking that Perl isn't already doing our work for us.

I'll do a little timing test to see if selecting a random key of a hash gets slower as the hash gets bigger:

```perl
#!/usr/bin/perl

use Benchmark;

for $i (1..10) {$little_hash{$i} = $i}
for $i (1..100) {$big_hash{$i} = $i}

timethese (10000, {
        little => sub {$foo = (keys %little_hash)[rand keys %little_hash]},
           big => sub {$foo = (keys %big_hash)[rand keys %big_hash]},
                    });
```

Benchmark::timethese is the standard way to compare the speed of code fragments. The first argument is the number of trials to run; the second argument is a reference to a hash that maps names to code fragments.

I should explain those code fragments. keys %hash returns an array of the keys of the hash; the tricky thing is that inside the square brackets, the return value is put in a scalar context to provide an argument for rand, turning it into the length of the array, which is the number of keys.

Anyway, here's the output I got:

```
Benchmark: timing 10000 iterations of big, little...
      big:  5.43 CPU secs ( 5.43 usr +  0.00 sys)
   little:  0.70 CPU secs ( 0.70 usr +  0.00 sys)
```

Here I can see that when I made the hash ten times as big, it took eight times as long to select a random key. So Perl hasn't already solved the problem for me.

See If a Solution Already Exists

Next (actually, I probably should have done this first!), I check if someone else has already solved the problem. The Perl FAQ and the Perl Cookbook are good places to start.

I didn't find any solutions there, but the Perl Cookbook did point me to Tie::IxHash, which implements an indexed hash, a data structure that combines many of the features of hashes and arrays. In fact, selecting a random key from a Tie::IxHash is O(1), but because it must do work to preserve the order of the keys, deletion is O(n).

A Working Data Structure

It looks like I'll have to find a solution myself. Can I get the best of both worlds by using both a hash and an array? The array just holds a list of keys, so that I can do my random key selection quickly. I do have to do some extra work on operations that modify the table (like insertion) to keep both of my data structures synchronized, but that's still constant time; it's just a bigger constant. When n gets big enough, the extra time I spend keeping the data structures in sync will pale next to the time I save on random key selection.

I'll check how complicated the operations actually are. Insertion is already O(1) for both cases. I get O(1) lookup by using the hash instead of the array, and O(1) random key selection by using the array instead of the hash.

The only tricky case is deletion. First of all, I need to actually find the key in the array so I can delete it (I didn't need to do that during lookup). To do that, for each key I'll have to store the corresponding array index in the hash, as well as the value, so I can get at the correct array element.

Secondly, I need to delete that key in constant time. I could splice it out by moving all the elements above it down one slot (and that's basically what Tie::IxHash does, since it has to preserve key order), but that takes linear time. The fast way to delete an element from an array is just to move the last element of the array into that slot. Since I don't have to preserve order, that works well; I just have to make sure the hash gets updated along with it.

Way up above in my original table, I claimed that deleting an element from an array is O(n). Was I lying? Well, sort of. Actually deleting the element, once you've found it, is an O(1) operation using the trick I just mentioned; it's finding that element in the first place that's the painful part. By using the hash, I'm able to find the element quickly, and the rest is gravy.

Implementation

Okay, it's time to implement it.

```perl
package RndHash1;

sub new {
    bless { arr => (), hash => {} }, $_[0];
}

sub insert {
    my ($self, $key, $val) = @_;
    push @{$self->{arr}}, $key; # update array
    $self->{hash}{$key} = [$val, $#{$self->{arr}}]; # update hash
}
```

```perl
sub get {
    my ($self, $key) = @_;
    $self->{hash}{$key}[0];                       # look up in hash
}

sub delete {
    my ($self, $key) = @_;
    my $idx = $self->{hash}{$key}[1];             # index in array to delete
    my $moved_key = $self->{arr}[-1];             # get last element
    $self->{arr}[$idx] = $moved_key;              # and move it here
    $self->{hash}{$moved_key}[1] = $idx;          # update hash
    --$#{$self->{arr}};                           # shorten array
    delete $self->{hash}{$key};                   # remove key from hash
}

sub rnd_key {
    my ($self) = @_;
    $self->{arr}[rand @{$self->{arr}}];
}

1;
```

If you've been scared away in the past from creating classes, cower no more. The only tricky part of writing a class is the new subroutine, which gets passed the class as the first argument. bless just takes the little hash reference I made and turns it into a reference that knows it's a RndHash1. Then each method of the class gets passed the object it's invoked with as its first argument.

The hash that I create has only two elements. arr is an array containing all the keys, and hash is the actual hash with the key-value mapping. Actually, as I noted above, the hash also needs to associate an array index with each key. So the value it associates with each key is a tiny two-element array: element 0 is the real value, and element 1 is the index of that key in arr.

Once you've gotten past that, delete is really the only interesting function here. I do have to catch a boundary case; what happens when the element I'm deleting is the last element of the array? The code here happens to work in that case too, though it does do a little unnecessary work.

Here's another little benchmarking program:

```perl
use RndHash1;
use Benchmark;

$rndhash1 = new RndHash1;

for $i (1..500) {$hash{$i} = $i}
for $i (1..500) {$rndhash1->insert($i, $i)}

$i = 1000;

timethese (5000, {
```

```
              hash => sub {$hash{$i++}='a';
                          @keys = keys %hash;
                          delete $hash{$keys[rand @keys]};},
           RndHash1 => sub {$rndhash1->insert ($i++, 'a');
                          $rndhash1->delete ($rndhash1->rnd_key());;},
           });
```

This benchmark tries to emulate typical use of the package; each time through the
(implicit) loop, I add a new element and randomly delete one of the existing ones.
Here are the results; yep, I speeded things up a lot!

```
Benchmark: timing 5000 iterations of RndHash1, hash...
  RndHash1:  1.22 CPU secs ( 1.19 usr +  0.03 sys)
      hash: 22.04 CPU secs (22.03 usr +  0.01 sys)
```

It's important to actually perform this timing comparison. It was possible that my
new implementation had enough overhead that it didn't actually perform better than
built-in hashes on normal-sized data sets. By timing it, I see that in fact, it *is* worthwhile to use RndHash.

Implementing a Tied Hash

I still have a few problems, though. For one thing, the implementation isn't robust at
all. insert doesn't check to see if the key already exists; delete doesn't check to
make sure that the key does exist.

Also, the syntax used to access the object isn't very idiomatic. It would be nice if I
could use a RndHash in the same way I can use a normal hash.

In fact, I can, using Perl's tie feature. tie allows me to override Perl's built-in implementation of a variable. For example, if I tie a variable to an object I've created, then
every time Perl would normally set the variable, it will instead call the STORE method
on our object. A standard example is a database on disk; by using tie, I can make
retrieving and updating values in the database look just like using a hash. Once the
tie is set up, the programmer needn't even know that it exists.

A complete hash tie implementation needs to support eight fundamental operations,
most of which I've already written in some form or another.

```
package RndHash2;

sub TIEHASH {
    bless { hash => {}, arr => (), iter => 0 }, $_[0];
}
```

TIEHASH is exactly analogous to new for a regular class. I'll use iter to implement the
code invoked when people write code like while (($key, $value) = each %hash).

```
sub STORE {
    my ($self, $key, $val) = @_;
    if (exists $self->{hash}{$key}) {
        $self->{hash}{$key}[0] = $val;
```

```
    } else {
        push @{$self->{arr}}, $key;
        $self->{hash}{$key} = [$val, $#{$self->{arr}}];
    }
}
```

STORE is called whenever code sets elements in the hash, such as $hash{$key} = $value.
That element may already exist in the hash, and if so, I only want to update the value,
not push a new key onto my array.

```
sub FETCH {
    my ($self, $key) = @_;
    return $self->{hash}{$key}[0];
}
```

FETCH is called in response to code that reads elements from the hash. I kind of have two
cases, since the element may or may not exist, but it turns out that one piece of code
handles both cases; if the key isn't in the hash, it returns undef, which is what I want.

```
sub DELETE {
    my ($self, $key) = @_;
    my $idx = $self->{hash}{$key}[1];
    if (defined $idx) {
        my $moved_key                = $self->{arr}[-1];
        $self->{arr}[$idx]           = $moved_key;
        $self->{hash}{$moved_key}[1] = $idx;
        --$#{$self->{arr}};
        delete $self->{hash}{$key};
    } else {
        return undef;
    }
}
```

DELETE now has to check whether the key that's passed already exists in the hash. If
not, it returns undef, since that's how built-in hashes operate.

```
sub EXISTS {
    exists $_[0]->{hash}{$_[1]};
}

sub CLEAR {
    %{$_[0]->{hash}} = ();
    @{$_[0]->{arr}}  = ();
    $_[0]->{iter}    = 0;
}
```

Here are a couple of methods needed for completeness that I hadn't bothered with
before. The EXISTS subroutine implements Perl's exists function; I just pass the
arguments on to the underlying hash I'm using. CLEAR destroys the hash; I just set my
underlying data structures to be empty.

```
sub FIRSTKEY {
    $_[0]->{iter} = 0;
    return $_[0]->NEXTKEY();
}
```

```
sub NEXTKEY {
    my ($self) = @_;
    if ($self->{iter} <= $#{$self->{arr}}) {
        return $self->{arr}[$self->{iter}++];
    } else {
        return undef;
    }
}
```

FIRSTKEY and NEXTKEY are used to implement Perl's each function. They are also used to implement keys and values, since Perl has no other way to find out the contents of a RndHash. Calling FIRSTKEY once and then NEXTKEY until undef is returned provides the complete list of keys. I don't have to return them in any particular order, but I'd be a fool not to use the order I'm already using internally.

To keep state, I use an object variable iter, which is the index of the next key to provide. All FIRSTKEY has to do is prime the index and hand off to NEXTKEY.

It does seem rather silly that when someone calls keys %hash, Perl calls NEXTKEY a gazillion times. I already have that list lying around; wouldn't it be easier and more efficient to just be able to return @{$self->{arr}} directly? Yes, it would, but I have no way of telling Perl that it's able to do that. The above eight methods constitute the only interface I need to fake built-in hash functionality. However, I can make my own interface analogous to keys, so that someone who knows about the fast access can do it:

```
sub get_keys {
    @{$_[0]->{arr}};
}

sub get_values {
    my ($self) = @_;
    map {$self->{hash}{$_}[0]} @{$self->{arr}};
}
```

get_keys returns the list of keys that I have lying around. If called in a scalar context, the @-expression automatically evaluates to the number of elements in the list, rather than the list itself. You might wonder why I'm passing back the entire array, rather than a reference to it. For one thing, I'm trying to emulate the behavior of keys, which returns an array rather than a reference. Also, if I passed back a reference, people would then have a handle into my internal data structure, and could modify it at will. Maybe you trust them not to do that. I don't.

Moving on, get_values takes that same list of keys, and uses map to replace each key with the value corresponding to it. If you're more comfortable with looping by hand than with using map, take a minute to see what's going on here; it's a perfect example of when map is much easier to use than an explicit loop.

Finally, here's the reason I wrote this class in the first place:

```
sub rnd_key {
    $_[0]->{arr}[rand @{$_[0]->{arr}}];
}

1;
```

Using a Tied Hash

Great, I've implemented it. Now, how am I going to use it? Like this:

```
use RndHash2;
$fruit_handle = tie %fruit, 'RndHash2';
```

Now I can use %fruit exactly like a normal hash, but under the hood, it's a
RndHash2.

```
$fruit{'a'} = 'apple';
$fruit{'b'} = 'banana';
$fruit{'c'} = 'cantaloupe';
delete $fruit{'b'};
```

But how do I call rnd_key? There's no standard hash interface for that. Conveniently, tie returns the actual object created by TIEHASH, so I can call methods on
that just as on any other object.

```
print "My favorite fruit is a ", $fruit_handle->rnd_key(), "\n";
```

I actually like to use $fruit instead of $fruit_handle; because of the way Perl handles names, the scalar $fruit exists independently of the hash %fruit. But that's
potentially confusing, and I probably shouldn't encourage it.

Super! Let's benchmark again, just for fun:

```
use RndHash1;
use RndHash2;
use Benchmark;

$rndhash1 = new RndHash1;
$rndhash2_handle = tie %rndhash2, 'RndHash2';

for $i (1..500) {$hash{$i} = $i}
for $i (1..500) {$rndhash1->insert($i, $i)}
for $i (1..500) {$rndhash2{$i} = $i}

$i = 1000;

timethese (5000, {
        hash => sub { $hash{$i++}='a';
                    @keys = keys %hash;
                    delete $hash{$keys[rand @keys]}; },
        RndHash1 => sub { $rndhash1->insert ($i++, 'a');
                    $rndhash1->delete ($rndhash1->rnd_key()); },
        RndHash2 => sub { $rndhash2{$i++}='a';
                    delete $rndhash2{$rndhash2_handle->rnd_key()}; }
            });
```

The results:

```
Benchmark: timing 5000 iterations of RndHash1, RndHash2, hash...
  RndHash1:  1.07 CPU secs ( 1.02 usr +  0.05 sys)
  RndHash2:  1.47 CPU secs ( 1.38 usr +  0.09 sys)
      hash: 22.09 CPU secs (22.08 usr +  0.01 sys)
```

Ugh, I've slowed things down by almost 40%. I've changed two things since RndHash1: I made the implementation more robust by doing things such as checking if a key already exists, and I hooked it up to a tie. I'll try to isolate the two effects by timing what happens when I call the methods explicitly, rather than through the tie functionality:

```perl
use RndHash1;
use RndHash2;
use Benchmark;

$rndhash1 = new RndHash1;
$rndhash2_handle = tie %rndhash2, 'RndHash2';
$rh3 = tie %rndhash3, 'RndHash2';

for $i (1..500) {$rndhash1->insert($i, $i)}
for $i (1..500) {$rndhash2{$i} = $i}
for $i (1..500) {$rndhash3{$i} = $i}

$i = 1000;

timethese (25000, {
    RndHash1 => sub { $rndhash1->insert ($i++, 'a');
                      $rndhash1->delete ($rndhash1->rnd_key()); },
    RndHash2 => sub { $rndhash2{$i++}='a';
                      delete $rndhash2{$rndhash2_handle->rnd_key()}; },
    RndHash3 => sub { $rh3->STORE($i++, 'a');
                      $rh3->DELETE($rh3->rnd_key()); }
              });
```

The results:

```
RndHash1:  5.58 CPU secs ( 5.40 usr +  0.18 sys)
RndHash2:  7.64 CPU secs ( 7.23 usr +  0.41 sys)
RndHash3:  5.61 CPU secs ( 5.34 usr +  0.27 sys)
```

Hmm—when I didn't go through the indirection of tie, my new code was just as fast as before. So it looks like the slowdown is due almost entirely due to tie. Every time I do a hash access, Perl has to see what it's tied to and then call a method on that object.

It looks like that's the price I'll have to pay for the convenience of tie. Even the new, slower code is a lot faster than using a regular hash, so it's not too worrisome.

Testing

Great, I'm done! Well, I'm done with the first draft. Now I have to make sure that it works. It's easy to eyeball the code, decide it looks reasonable, try it on a few test cases, and ship it out, but there are often little (and big) bugs lurking. In fact, I made a few stupid mistakes when I first coded this up. Here's how I caught them.

The easiest way to check whether a class is working is to figure out how you could tell if an object of that class were broken. For example, if some key is in @{$self->{arr}} but not in %{$self->{hash}}, that's obviously a problem. I can write a little method to check for this kind of obvious brokenness, and see if it ever squawks. I'm going to call this "verification;" you may know it as "sanity checking." If you see a discussion of *representation invariants* in some object-oriented textbook, this is what they're talking about.

```
sub verify {
    my ($self) = @_;

    my $arr_size  = @{$self->{arr}};
    my $hash_size = keys %{$self->{hash}};
    if ($arr_size != $hash_size) {
        die "RndHash: sizes of 'arr' and 'hash' don't match!\n" .
                                        "$arr_size vs $hash_size\n";
    }

    for (my $key_idx = 0, my $key = $self->{arr}[0];
        $key_idx <= $#{$self->{arr}};
        ++$key_idx, $key = $self->{arr}[$key_idx]) {
        if (!exists $self->{hash}{$key}) {
            die "RndHash: $key is in 'arr' but not in 'hash'!\n";
        }
        if ($self->{hash}{$key}->[1] != $key_idx) {
            die "RndHash: index for $key in 'hash' is incorrect!\n" .
                "Should be $key_idx but is $self->{hash}{$key}->[1]\n";
        }
    }
}
```

verify confirms that my data structure is self-consistent. First, I check that the array and the hash are the same size. Then, I make sure that each element in the array also exists in the hash, and that the array index stored in the hash is correct.

I don't have to check that the array is missing any elements, since each element in the array checked out, and I already confirmed that the number of array elements is the same as the number of hash elements.

Here's the start of a little testing program:

```
use RndHash2;

$rndhash2_handle = tie %rndhash2, 'RndHash2';

for $i (1..500) {$rndhash2{$i} = $i}
```

```
for $i (450..600) {
    print "insert $i / 'a'\n";
    $rndhash2{$i} = 'a';
    $rndhash2_handle->verify();
    $rnd_key = $rndhash2_handle->rnd_key();
    print "delete $rnd_key\n";
    delete $rndhash2{$rnd_key};
    $rndhash2_handle->verify();
}
```

I made $i go from 450 to 600 to exercise the STORE code that updates already exist-ing keys. After each RndHash operation, I call verify to see if the object still makes sense.

A complete test suite for RndHash would also need to check that each operation does what it's supposed to. For example, the list of keys after doing a STORE of a new element should be the same as the old list, with that element added. I will also check to make sure that the package functions in degenerate cases, such as when there's only one element.

Lest you think I'm just recommending testing to be politically correct, I caught a couple of embarrassing bugs. One was that in DELETE, I was forgot to actually remove the element from the hash. Also, in one place I forgot that %{$self->{hash}} stores [value, index] pairs, not just values.

Optimizations

There are two common dimensions that programmers worry about optimizing: time and space. I'll cover each in this section.

Time

My data structure is fast, but there are still some improvements I could make. For one thing, it seems kind of slow to be constantly performing hash lookups on the strings hash and arr every time I want get any information out of my class. I could just use an array instead of a hash, and then index by 0, 1, and 2, instead of by hash, arr, and iter.

I'll just include a couple of methods here, so you get the idea:

```
sub TIEHASH {
    bless [
            {},    # 0: hash
            [],    # 1: arr
            0      # 2: iter
        ], $_[0];
}

sub STORE {
    my ($self, $key, $val) = @_;
    if (exists $self->[0]{$key}) {
```

```
        $self->[0]{$key}[0] = $val;
    } else {
        push @{$self->[1]}, $key;
        $self->[0]{$key} = [$val, $#{$self->[1]}];
    }
}
```

That's not very readable. It would be handy if Perl could do this kind of thing for me, turning hash accesses into array accesses automatically in the appropriate places. Well, it turns out that it can, in Perl 5.005, using the use fields directive. I want this code to work in earlier versions, so I'm not going to use it.

Anyway, I should make sure that I'm actually getting some speed increase out of this. I'll spare you the benchmarking program and just show the results:

```
Benchmark: timing 25000 iterations of RndHash1, RndHash2, RndHash4...
  RndHash1:  6.35 CPU secs ( 6.35 usr +  0.00 sys)
  RndHash2: 10.50 CPU secs (10.50 usr +  0.00 sys)
  RndHash4:  9.81 CPU secs ( 9.81 usr +  0.00 sys)
```

Not earth-shattering, but definitely an improvement. Whether to sacrifice readability is a judgment call; I decided to go for it.

Space

There's another kind of waste going on. Every element of the hash part contains a reference to a two-element array. Perl's arrays are really flexible; unfortunately, one of the prices for that flexibility is that they take a lot of space. For one thing, Perl doesn't know that I have an array with exactly two elements that will never have to grow, so it starts out by allocating some extra space for it. That's not a big deal if I have a few arrays around, but with one for each key, it can add up.

There's a way I could save some of that space. Instead of keeping both an array index and a value in the hash element, I can just store the array index. Then I have an array of values, parallel to the array of keys, so that the value of $self->{key_arr}[$i] is $self->{val_arr}[$i].

Here's a new constructor and a couple of methods with this new structure:

```
sub TIEHASH {
    bless [
            {},  # 0: hash mapping keys to indices
            [],  # 1: array of keys
            [],  # 2: array of values
            0,   # 3: iterator index
        ],
        $_[0];
}
```

STORE now puts the value in the array @{$self->[2]}, not the hash %{$self->[0]}:

```
sub STORE {
    my ($self, $key, $val) = @_;
```

```
        if (exists $self->[0]{$key}) {
            # update
            $self->[2][$self->[0]{$key}] = $val;
        } else {
            # new key
            push @{$self->[1]}, $key;
            push @{$self->[2]}, $val;
            $self->[0]{$key} = $#{$self->[1]};
        }
    }
}
```

And FETCH has to go through one more level of indirection; it finds the array index through the hash, and then looks up the value at that array index.

```
sub FETCH {
    my ($self, $key) = @_;
    if (exists $self->[0]{$key}) {
        return $self->[2][$self->[0]{$key}];
    } else {
        return undef;
    }
}
```

I can see how much space this saves by writing a program that makes a hash with lots of keys and then hangs out. The Unix program ps tells us how much space is being used.

```
use RndHash4;
tie %rndhash4, 'RndHash4';
for $i (1..5000) { $rndhash4{$i} = $i };
print "OK\n";
$wait = <>;
```

I ran the above test once with RndHash4 and once with RndHash5 (the double-array implementation). The results:

```
~/Doc/TPJ $ ps aux | grep [p]erl
dfan      2949  6.8  5.5  3416  2628  p0 S    22:50   0:00 perl sizetest.pl
~/Doc/TPJ $ ps aux | grep [p]erl
dfan      2953 16.6  5.1  3164  2400  p0 S    22:51   0:00 perl sizetest.pl
```

The fourth column tells how much space the program is taking, in kilobytes. The difference in memory, per hash element, comes out to $(3416 - 3164) \times 1024 / 5000 = 52$ bytes. That's not particularly exact, but it gives me some idea of how much memory is being saved. It did slow things down by around 14%, though:

```
Benchmark: timing 15000 iterations of RndHash4, RndHash5...
   RndHash4:  5.71 CPU secs ( 5.71 usr +  0.00 sys)
   RndHash5:  6.49 CPU secs ( 6.49 usr +  0.00 sys)
```

As usual, it's a tradeoff: in this case, space versus speed. I decided that 50 bytes per element is peanuts compared to the 3+ megabytes that Perl is already taking up, so I kept the fast one.

Making It a Module

Great, I'm done! Well, now that I've solved this earth-shattering problem, maybe I should make it available for everyone else to use. The next step is to put it on CPAN, the Comprehensive Perl Archive Network.

The entire step-by-step procedure for making a module and submitting it to CPAN is outside the scope of this article, but I'll outline a couple of steps here. There are really only two main things I have to do to make it a well-behaved module. One is to make a $VERSION variable, which can be accessed by the CPAN software and which I'll use to keep track of public releases. The other is to write some documentation so that anyone can use it. The documentation is written in pod format (see the perlpod documentation bundled with Perl). I won't include the finished documentation here, but you can see it by looking up the module on CPAN.

Summing Up

Well, it's been quite a journey. Hopefully, you're more comfortable with some of the issues involved in making a module, and will consider going the extra mile the next time you come up with a generalizable solution to a problem you encounter.

The final (for now) version of RndHash can be found on CPAN, with the name Tie::RndHash. Already I'm thinking of further extensions. How about letting the user assign weights to each element, so he can change the selection probability associated with each key? Hmm.

Thanks to Tuomas J. Lukka for the original problem statement, and for coming up with the idea for the space optimization.

References

Sources of information about data structures and algorithms, optimization, ties, internals, and modules follow.

Data structures and algorithms
> You can't go wrong with Sedgewick's *Algorithms in C, Third Edition* (Addison-Wesley). There are also C++ and Java versions. This book just keeps on getting better each time he revises it. If you want a more rigorous approach, I recommend Cormen, Leiserson, and Rivest's *Introduction to Algorithms* (MIT Press & McGraw Hill). Of course, Knuth's *The Art of Computer Programming* (Addison-Wesley) is known as the bible of data structures and algorithms, because it's old and hard to read. Actually, it's not that bad if you don't try to read it straight through, and Chapter 2 (found in Volume I) is essential reading (and quite understandable). I'd also like to mention Skiena's *The Algorithm Design Manual* (Springer-Verlag), since it is excellent and not well known; it has many case studies and a great gazetteer of algorithmic topics. It's a good first place to look.

And of course, Orwant, Hietaniemi, and Macdonald's *Mastering Algorithms with Perl* (O'Reilly) focuses on algorithms from a Perl viewpoint.

Optimization

The best optimization book I know of is Bentley's *Writing Efficient Programs* (Prentice-Hall), a slim, clear, information-packed book that is, incredibly, out of print. Snatch it up if you ever find it. Bentley's other books, *Programming Pearls* and *More Programming Pearls* (both published by Addison-Wesley), are fine collections of case studies.

Ties

The `perltie` documentation is obviously the definitive reference. Srinivasan's *Advanced Perl Programming* (O'Reilly) has a fine chapter on `tie` as well.

Internals

If you want to see why arrays are big, *Advanced Perl Programming* has a good overview chapter on the Perl implementation.

Modules

The "Guidelines for Module Creation" section in *http://www.perl.com/CPAN/ modules/00modlist.long.html* is the best documentation for submitting modules.

## CHAPTER 33

Source Filters

Paul Marquess

 Looking back at this article a number of years after it was written, it strikes me that source filters were a cool idea waiting for a killer application to come along. Things would probably have stayed that way if Damian Conway hadn't stumbled across them, because he has certainly put them to good use.

Damian currently has five CPAN modules using source filters. The cornerstone module is undoubtedly Filter::Simple, and anyone wanting to play further with source filters *must* have copy of this module. The interface it provides is much easier to use than the Filter::Util::Call module described in this article and will be adequate for 95% of applications.

Another module worth checking out for a real-life source filter is Switch, which adds a switch statement to Perl 5. The switch statement destined to be included in Perl 6 bears a striking resemblance to this one.

This article is about a little-known feature of Perl called *source filters*. Source filters alter the program text of a module before Perl sees it, much as a C preprocessor alters the source text of a C program before the compiler sees it. This article tells you more about what source filters are, how they work, and how to write your own.

The original purpose of source filters was to let you encrypt your program source to prevent casual piracy. This isn't all they can do, as you'll soon learn. But first, the basics.

Concepts

Before the Perl interpreter can execute a Perl script, the interpreter must first read the script from a file into memory for parsing and compilation. (Even scripts specified on the command line with the -e option are stored in a temporary file for the parser to process.) If that script itself includes other scripts with a use or require statement, then each of those scripts will have to be read from their respective files as well.

Think of each logical connection between the Perl parser and an individual file as a *source stream*. A source stream is created when the Perl parser opens a file, it continues to exist as the source code is read into memory, and it is destroyed when Perl is finished parsing the file. If the parser encounters a `require` or use statement in a source stream, a new and distinct stream is created just for that file. See Figure 33-1.

Figure 33-1. Conventional parsing

There are two important points to remember:

1. Although there can be any number of source streams in existence at any given time, only one will be active.

2. Every source stream is associated with only one file.

A source filter is a special kind of Perl module that intercepts and modifies a source stream before it reaches the parser. A source filter changes the diagram, as shown in Figure 33-2.

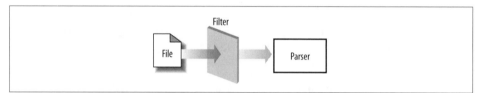

Figure 33-2. Source filters intercept data before it is parsed

If that doesn't make much sense, consider the analogy of a command pipeline. Say you have a shell script stored in the compressed file *trial.gz*. The simple pipeline command below runs the script without needing to create a temporary file to hold the uncompressed file.

```
gunzip -c trial.gz | sh
```

In this case, the data flow from the pipeline can be represented as shown in Figure 33-3.

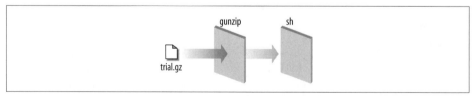

Figure 33-3. gunzip intercepting the data before sh can read it

With source filters, you can store the text of your script compressed and use a source filter to uncompress it for Perl's parser (Figure 33-4).

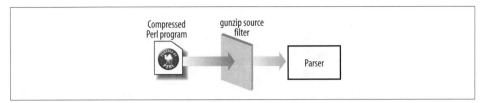

Figure 33-4. A gunzip source filter interpreting a compressed Perl program

Using Filters

So how do you use a source filter in a Perl script? Above, I said that a source filter is just a special kind of module. Like all Perl modules, a source filter is invoked with a use statement.

Say you want to pass your Perl source through the C preprocessor before execution. You could use the existing -P command-line option to do this, but as it happens, the source filter distribution comes with a C preprocessor filter module called Filter::cpp. Let's use that instead.

Below is an example program, cpp_test, that uses this filter. Line numbers have been added to allow specific lines to be referenced easily.

```
1 use Filter::cpp;
2 #define TRUE 1
3 $a = TRUE;
4 print "a = $a\n";
```

When you execute this script, Perl creates a source stream for the file. Before the parser processes any of the lines from the file, the source stream looks like Figure 33-5.

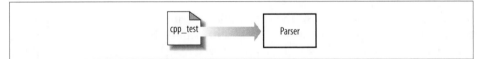

Figure 33-5. Parsing cpp_test (before Filter::cpp is invoked)

Line 1, use `Filter::cpp`, includes and installs the cpp filter module. All source filters work this way. The use statement is compiled and executed at compile time, before any more of the file is read, and it attaches the cpp filter to the source stream behind the scenes. Now the data flow looks like Figure 33-6.

As the parser reads the second and subsequent lines from the source stream, it feeds those lines through the cpp source filter before processing them. The cpp filter simply passes each line through the real C preprocessor. The output from the C preprocessor is then inserted back into the source stream by the filter (Figure 33-7).

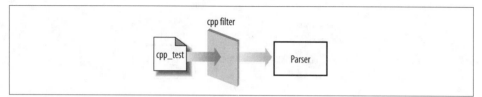

Figure 33-6. The cpp filter intercepts the cpp_test source stream

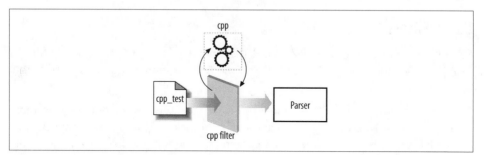

Figure 33-7. The cpp filter invokes cpp before the parser can read the remainder of cpp_test

The parser then sees the following code:

```
use Filter::cpp;
$a = 1;
print "a = $a\n";
```

Let's consider what happens when the filtered code includes another module with use:

```
1 use Filter::cpp;
2 #define TRUE 1
3 use Fred;
4 $a = TRUE;
5 print "a = $a\n";
```

The cpp filter does not apply to the text of the Fred module, only to the text of the file that used it (*cpp_test*). Although the use statement on line 3 will pass through the cpp filter, the module that gets included (Fred) will not. The source streams look like Figure 33-8 after line 3 has been parsed and before line 4 is parsed.

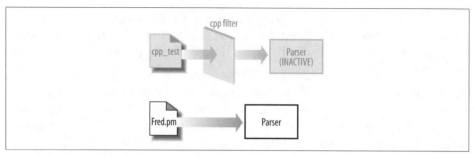

Figure 33-8. The cpp filter lets Fred.pm through unscathed

As you can see, a new stream has been created for reading the source from *Fred.pm*. This stream will remain active until all of *Fred.pm* has been parsed. The source stream for cpp_test will still exist, but is inactive. Once the parser has finished reading *Fred.pm*, the source stream associated with it will be destroyed. The source stream for cpp_test then becomes active again and the parser reads line 4 and subsequent lines from cpp_test.

You can use more than one source filter on a single file. Similarly, you can reuse the same filter in as many files as you like.

For example, if you have a uuencoded and compressed source file, it is possible to stack a uudecode filter and an uncompression filter like this:

```
use Filter::uudecode; use Filter::uncompress;
M'XL(".US4'\QV9I;F%L')Q;7/;1I;_I3=;;0&%E=%:F*'I"T?22Q/
M66]9*P*IQ+QXO0&GE) /30 (30
...
```

Once the first line has been processed, the flow will look like Figure 33-9.

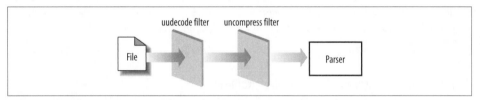

Figure 33-9. Cascaded source filters uudecoding and uncompressing a source stream

Data flows through filters in the same order that they appear in the source file. The uudecode filter appeared before the uncompress filter, so the source file will be uudecoded before it's uncompressed.

Writing a Source Filter

There are three ways to write your own source filter. You can write it in C, use an external program as a filter, or write the filter in Perl. I won't cover the first two in any great detail, so I'll get them out of the way first. Writing the filter in Perl is most convenient, so I'll devote the most space to it.

Writing a Source Filter in C

The first of the three available techniques is to write the filter completely in C. The external module you create interfaces directly with the source filter hooks provided by Perl.

The advantage of this technique is that you have complete control over the implementation of your filter. The big disadvantage is the increased complexity required to write the filter—not only do you need to understand the source filter hooks, but you also need a reasonable knowledge of Perl guts. One of the few times it is worth going to this trouble is when writing a source scrambler. The decrypt filter (which unscrambles the source before Perl parses it) included with the source filter distribution is an example of a C source filter.

Decryption Filters

All decryption filters work on the principle of "security through obscurity." Regardless of how well you write a decryption filter or how strong your encryption algorithm is, anyone determined enough can retrieve the original source code. The reason is quite simple: once the decryption filter has decrypted the source back to its original form, fragments of it will be stored in the computer's memory as Perl parses it. The source might only be in memory for a short period of time, but anyone possessing a debugger, skill, and a lot of patience can eventually reconstruct your program.

That said, there are a number of steps that can make life difficult for the potential cracker. The most important: write your decryption filter in C and statically link the decryption module into the Perl binary. For further tips to make life difficult for the potential cracker, see the file *decrypt.pm* in the source filters module.

Creating a Source Filter as a Separate Executable

An alternative to writing the filter in C is to create a separate executable in the language of your choice. The separate executable reads from standard input, does whatever processing is necessary, and writes the filtered data to standard output. Filter::cpp is an example of a source filter implemented as a separate executable—the executable is the C preprocessor bundled with your C compiler.

The source filter distribution includes two modules that simplify this task: Filter::exec and Filter::sh. Both allow you to run any external executable. Both use a *coprocess* to control the flow of data into and out of the external executable.[*] The difference between them is that Filter::exec spawns the external command directly, while Filter::sh spawns a shell to execute the external command. (Unix uses the Bourne shell; NT uses the cmd shell.) Spawning a shell allows you to make use of the shell metacharacters and redirection facilities.

Here is an example script that uses Filter::sh:

```
use Filter::sh 'tr XYZ PQR';
$a = 1;
print "XYZ a = $a\n";
```

Here's the output you'll get when the script is executed:

```
PQR a = 1
```

---

[*] For details on coprocesses, see Stevens's *Advanced Programming in the UNIX Environment* (Addison-Wesley).

Writing a source filter as a separate executable works fine, but it incurs a small performance penalty. For example, if you execute the small example above, a separate subprocess will be created to run the Unix `tr` command. Each use of the filter requires its own subprocess. If creating subprocesses is expensive on your system, you might want to consider one of the other options for creating source filters.

Writing a Source Filter in Perl

The easiest and most portable option available for creating your own source filter is to write it completely in Perl. To distinguish this from the previous two techniques, I'll call it a Perl source filter.

To help understand how to write a Perl source filter you need an example to study. Here is a complete source filter that performs rot13 decoding. (Rot13 is a very simple encryption scheme used in Usenet postings to hide the contents of offensive posts. It moves every letter forward thirteen places, so that A becomes N, B becomes O, and Z becomes M.)

```perl
package Rot13;

use Filter::Util::Call;

sub import {
    my ($type) = @_;
    my ($ref) = [];
    filter_add(bless $ref);
}

sub filter {
    my ($self) = @_;
    my ($status);
    tr/n-za-mN-ZA-M/a-zA-Z/ if ($status = filter_read()) > 0;
    $status;
}

1;
```

All Perl source filters are implemented as Perl classes and have the same basic structure as the example above.

First, you include the Filter::Util::Call module, which exports a number of functions into your filter's namespace. The filter shown above uses two of these functions, `filter_add` and `filter_read`.

Next, create the filter object and associate it with the source stream by defining the `import` function. If you know Perl well enough, you know that `import` is called automatically every time a module is included with a `use` statement. This makes `import` the ideal place to both create and install a filter object.

In the example filter, the object ($ref) is blessed just like any other Perl object. The example uses an anonymous array, but it isn't a requirement. Because this example doesn't need to store any context information, you could have used a scalar or hash reference just as well. The next section demonstrates context data.

The association between the filter object and the source stream is made with the filter_add function. This function takes a filter object as a parameter ($ref in this case) and installs it in the source stream.

Finally, there is the code that actually does the filtering. For this type of Perl source filter, all the filtering is done in a method called filter.* It's called every time the Perl parser needs another line of source to process. The filter method, in turn, reads lines from the source stream using the filter_read function.

If a line was available from the source stream, filter_read returns a status value greater than zero and appends the line to $_. A status value of zero indicates end-of-file; less than zero means an error. The filter function itself is expected to return its status in the same way, and put the filtered line it wants written to the source stream in $_. The use of $_ accounts for the brevity of most Perl source filters.

In order to make use of the rot13 filter, you need some way of encoding the source file in rot13 format. The script below, mkrot13, does just that.

```
die "usage mkrot13 filename\n" unless @ARGV;
my $in = $ARGV[0];
my $out = "$in.tmp";
open(IN,  "<$in")  or die "Cannot open file $in: $!\n";
open(OUT, ">$out") or die "Cannot open file $out: $!\n";

print OUT "use Rot13;\n";
while (<IN>) {
    tr/a-zA-Z/n-za-mN-ZA-M/;
    print OUT;
}

close IN;
close OUT;
unlink $in;
rename $out, $in;
```

If you encrypt this with mkrot13:

```
print "hello fred\n";
```

the result will be this:

```
use Rot13;
cevag "uryyb serq\a";
```

Running it produces this output:

```
hello fred
```

---

* It is also possible to write a Perl source filter using a closure. See the Filter::Util::Call documentation for details.

The Debug Filter

The rot13 example was trivial. Here's another demonstration that shows a few more features.

Suppose you wanted to include a lot of debugging code in your Perl script during development, but you didn't want it available in the released product. Source filters offer a solution. In order to keep the example simple, let's say you wanted the debugging output to be controlled by an environment variable, DEBUG. Debugging code is enabled if the variable exists; otherwise, it is disabled.

Two special marker lines will bracket debugging code, like this:

```
## DEBUG_BEGIN
if ($year > 1999) {
    warn "Debug: millennium bug in year $year\n";
}
## DEBUG_END
```

When the DEBUG environment variable exists, the filter ensures that Perl parses only the code between the DEBUG_BEGIN and DEBUG_END markers. That means when DEBUG doesn't exist, the code above should be passed through the filter unchanged. The marker lines can also be passed through as-is, because the Perl parser will see them as comment lines. You need a way to disable the debug code when DEBUG isn't set. A simple way to achieve that is to convert the lines between the two markers into comments:

```
## DEBUG_BEGIN
#if ($year > 1999) {
#    warn "Debug: millennium bug in year $year\n";
#}
## DEBUG_END
```

Here is the complete Debug filter:

```
package Debug;

use strict;
use Filter::Util::Call;

use constant TRUE  => 1;
use constant FALSE => 0;

sub import {
    my ($type) = @_;
    my (%context) = (    Enabled => defined $ENV{DEBUG},
                      InTraceBlock => FALSE,
                          Filename => (caller)[1],
                            LineNo => 0,
                         LastBegin => 0,
    );
    filter_add(bless \%context);
}
```

```
sub Die {
    my ($self)    = shift;
    my ($message) = shift;
    my ($line_no) = shift || $self->{LastBegin};
    die "$message at $self->{Filename} line $line_no.\n"
}

sub filter {
    my ($self) = @_;
    my ($status);
    $status = filter_read( );
    ++ $self->{LineNo};

    # deal with EOF/error first
    if ($status <= 0) {
        $self->Die("DEBUG_BEGIN has no DEBUG_END") if $self->{InTraceBlock};
        return $status;
    }

    if ($self->{InTraceBlock}) {
        if (/^\s*##\s*DEBUG_BEGIN/ ) {
            $self->Die("Nested DEBUG_BEGIN", $self->{LineNo})
        } elsif (/^\s*##\s*DEBUG_END/) {
            $self->{InTraceBlock} = FALSE;
        }

        # comment out the debug lines when the filter is disabled
        s/^/#/ if ! $self->{Enabled};
    } elsif ( /^\s*##\s*DEBUG_BEGIN/ ) {
        $self->{InTraceBlock} = TRUE;
        $self->{LastBegin} = $self->{LineNo};
    } elsif ( /^\s*##\s*DEBUG_END/ ) {
        $self->Die("DEBUG_END has no DEBUG_BEGIN", $self->{LineNo});
    }
    return $status;
}
1;
```

The big difference between this filter and the previous example is the use of context data in the filter object. The filter object is based on a hash reference, and is used to keep various pieces of context information between calls to the filter function. All but two of the hash fields are used for error reporting. The first of those two, Enabled, is used by the filter to determine whether the debugging code should be given to the Perl parser. The second, InTraceBlock, is true when the filter has encountered a DEBUG_BEGIN line, but has not yet encountered the following DEBUG_END line.

If you ignore all the error-checking that most of the code does, the essence of the filter is as follows:

```
sub filter {
    my ($self) = @_;
    my ($status);
    $status = filter_read( );
```

```
        # deal with EOF/error first
        return $status if $status <= 0;

        if ($self->{InTraceBlock}) {
            if (/^\s*##\s*DEBUG_END/) {
                $self->{InTraceBlock} = FALSE
            }

            # comment out debug lines when the filter is disabled
            s/^/#/ if !$self->{Enabled};

        } elsif ( /^\s*##\s*DEBUG_BEGIN/ ) {
            $self->{InTraceBlock} = TRUE;
        }
        return $status;
    }
```

Be warned: just as the C preprocessor doesn't know C, the Debug filter doesn't know Perl. It can be fooled quite easily:

```
print <<EOM;
##DEBUG_BEGIN
EOM
```

Aside from situations like this, a lot can be achieved with a modest amount of code.

Conclusion

You now have better understanding of what a source filter is, and you might even have a possible use for them. If you feel like playing with source filters but need a bit of inspiration, here are some extra features you could add to the Debug filter.

First, an easy one. Rather than having debugging code that is all-or-nothing, it is much more useful to control which specific blocks of debugging code are included. Try extending the syntax for debug blocks to allow each to be identified. The contents of the DEBUG environment variable can then be used to control which blocks get included.

Once you can identify individual blocks, try allowing them to be nested. That isn't difficult either.

Here is a interesting idea that doesn't involve the Debug filter. Currently, Perl subroutines have fairly limited support for formal parameter lists. You can specify the number of parameters and their type, but you still have to manually take them out of the @_ array yourself. Write a source filter that allows you to have a named parameter list. Such a filter would turn this:

```
sub MySub ($first, $second, @rest) { ... }
```

into this:

```
sub MySub ($$@) {
    my ($first) = shift;
    my ($second) = shift;
```

```
        my (@rest) = @_;
        ...
}
```

Finally, if you feel like a real challenge, have a go at writing a full-blown Perl macro preprocessor as a source filter. Borrow the useful features from the C preprocessor and any other macro processors you know. The tricky bit will be choosing how much knowledge of Perl's syntax you want your filter to have.

## CHAPTER 34

Overloading

Hildo Biersma

This article describes Perl's *operator overloading*, a feature that allows user-defined types to act in the same way as built-in types such as strings and numbers. It's one of the main strengths of C++, and one of the most glaring omissions in Java.

If you've been debugging your program with Data::Dumper and suffering output that looks like MyType=HASH(0xDEADBEEF), or if you're still invoking compare($first, $second) when you'd prefer to say $first == $second or $first eq $second, operator overloading can help.

This article starts by creating a simple user-defined type and then extends it to act as much like a built-in type as possible. After I'm done, you'll be able to decide how and when operator overloading should be used, and how to implement these features for your own types.

Defining Your Own Types

Perl 5 has always allowed you to add your own data types to the language via object-oriented programming. In this article, I'll define my own Date type that stores date stamps with a resolution of one day. It will support easy formatting in textual, European, and U.S. formats, provide easy comparison between dates, and allow simple arithmetic on dates.

Start by defining a simple Date class, in its own module. The class contains a new method, shown below:

```perl
# Constructor: get day, month, year, return object
sub new {
    my ($class, %args) = @_;        # Argument checking
    $args{'month'} -= 1;            # should be done here
    $args{'year'}  -= 1900;         # and here

    my $ctime = timelocal(0, 0, 0, $args{'day'}, $args{'month'}, $args{'year'});
    my $this = { 'ctime' => $ctime };
    return bless $this, $class;
}
```

This constructor computes a Unix timestamp (the return value of `timelocal`) and stores it inside the object. This is an implementation detail, of course; the object might as well store the day, month, and year values instead of the Unix time. A full implementation would also perform error-checking and throw an exception if the arguments are invalid or incomplete.

The Date class can be used as shown below:

```
use Date;

my $d1 = new Date('day' => 31,  'month' => 12, 'year' => 1999);
my $d2 = new Date('month' => 2, 'day' => 29,  'year' => 2000);
```

Adding Methods to the Date Class

Now, to make the class a bit more useful, I add three formatting methods that allow me to show the date in the three formats: text, U.S., European:

```
# Create a nice string for a date, like "Dec 31, 1999"
sub as_string {
    my ($this) = @_;

    my ($dd, $mm, $yy) = (localtime($this->{'ctime'}))[3,4,5];
    $mm = (qw(Jan Feb Mar Apr May Jun Jul Aug Sep Oct Nov Dec))[$mm];
    $yy += 1900;
    return "$mm $dd, $yy";
}


# Return in US format, e.g. 12-31-1999
sub us_fmt {
    my ($this) = @_;

    my ($dd, $mm, $yy) = (localtime($this->{'ctime'}))[3,4,5];
    $mm += 1;
    $yy += 1900;
    return "$mm-$dd-$yy";
}


# Return in European format, e.g. 31-12-1999
sub euro_fmt {
    my ($this) = @_;

    my ($dd, $mm, $yy) = (localtime($this->{'ctime'}))[3,4,5];
    $mm += 1;
    $yy += 1900;
    return "$dd-$mm-$yy";
}
```

These methods can be used as shown below:

```
use Date;

my $d1 = new Date('day'   => 31, 'month' => 12, 'year' => 1999);
my $d2 = new Date('month' => 2,  'day'   => 29, 'year' => 2000);
```

```
foreach my $dateval ($d1, $d2) {
    my $sd = $dateval->as_string();
    my $ed = $dateval->euro_fmt();
    my $ud = $dateval->us_fmt();
    print "Text: $sd; US format: $ud; Euro format: $ed\n";
}
```

The script generates the following output:

```
Text: Dec 31, 1999; US format: 12-31-1999; Euro format: 31-12-1999
Text: Feb 29, 2000; US format: 2-29-2000; Euro format: 29-2-2000
```

A Minor Problem

A minor problem occurs when I display date values without using any of the formatting methods displayed above. If I print $d1, I will get a string that indicates the class, the implementation, and the memory address of my object, like this: Date=HASH(0x80f11fc). That's not too informative.

When I use the date values with other operations such as numerical addition, numerical subtraction, comparison, or sorting, I get unfortunate effects: Perl operates on the values generated by converting my object to a string like Date=HASH(0x80f11fc).

Introducing Overloading

Operator overloading circumvents these problems, because it lets me provide my own versions of built-in operations like addition and subtraction. My new (overloaded) versions are automatically invoked in any expression involving objects of my class.

With my Date class, overloading can be applied to the built-in operators such as conversion-to-text ("stringification"), comparison, addition, and subtraction. All operator overloading features in Perl use the overload module, which is a standard part of Perl 5.004 and later versions.

I'll start by adding overloading for the conversion-to-string operator. Whenever this is called, I don't want to see things like Date=HASH(0x80f11fc); instead, I want to invoke the as_string method. I start by altering the Date class as follows:

```
package Date;

use overload ('""' => 'as_string');
```

That's all I need! From now on, printing a date object displays the proper value.

The syntax for the overload module is quite simple: following the use overload, list the operations to be overloaded, followed by their implementation. The implementation can either be a reference to a subroutine (\&as_string), or a string with the name of a method to be called ('as_string').

The difference between supplying a subroutine reference and a method name has to do with inheritance: when I supply a reference, I make sure the overloaded operator calls that exact subroutine, inheritance be damned. When I supply a method name, the overloaded operator will call that name and respect inheritance. In general, method names are preferable.

Overloading More Methods

Now that you've seen how to overload the stringification operator, let's do more. It would be useful if I could add a number of days to a date such as $day + 2, and have that work properly.

I start by adding an add method to my Date class:

```
# Add an integer number of days to a date
sub add {
    my ($this, $days) = @_;

    my $retval = { 'ctime' => $this->{'ctime'} };
    $retval->{'ctime'} += $days * 24 * 60 * 60;
    bless $retval, ref($this);

    return $retval;
}
```

The add method must take care to build a new object, which it modifies and returns. Users wouldn't be happy if $b = $a + 1 modified $a! Also, the object is built using the two-argument form of bless, making this code safe for inheritance. (When called with a derived object, I create a new object of the exact same class.) Combined with the appropriate change to the use overload instruction, this allows me to run the program below:

```
use Date;

my $d1 = new Date('day' => 31,  'month' => 12, 'year' => 1999);
my $d2 = $d1 + 1;
my $d3 = 100 + $d1;
print "$d1 $d2 $d3";
```

The output is shown here:

```
Dec 31, 1999 Jan 1, 2000 Apr 9, 2000
```

But wait! I have $d1 + 1 as well as 100 + $d1. How does that work?

Overloading and Associativity

Whether I call $object + number or number + $object, the same method is called. Obviously, the number cannot be asked to add a date value to itself and return a new date. This works for commutative operators such as + and *, where the order of the operands doesn't matter. For noncommutative operators like -, this result is obviously not desired. So Perl adds a third parameter to the method being called. The parameter is false if the arguments are in the proper order, but true if the parameters are reversed, as in the case of 100 + $date.

This allows me to build a proper implementation of the subtraction operator. I want to support the following:

- Subtract a number of days from a date, giving a new date.
- Complain when someone tries to subtract a date from a number.
- When two dates are subtracted from each other, show the difference in days.

The code below shows how to do this. Note that I've moved the cloning of a date into its own method, copy, which is also invoked from add. This is just for convenience. An alternative design strategy would be to require the Date class and all derived classes to support a less messy clone method.

```perl
# Add an integer number of days to a date
sub add {
    my ($this, $days) = @_;

    my $retval = $this->copy();
    $retval->{'ctime'} += $days * 24 * 60 * 60;

    return $retval;
}

# Subtract a number of days from a date or subtract two dates
sub subtract {
    my ($first, $second, $reverse) = @_;

    if (ref($second)) {          # Second parameter is a reference
        if (UNIVERSAL::isa($second, 'Date')) {
            my $val = $first->{'ctime'} - $second->{'ctime'};
            $val /= 24 * 60 * 60;
            return $val;
        }
        confess "Cannot subtract non-date [$second] from [$first]";
    } else {                    # Second parameter not a reference
        if ($reverse) {
            confess "Cannot call [[$second - $first]";
        }
        my $retval = $first->copy();
        $retval->{'ctime'} -= $second * 24 * 60 * 60;
        return $retval;
    }
}


# Copy constructor
sub copy {
    my ($this) = @_;
    return bless { %$this }, ref($this);
}
```

The subtract method shown above uses the UNIVERSAL class to determine whether the second object is a Date object or a derived class before accessing the ctime field inside the object. This code is careful to check the type (is this really a Date object?), while still allowing other classes to be derived from Date. Alternately, I could support "interfaces" (in the Java design style) and assume a ctime method is supported by the second object. It all depends on the programming and design style.

Let's use these methods with the following code:

```
use Date;

my $d1 = new Date('day' => 1,   'month' => 1,  'year' => 1999);
my $d2 = new Date('day' => 31,  'month' => 12, 'year' => 1999);
my $d3 = $d1 - 1;
my $days = $d1 - $d2;
print "$d1 / $d2 / $d3 / $days\n";

# The next one dies, so let's see...
eval { 100 - $d1 };
print $@;
```

Here is the output:

```
Jan 1, 1999 / Dec 31, 1999 / Dec 31, 1998 / -364
Cannot call [[100 - Jan 1, 1999] at Date.pm line 80
        Date::subtract('Jan 1, 1999', 100, 1) called at date1.pl line 10
        eval {...} called at date1.pl line 10
```

Full Overloading Implementations

A fully overloaded user-defined data type needs far more than this. Besides mere string conversion and simple arithmetic, I want to be able to compare two date objects using ==, >, or gt, sort objects using Perl's built-in sort function, use more complex operators such as += and ++, and cope with calls to undefined methods.

Please refer to the overload documentation bundled with Perl to see which operators can be overloaded: more than fifty are supported. In many cases, this is so much work it's not worth the effort. Of course, Perl can help with this as well.

Automatically Generating Overloaded Methods

Suppose that I do not change the Date class above, but invoke:

```
use Date;

my $d1 = new Date('day' => 1, 'month' => 1, 'year' => 1999);
$d1++;
$d1 += 5;
print "Date: $d1\n";
```

Possibly to your surprise, this will work properly. The reason is quite simple: Perl is able to build its own implementation of the ++ and += operators using the + operator that has been defined. As you can guess, the efficiency of these generated operators is slightly less than that of handcrafted methods that just modify an existing object, but hey, you get them for free.

In a similar fashion, Perl autogenerates all comparison operators if I provide cmp and <=>. It creates unary minus (negation) from the subtraction operator, and supports concatenation using string conversion. This magic drastically cuts down the amount of operators I need to write.

The code below defines a single compare method, used for string and numerical comparisons. Once this has been defined, all Perl comparison operators work properly.

```perl
package Date;

use overload ('cmp' => 'compare',
              '<=>' => 'compare',
              '""'  => 'as_string',
              '-'   => 'subtract',
              '+'   => 'add');

# Compare two values by comparing their ctimes
sub compare {
    my ($first, $second) = @_;

    unless (UNIVERSAL::isa($second, 'Date')) {
      confess "Can only compare two Date objects, not $second";
    }
    return ($first->{'ctime'} <=> $second->{'ctime'});
}
```

The Fallback Mechanism

A question remains: what will Perl do if I try to use an operator I haven't defined? Normally, Perl will complain and throw a fatal exception. Witness the output produced by trying to use the exponentiation operator on a Date:

```
Operation '**': no method found,
        left argument in overloaded package Date,
        right argument has no overloaded magic at date2.pl line 4.
```

As you can see, Perl dies. If I define a numerical conversion operator called 0+ for my class, all normal numerical operators could act on that converted numerical value. (Obviously, no such useful conversion exists for the Date class.) This is done through a *fallback* mechanism that allows Perl to use conversions. The fallback mechanism is enabled at the use overload line, and can be set to the following values:

- undef, to automatically generate ++ and += from +, but to throw an exception for unknown cases such as **.
- A *true* value, to generate operators and then fall back to the normal Perl operators on failure.
- A *false* value, to neither generate methods nor fall back to normal Perl operators.

As a silly example, the code below alters the Date class to turn on fallback and use a numerical conversion that generates the weekday number. Now ** will exponentiate using the weekday number.

```
package Date;

use overload ('fallback' => 1,        # true value
              '0+'                => 'to_number',
              'cmp'               => 'compare',
              '<=>'               => 'compare',
              '""'                => 'as_string',
              '-'                 => 'subtract',
              '+'                 => 'add');

# Silly numerical conversion operator
sub to_number {
    my ($this) = @_;

    return (localtime($this->{'ctime'}))[6];
}
```

Overloading and Inheritance

Overloading can be combined with inheritance as you wish. Any subclass automatically inherits all methods from the parent class and can then go on to override or add any operator at will. As an example of this, I'll define a EuroDate class that behaves exactly the same way as the normal Date class, except that the string representation is now in European format, not text format.

```
package EuroDate;

use strict;
use Date;
use vars qw(@ISA);

@ISA = qw(Date);

use overload ('""'  => 'euro_fmt');

1;
```

Everything behaves exactly as expected.

In the case of inheritance, there are a few traps to avoid:

- Overload methods by supplying a method name, not a subroutine reference. If you supply a code reference, virtual methods provided by derived classes will not be invoked.

- When you create new objects, as in the add and subtract methods above, make sure you use the two-argument form of bless to create objects of the proper class.

- When you check the class of an object, don't check the ref value; use the isa method from the UNIVERSAL class instead.

Limitations of Operator Overloading

However simple and elegant the Perl operator overloading mechanism may be, it has some limitations that C++ doesn't. The most important of these follow:

- There is no support for a proper assignment operator or copy constructor. Assignment of a reference is therefore always a shallow copy. If you define an assignment operator, it is only invoked in special circumstances: when you have multiple references to the same underlying object, and a mutating operator such as += is invoked, then a copy is made first.
- You can't override the arrow operator -> used for method calls and dereferencing.
- You *can* override array and hash indexing, but you must use a different and conflicting mechanism called tie.
- Since there is no proper copy constructor, the difference between pre-increment and post-increment ++ is largely academic.

Conclusion

This article shows how to use operator overloading for your own datatypes. As you've seen, simple things can be done very easily, and complex behavior can be created when you need it. The Perl overloading mechanism is general, yet flexible enough to be applied to your own classes as well.

References

For Perl, the bundled overload documentation (perldoc overload) is the definitive reference. For operator overloading in general, the C++ language reference (Stroustrup) introduces all the concepts you need, as well as the C++ implementation, which is both more powerful and less elegant than the Perl version.

The Math::Complex, Math::BigInt, and Math::BigFloat modules all use operator overloading.

CHAPTER 35

Building Objects Out of Arrays

Greg Bacon

Object-oriented programming is an approach to software design that most programmers simultaneously love and hate. OOP is just so adorable because it provides a simple conceptual model and code that often reads very similarly to natural language:

```
my $dog = new Dog;   ## create a new dog
$dog->bark;          ## Speak, Fido!
```

The misconception that object-oriented design is the proper ritual to drive out bugs and maintenance problems causes most most programmers to hang their heads and sigh when someone touts the latest Magic Object-Oriented Toaster. But the OOP Establishment thrives on rituals. In the tradition of Galileo, I will challenge the Establishment and repudiate one of those rituals:

> Objects in Perl need not be represented with hashes.

This article assumes at least some knowledge of how to implement objects in Perl. If you don't currently possess the prerequisite knowledge, fear not! You are but a short reading of the `perltoot` documentation away. This article explores how using arrays as objects can be more efficient (both timewise and spacewise) and encourage nicer style, while refraining from violating this principle given in the `perlmodlib` documentation:

> Perl doesn't have an infatuation with enforced privacy. It would prefer that you stayed out of its living room because you weren't invited, not because it has a shotgun.

We'll call this the Graciousness Principle.

OO Basics

There are several ways to create objects in Perl, but they all have the same effect: they store the state of the world (or at least the way they see it) in a data structure and return a reference to it. As the `perltoot` examples show, that data structure can be a scalar, array, hash, typeglob, or even an anonymous subroutine. Each of these makes different tradeoffs between flexibility, speed, size, and readability. As a quick browse of CPAN confirms, Perl programmers prefer hashes as their structure of choice, probably because of hashes' high score on the flexibility scale.

Let's say we want to create objects to represent people. In OO parlance, we would say that we want to create instances of the Person class. Think of a class as a definition of what objects "know" about themselves. For example, every person knows his name. If we can say something about the entire class, then that is said to be part of the class definition. Now, let's think of a particular person—Larry Wall, for instance. Larry knows his name, and he could tell us if we asked him. We can think of Larry as an instance of class Person.

This is how we might implement a Person class in Perl:

```perl
package Person;

# create a new Person object whose name is provided in @_
# e.g. my $person = new Person 'Larry';
sub new {
    my $class = shift;
    my $self  = {};
    $self->{NAME} = shift;
    bless $self => $class;
}

# A method to get or set the NAME
sub name {
    my $self = shift;
    $self->{NAME} = shift if @_;
    $self->{NAME};
}

1;
```

Before we attack this code, a little terminology. The new subroutine above is called a *constructor* because we invoke it whenever we want to create a new Person object. Subroutines that know how to operate on objects are called *methods*. (We might think of addition and subtraction as methods on the class of Integers, for example.) If a method is used only to store and retrieve an attribute (NAME, above) of an object, it's called an *accessor*. name is an accessor.

Say we want to have our Person objects come to the microphone and introduce themselves:

```perl
my $lwall   = new Person 'Larry';
my $tchrist = new Person 'Tom';

for $person ($lwall, $tchrist) {
    print "Hi, my name is ", $person->name, ".\n";
}
```

Because of the way we generalized the notion of what a person is and how to coax information out of them, we are able to use generic code to get people to speak up.

One of the tenets of OO is that we should be able to write code like this independently of how new and name are defined. When we peer inside the black box of a Person object, we see a hash: the my $self = {} makes $self into a reference to an anonymous hash, and the bless at the end of the constructor makes that into an object. Everywhere we look, we'll see constructors like this.

However, if we're willing to write our accessors differently, we can say my $self = [] and build objects out of arrays. Here's a new new that creates an object out of an array:

```
sub new {
    my $class = shift;
    my $self = [];
    $self->[NAME] = shift;
    bless $self => class;
}
```

Our new name also just trades braces for brackets:

```
sub name {
    my $self = shift;
    $self->[NAME] = shift if @_;
    $self->[NAME];
}
```

There are four reasons why arrays are preferable to hashes:

1. Arrays are faster.
2. They use less space.
3. They can prevent attribute collisions.
4. And arrays can prevent us from misspelling attribute names.

The first two are general truths, and the last two are specific to a technique for manipulating attributes, described later. In this article, we'll examine each of these reasons one by one.

Arrays Are Faster

We've only exchanged braces for brackets, but Graham Barr (author of the popular IO and libnet packages) reported that when he reworked Convert::BER to use arrays instead of hashes, he saw a speed improvement of better than twenty percent. To test this claim, I used a base class with two attributes and a subclass with one. The benchmark program used both arrays and hashes to construct new objects and read and write those attributes. My simple benchmarks found a comparable speedup.

The increase is because an element can be retrieved from an array faster than a hash, although as perltoot points out, the savings aren't as substantial as might be hoped:

> You might guess that the array access would be a lot faster than the hash access, but they're actually comparable. The array is a little bit faster, but not more than ten or fifteen percent, even when you replace the variables above like $AGE with literal numbers, like 1.

Arrays Use Less Space

My benchmark program created large arrays of subclassed objects. Using the PERL_DEBUG_MSTATS feature to measure the space, I found that arrays used a little more space initially, but for large numbers of objects, hashes used about 40% more memory in the Perl 5.005 days. Under Perl 5.6, the space savings is about 20%. perltoot continues:

> A bigger difference between the two approaches can be found in memory use. A hash representation takes up more memory than an array representation because you have to allocate memory for the keys as well as for the values.

Although space and time requirements should not be the standards by which all implementations are judged, they become increasingly important as an application creates more and more objects.

Arrays Can Prevent Attribute Collisions

Let's say we define a subclass of the Person class: Child. Any Person can have an email address, even children, so we make EMAIL an attribute of all Person objects. An email accessor is used to get and set the email address. And if we implement our objects as hashes, the attribute would be stored as $object->{EMAIL}. So far, so good.

The sharp reader will wonder what prevents a subclass from inadvertently accessing the attribute of a superclass. Envision a collaborative software project in which different people implement different classes. The author of the Child class didn't remember that the author of the Person class implemented an EMAIL attribute, and in a late night coding frenzy he used $object->{EMAIL} as a Boolean to keep track of whether the Child is old enough to read email. That's a *collision*, and it's a common problem in large software projects.

Unfortunately, there's no easy way to prevent collisions: this is one of the biggest problems with hashes as objects. It might be possible to represent the object with a tied hash whose FETCH and STORE methods (see the perltie documentation) maintained a registry of which classes are allowed to access which keys, but this would be cumbersome and slow. Such a solution would also violate the Graciousness Principle.

We're going to solve the collision problem by ensuring that each attribute is assigned a unique number. That shouldn't come as a surprise; the big difference between hashes and arrays is that hashes let us name elements, while arrays only let us number them. Naming is more convenient and readable (at least for the programmer)— but as we'll see, there's a clever workaround that allows us to name the elements of our array *and* avoid collisions.

The perlsub documentation describes how we can create constants at compile time. Here's the common example:

```
sub PI () { 3.14159 }      # define constant PI
use constant PI => 3.14159;  # has the same effect
```

Subroutines like this are a hint to the Perl compiler that it's okay to inline the subroutine's return value—to substitute 3.14159 wherever it sees PI, just like the C preprocessor.

We can use this for our attributes, converting names into numbers with subroutines like sub NAME { 0 } and sub EMAIL { 1 }.

What we'll do is generate those numbers automatically to preclude collisions beween names. Our collision protection for root classes (that is, classes with no superclasses) goes near the top of the class:

```
package Person;

my @Attributes;
BEGIN {                      # executed at compile time
    @Attributes = qw( NAME EMAIL );

    my $i = 0;
    for (@Attributes) {
        eval "sub $_ () { $i }";
        $i++;
    }
}


sub ATTRIBUTES { @Attributes }
```

The Child subclass looks like this:

```
package Child;

use Person;

my @Attributes;
BEGIN {
    @Child::ISA = qw( Person );
    @Attributes = qw( PARENT EMAIL );

    my $class = 'Child';

    # Set $i to the number of known attributes,
    # which is also the next free index in the array.
    my $i = $class->SUPER::ATTRIBUTES;

    for (@Attributes) {
        eval "sub $_ () { $i }";
        $i++;
    }
}

sub ATTRIBUTES {
    my $class = shift;
    my @a = ($class->SUPER::ATTRIBUTES, @Attributes);
    return @a;
}
```

```
sub parent {
    my $self = shift;
    $self->[PARENT] = shift if @_;
    $self->[PARENT];
}

1;
```

The purpose of all this ATTRIBUTE code is to ensure that every attribute throughout the class hierarchy has a unique integer. That integer corresponds to its index in the array, which is how we can get away with the illusion of having conveniently named attributes instead of unintuitive integers. Thanks to the constants created by our eval statement, it's speedy. And we have observed the Graciousness Principle: anyone can "cheat" and access the array directly, or even recover the symbol associated with a particular index.

Arrays Can Prevent Misspellings

If we were really determined to use hashes, we could do what Graham Barr did to avoid collisions and always put the class name in the keys to avoid ambiguity. So a Child's email address would be $obj->{CHILD_EMAIL}. This works, but it's cumbersome and involves a lot of extra typing. Furthermore, deep subclasses will have extremely long keys, such as Person_Worker_Blue_Collar_Construction. The longer the name, the more opportunities there are to misspell it.

People—especially programmers—are lazy. If we want someone to go along with our idea, we have to show him how we can help him save some effort. Our shortened attribute names are simpler to spell. And there's an added bonus: if our class uses the strict pragma, we'll be notified at compile time if we misspell a key!

Disadvantages

This technique for collision avoidance won't work for multiple inheritance. Depending on your opinion of MI, this is either a Good Thing or a Big Loss. Given that forcing people to do things isn't nice, this approach would be better if there were a way to reconcile it with multiple inheritance.

Furthermore, this approach requires that all attributes be known in advance; you can't add attributes at runtime. If you do, you run the risk of two attributes being awarded the same index number, causing colliions.

The biggest disadvantage to this approach is the inertia that the hash representation has gained over the past few years. One criticism of Perl's OO is that subclasses are forced to use the same representation as the superclass. Using the array representation described here means retrofitting lots of old code, and the path of least resistance dictates that people will happily stay where they are. Of course, that doesn't stop anyone from using this approach in *new* code, and I hope they will, because it makes the right tradeoffs between flexibility, speed, size, and readability.

Other Approaches

As the number of elements in an array grows, the space costs become more and more expensive. When it becomes untenable, you could store your arrays in a packed string, or even a simple string like `$obj = join $;, @array;`. Some details are hazy; for instance, how do you assign to the middle of your scalar efficiently? Repeatedly inflating and deflating the string would probably kill any gain. However, if the object is write-one-read-many, it might be a reasonable tradeoff.

Abigail's brilliant OO::Closures module makes use of closures to create a simple and elegant OOP environment; see also the next article, *Hiding Objects with Closures*.

This new approach to implementing objects illustrates that you don't have to do what everyone else does to do your job well. When you can build your objects out of arrays, you benefit from a cleaner style, attribute spellchecking, collision protection, and you use less memory and access time. If arrays aren't feasible, remember that There's More Than One Way To Do It, and take advantage of Perl's empowering flexibility to craft a solution that works for you.

## CHAPTER 36

Hiding Objects with Closures

Nigel Chapman

Tom Christiansen's object-oriented Perl tutorial (the *perltoot* documentation bundled with Perl) describes a way of using closures to hide data stored in an object. It's a technique that deserves to be better known, so in this article I will elaborate on Tom's description and add a little background.

First of all, a warning. The three great object-oriented virtues are correctness, maintainability, and re-usability—efficiency isn't included. The techniques I'm going to describe are not the fastest. If that bothers you, don't use them.

Those who like to use objects and classes do so, in part, in order to manage the complexity of medium to large programs by breaking them into pieces and restricting the way in which separate pieces interact with one another. An extra benefit is that other people can take some of our pieces and use them in their programs, too.

The basic idea is to organize a program as a set of objects that know various things about their own state, and can perform certain actions in response to messages. There is no other way the object's state can be changed. In anthropomorphic terms, the object takes responsibility for organizing its own internal state, and doesn't allow any other object or function to change it directly.

The set of actions an object can perform—that is, the set of messages it responds to—depends on what sort of object it is, so objects can be grouped into classes according to the actions they perform. A program can be designed by thinking about the sorts of things that it models. These sorts of things are then characterized by their behavior, leading to a specification of some classes. A particular program performs a task by creating some objects belonging to these classes, which carry out the desired computation by exchanging messages that cause them to carry out actions.

The well-known object-oriented programming languages such as C++ and Java implement objects as structures (or records) that hold the data representing the object's state, ensuring that these values can only be altered by the functions—or *methods*, as they are more often called—that implement the actions provided by the class. The methods provide a well defined interface to the object. The user of the object can only affect it by calling methods (or "sending it messages," if you prefer), and never by directly altering the values stored in the object structure. This means the user doesn't need to know how the values are stored, because only the external effect of the method matters. (In some languages, it is possible to write down a set of equations, or *axioms*, that define the effect of the methods purely in terms of each other, without reference to any internal representation at all. You can't do this in C++ or Java, though. Or in Perl.)

This *data hiding* has several advantages. It leaves the implementor of the class free to change the representation at any time. As long as the interface is left in place and the methods provide the same external behavior, the user of the class will be none the wiser.

Thus, if there is some compelling reason to change the representation of a class, the changes are entirely confined to the definition of the class itself. An example is a class for storing dates; if a hapless programmer had decided to store the year as two decimal digits, when the truth finally dawned the necessary changes would be confined to the date class and its methods, not scattered around every program that manipulated dates.

Another advantage concerns debugging. If a program misbehaves and preliminary investigations show that some object has an unexpected value that is causing the problem, you know that the only place you need to look is in the methods of the class to which the offending object belongs, because that is the only code that can alter the value. If any function at all is able to alter the values stored in an object, then all functions are potentially suspect (especially if you use global variables).

Perl has facilities for defining classes and creating objects belonging to the classes, but unlike other object-oriented languages it provides no special linguistic support for data hiding. Usually, Perl programmers rely on documentation, a bit of convention, and common sense.

A Simple Example

To see how this works, consider a simple example. Suppose you're writing a collection of Perl programs to control event scheduling, and you want to provide an interface resembling the controls of a VCR. That is, to set up an event, your user sees a display showing hours and minutes, and can cycle through them using up and down arrows to set a time for something to happen. (If you want to be extravagant, let's suppose that the system provides an integrated environmental control for all the timed devices in someone's house: central heating, VCR, microwave oven, and so on.)

Don't be concerned with the details of the display here—it can be done with Perl/Tk. The program will manipulate a representation of time that I'll call a "time setting," and it will need to be able to increase, decrease, and display these time settings.

Hence, I want a class TimeSetting, with methods hrs_up, hrs_down, mins_up, mins_down, and value. I also need a constructor, which I'll call new, to create TimeSetting objects. I'll give it an initial pair of integer values as arguments. (It's trivial to test whether these are supplied and set a default otherwise.) Having decided on those methods, I know how to use TimeSetting objects even though I haven't yet decided how to store their values, or how to implement the methods.

Conceptually, there are two sorts of methods: *object methods* and *class methods*. Object methods are called with an object as their first argument, and typically use the data stored in that particular object. To distinguish method calls from ordinary subroutine calls, a different syntax is employed. If $t is a TimeSetting object, then I would increment the hours component like this:

```
$t->hrs_up();
```

This passes $t to the hrs_up method as its first (in this case, its only) argument. For constructors, this doesn't work; there's no object to pass, since the whole point of a constructor is to create it. Instead, the name of the class is passed as an implicit argument to the method:

```
$t = TimeSetting->new(23, 58);     # two minutes to midnight
```

A more readable alternative, called *indirect object syntax*, is sometimes used, where the class name is written between the method name and any arguments:

```
my $t = new TimeSetting 23, 58;
```

Now that we know how to use our class, let's implement it. I'll store the pair of values in a hash, using HOURS and MINUTES as keys, so the hash looks like a structure. All the methods live in a package called TimeSetting, stored in *TimeSetting.pm*. The constructor initializes the hash (it should check whether the arguments are valid, but I've omitted the test to keep the code uncluttered) and returns a blessed reference to it, which will serve as the object.

If you have never worked with Perl's object-oriented features before, this may be a little obscure, but it's quite simple. Blessing a reference marks the thing it refers to as belonging to a class. This means methods can be called through the reference using the object-oriented syntax, and their names will be looked up in the class.

Apart from the constructor, the other methods are straightforward. Each shifts its first argument, which will be the object reference. That is then dereferenced, and the value-changing methods perform some arithmetic on one of the values, while value formats them with sprintf.

```
package TimeSetting;

sub new {
    my $class = shift;
    my ($h, $m) = @_;
    return bless {
        HOURS => $h,
        MINUTES => $m
    }, $class;
}
```

```perl
sub hrs_up {
    my $this = shift;
    ++$this->{HOURS} < 24 or $this->{HOURS} = 0;
}

sub hrs_down {
    my $this = shift;
    --$this->{HOURS} >= 0 or $this->{HOURS} = 23;
}

sub mins_up {
    my $this = shift;
    ++$this->{MINUTES} < 60 or $this->{MINUTES} = 0;
}

sub mins_down {
    my $this = shift;
    --$this->{MINUTES} >= 0 or $this->{MINUTES} = 59;
}

sub value {
    my $this = shift;
    return sprintf("%02d:%02d", $this->{HOURS},
                                 $this->{MINUTES});
}

1;
```

TimeSetting is certainly a class, and provided you play by the rules, all the benefits I've advertised will follow from its use. For example, I could change the stored representation of the time to a number of minutes past midnight, without requiring any program that uses a TimeSetting to be changed. Any weird values such as 199:88 can only be generated by the methods in this class; should such a value get thrown out during debugging, I would know where to look.[*] But Perl cannot offer any guarantees: the blessed reference is still a reference to a hash, as well as being blessed, and it can still be dereferenced and indexed. This is legal, if unwise:

```perl
my $t = new TimeSetting 23, 58;
$t->{HOURS} = 199;
$t->{MINUTES} = 88;
```

The Perl world says that anybody who does something like that either deserves anything they get or knows what they're doing and should not be constrained by repressive rules. I have a lot of sympathy for this point of view, but I also have some sympathy for the notion that if a programming language can help you avoid mistakes, you should let it do so. Remember that object-oriented techniques are only really relevant in large programs, or when we are re-using software components. It is conceivable that deep in a chain of subroutine calls, someone might mistake a

---

[*] Remember, I've elided some range-checking code from the constructor.

reference to a TimeSetting for some other sort of reference, and use it in such a way as to violate the TimeSetting axioms.

And then there is deliberate interference. In the Perl community, we usually dismiss worries about people interfering with our code as paranoia, but there are occasions when such worries are justified. The typical scenario is some programmer feeling that it's necessary to use an object in a way its designer didn't intend, but seems to be consistent with its semantics. For example, somebody might want to extract the hours from a TimeSetting. Even if they do this in a respectable way by deriving their own class and adding the new method there, their code will still break if a new version of the TimeSetting class is produced that uses the seconds-after-midnight representation. For a widely-distributed class, this could mean a maintenance nightmare for the original programmer.

For circumstances where it might matter if the representation of an object is accessed other than through its class's methods, there is a better way of storing data in objects in Perl. It's based on closures, and since not everybody is familiar with closures, I will briefly review them.

Closures

In Perl, you can create references to subroutines; in particular, you can create references to anonymous subroutines, using an expression like this:

```
sub { BODY }
```

Much like pointers to functions in C, references to subroutines effectively allow you to assign a subroutine to a scalar variable, store it in an array or hash, pass it as an argument to a subroutine, or return it as a result. Perl's references to subroutines are more powerful than C's function pointers, because of the way free variables are treated. A free variable is one that is not local. (I use the word "local" in its conventional, lexically scoped, sense, which has little to do with Perl's local function; see the article entitled *Scoping* for an explanation of the difference.) Since a reference to an anonymous subroutine can be created in any context in which an expression can be used, it may access the local variables of an enclosing block. Consider the following:

```
sub multiplier {
    my $x = shift;
    return sub { return $x * shift }
}
```

The $x used inside the anonymous subroutine is the local variable $x of multiplier. It continues to refer to this variable, even after the anonymous subroutine has been returned as the result, and even when it is subsequently used. If, for example, I call multiplier like this:

```
$doubler = multiplier(2);
```

then $x will be initialized to 2 within multiplier. Hence, the value returned by multiplier is a reference to a subroutine that multiplies its argument by 2—a doubler, in fact, so that &$doubler(5) is 10. On the other hand, this sets $quadrupler to a subroutine that multiplies its argument by four:

```
$quadrupler = multiplier(4);
```

$doubler and $quadrupler do not interfere with each other. The free variable is bound *dynamically* at the time the anonymous subroutine is created, so each value returned by multiplier has its own $x, set to the value of multiplier's argument.

If you are used to C's model of function calls, this may seem very strange—C functions can't access free variables, and the locals of a function cease to exist once control returns from the function.

However, once you grant that it makes sense to refer to free variables (and many programming languages sanction the practice) it also makes sense for a subroutine that is returned in this way to go on referring to them. Obviously, arranging for everything to work properly is a slight headache for the language implementors, but it can be done. The value of an anonymous subroutine is a thing called a *closure*, which not only holds the code to be executed, but also contains the environment in which the closure was created—that is, the free variables.

Closures have many uses. In Perl, one of them is the topic of this article: protecting an object's data from outside interference. The key observation is that the free variables of a closure created inside a subroutine are local to that subroutine, and these are out of scope, and therefore truly inaccessible anywhere else. In the example above, the name $x cannot be used at all outside multiplier to refer to the variable initialized at the beginning of that subroutine.

There are only two ways to access the value of a subroutine's local variables from outside the subroutine: one is to create a reference to them and pass that out of the subroutine, which is inviting interference; and the other is to pass out a closure that accesses them, which means access is only provided through the code of that closure. And this is just what you want with objects: access to the data should only be possible through methods.

There is more than one way to organize the details, but the strategy is to store the object's data in local variables of the constructor, and use closures created inside the constructor and called from the methods to perform the actions of the class. To make the closures available for subsequent use, I'll store them in a hash, and bless a reference to that hash to return as the object. My constructor looks like this:

```
sub new {
    my $class = shift;
    my ($h, $m) = @_;
    my %methods;

    $methods{HRS_UP}    = sub { ++$h < 24 or $h = 0  };
    $methods{HRS_DOWN}  = sub { --$h >= 0 or $h = 23 };
    $methods{MINS_UP}   = sub { ++$m < 60 or $m = 0  };
```

```
        $methods{MINS_DOWN} = sub { --$m >= 0 or $m = 59 };
        $methods{VALUE}     = sub { return sprintf("%02d:%02d", $h, $m) };
        return bless \%methods, $class;
    }
```

The methods now look very simple:

```
sub hrs_up {
    my $this = shift;
    &{$this->{HRS_UP}}( );
}
```

And so on. This class can be used in exactly the same way as the previous implementation by programs that only use its methods to access objects. Programs that dereference the object and change its data directly will no longer work.

The scheme is not bulletproof. It is certainly the case that the variables $h and $m can only be changed using the methods of this class, which is what I wanted. But like any object reference, one returned by this constructor can be dereferenced, which leads to some entertaining possibilities:

```
my $t = new TimeSetting 10, 30;
my $hu = $t->{HRS_UP};
&$hu( );
```

$hu->value now returns 11:30. I could call this a feature, like a with statement, but updating an object without the object is not really in the spirit of the game. At this point, I would be inclined to revert to the Perl establishment's approach, and say that anyone who does this wants their head examined. But it is possible to guard against this.

The closures *could* check the name of the calling package with caller to ensure that it was called from TimeSetting. Unfortunately, this check can only be made at runtime.

It's also possible for someone to assign new closures to elements of the hash inside a TimeSetting object or add new elements. Again, I could call this a feature. Doing so would not compromise the object's data, but it would change its class. There are programming languages in which you can do this—JavaScript, for example. I can't think of a sensible reason to do so (I can't even think of a silly reason), but I am aware that some people program in a style radically different from mine, so I'm prepared to believe that it might be a useful feature.

You can, however, prevent this by using a variation on the implementation just given.* Instead of building a separate closure for each method, just build one that selects a different branch to execute depending on a key passed as an argument, and return a blessed reference to the closure as the object.

```
sub new {
    my $class = shift;
    my ($h, $m) = @_;
```

---

* It is essentially this variation that is described in the *perltoot* documentation, although there only get/set methods are being used, so the methods can be collapsed into a single piece of code.

```
    my $methods = sub {
        my $key = shift;
        if    ($key eq HRS_UP)    { ++$h < 24 or $h = 0  }
        elsif ($key eq HRS_DOWN)  { --$h >= 0 or $h = 23 }
        elsif ($key eq MINS_UP)   { ++$m < 60 or $m = 0  }
        elsif ($key eq MINS_DOWN) { --$m >= 0 or $m = 59 }
        elsif ($key eq VALUE)     { return sprintf("%02d:%02d", $h, $m) }
    };
    return bless $methods, $class;
}

sub hrs_up {
    my $this = shift;
    &$this(HRS_UP);
}
```

And so on.

What About Inheritance?

My original scheme presents no problems for inheritance. Additional closures can be added to the hash, and methods to call them can be added to the interface. You can't sensibly derive anything from a TimeSetting, so consider a new example.

Suppose I want to create objects to connect to different network resources—to keep things manageable, say web pages and FTP sites. A very simple (too simple) model could be built by deriving classes for the two resources from a common base class that stored the host and pathname components of a URL. Using closures and local variables, this might be defined as follows:

```
package NetResource;

sub new {
    my $class = shift;
    my ($host, $path) = @_;
    my %methods;

    $methods{GET_HOST} = sub { return $host };
    $methods{GET_PATH} = sub { return $path };
    return bless \%methods, $class;
}

sub get_host {
    my $this = shift;
    &{$this->{GET_HOST}}();
}

sub get_path {
    my $this = shift;
    &{$this->{GET_PATH}}();
}

1;
```

I won't let you change the data once a NetResource object has been constructed, so there are no methods to assign new values to $host and $path.

From NetResource, I can derive a HTTPResource that adds a connect method:

```
package HTTPResource;

use NetResource;
@ISA = qw(NetResource);

sub new {
    my $class = shift;
    my $this = SUPER::new $class @_;

    $this->{CONNECT} = sub {

        # Make the connection using $this->get_host() and
        # $this->get_path() to find the components of the URL

    };
    return $this;
}

sub connect {
    my $this = shift;
    &{$this->{CONNECT}}();
}

1;
```

Here, I gain nothing from the use of closures, because there is no private data in the derived class. For an FTP resource, I might want to store a username and password, which makes the FTPResource class more interesting:

```
package FTPResource;

use NetResource;
@ISA = qw(NetResource);

sub new {
    my $class = shift;
    my $this = SUPER::new $class @_;
    my ($user_id, $password) = ($_[2], $_[3]);

    $this->{CONNECT} = sub {
    # Make the connection using $this->get_host() and
    # $this->get_path() to find the components of the URL
    # and $user_id and $password for identification

    };
    return $this;
}
```

```
sub connect {
    my $this = shift;
    &{$this->{CONNECT}}();
}

1;
```

I can use these classes in this manner:

```
my $web_page = new HTTPResource 'www.macavon.demon.co.uk', 'index.html';
# Use methods from the base class
print "host: ", $web_page->get_host(), "\n";
print "path: ", $web_page->get_path(), "\n";
# Use a method from the derived class
$web_page->connect();

my $cpan = new FTPResource 'ftp.demon.co.uk', 'pub/mirrors/perl/CPAN',
              'Groucho', 'swordfish';
# use a method from the other derived class
$cpan->connect();
```

I can even do something very C++-like, and move the connect method up into the base class, like this:

```
package NetResource;

sub new {
    my $class = shift;
    my ($host, $path) = @_;
    my %methods;

    # $methods{GET_HOST}, $methods{GET_PATH} as before
    $methods{CONNECT} = sub {
        die "Cannot connect to an abstract net resource\n";
    };
    return bless \%methods, $class;
}

sub connect {
    my $this = shift;
    &{$this->{CONNECT}}();
}

# Other methods as before

1;
```

The derived classes no longer need to define a connect method (calls to it through HTTPResource and FTPResource objects will find NetResource::connect via @ISA) but they still must assign their closures to the CONNECT element of %methods. This saves you a little typing, but doesn't gain you much else in the absence of statically typed objects in Perl. (If you like the idea that Perl has a postmodern architecture, you could claim that you are making an "ironic reference" to pure virtual functions in C++.)

One thing that may seem worrisome to a conventional object-oriented Perl programmer is that methods in derived classes cannot access the data in the base class. This is deliberate. There's little point in protecting this data if all a programmer needs to do to gain access to it is derive a new class. Derived classes should only be able to access data in their base class through the class's methods, just like any other code. This means more thought has to go into the design of base classes, but object-oriented design is not easy if it is done properly.

The more robust variation of the data hiding scheme—using a closure as the object itself—is less amenable to inheritance, since the closure returned by new cannot be extended. Instead, the object has to store a reference to its parent closure, and defer method calls it could not handle to that closure, effectively duplicating the built-in inheritance mechanism @ISA. For this reason, I prefer the original implementation.

Conclusion

You're probably concerned about the efficiency of the schemes I have described. Basically, you get one method call for the price of two, which doesn't sound like a good deal. This is only a linear slowdown, and a sufficiently aggressive optimizer could eliminate the extra call, but it's worth emphasizing that this approach to objects is only worthwhile when correctness, maintainability, and re-usability are more important than runtime efficiency or ease of hacking.

Traditionally, this has not been the case. Most Perl scripts are short, sharp, and to the point. However, as Perl becomes more widely accepted as a serious programming language and is used for more complex tasks, these concerns will become more relevant, and where object-oriented features are used, protecting data using closures will be seen as a worthwhile precaution. What is interesting to the programming language devotee is that the technique described in this article provides protection not by some special feature based on operating system access permissions, but by old-fashioned scope alone. Whereas the data hiding facilities of C++ can be undermined in a host of ways, there is no way around the fact that if a variable is out of scope, you just can't get at it.

Although the *perltoot* documentation is the immediate source of the data hiding scheme described in this article, it is not the first example of traditional scope rules being applied in a similar way. In particular, Malcolm Atkinson and Ron Morrison have described using the "first class" functions and lexical scoping of their programming language PS-Algol to provide an effective separation of a class's interface from its implementation.

## CHAPTER 37

Multiple Dispatch in Perl

Damian Conway

I can still remember the precise moment I first fell in love with polymorphism.

I had just delivered the final version of a medium-sized system (20,000 lines of C++) for running psychophysical visual perception experiments. The system could generate and animate a wide range of visual stimuli in 3D, using left-right stereograms viewed through LCD-shuttered glasses. It had its own scripting language and could run a controlled series of experiments, record a subject's responses, and generate reports and statistics on the results. It had real-time feedback mechanisms. It optimized its graphics to ensure that minimal frame-rates were always met. It was just what the doctors ordered.

Naturally, I got a phone call the very next day: "It's a great system, Damian. Works like a charm. Easy to use. Does everything we'd hoped. It's just what we ordered. Now, could we just add…"

Of course what they wanted was an entirely new category of visual stimulus. As well as the ability to investigate stereo perception (by sending a slightly offset version of the same signal to both eyes), they now wanted to study differences in left-brain/right-brain neurophysiology, by sending *completely different* signals to each eye. And could they have it by Friday?

As it turned out, they could.

The main stimulus-display subsystem was based on a tightly coded while loop that did little more than call the draw_me method of the current Stimulus object. Normally, this object was of the subclass StereoStimulus, but it took all of 20 minutes and about 40 lines of code to derive a new subclass called LeftRightStimulus, instantiate an object of that type, and plug it into the display loop. The LeftRightStimulus object encapsulated two subobjects (left_stim and right_stim), each of the existing type MonoStimulus. The complete LeftRightStimulus::draw_me method looked like this:

```
// Warning: C++ code!

void LeftRightStimulus::draw_me(Viewpoint* vp)
{
```

```
        left_stim->draw_me(vp->left_eye());
        right_stim->draw_me(vp->right_eye());
}
```

The new behavior worked the first time. The display loop didn't miss a beat, the graphics optimizer didn't bat an eye, the LCD shutter synchronization mechanism didn't even notice. Every one of the original 20,000 lines of code continued to work as smoothly as before, except now they could handle the new stimulus as well.

The kind of cleverness that allowed me to replace one object with another—and thereby invoke new behaviors with old code—is known as *polymorphism* (literally, "many forms"). It's a feature of any language in which the same method call can be applied to many types of objects, which then respond uniquely, each according to its class. And as you can see, it's a mighty useful and powerful technique.

Unfortunately, I can also remember the precise moment (a few short weeks later) when I fell out of love with polymorphism.

Several "Can you just adds..." down the line, the psychologists decided they now wanted to do what they called "motion tracking under distraction." That is, they wanted to have a subject follow one stimulus with a cursor while other stimuli appeared randomly on the screen (perhaps in another window), and they wanted the subject to respond in various ways (i.e., click the mouse, press a button, select the window) when certain conditions were detected. (Psychologists generally run these kinds of tests on their students—that is, future psychologists—which explains a great deal.)

The problem was that this kind of interaction requires the system to respond appropriately to events of various types, applied to stimuli of various sorts, in windows of various kinds. But you can't just call the handle_me method of some Event object, because that won't distinguish between the different types of stimuli and windows. Likewise, you can't call the handle_event of a Stimulus object, because that won't identify the specific kind of event and window involved.

So the standard polymorphic mechanism fails, because methods are selected using just a single piece of information—the class of the object on which a method is called. That's known as *single dispatch*, and it's all you get with most object-oriented programming languages. If your program needs to decide what to do based on the classes of two or more objects at once, you're out of luck.

In the end, giving the boffins their "motion tracking under distraction" involved a large amount of recoding of the existing system, a number of ugly hacks around the limitations of single dispatch,[*] and a sense of tragic disillusionment. What I needed

---

[*] Most of which are reported in: Chatterton, D.F. & Conway, D.M., *Multiple dispatch in C++ and Java*, Proc. TOOLS Pacific 1996, Monash University, Melbourne Australia, pp 75-87, 1996.

was a generic way of selecting the right method to handle the specific combination of event, stimulus, and window objects. And regular polymorphism just couldn't cut it.

Multiple Dispatch

Like most object-oriented languages, Perl polymorphically selects the subroutine to invoke in response to a method call. The subroutine is the one belonging to the invoking object's class. So, a call to `$objref->method(@args)` invokes *CLASSNAME*::method, where *CLASSNAME* is the class into which the `$objref` object was blessed.

If the class in question doesn't *have* a suitable method, then the dispatch procedure searches "upwards" through the various superclasses of the object's class, looking for an appropriate subroutine. If that search fails, the dispatch procedure searches the complete inheritance hierarchy again, looking for an AUTOLOAD subroutine instead.

The important point is that no matter which subroutine the method dispatcher eventually selects, it is all determined by the class of the original object on which the method was invoked. That is, according to the type of the first argument only.

As the anecdote above indicates, the ability to select behavior based on a single type is sufficient for most applications. In terms of their expressive power, such single dispatch mechanisms provide the same functionality as a "case" statement. The dispatch mechanism uses the class of the method's first argument like the selector of a switch statement in C, and the various polymorphic methods that can be invoked correspond to the various cases that could be selected. Alternatively, you can think of a polymorphic method as a 1D lookup table, where the first argument's type is the key and the method to be invoked is the corresponding value. In fact, many languages (including Perl) use such lookup tables to implement, or optimize, calls to polymorphic methods.

However, applications such as the motion tracking experiment mentioned above need to select the best polymorphic method on the basis of more than one argument. Hence they require a more complex dispatching behavior: something equivalent to nested switches or multidimensional tables. The object-oriented equivalent of those constructs is called *multiple dispatch*.

Whereas single dispatch considers only the first argument and searches for a subroutine compatible with it alone, multiple dispatch works by considering the actual class of *every one of a method's arguments*, and searching for a subroutine with a set of (typed) parameters compatible with them all.

Typical situations where multiple dispatch is needed include:

- Processing events in a graphical user interface, in which the correct response to an event depends not just on the graphical object that receives it, but also on the type of event, and the current mode of the interface (i.e., whether it's active or not, what types of events are enabled, and so on).

- Performing image-processing operations between heterogeneous images, such as a blend between two images that may be in different formats. Using multiple dispatch, the common case where the two images are in the same format can be handled by one (optimized) subroutine, and cases where conversions are required can be delegated to a more general (but probably less efficient) method.

- Handling binary operations on different numerical types (integer, rational, arbitrary-precision, etc.) Often the return type of such an operation will depend on the types of both operands: *integer* + *integer* gives *integer*, *integer* + *rational* gives *rational*, *arbitrary-precision* + *rational* gives *arbitrary-precision*. Multiple dispatch lets you supply a separate method for each combination of operands, and then enables the program to automatically find the right one each time.

- Implementing simulations in which a diversity of objects interact. For example, in a physical simulation, the interaction of two objects colliding will depend on the nature of both (hard/hard, hard/brittle, soft/hard, brittle/sticky, and so on). Using multiple dispatch, handlers for each type of object-object interaction can be coded separately, and the correct handler selected automatically, based on the types of objects involved.

Generally speaking, multiple dispatch is needed whenever two or more objects belonging to different class hierarchies need to interact, and you find yourself doing different things depending on which objects are being combined.

Note that multiple dispatch *isn't* the same thing as overloaded functions (in C++ or Java). In those languages, you can define two or more methods with the same name but different parameter lists, and the compiler works out which one to call based on the nominal types of the arguments you specify. In other words, the compiler analyzes the argument type information, selects the corresponding target method, and hardcodes a call to it. That means if you then call the overloaded method with a set of arguments belonging to derived classes, you still invoke the method that handles the original base class arguments.

In multiple dispatch, on the other hand, the method is always chosen polymorphically by examining the actual runtime types of the objects you passed as arguments, *not* the compile-time types of the pointers or references through which those arguments were passed. Hence, if you pass derived objects as arguments, you get the method that handles derived objects.

Multiple Dispatch via "Tests-in-Methods"

Let's consider the example of an object-oriented GUI, since that's probably the most familiar application that can make good use of multiple dispatch. In such a system, there would be classes for various types of windows:

```
package Window;
package ModalWindow;      @ISA = qw( Window );
package MovableWindow;    @ISA = qw( Window );
package ResizableWindow;  @ISA = qw( MovableWindow );
```

and for various types of events:

```
package Event;
package ReshapeEvent;        @ISA = qw( Event );
package AcceptEvent;         @ISA = qw( Event );
package MoveEvent;           @ISA = qw( ReshapeEvent );
package ResizeEvent;         @ISA = qw( ReshapeEvent );
package MoveAndResizeEvent;  @ISA = qw( MoveEvent ResizeEvent );
```

and for various modes that the entire interface may be in:

```
package Mode;
package OnMode;     @ISA = qw( Mode );
package ModalMode;  @ISA = qw( Mode );
package OffMode;    @ISA = qw( Mode );
```

But what happens when a Window has to handle a specific Event in a certain Mode? That will happen repeatedly in the GUI's event loop:

```
while ($next_event = shift @event_queue) {
    $focus_window->receive_event($next_event, $current_mode);
}
```

Each of the classes in the Window hierarchy needs a polymorphic method (receive_event) that expects two arguments (an Event and a Mode) and determines how to handle the resulting combination. Example 37-1 shows an implementation of the Window hierarchy with suitable handler methods.

Example 37-1. Window subclasses with polymorphic receive_event methods

```
package Window;

my $_id = 1;
sub new { bless { _id => $_id++ }, $_[0] }

sub receive_event {
    my ($self, $event, $mode) = @_;
    if ($event->isa(Event) && $mode->isa(OffMode))
      { print "No window operations available in OffMode\n" }
    else
      { print "Window $self->{_id} can't handle a ",  ref($event),
            " event in ", ref($mode), " mode\n" }
}

package ModalWindow; @ISA = qw( Window );

sub receive_event {
    my ($self, $event, $mode) = @_;
    if ($event->isa(AcceptEvent)) {
      if ($mode->isa(OffMode))
        { print "Modal window $self->{_id} can't accept in OffMode!\n" }
      else
        { print "Modal window $self->{_id} accepts!\n" }
    }
    elsif ($event->isa(ReshapeEvent))
      { print "Modal windows can't handle reshape events\n" }
```

```
        else
          { $self->SUPER::receive_event($event,$mode) }
    }

    package MovableWindow; @ISA = qw( Window );

    sub receive_event {
        my ($self, $event, $mode) = @_;
        if ($event->isa(MoveEvent) && $mode->isa(OnMode))
          { print "Moving window $self->{_id}!\n" }
        else
          { $self->SUPER::receive_event($event,$mode) }
    }

    package ResizableWindow; @ISA = qw( MovableWindow );

    sub receive_event {
        my ($self, $event, $mode) = @_;
        if ($event->isa(MoveAndResizeEvent) && $mode->isa(OnMode))
          { print "Moving and resizing window $self->{_id}!\n" }
        elsif ($event->isa(ResizeEvent) && $mode->isa(OnMode))
          { print "Resizing window $self->{_id}!\n" }
        else
          { $self->SUPER::receive_event($event,$mode) }
    }
```

Notice that each `receive_event` method of the various classes has what amounts to a nested case statement inside it (hence the description "tests-in-methods"). These `if` statements are needed to work out which combination of argument types has actually been received, and what action to take as a result. Also note that the last alternative in each method is always the same: give up and pass the arguments to the parent class, in the hope that it will be able to handle them.

The various cases that are directly tested don't explicitly cover all possible combinations of argument types. To do so would require a total of 96 alternatives (4 window classes × 6 event types × 4 modes). Instead, the handlers rely on the inheritance relationships of the various classes. For example, there is no specific test to detect a `ResizableWindow` object receiving a `MoveEvent` in `OffMode`. If that actually ever happens, the following sequence ensues:

- `ResizableWindow::receive_event` is called, and tests for the various cases it handles. None match, so it executes the `else` block, invoking its parent class's `receive_event` method on the same set of arguments.

- In response, `MovableWindow::receive_event` is called, and tests for the various cases that it handles. Once again, none match, so the `else` block is selected and invokes the grandparental `receive_event` method on the same arguments.

- That means `Window::receive_event` is called, and it too tests its various cases. The first case discovers that the `MoveEvent` argument can be treated as a `Event` (since the MoveEvent class inherits from Event). Then it discovers that the modes also match exactly. Consequently, it executes the code of the first case.

The result is that the set of arguments (ResizableWindow, MoveEvent, OffMode) have *collectively* been treated polymorphically, as if their types were Window, Event, and OffMode. Since there was no case to explicitly handle the actual combination, receive_event has located a case that will handle it more generally—by abstracting the first two arguments.

This type of "best fit" behavior is extremely useful, because it means you can code the cases you want to handle specially, and then provide one or more catch-all cases (handlers that take base-class parameter types) to deal with other argument combinations.

Normally, a polymorphic method like receive_event selects the subroutine to call by the type of its first argument alone and, if necessary, works its way up that argument's inheritance tree to find a suitable method. Here, in contrast, it's as if the receive_event was able to select the appropriate action on the basis of the combined types of *all three* arguments, working its way up *all three* inheritance hierarchies at once to find a suitable response.

That's polymorphism with a vengeance!

Multiple Dispatch via a Table

Of course, vengeance always comes at a price. In this instance, instead of the (already high) cost of doing a single polymorphic dispatch on the receive_event method, the dispatch mechanism now has to do that dispatch, test the various cases, perhaps redispatch receive_event to a parent class, and then repeat the tests there as well. You can feel the performance of your application ebbing away.

It would be far better if the call to receive_event went directly to a single method, which then determined the classes of the arguments involved, looked up the appropriate handler in some table, and invoked that handler directly. No multiple tests, no redispatch; just one subroutine call, one table lookup, and the handler is invoked. Example 37-2 illustrates the implementation of just such a method.

Example 37-2. A table-based implementation of the receive_event method

```
package Window;

my $_id = 1;
sub new { bless { _id => $_id++ }, $_[0] }

my %table;

sub init {
    my ($param1,$param2,$param3,$handler) = @_;
    foreach my $p1 ( @$param1 ) {
        foreach my $p2 ( @$param2) {
```

```perl
            foreach my $p3 ( @$param3 ) {
                $table{$p1}{$p2}{$p3} = $handler;
            }
        }
    }
}

my $windows  = [qw(Window ModalWindow MovableWindow ResizableWindow )];
my $events   = [qw(Event ReshapeEvent AcceptEvent MoveEvent
                   ResizeEvent MoveAndResizeEvent )];
my $modes    = [qw(Mode OnMode OffMode ModalMode )];

init $windows, $events, $modes                              # Case 0
    => sub { print "Window $_[0]->{_id} can't handle a ",
                   ref($_[1]), " event in ", ref($_[2]), " mode\n" };

init $windows, $events, [qw(OffMode)]                       # Case 1
    => sub { print "No window operations available in OffMode\n" };

init [qw(ModalWindow)],                                     # Case 2
     [qw(ReshapeEvent ResizeEvent MoveEvent MoveAndResizeEvent)],
     $modes
    => sub { print "Modal windows can't handle reshape events\n" };

init [qw(ModalWindow)], [qw(AcceptEvent)], $modes           # Case 3
    => sub { print "Modal window $_[0]->{_id} accepts!\n" };

init [qw(ModalWindow)], [qw(AcceptEvent)], [qw(OffMode)]    # Case 4
    => sub { print "Modal window $_[0]->{_id} can't accept in OffMode!\n" };

init [qw(MovableWindow ResizableWindow)],                   # Case 5
     [qw(MoveEvent MoveAndResizeEvent)],
     [qw(OnMode)]
    => sub { print "Moving window $_[0]->{_id}!\n" };

init [qw(ResizableWindow)], [qw(ResizeEvent)], [qw(OnMode)] # Case 6
    => sub { print "Resizing window $_[0]->{_id}!\n" };

init [qw(ResizableWindow)], [qw(MoveAndResizeEvent)], [qw(OnMode)] # Case 7
    => sub { print "Moving and resizing window $_[0]->{_id}!\n" };

sub receive_event {
    my ($type1, $type2, $type3) = map {ref} @_;
    my $handler = $table{$type1}{$type2}{$type3};
    die "No suitable handler found" unless $handler;
    $handler->(@_);
}

package ModalWindow;     @ISA = qw( Window );
package MovableWindow;    @ISA = qw( Window );
package ResizableWindow; @ISA = qw( MovableWindow );
```

This version of the Window hierarchy uses a three-dimensional *dispatch table*, stored in the lexical hash %table. Each dimension of the dispatch table represents the range of possible parameter types of one of the three arguments passed to the receive_event method: the first dimension represents the Window argument; the second represents the Event argument; and the third represents the Mode argument.

The table must have entries for each possible combination of the Window, Event, and Mode subclasses. To make this less tedious (remember, there are 96 distinct combinations), the init subroutine is provided. This subroutine takes three references to arrays and a reference to an anonymous subroutine. The three arrays specify the respective sets of parameter types for which the anonymous subroutine should be used as a handler.

Consider this call to init:

```
init [qw(ModalWindow)],
     [qw(ReshapeEvent ResizeEvent MoveEvent MoveAndResizeEvent)],
     [qw(Mode OnMode ModalMode OffMode)]
          => sub { print "Modal windows can't handle reshape events\n" };
```

This can be interpreted as:

> Locate every dispatch table entry for calls in which the first argument is a ModalWindow, the second argument is a ReshapeEvent, ResizeEvent, MoveEvent, or MoveAndResizeEvent, and the third argument is any mode (Mode, OnMode, OffMode, or ModalMode). To each such entry, assign a reference to the specified anonymous subroutine.

The nested foreach loops in init iterate through the class names in each array, installing a reference to the handler subroutine ($handler) in the corresponding entries in the dispatch table. In other words, each of the arrays specifies a set of parameter classes, whose objects may appear as the corresponding argument, and the specified handler is called for every combination of parameters in those classes.

Typically, there will be no special handler for most combinations of parameter types, so most of the dispatch table entries will correspond to cases that use the most generic possible behavior. Thus, the first step in setting up the dispatch table is to initialize the entire table to point to a general handler (#case 0). That is:

```
init $windows, $events, $modes =>
        sub { print "Window $_[0]->{_id} can't handle a ",
             ref($_[1]), " event in ", ref($_[2]), " mode\n" };
```

Note that the three lexical variables ($windows, $events, and $modes) were set up with complete lists of the various subclasses of each hierarchy, specifically to make this general initialization easier.

Once the universal "catch-all" case has been set up, particular table entries can be overwritten to redirect them to more specific handlers. First (Case 1), every combination that includes an OffMode parameter is reinitialized to refer to the handler specific to OffMode. Then (Case 2), every combination of arguments with a ModalWindow, a ReshapeEvent (or any derived class), and a Mode (or any derived class) is given a special handler. Next (Case 3), a handler is installed for the ModalWindow, AcceptEvent, *any-kind-of-mode* combination, and finally (Case 4), one for the more specific ModalWindow, AcceptEvent, OffMode combination is installed. The initialization process continues until all the handlers are correctly set up.

Once the table is complete, implementing the actual receive_event method is straightforward. The method simply determines the class of the three arguments (by applying ref to each of them), and then looks up the corresponding entry in %table to retrieve the appropriate handler. If the entry isn't defined, an exception is thrown. Otherwise, the handler is called and passed the original argument list.

As promised, there is only a single receive_event method, which handles every call on any type of Window object. To make sure that happens, the method is defined in the base class (i.e., in Window) and the derived classes simply inherit it unchanged.

Also note that because this change to the internals of the multiple dispatch mechanism is safely encapsulated within the receive_event method, the GUI's event loop doesn't have to change at all when a dispatch table is used instead of "tests-in-methods."

```
while ($next_event = shift @event_queue) {
    $focus_window->receive_event($next_event, $current_mode);
}
```

Ah, the joys of object-orientation!

Initializing the Dispatch Table

Obviously, the whole technique will only work if the dispatch table is set up correctly, which in turn requires that the various table entries must be initialized in the right order. That order is determined by the relationships within and between the set of classes that each argument accepts.

For example, consider the following two initializations:

```
# initialization A
init [qw(Window)], [qw(Event)], [qw(Mode OnMode OffMode ModalMode)]
    => sub { print "universal handler" };

# initialization B
init [qw(Window)], [qw(Event ResizeEvent)], [qw(OffMode)]
    => sub { print "specific OffMode handler" };
```

If these initializations had occurred in the opposite order, then the dispatch table entry for the combination ModalWindow, Event, OffMode would initially be set up to refer to the OffMode handler, only to be immediately—and incorrectly—overwritten with a reference to the more general, "universal" handler.

This same problem may occur wherever there is an overlap in the set of cases covered by two handlers. Obviously, some kind of rule is needed to determine the order in which a given set of table initializations should be performed.

The way to determine the correct order for any two initializations is to work out which of the handlers covers the widest range of cases. Typically, either one handler will cover a superset of the other handler's cases (in which case, it's obviously the more general of the two and should be initialized first), or each handler will cover a nonoverlapping set of cases (in which case, the initialization order doesn't matter), or else there will be some noninclusive overlap in the cases covered (which is a damn nuisance—so I'll leave it to the next section).

Ignoring the problem of overlapping coverage for the moment, it's relatively straightforward to determine which of two handlers should be initialized first. To do so, you have to ascertain the *least-derived* class name in the parameter set of each handler. That is, for each argument of each handler, you have to determine the one class within its parameter set that is an ancestor for all the other classes in the same set. For example, within a set such as [qw(ReshapeEvent Event ResizeEvent)], the least-derived class is Event, since it's the ancestor of the other two.

Once you've determined the two lists of least-derived parameter types, you use them to compare the two handlers in question argument-by-argument. The goal is to find an argument position for which the least-derived parameter in one handler is an ancestral class of the least-derived parameter in the other handler.

Huh?

Well, looking at initializations A and B above, you can see that for A, the least-derived parameter classes of the three arguments are Window, Event, Mode. That's because the first two parameter sets have only one candidate each (Window and Event, respectively), so those classes are automatically the least-derived for those parameters. For the third parameter set, there are four candidates, but Mode is the base class of the other three, so it's clearly the least-derived. By similar logic, the least-derived parameter classes in initialization B are Window, Event, OffMode.

Having now determined the least-derived parameter class in each argument position of both handlers, you can compare them, one argument position at a time. For their first arguments, the least-derived class of each handler is Window, so they're "equal" at that point. Likewise, the least-derived class for both handlers' second arguments is Event, so they're still equal. Only when you compare the final arguments is there a difference: Mode versus OffMode. Since Mode is an ancestor of OffMode, initialization A wins. Winning implies that initialization A sets up the more general of the two handlers; hence, it should be performed first.

Choosing the Initialization Order

Working out the ordering of two (or more) initializations isn't always so easy, even when each parameter set has only a single element. Consider the following case:

```
# initialization C
init [qw(Window)], [qw(AcceptEvent)], [qw(OffMode)],
    => sub { print "Window $_[0]->{_id} can't accept in OffMode!\n" };
```

```
# initialization D
init [qw(ModalWindow)], [qw(Event)], [qw(Mode)]
    => sub { print "Modal window $_[0]->{_id} can't handle event!\n" };
```

Comparing the parameter sets for the first argument position suggests that initialization C should be done first (since `Window` is an ancestor of `ModalWindow`). However, the opposite conclusion is reached when you compare the parameters for the second argument: `Event` is the base class of `AcceptEvent`, so initialization D should come first. The parameter types for the third arguments also suggest that initialization D should be done first (since `OffMode` is derived from `Mode`).

Cases such as this are inherently ambiguous. Suppose, for example, that the actual set of arguments passed to `receive_event` was `ModalWindow`, `AcceptEvent`, `OffMode`. Clearly the handler for `Window`, `AcceptEvent`, `OffMode` could handle these arguments: it would just treat the `ModalWindow` argument polymorphically as a `Window`. Equally clearly, the `ModalWindow`, `Event`, `Mode` handler could handle the call, by treating the `AcceptEvent` argument polymorphically as a `Event` and the `OffMode` argument polymorphically as a `Mode`.

There are several ways to resolve this ambiguity. You might decide that the initialization with the greatest number of more general arguments should come first, in which case initialization D wins (with two ancestral parameter types to C's one). This is known as the "most specific first" policy.

Or you might still follow the algorithm described in the previous section, and effectively give priority to the leftmost parameter where there is a difference. In that case, initialization C wins since the difference in the first parameters favors it. This approach is known as the "leftmost argument wins" policy.

Or you might choose to complain that the two handlers really do make the `ModalWindow`, `AcceptEvent`, `OffMode` combination ambiguous, and demand that a third handler be provided specifically for that case. This policy is known as *noli accipere nullum stercum*.

Generally speaking, it doesn't matter which resolution policy you choose to apply, as long as it's well documented and used consistently. The few languages with built-in support for multiple dispatch generally opt to give leftmost arguments priority, mainly because it's an easy rule for language designers to implement and programmers to remember; it doesn't necessarily lead to more predictable or appropriate dispatching behavior.

Comparing the Two Approaches

Having now looked at two very different approaches to implementing multiple dispatch—tests-in-methods and dispatch tables—the obvious question is: which approach is better?

Multiple dispatching via tables is clearly superior in terms of execution speed. For the implementations shown above, a single call to a handler is dispatched through a dispatch table approximately twice as fast as through a method with embedded tests. That translates to an average improvement of around 20% in real applications, where the cost of actually executing the handler typically dominates the cost of invoking it.

Many developers also find dispatch tables easier to maintain, since the various calls to init explicitly document the expected behavior for every combination of argument classes. On the other hand, experienced object-oriented programmers may find the use of methods with nested tests more illuminating, because the polymorphism of the initial single dispatch and the subsequent calls to isa allow them to reason abstractly about the overall behavior of the handlers.

Despite its poorer runtime performance, the tests-in-methods approach has one indisputable advantage over a fixed dispatch table: it is able to handle requests involving arguments of classes that are not explicitly named in the handlers.

For example, suppose you derived a new type of window from ResizableWindow—let's call it CollapsibleWindow—and a new mode from OnMode—say, ActiveMode. If the GUI event handler were called on a set of arguments with classes CollapsibleWindow, ResizeEvent, ActiveMode, then the tests-in-methods version of the handler would initially call the inherited method ResizableWindow::receive_event, because that's the one that CollapsibleWindow inherits:

```
sub ResizableWindow::receive_event {
    my ($self, $event, $mode) = @_;
    if ($event->isa(MoveAndResizeEvent) && $mode->isa(OnMode))
        { print "Moving and resizing window $self->{_id}!\n" }
    elsif ($event->isa(ResizeEvent) && $mode->isa(OnMode))
        { print "Resizing window $self->{_id}!\n" }
    else { $self->SUPER::receive_event($event,$mode) }
}
```

That method will try each of its tests and discover that the second test suceeds, because the ResizeEvent object *is-a* ResizeEvent (obviously), and the ActiveMode object *is-a* OnMode (since it inherits directly from that class). Even though there's no specific code to handle the many new argument combinations created by adding the two new classes, the existing handlers can still make use of inheritance relationships to treat all three arguments polymorphically.

In contrast, if you were using the dispatch table approach, then the receive_event method inherited from class Window would be called:

```
sub receive_event {
    my ($type1, $type2, $type3) = map {ref} @_;
    my $handler = $table{$type1}{$type2}{$type3};
    die "No suitable handler found" unless $handler;
    $handler->(@_);
}
```

It would attempt to look up the entry for the new combination in %table, but fail to find it (since no entries for either CollapsibleWindow or ActiveMode were ever initialized). Instead of handling the request in some reasonable way, this version of receive_event will throw a tantrum.

To add the new classes into the table-dispatched application, you have to ensure that you've also covered all possible combinations of those classes with appropriate extra initializations. For example, to cover the CollapsibleWindow, ResizeEvent, ActiveMode combination you could extend the initialization from this:

```
init [qw(ResizableWindow)], [qw(ResizeEvent)],
    [qw(OnMode)] => sub {print "Resizing window $_[0]->{_id}\n"};
```

to this:

```
init [qw(ResizableWindow CollapsibleWindow)], [qw(ResizeEvent)],
    [qw(OnMode ActiveMode)] => sub {print "Resizing window $_[0]->{_id}\n"};
```

Dynamic Dispatch Tables

Of course, it's not particularly difficult to redesign the dispatch table mechanism so that it can automatically treat unfamiliar argument types polymorphically. To do so, you just need to supply a means of extending the dispatch table whenever it's asked for an unknown combination of types.

On failing to find a suitable entry in the dispatch table, receive_event will have to search upwards through the various argument hierarchies until it finds a combination of ancestral parameter classes that *does* have an entry in the table. Example 37-3 illustrates the surprisingly extensive changes (in bold) required to provide this new behavior.

Example 37-3. Implementing the receive_event method via a dynamic dispatch-table

```
package Window;

my $_id = 1;
sub new { bless { _id => $_id++ }, $_[0] }

my %table;

sub init {
    my ($param1,$param2,$param3,$handler) = @_;
    $table{$param1}{$param2}{$param3} = $handler;
}

init "Window", "Event", "Mode"
    => sub { print "Window $_[0]->{_id} can't handle a ",
               ref($_[1]), " event in ", ref($_[2]), " mode\n" };

init "Window", "Event", "OffMode"
    => sub { print "No window operations available in OffMode\n" };

init "ModalWindow", "ReshapeEvent", "Mode"
```

```perl
                    => sub { print "Modal windows can't handle reshape events\n" };

    init "ModalWindow", "AcceptEvent", "Mode"
        => sub { print "Modal window $_[0]->{_id} accepts!\n" };

    init "ModalWindow", "AcceptEvent", "OffMode"
        => sub { print "Modal window $_[0]->{_id} can't accept in OffMode!\n" };

    init "MovableWindow", "MoveEvent", "OnMode"
        => sub { print "Moving window $_[0]->{_id}!\n" };

    init "ResizableWindow", "ResizeEvent", "OnMode"
        => sub { print "Resizing window $_[0]->{_id}!\n" };

    init "ResizableWindow", "MoveAndResizeEvent", "OnMode"
        => sub { print "Moving and resizing window $_[0]->{_id}!\n" };

sub ancestors {
    no strict "refs";
    my @ancestors = @_;
    for (my $i=0; $i<@ancestors; $i++)
        { splice @ancestors, $i+1, 0, @{"$ancestors[$i]::ISA"} }
    return @ancestors;
}


sub receive_event {
    my ($type1, $type2, $type3) = map {ref} @_;
    my $handler = $table{$type1}{$type2}{$type3};
    if (!$handler) {
        my @ancestors1 = ancestors($type1);
        my @ancestors2 = ancestors($type2);
        my @ancestors3 = ancestors($type3);

        SEARCH: foreach my $anc1 ( @ancestors1 ) {
                    foreach my $anc2 ( @ancestors2 )  {
                      foreach my $anc3 ( @ancestors3 ) {
                          $handler = $table{$anc1}{$anc2}{$anc3};
                          next unless $handler;
                          $table{$type1}{$type2}{$type3} = $handler;
                          last SEARCH;
                      }
                    }
                }
    }
    die "No handler defined for ($type1,$type2,$type3)"
        unless $handler;
    $handler->(@_);
}

package ModalWindow;      @ISA = qw( Window );
package MovableWindow;    @ISA = qw( Window );
package ResizableWindow;  @ISA = qw( MovableWindow );
```

The central concern of those changes is what happens when the table doesn't specify a handler for a particular set of arguments. What happens is that receive_event compiles a list of the ancestral classes of each argument, and then searches through the full set of combinations of those ancestors (in three nested foreach loops), looking for a combination with an entry in the table. If such an entry is found, it's guaranteed to handle the actual argument types.[*]

The ancestors subroutine computes the set of ancestral classes for each argument. Starting with a list consisting of just the class itself, it iteratively splices the parents of each class into the list, using the symbolic reference @{"$ancestors[$i]::ISA"} (hence the need for no strict "refs"). Each parent list is spliced in just after the class itself, and this eventually produces a depth-first, left-to-right listing of the various ancestors of the original class.

Note that instead of rolling your own hierarchy traversal mechanism, you could use the Class::ISA module (*CPAN/authors/id/S/SB/SBURKE*) to generate the very same ancestry lists. You could also use *memoization* (see Chapter 20) to improve the overall performance of ancestors by caching the various ancestor lists it returns.

In any case, having determined the ancestry of each of its arguments, the receive_event method then iterates through three nested foreach loops, stepping through each combination of possible argument types until it finds a suitable handler. The order of the nested loops (i.e., foreach (@ancestors1)...foreach (@ancestors2)...foreach (@ancestors3)) is important here because that nesting gives priority to the leftmost argument. In other words, combinations featuring the most-derived classes of the leftmost arguments are tried first. This is an extension of the "leftmost argument wins" ambiguity resolution policy described earlier.

Most importantly, once a handler is found for a previously unknown set of argument types, that handler is assigned to the corresponding entry of the dispatch table. That way, the search won't have to be repeated the next time the same set of argument types is encountered.

Because receive_event can now cope with missing table entries, the initialization process can be made much simpler. It's no longer necessary to ensure that every possible combination of argument classes has a handler, since a suitable polymorphic substitute for any missing combination will be automatically located when the table is forced to extend. As long as you remember to initialize the critical default case Window, Event, Mode, every actual combination of arguments will find its way back there if no more appropriate handler is found.

---

[*] Because one of the consequences of an inheritance relationship is that each object is conceptually an instance of every one of its ancestral types, and can be treated as such whenever necessary.

Hence the init subroutine can be simplified so that it merely initializes the entry for the three least-derived classes handled by a particular handler. And those single class names can now be passed as scalar strings rather than as anonymous arrays.

The Costs of Extending the Dispatch Table

It's important to recognize that extending the dispatch table mechanism in this way comes at a cost. For a start, it greatly complicates receive_event, which is unfortunate if you're planning to use a number of different multiply-dispatched methods, and will need to implement a distinct dispatch table mechanism for each.

The greater complexity of the mechanism also reduces the dispatch table's raw performance by around 60% for each call in which the table has to be extended. Amortized over a large number of calls, this reduces the real-world performance by around 15–20% (once all combinations have been handled at least once and the table is fully extended).

Of course, the simplified initialization process compensates somewhat for this loss of performance. Unlike the tests-in-methods approach, which distributes the various possible handlers amongst numerous methods throughout the first argument's hierarchy, the dynamic table-driven dispatch collects all the alternatives together and specifies them in a generic way that makes the dispatch process much easier to predict. Better still, since each initialization sets up only a single table entry, it doesn't matter what order they're applied in.

Multiple Dispatch and Subroutine Overloading

Although multiple dispatch is not the same as subroutine overloading in statically-typed languages like C++, under Perl's dynamic typing system the two concepts *are* more-or-less equivalent. Example 37-4, for example, shows an implementation of a subroutine called debug, which invokes different anonymous subroutines depending on the type of argument it receives. (Perl puritans should avert their eyes at this point. The following section contains strong typing, explicit parameter names, and graphic depictions of overloading.)

Example 37-4. Multimethods + subroutines = overloading

```
my %table;

sub debug {
    my $argtype = ref($_[0]);
    my $handler = $table{$argtype};
    if (!$handler) {
        foreach my $anc ( ancestors($argtype) ) {
            $handler = $table{$anc};
            next unless $handler;
            $table{$argtype} = $handler;
            last;
        }
    }
```

Example 37-4. Multimethods + subroutines = overloading (continued)

```
        die "No handler defined for $arg" unless $handler;
        $handler->(@_);
    }

    sub debug_for {
        my ($argtype,$handler) = @_;
        $table{$argtype} = $handler;
    }

    debug_for ""
        => sub { print "Scalar value is: $_[0]\n" };

    debug_for "Window"
        => sub { print "Reference to Window: $_[0]->{_id}\n" };

    debug_for "SCALAR"
        => sub { print "Scalar reference to value: ${$_[0]}\n" };

    debug_for "ARRAY"
        => sub { print "ARRAY:\n";
                foreach ( @{$_[0]} )
                    { print "ELEMENT: "; debug($_) }
            };

    debug_for "HASH"
        => sub { print "HASH:\n";
                foreach ( keys %{$_[0]} )
                    { print "KEY: "; debug($_);
                        print "VAL: "; debug($_[0]->{$_}); }
            };

    debug_for "CODE"
        => sub { print "CODE\n" };
```

The overall structure of the debug subroutine is identical to the receive_event method in Example 37-3 except that, because the subroutine takes only a single parameter, the table extension mechanism is considerably simplified. The debug_for subroutine takes the place of init in previous examples, and is used to initialize the (one-dimensional) dispatch table.

The rest of the code consists of initializations of handlers for various cases. The first case is interesting in that the specified parameter type is the empty string. This indicates that the handler is to be used when the argument passed is a scalar value, rather than a reference. That's because the ref function returns undef when applied to a nonreference, which is then converted to the empty string when $argtype is used as a key into the %table hash.

The second initializer sets up a handler for objects of class Window. Of course, this case also covers objects of any class derived from Window (courtesy of the dispatch table extension mechanism).

The last four cases set up handlers for references to standard Perl scalars, arrays, hashes, and subroutines. This is interesting because it highlights the fact that the table-driven dispatch doesn't really know anything about classes per se. It just dispatches to the handler the ref function tells it to use.

Also note that the handlers for array and hash references recursively call debug to display their contents, thereby ensuring that the debug subroutine can handle nested data structures correctly (arrays of arrays, hashes of hashes, hashes of arrays of subs, and so on). Best of all, the handlers don't even need to detect what kind of hierarchical data structure their array or hash is storing, because the overloaded debug method sorts it out automatically.

The Class::Multimethods Module

The handcrafted approaches to multiple dispatch shown above are fine for small applications in which it's relatively easy to work out the necessary tests (in the tests-in-methods approach) or to construct suitable dispatching mechanisms (for a dispatch table).

But the number of possible cases (and potential handlers) grows with the product of the size of the various class hierarchies involved, and that way lies madness. For example, adding a single new type of window to the GUI adds 24 extra cases (1 new window type × 6 existing events × 4 existing modes). By adding a single class, you just made the already complex task of setting up handlers about 25% more difficult.

Moreover, most of us simply aren't able to directly comprehend the consequences of simultaneous changes in multiple interacting hierarchies. (Consider, for example, the many unforeseen consequences to England's monarchy when the Windsor hierarchy started interacting with the Spenser and Ferguson family trees.) Imagine adding that one extra window subclass, *and* a few extra events specific to it, *and* throwing in another possible mode. Do any of the existing handlers become ambiguous? If so, the dispatch of *existing* method calls may also be affected. How many additional handlers will be required? If you're using tests-in-methods, will the order of testing have to change? And what happens if that new window subclass inherits from *two* existing classes (for example, combining MovableWindow and ModalWindow to create a MovableModalWindow)?

In such cases, it can be particularly hard to ensure that all possible combinations of arguments are covered, and dispatched in a consistent and predictable manner. Even if you do manage to encode the correct set of choices, testing and maintenance can become a nightmare. On top of everything else, you still have to rebuild a separate dispatch table, lookup method, and extension mechanism for each new multiply-dispatched method you add.

As usual, CPAN offers you some Applied Laziness that solves these problems. The Class::Multimethods module (*CPAN/authors/id/DCONWAY*) generalizes and automates the dynamic dispatch table technique described above. It exports a subroutine called multimethod that can be used to specify multiply-dispatched methods without the need to manually implement the underlying multiple dispatch mechanisms.

For example, Example 37-5 shows the multiply-dispatched receive_event method from Example 37-3, but implemented using Class::Multimethods. Note that there's no explicit handler subroutine, no ancestors subroutine, no %table hash, no hard-coded extension mechanism, and no table initializations.* Instead, you just say what you mean, and get what you want, with a syntax that's temptingly like subroutine overloading.

Example 37-5. Implementing the receive_event method via Class::Multimethods

```perl
package Window;

my $_id = 1;
sub new { bless { _id => $_id++ }, $_[0] }

use Class::Multimethods;

multimethod receive_event => ("Window", "Event", "Mode")
    => sub { print "Window $_[0]->{_id} can't handle a ",
             ref($_[1]), " event in ", ref($_[2]), " mode\n" };

multimethod receive_event => ("Window", "Event", "OffMode")
    => sub { print "No window operations available in OffMode\n" };

multimethod receive_event => ("ModalWindow", "ReshapeEvent", "Mode")
    => sub { print "Modal windows can't handle reshape events\n" };

multimethod receive_event => ("ModalWindow", "AcceptEvent", "Mode")
    => sub { print "Modal window $_[0]->{_id} accepts!\n" };

multimethod receive_event => ("ModalWindow", "AcceptEvent", "OffMode")
    => sub { print "Modal window $_[0]->{_id} can't accept in OffMode!\n" };

multimethod receive_event => ("MovableWindow", "MoveEvent", "OnMode")
    => sub { print "Moving window $_[0]->{_id}!\n" };

multimethod receive_event => ("ResizableWindow", "ResizeEvent", "OnMode")
    => sub { print "Resizing window $_[0]->{_id}!\n" };

multimethod receive_event => ("ResizableWindow", "MoveAndResizeEvent", "OnMode")
    => sub { print "Moving and resizing window $_[0]->{_id}!\n" };

package ModalWindow;     @ISA = qw( Window );
package MovableWindow;   @ISA = qw( Window );
package ResizableWindow; @ISA = qw( MovableWindow );
```

---

* Although the various calls to multimethod look suspiciously familiar in that regard.

The Class::Multimethods module also provides mechanisms to distinguish different types of scalar arguments (numeric versus string, for instance), to ignore certain arguments entirely, to specify how ambiguous calls are handled, to recover when no handler can be found, and to test the consistency of a given set of multiply-dispatched handlers. All these features are fully described in its extensive documentation.

PART V

Software Development

This section features seven articles that will help you with the mechanics of creating Perl programs. The first two articles show how to take code already written in another language and use it from Perl. Brian Ingerson explains his popular Inline module in *Using Other Languages from Perl*, and Scott Bolte shows how to use the SWIG system for generating XS code in the article of the same name.

In the third article, *Benchmarking* the oddly typeset brian d foy demonstrates how to measure the speed of snippets of Perl code, and Bob Sidebotham then explains his extraordinary replacement for make in *Building Software with Cons*.

Randy Ray concludes the section with a triumvirate of software development articles. *MakeMaker* navigates through the sometimes confusing MakeMaker system for generating Makefiles; *Autoloading Perl Code* illustrates how you can create a module that loads portions of code on demand instead of all at once; and *Debugging and Devel::* tours the various Devel:: modules bundled with the Perl distribution, some of which can help you debug your Perl programs. (For more on debugging, see *Perfect Programming* in the first section of this book, and *Debugging Perl Programs with –D* in the last.)

## CHAPTER 38

Using Other Languages from Perl

Brian Ingerson

Inline is a Perl module that allows you to use other programming languages from within Perl code. Initially, I created it to use C from within my Perl programs, and thanks to the efforts of a number of developers, it can now handle not just C but awk, BASIC, C++, Java, Python, Ruby, Tcl, and even assembly language.

I started out as an IBM assembly language programmer: hexadecimal arithmetic, bit-level operations, debugging 500 page core dumps printed on greenbar paper, and so on. The cool thing about assembly language is that you can do *anything*. You could write a nice menu-based hyperlinking user interface that stores its data on your own homemade mass-storage device. What sucks about assembly language is that you *have* to do *everything*. Programming A = B + C takes more than one punch card.

After a while, I spent most of my time developing programming tools and language extensions. Any hacker worth his salt can't code something the same way more than three times without writing an abstraction to eliminate the repetition. I wrote things to turn concepts like memory allocation, I/O, and database access into assembly language one-liners with a touch of object-oriented behavior.

When I switched to Perl around 1997, it was a natural transition. I found I could do everything I needed, with a lot less work. Perl has many powerful built-in features and extensions: regular expressions, runtime evaluation, LWP, and CGI, to name a few. If I needed to write my own protocol or device level stuff, I could generally do that, too.

Everything proceeded swimmingly. Then one day, I needed to make my Perl code work with someone else's C code. I heard Perl had facilities for doing such things. I assumed that since Perl was so awesome, it must be really easy. Something like this:

```
$question = "How soon is now?";
print "And the answer is: ", &ask_Mr_Wizard($question);
exit;
BEGIN :C {
    char* ask_Mr_Wizard(char* q) {
    /* omniscient C code omitted */
        return a;
    }
}
```

Unfortunately, it turned out that I needed to create a separate module, a separate C file, a "glue code" file in a language called XS, a type-mapping file, and a *Makefile* generating file. (Actually, the h2xs utility creates all of these for you, but it's up to you to modify and maintain them.) Then I needed to absorb the content of over a half dozen lengthy perldoc manual pages, read a couple of books, and muck about in the Perl source code for examples. Captivating stuff, I assure you, but all I wanted to do was ask Mr. Wizard a question. If Perl is supposed to make simple things simple, and hard things possible, this was bordering on the impossible.

Introducing Inline.pm

Inspired by the many presentations of Damian Conway at the Perl Conference 4.0, I decided to create a module that would let me include other programming languages directly in my Perl code in much the same manner shown above. What impressed me about Damian's modules was that he coupled problems of immense magnitude with solutions of equal simplicity, or in Damian's words "DWIMity" (Do What I Mean). I decided to call this module "Inline." It is fitting that much of the work done by this module is accomplished with Damian's Parse::RecDescent module, described in the article *Parsing*.

Inline works on all flavors of Unix, Linux, and Windows. Read the Inline documentation for installation information.

Enough talk. Let's check this thing out. Here's a simple but complete program:

```
# rithmatick.pl
print "9 + 16 = ", add(9, 16), "\n";
print "9 - 16 = ", subtract(9, 16), "\n";

use Inline C => <<'END_OF_C_CODE';

int add(int x, int y) {
  return x + y;
}

int subtract(int x, int y) {
  return x - y;
}

END_OF_C_CODE
```

That's it! Just run it like any other Perl program and it will print:

```
9 + 16 = 25
9 - 16 = -7
```

I've managed to accomplish something in ten lines that used to take two. But it's just an example; the point is that you can now jump painlessly from Perl-space to C-space and back. Once you're in C-space, you can do whatever floats your boat, like write a super-speedy algorithm, invoke legacy code through an API, or access all of Perl's internals.

How is this possible? Don't you need to compile and link the C code? Wouldn't that make the program extremely slow? How do the Perl variables get converted to C variables and back? How can C functions be called like Perl subroutines?

That's the DWIMity kicking in: all the hairy details are handled for you by the module. You just say what you need to say and let Inline do the rest. Here's how it works.

The first time you run this program, Inline does everything the hard way. It analyzes your C code, creates all those different files, compiles the code, links it, and finally loads the executable object. On my Linux box, this causes a three to four second delay in execution time. The second time you run it, it's lightning fast. That's because Inline caches the executable object on disk. You can change your program as much as you like, and as long as you don't touch the C code, Inline will use the cached version. As soon as you *do* change the C code, Inline will recompile it on the next run.

A More Complex Example

Let's look at a slightly more complex example. The program, vowels.pl (Example 38-1), takes a filename from the command line and prints the ratio of vowels to letters in that file. vowels.pl uses an inlined C function called vowel_scan that takes a string argument and returns the percentage of vowels as a floating point number between zero and one. It handles upper and lowercase letters, and (true to my IBM roots) both ASCII and EBCDIC. (It is also quite fast; check out the benchmarks at the end of the article.)

Example 38-1. vowels.pl

```
use Inline C => 'DATA';

$filename = $ARGV[0];
die "Usage: perl vowels.pl filename\n" unless -f $filename;

$text = join '', <>;           # slurp input file
$vp = vowel_scan($text);       # call our function
$vp = sprintf("%03.1f", $vp * 100);  # format for printing
print "The letters in $filename are $vp% vowels.\n";

__END__
__C__
/* Find percentage of vowels to letters */
double vowel_scan(char* str) {
  int letters = 0;
  int vowels = 0;
  int i = 0;
  char c;
```

Example 38-1. vowels.pl (continued)

```
    char normalize = 'a' ^ 'A';  /* Assembly programmer trick :-) */
    /* normalize forces lower case in ASCII; upper in EBCDIC */
    char A = normalize | 'a';
    char E = normalize | 'e';
    char I = normalize | 'i';
    char O = normalize | 'o';
    char U = normalize | 'u';
    char Z = normalize | 'z';

    while(c = str[i++]) {
      c |= normalize;
      if (c >= A && c <= Z) {
        letters++;
        if (c == A || c == E || c == I || c == O || c == U)
          vowels++;
      }
    }

    return letters ? ((double) vowels / letters) : 0.0;
}
```

Here's how to count the vowels in the Unix word list:

```
% perl vowels.pl /usr/dict/words
The letters in /usr/dict/words are 37.5% vowels.
```

Although this is just another example of calling a C function as if it were a Perl sub-routine, it introduces a couple of new concepts.

First, notice that the syntax for invoking Inline is different. The C source code is stored after the __C__ token, which means it is accessible to the program through the DATA filehandle. Unfortunately, you can only read from the DATA filehandle at run-time, and use is a compile time directive. Fortunately, in Perl, TMTOWTDI.

When the special keyword 'DATA' is used where the source code should be, Inline remembers the invocation and handles the request as an INIT block. This happens just before runtime, but after the DATA filehandle is available.

The DATA section lets you put all of your C code at the bottom of the source file. It can be mixed with Pod and Autoloader subroutines that normally go down there. This gives you a clean way to organize your Inline source code.

Second, there are two new data types in our C program: double and char*. Luckily, those are two of the five data types Inline supports:

```
int
long
double
char*
SV*
```

Those five are all you need! int and long are for integer scalars, double is for floating point scalars, and char* (usually pronounced "Char Star" in social settings) is for strings. SV* is a generic Perl type that covers "anything else" (hash references, for instance). It will be covered in detail in the following sections. These types provide a simple interface that can be expanded to handle the most complex situations. (Just like Perl itself.)

At this point, your optimism about Inline solving your real life needs is probably inversely proportional to your knowledge of C, XS, and Perl internals. "XS provides a lot more type-mapping and functionality," you say. If you're skeptical, that's good. Stick with me.

In more recent versions, any type can be used as long as there is typemap support for it. Perl has a default typemap with nearly 40 types.

Calling C Functions from Perl

There are four ways to call C functions from Perl. C functions typically take a fixed number of arguments as input, and produce one or zero return values. When a C function needs to return multiple values, it has the caller pass in the return values by reference. Perl, on the other hand, almost always returns multiple values as a list. This provides you with four different situations for Inline:

int foo(int i, double n, char* str) {
> This is the simplest case. The function, foo, takes an exact number of input arguments and returns one value, an integer. All of the Perl to C conversions happen automatically. The examples shown earlier in the article are like this.

void foo(int i, double n, char* str) {
> In C, void normally means that the function doesn't return anything. Inline uses void to indicate that the function will return a list to Perl. You'll need to manage the Perl internal stack yourself. Read on.

int foo(SV*, ...) {
> Just like in C, the ellipsis syntax indicates that an unknown number of arguments will be passed in. Again you will need to access Perl's internal stack manually. Inline provides a bunch of C macros to make this easier.

void foo(SV*, ...) {
> This is just a combination of calls 2 and 3 above. It's another way of saying, "I can handle everything myself, thank you."

Manipulating Perl's Stack

Internally, Perl is centered around a stack, which is just an array that you only access from one end. Computer scientists like to compare it to a spring-loaded stack of dinner plates in a cafeteria: you can push plates onto the stack or pop them off, and that's all you can do. Perl uses the stack to pass scalar arguments to a subroutine.

When the subroutine takes control, it pops the plates from the stack. Before the subroutine returns control, it pushes the return values back onto the stack. You do this all the time in Perl without knowing it, using @_ and return. With Inline, you need to delve a bit into Perl's internals.

Inline provides the following C macros for dealing with the stack:

Inline_Stack_Vars
> Use this macro if you want to use any of the others. It sets up a few local variables for use by the other macros: sp, items, ax, and mark. It's not important to know what they do; I'm mentioning them so you can avoid naming conflicts.

Inline_Stack_Items
> Returns the number of arguments passed in on the stack.

Inline_Stack_Item(i)
> Refers to a particular SV* in the stack, where i is an index number starting from zero. It can be used to get or set the value.

Inline_Stack_Reset
> Use this macro before pushing anything back onto the stack. It resets the internal stack pointer to the beginning of the stack.

Inline_Stack_Push(sv)
> Pushes a return value back onto the stack. The value must be of type SV*.

Inline_Stack_Done
> After you have pushed all of your return values, you must call this macro.

Inline_Stack_Return(n)
> Returns n items on the stack.

Inline_Stack_Void
> This is a special macro that indicates you really don't want to return anything. It's the same as Inline_Stack_Return(0).

The C type SV* deserves an explanation. SV, which stands for *scalar value*, is simply the name of the internal structure that Perl uses to hold scalars. The stack, therefore, is an array of pointers to SVs. Perl provides a slew of helper macros for getting data in and out of SVs (and AVs, HVs, RVs, GVs, and so on). See the *perlapi* and *perlguts* documentation bundled with Perl for all the details.

Another example should help clear the fog. In scalars.pl, shown in Example 38-2, the get_scalars function takes a list of names of Perl global scalars and returns the values of the ones that actually exist and contain a string.

Example 38-2. scalars.pl

```
use Inline 'C';

$, = '/';      # Set print list separator

($scalar1, $scalar2, $scalar3) = ('paper', 'scissors', 42);
```

Example 38-2. scalars.pl (continued)

```
  print get_scalars(qw(main::scalar2 main::scalar4 main::scalar3 main::scalar1));
  print "\n";
  __END__
  __C__
  void get_scalars(SV* sv, ...) {
    Inline_Stack_Vars;
    int i;
    SV* name_sv;
    SV* value_sv;
    char* name;

    Inline_Stack_Reset;
    for (i = 0; i < Inline_Stack_Items; i++) {
      name_sv = Inline_Stack_Item(i);
      name = SvPVX(name_sv);
      value_sv = perl_get_sv(name, FALSE);
      if (value_sv && SvPOK(value_sv))
        Inline_Stack_Push(value_sv);
    }

    Inline_Stack_Done;
  }
```

Here's what Example 38-2 prints:

```
% perl scalars.pl
scissors/paper
scissors/Inline/42
```

The first time you call get_scalars, it fails to return $scalar4 because it is not defined, and $scalar3 because it's not a string. In the second case, $scalar4 is defined (and thus returned), $scalar1 is undefined (and thus ignored), and $scalar3 is returned because it is now a string.

More important, you can handle list input and list output with relative ease. You'll notice I snuck in a few Perl internal macro calls. SvPVX returns the string (char*) from an SV variable. SvPOK indicates whether an SV has a string component or not, and perl_get_sv (get_sv in Perl 5.6) returns an SV from Perl's internal symbol table. You can read about these and many, many more in the *perlapi* documentation bundled with Perl.

How Inline Works

Let's take a break from using Inline and examine how it does its magic. The module lets you take C source code and effectively eval it into Perl at runtime. What, exactly, is going on under the hood to make all of this work? Here's a basic outline of what happens when you invoke Inline.

1. Receive the source code. Inline gets the source code from your program or module with a statement like the following:

   ```
   use Inline C => 'source code';
   ```

in which "C" is the programming language used, and 'source code' is the actual source code itself in the form of a string. 'source code' can also be a filename, a reference to a subroutine, or anything else that returns source code. Inline then prepends the following header includes to your source code:

```
#include "EXTERN.h"
#include "perl.h"
#include "XSUB.h"
#include "INLINE.h"
```

This should be all the headers you need for regular situations. (The *perl.h* file includes all the standard C header files, such as *stdio.h*.)

2. Check if the source code has been compiled. Inline only needs to compile the source code if it has not yet been compiled. But how can it tell if the source code has changed? It accomplishes this seemingly magical task by running the source text through the Digest::MD5 module to produce a virtually unique 128-bit hexadecimal "fingerprint" of the source code. The fingerprint is mangled together with the current package name and the name of the programming language. If the package is main, then the program name is added; otherwise, the module version number is used. This procedure forms a unique name for the executable object. For instance, the *vowels.pl* example produces a cached executable object called (on a Unix system):

```
main_C_vowels_pl_bcc13cd1d188b32fc216cea883239ee3.so
```

If an object with that name already exists, then skip to step 8, because no compilation is necessary.

3. Find a place to build and install. At this point Inline knows it needs to compile the source code. The first thing to figure out is where to create the great big mess of files associated with compilation, and where to put the object when it's done.

By default, Inline will try to build and install under the first of the following places that is a writable directory:

$ENV{PERL_INLINE_BLIB}
> The PERL_INLINE_BLIB environment variable overrides all else.

./blib_I/
> Inside the current directory, unless you're in your home directory.

$bin/blib_I/
> Where $bin is the directory the program is in.

$ENV{HOME}/blib_I/
> Under your home directory.

$ENV{HOME}/.blib_I/
> Same as above, but more discreet.

blib stands for "build library" in Perl-speak. It is a temporary staging directory created when you install a Perl module on your system. blib_I is the Inline version of the same concept.

If none of these directories exist, Inline attempts to create and use $bin/blib_I/ or ./blib_I/, in that order. Optionally, you can configure Inline to build and install exactly where you want it, using Inline::Config. In the unlikely event that Inline cannot find a place to build, it croaks.

4. Parse the source for semantic cues. Inline uses the Parse::RecDescent module to parse your chunks of source code and identify things that need runtime bindings. For instance, in C it looks for all of the function definitions and breaks them down into names and data types. These elements are used to bind the C function to a Perl subroutine.

5. Create the build environment. Inline takes all of the gathered information and creates an environment to build your source code into an executable object, creating all the appropriate directories and source files.

6. Compile the code and install the executable. The planets are in alignment, and all that's left is the easy part. Inline just does what users normally do to install a module on Unix systems:

```
% perl Makefile.PL
% make
% make test      # (Inline skips this one)
% make install
```

If something goes awry, Inline croaks with a message indicating where to look for more info.

7. Tidy up. By default, Inline removes the mess created by the build process, assuming that everything worked. If the compile fails, Inline leaves everything intact so you can debug your program. Running something like this:

```
% perl -MInline=NOCLEAN example.pl
```

prevents Inline from cleaning up, in case you want to poke around in the blib_I directory.

8. DynaLoad the executable. Inline uses Perl's DynaLoader module to pull your external object into Perl-space. Now you can call all of your C functions like Perl subroutines!

Creating Perl Extensions

So far, all the examples in this article have been Perl *programs*, but Inline can also create Perl modules like the ones found on CPAN. Modules that use C code as well as Perl are called *extension modules*. This section describes how to create an extension module that can be uploaded to CPAN.

Let's create a module called Math::Simple that provides four functions: add, subtract, multiply, and divide. I'll assume you're using some kind of Unix. Execute the following commands:

```
% h2xs -PAXn Math::Simple
Writing Math/Simple/Simple.pm
```

```
Writing Math/Simple/Makefile.PL
Writing Math/Simple/test.pl
Writing Math/Simple/Changes
Writing Math/Simple/MANIFEST
% cd Math/Simple
% ls
Changes  MANIFEST  Makefile.PL  Simple.pm  test.pl
```

The h2xs program is useful even if you're not using XS; it generates all of the files
you'll need to distribute your module. The -X and -A switches prevent it from generating a lot of XS-specific stuff that you won't need. The -P switch prevents the generation of sample pod documentation. Documentation is important for a distributed
module, but it gets in the way of the Inline code. Put your documentation in a separate file called *Simple.pod* and add an entry for it in the *MANIFEST* file, or use pod
normally but put the C source code inside a string instead of after the __DATA__
token.

Edit *Simple.pm* to look something like Example 38-3.

Example 38-3. The Simple.pm module

```
package Math::Simple;

use strict;
use vars qw($VERSION @ISA @EXPORT_OK);
$VERSION = '1.23';
require Exporter;
@ISA = qw(Exporter);
@EXPORT_OK = qw(add subtract multiply divide);

use Inline C => DATA =>
    NAME => 'Math::Simple',
    VERSION => '1.23';
1;

__DATA__
__C__
double add(double x, double y) {
  return x + y;
}

double subtract(double x, double y) {
  return x - y;
}

double multiply(double x, double y) {
  return x * y;
}

double divide(double x, double y) {
  if (! y)
    croak("Error! Attempt to divide by zero\n");
  return x / y;
}
```

By using the NAME and VERSION configuration parameters, you are letting Inline know that this module is meant to be installed like any other CPAN module. It is important that the NAME be the same as the package name and VERSION be the same as $VERSION.

You must also use a slightly modified *Makefile.PL*:

```
use Inline::MakeMaker;
WriteMakefile ( NAME => 'Math::Simple',
               VERSION_FROM => 'Simple.pm',
             );
```

The only real difference is that you replace ExtUtils::MakeMaker with Inline::Make-Maker. The latter is just a small wrapper around the former. It ensures that the Makefile has a special rule to force the Inline code to be compiled at make time.

Finally, run these commands:

```
% perl Makefile.PL
% make
% make test
% make install  # Optional
% make dist
```

The make install command will install the module on your local system. When it's all working, the make dist command will produce the file *Math-Simple-1.23.tar.gz*. This is your complete distribution package, ready for CPAN.

Inline::Config

Inline tries to do the right thing as often as possible. But sometimes you may need to override the default actions, and that's where Inline::Config comes in handy. It gives you fine-grained control over the entire process.

An important point to remember is that the configuration settings must be done *before* Inline receives the source code. Since use happens during compile time, you may need to do something like this to use Inline::Config.

```
BEGIN {
    use Inline;
    $Inline::Config::PRINT_INFO = 1;
    Inline::Config::Force_Build(1);
    Inline::Config->makefile('LIBS' => ['-lm']);
}

use Inline C => "C code goes here...";
```

This demonstrates the three different syntaxes for setting options. You can also set options on the command line; to cut down on typing, several options have terse (and case-insensitive) command-line versions. Some examples:

```
% perl -MInline=Info program.pl
% perl -MInline=Force,Noclean,Info program.pl
% perl -MInline=Clean program.pl
```

Info tells Inline to print a small report about the status of the Inlined code. Force forces a build to happen even if the cached object is up to date, and Noclean leaves the build mess intact so that you can inspect it. The Clean option tells Inline to clean up all previous messes that it knows about. (Remember, everything is under one blib_I directory, so it's a manageable mess.)

You can even get information about any installed module that uses Inline with a one-liner like this:

```
% perl -MInline=Info -MMath::Simple -e 42
<---------------------Information Section---------------------->

Information about the processing of your Inline C code:

Your module is already compiled. It is located at:
/usr/local/lib/perl5/site_perl/5.6.0/i686-linux/auto/Math/Simple_C_1_23_9cddc
5e3bf29ec8e1b4218f2de670c59/Simple_C_1_23_9cddc5e3bf29ec8e1b4218f2de670c59.so

The following Inline C function(s) have been successfully bound to Perl:
        double add(double x, double y)
        double divide(double x, double y)
        double multiply(double x, double y)
        double subtract(double x, double y)


<------------------End of Information Section-------------------->
```

There is a special option called Reportbug. When you run into a problem and suspect that it is Inline's fault, just issue the following command:

```
% perl -MInline=Reportbug program.pl
```

Explicit instructions will be displayed telling you how to report the problem. For more information about configuration issues, see the Inline::Config documentation.

> NOTE: Inline::Config was long ago replaced by an easier configuration syntax.

XS and SWIG

Here is my opinionated rant on why Inline is better than XS and SWIG. If you're already convinced that Inline is the best way to extend Perl, feel free to skip this section. SWIG (Simplified Wrapper and Interface Generator) is more or less a generic version of XS that supports other scripting languages as well. Since this rant applies equally to both methods, I will only talk about XS.

XS is a small glue language that works with the h2xs template-generating tool and the xsubpp translating compiler. The basic idea is to run h2xs against some existing C library's header files. This creates a Perl module, an XS interface file, and a *Makefile. PL*. Then you run the normal Perl install commands and presto, you have a Perl module that gives you full access to that library's API. Some of this process is shown in the article *Random Number Generators and XS*.

If you can get it to work that easily, by all means use XS.

The first problem that you will undoubtedly run into is that you'll need to tweak each of the generated files. A lot. That means you'll need to read a lot of documentation about the format of those files. You'll do most of the tweaking in the *Foo.xs* file. XS gives you a dozen or so special keywords to help you tweak. Keywords like INIT, PREINIT, CODE, and PPCODE allow you to sprinkle bits of C code around the calling of the function. Knowing how all of these bits get pasted together at compile time is the stuff of legends.

Another problem you'll find is with typemaps, which translate Perl data types to C and vice versa. XS provides a lot of defaults, but some of them actually update the input arguments themselves. That's good in C, but horrible in Perl. If you use these literally mapped function calls, you'll end up providing a very confusing interface from the perspective of a Perl programmer. Also, if your existing library uses any but the simplest types and typedefs, you'll have to write your own typemaps in yet another file called *typemaps*.

To make Inline use an existing API, you'll need to write your own wrapper function for each function you want to expose. If this seems crummy at first, consider that all of your code will be in your module, and that it will be laid out in the true order of execution, instead of being masked by a lot of extra syntax. And you don't have to run make every time you tweak.

If you're not using an existing API, choosing Inline should be a no-brainer. One of the best things about Inline is that you can use it from a program. With XS and SWIG, you always need to create a full-blown module.

Using Perl as C's Memory Manager

As you journey beyond the examples and into more complex C programming, you may find yourself clicking your heels from time to time. "I'm not in Perl anymore!" you might say. But if you think about it, you never really left. You're merely on the dark side now. Use the force.

The full power of Perl remains at your fingertips. For example, in Perl memory is automatically allocated each time you mention a new variable. If you add text to a string variable, Perl automatically allocates more memory. When the variable goes out of scope, all the memory is automatically freed. But in C, you need to use malloc and realloc and free to manage memory.

Now you can use Perl's memory management from C. You can ask Perl for a new anonymous scalar (SV) at any time. You can ask Perl to extend it for you, and you can even tell Perl to free it at some point *after* your C function returns.

Example 38-4 demonstrates a function that takes a hash reference and returns its values as a comma separated string. Of course, we'll need to build the return value in a buffer of unknown size.

Example 38-4. Accessing Perl hashes from C

```
use Inline C => <<'END_OF_C_CODE';

void hash_values(SV* hash_ref) {
  Inline_Stack_Vars;
  HV* hash;
  HE* hash_entry;
  int num_keys, i;
  SV* buffer;
  SV* sv_val;

  if (! (SvROK(hash_ref) && SvTYPE(SvRV(hash_ref)) == SVt_PVHV))
    croak("Error. Expected a hash reference");
  hash = (HV*)SvRV(hash_ref);
  num_keys = hv_iterinit(hash);

  buffer = NEWSV(0, 0);
  for (i = 0; i++ < num_keys;) {
    hash_entry = hv_iternext(hash);
    sv_val = hv_iterval(hash, hash_entry);
    sv_catpvf(buffer, "%s%s", SvPV(sv_val, PL_na),
            (i < num_keys) ? "," : "");
  }

  Inline_Stack_Item(0) = sv_2mortal(buffer);
  Inline_Stack_Return(1);
}

END_OF_C_CODE

%hash = ( Who  => 'Ingy',
          What => 'Loves',
          Whom => 'Perl'  );

print hash_values(\%hash), "\n";
```

If you run the code in Example 38-4, you'll get:

```
% perl ./hash_keys.pl
Perl,Loves,Ingy
```

I've just presented you with dozen or so new calls. I'll leave it you to find out how they all work — they're described in the documentation bundled with Inline.

Benchmarks

I did some benchmark testing on the *vowels.pl* program. The vowel_scan subroutine was called 1,000 times with the contents of */usr/dict/words* as its input string. This is a huge string (409,093 bytes). It took 16.0 secs to run. That's 0.0160 secs/call.

A similar subroutine written in Perl took 2.96 secs/call, 186 times slower than C. An optimized version of this routine, which used only numeric comparisons, took 2.54 secs/call. Better, but not much.

However, if you think this an argument against Perl, think again. The algorithm was then coded as a Perl one-liner with creative use of the tr command.

```
sub vowel_scan { $_[0]=~tr/aeiouAEIOU// / $_[0]=~tr/a-zA-Z// }
```

Pretty? Maybe not. Fast? This ran at 0.0169 secs/call. Less than a millisecond slower than the C function.

CHAPTER 39
SWIG

Scott Bolte

 When this article was written, the Inline module discussed in *Using Other Languages from Perl* didn't exist. When you want to use C from Perl, you should consider Inline, SWIG, and XS, in that order.

Tired of the "which interpreter is best for the job" debates? Want something that makes the speed and power of C and C++ available to several common interpreters automatically? There's a new tool that does exactly that: SWIG, the Simplified Wrapper and Interface Generator.

SWIG is a freely available compiler developed by Dave Beazley, now at the University of Chicago. It works on many Unix variants, as well as Windows and Mac OS, although the Windows versions are less polished. It converts C and C++ files into interface code (called a *wrapper*) that makes the contents available to Perl, Tcl, Guile, Java, Ruby, and Python—all automatically. Like Perl's own XS language, SWIG creates Perl wrappers around C code. Unlike XS, SWIG requires little or no programming effort.

I'm not going to describe the mechanics of SWIG in detail; a more thorough treatment would address function prototypes, complex data structures, multiple inheritance, Perl classes, Tcl 8 modules, exception handling, Makefile generation, strict type checking in the interpreter, conditional compilation, and automatic generation of documentation. There's an excellent user guide bundled with SWIG that covers all of these topics. In this article, I'll just show you the basics: how to take an existing application and create a Perl wrapper around it.

This tutorial is divided into three sections. First, I'll show you a simple use of SWIG: creating a Perl wrapper around a lone C function. Second, you'll see how to make C data structures available to Perl via what SWIG calls an interface file. Finally, I'll take the source code for an entire utility and "port" it to Perl.

Along the way, you'll see examples of how SWIG is invoked, how shared libraries are built, and how the resulting Perl modules are used. Finally, I'll demonstrate how to write a Perl script that does a great job of imitating top (a widely-used process monitor) using the actual top source code.

SWIG's home page is *http://www.swig.org*. Don't try to use the original SWIG module in CPAN, since it is out of date. You can join the SWIG mailing list at *http://mailman.cs.uchicago.edu/mailman/listinfo/swig*. The message volume is low and the signal-to-noise ratio is high.

Hooks by Hand

I first started using Perl and Tcl in the early 1990s when both were new. Perl was an immediate hit and I happily used a2p and s2p to convert all my awk and sed scripts to Perl. Then, looking at the generated Perl for clues, I converted my sh scripts, too. Tcl, while not nearly as powerful as Perl, had the nifty feature of allowing user-defined C functions to be exported to the interpreter. While Perl would eventually do that as well, it was still years away. (I was using Perl 3, after all.)

I spent an inordinate amount of time trying to simplify the writing of Tcl glue code. Eventually an entire library was developed that used a C template structure to convert a vector of Tcl string arguments into C data structures. This made it much easier to call C functions without an argc/argv-style interface. Even so, the linkage between C and Tcl was still a hassle.

Perl caught up with Tcl when XS was introduced. Not only could developers specify how to convert between the compiled and interpreted worlds, but the compiled code could be dynamically loaded via a shared library. On the surface, this seemed a wonderful solution. The problem with interface code is that, well, you have to write it. That might be acceptable if you're creating entirely new code to be made available via a Perl wrapper, but what about legacy code? Wouldn't you rather develop new programs than spend your time creating wrappers around old code?

Wrapping a C Function

Let's start out with a simple example. Many people who post to the Usenet newsgroup comp.lang.perl.misc ask how to determine the amount of time used by chunks of their Perl programs. The typical solution is to use one of the timing modules, such as Benchmark.pm (described in the next article, *Benchmarking*). To demonstrate SWIG, I'll create and use a C function instead.

In Example 39-1, you'll see *elapsed.c*, which contains nothing but the elapsed_seconds function.

Example 39-1. elapsed.c: a C function to be wrapped by SWIG

```
#include <sys/time.h>
/*
  Return the number of seconds since the first time
```

Example 39-1. elapsed.c: a C function to be wrapped by SWIG (continued)

```
    elapsed_seconds() was called.
 */

float
elapsed_seconds(void)
{
  static struct timeval then = {0, 0};
  struct timeval now;

/* The first time we're called note the time and then return 0.
 */

if (then.tv_sec == 0) {
  (void) gettimeofday(&then, 0);
  return (0);
}

/*
 * Return the elapsed time as a floating point number
 * on subsequent calls.
 */

(void) gettimeofday(&now, 0);
return (now.tv_sec - then.tv_sec
        + (now.tv_usec - then.tv_usec) / 1000000.0);
}
```

Since *elapsed.c* is so simple, you can feed it directly to SWIG:

```
% swig -perl5 -shadow -module Elapsed elapsed.c
Generating wrappers for Perl 5
```

This generates three files: the Perl modules in *Elapsed.pm*, the XS wrapper code in *elapsed_wrap.c*, and the documentation in *elapsed_wrap.doc*.

I won't discuss *elapsed_wrap.doc*. It's enough to say that SWIG's surprisingly rich documentation generation can create plain ASCII, HTML, or LaTeX. There are options to locate, extract, and format comments from the source code. As with most configuration preferences, the options can be selected either by the SWIG command line or via directives embedded in the source code.

SWIG isn't a full C/C++ parser; many snippets of code will give it fits. Instead of throwing full-fledged C programs at it, it's more common to process merely a header (*.h*) file. If you're going to be intermixing C/C++ source code with SWIG directives, then an interface file (ending in *.i* by convention) would be a better choice. SWIG defines the *SWIG preprocessor token*, so you can make a portion of the C source code visible only to SWIG by enclosing it between #ifdef SWIG and #endif lines, or render it invisible to SWIG with #ifndef SWIG and #endif.

In addition to providing the name of the source module, you need to tell SWIG a few other things. In the command line shown above, you set the output language to Perl, request shadow classes (more on those later), and set the module name to Elapsed.

The *Elapsed.pm* and *elapsed_wrap.c* files generated by SWIG constitute a full-fledged Perl extension. They verify function arguments, translate them into C data structures, invoke the functions, and translate return values into a form palatable by Perl. It handles not only functions, but global variables and read-only constants as well. The wrapper, along with the original source file, is compiled and turned into a shared library.

One of the obstacles to using SWIG (and nearly everything else) on different platforms is the variety of ways to create shared libraries. Here's the particular incantation for FreeBSD:

```
% gcc -DPIC -fpic -I/opt/perl5.004/lib/ i386-freebsd/5.00403/CORE -c elapsed_wrap.c

% gcc -DPIC -fpic -Wall -c elapsed.c

% ld -Bshareable -L/usr/local/lib -o Elapsed.so elapsed_wrap.o elapsed.o
```

You'll need to figure out the commands and options your platform requires. This information should be available from your Perl configuration; here's an ugly but effective make rule that appends the pertinent variables to the Makefile. Whenever I move to a new platform, make localvars deletes the old variables and adds the new ones. It's not pretty, but it works.

```
localvars:
    perl -MConfig -e 'printf("LD = %s %s\n", $$Config{ld}, $$Config{lddlflags});
                      printf("CC = %s %s\n", $$Config{cc}, $$Config{cccdlflags});
                      printf("PERLINC =-I%s/CORE\n", $$INC[0]);'
    >> Makefile
```

The test of elapsed_seconds is encapsulated in a Perl program called *elapsed*, shown in Example 39-2. This program computes the Fibonacci sequence and the ratio between successive numbers in the sequence, which converges to the Golden Mean. I'll use elapsed_seconds to time this program. (Remember, this is only so you can demonstrate SWIG; to time Perl code, you can always use Perl's own Benchmark module, bundled with the standard distribution.)

Example 39-2. elapsed: using a wrappered C function

```
#!/usr/bin/perl -w

# Use the first N elements of the Fibonacci sequence
# to approximate the Golden Mean.

use strict;
use Elapsed;
my $before = Elapsed::elapsed_seconds();
```

Example 39-2. elapsed: using a wrapped C function (continued)

```perl
my $N = shift || 20; # Take either first argument or 20.
my ($n1, $n2) = (1, 1);

printf("%2d: %10d\n", 1, $n1);
printf("%2d: %10d %.10g\n", 2, $n2, $n2/$n1);

for (3..$N) {
    ($n1, $n2) = ($n2, $n1 + $n2);
    printf("%2d: %10d %.10g\n", $_, $n2, $n2/$n1);
}

my $after = Elapsed::elapsed_seconds();

printf("Elapsed time is %g seconds.\n", $after - $before);
```

As you'd hope, the calls to the C function elapsed_seconds and the assignments of $before and $after look like regular Perl. Once you include the C function with use Elapsed, you can treat it like any other Perl subroutine; the fact that the underlying code happens to be written in C makes no difference.

Here's the output of the *elapsed* program:

```
 1: 1
 2: 1 1
 3: 2 2
 4: 3 1.5
 5: 5 1.666666667
 6: 8 1.6
 7: 13 1.625
 8: 21 1.615384615
 9: 34 1.619047619
10: 55 1.617647059
11: 89 1.618181818
12: 144 1.617977528
13: 233 1.618055556
14: 377 1.618025751
15: 610 1.618037135
16: 987 1.618032787
17: 1597 1.618034448
18: 2584 1.618033813
19: 4181 1.618034056
20: 6765 1.618033963
Elapsed time is 0.001777 seconds.
```

Interface Files

Now I'll provide SWIG with an interface file, which lets me use SWIG pragmas. I'll skip over compilation and linking, and look at a few complex data structures instead.

In *gettime.i*, shown below, I set the module name, make the global variable errno read-only, and ask for default structure constructors. I also define two time structures and provide the prototypes for gettimeofday and settimeofday.

```
%module Gettime;          // Alternative to command line
                          // arguments (for naming)

%readonly                 // Make all variables read only.
int errno;
%readwrite                // Restore default behavior.

%pragma make_default;     // Generate default constructors.
struct timeval {
  long tv_sec;            // seconds
  long tv_usec;           // and microseconds
};

struct timezone {
  int tz_minuteswest;     // minutes west of Greenwich
  int tz_dsttime;         // type of dst correction
};

int gettimeofday(struct timeval * tp,
                 struct timezone * tzp);

int settimeofday(const struct timeval * tp,
                 const struct timezone * tzp);
```

I can now build the module much as before. I don't need the -module option, since the name of the module is set in the interface file with the statement %module Gettime.

```
% swig -perl5 -shadow gettime.i
Generating wrappers for Perl 5

% gcc -DPIC -fpic -I/opt/perl5.004/lib
  i386-freebsd/5.00403/CORE -c gettime_wrap.c

% ld -Bshareable -L/usr/local/lib -o Gettime.so gettime_wrap.o
```

Now using gettimeofday is easy:

```
#!/usr/bin/perl -w
use Gettime;
my $tv = new timeval();  # Allocate a timeval structure

# Below, undef maps to a null pointer
Gettime::gettimeofday($tv, undef)
   && warn("gettimeofday() failed, errno = $Gettime::errno.\n");

# The shadow option is what allows these symbolic references
# to structure fields.
printf("Time is %d.%06d\n", $tv->{tv_sec}, $tv->{tv_usec});
```

Here is the script's output:

```
Time is 877438914.248738
```

Let's look at a program that doesn't work. The following script tries to set the time, but fails because it wasn't run by the superuser. Then it fails again because I made $errno read-only.

```perl
#!/usr/bin/perl -w
use Gettime;

my $tv = new timeval();              # Allocate timeval structure.
$tv->{tv_sec} = $tv->{tv_usec} = 0; # Turn back the clock.

# This if statement will fail unless you're root
if (Gettime::settimeofday($tv, undef)) {
    warn("settimeofday() failed, errno = $Gettime::errno.\n");
    $Gettime::errno = 0;             # This fails since it's read-only
}
```

The output is:

```
settimeofday() failed, errno = 1.
Value is read-only. at ./Gettime-test.pl line 9.
```

An In-Depth Example: Emulating top

The remainder of this article shows how the power of top can be made available to Perl. The top utility, developed by William LeFebvre and a cast of dozens for more than a decade, is a great system utility similar to ps: it displays a system summary followed by a listing of processes. Unlike ps, the display is updated at regular intervals. There are various other nifty features, but the kicker is that top is portable. Source code is available from *ftp://ftp.groupsys.com/pub/top*.

There are three reasons I chose top. First, since I didn't write it, it serves as a good test of adapting legacy code to a new environment. Second, top was written with portability in mind, and that makes my job easier. Version 3.4 runs on over two dozen Unix variants—pretty unusual for a program that's so sensitive to internal kernel structures. top's portability makes it an ideal candidate for SWIG. Finally, I've always wanted to have access to top's information in my system monitoring scripts without having to decode the internal structures of yet another operating system.

One of top's header files, *machine.h* (shown in Example 39-3), contains three structure definitions and a few function prototypes. That's it. The operating system-specific code for each port need only populate an array of those structures. Those three structures and a few functions are all SWIG needs to know about.

Example 39-3. machine.h: one of top's header files

```c
/* This file defines the interface between top and the machine-dependent
 * module. It is NOT machine dependent and should not need to be changed
 * for any specific machine.
 */
```

Example 39-3. machine.h: one of top's header files (continued)

```
/* The statics struct is filled in by machine_init */
struct statics
{
  char **procstate_names;
  char **cpustate_names;
  char **memory_names;
};

/* The system_info struct is filled in by a machine-dependent routine. */
struct system_info
{
  int last_pid;
  double load_avg[NUM_AVERAGES];
  int p_total;
  int p_active; /* number of procs considered "active" */
  int *procstates;
  int *cpustates;
  int *memory;
};

/* cpu_states is an array of percentages * 10. For example,
 *   the (integer) value 105 is 10.5% (or .105).
 */

/* The process_select struct tells get_process_info what processes interest us */
struct process_select
{
  int idle;      /* show idle processes */
  int system;    /* show system processes */
  int uid;       /* only this uid (unless uid == -1) */
  char *command; /* only this command (unless == NULL) */
};

/* Routines defined by the machine dependent module */
char *format_header( );
char *format_next_process( );

/* non-int routines typically used by the machine-dependent module */
char *printable( );
```

My interface file, *top.i* (Example 39-4) has two sections. The first section, delimited by %{ and %}, is literal source code that will be needed by the Perl extension generated by SWIG. This section is opaque to SWIG and can be as complex as necessary. The code after the %} is almost straight C as well; in fact, if the special %include statements weren't necessary, the entire interface file could be nothing but C code.

Example 39-4. top.i: a SWIG interface file

```
%{
  #include "top.h"
  #include "machine.h"
```

Example 39-4. top.i: a SWIG interface file (continued)

```
  char *printable(str)
  char *str;
  {
    int c;
    for (c = 0; str[c] != '\0'; c++) {
      if (!isprint(str[c]))
        str[c] = '?';
    }
    return (str);
  }

  char *full_format_header(char *uname_field)
  {
    return (format_header(uname_field));
  }

  char *full_format_next_process(caddr_t handle)
  {
    extern char *username(int uid);
    return (format_next_process(handle, username));
  }
%}

%include pointer.i
%include typemaps.i
%include "top.h"
%pragma make_default
%include "machine.h"

extern char    *full_format_header(char *uname_field);
extern char    *full_format_next_process(caddr_t handle);

extern int     machine_init(struct statics * statics);
extern void    get_system_info(struct system_info * si);
extern caddr_t get_process_info(struct system_info * si,
                           struct process_select * sel, int fake = 0);
```

From %{ to %}

This section contains three functions to be included in the Perl extension. The printable function mimics a function in the top source code. The original is in a file that, if compiled and linked, introduces many more platform dependencies. To keep the number of dependencies to a minimum, I just duplicated what I needed.

The two functions after printable (full_format_header and full_format_next_process) are only needed in the interface file for their complete prototype definitions. As you can tell, the original prototypes in *machine.h* lack arguments, so you have to provide them here. (As LeFebvre points out, this code predates ANSI C and is due for an overhaul.)

Complete prototypes are required, and for a good reason. SWIG isn't as permissive as Perl. It doesn't have Perl's anything-goes attitude, and in fact performs extensive type-checking of function arguments. This should be reassuring to people leery of integrating a low-level application into a typeless language.

After the %{ ... %} Block

The next lines in *top.i* are a few %include statements. The first two import a couple of SWIG's built-in interface files: *pointer.i* and *typemaps.i*. SWIG supports basic data types, but more sophisticated structures (structures, arrays, complex pointers, and the like) require additional help. These built-in interface files handle common C constructs, such as a null-terminated array of strings represented as a char **.

The next two include statements pull in two *top* header files: *top.h* and *machine.h*. The first contains some constants, and the second, as you've already seen, contains the portable structures used by top.

Finally, the five extern declarations at the bottom of *top.i* are function prototypes. The first two should look familiar; they need to be included so SWIG will know to generate wrappers. (Remember, the earlier code block was opaque to SWIG.) The last three statements are prototypes for the top functions we'll be calling from the Perl program.

If this interface file seems overly complex, it's due to my desire to leave the legacy top source code untouched. If this were new code, the interface file might have been just a few include statements—or the *.h* files might even have been used directly.

You can have SWIG process the interface file as follows (assuming you're in the same directory as the code). The only new option, -Itop-3.4, indicates where to look for include files. The other options should all look familiar:

```
% swig -Itop-3.4 -perl5 -shadow -module Top top.i
```

SWIG then creates three files: *top_wrap.c*, *Top.pm*, and *top_wrap.doc*. The wrapper source file contains all the Perl to C interfaces—well over 2,000 lines of code that you, thankfully, don't have to write. This may seem like a lot; it's because of SWIG's type-checking and its tests for end cases. You might be able to do as good a job by hand, but I doubt it.

Top.pm is the Perl module proper. It uses Perl's built-in DynaLoader module to load the top shared library dynamically (assuming your system supports shared libraries). This makes the functions and C constants in *top.h* available to the module.

The final step is to compile the C code. *top_wrap.c* is compiled along with three files from the top sources. They're linked together into a shared library (*Top.so* on my system) and we're ready to go.

```
% swig -Itop-3.4 -perl5 -shadow -module Top top.i
top-3.4/machine.h : Line 28. Warning. Array member will be read-only.
Generating wrappers for Perl 5
```

```
% gcc -DPIC -fpic -Itop-3.4 -I/opt/perl5.004/lib/ i386-freebsd/5.00403/CORE -c top_wrap.c
% gcc -DPIC -fpic -Itop-3.4 -c top-3.4/machine.c
% gcc -DPIC -fpic -Itop-3.4 -c top-3.4/utils.c
% gcc -DPIC -fpic -Itop-3.4 -c top-3.4/username.c
% ld -Bshareable -L/usr/local/lib -o Top.so>> top_wrap.o machine.o utils.o username.o
-lkvm
```

The warning from line 28 about the read-only array member (in the source code, the line with double load_avg[NUM_AVERAGES]) is telling; the distinction between an array and a pointer is subtle in C. To avoid such problems, SWIG treats references as read-only by default. You can usually create unambiguous types with typedef if you need to.

The last line above uses ld to link the four .o files with the KVM library. KVM is the kernel memory interface for FreeBSD; it will be loaded along with the top library at the first call to the top module. Since the module opens sensitive kernel structures, you'll most likely need to run it as the superuser.

The top Emulator

A Perl program that emulates top is shown in Example 39-5. There are a few new aspects to it, notably the ptrvalue calls, but most of the program is straightforward.

Example 39-5. A SWIG-enabled top emulator

```perl
#!/usr/bin/perl -w
use strict;
use Top; # treated like any other module

sub memfix ($) {
    my $label = shift;
    if ($label =~ m/(\d+)K/ && $1 > 8192) {
        my $M = int($1 / 1024);
        $label =~ s#$1K#${M}M#;
    }
    return $label;
}

sub names ($) {
    my $ref = shift;
    my @names = ();
    for (my $i = 0; $val ne "NULL"; $i++) {
        my $val = Top::ptrvalue($ref, $i);
        push(@names, $val);
    }
    return(@names);
}

my $clear = `clear`;
my($statics) = new statics();      # contains the OS specific field names
my($si)      = new system_info(); # contains the raw system information
my($ps)      = new process_select(); # used to store process information
$ps->{idle}     = 1;
$ps->{"system"} = 0;
$ps->{uid}      = -1;
```

Example 39-5. A SWIG-enabled top emulator (continued)

```
# Extract field names from their respective null-terminated lists.
Top::machine_init($statics);
my(@procstates) = names($statics->{procstate_names});
my(@cpustates) = names($statics->{cpustate_names});
my(@memory) = names($statics->{memory_names});

# We'll emulate top's basic display sixty times.
Top::get_system_info($si);
for (1 .. 60) {
    sleep(1);

    # Get the info and clear the screen
    Top::get_system_info($si);
    my $handle = Top::get_process_info($si, $ps);
    print $clear;

    # "load averages: 0.02, 0.05, 0.01 20:43:09"
    print("load averages");
    for my $i (0 .. 2) {
        my $value = Top::ptrvalue($si->{load_avg},$i);
        printf("%s %5.2f", $i == 0 ? ":" : ",", $value);
    }

    printf("\t\t\t\t    %2d:%02d:%02d\n", reverse((localtime()))[0..2]));

    # "34 processes: 1 running, 32 sleeping, 1 stopped"
    printf("%d processes: ", $si->{p_total});
    for my $i (0 .. $#procstates) {
        my $value = Top::ptrvalue($si->{procstates},$i);
        next unless $value;
        printf("%d%s", $value, $procstates[$i]);
    }
    print("\n");

    # "CPU states: 2.3% user, 0.0% nice, 1.5% system, 0.0% interrupt, 96.2% idle"
    my $sum = 0;
    for my $i (0 .. $#cpustates) { $sum += Top::ptrvalue($si->{cpustates}, $i) },
    $sum /= 100.0;
    for my $i (0 .. $#cpustates) {
        my $percent = Top::ptrvalue($si->{cpustates},$i)/$sum;
        my $value = $percent == 100.0 ? "100" : sprintf("%4.1f", $percent);
        printf("%s %4s%% %s", $i == 0 ? "CPU states:" : ",", $value,
    }
    print("\n");

    # "Mem: 25M Active, 3752K Inact, 14M Wired, 8M Cache, 7323K Buf, 8M Free"
    print("Mem: ");
    for my $i (0 .. $#memory) {
        my $value = Top::ptrvalue($si->{memory},$i);
        next if $value == 0;
        print(memfix("$value$memory[$i]"));
    }
    print("\n");
```

Example 39-5. A SWIG-enabled top emulator (continued)

```
    # "29938 root 28 0 1204K 1648K RUN 0:00 20.31% 0.99% perl"
    print("\n");
    print(Top::full_format_header("USERNAME"), "\n");
    for my $p (1 .. $si->{p_total}) {
        print(Top::full_format_next_process($handle), "\n");
    }
}
```

Look back at *machine.h*; you'll see that the static structure has pointers to character arrays. Normally, the potential ambiguity of pointers to pointers would cause SWIG to punt unless it had explicit directions for what to do. However, the array-of-strings construct is so common that SWIG provides support via the *pointer.i* interface file.

The names subroutine steps through the char ** array, pulling off the strings one by one until NULL is reached. ptrvalue is a standard SWIG function that requires an array reference and an index; it returns the element at that index. The assembled array is then returned by names. The memfix routine is more mundane. It just converts a number from kilobytes to megabytes.

The initialization section of the script creates three structures ($statics, $si, and $ps) via calls to new. SWIG's %make_default pragma (back in *top.i*) automatically allocated the structures and created the new methods for you.

The ps structure is initialized by hand so that its values make sense the first time they are used, and the Top::machine_init method populates the statics structure. The three calls to names extract the respective names into arrays.

The remainder of the script is just a loop that repeats 60 times. On each iteration, the script pauses, gathers current statistics, and prints a top-style report. The output of the emulator is shown below.

```
    load averages: 0.14, 0.03, 0.01                              22:44:41
    30 processes: 1 running, 29 sleeping,
    CPU states: 5.3% user, 0.0% nice, 1.5% system, 0.8% interrupt, 92.4% idle
    Mem: 27M Active, 8M Inact, 14M Wired, 5060K Cache, 7640K Buf, 6952K Free
```

```
      PID USERNAME PRI NICE SIZE   RES STATE  TIME  WCPU    CPU COMMAND
    15121 root      28   0 1276K 1748K RUN    0:00  2.13%  0.84% perl
    14499 root      18   0  684K  896K pause  0:00  0.00%  0.00% tcsh
    14498 scott      2   0  608K 1828K select 0:00  0.04%  0.04% xterm
    13917 scott      3   0 1448K 1652K ttyin  0:02  0.00%  0.00% vi
      242 scott     18   0  828K 1016K pause  0:04  0.00%  0.00% tcsh
      241 scott      3   0  652K  944K ttyin  0:00  0.00%  0.00% tcsh
      240 scott      3   0  664K  952K ttyin  0:00  0.00%  0.00% tcsh
      239 root       2   0 1244K 1380K select 1:08  0.00%  0.00% perl
      233 scott      2   0  532K 1408K select 0:19  0.00%  0.00% xterm
      232 scott      2   0  208K 1172K select 0:02  0.00%  0.00% xclock
```

It runs equally well on all top-ready operating systems. The only feature missing is the ability to sort processes according to their CPU usage. More sophisticated scripts might extend top in different ways, including data trending, event triggers, real-time plots of system data, and so on.

Conclusion

SWIG's 300-page user manual goes into great detail about features not covered in this article: pointers, input constraints, typemaps for complex data types, exception handling, and further customization. It also covers C++ and Objective C.

Other common uses of SWIG include rapid prototyping, interactive debugging, script-based testing of systems, and optimization of existing scripts by implementing slow portions in C or C++. SWIG makes it simple to embed C and C++ code in your favorite interpreter. In addition to Perl, SWIG can just as easily generate interface code for Tcl, Guile, and Python. Best of all, SWIG is portable and free.

CHAPTER 40

Benchmarking

brian d foy

Perl's motto is "There Is More Than One Way To Do It." Some ways are easy to read, some are fast, and some are just plain incomprehensible. Often I'll need to know how long it takes for my program to execute, and I'll use the Benchmark module to find out. The Benchmark module comes with the standard Perl distribution and is written completely in Perl, so you can use it right away.

The Trouble with time( )

Before I discuss the Benchmark module, let's examine what's involved in timing an event. I need to know when the event started and when the event ended. Once I have those details, timing the event is a simple matter of subtraction.

If I want to time one of my programs, I could use my stopwatch to figure out how long it takes to execute. If the program takes more than several seconds, I might actually be able to do that. However, I don't need my watch, since Perl already provides a way to do this with the built-in time function, which returns the system time. I can record the system time twice and take the difference:

```
my $start_time = time;
# My code here
my $end_time = time;

my $difference = $end_time - $start_time;
print "My code took $difference seconds.\n";
```

Since time returns an integral number of seconds, this method can only record times and differences with one-second precision. That might be too coarse a granularity for the really fast code that I've written. Also, the CPU works on other things before it finishes my program, so the stopwatch approach doesn't tell me how long the CPU actually spent on *my* program. When the CPU is more heavily loaded, the time to execute might be longer. A program might take ten seconds to execute, but only use two seconds of actual CPU time.

Better Resolution with times

Perl's built-in times function provides more information: a list of the user time, system time, children's user time, and children's system time, all with a finer granularity than time. Better still, it only records the time actually spent on my process—an important distinction for multitasking operating systems. I can use the same technique that I used before to time my program:

```perl
my @start_times = times;
# My code here
my @end_time = times;

my @differences = map { $end_time[$_] - $start_time[$_] } (0..$#start_time);

my $difference = join ', ', @differences;
print " My code took ($difference) seconds\n";
```

My code might still run a lot faster than the smallest time that I can measure, even with times, so what I should do is run my code many times and compute the average. This makes the situation much more complicated: not only I will I need to make a loop to run the code several times, but I will need to figure out how the addition of the loop increased the time. You don't have to worry about any of this if you use the Benchmark module.

The Benchmark Module

Now I want to rewrite my previous examples using Benchmark. To record a time, I construct a Benchmark object. The constructor creates a list of the times returned by time and times, although I don't need to worry about that, since I just use the object-oriented interface.

```perl
use Benchmark;

my $start_time = new Benchmark;

# My code here

my @array = (1 .. 1000000);
foreach my $element ( @array ) { $_ += $element }

my $end_time = new Benchmark;
```

I also need a way to determine the time difference, which I can do with the timediff function:

```perl
my $difference = timediff($end_time, $start_time);
```

This returns another Benchmark object. When I want to see the times that I have measured, I use the timestr method:

```perl
print "It took ", timestr($difference), "\n";
```

This function provides several ways to print the time using optional FORMAT and STYLE parameters, explained in the documentation embedded in the Benchmark module (type perldoc Benchmark or man Benchmark). After running this code I get:

```
It took 40 secs (17.53 usr 6.39 sys = 23.92 cpu)
```

The first number, 40 seconds, is the real time it took to execute—exactly what my stopwatch would have revealed. The module takes this directly from time. The next numbers are the values from times giving the user and system times, which, when summed, give the total CPU time.

I can also measure the time it takes to perform several iterations of the code by using the timeit method, which takes either a code reference (a reference to an anonymous subroutine) or a string. The function returns a Benchmark object that I can print as before.

```perl
#!/usr/bin/perl
use Benchmark;

my $ITERATIONS = 1000;

my $code = 'foreach my $element ( 1 .. 1000 ) { $_ += $element }';

my $time = timeit($ITERATIONS, $code);

print "It took ", timestr($time), "\n";
```

On my computer, this program prints:

```
It took 14 secs ( 8.49 usr 0.00 sys = 8.49 cpu)
```

Here, I'm providing code to Benchmark as a string. I could have provided it as a code reference instead, but it's important never to mix them in a single benchmark, since there's extra overhead with the eval needed to benchmark a string.

As I mentioned before, running a snippet of code several times has additional overhead unrelated to the speediness of my code—the time required to set up the loop constructs, for instance. One of the advantages of the Benchmark module is that timeit tests how long it takes to execute an empty string and subtracts that time from the time needed to run your code; this step compensates for the extra overhead introduced by the act of benchmarking code. There are several methods that let you exert finer control over this feature; they're described in the documentation embedded in the module.

The function timethis is similar to timeit, but has optional parameters for TITLE and STYLE. The TITLE parameter allows you to give your snippet a name, and STYLE affects the format of the output. The results are automatically sent to STDOUT, although timethis still returns a Benchmark object. Internally, timethis uses timeit.

Example: Summing an Array

Now that I know how long it took to run my bit of code, I'm curious if I can make that time shorter. Can I come up with another way to do the same task, and, if I can, how does its time compare to other ways? Using the Benchmark module, I can use timeit for each bit of code. However, the Benchmark module anticipates this need, providing a function that compares several chunks of code: timethese.

The timethese function is a wrapper around timethis. The %SNIPPETS hash contains snippet names as keys, and either CODE references or strings as values. The function returns a list of Benchmark objects for each chunk of code.

```
my @benchmarks = timethese($ITERATIONS, \%SNIPPETS);
```

timethese doesn't guarantee any particular order for testing the snippets, so I have to keep track of the order in which timethis reports the results. If I wanted to do further programmatic calculations with the times, I could store the list returned by timethese, but for now I will rely on the information printed from timethis. Now I just need something to compare.

To demonstrate timethese, I want to compare five different ways to sum an array. I gave each snippet a name based on my impression of it. The Idiomatic method is the standard use of foreach. Even if this technique turns out to be slower than another, I'd still prefer it because it's the most straightforward solution. The Evil use of map in a void context seems like it might be really clever and preferred by some Perl pedants, but how fast is it? The Iterator technique uses the sum function from Graham Barr's List::Util module, which uses XS to tie C code to a Perl function. I think Iterator might be very competitive. I expect the Curious and Silly methods to be very slow, but at the very least they'll make me appreciate the speed of the other techniques.

Idiomatic
```
foreach (@array) { $sum += $_ }
```
Evil (use of map in void context)
```
map { $sum += $_ } @array;
```
Iterator
```
$sum = sum @array;
```
Curious
```
grep { /^(\d+)$/ and $sum += $1 } @array
```
Silly
```
$_ = join 'just another new york perl hacker', @array_name;
while (m/(\d+)/g ) { $sum += $1 }
```

Our program to test all five techniques:

```perl
#!/usr/bin/perl
use Benchmark qw(timethese);
use List::Util qw(sum);

my $iterations = 100000;
@array = (1 .. 10);

my %SNIPPETS = (
    Idiomatic => '$sum=0; foreach (@array) { $sum += $_ }',
         Evil => '$sum=0; map { $sum += $_ } @array',
     Iterator => '$sum=0; $sum = sum @array'
      Curious => '$sum=0; grep { /^(\d+)$/ and $sum += $1 } @array',
        Silly => q|$sum=0; $_ = join 'just another new york perl
                    hacker', @array; while( m/(\d+)/g ) {  $sum += $1 }| );

timethese($iterations, \%SNIPPETS);
```

I get the following output on my Powerbook G3 running Mac OS 10.1.2 with Perl 5.6.1:

```
Benchmark: timing 100000 iterations of Curious, Evil, Idiomatic, Iterator, Silly...
  Curious: 20 wallclock secs (12.84 usr + 0.00 sys = 12.84 CPU) @ 7788.16/s
     Evil: 6 wallclock secs ( 3.87 usr + 0.00 sys =  3.87 CPU) @ 25839.79/s
Idiomatic: 1 wallclock secs ( 1.01 usr + 0.00 sys =  1.01 CPU) @ 99009.90/s
 Iterator: 1 wallclock secs ( 0.25 usr + 0.00 sys =  0.25 CPU) @ 400000.00/s
            (warning: too few iterations for a reliable count)
    Silly: 15 wallclock secs ( 9.52 usr + 0.00 sys =  9.52 CPU) @ 10504.20/s
```

The sum function from List::Util is *very* fast. In fact, it was so fast that for 100,000 iterations the Benchmark module couldn't measure a reliable time. The idiomatic foreach loop is slightly faster than the "clever" use of map, but both are significantly slower than List::Util's sum. The other methods, which I never expected to be fast, are indeed quite slow.

However, this comparison doesn't satisfy me. What happens as the size of the array and the number of iterations changes? Over several weeks I ran several combinations of array size and iterations for each of the methods. Since I don't really care about the Curious and Silly methods, I'll only report the results for the Idiomatic, Evil, and Iterator methods. I ran each with arrays of sizes from 10 to 10,000 elements, for 1,000 to 1,000,000 iterations. The longest time took about 86,000 CPU seconds of a Sparc20 (96 Mb RAM, Perl 5.004)—that's about 1 CPU day! The results are pictured in Figure 40-1. Don't try this without telling the system administrator what you are doing, especially if you called your script test. It's no fun to get email nastygrams from an administrator who thinks you have a script running amok when it's really doing exactly what you want it to do. Not that this happened to me and you can't prove it anyway.

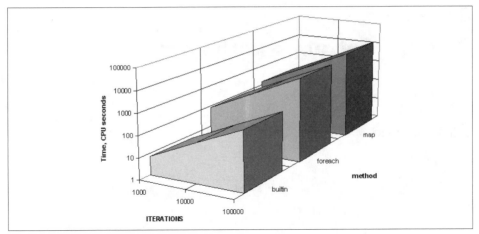

Figure 40-1. Total CPU time for three different methods summing an array of 10,000 integers

Conclusion

Stopwatches aren't very effective for timing a piece of code because the CPU might work on other things before it finishes your task. The `times` function is a little better, but my code might run faster than it can measure. I don't have to worry about these issues when I use the Benchmark module, which averages the time needed over many iterations.

In my summing example, I discovered that the "clever" use of `map` was consistently slower than the idiomatic `foreach`, which in turn was much slower than `sum`. Although `foreach` is the conventional way to sum an array, I am hard-pressed to justify the order of magnitude speed penalty—I'll be using `sum` from now on. If you think that you have a faster method, you now have the tools to test it. If your method beats `sum`, send me a note (and Graham too)!

 I haven't shown all of the things you can do with the Benchmark module. Since this article was first published, another set of Benchmark functions has become available, allowing you to turn the benchmarks "inside out"—you can specify how long you want the benchmark to run, and it tells you how many iterations it was able to accomplish in that time.

CHAPTER 41
Building Software with Cons

Bob Sidebotham

 Since this article was written, Cons has grown up considerably. It's now been GPL'd, and the copyright transferred to the Free Software Foundation. An energetic community has contributed many useful enhancements; Rajesh Vaidheeswarran and Steven Knight deserve special thanks for all the excellent work that they've put into maintaining, enhancing, and improving so many aspects of Cons. Steve's Cons derivative, Sc-cons, won the Software Carpentry design competition's Build category, and is now in active development over on SourceForge (as Scons). Despite the changes, the description of Cons in this article is still sound. Please note, however, that there may be minor differences in the signature handling in the current version of Cons.

Understandably, many Perl programmers don't like having to program in low-level languages like C and C++. Writing the Makefiles necessary to compile and install those programs with the Unix make utility is even more irritating. Worse still is being saddled with maintaining someone else's Makefiles.

You might have reached an uneasy truce with make, and you might even have doubts about the statements above. Reading this article will likely shatter your illusions. You have been warned! In this article I introduce Cons, a Perl alternative to make. First, I'll explain why it's necessary.

Make Doesn't Do the Right Thing

Perhaps the most egregious aspect of make is the make language itself. In fairness, make has been around for a long time, predating even Perl. The standard for scripting in the Unix community at the time of make's emergence was the Bourne shell, and make represented a considerable advance over the then-common practice of using shell scripts to build software.

As a scripting vehicle, Makefiles are really just glorified collections of macros with no control flow, sophisticated substitutions, or variable scoping, and poor control over import/export of environment variables and command arguments. If you want proof that make is inadequate, just look at the plethora of utilities that people use to avoid writing their own Makefiles, like MakeMaker and imake. I could provide a long list of the shortcomings of the make language, but I'd be surprised if any Perl programmer needs much persuasion.

Software construction systems like make need to know not only how to build the final target, but when particular components need to be rebuilt. You might think that make does this well. You'd be wrong.

In typical C-based software systems, an executable program depends on libraries, the libraries depend on object files, the object files depend on C programs, and the C programs depend on C header files. Managing these dependencies is trickier than it might seem; even systems that automate dependency generation seldom get it right.

One approach is to use the C compiler to find dependencies. However, this won't find dependencies for intermediate files, such as interface files generated by a separate interface definition utility. This approach also suffers because the entire system has to be built from scratch before it's possible to determine the dependencies.

Global dependencies (such as make depend) are typically mishandled by make. The process is usually slow and cumbersome, and thus often avoided by impatient users. If a dependency is wrong, or if the dependency calculations are circumvented (for example, by building a lone subdirectory without first building its dependencies), you're already a goner, because once a file is built—whether correctly or incorrectly—its modification time is updated. Now it's more up-to-date than its dependencies, and no amount of after-the-fact analysis will reveal this.

Partly to address this problem, and partly to get around the need to recompile too much of the tree, many Makefiles or make-like programs let you touch all the files controlled by the Makefile, causing them to be presumed to be up-to-date, while files that depend upon them are presumed not to be up-to-date. (touch is a Unix command that sets the last modification time of the file to the current moment.) This is a contrived and error-prone practice because a touched file will not be rebuilt, regardless of whether it needs to be.

Problems result when a subset of modules are built in a particular way. Perhaps debugging is enabled in a subset of modules, but then must be removed in the final target. In this situation there is no reliable way to determine which files need to be rebuilt. A great burden falls on the developer, who must remember exactly what she has done. A similar problem occurs from changes to rules that affect the way derived files are built. Attempts are occasionally made to deal with this by having derived files depend upon their Makefiles, but this is a heavyweight solution which invites the unsafe use of touch or other hacks to prevent unwanted rebuilds.

The result is that particular build trees become less likely to have been built correctly: in the right order, with the right parameters, by the right compilers, and with the right environment. When the developer has lost confidence in the tree, often after much wasted time chasing build-related problems masquerading as bugs, a make clean must be performed. The complete build from scratch wastes additional time.

Problems also arise from implicit rules, wildcards, and *vpaths* (lists of alternate directories to be searched for targets or dependencies). The unrestricted import of environment variables also causes confusion, with builds working correctly for one user but not another. And it's not unusual for a manually invoked Makefile to behave differently than when it's invoked by another Makefile.

Using file modification times as the sole determinant of whether a file is up-to-date is perilous. It causes problems in distributed systems if time is not carefully synchronized over all hosts. Library release management can also expose the fragility of this approach; if users have performed builds prior to the release date of the library, but after the library was built, make can be fooled into thinking that the users' builds are up-to-date. The central problem with the use of file modification times, however, is that a file's modification time says *when* the file was built, but not *how* the file was built. This is insufficient information for determining whether it's current.

Build Sequencing

Another difficulty with make is build sequencing. If you manage to get dependencies correct, make is pretty good about sequencing the build steps within each directory. However, between directories, the picture is murkier. In large systems, a common approach is to build the whole system in several passes. The first pass might install some include files; the second might build some tools and install them; a third pass might use these tools to build a set of interface files from interface description files, and so on.

Setting up the appropriate sequencing in a maintainable and understandable manner can be quite a challenge, typically resulting in complexity and inflexibility. Because of the perceived performance hit from multiple passes through trees of Makefiles, a full recursive build is often circumvented, compromising the build for the reasons cited earlier.

Variant Builds

make offers little support for parallel variant builds. You might wish to build a system for multiple target platforms or architectures, or maintain separate versions of libraries—one with debugging symbols and one without. It's also desirable to be able to change the way the system is built temporarily. Once again, make is no help.

Complexity

Perhaps the most serious issue with make is complexity. The complexity arises from many sources, most of all from the make language itself. Dependencies are hard to maintain, because the dependency information is frequently written in at least two places: once in the Makefile and once, implicitly, in the source file (e.g., #include declarations). Automated dependency add-ons can be difficult to use, unreliable, and difficult to understand. Build sequencing can require extra baggage in each Makefile. Recursive invocations of make in multiple passes can be hard to understand and maintain. Implicit rules, vpaths, and wildcards all increase the cognitive load on the developer or maintainer.

The Solution: Cons

My relationship with make got off to a bad start back in the early 1980s, and went downhill from there. A couple of years ago, my frustration level peaking, I looked at alternatives to make such as Odin, Shape Tools, and Jam. Of these, only Jam was close to what I wanted. It had a small footprint, didn't try to do too much, and was fast. But none of the alternatives was as flexible as I wanted. Eventually, I realized that I didn't have to be a slave to any of these systems; I could roll my own with Perl.

The result is Cons, so called because it can be used to cons-struct software. All the other building words like bake, make, and build were already taken. Cons addresses all of the issues raised above and provides superior solutions in a very simple and user-friendly package. Strong claims? Read on.

Cons Scripts Are Perl Scripts

The key to building a powerful construction system turned out to be Perl. Not only is Cons written in Perl (it's a single 1,500-line program) but all user-supplied construction scripts are also written in Perl. Here's an example of a trivial script:

```
$cons = new cons();
Program $cons "foo", "foo.c";
```

The first line creates a *construction environment*, a Perl object that encapsulates how to construct derived files. A construction environment has a set of methods, such as the Program method shown above, and a set of key/value pairs used by the methods. If I place this code in a file called *Construct*, making sure that the source file *foo.c* is in the same directory, then I build foo like this:

```
% cons foo
cc -c foo.c -o foo.o
cc -o foo foo.o
```

The default implementation of Program never builds a program in one step. It easily could, but there didn't seem to be any great need for it, so it doesn't.

I can elaborate this script to enable debugging and use the GNU C compiler, gcc:

```
$cons = new cons(
  CC => 'gcc',
  CFLAGS => '-g'
);

Program $cons "foo", "foo.c";
```

Then recompile it like this:

```
% cons foo
gcc -g -c foo.c -o foo.o
gcc -o foo foo.o
```

Since I have Perl scripting at my fingertips, I can get fancier and control compile-time options via command-line arguments. Here's a somewhat trivial example:

```
$opt = "-O$ARG{opt}" if $ARG{opt};
$dbg = "-g" unless $opt;

$cons = new cons(
  CC => 'gcc',
  CFLAGS => "$dbg $opt"
);
```

Any arguments with embedded equal signs are passed to the top-level *Construct* file via the %ARG hash. Here's the result:

```
% cons foo opt=4
gcc -O4 -c foo.c -o foo.o
gcc -o foo foo.o
```

If I rebuild again without opt=4, I get:

```
% cons foo
gcc -g -c foo.c -o foo.o
gcc -o foo foo.o
```

This tiny example hints at the flexibility Perl provides Cons scripts. With Perl, scripts can do exactly what you want them to do in the most straightforward possible manner. It's especially useful for adapting to multiple machine architectures or environments. There's never any need for preprocessors like imake: everything can be done directly within Perl. All the things that make Perl a great language also make it a good choice for a software construction tool.

Cons Does the Right Thing

It doesn't matter who builds the system, what has been built before, or what has changed: *Cons will always build the system correctly.* Period. Several techniques help ensure this. Cons performs global automatic dependency analysis, and considers everything that goes into the file and how all those pieces were built.

With Cons, the golden rule for dependency handling, is, ideally, that *every* dependency is written down exactly once. If a C file #includes a header file, there's your dependency. In the previous example, *foo.c* includes the file *foo.h*, and this dependency is automatically recognized by Cons:

```
% cons foo
cons: "foo" is up-to-date.
% cp /etc/passwd foo.h
% cons foo
gcc -g -c foo.c -o foo.o
gcc -o foo foo.o
```

In the following example, you can see that the file *foo.o* is not only dependent on the files *foo.c*, and *foo.h*, but it is also dependent on the actual commands that were used to produce it. Notice what happens if I change the optimization level:

```
% cons foo opt=1
gcc -O1 -c foo.c -o foo.o
gcc -o foo foo.o
% cons foo opt=1
cons: "foo" is up-to-date.
% cons foo
gcc -g -c foo.c -o foo.o
gcc -o foo foo.o
% cons foo
cons: "foo" is up-to-date.
```

As long as I leave the optimization level alone, Cons will not recompile. As soon as the optimization level is changed, foo is rebuilt.

Notice what happens if the target file is modified outside of the construction system since the last Cons-directed build:

```
% cons foo
cons: "foo" is up-to-date.
% cp /etc/passwd foo
% cons foo
gcc -o foo foo.o
```

If I'd been using make, foo would have been considered up-to-date because it was modified more recently than its dependencies.

Now consider what happens if *foo.o* is modified behind Cons's back:

```
% cons foo
cons: "foo" is up-to-date.
% cp /etc/passwd foo.o
% cons foo
gcc -c foo.c -o foo.o
cons: "foo" is up-to-date.
```

This one is, perhaps, surprising: Cons detects that *foo.o* needs to be rebuilt. After doing this, however, Cons does not relink foo because it discovers that it was previously linked with an identical version of *foo.o*. It's worth observing that make, in the same situation, would have attempted to rebuild foo from the corrupted *foo.o*. Since the object file was newer than *foo.c*, make would have made no attempt to rebuild.

Explicit and Implicit Dependencies

How can Cons be this smart? If you go back to the construction script, you see that the crux of the script is:

```
Program $cons "foo", "foo.c";
```

The Program method expects a target filename and a set of object files. When it's given a file without the standard object extension (e.g., .o, identified by SUFOBJ in the $cons object), it implicitly invokes the Objects method. So this script is equivalent to:

```
Program $cons "foo", "foo.o";
Objects $cons "foo.c";
```

The Program method sets up an explicit dependency of foo on *foo.o*. The Objects method knows, for the specified environment $cons, how to derive a corresponding object file for each file mentioned, and uses the file's extension to determine precisely how to do this. Cons uses SUFOBJ in the $cons environment to determine the resulting file extension. It sets up an additional explicit dependency of *foo.o* on *foo.c* and associates a builder object for C files with *foo.o* as the output and *foo.c* as the input. This builder object, in turn, recognizes that *foo.c* may reference other sources, and it provides a *scanner*, responsible for scanning *foo.c* for #include lines, and, recursively, scanning any include files that are included by *foo.c*. The files returned by this scanner are implicit dependencies of *foo.o*.

When the user types cons foo, Cons descends the dependency tree, starting from the file foo. Cons determines that *foo.o* depends on foo, and determines how to build that. The request to build *foo.o* causes the dependency scanner for *foo.c* to be invoked, returning the list of additional, dynamically determined dependencies of *foo.o*. In this case, as you know, at least *foo.h* must be returned.

Up to this point, make would have done a similar analysis, with some key differences. In both systems, the dependency of foo on *foo.o* is listed explicitly. In contrast to make, the dependency of *foo.o* on *foo.c* is explicit in Cons. The user might not remember to include the dependency in his script, but it is explicitly defined by the script because the Objects method is invoked, and the method doesn't care what files happen to be sitting in the directory at that moment. In Cons, if *foo.c* doesn't exist, an error will occur if *foo.o* is needed; in make, a missing *foo.c* does not necessarily mean the build will fail: it might choose another, probably inappropriate way to build it. That might sound unlikely, but it's happened to me. In make, of course, the dependency of *foo.o* on *foo.h* is not determined automatically and must be listed explicitly by other means.

MD5 Cryptographic Signatures

Once the dependencies are determined, make decides what to rebuild based solely on the dependency hierarchy and the relative modification times of the files involved. Cons abandons relative modification times and introduces *cryptographic file signatures* instead. Cons uses the MD5 algorithm to compress information about the file into a unique signature. MD5 takes an input string of arbitrary length (such as a source file) and generates a "fingerprint" that identifies the string. The fingerprint is always 128 bits long, no matter how large the input string is. Cons uses the MD5 Perl module, available on CPAN.

Filesystems commonly do not provide any way of adding annotations to files, so the signatures are recorded separately. Cons stores the signatures in a *.consign* file, one for each directory containing files under the control of Cons. In my directory for the example I've been working with, the *.consign* file contains the following lines:

```
foo.o:867019197 e08563e22a97ea75de433949381ebdea
foo:867019197 c9cda7211523e4b17aeb8d7850790f47
```

The first number of each entry is a validation timestamp, and the second number is the file's signature: a 128-bit MD5 checksum. An entry is valid if its validation timestamp matches the corresponding file's modification time, as returned by the Perl stat function.

Notice what happens to the signatures if I recompile foo at a different optimization level:

```
% cons foo opt=2
gcc -O2 -c foo.c -o foo.o
gcc -o foo foo.o
% cat .consign
foo.o:867038502 a5ee7b74ca613efe91f193f1e2d3b27b
foo:867038503 a9e138331c31b8c5f41f95cfdd89569a
```

Both the validation timestamps and the signatures have changed. If I recompile without optimization:

```
% cons foo
gcc -g -c foo.c -o foo.o
gcc -o foo foo.o
% cat .consign
foo.o:867038521 e08563e22a97ea75de433949381ebdea
foo:867038521 c9cda7211523e4b17aeb8d7850790f47
```

I get the original signatures back, but with new validation stamps, representing the times the files were most recently derived.

Cons dumps everything it knows about a file into the signature. The signature thus reflects the way a file was built and all dependencies of the file. The signatures of the dependencies, in turn, include the command lines that were used to build them and their dependencies. For a source file that is not derived and for which no pre-existing signature exists, Cons uses the MD5 checksum of the file contents as its signature.

The algorithm used to determine whether a file must be rebuilt is simple. First, determine the file's signature. This is a recursive operation that will build, if necessary, any dependencies of the file. Second, compare the file's signature with that stored in the appropriate *.consign* file. If no valid signature can be found, or if the modification time of the file does not match the validation timestamp in the signature, the file is assumed to be out of date. If the signature does not match, the file is also assumed to be out-of-date. To rebuild the file, Cons uses whatever rules have been specified in the construction script. If the rebuild is successful, a new *.consign* entry is created accordingly.

A further benefit of file signatures is that Cons never has to remove files after an interrupted build! Since Cons only updates the signature *after* the file is built, there is no way that a newly modified file can have a valid signature if Cons is interrupted before completion of the processing step that creates the file.

Automatic, Global Sequencing of Builds

Because Cons does full and accurate dependency analysis, and because it's global across the entire build, it can use this information to take full control of the build sequencing. This sequencing is evident in the above examples, and is equivalent to what you would expect from make if you had a full set of dependencies. With Cons, however, this sequencing extends to larger, multidirectory builds.

A build is organized by creating a hierarchy of build scripts, starting with the top-level Construct file, and including multiple Conscript files from various directories. These scripts are tied together by the Cons-provided functions Build, Export, and Import. In make, subsidiary scripts are evaluated in a separate invocation. With Cons, only a single invocation is needed: Cons executes all of the scripts in the tree as part of the same Perl program. Note that the exact set of scripts read is under the control of Cons, and thus might change to accommodate different building arrangements.

To illustrate this procedure, consider a simple system with a top-level directory and beneath it a directory called *src* containing all the source code for the build. This directory is organized hierarchically. I'll consider just a small part of a system, with subdirectories *tpj* and *app*. The first directory contains a library of code used by the application in the *app* directory. Rather than teach the application the location of the library's source directory, I'll arrange for the library directory to install its products in known locations in a shared hierarchy called *build* instead. Files will be installed in *build/include*, *build/lib*, and *build/bin*. The *Construct* file might look like this:

```
# Define the various build directories
$build   = "#build";   # Pathnames starting with '#' are relative names
$LIB     = "$build/lib";
$INCLUDE = "$build/include";
$BIN     = "$build/bin";

# Define an environment for building programs
# linked against libtpj.a.
$CONS = new cons(      CC => 'gcc',
                     LIBS => '-ltpj',
                  LIBPATH => $LIB,
                  CPPPATH => $INCLUDE );

# Export the environment and build directories to our subsidiary scripts.
Export qw( CONS LIB INCLUDE BIN );

# Read and execute the subsidiary Conscript files.
for ("app", "tpj") { Build "src/$_/Conscript"; }
```

The file *src/tpj/Conscript* looks like this:

```
# Import these variables from our invoking script.
Import qw( CONS INCLUDE LIB );

# Arrange to build the library from these source files
Library $CONS "libtpj.a", qw( tpj.c jon.c );

# Arrange to install the library in the $LIB directory
Install $CONS $LIB, "libtpj.a";

# Arrange to install the header file in $INCLUDE.
Install $CONS $INCLUDE, "tpj.h";
```

And the file *src/app/Conscript* looks like this:

```
# Import these variables from our invoking script
Import qw( CONS BIN );

# Arrange to build the "app" program.
Program $CONS "app", "app.c";

# Arrange to install the app program in $BIN.
Install $CONS $BIN, "app";
```

These scripts result in a *build tree*: for every derivable file in the tree, Cons records the explicit dependencies and a method for dynamically determining the implicit dependencies, if any. Cons also determines a method for actually deriving the file, should it be necessary. In most cases, this method comes down to one or more commands to pass to the shell.

I can ask Cons for a list of products in the build tree:

```
% cons -p .
build/bin/app
build/include/tpj.h
build/lib/libtpj.a
src/app/app src/app/app.o
src/tpj/jon.o
src/tpj/libtpj.a
src/tpj/tpj.o
```

Or how they're built:

```
% cons -pa .
build/bin/app:
... Install src/app/app as build/bin/app
build/include/tpj.h:
... Install src/tpj/tpj.h as build/include/tpj.h
build/lib/libtpj.a:
... Install src/tpj/libtpj.a as build/lib/libtpj.a
src/app/app:
... gcc -o src/app/app src/app/app.o -Lbuild/lib -ltpj
src/app/app.o:
... gcc -Ibuild/include -c src/app/app.c -o src/app/app.o
```

```
src/tpj/jon.o:
... gcc -Ibuild/include -c src/tpj/jon.c -o src/tpj/jon.o
src/tpj/libtpj.a:
... ar r src/tpj/libtpj.a src/tpj/tpj.o
src/tpj/jon.o
... ranlib src/tpj/libtpj.a
src/tpj/tpj.o:
... gcc -Ibuild/include -c src/tpj/tpj.c -o src/tpj/tpj.o
```

Or which build scripts define them:

```
% cons -pw .
build/bin/app: cons::Install in "src/app/Conscript", line 8
build/include/tpj.h: cons::Install in "src/tpj/Conscript", line 11
build/lib/libtpj.a: cons::Install in "src/tpj/Conscript",line 8
src/app/app: cons::Program in "src/app/Conscript", line 5
src/app/app.o: cons::Program in "src/app/Conscript", line 5
src/tpj/jon.o: cons::Library in "src/tpj/Conscript", line 5
src/tpj/libtpj.a: cons::Library in "src/tpj/Conscript", line 5
src/tpj/tpj.o: cons::Library in "src/tpj/Conscript", line 5
```

So how is the build sequenced? It's very simple: Cons processes the target arguments one by one, and looks them up in the build tree. For each argument, it first determines the dependencies (which might involve other recursive build steps), and recursively builds any dependencies with signatures that don't match their computed signature. It then builds the target argument itself, if necessary. This process is sufficient to build any target, with any dependencies, at any location in the tree.

Summary

The best feature of Cons is its use of Perl as a scripting language. Automatic dependency analysis, cryptographic file signatures, detailed control of the command execution environment, and explicit construction directives further simplify construction scripts and ensure that Cons reliably builds software. Construction environments encapsulate and localize knowledge of how to build target files. Automatic build sequencing makes writing and building scripts dead easy. Parallel, variant builds are especially easy to arrange.

Cons is effective. It is used in a number of projects with several thousand source files. The "from scratch" build time of large projects decreased significantly whenever Cons was employed. More importantly, these projects no longer suffer from what used to be daily build-related problems: the builds are now consistently correct.

All of this is accomplished with a single portable program in a simple and easy to use package. But you don't have to take my word for it; try it out! Cons is freely available at *http://www.dsmit.com/cons*.

## CHAPTER 42

MakeMaker

Randy J. Ray

 As this book goes to print, there is a nascent effort to replace Make-Maker with a program tentatively called makepmdist. No one can say yet whether this new program will unseat MakeMaker, but whatever happens, MakeMaker will remain a valid option for creating CPAN module distributions in the years ahead.

MakeMaker is one of the most-used modules among Perl developers. It creates a *Makefile* for your own modules so that they can be compiled and installed by other people on other platforms. MakeMaker insulates you from the vagaries of different operating systems such as compiler flags or the construction of dynamic libraries. It frees you to focus on the module itself rather than the installation process. If you're writing a module that will be distributed on CPAN, or that needs to run on more than one architecture, MakeMaker is essential. This article assumes knowledge of basic configuration issues and the make command.

MakeMaker is the colloquial name for the ExtUtils::MakeMaker module. When loaded, it imports a set of core routines and a platform-specific library of routines. To MakeMaker, all Unix platforms are similar, since the Perl configuration process will already have identified the relevant differences between them. Thanks to Make-Maker, packages as operating-system–dependent as Perl/Tk will automatically build on platforms as diverse as VMS, Windows 98, Linux, and OS/2.

Reasons to Use MakeMaker

MakeMaker is absolutely necessary only when your module requires compilation of non-Perl code with XS. But there are several reasons you might want to use Make-Maker even when your module is pure, portable Perl:

- Your module requires the presence of other Perl modules, and you want to ensure they're available.
- You've got some computation to perform when your module is configured.

- You want your package to be installed into the standard area, wherever that might be. These paths are available to MakeMaker using Perl's configuration.
- Your module consists of several .*pm* files set up for autoloading. You don't want to manually split them, so you have MakeMaker do it for you.
- Users are accustomed to installing CPAN modules with `perl Makefile.PL` and a make. Why surprise them?

h2xs

The `h2xs` program bundled with the Perl distribution is indispensable for module developers. Although it was designed primarily for creating an module framework from a C header file, it's flexible enough to serve the needs of most modules whether or not they use C.

h2xs creates a basic .*pm* file, a *MANIFEST* file, a *Changes* file, a simple *test.pl* script, and, most importantly, a skeletal *Makefile.PL*. Here's the *Makefile.PL* generated by `h2xs -n Test`:

```
use ExtUtils::MakeMaker;
# See lib/ExtUtils/MakeMaker.pm for details of how to influence
# the contents of the Makefile that is written.
WriteMakefile(
    'NAME' => 'Test',
    'VERSION_FROM' => 'Test.pm',    # finds $VERSION
    'LIBS' => [''],                 # e.g., '-lm'
    'DEFINE' => '',                 # e.g., '-DHAVE_SOMETHING'
    'INC' => '',                    # e.g., '-I/usr/include/other'
);
```

There's not much here, but it does a great deal. It contains the information necessary for ExtUtils::MakeMaker to obtain the release version from your .*pm* file, notice whether your module uses XS (to link in C or C++ code), build shared libraries from compiled code, create a distribution tar file, and more. (The above snippet affects both *Test.pm* and *Test.xs*.

Invoking h2xs with the -X option would have suppressed the XS aspects and removed references to *Test.xs* from *Test.pm*—if your module (like most modules) makes no use of XS, you should use the -X option. Consider using h2xs even if your module makes no use at all of XS code; MakeMaker is easily tamed with it. See the h2xs documentation for more information.

On to the components of the file itself.

Components of Makefile.PL

MakeMaker allows people who download your module to prepare for compilation with one command: `perl Makefile.PL`. Ideally, this results in a module that compiles without problems and can be merged seamlessly with the user's existing Perl installation.

Makefile.PL is a Perl script, but it can't make any assumptions about, say, where your Perl executable is. Thus, it immediately imports the ExtUtils::MakeMaker module. The rest of the module is merely a call to that module's `WriteMakefile` subroutine. `WriteMakefile` is given some basic attributes of your module: its name, the version number (if any), and whether extra libraries, compile-time definitions, or include paths are needed. Other attributes can be supplied; five of the most common are listed in Table 42-1. See the ExtUtils::MakeMaker documentation for the complete list.

Table 42-1. Common attributes inside a Makefile.PL file

Attribute	What to pass	What it does
CONFIGURE	Code reference	The code reference is executed, and is expected to return a hash reference with other attributes for Makefile generation.
INSTALLSCRIPT	Scalar	The installation directory for scripts.
INSTALLSITELIB	Scalar	The installation directory for libraries. This assumes that you're not building within the Perl distribution; it defaults to the `site_lib` set when Perl was built.
PL_FILES	Hash reference	Maps *.PL* files to their full filenames.
PREREQ_PM	Hash reference	A list of modules required for this module to work, such as Fcntl for SDBM_File. The hash should map module names to the version number you need.

If you provide the attributes shown in Table 42-2 to `WriteMakefile`, the appropriate Makefile commands will be generated.

Table 42-2. Makefile commands controlled via Makefile.PL

Attribute	What to pass	What it does
clean	Hash reference	The key FILES should map to an anonymous list of files to be removed during make clean.
realclean	Hash reference	As above, for `make realclean`.
dist	Hash reference	Contains keys for bundling and unbundling the module (more on this later).

A Deeper Example

To see some of these items at work, consider the *Makefile.PL* from my X11::Fvwm module on CPAN, shown in Example 42-1. (The X11::Fvwm module provides access to Fvwm, a popular window manager for the X11 Window System. It's available on CPAN.)

Example 42-1. A sample Makefile.PL

```
require 5.002;
use ExtUtils::MakeMaker;
```

Example 42-1. A sample Makefile.PL (continued)

```
# This is borrowed almost verbatim from Graham Barr's MailTools package
sub chk_version {
    my ($pkg, $wanted) = @_;
    $| = 1;
    print "Checking for $pkg...";

    eval { my $p; ($p = $pkg . ".pm") =~ s!::!/!g; require $p; };

    my $vstr = ${"${pkg}::VERSION"} ? "found v" . ${"${pkg}::VERSION"} : "not found";
    my $vnum = ${"${pkg}::VERSION"} || 0;

    print $vnum >= $wanted ? "ok\n" : " " . $vstr . "\n";
    $vnum >= $wanted;
}

chk_version(Tk => 400.200) or
    warn "\n\tTk (400.200 or newer) wasn't found. You won't be able\n" .
    "\tto use Tk as a GUI (via X11::Fvwm::Tk) without it.\n\n";

chk_version(X11::Xforms => 0.7) or
    warn "\n\tX11::Xforms (0.7 or newer) was not found.\n" .
    "\tYou won't be able to use X11::Xforms as a GUI\n" .
    "\t(via X11::Fvwm::Xforms) without it.\n\n";

@DEMO_SCRIPTS = qw(scripts/PerlTkWL scripts/PerlWinList scripts/pDebug);

%PL_SCRIPTS = map { sprintf("%s.PL", $_) => "$_" } @DEMO_SCRIPTS;

WriteMakefile( NAME => 'X11::Fvwm',
               VERSION_FROM => 'Fvwm.pm',
               LIBS => [''],
               DEFINE => '',
               INSTALLSCRIPT => '/usr/local/lib/X11/fvwm2',
               INC => '-I$(FVWMSRCDIR)',
               macro => { 'FVWMSRCDIR' => '/usr/local/src/fvwm' },
               dist => { COMPRESS => 'gzip -9f', SUFFIX => 'gz' },
               EXE_FILES => [@DEMO_SCRIPTS],
               PL_FILES => \%PL_SCRIPTS,
               PMLIBDIRS => ['Fvwm'],
               clean => { FILES => join(' ', @DEMO_SCRIPTS) },
               realclean => { FILES => join(' ', @DEMO_SCRIPTS) } );
```

The require 5.002 ensures that users are running Perl 5.002 or newer. After the use ExtUtils::MakeMaker, the chk_version subroutine (adopted from Graham Barr's MailTools package) is defined. It checks whether a package is present and sufficiently recent, printing ok if so, or a diagnostic message if not: either not found or the version it found but couldn't accept. Unlike the PREREQ_PM attribute, it doesn't die if the package can't be found; it only warns the user that some features might not be available. (The return code could also be used to configure some parts of the module, if the absence of the package makes this appealing.)

After Tk and X11::Forms are checked, the scripts provided by the module are declared in @DEMO_SCRIPTS, and the mapping from .PL files to actual names is created in %PL_SCRIPTS. The hash is passed (as a reference) to WriteMakefile via the PL_FILES attribute. The original list will also be used in the definitions for clean and realclean, and is explicitly listed in EXE_FILES to ensure delivery into the appropriate install directory (INSTALLSCRIPT, since all four are scripts).

The WriteMakefile subroutine provides the NAME of the module, and the version number for the distribution is gleaned from *Fvwm.pm*. There are no extra libraries to be linked, nor defines for the C compiler lines. In this example, INSTALLSCRIPT is hard-coded to */usr/local/lib/X11/fvwm2*, and both INC and the attributes for macro utilize it. The macro attributes define a make macro called FVWMSRCDIR that the XS code needs in its include path for a few header files.

The two dist attributes fine-tune the results of make dist. COMPRESS identifies which compression utility to use, and SUFFIX identifies the suffix for the final filename. (If you specify COMPRESS, you must also specify SUFFIX.) Other keys that can be used here include TAR to specify a tar utility, TARFLAGS to pass to tar, SHAR to define the shell archive utility, PREOP to define make commands to execute before creating the distribution, and POSTOP to define commands to be run after creating the distribution. There's also DIST_DEFAULT, which can be one of tardist, shdist, zipdist, or uutardist. This defines which action is performed upon make dist; the default is tardist.

Advanced Makefile Features

Perhaps this still isn't enough flexibility for you; MakeMaker can oblige. Some of the methods used by MakeMaker (in the MM class) can be overridden if you provide a method of the same name in the MY class. This is the last resort for tailoring your Makefile; the documentation for ExtUtils::MM_Unix (the subclass of MM that provides Unix-based methods) encourages those who need to write their own methods to mail the MakeMaker authors and let them know why MakeMaker wasn't up to snuff. I'll cover some of the more common methods that can be overloaded.

I'll explore a few methods that actually produce chunks of text for the resulting Makefile. Most of these take only the object reference as an argument and rely on other method calls for access to information as shown in Table 42-3.

Table 42-3. MakeMaker method calls

Method	What does it do?
constants	Produces a code block that defines most of the make constants. Most of these pertain to system tools (ar, linkers, etc.) and Perl-related version strings and paths.
dist	Produces the macros for making the dist targets.
macro	Produces macros derived from the macro attribute passed into MakeMaker.

Table 42-3. MakeMaker method calls (continued)

Method	What does it do?
post_constants	Lets the user place override constants immediately after MakeMaker executes the `constants` method.
postamble	Allows the user to specify some text for the end of the Makefile.

There are many more than these five methods. In the documentation for both Make-Maker and the operating-system–specific variants (e.g., *ExtUtils::MM_Unix.pm*, *ExtUtils::MM_Win32.pm*), the methods that can be overridden are marked with an o. When overriding a method, you simply define it in *Makefile.PL* like so:

```
sub MY::post_constants {
    my $self = shift;
    my @m;

    push(@m,"PURIFY_DIR = /usr/local/pure/purify/purify-4.0-hpux/\n",
            "PURIFY = $(PURIFY_DIR)/purify\n");

    join "", @m;
}
```

Or, if you intend to reference the original method (or any other methods from the MM package), use the MY package:

```
sub MY::constants {
    package MY;        # To help SUPER work right
    my $self = shift;
    my @m;

    push(@m, $self->SUPER::constants(@_));
    push(@m, "PURIFY_DIR = /usr/local/pure/purify/purify-4.0-hpux/\n",
            "PURIFY = $(PURIFY_DIR)/purify\n");

    join "", @m;
}
```

MakeMaker and Installation of Modules

As mentioned earlier, MakeMaker manages the rules associated with installing your module and its files, letting you control where those files are placed.

The destination directories for files are based on the file type and whether Make-Maker is operating within the Perl source tree. The important directories are shown in Table 42-4.

Table 42-4. Destination directories used by MakeMaker

Directory	What's stored there
INSTALLSITESEARCH	Architecture-dependent files (such as dynamic libraries)
INSTALLSITELIB	Other library files (such as *.pm* files)

Table 42-4. Destination directories used by MakeMaker (continued)

Directory	What's stored there
INSTALLBIN	Binary executables (used if an extension provides the option of creating a new Perl with the extension built in)
INSTALLSCRIPT	Runnable scripts
INSTALLMAN1DIR	Section 1 manual pages (from scripts or standalone pods)
INSTALLMAN3DIR	Section 3 manual pages (from *.pm* files)

Two caveats: First, INSTALLSITESARCH and INSTALLSITELIB assume that you, the module author, want the end product to be installed in the site-local area where non-core modules are meant to go. If users prefer to have their Perl installation keep all modules in the same place, they can force that by setting INSTALLDIRS to perl when they create the Makefile: perl Makefile.PL INSTALLDIRS=perl.

Second, if you explicitly set either INSTALLSITESARCH or INSTALLSITELIB, then INSTALLDIRS will take precedence. Installation directories are only defined for section 1 and section 3 manual pages. If you have manual pages that belong in other sections, you'll have to encode those rules yourself, probably by overloading one of the MM methods such as postamble.

For users who want to build MakeMaker-based packages but don't have the necessary access to install them, MakeMaker supports the use of either LIB or PREFIX settings on the command line. Do *not* provide them to WriteMakefile; it's LIB that should dictate where the *.pm* files go: perl Makefile.PL LIB=~/perl_lib. This causes ~/perl_lib to be used for all the non-architecture–specific files. Architecture-specific files will be deposited in ~/perl_lib/$arch, where $arch is the configured architecture name (PA-RISC1.1 on my HP/UX machine). This affects only the library code, however; it doesn't affect any scripts you provide in your package. If the user instead sets PREFIX with, for example, perl Makefile.PL PREFIX=~, all of the installation-related values will be set relative to ~. This overloads the configuration value prefix, which is often something like */usr/local* or */opt/perl*.

My home directory is */home/tremere/rjray*, and my Perl is installed below */usr/local*. Here are the six installation paths for my machine, with and without the PREFIX=~ override:

INSTALLSITEARCH

    Without PREFIX: */usr/local/lib/perl5/site_perl/PA-RISC1.1*

    With PREFIX: */home/tremere/rjray/lib/perl5/site_perl/PA-RISC1.1*

INSTALLSITELIB

    Without PREFIX: */usr/local/lib/perl5/site_perl*

    With PREFIX: */home/tremere/rjray/lib/perl5/site_perl*

INSTALLBIN

    Without PREFIX: */usr/local/bin*

    With PREFIX: */home/tremere/rjray/bin*

INSTALLSCRIPT

Without PREFIX: */usr/local/bin*

With PREFIX: */home/tremere/rjray/bin*

INSTALLMAN1DIR

Without PREFIX: */usr/local/man/man1*

With PREFIX: */home/tremere/rjray/man/man1*

INSTALLMAN3DIR

Without PREFIX: */usr/local/lib/perl5/man/man3*

With PREFIX: */home/tremere/rjray/lib/perl5/man/man3*

Any of these six could be overridden in the call to WriteMakefile. For instance, the X11::Fvwm *Makefile.PL* shown earlier overrides INSTALLSCRIPT to force the scripts into the directory preferred by Fvwm. To look at the values from your configuration, try perl "-V:install.*".

perllocal.pod

You might not have known that Perl keeps a list of the packages installed with Make-Maker. Several lines are appended to *INSTALLARCHLIB/perllocal.pod* upon success-ful installation, noting the package that was installed, a few details about it, and when the installation occurred. A tidy little cron job could give you a web-browsable record of what modules have been installed on your system. Read *perllocal.pod* on your system and see what's there.

More detail can be found in the documentation for ExtUtils::MakeMaker, your sys-tem's MM methods (ExtUtils::MM_Unix for me), and h2xs. The MakeMaker package has recently been refactored to enable maintenance and development independent of Perl; the latest version can now be found on CPAN, and downloaded without forc-ing an upgrade to a newer Perl as a side effect.

## CHAPTER 43

Autoloading Perl Code

Randy J. Ray

Would you prefer to load a library of 10, 20, or more routines all at once, or only as needed? Perl provides a procedure called *autoloading* that specifies what happens when a program encounters a subroutine that is not currently defined. You do this using two modules: AutoLoader and AutoSplit.

Why Autoload?

I first took an interest in the AutoLoader when converting a lot of legacy code from Perl 4 to 5. One of the libraries that particularly frustrated me was a front end to some RCS utilities. The overhead was too high; in a library of 40–50 subroutines, I rarely needed more than two-thirds in a given execution, and sometimes just a few. Not only did I want to avoid the penalty of loading and parsing the whole library, I wanted to keep the unneeded routines from being loaded in the first place.

One of the ways in which use differs from require is that it loads (that is, reads and compiles) the module at compile time, before Perl runs the script. In Perl 4, which doesn't have use, I deferred loading the RCS library as long as possible by performing other tasks first, such as validating command-line usage, and so on. But as I upgraded, I realized that to take advantage of Perl 5, I needed to turn libraries into modules, and design my modules around the tools that Perl provides. As a result, I turned to the AutoLoader and AutoSplit libraries.

I'll use a smaller example for this article, a module I maintain called Image::Size (available on CPAN). It's a general-purpose utility that reads the height and width of an image file, and enables CGI scripts to generate HTML height and width attributes for image tags. Image::Size supports many image formats, inlcuding GIF, JPEG, XBM, XPM, PPM, and PNG. However, few of these are recognized by web browsers, and the odds of finding more than two or three in a given document are not high. So this was a logical use of the AutoLoader and AutoSplit libraries, and I wrote my library from the start with the intent of using them.

Using the AutoLoader

To make your module autoload, first add this line to the beginning:

```
use AutoLoader 'AUTOLOAD';
```

The use statement includes the AutoLoader module, and specifically imports the AUTOLOAD subroutine from that package into your module's package. As its name suggests, AUTOLOAD handles a lot of the dirty work of autoloading. Whenever Perl can't find a subroutine, it looks to see if there's an AUTOLOAD subroutine, and uses that instead.

The next step is to decide which routines should and should not be autoloaded. Code that initializes things, such as the new method of a class, will almost certainly be called every time the module is loaded, so there's nothing to be gained from autoloading—in fact, it slows down the first call slightly. Cluster the subroutines that need not be autoloaded at the top of the module. In Image::Size, there are three such subroutines:

```
imgsize()
html_imgsize()
attr_imgsize()
```

imgsize will always be called at least once, and the other two subroutines are just wrappers around it. In addition, Image::Size contains one subroutine for each of the supported image formats:

```
gifsize()
jpegsize()
xbmsize()
xpmsize()
ppmsize()
pngsize()
```

And so on. I didn't want Image::Size to load and parse any of these subroutines unless the user had an image in the corresponding format. So the next step was to place the special Perl token __END__ before all of those subroutines:

```
sub imgsize { ... }
sub html_imgsize { ... }
sub attr_imgsize { ... }

__END__

sub gifsize { ... }
sub jpegsize { ... }
...
```

Perl stops reading whenever it encounters an __END__. However, a program called AutoSplit (described later) knows to look for your module definitions there. Figure 43-1 shows what Image::Size looks like after AutoSplitting.

AutoSplit "splits out" the subroutines after __END__, placing each into its own *.al* file, as Figure 43-1 shows. Though the subroutines still exist in the original *Image/Size.pm*, Perl will ignore them in favor of the *.al* files. We'll come back to *autosplit.ix* shortly.

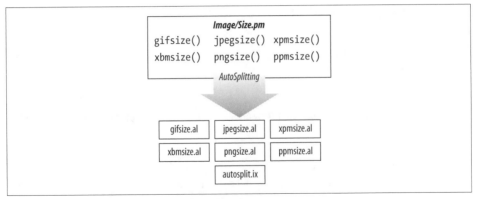

Figure 43-1. The Image::Size module after autosplitting

The next section explains what happens to the subroutines following __END__, and how they're loaded into memory and made accessible to your program.

How Autoloading Works

The AUTOLOAD subroutine provided by the AutoLoader module searches all the directories in @INC (the special list of directories that Perl uses to locate modules and library files), looking for subdirectories called auto. On the first call to gifsize, this subroutine tries to find an *auto/Image/Size* directory somewhere in @INC, and then tries to find a file named *gifsize.al* in that directory. If found, it's read in and compiled. Presuming the compilation succeeds, Perl uses a special form of the goto statement to switch execution to the new routine without altering the runtime stack. (This in itself is important—if you are running under the debugger, or if you use the Carp module to handle warnings and error reports, your subroutine call stack is crucial for tracing execution of your program. However, after autoloading, there will be no trace of AUTOLOAD in your stack.)

The index created by AutoSplit, *autosplit.ix*, declares the package namespace (which is Image::Size in our example) and predeclares the subroutines to be loaded on demand (the subroutines following the __END__).

If you install Image::Size and then type something like this from your prompt, the imgsize subroutine in Image::Size will automatically call gifsize.

```
% perl -e 'use Image::Size; print imgsize("TPJ.gif")'
```

Since that subroutine wasn't immediately available, the AutoLoader loaded it from *lib/site_perl/auto/Image/Size/gifsize.al*.

For a more hands-on example, visit your Perl's *lib* directory and find *auto/POSIX*. This package is too large to use as an example here, but that's exactly what makes it a prime candidate for autoloading: it's a hundred functions strong, but usually only a few will be desired at any one time.

AutoSplitting Your Module

There's one step I haven't told you about yet: how do you create the *.al* and *autosplit.ix* files that AUTOLOAD looks for? You know that's done by the AutoSplitter, but how is *that* invoked?

You could invoke it manually:

```
% perl -e 'use AutoSplit; autosplit("YourModule.pm", "YourLibAutoDirectory", 0, 1, 1);
```

This does five things:

- Checks that the module does in fact use AutoLoader.
- Extracts each subroutine after the __END__ and places it in its own *.al* file.
- Removes any *.al* files not referenced in the current module, presuming them to be obsolete.
- Creates the *autosplit.ix* file declaring the autoloadable subroutines.
- Splits the module only if any previously existing *autosplit.ix* file is older than the module.

Or, if you're using MakeMaker (the Perl utility that lets module users create make-files for their particular platform, described in the article *MakeMaker*), the Makefile generated by MakeMaker's *Makefile.PL* will contain rules to invoke AutoSplit automatically. However, since MakeMaker isn't always available, you can embed the rules in your Makefile yourself:

```
PERL = /usr/local/bin/perl
PERL_LIB = /usr/local/lib/perl5
PERL_ARCHLIB = /usr/local/lib/perl5/PA-RISC1.1/5.003
AUTOSPLITFILE = ${PERL} -MAutoSplit -I$(PERL_ARCHLIB)
                        -I$(PERL_LIB) -e 'autosplit($$ARGV[0], $$ARGV[1], 0, 1, 1)'
```

That's for my HP 712 running HP/UX 9.05. Your paths and architecture will certainly be different. Use perl -V to determine your settings:

```
% perl -V:perlpath
```

```
% perl -V:installsitelib
```

```
% perl -V:installarchlib
```

Inside your Makefile, you'll need to add an "action line" such as this, causing the file *Module.pm* to be split into the directory */my/perllib/auto*:

```
$(AUTOSPLITFILE) Module.pm /my/perllib/auto
```

AutoLoading Scripts

The AutoLoader/AutoSplit combination was designed to work only on modules, but the notion of deferring work is useful for scripts as well. I often combine multiple CGI scripts into a single, self-referencing script that needs only one or two subroutines, depending on the CGI parameters. Why waste cycles parsing code that won't be executed?

Enter a cousin of AutoLoader called SelfLoader. The SelfLoader module is similar to AutoLoader, pulling in and compiling routines on demand. But unlike AutoLoader, it's meant to work within an executing script, and it uses the __DATA__ token rather than __END__.

AutoLoading C Programs

Modern operating systems support the notion of *dynamic linking*: loading chunks of object code (usually compiled from C) only when needed. If you want to do this from Perl, use Perl's DynaLoader module. However, DynaLoader doesn't provide the Perl-to-C bridge code. For that, you need to create stub functions in a language called XS; see *Random Number Generators and XS* or read about how to use other languages from Perl in *Using Other Languages from Perl*.

Summary

At this point, you know everything you need to use autoloading in your modules. Take that 2,000-line module, slice it up, improve your application's startup time, and show your boss that you deserve a raise. If Image::Size and POSIX don't slake your thirst, there are many other CPAN-retrievable packages that are good examples of autoloading: Tk, MailTools, and LWP, to name a few.

There are a few other autoloading tidbits I'd like to share. First, a caveat: autoloading does incur a load and compile penalty for each subroutine loaded on demand. Second, each autoloaded subroutine results in an extra file containing some of the same code that already exists in the module. Third, autoloading isn't the only way to dynamically load subroutines.

Lincoln Stein's CGI.pm module uses a self-contained autoload scheme that is efficient, ingenious, and obfuscated all at once, making use of AUTOLOAD but not the AutoLoader. Remember that when Perl encounters a call to an undefined subroutine, it tries to substitute AUTOLOAD, if such a subroutine exists in the current package. That subroutine can do anything you want. When AUTOLOAD is invoked, a variable called $AUTOLOAD will have been set to the full package-qualified name of the desired subroutine (for example, Image::Size::gifsize). The special array @_ contains the arguments intended for the subroutine. AUTOLOAD isn't expected to return a result (except on error), but instead to transparently pass execution to the newly-loaded code.

Several packages (such as POSIX and DB_File in the core Perl distribution) use their own AUTOLOAD function, and that function calls the AUTOLOAD inside *AutoLoader.pm*. This allows local handling of such things as package constants or pseudoroutines, while still letting AutoLoader handle the more detailed loading tasks.

CHAPTER 44
Debugging and Devel::

Randy J. Ray

 Since the initial publication of this article, the Devel::* group of modules has flourished, now numbering well over 60 modules. However, all of the information in this article remains current.

You might have learned about Perl's -d switch, which launches Perl's internal symbolic debugger. If not, read the perldebug documentation and get started; it lets you set breakpoints and step through your programs line-by-line. The debugger is one of Perl's most attractive tools for developers, in part because it's not so much a debugger as a debugging system into which you can place the debugger of your choice. The debuggers can be found in the Devel:: category of the CPAN. In this article, I'd like to describe some of the modules you can find there (listed in Table 44-1).

Table 44-1. Some of the Devel:: modules

Module	Purpose
Devel::DProf	Reports the time used by the program and its subroutines.
Devel::Peek	Displays Perl values and structures.
Devel::SmallProf	Profiles individual lines.
Devel::TraceFuncs	Provides call sequences of subroutines.
Devel::Symdump	Provides symbolic dumps for variables and symbol tables.
Devel::WeakRef	Creates weak references to objects.
Devel::DumpStack	Displays the current subroutine's stack in human-readable format.
Devel::DebugInit	Creates initialization files for C/C++ symbolic debuggers.
Devel::Coverage	Coverage analysis of Perl scripts and libraries.
Devel::CoreStack	Generates a stack trace from a core dump using the best available debugger.

Not all of these modules are debuggers, but the ones that are debuggers can be launched as perl -d:*ModuleName*. DProf, SmallProf, and Coverage can be used in this way; the rest can't.

Runtime Examination of Data

Devel::Peek and Devel::Symdump help you examine Perl data as your program runs. Devel::Peek, by Ilya Zakharevich, reveals Perl's internal representation of your data, letting you verify that XS subroutines are operating correctly. The Devel::Symdump module, by Andreas Koenig and Tom Christiansen, lets you examine your variables—and entire symbol tables. The Devel::Symdump package is used by mod_perl to provide runtime status of the Perl interpreter in a running Apache web server. This is highly recommended.

Devel::TraceFuncs and Devel::DumpStack are handy for inspecting the subroutine stack or following the paths to subroutines. Devel::TraceFuncs, by Joe Hildebrand, allows selective enabling of the tracing of function entry, useful when you need to confirm that a subroutine is being called in the right sequence with respect to other routines. Jack Shirazi's Devel::DumpStack provides neatly-formatted stack traces. It lets you tune the depth of the trace and the formatting indentation.

All four of these modules can be brought in on demand from the debugger. You can load them at any time with use *ModuleName*.

Profiling and Coverage Testing

Devel::DProf and Devel::SmallProf tell you how much time is spent executing different portions of your program. Devel::DProf, by Dean Roehrich, measures time spent by the application itself, as well as time spent in individual subroutines. Ted Ashton's Devel::SmallProf module profiles individual lines, determining how often each was executed and how long each line took. Both tools write the profile information to an external file. DProf writes it in a binary format, providing a utility (`dprofpp`) to interpret the information. SmallProf generates human-readable ASCII.

Devel::Coverage provides coverage analysis, which is a cousin of profiling. The module tells you how often lines and subroutines are reached, with an eye toward identifying sections that are never reached. Coverage analysis helps you develop test suites guaranteed to exercise every line of your code. The module writes results to an external file (readable with `coverperl`, provided with the module) and can monitor multiple runs of your program.

Reference Manipulation

The Devel::WeakRef module, by Jesse Glick, enables the creation of *weak references* to data, duplicating an existing reference without changing Perl's internal reference count. These weak references can still be used to access the data, but deleting them poses no threat to the data, and deleting the data itself will proceed regardless of how many weak references still exist.

Helping C and C++ Programmers

Devel::CoreStack and Devel::DebugInit aid C and C++ development. Neither of these is a Perl debugger, so they should be invoked with use or Perl's -M switch. Jason Stewart's Devel::DebugInit module parses C and C++ header files and creates an initialization file for symbolic debuggers (currently only gdb) that identify the macro definitions. Devel::CoreStack, by Alligator Descartes and Tim Bunce, takes a core file from a recent program crash, locates the best available debugger, and fashions a short command-file to produce a stack trace of what the program was thinking when it crashed.

Rolling Your Own

Writing your own development tools can be tricky. If the tool you're designing is similar to Devel::Symdump or Devel::TraceFuncs, write it as you would any other module. If you want a module more like the profilers or Devel::Coverage, read on.

The DB:: Namespace

The debugger resides in a special namespace called DB. Tools that need to operate on programs line-by-line can install themselves into this namespace to get the debugger's capabilities for line-by-line stepping, subroutine breakpoints, and so on. These features are enabled by the -d switch. By itself, -d loads Perl's default debugger from *perl5db.pl*. If you combine the switch with a module name (e.g., -d:SmallProf), Perl looks for the module in the *Devel/* directory (e.g., *Devel/SmallProf.pm*). Any module loaded in this way is expected to provide certain functions.

The most basic function is DB::DB, which is called for every executable line just as it's about to be executed. Perl's caller function is used to identify the package name, filename, and line number; debuggers can use this information to prompt for commands if the user is single-stepping through the program. (Devel::Coverage uses it to increment the hit count for the line.)

Whenever a subroutine is entered, DB::sub is called. $DB::sub will have been set to the name of the subroutine. The debugger system maintains a hash, %DB::sub, with keys that are the fully-qualified subroutine names, and with values that are of the form *FILE:STARTLINE-ENDLINE*. The argument list for DB::sub is the same argument list passed to the subroutine. Don't modify it unless you know what you're doing.

DB::postponed is called whenever a file (a program or a module) has been compiled. (It can also be called after individual subroutines have been compiled, if the subroutine names exist in %DB::postponed.) When DB::postponed is called, the only argument is a reference to a glob containing the debugger information for the file. The scalar instantiation of the glob is _<*FILENAME*. Interpreted as a list, the glob contains all lines of the file, with a strange and useful property: if compared to 0 with ==, the result is true if the line might conceivably have a breakpoint, and false otherwise.

(You might want to include the statement local $W = 0 beforehand to suppress warnings.) The profilers and Devel::Coverage use this feature to identify lines that needn't be tracked. The hash instantiation of the glob contains breakpoint information for the file, keyed by line number.

Whenever a line is reached that might conceivably have a breakpoint, DB::DB is called if any of $DB::trace, $DB::signal, or $DB::single are true. $DB::trace, if set to true, simulates the user typing the t command in the debugger. $DB::signal simulates a conditional breakpoint, and $DB::single simulates an s command for single-stepping lines. Given the interpreter's name for a file (those files located in @INC will be full pathnames, those that are relative to the process running directory will be relative paths), *{"_<FILENAME"} will give you access to the debugger data for FILENAME.

For more on this topic, read the perldebug documentation, *perl5db.pl*, and any of Devel::DProf, Devel::SmallProf, or Devel::Coverage.

Which Should You Use?

If you need to improve runtime performance, use one of the profilers. If you're building test suites, use my coverage tool. For general debugging, Devel::Peek is invaluable.

PART VI

Networking

Perl is sometimes called a "glue language" because of its utility for creating connections between things. In this section, 13 articles show how to get some of those things (servers, programs, web sites, languages, telephones, people) talking to one another.

To begin, three articles explore email manipulation with Perl: two by Dan Sugalski on sending mail, and one by Simon Cozens on blocking spam and filtering mail. Jay Rogers then describes his Net::Telnet module, which you can use to automate network sessions, such as when you telnet to another computer. Tim Meadowcroft follows with an article about how to expose a Perl interpreter as a Microsoft COM object, enabling you to control Microsoft Office applications from your Perl program, wherever it might be.

Lincoln D. Stein follows with three articles on networking. His first article, *Client-Server Applications*, shows you how to create network applications with Perl. In *Managing Streaming Audio*, Lincoln demonstrates how to use Perl to stream audio over the Internet. Lincoln then demonstrates his networking chops by implementing an Internet telephone in 74 lines of Perl, which he walks through in *A 74-Line IP Telephone*. Bill Birthisel continues the telephone theme with an article showing how to control modems from Perl programs.

In the next two articles, Graham Barr talks about Net::NNTP and Net::FTP, followed by Gerard Lanois showing how to use Net::FTP to traverse an entire FTP site for mirroring, downloading, searching, and more. Finally, Jon Drukman closes out the section with *DNS Updates with Perl*, which demonstrates how to use the Net::DNS::Update module to programmatically change how your hostnames (e.g., "www.oreilly.com") are mapped to IP addresses (e.g., "172.17.146.22")—frequently needed by systems such as load-balancing web servers.

## CHAPTER 45

Email with Attachments

Dan Sugalski

You know the drill. Someone in accounting has asked that daily reports get emailed to him, or your manager has decided that your sales email autoresponder needs to be sending off Microsoft Word documents, or marketing has this great idea for an email newsletter *just* like the one that Amazon sends out, HTML and all. To do that, of course, you need to send out MIME-encoded mail. But MIME is a dark and mysterious thing, almost impossible to do properly, right?

Well, no. It's pretty easy to MIME-encode mail, far simpler than you'd think given how many programmers get it wrong. What I'm going to do in this article is cover the basics of MIME and show you how to build and send your own MIME mail.

One thing this article *isn't* going to do is show you how to build a MIME mail body by hand. While building MIME mail isn't enormously tough, there are a couple of modules available on CPAN that'll do it for you. Since there's no pressing reason to rewrite one, I won't. Instead, I'll use MIME::Lite, available from CPAN. If you need heavier-duty tools, or need to decode MIME messages, check out MIME::Tools instead.

What Is MIME, and Why Do I Care?

MIME is short for Multipurpose Internet Mail Extensions. It's an Internet standard, documented in RFCs 2045 through 2048. If you want to read them yourself, and you probably should if you're going to do a lot of work with MIME, the RFCs are available on the web at *http://www.rfc-editor.org*, or via FTP at *ftp://ftp.isi.edu/in-notes*.

Put simply, MIME is a way of imposing structure and encoding data in the body of a mail message. When mail was standardized in 1982 with RFC 822, most of the attention was focused on the mail headers. The body of a mail message was intentionally left alone. The only limits placed on the body were the character set (7-bit ASCII) and the maximum line length (1,000 characters).

The MIME standard covers the encoding and the structure of a mail message. There are two times when you'd want to use MIME mail: when your message isn't entirely plain 7-bit US-ASCII (mail sent by most of the world), or when you need to attach files to a mail message. I'll show you how to do both.

How Does MIME Encode Data?

Since normal mail is restricted to the 7-bit US-ASCII character set, there's obviously a lot of data that can't go into a mail message. To get around this problem, MIME encodes the data to make it safe to use in mail. There are three different major types of MIME encodings: quoted-printable, base 64, and no encoding at all. These *content transfer encodings* are listed in Table 45-1.

Table 45-1. MIME content transfer encodings

Encoding	Meaning
7bit	7-bit text, no encoding
8bit	8-bit text, no encoding
binary	Raw binary data, no encoding
quoted-printable	Plain text with characters outside the printable range hex escaped
base64	Binary data encoded into base64 format

The "no encoding" type is the simplest encoding method, because it's not really an encoding method at all. It's used for multipart messages that have a text component, or for folks willing to take the chance that their mail server handles 8-bit data. It's also used by web servers when they transfer data to clients. (HTTP transfers use MIME encoded data.) There are three different keywords: 7bit, 8bit, and binary, that tell the recipient program how to interpret the message at its lowest level: byte-by-byte.

Quoted-printable encoding hex-escapes illegal bytes. Any byte outside the printable 7-bit US-ASCII set is replaced by an equals sign and a two-digit hex value. Space, for example, can be encoded as =20, and an equals sign as =3D. Data that's been encoded as quoted-printable must have lines no longer than 76 characters.

Finally, base64 encoding takes arbitrary data and encodes it using a set of 65 characters. The encoded data ends up one-third larger, and unlike quoted-printable encodings, is unreadable by humans. The encoded data is guaranteed to go through gateways unmangled, and will even travel through EBCDIC systems unscathed.

In addition to encoding data, MIME tags it with a *media type* that indicates exactly what has been encoded. You've probably seen these in mail, or as messages from your web broswer—things like application/x-zip or image/jpeg. The media type is the first part of the Content-type header. Table 45-2 shows a list of media types and their meanings.

Table 45-2. MIME media types

Media type	Meaning
text	Textual things, including HTML
image	Pictures
audio	Encoded audio
video	Encoded video (which may include encoded audio)
application	Application-specific data
multipart	Used when there is more than one media type

MIME marks data with both a media type and subtype. Each of the types in Table 45-2 can have a list of different subtypes. The full list can be found at *ftp://ftp. isi.edu/in-notes-iana/assignments/media-types/media-types*. Table 45-3 lists the most common type/subtype combinations.

Table 45-3. MIME Type/subtype combinations

Media type	Meaning
text/plain	Plain text
text/html	An HTML document
text/enriched	A rich-text document (*not* a MS RTF document)
application/octet-stream	Generic binary data
application/pdf	Acrobat document
application/msword	A Microsoft Word document of some sort
application/x-anything	All the x- subtypes are reserved for anyone to do whatever they want with
image/gif	A GIF image
image/jpeg	A JPEG image
video/mpeg	An MPEG movie
video/quicktime	A Quicktime video
multipart/mixed	Indicates that there's more than one part
multipart/alternative	The same file multiple times, in multiple formats
multipart/digest	Indicates that there's more than one part, and that each part is a mail message (usually of type message/RFC822)
message/rfc822	A normal mail message in its entirety, including headers

It's important that you use the right MIME media type when you're building a MIME message. A good, standards-conforming MIME decoder will use this information to determine how it should handle each chunk of a MIME message. Unfortunately, there are a depressingly large number of noncompliant MIME decoders, and on most systems the media type information is lost as soon as the file is saved, so it's a good idea to tag individual pieces with filenames that have standard extensions.

A subtype of octet-stream indicates that this part of the MIME message is filled with data of some sort, and any MIME application that deals with it should treat it like a raw stream of bytes with no intrinsic meaning. A good MIME application is also supposed to treat any subtype that it doesn't understand as if it were octet-stream.

If you find that you need a media subtype not on the standard list, it's perfectly acceptable to roll your own. All subtypes beginning with x- are reserved for general use, much like the X- mail headers. So if, for example, you were MIME-encoding a *tar* file, it'd be reasonable to tag it as application/x-tar.

Figure 45-1 shows a symbolic representation of a one-part MIME message.

```
Content-Type: text/plain
Content-transfer-encoding: 7bit

This is just a plain old piece of text
```

Figure 45-1. A one-part MIME message

Multiple Pieces of MIME

Encoding and media typing are useful, and are some of the underpinnings of the web, but one of the main uses for MIME in mail is to send attachments. There are two media types, multipart/mixed and multipart/alternative. Both indicate that the MIME message has multiple parts. Figure 45-2 shows an example.

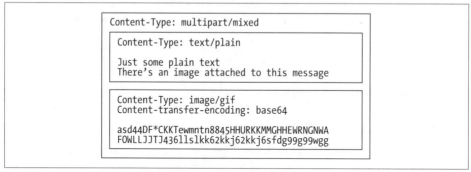

Figure 45-2. A sample multipart/mixed MIME message

If you do nest them, each multipart/mixed section (not the pieces inside, mind you, but the thing as a whole) can't be encoded with quoted-printable or base64. That'd require the MIME client to decode the multipart/mixed section and then handle each individual piece inside, which might themselves be multipart/mixed. The folks that wrote the standards decided this was too much to expect of a client, so it's explicitly forbidden. Figure 45-3 shows an HTML message expressed in MIME.

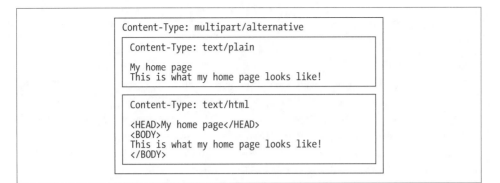

Figure 45-3. An HTML message expressed in MIME

How to Create a Mime Message

Creating a MIME message is pretty simple with MIME::Lite. In fact, it can be as simple as three Perl statements:

```
# Build the message
$message = MIME::Lite->new(     From => 'me@here.org',
                                  To => 'you@there.com',
                             Subject => "A test",
                                Type => "text/plain",
                            Encoding => '7bit',
                                Data => "Just a test message");

# Tell MIME::Lite to use Net::SMTP instead of sendmail
MIME::Lite->send('smtp', 'localhost', Timeout => 20);

# Send the message
$message->send;
```

This code builds and sends a mail message via Net::SMTP. If you prefer to use sendmail, you can omit the second line of code. It's okay to have multiple folks in the To list—just pass them in an anonymous array. MIME::Lite::new takes the standard RFC 822 headers, so if you want to specify a Cc or Bcc list, or set the Sender field, you can.

In that last example, the message I was sending was specified explicitly with Data. If you'd like to get fancier, try something like this:

```
# Build the message
$message = MIME::Lite->new(     From => 'me@here.org',
                                  To => 'you@there.com',
                             Subject => "The Net::SMTP docs",
                                Type => "text/plain",
                            Encoding => '7bit',
                            Filename => 'Net_SMTP.txt'
                                Path => 'perldoc Net::SMTP |');
```

```
# Tell MIME::Lite to use Net::SMTP instead of sendmail
MIME::Lite->send('smtp', 'localhost', Timeout => 20);

# Send the message
$message->send;
```

In this example, I've substituted `Path` for `Data`. `Path` specifies the full path to be passed to open. It can be a plain file but, as the example shows, it doesn't have to be. In this case, I'm spawning `perldoc` to extract the plain text version of the Net::SMTP docs. The `Filename` option tags the MIME section that's created with a filename of *Net_SMTP.txt*. While this doesn't affect where the data comes from, MIME clients often use it as a default filename to extract the data.

There's no real reason that the message you build needs to be text, of course. You could use a JPEG image or PDF file instead. Normally, though, you'll start with plain text and, if you need to send nontext stuff, attach other things to the end.

Building a mail message with attachments is nearly as simple as building a single-part mail message. For example, take this chunk of code from a mythical tech support autoresponder:

```
# Build the message
$message = MIME::Lite->new(From => 'me@here.org',
                             To => 'you@there.com',
                        Subject => "Technote PDF Autoresponder",
                           Type => "text/plain",
                       Encoding => '7bit',
                           Data => "This is the technote you requested");

# Add the attachment
$message->attach(   Type => "application/pdf",
                Encoding => "base64",
                    Path => $technote_requested,
                Filename => "Technote.pdf");

# Tell MIME::Lite to use Net::SMTP instead of sendmail
MIME::Lite->send('smtp', 'localhost', Timeout => 20);

# Send the message
$message->send;
```

Pretty simple. You can attach as many files as you like this way just by adding extra calls to attach.

An Alternate Route

You can save messages for later use, or send them with an alternate mailer that has less overhead, such as the simple SMTP subroutine that appears in the next article, *Sending Mail Without sendmail*.

The easiest way to extract the message is with the as_string method, like so:

```
# Build the message
$message = MIME::Lite->new(    From => 'me@here.org',
                                 To => 'you@there.com;,
                            Subject => "A test",
                               Type => "text/plain",
                           Encoding => '7bit',
                               Data => "Just a test message");
$message_text = $message->as_string;
```

This sticks the entire message, headers and all, into $message_text. From there you can do what you like with it. If you'd rather have just the headers, or just the body, you can use the header_as_string or body_as_string methods, respectively.

A Full-Blown Example

Finally, let's take a look at a full program that sends MIME mail. The program in Example 45-1 is *mail_attach.pl*, a variation of which I've got in production on my VMS cluster. We use it for email delivery of some daily reports, but it can be easily modified to do most anything you like.

Example 45-1. mail_attach.pl

```
#!/usr/bin/perl -w
# mail_attach.pl -- Mail files as attachments
#
# $ARGV[0]: The sender email address
# $ARGV[1]: Filename with main message in it.
# $ARGV[2]: Filename to attach. If >1, separate with commas and *no* spaces
# $ARGV[3]: Subject
# $ARGV[4..$#ARGV]: Destination email addresses. If there are spaces in
#                an address, then enclose it in quotes

use strict;
use Socket;
use MIME::Lite;
use Net::SMTP;

my %ending_map = (      crt => ['application/x-x509-ca-cert' , 'base64'],
                       aiff => ['audio/x-aiff' , 'base64'],
                        gif => ['image/gif' , 'base64'],
                        txt => ['text/plain' , '8bit'],
                        com => ['text/plain' , '8bit'],
                      class => ['application/octet-stream' , 'base64'],
                        htm => ['text/html' , '8bit'],
                       html => ['text/html' , '8bit'],
                      htmlx => ['text/html' , '8bit'],
                        htx => ['text/html' , '8bit'],
                        jpg => ['image/jpeg' , 'base64'],
                        dat => ['text/plain' , '8bit'],
                        hlp => ['text/plain' , '8bit'],
                         ps => ['application/postscript' , '8bit'],
                     'ps-z' => ['application/postscript' , 'base64'],
```

Example 45-1. mail_attach.pl (continued)

```
                         dvi => ['application/x-dvi' , 'base64'],
                         pdf => ['application/pdf' , 'base64'],
                         mcd => ['application/mathcad' , 'base64'],
                        mpeg => ['video/mpeg' , 'base64'],
                         mov => ['video/quicktime' , 'base64'],
                         exe => ['application/octet-stream' , 'base64'],
                         zip => ['application/zip' , 'base64'],
                         bck => ['application/VMSBACKUP' , 'base64'],
                          au => ['audio/basic' , 'base64'],
                         mid => ['audio/midi' , 'base64'],
                        midi => ['audio/midi' , 'base64'],
                       bleep => ['application/bleeper' , '8bit'],
                         wav => ['audio/x-wav' , 'base64'],
                         xbm => ['image/x-xbm' , '7bit'],
                         tar => ['application/tar' , 'base64'],
                    imagemap => ['application/imagemap' , '8bit'],
                         sit => ['application/x-stuffit' , 'base64'],
                         bin => ['application/x-macbase64'],
                         hqx => ['application/mac-binhex40' , 'base64'],
);

my $mail_from     = shift @ARGV;
my $message_file  = shift @ARGV;
my @mail_file     = split(",", shift(@ARGV));
my $subject       = shift @ARGV;
my @mail_to       = @ARGV;

my $mime;                                  # The MIME object

# Slurp in the message text and build up the main part of the mail.
{
    local $/;
    $/ = undef;
    local @ARGV;
    @ARGV = $message_file;
    my $main_message = <>;
    $mime = new MIME::Lite( From => $mail_from,
                              To => [@mail_to],
                         Subject => $subject,
                            Type => 'text/plain',
                            Data => $main_message );
}

foreach (@mail_file) {                      # Attach each file in turn
    my($type, $ending);
    /.*\.(.+)$/;                            # Snag the ending
    $ending = $1;
    if (exists($ending_map{$ending})) {    # Is it in our list?
        $type = $ending_map{$ending};
    } else {
        $type = ['text/plain', '8bit'];
    }
```

Example 45-1. mail_attach.pl (continued)

```
    # Attach it to the message
    $mime->attach(    Type => $type->[0],
                  Encoding => $type->[1],
                      Path => $_);
}

# Tell MIME::Lite to use Net::SMTP instead of sendmail.
MIME::Lite->send('smtp', 'localhost', Timeout => 20);
$mime->send;
```

At the top of the program, there's a hash with a set of common extensions and their associated media types. This list was lifted out of the configuration files for the webserver I run on my cluster and works well for me, but you might want to tweak it for the sorts of files you're sending. Embedding the list in the program saves you from having to educate every analyst on which MIME types go with which files.

Next, the program takes the parameters off the command line. It could (and probably should) use switches rather than positional parameters, but this way works, and the folks I work with consider positional parameters the norm.

I then read in the file with the body text of the message I'm sending and create the MIME::Lite object. This text doesn't need to be anything fancy, but it's a good idea to give the recipient at least some idea of what the attachments are. This is especially useful for things that get mailed out less than once a week.

The program runs through all the files that need to be attached. A regex extracts the extension and I run it through the extension hash to see if I've got an entry. If so, I use the media type and encoding that goes with it. Otherwise, I default to text/plain and 8bit. A different default, such as application/octet-stream and base64, might be desirable depending on what I'm mailing out.

Finally, I send the message. This version uses Net::SMTP to do the sending. You might perfer to use sendmail if you're on a Unix box, or another mail routine entirely, depending on your setup. My production copy uses a variation on the standalone mail subroutine (appearing in the next article) to avoid loading in Net::SMTP and the entire IO:: family of modules. While they're quite nice, the overhead really isn't justified for a simple mailing program like this.

Conclusion

Well, that's it. Sending MIME mail is pretty straightforward, but if you peek under the hood of *MIME/Lite.pm* you'll see the details are tricky enough to justify not rolling your own.

In the next article, I'll show how your Perl programs deliver email even when the venerable sendmail program isn't available.

## CHAPTER 46

Sending Mail Without sendmail

Dan Sugalski

Sooner or later, most Perl programmers need to send electronic mail from a program. It might be for a CGI application, sending out autoconfirmations, generating monthly email invoices, or sending reports to the payroll department.

The normal way to send email from Perl is to use the Mail::Sendmail module, or to do something like this:

```
open (SENDMAIL, "|/usr/lib/sendmail -t") or die "Can't start sendmail";
print SENDMAIL "From: (goes here)\n";
print SENDMAIL "To: (goes here)\n";
print SENDMAIL "Subject: Test mail\n\n";
print SENDMAIL "Message body goes here";
close SENDMAIL or die "Hey, sendmail failed!";
```

Nice, simple, and straightforward—but not if you're on a non-Unix machine (such as Windows, VMS, OS/390, or the Mac) or you don't have sendmail or a reasonable fascimile installed. And even if you do have sendmail, you might not want to pay the cost to invoke it just to send a single mail message. It is, after all, a fairly big program, and the last thing you want is your system monitoring program to drop dead because it couldn't fork off sendmail to tell you it was out of process slots.

In this article, I'm going to build a sendmail replacement suitable both for use in place of a real sendmail and as donor code that you will undoubtedly gut for your own use. (I use the mail-sending routines in some system monitoring programs, for example.)

Some Email Background

Before I go into the code that actually sends the mail, I need to talk about what exactly email is and how it works.

A Store-and-Forward System

The single most important thing about email that anyone can know is that email is *not* a direct delivery, point-to-point system like, for example, the web. Instead, email is a store-and-forward system. When you send mail to someone it doesn't go directly to their mail host. Instead, it goes to some intermediate machine, which itself might forward the mail to another machine before the mail gets to its final destination.

In many cases, the machine you think is the final delivery system isn't. It's common for the machine publicly advertised in an email address to be a gateway to another mail system. Corporate mail systems are often like this, as the host you think is the final destination is really a gateway through a firewall, a gateway to a completely different mail system (such as Groupwise or Lotus CC:Mail), or both.

There's More Than One Way to Deliver Mail

The standards for email, like the standards for most everything else on the Internet, are set down in a series of documents called RFCs. (Short for Request for Comments, although the standards set down are quite a bit stronger than the name might imply. See *ftp://ftpeng.cisco.com/fred/rfc-index/rfc.html* for a comprehensive list.) The standards for SMTP, the Simple Mail Transport Protocol, are set down in RFC 821, while the standards for email headers are set down in RFC 822.

The most common way to deliver mail from one system to another is via SMTP, which requires a network connection. Usually that connection is TCP/IP, but SMTP will work over a variety of other network protocols.

The other main delivery method is UUCP. UUCP normally operates over a dialup connection, and doesn't require constant connectivity between hosts. With UUCP, the client system occasionally polls a host system for any pending work. (UUCP is used to transfer more than just mail. It's designed to transfer arbitrary files between two systems, and is often used to move Usenet news in addition to mail.)

Standards Governing Email

There are many different email systems kicking around, but I'm going to talk about the most common type, usually called "Internet email." It's a bit of a misnomer, though, since it's certainly not restricted to machines on the internet.

Since the code I'm going to work with sends mail over the network via SMTP, I need to make sure it follows the standards properly. Not to worry, though—SMTP is simple.

The Mail Itself

Finally, let's talk a bit about the actual message, which from our perspective is the least interesting part of mail delivery.

Email sent via SMTP has three parts—which is probably one part more than you were expecting. The contents of email is also governed by standards, in this case RFC 822 and its descendants. (If you're going to be building email messages, you should definitely read this RFC. You might also want to read some of the RFCs that extend 822.)

The Message Body

The least interesting part of a mail message, at least as far as we're concerned, is the message body. While the people receiving the mail care most about this part, the mail transport software doesn't care in the least about it. It's just data that needs to be sent on its way. The body consists of everything after the first blank line in the message.

The Message Headers

All the lines up to the first blank line in the message are considered the message headers. In general, mail transport software doesn't care very much about the message headers. With one exception, the mail software isn't supposed to mess with the headers at all. Nor is it supposed to pay any attention to them.

The single exception to the "leave the headers alone" rule is the Received: header. Each mail system that relays a message is supposed to add a Received: header at the top of each message. You can use these headers to track the systems that a message has passed through.

RFC 822 does mandate a minimum set of headers. To be fully compliant, all mail should have at least a From:, Date:, and either a To: or Bcc: header. There are others, of course, listed in the various RFCs. The standards mandate that *only* headers listed in the RFCs can be in a header—you can't make up your own. RFC 822 grants a single exception: headers that begin with X- are allowed.

The Message Envelope

When one system sends mail to another, it doesn't just open up a connection and start pumping data across. There's a conversation that takes place: the sender tells the receiver who it is, who the mail is for, and who the mail is from. This information is called the *envelope* because it acts like an envelope for a letter; it encloses the letter but isn't actually a part of it.

The information in the envelope is the only information used by the receiving system to determine what it should do with the mail and who should receive it. The recipients listed in the mail headers don't have anything to do with who the mail is ultimately delivered to.

Sending Mail in Six Easy Steps

An SMTP transaction is a reasonably simple thing. Your program connects to the remote server, identifies itself, tells the remote machine who the mail is from, who it's to, and then sends the message. Simple, huh? All the details are specified in RFC 821, and if you're going to be writing an SMTP client, you should definitely read it before writing any code.

There are two gotchas involved in SMTP conversations that might slip past a quick reading of the RFC. First, all lines end with a CRLF (carriage-return and linefeed) pair, *not* a bare linefeed, so is not appropriate as a line ending. Use \cM\cJ instead. Second, RFC 821 says that the SMTP channel is 7-bit and the high bits of all bytes should be cleared. This restriction is lifted in a later RFC, but it requires a slightly different and somewhat more complex conversation between client and server.

Otherwise, conversations between client and server are fairly straightforward. The client sends a command with an optional parameter and then a CRLF. The server responds with a three-digit status code and a one-line message describing the status. The first digit provides the general message class: 2*xx* for OKs, 3*xx* for start mail transmission, 4*xx* for temporary errors, and 5*xx* for permanent errors. You can check the first digit for the general status of the request and proceed accordingly.

It's best to abort the transaction and try again later on 4*xx* errors, but abort the transaction and give up on 5*xx* errors—except in special cases. It's silly to toss a whole mail message if one recipient in a list of a dozen fails, for example.

SMTP places some limits on the transmission of commands and messages; they're listed in Table 46-1. These numbers are what RFC821 requires from a conformant SMTP server and client. Servers can accept larger values, but they don't have to.

Table 46-1. Minimum maximums mandated by RFC 821

Field	Length
Username	64 characters
Domain	64 characters
Path	256 characters
Command line	512 characters (including the command and the CRLF terminator)
Reply line	512 characters (including the status code and the CRLF terminator)
Text line	1,000 characters (including the CRLF terminator)
Number of recipients	100

Step One: Connecting to the Remote SMTP Server

According to the standard, SMTP servers are supposed to be listening on TCP port 25, so the client should open a connection there. When the connection is successfully made, the server will send out a single-line message with a status code.

Step Two: Identifying Yourself

After connecting, the next step is to identify yourself. This is done with the HELO command (no, that's not a typo). The full command is:

```
HELO name.of.connecting.machineCRLF
```

While many servers will still accept a HELO with no (or a bogus) name, many don't anymore. A common spammer trick was to leave off the name or mis-identify themselves to try to slip past security measures.

Step Three: Identifying the Mail Sender

Next, your program needs to say who's sending the mail. This is done with the MAIL command, which looks like this:

```
MAIL FROM: <user@host.com>CRLF
```

Note that the contents of <> are real—you need to store the sending email address there. This is the address that all bounced mail will go to. If the mail being sent cannot be bounced (because, for example, it's a bounce notice itself and thus bouncing it would set up a nasty loop) the address can be an empty <>.

Step Four: Identifying the Mail Recipients

After telling the remote system who the mail is from, you need to tell it who the mail is going to. This is done with the RCPT command. Your program sends out one or more RCPTs, which look like this:

```
RCPT TO: <user@host.com>CRLF
```

Once again, the addresses must be enclosed in angle brackets. You may send up to 100 RCPTs per mail message, and the server will send back a status on each one.

Step Five: Sending the Mail

Once you've identified the sender and recipients, it's time to send out the mail itself. The DATA command marks the start of the message itself, which continues until you send a line with just a period. If you need to send a line with just a period on it for some reason, the protocol allows you to send a doubled period, which the server converts to a single period.

If you do send out a line with a single period to end the mail message, the server will respond with a status message that tells you what it thinks of your mail.

Step Six: Closing the Connection

Finally, you need to close the connection by sending the QUIT command. While it's not uncommon to see programs send out a QUIT and drop the connection, you should wait for the final status to make sure that things went properly.

What Next?

Now that you know the theory, it's time for the practice: sending mail from your Perl program. There are three common ways: Mail::Mailer, Net::SMTP, and talking directly to the mail host. I'll go over each of these methods in turn. I'll present an example of sending mail with each of the three different methods.

Sending Mail with Mail::Mailer

Mail::Mailer, included as part of the MailTools module, sits on top of Net::SMTP, so it requires the libnet bundle to run. Both modules are well worth the time, so install (or get your sysadmin to install) them into your production tree. Example 46-1 shows Mail::Mailer in action.

Example 46-1. Sending mail with Mail::Mailer

```
#!/usr/bin/perl -w
# mail_mailer.pl - sample mail sending routine using Mail::Mailer
use Mail::Mailer qw(smtp);

my $mailer = new Mail::Mailer 'smtp';

# Hash keys are headers in the outgoing mail
$mailer->open(    To => ['you@localhost'],
                  Cc => ['me@localhost'],
                From => 'me@localhost',
             Subject => 'Some test mail');

print $mailer "Hi! This is some test mail. Boring, huh? :-)\n";

$mailer->close;
```

As you can see from Example 46-1, sending mail with Mail::Mailer is pretty straightforward. The whole thing's only 14 lines, and that's with comments.

The one thing to keep in mind with Mail::Mailer is that it figures out the sender and recipients from the headers of the mail message, so you lose the separation of the envelope and headers. That's not necessarily a bad thing, but something to remember.

Sending Mail with Net::SMTP

Net::SMTP, which is included as part of the libnet bundle, puts a fairly thin wrapper around the SMTP conversation, just barely encapsulating it. There's one function call for each step of the SMTP conversation, with just enough code wrapped around the conversation to do error checking and similar things. Example 46-2 demonstrates sending mail with Net::SMTP.

Example 46-2. Sending mail with Net::SMTP

```
#!/usr/bin/perl -w
use Net::SMTP;

# use the default mailhost configured into the libnet package
my $smtp = Net::SMTP->new;
```

Example 46-2. Sending mail with Net::SMTP (continued)

```
# First the envelope bits
$smtp->mail('me@localhost');
$smtp->to('me@localhost');
$smtp->to('you@localhost');

# Now for the message itself
$smtp->data();
$smtp->datasend("From: me^localhost\n");
$smtp->datasend("To: you^localhost\n");
$smtp->datasend("Cc: me^localhost\n");
$smtp->datasend("Subject: Some test mail\n");
$smtp->datasend("\n");
$smtp->datasend("Hi! This is some test mail. Boring, huh? :-)\n");
$smtp->dataend();

$smtp->quit;
```

As you can see from Example 46-2, Net::SMTP is a bit more verbose than Mail::Mailer, though not by much. You've got full control over the SMTP conversation this way, although you don't get fine-grained response codes.

Talking Directly to the Mail Host

Finally, there's the fully manual way. It's significantly longer than the other methods—too long for this article. You can find my *smailer.pl* program on the web page for this book. The reason it's so long is that I include the code that actually sends the mail out. In the other examples, that code is encapsulated in other modules.

I'm not going to spend too much time going over this code, since you can't see it here anyway. However, I'll touch on a few high points. You'll notice, for example, that I use syswrite to write the data out, while I use <> to read it in, and on two different filehandles to boot. The question, of course, is why?

The main reason is to compensate for a variety of odd socket and stdio implementations on the platforms on which Perl runs. syswrite is guaranteed to work for writing, and <> works okay for reading. They each use a separate filehandle to make sure there aren't any underlying stdio buffer collisions or anything.

You'll also note that the code doesn't care which non-2xx response code it gets—it considers them all errors and returns the status to the caller of the subroutine, who can hopefully do something reasonable with the return values.

Other than that, the code's pretty straightforward. The smailer subroutine is written such that you ought to be able to cut and paste it into your own code and have it ready to run. (You can, for example, fill in some of the empty variables at the top of the subroutine if you want to avoid the overhead of computing them on every invocation.)

Which Should You Choose?

Now that I've covered the three different methods, which one is the right one? The answer, of course, is "it depends."

The hand-rolled method is the lightest of the three methods: it's snappy and takes up very little memory, although it does sacrifice some flexibility. For instance, it doesn't handle ESMTP, the extension to SMTP allowing delivery notifications and 8-bit characters in mail messages.

Net::SMTP is more flexible than the hand-rolled way, but you pay for that increased flexibility. It's fully object-oriented, which means that it incurs Perl's substantial method call overhead. It's also layered on top of the IO modules, which are themselves quite large. (This is only a consideration if you're not already using them, of course.) On the other hand, it does talk ESMTP, and exposes SMTP in easy-to-use pieces.

Mail::Mailer is the most flexible of the three methods. In addition to connecting via SMTP, it can send mail by invoking `sendmail`, or by firing off `mail` or an equivalent. It's also got the highest overhead in terms of both speed and memory usage. It's layered on top of Net::SMTP, and so inherits the Net::SMTP overhead as well as generating some of its own.

In general, I'd recommend using Mail::Mailer for general-purpose mailing work. While it's got some overhead, the delays you might incur will be far less than typical network latency. Its extra flexibility and robustness are worth it.

If you find the overhead of Mail::Mailer is a bit much, especially if you need to send mail using minimal computational resources, go for the hand-rolled approach. Also, if you're not using any of the IO modules, and you're not sending mail that's got 8-bit characters in it, the hand-rolled method should work well.

Finally, for the very curious, it is possible to write a reasonable emulation of `sendmail` with Perl and these mail routines, at least enough to send mail with. I have an implementation that I mess with on and off. Versions occasionally make it to my CPAN directory, so you can always check there to see how it's going.

Filtering Mail

Simon Cozens

Let's face it. procmail is horrid. But for most of us, it's the only sensible way to handle mail filtering. I used to tolerate procmail, with its grotesque syntax and its less-than-helpful error messages, because it was the only way I knew to separate out my mail. One day, however, I decided that I'd been told "delivery failed, couldn't get lock" or similar garbage for the very last time, and I sat down to write a procmail replacement.

That's when it dawned on me that what I really disliked about procmail was the recipe format. I didn't want to handle my mail with a collection of colons, zeroes, and single-letter commands that made *sendmail.cf* look like a Shakespearean sonnet; I wanted to program my mail routing in a nice, high-level language. Something like Perl, for instance.

The result is the astonishingly simple Mail::Audit module. In this article, I'll examine what can be done with Mail::Audit and how to use it to create mail filters. I'll also look at the News::Gateway module for turning mailing lists into newsgroups and back again.

What Is It?

Mail::Audit itself isn't a mail filter—it's a toolkit that makes it very easy for you to build mail filters. You write a program that describes what should happen to your mail, and this replaces your procmail command in your *.forward* or *.qmail* file.

Mail::Audit provides the functionality for extracting mail headers, bouncing, accepting, rejecting, forwarding, and filtering incoming mail.

A Very Simple Mail Filter

Here's the simplest filter program you can make with Mail::Audit.

```
use Mail::Audit;
my $incoming = Mail::Audit->new;
$incoming->reject;
```

If you save this as ~/bin/chuckmail, you can put the following in a .forward file:

```
|~/bin/chuckmail
```

or in a .qmail file:

```
preline ~/bin/chuckmail
```

Every mail message you receive will now pass through this program. The mail comes into the program via STDIN, and the new method takes it from there and turns it into a Mail::Audit object:

```
my $incoming = Mail::Audit->new;
```

Next, bounce it as undeliverable:

```
$incoming->reject;
```

You could even get fancy, and supply a reason with the bounce:

```
$incoming->reject(<<EOF);
    The local user was silly enough to leave chuckmail as his
    mail filter.  Too bad you can't mail him to let him know.
EOF
```

This reason will be relayed back to the sender as part of the bounce message.

Separating Mail into Folders

The one thing most people use procmail for is to separate mail into several mail folders. Here's an example of how I'd do this:

```
use Mail::Audit;
my $item = Mail::Audit->new;

if ($item->from =~ /perl5-porters/) {
    $item->accept("/home/simon/mail/p5p")
}

$item->accept;
```

Now any mail with perl5-porters in the From: line will be added to the file *mail/p5p* under my home directory. Any other mail will be accepted into my inbox as normal.

Two things to note here:

- Once the mail has been filed to *mail/p5p* via accept, it leaves the program. Game over, end of story. The same goes for the other methods such as reject, pipe, and bounce.

- The last line in the program should probably be an accept call; mail that reaches the end of the program without being deposited in a mailbox or rejected will be silently ignored. (This may change to an implicit accept in a later version, to be more procmail-like.)

If I've got a few mailing lists or people I want to filter, I could do this:

```
use Mail::Audit;
my $item    = Mail::Audit->new;
my $maildir = "/home/simon/mail/";

my %lists = (
    perl5-porters    => "p5p",
    helixcode        => "gnome",
    uclinux          => "uclinux",
    'infobot\.org'   => "infobot",
    '@dion\.ne\.jp'  => "yamachan"
);

for my $pattern (keys %lists) {
    $item->accept($maildir.$lists{$pattern})
        if $item->from =~ /$pattern/ or $item->to =~ /$pattern/;
}

$item->accept;
```

This time, I perform a regular expression match to see if either the From: line or the To: line match any of the patterns in our hash keys, and if they do, direct the mail to the corresponding folder. Since I'm using ordinary Perl regular expressions, I can do this sort of thing:

```
'\bxxx.*\.com$'  => "spam"
```

(And you'd be surprised at quite how much junk mail that one traps.)

Here's another simple but remarkably effective spamtrap recipe:

```
$item->accept("questionable") if $item->from !~ /simon/i and $item->cc !~ /simon/i;
```

I check the From: and CC: headers for my name, and if it's not in either, the mail probably isn't to me. This one only makes sense after I've filtered out mailing list messages, which could reasonably be sent from a subscriber to a generic list address.

Mail and News

I much prefer reading mailing lists as newsgroups; while a good mail client like mutt can display mail as threaded discussions, I personally prefer navigating in a news-reader. So how do I gate mailing lists to newsgroups and back?

Russ Allbery's News::Gateway module does just that: it provides a program called listgate, which takes an incoming mailing list message, reformats it as a valid news article, and then posts it to the news server. I can plug this into my mail filter quite easily; assuming I've got the group lists.p5p set up on the local newsserver and I've configured listgate appropriately, I can just say:

```
$item->pipe("listgate p5p") if $item->from =~ /perl5-porters/;
```

Again, if I have multiple groups, I can use a hash to correlate patterns to groups as I did with mailing lists above.

So much for getting incoming mail to news. What about getting posted articles back into the mailing list? The key to this is in the newsgroup moderation system—when you post to a moderated newsgroup, the article is mailed to a moderator for approval. If you set the moderator of lists.p5p to the list address, you can get your outgoing posts sent to the list. In */usr/news/etc/moderators*, you'd say:

```
lists.p5p:  perl5-porters@perl.org
```

Very easy. The only problem is that it doesn't work. Mail messages and news articles have a slightly different format, and some mailing list managers reject mail messages that resemble news articles, so you need to send your message through a clean-up phase first. Instead of sending it to perl5-porters@perl.org, you should send it to news-outgoing@localhost instead:

```
lists.*:    news-outgoing@localhost
```

Mail arriving at that account needs to go through another Perl program to clean up and dispatch the outgoing article, and that looks like this:

```
#!/usr/bin/perl

use News::Gateway;
my $gw=News::Gateway->new(0);

$gw->modules('newstomail', 'headers');
$gw->config_line("newstomail /home/simon/bin/news2mail.h");
$gw->config_line("header newsgroups drop");
$gw->config_line("header organisation drop");
$gw->config_line("header nntp-posting-host drop");
$gw->read(*STDIN) or die $!;
$gw->apply();
$gw->mail();
```

This reads an article from standard input, drops the Newsgroups, Organisation, and NNTP-Posting-Host headers, reformats it as a mail message using the configuration file */home/simon/bin/news2mail.h* to find the address, and then sends it. That config file is just a list of newsgroups and the addresses they belong to:

```
lists.p5p perl5-porters@perl.org
lists.tlug tlug@tlug.gr.jp
lists.advocacy advocacy@perl.org
lists.linux-kernel linux-kernel@vger.rutgers.edu
lists.perl-friends perl-friends@perlsupport.com
```

Here's the recipe for filtering news to mail and back again:

Incoming messages

Trapped by a rule in your mail filter, and piped to listgate via a line like:

```
$item->pipe("listgate p5p") if $item->from =~ /perl5-porters/;
```

listgate will then post them to your news server, to the group lists.p5p.

Outgoing articles

Sent to the moderator address, news-outgoing@localhost, for clean-up. The clean-up program will drop unnecessary headers, reformat as a mail message, and then look at the configuration file to determine where to send them on. They'll be sent to the mailing list, and sometime later will be returned to you by mail, to appear in the newsgroup as above.

A Complete Filter

To show off exactly what I do with Mail::Audit, here is a suitably anonymized and annotated version of the filter I currently use to process my incoming mail. The first three lines:

```
#!/usr/bin/perl
use Mail::Audit;
$folder = "/home/simon/mail/";
```

Anything that actually reaches me is going to be logged so that I can `tail -f` a summary of incoming mail to one of my terminals.

```
open (LOG, ">>/home/simon/.audit_log");
```

Read in the new mail message, and extract the important headers from it:

```
my $item = Mail::Audit->new;
my $from = $item->from();
study $from;
my $to = $item->to();
my $cc = $item->cc();
my $subject = $item->subject();
chomp($from, $to, $subject);
```

If I'm likely to be at the office, I appreciate a copy of all mail I receive, in case there's something I need to deal with immediately. So I need *time-controlled* filtering. Try doing this with procmail:

```
my ($hour, $wday) = (localtime)[2,6];
if ($wday !=0 and $wday !=6           # Not Saturday/Sunday
    and $hour > 9 and $hour < 18) {   # Between 9am and 6pm
    print LOG "$subject: $from: Bouncing to work\n";
    $item->resend('simon@theoffice.com');
    # resend is the only action which doesn't end the program.
}
```

One of my users didn't have their own email address for a while, so they had their friends send mail to me instead. Now he has his own address, so the mail is bounced across to him:

```
$item->bounce('ei@somewhere.com') if $subject =~ /^For Ei:/;
```

I maintain two FAQs, the perl5-porters FAQ and the Tokyo high speed connectivity FAQ. The mail comes to different email addresses, but it all ends up at my box. They need to go in separate folders.

```
$item->accept("$folder/p5p-faq")   if $to=~ /p5p-faq/;
$item->accept("$folder/tokyo-faq") if $to=~ /faq/;
```

I get some mail in Greek that needs to be processed with metamail to sort out the character sets. The pipe method squirts the mail to a separate program:

```
$item->pipe("metamail -B -x>> $folder/greek") if $from =~/hri\.org$/;
```

Some people I definitely want to hear from, so they get accepted at this stage to save time:

```
for (qw(goodguy dormouse locust)) {
    if ($from =~ /$_/) {
        print LOG "$from:$subject:Exception, accepting into inbox\n";
        $item->accept;
    }
}
```

Some people I very definitely do not want to hear from:

```
for (qw(badguy nasty enemy)) {
    if ($from =~ /$_/) {
        print LOG "$from:$subject:Dumped\n";
        $item->reject("Go away! Stop emailing me!");
    }
}
```

Some people or mailing lists I currently just don't have time for, so they get silently ignored:

```
for (qw(freshmeat.net microsoft news\@myhost cron)) {
    if ($from =~ /$_/) {
        print LOG "$from:$subject:Ignored\n";
        $item->ignore;
    }
}
```

Some mailing lists I want to stay in list form:

```
my %lists = (
    "pound.perl.org" => "purl",
    "helixcode"      => "gnome",
    "uclinux"        => "uclinux",
    "infobot"        => "infobot",
    "european-"      => "yapc",
    "tpm\@otherside" => "tpm",
    "hellenic"       => "greeknews",
);

for my $what (keys %lists) {
    next unless $from =~ /$what/i or $to =~ /$what/i or $cc =~/$what/i;
    my $where = $lists{$what};
    print LOG "$from:$subject:List, accepting to folder $where\n";
    $item->accept($folder.$where);
}
```

And some I want to pipe to `listgate` as newsgroups:

```perl
my %gated = (
    "tlug"          => "tlug",
    "advocacy"      => "advocacy",
    "security-sig"  => "security",
    "iss.net"       => "security",
    "securityfocus" => "security",
    "perl5-porters" => "p5p",
    "linux-kernel"  => "linux-kernel",
    "perlsupport"   => "perl-friends",
);

for my $what (keys %gated) {
    next unless $from =~ /$what/i or $to =~ /$what/i or $cc =~/$what/i;
    my $where=$gated{$what};
    print LOG "$from:$subject:Gated to lists.$where\n";
    $item->pipe("/usr/local/bin/listgate $where");
}
```

Some spammers just don't give up, so I actually reject their messages. I do this based on subject, which is a bit risky but seems to work:

```perl
for ("Invest", "nude asian"))  {
    $item->reject("No! Go away!") if $subject=~/\b$_\b/;
}
```

Before I allow the message, there's a long list of patterns at the end of the program that match known spam senders. I check the incoming mail against this list, and save it for analysis and reporting:

```perl
while (<DATA>) {
    chomp;
    next unless $from =~ /$_/i or $to =~ /$_/i;
    print LOG "$from:$subject:Spam?\n";
    $item->accept($folder."spam");
}
```

Now, a final check for mail that doesn't appear to be for me:

```perl
if ($item->from !~ /simon/i and $item->cc !~ /simon/i) {
    print LOG "$from:$subject:Badly addressed mail\n";
    $item->accept("questionable")
}
```

Finally, I let the mail in:

```perl
print LOG "INCOMING MAIL:$from:$subject:Accepting to inbox\n";
$item->accept();
```

Caveats

I'm perfectly happy to trust Mail::Audit with all my incoming email. For a while it was running alongside procmail, but now it rules the roost. However, there are some things you'll need to be careful about if you want to run it yourself.

Mail::Audit has been tested on qmail and postfix; it should work on other MTAs (Message Transfer Agents), so long as they believe that exit 100; means reject. If they don't, you can override the reject method like this:

```
$item = Mail::Audit->new( reject => sub { exit 67; } );
```

It also assumes that the default mail box is */var/spool/mail/name*, where name is the user ID of the current user. If this isn't the case (I believe mh doesn't work like this), say accept("Mailbox") or override accept with a subroutine of your own.

Mail::Audit isn't sophisticated. It's little more than a wrapper around Mail::Internet. While it's probably perfectly fine for most filters you want to write with it, don't expect it to do everything for you.

Conclusion

Mail::Audit and News::Gateway are both available from CPAN; together they allow you to easily construct mail filters and newsgroup gateways in Perl. It's a great way to filter your mail with Perl, and an excellent replacement for moldy old procmail.

## CHAPTER 48

Net::Telnet

Jay Rogers

This article introduces Net::Telnet, a module that allows your Perl program to communicate with networked hosts or devices such as workstations, terminal servers, routers, and the like. The dialog is established via a client connection to a TCP port—typically, to a port using the telnet protocol.

Simple I/O methods such as print, get, and getline are provided, of course, but more sophisticated interactive features are available as well—features tailored for communicating with programs intended solely for human interaction. This includes the ability to specify a timeout and to wait for a pattern to appear in the input stream, such as a shell prompt.

Net::Telnet is written entirely in Perl; it doesn't require a locally installed telnet program. This makes Net::Telnet especially easy to install and use on those ubiquitous Windows machines.

The Problem

Sounded easy when you first thought about it: your Perl program needs to monitor disk space on a remote machine named sparky, but it can access sparky only by connecting to it via telnet. You try something like this:

```
open  TELNET, "|telnet sparky";
print TELNET "joebob\n";
print TELNET "passwd-for-joebob\n";
print TELNET "df -k\n";
```

You find that piping commands to telnet's standard input doesn't work. The telnet program connects just fine, but sparky doesn't process any of the commands you send it. You discover that your telnet only reads from the terminal (also known as a *tty*) and not from its standard input.

You could use a package like *Comm.pl* to create a pseudoterminal (a *pty*) and make telnet read from that instead. But then you think, "Hey, why don't I just connect a socket directly to TCP port 23 on sparky and read and write directly to the telnet port? That way I don't even need a telnet program!"

Now you write some socket code—only to find out you still have the same problem. You can connect a socket to the TCP telnet port on sparky, but the remote side doesn't seem to respond to I/O.

After digging through the RFC documentation for the telnet protocol, you learn that telnet sends control information along with data in the same socket stream. The reason the remote side wasn't sending data was because you weren't responding properly to its control queries. In other words, you weren't speaking the telnet protocol.

The Solution

Net::Telnet solves this problem. It recognizes the telnet control commands, removes them from the data stream, and sends back an appropriate response. This allows you to read from and write to a port without having to worry about the vagaries of the telnet protocol.

Net::Telnet also provides sophisticated features to help you establish dialogs with programs designed for human interaction. "Human interaction" means an online conversation between you and some remote service (such as a shell, or a MUD, or IRC). What this boils down to is the ability to perform I/O with a specified timeout while waiting for patterns to appear in the input stream.

Telnetting the Hard Way

Here's some code that prints out a summary of disk usage on sparky. Net::Telnet is used to log in as user joebob and issue the *df* command to get the disk information. You assume that joebob's shell prompt is $.

```
use Net::Telnet ;
$remote = new Net::Telnet (Timeout => 10, Errmode => 'return');

$remote->open("sparky") or die $remote->errmsg;
$remote->waitfor('/login: $/i') or die $remote->errmsg;

$remote->print("joebob") or die $remote->errmsg;
$remote->waitfor('/password: $/i') or die $remote->errmsg;

$remote->print("passwd-for-joebob") or die $remote->errmsg;
$remote->waitfor('/\$ $/') or die $remote->errmsg;

$remote->print("df -k") or die $remote->errmsg;

($output) = $remote->waitfor('/\$ $/') or die $remote->errmsg;

print $output;
```

As with many of the Perl I/O modules, the first step is to create an object, with the new method. Afterwards, all actions are invoked via that object's methods. Here's what the output looks like:

```
df
Filesystem     1024-blocks    Used  Available  Capacity  Mounted on
/dev/hda2          11709       6184       4921      56%    /
/dev/hda5         298573     237172      45981      84%    /usr
/dev/hda6         435180     298877     113827      72%    /home
```

Net::Telnet has a flexible way of handling errors: the Errmode parameter. When Errmode is set to return as in the example above, any errors encountered in Net::Telnet methods are saved in the Net::Telnet object, and the method returns false. That error message can be obtained with $obj->errmsg.

Telnetting the Easy Way

If you always want to die on error and print out the error message as the code above does, you can set Errmode to die. Net::Telnet will kill your program for you, showing you the line where the error occurred. Let's clean up the above code a bit using an Errmode of die. That's the default, but we'll specify it anyway.

```
use Net::Telnet ();
$remote = new Net::Telnet (Timeout => 10, Errmode => 'die');

$remote->open("sparky");
$remote->waitfor('/login: $/i');

$remote->print("joebob")
$remote->waitfor('/password: $/i');

$remote->print("passwd-for-joebob")
$remote->waitfor('/\$ $/');

$remote->print("df -k");
($output) = $remote->waitfor('/\$ $/');

print $output;
```

Now look a bit closer at what this code does. The new creates a new object that has a base class of (that is, it inherits from) FileHandle or IO::Socket::INET, depending on whether you have the IO:: libraries installed. (The IO:: libraries now come standard with Perl 5.004.)

This means that the $remote object can be used as a filehandle anywhere a Perl filehandle would be used. If you have IO::Socket::INET installed, you have access to its routines via method inheritance. For example, you can call its peeraddr routine as $remote->peeraddr. (That returns the packed IP address of the remote host to which you're connected.)

In this code, you configured the object to use a ten-second timeout when connecting, reading, and writing. Connect to the remote telnet port using open and then use a series of waitfor and print routines to log in to the host. Three prompts must be waited for: the login prompt, the password prompt, and the shell prompt $.

The example above makes prominent use of `waitfor`. Let's examine it more closely. `waitfor` takes a string containing a Perl regular expression and waits for the pattern to appear in the data stream within `Timeout` seconds. Assuming the pattern appears, it reads and removes everything in the data stream, up to and including the matched string.

If the pattern doesn't occur before the timeout, Net::Telnet signals an error. For example, suppose the following command is issued, but the remote side doesn't print `login:` within ten seconds:

```
$remote->waitfor('/login: $/i');
```

That's an error, so `waitfor` will either print an error message and `die`, or just return with a false value depending on whether `Errmode` is set to `die` or `return`.

Once you're logged in and your shell prompt has appeared, issue the `df` command. Pause until `df` finishes, simply by waiting for the next shell prompt. Use the return value of `waitfor` to collect the output from the `df` command:

```
$remote->print("df -k");
($output) = $remote->waitfor('/\$ $/');
```

In a list context, `waitfor` returns two values akin to `$'` and `$&` (also known as `$PREMATCH` and `$MATCH` if you use `English`). The first value is all the characters before the matched string, and the second value is the matched string itself. In this example you use only one of the returned values—whatever matches up to the dollar sign and space at the end of the string. `$output` is thus exactly what you want: everything between the shell prompts, which, if all goes according to plan, will be the output from the `df` command.

Telnetting the Easiest Way

Because they're such common tasks, Net::Telnet provides a routine to log in (`login`) and a routine to send a command and retrieve the output (`cmd`). I'll rewrite the example one last time to use these routines.

Both `login` and `cmd` need to be able to recognize the remote shell's prompt, so I set the object's `Prompt` attribute when it's created.

```
use Net::Telnet ();
$remote = new Net::Telnet (Timeout => 10, Prompt => '/\$ $/'>);

$remote->open("sparky");
$remote->login("joebob", "passwd-for-joebob");
print $remote->cmd("df -k");
```

The `login` method expects the login prompt to look like either `/login[: ]*$/i` or `/username[: ]*$/i`. The password prompt must look like `/password[: ]*/i`.

If the thing you're connecting to doesn't use one of those prompts, you'll have to customize your own login using a series of `waitfor` and `print` commands.

Special Considerations

You may have noticed that none of the strings sent via print or cmd ends with a newline in this example. The Net::Telnet attribute output_record_separator is set to a newline as a convenience, because that's what you normally see at the end of each line. If for some reason you need to write characters without an ending newline, just change output_record_separator to the null string, "".

At some point, you might need to debug programs that use Net::Telnet. The typical symptom will be a timeout error because you've made incorrect assumptions about what the remote side is sending. The easiest way to reconcile the remote side with your expectations is to use the input_log or dump_log methods. dump_log allows you to see the data being sent from the remote side before any translation is done, while input_log shows you the results after translation.

The translation includes converting end of line characters. Typically, when you're communicating with a TCP port such as telnet or SMTP, newlines are designated using a two character ASCII sequence: a carriage return followed by a linefeed. For convenience, Net::Telnet converts sequences of carriage returns and linefeeds to native newline characters on input (that is, \n), and vice versa on output. You can control this translation with binmode.

The translation also includes stripping and responding to telnet commands embedded in the data stream. You can control this translation with telnetmode. For example, you might want to turn off this mode ($remote->telnetmode(0)) if you're connecting to a non-telnet port such as SMTP (port 25). For the curious, telnet commands are preceded by hexadecimal 255.

Other Features

Like the telnet program itself, Net::Telnet can be used to communicate with any TCP port, not just ports using the telnet protocol. Net::Telnet is frequently used to create the client side of client-server applications, because of its ability to time out when reading and writing.

You might also want to use Net::Telnet's interactive features with filehandles other than sockets. The fhopen method can be used to associate an already open filehandle with a telnet object:

```
$obj->fhopen(*STDIN);
```

Now, when you read from the object $obj, you're actually reading from standard input—with all the features of Net::Telnet available.

If you use Net::Telnet, be sure to read the embedded documentation, which includes several examples.

## CHAPTER 49

Microsoft Office

Tim Meadowcroft

Working in the Microsoft world of Windows, Office, Visual Basic, and loosely structured user documents, situations regularly appear in which you'd like to use Perl to tweak a piece of data or perform some task, but can't because you're deep in the Microsoft way of doing things. Normally, integration is hard to achieve, but this article describes how you can grab that little bit of Perl when you want it using tools from ActiveState's Perl Development Kit.

Microsoft tools tend to integrate well with other Microsoft tools, and not at all with anything else. And when it comes to writing code, you're often forced to use VB or a derivative, which aren't ideal tools for manipulating text. But invoking your favorite bit of Perl, simply and transparently, deep within the internals of Excel, Word, VB and the like is now much easier, thanks to ActiveState's PerlCOM and PerlCtrl, parts of their commercial Perl Development Kit available at *http://www.activestate.com*.

This article describes a scenario in which a complete Perl solution (using an external Perl script to automate Office) wasn't appropriate, but a hybrid Perl/non-Perl approach was, and how PerlCOM made that hybrid solution almost trivially simple.

 There is VB code in the following example. It's the subject of the article, so I can't really skip it. You don't need to know VB in order to read the examples; they're fairly simple, and as long as you get the gist of what the VB code does, you'll be fine.

Background

All too frequently, U.K. telephone numbers are subject to wide-reaching changes (combined with promises that "this will be the last time"). The most recent was the overnight change to London and five other city codes, covering a quarter of the U.K. population, and all mobile and pager numbers. (See *http:///www.numberchange.org/* for the gritty details.) For the sake of this article, I'll limit the discussion to just the London numbers, for which the seven-digit local codes became eight-digit codes overnight:

```
0171 xxx xxxx (Central London) became 020 7xxx xxxx
0181 xxx xxxx (Outer London) became 020 8xxx xxxx
```

In any large company, there are plenty of data sources that need updating, and it's the semi-structured and unstructured data sources that are hardest to change.

Databases with proper telephone number fields, in which area codes and numbers are correctly separated, are easy to change with one-time scripts. The trouble arises in the messy areas: text files, word processing documents, and all those ubiquitous spreadsheets (I work for investment banks; I've seen people write essays in Microsoft Excel because "it's the only program I understand"). If you blindly modify every cell, you risk converting data that shouldn't be touched.

The Problem

I have quite a few spreadsheets (such as telephone books) with contact information scattered throughout. Many of these had old-style (seven-digit) Central London telephone numbers, or were loosely formatted, as in Table 49-1.

Table 49-1. A spreadsheet of telephone information

Name	Number	Comment
Tim Meadowcroft	220 8537	(0171 implied)
Reception	8000	(0171 220 implied)
Tim's Fax	220-8375/6/7	(0171 implied, multiple numbers)
Tim's Department	800 0001	(Not a phone number, but a department code)

This is easy to convert with a cute application of a Perl regular expression or two. The usual approach is to automate Excel with Win32::OLE. *OLE Automation* is a system where Microsoft exposes all the innards of a program so that programs able to talk to OLE objects can operate the program. This is very powerful for the right type of problem, and the Win32::OLE module makes it possible. Effectively, your script drives the application, rather than the application invoking your script.

But I don't want to automate the entire process. If I blindly modify all the cells, it would cause a problem with the last example above. I could automate Excel and make it ask the user before each modification, but that would be tedious. What I'd really like to do is let users control the process from within Excel: let them select the cells they'd like to modify, and then invoke my conversion script on all those cells, whether it's a single cell or a thousand.

Microsoft provides a built-in programming environment for this, using VBA (Visual Basic for Applications) as an embedded scripting language based on VB (it used to be a subset, but now it has extra features and is best considered a different, but related, product). Because VBA is embedded in Office tools, it's great for putting a "fix the selected cells" button on the Excel Toolbar, but not so great for actually coding the change, as anyone who's tried to write text manipulation code in VB will tell you. But Perl and its regular expressions are ideally suited for the task. (The pedantic might note that the later versions of VBScript have a RegExp object, which *should* be callable from VBA, but after a couple hours downloading and registering objects I still couldn't call it from Excel. And there are plenty of other problems where Perl is going to be "just right" anyway.)

The basic VBA routine, shown below, is simple. It's written within Excel, and can be easily attached to a new button on an Excel toolbar. It loops over all the cells that are currently selected, and calls a FixPhone function with the contents of the cell. FixPhone returns a empty string if it can't convert the string, or the new value if it can. I then either replace the cell contents, or highlight it to signal an error to the user.

```
Sub FixPhoneOnSelection( )
  On Error Resume Next
  If TypeOf Selection Is Range Then
      'we don't try to fix a chart or similar... just cells
      Dim c As Range
      For Each c In Selection.Cells
          If Not IsEmpty(c.Value) Then
              dim t as string
              t = FixPhone(c.Text)
              If t <> "" Then
                  ' replace cell with new value - remove coloring
                  c.Value = t
                  c.Interior.ColorIndex = xlNone
              Else
                  ' leave the cell alone, but color it yellow to show error
                  c.Interior.Color = RGB(255, 255, 0)
              End If
          End If
      Next
  End If
End Sub
```

Now I just need to write FixPhone.

The Solution

Perl programmers are probably thinking that the ideal solution would be to spawn a Perl script and capture the output, using backticks or a similar mechanism, but unfortunately VB isn't very good at things like spawning a process and capturing and parsing the STDOUT stream. It can call DLLs, but stumbles if the call is complicated, and mapping parameter and return types can be complex and error-prone. One thing VB can do very well is make and use COM or OLE objects.[*]

---

[*] OLE was the original name for a compound document technology written by Microsoft. As OLE evolved, COM was written as a Component Object Model technology that OLE could be based upon. At this stage, the naming got a bit complex as Microsoft started referring to "OLE objects," "COM objects," "OLE technologies," and then also introduced the "ActiveX" name to mean the whole OLE/COM arena as it affected component developers. Today it is easier (and approximately correct) to consider all the names interchangable, with COM as the core name.

PerlCOM, part of the ActiveState Perl Development Kit, exposes a generic Perl interpreter as a COM object, which is an "object" as defined by most OO definitions (a combined chunk of data and functionality with a callable interface) that can be used by any environment that "talks COM." Functions defined in a Perl script, when given to the PerlCOM object, appear as methods on that PerlCOM object. They can be simply called from VB with parameters properly mapped and return values properly returned.

Given the a `FixPhone` function, here's the VB to make and invoke the relevant Perl:

```
sub FixPhone( byval text as string ) as string
   'Declare an object variable and make an instance of PerlCOM
   Dim perlObj as Object
   Set perlObj = CreateObject("PerlCOM.Script")

   'OK then, check it worked
   If perlObj Is Nothing Then
      MsgBox ("Sorry, No PerlCOM on this machine")
      exit
   End If

   'Make a nice Perl routine (trivial body for a simple example...)
   Call perlObj.EvalScript("sub PerlFixPhone { return '020 7'.$_[0]; }")

   'Invoke my perl subroutine (parameters and return value seamlessly done)
   Dim t as String
   t = perlObj.PerlFixPhone(text)
   FixPhone = t
end sub
```

Notice that for the sake of simplicity, I make a PerlCOM object, give it a small inline script to parse, and then I can invoke the Perl function I want as a new method on the PerlCOM object. The implementation of `PerlFixPhone` above is very simple; notice how the PerlCOM layer automatically maps parameter and return types between the languages.

Writing a bit of Perl to fix up the numbers is fairly simple. The neat thing is that I can invoke a Perl subroutine as if it were VB by creating new methods on a COM object.

Of course, in the real code I don't want to make a new Perl interpreter and then destroy it for every cell, so I hide the "create the Perl object and initialize the code" in a separate routine that creates the object on first invocation and caches it thereafter:

```
function GetMyPerlObj as Object
   'Declare an object variable and make it on first call only
   static perlObj as Object
   if perlObj is nothing then
     Set perlObj = CreateObject("PerlCOM.Script")

     'OK then, check it worked
     If perlObj Is Nothing Then
       MsgBox ("Sorry, no PerlCOM on this machine")
       exit
     End If
```

```
    'Make a nice Perl routine (trivial body for a simple example...)
    Call perlObj.EvalScript("sub PerlFixPhone { return '020 7'.$_[0]; }")
  end if

  ' this "assign to name of function" is how you return a value in VB...
  set GetMyPerlObj = perlObj
end function
```

Then, in the original routine, where I had:

```
t = FixPhone(c.Text)
```

I can now simply call:

```
t = GetMyPerlObj.PerlFixPhone( c.text )
```

Those with a purist OO background may raise complaints here that a COM object is effectively changing its interface by having new methods made suddenly available. Well, that's how it's done in the COM world. It looks a little unusual, but anyone who's used to AUTOLOAD methods in Perl shouldn't have a problem reading the code.

To do the same from Microsoft Word (or Powerpoint, Publisher, Visio, or any other VBA enabled product), simply write a new outer routine that grabs and modifies the appropriate selected item. That is, you have a nice separation of the part that finds and replaces the data (in VBA) and the the part that transforms the data (in Perl).

An example for Word is shown below (this assumes the same GetMyPerlObj function has been included).

```
Sub FixPhoneOnWordSelection( )
  If Selection.Text <> "" Then
    Dim t As String
    t = GetMyPerlObj.FixPhone(Selection.Text)
    If t <> "" Then
        ' replace selection with new value
        Selection.Text = t
    Else
        ' couldn't convert - popup a message
        MsgBox ("Couldn't find a suitable phone number to convert")
    End If
  End If
End Sub
```

This is a much simpler routine than the Excel example, as there's only one selection to fix, and no cells to enumerate. Accordingly, I've decided to report errors directly to the user, whereas in the Excel code I changed the coloring of cells to indicate errors. (This is important: if the user selects the wrong column for changes, you don't want him to have to dismiss a thousand dialog boxes, one for each cell, whereas in Word the selction is a span of text.)

For those who are really interested, the Perl code I actually used to fix up the phone numbers (as opposed to the trivial version above) looked like this. It's not very complex and it doesn't solve everything, but it saved time converting a lot of numbers.

```
# Tests:
#   020 xxxx xxxx : fine as is
#   xxx xxxx      : assume 020 7xxx xxxx
#   2xxx          : Building 1 extension, assume 020 7457 2xxx
#   8xxx          : Building 2 extension, assume 020 7220 8xxx
#   0171 xxx xxxx : convert to 020 7xxx xxxx
#   0181 xxx xxxx : convert to 020 8xxx xxxx
# Anything else is an error and should be hand converted....
#
sub PerlFixPhone {
    local $_ = shift;
    return $_ if /^020 \d{4} \d{4}$/;
    return $_ if s/^\s*(\d{3})[-\s]+(\d{4})\s*$/020 7$1 $2/;
    return $_ if s/^\s*(\d{3})[-\s]+(\d{4})[-\s]+(\d{4})\s*$/$1 $2 $3/;
    return $_ if s/^\s*(2\d{3})\s*$/020 7457 $1/;
    return $_ if s/^\s*(8\d{3})\s*$/020 7220 $1/;
    return $_ if s/^\s*0171[-\s]+(\d{3})[-\s]+(\d{4})\s*$/020 7$1 $2/;
    return $_ if s/^\s*0181[-\s]+(\d{3})[-\s]+(\d{4})\s*$/020 8$1 $2/;
    return '';
}
```

Wait, There's More

PerlCOM exposes much more than I've shown here. It provides simple mechanisms for loading modules and calling functions in a scalar or array context. It can make and return instances of a Perl object, and even makes the raw hash datatype available to poor VB programmers who've suffered with the atrocious Collection class for so long:

```
dim hash as Object
set hash = perlObj.CreateHash    'imagine this as $hash = { };
hash.name = "Tim"                '$hash{name} = "Tim"
hash.surname = "Meadowcroft"
```

As wordy as this is, it's nothing compared to a VB Collection object!

For the examples I've shown so far, I needed a licensed PDK on the machine running the scripts. But if I wanted to make a VB/Perl hybrid that I could distribute to others, what would I do?

The PDK also includes PerlCtrl, which makes ActiveX components from a script. Whereas PerlCOM exposes a generic Perl interpreter, PerlCtrl wraps a selected script into an ActiveX DLL that can be distributed freely and invoked in a manner similar to the above example (but without the EvalScript call).[*]

I won't go into much detail about PerlCtrl. When you've written some useful functions (say, invoking WWW::Search on the selected words in a document) that you

---

[*] There's that jargon again. An *ActiveX DLL* is a Dynamically Linked Library containing one or more COM objects. It registers itself under Windows so that when someone asks for an instance of the appropriate object, Windows knows how to load the DLL and create the object automatically without the caller needing to know where the object came from.

want to use from inside some visually pretty (but feature poor) VB GUI, PerlCtrl comes in handy. Much like PerlApp compiles a Perl script into a standalone EXE file, PerlCtrl compiles Perl code into DLL components. I've used this to produce a VB prototype of a GUI, that itself uses a Perl prototype of a specialized multitier TCP/IP messaging system. The system combined rapid frontend development and rapid framework development tools to demonstrate complete front-to-back feasibility with a minimum of coding effort.

Other tools are included in the PDK. PerlApp, for example, compiles a Perl script into a standalone executable. Unix hackers may wonder what all the fuss is about, but for those of us locked behind Windows these tools are a breath of fresh air.

If you start working with the innards of Microsoft products, you're going to need some help. In the "integrate with anything as long as it's Microsoft" world of Win32 programming, which a lot of us unfortunately inhabit, the COM integration that the PDK offers is well worth the money.

CHAPTER 50

Client-Server Applications

Lincoln D. Stein

Ah, for the good old days, when real programmers used vi, networking software was written in C, and monolithic client/server applications ruled the Internet. Today, it's easy to slap up a network application in a matter of minutes with a little CGI scripting, and if you are using a web authoring tool like Microsoft FrontPage, you can even write a serviceable network application without knowing any programming whatsoever.

Still, there are times when the web paradigm breaks down, and you need an application that has the immediacy and interactivity of an old-style client/server application, in which custom software on both sides of the connection exchange data using protocols designed specifically for the purpose at hand. The ease of writing client/server applications in Perl isn't generally appreciated. In this article, I'll show you how to do it.

Our running example uses the Chatbot::Eliza module, John Nolan's marvelous pure-Perl clone of Joseph Weizenbaum's classic psychotherapist simulation and the subject of his article in the third Best of TPJ book, *Games, Diversions & Perl Culture*. Chatbot::Eliza is available on CPAN and works very simply. It accepts a line of input from the user, transforms it according to a clever set of transformational rules, and echoes it back to the user in the form of a question. The effect is a lot like talking to a Freudian psychoanalyst, except that the conversation never seems to go anywhere.

Although Chatbot::Eliza can be customized extensively, most people will use its command-line interface, which can be invoked in just four lines of code (see Example 50-1). The program begins by loading the Chatbot::Eliza module. Line 3, which puts STDOUT into autoflush mode, isn't strictly necessary for this example, but comes in handy when we turn the script into a server in the next section.

Example 50-1. eliza.pl

```
0 #!/usr/bin/perl
1
2 use Chatbot::Eliza;
3 $| = 1;
4 my $bot = Chatbot::Eliza->new;
5 $bot->command_interface;
```

The script creates a new Chatbot::Eliza object, which is stored in the $bot variable, and invokes the object's command_interface method. This method now takes over the show, reading user input from STDIN, and writing transformed text to STDOUT. When we run the script, the conversation might go something like this:

```
% eliza.pl
Eliza:      Is something troubling you?
you:        Yes, my mother is getting on my nerves.
Eliza:      What else comes to mind when you think of your mother?
you:        I think of my father, of course.
Eliza:      Your father?
you:        Yes, the husband of my mother.
Eliza:      Your mother?
you:        Yes, the wife of my father.
Eliza:      Your father?
you:        Yes, the father of my brother.
Eliza:      Tell me more about your family.
you:        I have a dog too.
Eliza:      That's quite interesting.
you:        quit
Eliza:      Life is tough.  Hang in there!
```

What if we wanted to make Chatbot::Eliza available via the Internet? We could probably write a CGI wrapper around the module and use text entry fields to input lines of text, but it wouldn't be entirely straightforward. For one thing, there would be the overhead of receiving and rendering the entire HTML page for each line of the conversation, and the rendering delay would make the conversation feel less spontaneous. For another, the Chatbot object maintains a certain amount of state. That is, it remembers portions of the session, allowing it to return to previous topics and restart stalled conversations. But web sessions are not stateful, and in order to create a CGI interface to Chatbot::Eliza, we'd have to maintain a pool of Chatbot::Eliza objects in memory or disk, and associate them with users so one user doesn't end up in the middle of another user's session. This can be done, but it's not short or elegant.

Using the inetd Super-Daemon

In contrast, we can turn Example 50-1 into a server without changing a line of code. If you are using a Unix (or Linux) system, the inetd super-daemon will do all the dirty work. Just add the following line to the bottom of the /etc/inetd.conf configuration file:

```
12000 stream tcp nowait lstein /tmp/eliza/eliza.pl eliza.pl
```

You must have superuser access to edit this file. Replace the username lstein with your own login name, and adjust the path to the eliza.pl script to reflect its actual location. When you're done editing the file, restart the inetd daemon by sending it a HUP signal. You can do this by finding its process ID (PID) using the ps command and then using the kill command to send the signal. For example:

```
% ps aux | grep inetd
root       657  0.0  0.8  1220  552 ?       S   07:07  0:00 inetd
lstein     914  0.0  0.5   948  352 pts/1   S   08:07  0:00 grep inetd
% kill -HUP 657
```

Two shortcuts that work on many Linux systems are shown below:

```
% kill -HUP `cat /var/run/inetd.pid`
% killall -HUP inetd
```

Now you can use the vanilla telnet program to talk to Eliza. telnet acts as the client, and *eliza.pl* is the server:

```
% telnet localhost 12000
Trying 127.0.0.1...
Connected to localhost.
Escape character is '^]'.
Eliza:  Hello, I am a computer program.
you:    I am a human being.
Eliza:  How long have you been a human being?
you:    About 39 years.
Eliza:  That is interesting. Please continue.
you:    It started when I was born...
Eliza:  Why do you tell me you were born now?
you:    Because you asked.
Eliza:  We were discussing you -- not me.
you:    bye
Eliza:  Goodbye.  It was nice talking to you.
Connection closed by foreign host.
```

If you aren't on a Unix system, or don't have superuser access, don't worry. A Chatbot::Eliza server that will work for you is coming up soon.

Let's look at that *inetd.conf* line in more detail. It's divided into seven fields delimited by whitespace (tabs or spaces):

12000

> The port number that the server will listen to. It can be any number between 1024 and 65536. Numbers between 1–1023 are reserved for use by standard services like email and the web. Port numbers above this range can be used by any program, but only one program can use a given port at a time. Be sure to check that your system doesn't already use a particular port for some service before adding a new server (you can use the netstat program for this). 12000 is usually a pretty safe bet. This number can be replaced by a symbolic name taken from the file */etc/services*.

stream

> Specifies the server type, and can either be stream for connection-oriented services that send and receive data as continuous streams of data, or dgram, for services that send and receive short fixed-length messages. Any program that reads STDIN and writes STDOUT is a stream-based service, so use stream here.

tcp

> Specifies the communications protocol, and may be either tcp or udp (many systems also support a few more esoteric protocols, but I won't discuss them here). The TCP protocol is a connection-oriented, reliable protocol that is used for stream-type communication. UDP is used for message-oriented datagrams. Stream-based services will use tcp.

`nowait`

Tells `inetd` what to do after launching the server program. It can be `wait`, to tell `inetd` to wait until the server is done before launching the program again to handle a new incoming connection, or `nowait`, which allows `inetd` to launch the program multiple times to handle several incoming connections at once. The typical value for stream-based services is `nowait`, since communications sessions may be minutes or hours long. The implication of this value, however, is that there may be several copies of the script running at once. Some versions of `inetd` allow you to place a ceiling on this value.

/tmp/eliza/eliza.pl

The full path to the program. */tmp* is not the best place to put executables, since many systems clear */tmp* when they boot, but it suffices for tests and demos like this one. You'll want to choose a more stable directory, such as */usr/local/bin*, or */usr/local/sbin*.

eliza.pl

The seventh and subsequent fields are command-line arguments for the script. This can be any number of space-delimited command-line arguments and switches. By convention, the first field is the name of the program itself. You can use the actual script name, as shown here, or make up your own name, such as "elizabot". This value will show up in the script in the $0 variable. Other command-line switches will appear in the @ARGV array in the usual manner.

`inetd`

Allows you to take any program written in Perl (or another language for that matter) and turn it into a server. The main restriction is that the program must use standard input, standard output, and standard error for its interface. Fancy stuff, such as Curses-based graphics, will probably not work. There are a few gotchas, primarily output buffering issues. By default, when Perl detects that STDOUT is not connected directly to the user's screen, it will buffer its `print` statements to make them more efficient. This is OK when Perl is writing to a file, but not OK when it's writing to the network under the control of `inetd`. The Chatbot::Eliza object will write its initial greeting, but because the greeting is short it just gets buffered on the server side of the connection and the user never sees it.

The solution to this problem is simple: turn on autoflushing by setting $| to a true value.

A Standalone Server

What if you don't have superuser access, or are using a system that doesn't support the `inetd` super-daemon? Or what if the script has to load a lot of modules at startup time, making the launch time delay unacceptable for your application?

Under these circumstances, you can write a standalone server that does all the networking stuff itself. Thanks to Graham Barr's wonderful IO::Socket module (included with Perl), the code is not much more complicated than the original script.

Before I walk through the code, some socket theory. Much of the Internet runs across Berkeley sockets, a networking API (application programming interface) that was part of one of the early Berkeley Standard Distribution releases of Unix. A *socket* is a communications endpoint that can be connected to another socket somewhere else on the same machine or Internet. There are different types of sockets corresponding to different network protocols, each with a unique addressing scheme. The most familiar kind, the TCP/IP socket, uses an address consisting of an IP address and a port number.

Once connected, data sent to the socket at one end appears at the other. From Perl's point of view, sockets are filehandles, just like the more conventional ones that are connected to files and pipes. This makes writing networked applications extremely straightforward.

Consider this complete networking client:

```
use IO::Socket;
my $s = IO::Socket::INET->new( PeerAddr => 'phage.cshl.org',
                               PeerPort => 'daytime');
die "Can't connect: $@" unless $s;
print <$s>;
```

The first line loads the IO::Socket module, defining a number of new object classes for dealing with sockets and a number of handy constants. The second line attempts to create a new IO::Socket object. There are currently two subclasses of IO::Socket. One, called IO::Socket::INET, is used for Internet communications using TCP/IP. The other, used for communications between two processes on the same machine, is called IO::Socket::UNIX.

Because I want an Internet connection, I attempt to create an IO::Socket::INET object by calling its new method. new recognizes multiple named arguments. In this case, I need just two: PeerAddr gives the name of the remote host to contact (in this case, *phage.cshl.org*) and PeerPort gives the port number or symbolic name of the service to connect to (in this case, the daytime service that runs on many Unix machines). new attempts to connect to the indicated machine and port. If successful, it returns a new IO::Socket object. Otherwise, new returns an undefined value and leaves an error message in $@.

Once created, a socket object looks and feels a lot like a read/write filehandle. You can use it as the argument to print, or read lines from it using the angle-bracket operator (<>). Socket objects also support a large number of input/output methods inherited from the IO::Handle base class. For example, you can call $socket->print to transmit some data across the connection, or $socket->getline to fetch a line of text.

The daytime service waits for incoming connections and then transmits its idea of the current day and time. You read whatever text it sends you using the <> operator, and immediately print it.

If you run the program, you'll see this (adjusted for the correct time, of course):

```
% daytime.pl
Thu Apr 18 09:50:48 2002
```

Servers are not much harder to write. Example 50-2 provides the source code for *eliza_server.pl*, a network-ready pseudopsychoanalyst. It begins by importing the Chatbot::Eliza and IO::Socket modules, and brings in the WNOHANG constant from the POSIX module (used by the CHLD signal handler, see below).

Example 50-2. eliza_server.pl

```
 0  #!/usr/bin/perl
 1
 2  use Chatbot::Eliza;
 3  use IO::Socket;
 4  use POSIX 'WNOHANG';

 5  use constant PORT => 12000;

 6  # signal handler for child die events
 7  $SIG{CHLD} = sub { while ( waitpid(-1,WNOHANG)>0 ) { } };

 8  my $listen_socket = IO::Socket::INET->new(LocalPort => PORT,
 9                                            Listen    => 20,
10                                            Proto     => 'tcp',
11                                            Reuse     => 1);
12  die "Can't create a listening socket: $@" unless $listen_socket;
13  warn "Server ready.  Waiting for connections...\n";

14  while (my $connection = $listen_socket->accept) {
15    die "Can't fork: $!" unless defined (my $child = fork());
16    if ($child == 0) {
17      $listen_socket->close;
18      interact($connection);
19      exit 0;
20    }
21  } continue {
22    $connection->close;
23  }

24  sub interact {
25    my $sock = shift;
26    STDIN->fdopen($sock,"r")  || die "Can't reopen STDIN: $!";
27    STDOUT->fdopen($sock,"w") || die "Can't reopen STDOUT: $!";
28    STDERR->fdopen($sock,"w") || die "Can't reopen STDERR: $!";
29    STDOUT->autoflush(1);
30    Chatbot::Eliza->new->command_interface;
31  }
```

The code then defines a constant containing the port number to run on. I use 12000 again. Be careful if you've already installed the inetd version of the script, because they can't share the same port. You should either deactivate the inetd configuration line (by commenting it out and sending inetd a HUP signal), or change the constant to an unused port.

Line 6 sets a handler for the CHLD handler. I will explain this technical detail after the main code walkthrough.

The real fun begins in line 8, where a new IO::Socket object is created to accept incoming connections. Again, I call the IO::Socket::INET class's new method, but the arguments are quite different. Instead of providing new with PeerAddr and PeerPort arguments, I hand it LocalPort and Listen arguments. LocalPort tells new that it is to "bind to" (associate itself with) local port 12000, and Listen tells new that the socket will be used to accept incoming connections. The numeric argument to Listen specifies how many incoming requests can be queued up while waiting the server to call accept (more on this below). For this presumably low-volume service, 20 simultaneous connections is a very generous assumption! The other two arguments are not strictly necessary. Proto specifies the communications protocol, in this case tcp. Since stream-based TCP servers are much more common than message-based UDP servers, IO::Socket::INET's new method will default to TCP unless otherwise specified.

The Reuse argument tells new that it is okay to reuse the port number if the program is killed and immediately restarted. Ordinarily, the operating system will impose a small delay of about 90 seconds between the time a socket is killed and the time its port can be reused. During this time, new will be unable to create a new socket. The delay is protection against one program accidentally inheriting another program's delayed incoming connections. This protection is irrelevant when it's the same program opening the socket, so servers generally set Reuse to a true value in order to disable this delay.

Another optional argument, not used in this example, is LocalAddr, which takes a local hostname or IP address. In the event that your machine has more than one network interface (or multiple IP addresses associated with the same interface), you can use LocalAddr to choose which interface the socket should listen to. If not specified, the socket will accept incoming connections bound to any of your machine's IP addresses.

If something goes wrong, new returns undef and places a description of the error in the $@) global. I die with a suitable message (line 12). Otherwise, I store the returned socket object in the variable $listen_socket. Technically, the socket returned by this call is a *listen socket*, as opposed to the *connected socket* that was returned by new in the short example earlier.

The loop between lines 14 through 23 is where all the action happens. Multiple clients are going to connect to the server, and I must service each one in turn. Since I don't know in advance when a connection is going to come in, the most efficient way to do this is to go to sleep and let the operating system tell me that a new connection is ready for servicing. The accept method does this. It suspends the process until an incoming connection is attempted, at which point it completes the connection and returns to the server a brand new socket object connected to the remote client. The server uses this connected socket to talk to the client. When it's finished, it closes the connected socket. Meanwhile, the original listening socket is still available to accept new incoming connections.

At the top of the loop (line 14), I call the listen socket's accept method, and some time later it returns a connected socket. I could now go ahead and work with the connected socket, but there would be a slight problem. While I was working with the connected socket, other clients might be trying to connect, and wouldn't get an answer from the server until it called accept again. The server wants to call accept again as soon as possible—preferably at the same time that it's servicing the current connection.

To do this requires the server to walk and chew gum at the same time. On Unix systems, fork is the way to do multiprocessing (I'll cover Windows systems soon). The fork call spawns a duplicate process called the *child*. The child is identical in every respect to its parent, with one difference. In the parent process, the fork call's return value is the process ID of the child. In the child process, fork returns numeric 0. In case of an error, fork returns undef. The strategy here is for the child process to handle the task of talking to the connected client, while the parent goes back to the top of the loop and calls accept. This way many clients can connect simultaneously. Each will have a dedicated child process to talk to.

Line 15 calls fork and saves the result code to the variable $child. If $child is undefined, then the fork failed for some reason, and the server dies. Otherwise, it looks at the return value. If the value is equal to numeric 0, then the server knows it's in the child process. The child won't be calling accept again. It doesn't need the listen socket, so it closes it by calling the socket's close method. While this closing is not strictly necessary, it's always a good idea to tidy up unneeded resources in network communications, and it avoids the possibility of the child inadvertently trying to perform operations on the listen socket.

The child now calls a subroutine named interact, passing it the connected socket object. interact will manage the Eliza conversation and return when the user terminates the connection (by typing bye, for example). After interact returns, the child process itself terminates by calling exit.

Meanwhile, back in the parent process, the main loop closes the connected socket by calling its close method (line 22) and goes back to the top of the loop to accept more connections. Explicitly closing the connected socket in this way is good practice because it avoids the possibility of the parent inadvertently interfering with the child's I/O.

The actual input/output operations are performed in the interact subroutine, lines 24–31. There's a slight problem with wiring Chatbot::Eliza up to the network, because Eliza's command_interface method is hardwired to read and write to STDIN and STDOUT, whereas I want it to communicate via the connected socket. I could fix this by reaching into the chatbot's published lower-level methods and calling the routines to print the prompts and transform strings myself. This isn't much work, but there's an even lazier way to do it. I simply replace the default STDIN and STDOUT filehandles with the connected socket by reopening them.

When I loaded IO::Socket, it brought in methods from its parent class, IO::Handle. Among these methods is a filehandle method called fdopen, which allows me to do a brain transplant on any previously opened filehandle, including the standard ones. Essentially, fdopen closes the existing filehandle and reopens it using information from another filehandle that I give it. I call fdopen three times, once each for STDIN and STDOUT, and once for STDERR for good measure. Each time I call fdopen, I pass the socket object and a symbolic file access code. STDIN is reopened for reading with a mode of r, while STDOUT and STDERR are both reopened for writing with a mode of w. Now, almost as if by magic, writing to STDOUT and STDERR will send data flying down the socket, and reading from STDIN will perform a read on the socket.

The last detail is to call STDOUT's autoflush method. This is equivalent to setting $| to true, but is a bit easier to understand. At this point, I create a new Chatbot::Eliza object and invoke its command_interface method.

When you run this program, it prints out a message saying that it's waiting for connections, and then it will appear to hang. Go to a second command-line window, telnet to port 12000, and talk to the psychiatrist for awhile. Leaving the session open, go to another window, and telnet to the server again. The server should be able to handle both sessions simultaneously. If you go to a fourth window and run the ps command, you should see three copies of the script running. One is the parent server waiting in the accept method for incoming connections. The other two are the children spawned to deal with the two running sessions.

To stop the server, go back to the original window and press the interrupt key (usually Ctrl-C).

Now to explain the CHLD signal handler. Whenever a parent process forks a child, and the child exits before the parent does, the Unix operating system gives the parent a chance to examine the status code from the child to see if it exited normally or as the result of an error. The CHLD signal is used to alert the parent that something has happened to its child, and the wait and waitpid calls are used to retrieve the status code, a process known as *reaping*. In this particular case, you don't care about the childrens' exit status codes, but the operating system doesn't know that. If a child exits and the parent doesn't wait on it, a mummified version of the child process will hang around in the system process table until the parent either waits on it, or the parent exits. These so-called *zombie processes* can take up system resources and are generally undesirable.

The general technique of avoiding this problem is to install a CHLD signal handler in the parent. The handler calls wait or waitpid to retrieve the status code of the exited process and allow the zombie to go to its eternal reward. For a variety of reasons involving the handling of stopped processes and the rare event in which two children exit at nearly the same moment, the best technique is to call waitpid in a tight loop with a first argument of -1 and a second argument of WNOHANG. Together these arguments tell waitpid to reap the next child that's available, and prevent the call from blocking if there happens to be no child ready for reaping. The handler will loop until waitpid returns a negative number or zero, indicating that no more reapable children remain.

A Threaded Server

Microsoft Windows and Macintosh (pre-OS X) users are probably fretting at this point, because neither of the server implementations I've shown so far will run on your platforms. You can't use inetd because there isn't one built into either operating system (though I understand there are plug-in replacements available on the Internet that you could try), and neither supports fork.

Although I have no solace for MacPerl developers (other than a suggesting that they upgrade to OS X), Windows users are in luck.[*] Recent ports of Perl can take advantage of multithreading capabilities, which in some ways are an improvement over fork. In this section, I will show the standalone server rewritten to use threading. It's worth emphasizing that Perl's multithreading facilities are still unstable. If you are on a Unix system, you're safer using fork rather than threads. Windows users must use multithreading for server applications because other options are limited.

Example 50-3 gives the code for the multithreaded version of the server. You must be using Perl 5.005_03 or higher for this program to work, and it must be compiled with thread support. It starts out similarly to the forking version, except that it brings in the Thread module and my own derivative of the Chatbot::Eliza module called Chatbot::Eliza::Server (line 4). The rationale for using this derivative class will be explained momentarily.

Example 50-3. eliza_thread.pl

```
0  #!/usr/bin/perl
1
2  use IO::Socket;
3  use Thread;
4  use Chatbot::Eliza::Server;

5  use constant PORT => 12000;
6  my $listen_socket = IO::Socket::INET->new(LocalPort => PORT,
7                                            Listen    => 20,
8                                            Proto     => 'tcp',
9                                            Reuse     => 1);
10 die "Can't create a listening socket: $@" unless $listen_socket;

11 warn "Listening for connections...\n";
12 while (my $connection = $listen_socket->accept) {
13   my $t = Thread->new(\&interact,$connection) || die "Can't start a thread: $!";
14   $t->detach;
15 }
```

---

[*] Pre-OS X Mac developers can use a technique known as *I/O multiplexing* to simulate the behavior of multithreading. This technique involves keeping track of multiple socket objects simultaneously and using select to distinguish which ones are ready for reading and writing. It's a bit tedious to write such a server, but the reward is a system that runs more efficiently than either the fork or the multithreading techniques. However, this is outside the scope of the article. For the gory details, see W. Richard Stevens' book, referenced at the end of this article.

Example 50-3. eliza_thread.pl (continued)

```
16  sub interact {
17      my $handle = shift;
18      Chatbot::Eliza::Server->new->command_interface($handle,$handle);
19      $handle->close();
20  }
```

The listening socket is created exactly as before (lines 6–9), but the accept loop and the interact subroutine are both rather different. After accept returns a new connected socket, the code creates a new thread of execution by calling the Thread class's new method. The arguments to new are a code subroutine reference and an optional list of arguments to pass to it. In this case, I pass Thread->new a reference to the interact subroutine and the connected socket object.

Perl launches a new thread of execution and immediately calls interact, returning a new Thread object, which I'll call the *session thread*. When interact is finished, the thread terminates. Back in the main thread, the Thread object can be used to monitor and control the session thread's activities.

Threads can either be *attached* or *detached*. If attached, they hang around indefinitely after they've finished execution waiting for the main thread to call their join method. This allows threads to return a result to the main thread. Detached threads go into the background and disappear as soon as they're finished executing. This is used for threads that don't have any useful information to return to the main process. The threads that handle connections are detached, so after creating the session thread, the main thread immediately calls the object's detach method. At this point, the main thread can go back to waiting for incoming connections with accept.

The interact method is shorter than the previous version. It recovers the connected socket from its argument list and places it in a variable named $handle. It creates a new Chatbot::Eliza::Server object and immediately invokes its command_interface method. Chatbot::Eliza::Server is a small subclass that I wrote for the purposes of supporting the multithreaded server. It is identical in all respects to Chatbot::Eliza, except that the command_interface method now takes two filehandles as arguments, one for reading user input and the other for writing psychoanalyst output.

The rationale for creating this subclass is that the previous trick of reopening STDIN and STDOUT won't work in a multithreaded environment. Unlike the multiprocess solution based on fork, where changes to global variables in the child don't affect the corresponding variables in the parent, each thread of execution in a multithreaded application shares exactly the same globals. Reopening STDIN in one session thread would affect the STDIN filehandle in all threads, with confusing results. For the same reason, you'll notice that the main thread doesn't close the connected socket, and the session thread doesn't close the listen socket. The main thread and each of the session threads are responsible for closing their own sockets when they are finished executing.

Example 50-4 shows the code to Chatbot::Eliza::Server. It is essentially a cut-and-paste job in which I took the command_interface method out of the Chatbot::Eliza code and overrode it with a version that reads and writes to filehandle objects that are passed to it at runtime. Essentially, I substituted the expression $in->getline everywhere that the original was reading from STDIN, and the expression $out->print everywhere that the original was printing to STDOUT. The bad news is that I had to subclass the Chatbot::Eliza object in order to get the multithreaded server to work. The good news is that Perl's object-oriented features allowed me to do this without messing with the other 99% of the Chatbot::Eliza code.

Example 50-4. Chatbot::Eliza::Server

```perl
0   package Chatbot::Eliza::Server;
1   use Chatbot::Eliza;

2   @ISA = 'Chatbot::Eliza';

3   sub command_interface {
4     my ($self,$in,$out) = @_;
5     die "usage: Chatbot::Eliza::Server->new(\$input_handle,\$output_handle)"
6         unless $in && $out;
7     my ($user_input, $previous_user_input, $reply);

8     $self->botprompt($self->name . ":\t");  # Set Eliza's prompt
9     $self->userprompt("you:\t");            # Set user's prompt

10    # Print an initial greeting
11    $out->print ($self->botprompt,
12                 $self->{initial}->[ int rand scalar @{ $self->{initial} } ],
13                 "\n");

14    while (1) {
15      $out->print ($self->userprompt);
16      $previous_user_input = $user_input;
17      chomp( $user_input = $in->getline );

18      # If the user wants to quit,
19      # print out a farewell and quit.
20      if ($self->_testquit($user_input) ) {
21        $reply = $self->{final}->[ int rand scalar @{ $prompt->{final} } ];
22        $out->print ($self->botprompt,$reply,"\n");
23        last;
24      }

25      # Invoke the transform method to generate a reply.
26
27      $reply = $self->transform( $user_input );

28      # Print the actual reply
29      $out->print ($self->botprompt,$reply,"\n");
30    }
31  }

32  1;
```

Launching Standalone Servers from inetd

If you've been following along so far, you may have felt dissatisfied with both the inetd and standalone server solutions. The problem with inetd is that a new version of the script must be launched every time a connection comes in. There will be a perceptible delay while the script is launched, and having many copies of the script running simultaneously consumes memory resources (in contrast, when a script forks, much of its memory space is shared).

The standalone server has its problems, too. First of all, you must launch it manually, or arrange for it to be launched at system startup time. This can be inconvenient, particularly if the service is used only occasionally. Secondly, there's actually a bit more work that must be done with the simple standalone server example before it's ready for production. The server must background itself automatically, dissociate itself from the controlling terminal, respond appropriately to HUP signals, write status messages to the system log, and so forth.

Fortunately, inetd provides a mechanism that combines the convenience of inetd with the performance of the standalone server. It's achieved by changing the nowait flag in the *inetd.conf* line to wait and making a few small changes to the standalone server.

To understand the effect of these changes, a brief discussion of inetd internals is in order. When inetd is first launched, it scans its configuration file and creates a whole bunch of listening sockets, one for each service defined in the configuration file. inetd monitors all these sockets simultaneously by using I/O multiplexing, a technique I haven't discussed in this article (see the earlier footnote). When a connection comes in, inetd calls accept to create a connected socket, and then uses the trick from Example 50-2 to make the standard input, output, and error file descriptors all point to the connected socket. It now invokes the appropriate server program, which inherits the modified file descriptors. For Perl programs, these file descriptors eventually become the STDIN, STDOUT, and STDERR filehandles seen by the script. So writing to STDOUT sends data to the connected socket, and reading from STDIN reads data from the socket. Meanwhile, inetd goes back to waiting for incoming connections on the original listen socket.

This scenario occurs if the fourth field of the *inetd.conf* line is nowait. What happens if the field is wait? In this case, when inetd detects that a client is trying to establish a connection on a socket, it does *not* call accept. Instead, it copies the listen socket into standard input, standard output, and standard error, and invokes the server program. The server must call accept itself and handle the session. It is free to call accept again as many times as it likes. inetd will wait politely for the server to finish and exit, at which point it will go back to listening on the socket.

Example 50-5 contains the last version of the chatbot server. This one is designed to conserve resources without sacrificing performance. It is launched by inetd using the wait mechanism described above. It services requests until a certain period of idle time goes by without any new incoming connections. At that point, the server exits and returns control to inetd.

Example 50-5. eliza_inetd_server.pl

```perl
0  #!/usr/bin/perl
1
2  use Chatbot::Eliza;
3  use IO::Socket;
4  use POSIX 'WNOHANG';

5  use constant TIMEOUT => 1; # 1 minute default
6  my $timeout = shift || TIMEOUT;

7  # signal handler for timeout
8  $SIG{ALRM} = sub { exit 0 };
9  # signal handler for child die events
10 $SIG{CHLD} = sub { while ( waitpid(-1,WNOHANG)>0 ) { } };

11 # retrieve socket from STDIN
12 die "STDIN is not a socket" unless -S STDIN;
13 my $listen_socket = IO::Socket->new_from_fd(STDIN,"r+")
14   || die "Can't create socket: $!";

15 warn "Server ready.  Waiting for connections...\n";

16 while (my $connection = $listen_socket->accept) {
17   die "Can't fork: $!" unless defined (my $child = fork());
18   if ($child == 0) {
19     alarm(0);
20     $listen_socket->close;
21     interact($connection);
22     exit 0;
23   }
24 } continue {
25   $connection->close;
26   alarm ($timeout * 60);
27 }

28 sub interact {
29   my $sock = shift;
30   STDIN->fdopen($sock,"r")  || die "Can't reopen STDIN: $!";
31   STDOUT->fdopen($sock,"w") || die "Can't reopen STDOUT: $!";
32   STDERR->fdopen($sock,"w") || die "Can't reopen STDERR: $!";
33   STDOUT->autoflush(1);
34   Chatbot::Eliza->new->command_interface;
35 }
```

The code is almost identical to the standalone server of Example 50-2. One new feature is a command-line argument indicating the number of minutes of idle time to allow before the server exits. Line 6 retrieves this argument and defaults to one minute if absent. Line 8 installs an ALRM handler. Every time through the main loop, the code will set a timer using the alarm call. If the alarm goes off before accept returns, this handler will be invoked, causing the server to exit.

Lines 12 and 13 retrieve the listen socket. Instead of creating a new socket by calling IO::Socket::INET's new method, the code checks STDIN with the -S operator. -S returns true if STDIN is actually a socket. If it's not a socket, then the server dies with an error. (This can happen if someone tries to run the server from the command line.) Otherwise, the code turns STDIN into an IO::Socket object by calling the IO::Socket class's new_from_fd method. This method is nearly identical to fdopen, except that it avoids having to first create the IO::Socket, and then reopen it. If this call is successful, the $listen_socket variable will contain a listening socket that is ready to accept an incoming connection.

The main loop (lines 16–27) is identical to Example 50-2, with the addition of two calls to alarm. Each time through the loop, the code calls alarm in the continue{} block with the value of the timeout expressed in seconds. If the code reaches this point before the alarm goes off, the server gets a new lease on life. Otherwise, the ALRM handler is called and the server exits. However, I don't want the alarm to go off within a child session, so the code carefully turns off the alarm each time it forks off a child (line 18).

To run this version of the chatbot server, enter a line like this one in *inetd.conf* and send inetd a HUP signal:

```
12000 stream tcp wait lstein /tmp/eliza/eliza_inetd_server.pl
                                     eliza_inetd_server.pl 2
```

While running ps or top in a separate window, telnet to port 12000 a few times and confirm that the same parent server is processing all the requests. Now refrain from connecting to the server for two minutes. You will see the parent disappear, leaving any active child sessions running. The next time you telnet to the port, a new parent server will be launched.

Further Information

Everything I know about Berkeley sockets I learned from W. Richard Stevens, *Unix Network Programming: Networking Apis: Sockets and Xti (Volume 1)* (Prentice Hall). It's written for C programmers, but there's nothing there that can't be applied to Perl immediately. Also read through the pod documentation for IO::Handle, IO::Socket, and perlipc.

## CHAPTER 51

Managing Streaming Audio

Lincoln D. Stein

Lately I've been playing with MPEG level 3 (MP3), that wonderful technology that allows me to take a huge CD audio file and reduce its size more than tenfold without perceptible loss of fidelity. The last year has seen an explosion of MP3-related web sites, encoding and playing software, Internet-based CD databases, and even hardware products such as the Diamond Multimedia Rio MP3 player.

One of the neat things that MP3 supports is streaming audio. Instead of downloading the entire MP3 file to disk and then launching a player application to play it, the player retrieves the audio stream directly from the network, playing the music in real time as it downloads. Provided that the available network bandwidth is sufficient, it is much more satisfying to click on a link and instantly hear the music than to wait for a long download to complete.

On the client side, streaming MP3 audio is supported by several of the more popular MP3 players, including WinAmp on Microsoft Windows systems, and the open source Xmms program for Unix machines. On the server side, streaming MP3 audio is supported by the commercial Shoutcast system on Windows platforms, and by the open source Icecast system on Linux and other Unix platforms. In addition to providing streaming MP3 audio to clients, the Shoutcast and Icecast systems implement a form of Internet broadcasting that allows people with the appropriate client software to send an audio stream to an Internet server. The server relays the broadcast along a set of replica servers, which in turn stream the audio to anyone who tunes in to the proper channel.

I played with the Icecast server for a while, but wasn't particularly interested in its broadcasting abilities. I really just wanted to stream static MP3 files from the comfort and convenience of my Apache web server. So I started looking into how Shoutcast/Icecast do MP3 streaming. The result was Apache::MP3, an Apache module written to run under the mod_perl embedded interpreter.

Playlists, Streams, and ID3 Tags

It turns out that the core of MP3 streaming is not difficult. All you have to do for a rudimentary form of streaming is put an MP3 file on a web server, fire up your favorite stream-savvy MP3 player, and tell the player to open the sound file's URL. The MP3 player contacts the web server, generates a correctly-formed GET request for the sound file, and plays it as soon as the data begins to appear.

Two things bothered me about this. The first problem was that I had to open up the URL from within the player application. Although WinAmp has a "mini-browser" built into it, its browser window is small and its abilities are extremely limited (and it displays advertising). Other players have no built-in browser at all, which required me to type in the URLs by hand, something I avoid whenever possible. Ideally, I would like to click on a link in Netscape Navigator or Internet Explorer, and have the player application pop up and immediately begin playing the audio stream.

A second annoyance was that when the player application opens an MP3 URL, it displays the *http://* URL in its playlist and title area. Call me compulsive, but I don't care to see the URL in the playlist. I'd rather see the artist's name, the title of the album, and the title of the track.

My initial solution to problem number one was to configure my web browser to use Xmms as the helper application for MP3 files, which I did by adding the line below to my .mailcap file. Mailcap files, often located in home directories, contain a list of MIME types and an application to launch upon encountering data of that type. This line makes audio/mpeg messages trigger the Xmms application.

```
audio/mpeg; xmms %s
```

This didn't work the way I wanted. Netscape downloaded the entire file to disk, and then launched Xmms to play it.

My next solution was only slightly better. I changed the .mailcap entry to read:

```
audio/mpeg; xmms %u
```

A little-known Netscape extension to the .mailcap file replaces %u with the URL being downloaded. This caused Xmms to stream the requested URL, which was great, but while the data was streaming, Netscape went ahead and downloaded the entire file to a temporary directory, which it then deleted as soon as the download was finished. There went half my bandwidth!

After poking about a bit in the Icecast sources, I discovered the *playlist*. A playlist is a list of one or more files or URLs that you can pass to an MP3 player. When an MP3 player is asked to open a playlist, it loads and plays each file or URL in the order specified. Playlists have a MIME type of audio/mpegurl and a straightforward format. A sample playlist is shown in Figure 51-1.

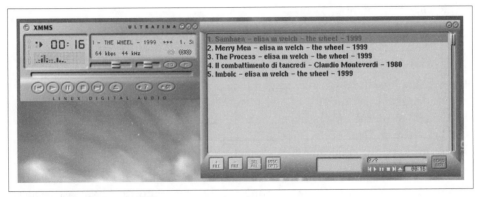

Figure 51-1. An Xmms playlist

With this knowledge, the solution to the first problem became clear. Arrange for Apache to generate playlists on the fly, and then declare the MP3 player to be the helper application for MIME type audio/mpegurl:

```
audio/mpegurl; xmms %s
```

As it turned out, the streaming audio players on Windows and Macintosh systems register themselves as audio/mpegurl helper applications when they are first installed, so this step is only necessary on Unix systems.

So much for the first problem. But what about the second? MP3 files ordinarily embed information about the artist, title, genre, and track in a data structure called an *ID3 tag*. The problem is that this information is located at the very end of the file, a position that is inconvenient for a streaming protocol that doesn't get to the end of the file until all its work is done. I knew that MP3 players were able to display title information while streaming Shoutcast/Icecast broadcasts, so there must be some way these servers transmitted the information at the very beginning of the broadcast.

Examining the Icecast source code revealed one such method. Before an Icecast server begins to transmit the MP3 data, it sends a series of headers that describe the audio stream. A typical set of headers is shown below. It begins with an HTTP-like status, ICY 200 OK, followed by a set of icy- lines. The important fields are icy-name, which provides the name of the work to display in the player window, icy-genre, which specifies the genre of the piece, icy-url, which causes WinAmp to display the specified page in its mini-browser window, and icy-br, which specifies the bitrate of the MP3 file. I'm not sure what icy-pub means, but presumably it has something to do with the broadcast aspect of the Shoutcast/Icecast protocol. (I don't know what the "icy" prefix means either; if the protocol is published, I haven't been able to find it.)

```
ICY 200 OK
icy-notice1:<BR>This stream requires <a href="http://www.winamp.com">WinAmp</a><BR>
icy-notice2:<BR>Icecast server version 1.2<BR>
icy-name:Samhain - elisa m welch - the wheel - 1999
icy-genre:Folk
```

```
icy-url:http://stein.cshl.org:8080
icy-pub:1
icy-br:64

[...music data follows...]
```

When a Shoutcast/Icecast server responds to a GET request from a player, it provides this header as a substitute for the standard HTTP header. In addition to providing this data up front, the servers also respond to clients that request the data via a UDP-based mechanism. This option is to satisfy clients that enter a musical broadcast half-way, so my application doesn't need to handle it.

Having accomplished this bit of reverse engineering, my last research task was to figure out how to read the ID3 tags in order to get them into the Shoutcast headers. Fortunately, this task was rendered trivial by Chris Nandor's MP3::Info, a Perl module capable of reading and writing ID3 tags.

Apache::MP3

Apache::MP3 is designed to respond to requests for a playlist document ending in the extension *.pls* (which is standard), or a streaming MP3 document ending in the extension *.mps* (which I made up for this application). Neither of these documents exist as static files, but are generated dynamically as needed from a directory structure containing MP3 files.

The rules for the playlist construction are a bit tricky. Consider a web root that contains a top-level directory named samples, and that contains four files arranged in the following manner:

```
/samples/the_wheel/Imbolc.mp3
/samples/the_wheel/Samhain.mp3
/samples/the_wheel/Merry_Men.mp3
/samples/the_wheel/The_Process.mp3
```

A request for the URL */samples/the_wheel/Merry_Men.pls* will make Apache::MP3 look at the */samples/the_wheel* directory, notice that there is a MP3 file with the same basename as the requested playlist, and autogenerate a playlist containing the single URL *http://my.site/samples/the_wheel/Merry_men.mps*. Notice the URL Apache::MP3 generates is a request for a .mps URL rather than for the MP3 file itself. The *.mps* URL will be used in a second request to generate an MP3 stream.

Apache::MP3 can also generate a playlist for an entire directory of MP3 files. Just take the directory name and add a *.pls* extension. For example, if the browser requests the URL */samples/the_wheel.pls*, Apache::MP3 will construct a playlist containing the four URLs */samples/the_wheel/Imbolc.mps* through */samples/the_wheel/ The_Process.mps*.

When Apache::MP3 receives a request for a URL ending in the extension *.mps*, it looks for the corresponding MP3 file, extracts its ID3 tags with MP3::Info, constructs a Shoutcast/Icecast header, and streams the file to the client.

Apache::MP3 is implemented as an Apache module using the mod_perl API. This makes it fast and flexible. If you are unfamiliar with the mod_perl API, I refer you to the introductory article that Doug MacEachern and I wrote for TPJ #9. (It's included in *Web, Graphics, & Perl/Tk: Best of the Perl Journal*.) To install Apache::MP3, copy *MP3.pm* to the directory where your Apache mod_perl modules live: either the Perl site-specific module directory, or one that was specifically configured for use by Apache. Then add the following directives to your Apache configuration file:

```
AddType audio/mpeg .mp3
AddType audio/mpegurl .pls
AddType audio/x-shoutcast-stream .mps

<Files ~ "\.(pls|mps)$">
 SetHandler perl-script
 PerlHandler Apache::MP3
</Files>
```

The AddType directives assign the appropriate MIME types to the three extensions we care about: *.mp3*, *.pls*, and *.mps*. The first two are standard, but the third one is new. The Shoutcast/Icecast system doesn't use MIME types for its audio streams, but I felt that there should be some MIME type entry for the purpose of documentation. This is followed by a <Files> section declaring that requests for files ending in *.pls* or *.mps* should be handled by mod_perl. The SetHandler directive tells Apache to pass the request to the mod_perl interpreter, and the PerlHandler directive tells mod_perl to run and load the Apache::MP3 module.

The code for Apache::MP3 is shown below. It begins by bringing in the various modules the code needs, including the list of commonly-used Apache server result codes, the MP3::Info module, the IO::Dir package for object-oriented directory handle access, and Apache::File, a lightweight alternative to the IO::File object-oriented file access class:

```
0  package Apache::MP3;
1  # file: Apache/MP3.pm

2  use strict;
3  use Apache::Constants qw(:common);
4  use MP3::Info;
5  use IO::Dir;
6  use Apache::File;

7  # Intercept requests for audio/mpegurl (.pls) files and convert them
8  # into an appropriately-formatted playlist.
9  # Intercept requests for audio/x-shoutcast-stream (.mps) and convert them
10  # into appropriate shoutcast/icecast output
11  # to install:
```

```
12   #
13   # AddType audio/mpeg .mp3
14   # AddType audio/mpegurl .pls
15   # AddType audio/x-shoutcast-stream .mps
16   #
17   # <Files ~ "\.(pls|mps)$">
18   #   SetHandler perl-script
19   #   PerlHandler Apache::MP3
20   # </Files>
```

The entry point for Apache::MP3 is a subroutine named handler, which extends from lines 22 to 51. It is called by mod_perl to process every request that comes in for a *.pls* or *.mps* URL. handler begins by storing the Apache request object from the subroutine stack into a variable named $r. The request object will be used for all communication with the Apache server. The code then reconstructs the URL for the server by calling various methods in the request object (lines 26–29). This server URL will be used later in various places.

```
21   # entry point for mod_perl
22   sub handler {
23     my $r = shift;
24     my $filename = $r->filename;

25     # Reconstruct the requested URL.  We need it at various places.
26     my $server_url = join '', 'http://',
27                               $r->server->server_hostname,
28                               ":",
29                               $r->get_server_port;
```

Lines 30–33 parse out the basename of the requested file (the name without the extension), the physical directory that the requested file lives in, and the virtual directory (in URL space) of the requested URL. I need both the physical and the virtual directory paths because I'll be retrieving information about files located on the physical filesystem, but transmitting back a playlist containing URLs. Notice the use of the request object's filename method to retrieve the request translated into a physical filesystem path, and uri to recover the same information expressed as a URL.

```
30     my $filename = $r->filename;
31     my ($basename)  = $filename  =~ m!([^/]+)\.[^/.]*$!;  # get basename
32     (my $directory  = $filename) =~ s!/[^/]+$!!;  # get the directory part
33     (my $virtual_dir = $r->uri)  =~ s!/[^/]+$!!;
```

Lines 34–44 deal with a request for a playlist. I call the request object's content_type method, and test to see if it matches MIME type audio/mpegurl. Testing the request indirectly via its MIME type is cleaner because it avoids hardcoding file extensions into the module. If the MIME type matches, then this is a request for a playlist. I now test to see whether the basename corresponds to a directory, and if so I call an internal routine named dir2playlist with arguments that make it generate a playlist for the entire directory. Otherwise, I generate a playlist that contains only a single entry by calling

dir2playlist with arguments that make the subroutine include only those MP3 files
that share the common basename.

```
34    if ($r->content_type eq 'audio/mpegurl') {
35      # If this is a request for a file of type audio/mpegurl, then
36      # strip off the extension and look for a directory
37      # containing the name.  Generate a playlist from all mp3 files
38      # in the directory.
39      return dir2playlist($r,"$directory/$basename",undef,"$server_url/$basename/")
40        if -d "$directory/$basename";

41      # If none found, then search for a file of type audio/mpeg that shares the
42      # basename, and generate a playlist from that.
43      return dir2playlist($r,$directory,$basename,"$server_url$virtual_dir/");
44    }
```

Lines 45–50 deal with a request for a streaming MP3 file, MIME content type audio/
x-shoutcast-stream. The code calls an internal subroutine named search4mp3 to
retrieve MP3 files in the directory that share the same basename. If no matching MP3
file is found, the handler aborts by returning an error code of DECLINED. Otherwise, it
calls a routine named send_stream to stream the file to the client.

```
45    # Otherwise is this a request for stream data?
46    elsif ($r->content_type eq 'audio/x-shoutcast-stream') {
47      my ($mp3_file) = search4mp3($r,$directory,$basename);
48      return DECLINED unless $mp3_file;
49      return send_stream($r,"$directory/$mp3_file",$server_url);
50    }
51  }
```

Lines 52–64 implement the search4mp3 function. It takes three arguments: the
request object, the directory to search in, and an optional search string containing
the basename to match. It searches through the indicated directory and returns all
files of type audio/mpeg with basenames that match the search string. The search
string may be undefined, in which case all MP3 files are returned. I search for MP3
files in this way rather than simply tacking a *.mp3* extension onto the basename in
the name of flexibility. Perhaps this module will need to support MPEG level 4 files
some day; or perhaps some of the files in the directory are generated by a DOS program that uses the uppercase *.MP3* extension.

```
52  # search for an mp3 file that matches a basename
53  sub search4mp3 {
54    my ($r,$dir,$basename) = @_;
55    my $pattern = quotemeta $basename;
56    my @mp3;
57    my $dh = IO::Dir->new($dir) || return;
58    while ( defined($_ = $dh->read) ) {
59      next if $pattern && !/^$pattern(\.\w+)?$/;
60      next if $r->lookup_file("$dir/$_")->content_type ne 'audio/mpeg';
61      push (@mp3,$_);
62    }
63    return @mp3;
64  }
```

The logic of search4mp3 is simple. It quotes metacharacters in the search string by calling Perl's quotemeta function (line 55) and stores the result in a variable named $pattern. It uses IO::Dir to create a new directory handle and loops through each entry in the directory. For each directory entry, it tests to see if its name matches the pattern, skipping the test if no basename is specified. It then calls the request object's lookup_file method to ask Apache what it thinks the file's MIME type is. If the entry matches audio/mpeg, then the entry is pushed onto a growing list. For searches in which no search string is specified, search4mp3 returns all MP3 files in the directory. Otherwise, search4mp3 usually returns a list of length zero (nothing found) or one (a single MP3 file found). If the web server allows several alternative extensions for MP3 audio files, however, it is possible for search4mp3 to return a list greater than length 1.

Lines 66–80 implement dir2playlist, which generates a playlist containing one or more MP3 URLs. It is called with the Apache request object, the directory to search in, the basename of the file to search for, and a URL prefix to prepend to the names of all matching files. This URL prefix contains the hostname and port, as well as the partial directory path. dir2playlist calls search4mp3 to retrieve the list of matching MP3 files and stores them into an array named @mp3 (lines 68–69). If this array is empty, the routine returns DECLINED, causing Apache to return the standard "File not found" error.

```
65  # send the playlist...
66  sub dir2playlist {
67      my ($r,$dir,$basename,$url) = @_;

68      my @mp3 = search4mp3($r, $dir, $basename);
69      return DECLINED unless @mp3;

70      $r->content_type('audio/mpegurl');
71      $r->send_http_header;
72      return OK if $r->header_only;

73      $r->print ("[playlist]\r\n\r\n");
74      $r->print ("NumberOfEntries=", scalar(@mp3), "\r\n");

75      for (my $i = 1; $i <= @mp3; $i++) {
76        (my $file = $mp3[$i-1]) =~ s/(\.[^.]+)?$/.mps/;
77        $r->print ("File$i=$url$file\r\n");
78      }
79      return OK;
80  }
```

Otherwise, dir2playlist sets the outgoing content type to audio/mpegurl and sends the HTTP header by calling the request object's send_http_header method (line 71). After calling the request object's header_only method to check whether the client wants the HTTP headers only (line 72), the subroutine proceeds to generate the playlist file a line at a time by calling the request object's print method repeatedly. Most of the action occurs in lines 75–78, in which the subroutine loops through all the MP3 files in the @mp3 array. Each one is transformed into a corresponding *.mps* file using a string substitution, and incorporated into the playlist, producing a format like this:

```
[playlist]

NumberOfEntries=4
File1=http://stein.cshl.org/samples/the_wheel/Imbolc.mp3
File2=http://stein.cshl.org/samples/the_wheel/Samhaen.mp3
File3=http://stein.cshl.org/samples/the_wheel/Merry_Men.mp3
File4=http://stein.cshl.org/samples/the_wheel/The_Process.mp3
```

The last and most interesting part of this module is the subroutine send_stream (lines 82–105), which is responsible for converting an MP3 file into a Shoutcast/Icecast-compatible stream. It receives three arguments: the request object, the physical path to the MP3 file to send, and the URL of the server. This last argument is required in order to satisfy WinAmp, which likes to pop up a mini-browser showing the home page of the streaming audio source.

```
81  # send the music stream...
82  sub send_stream {
83      my ($r,$file,$url) = @_;
84      my $tag  = get_mp3tag($file);
85      my $info = get_mp3info($file);
86      return DECLINED unless $info;  # not a legit mp3 file?

87      my $fh = Apache::File->new($file) || return DECLINED;

88      my $title = $tag->{TITLE} || $url . $r->uri;
89      foreach ( qw(ARTIST ALBUM YEAR COMMENT) ) {
90          $title .= ' - ' . $tag->{$_} if $tag->{$_};
91      }
92      my $genre = $tag->{GENRE} || 'unknown';

93      $r->print("ICY 200 OK\r\n");
94      $r->print("icy-notice1:<BR>This stream requires a shoutcast/icecast
                                            compatible player.<BR>\r\n");
95      $r->print("icy-notice2:Apache::MP3 module<BR>\r\n");
96      $r->print("icy-name:$title\r\n");
97      $r->print("icy-genre:$genre\r\n");
98      $r->print("icy-url:$url\r\n");
99      $r->print("icy-pub:1\r\n");
100     $r->print("icy-br:$info->{BITRATE}\r\n");
101     $r->print("\r\n");
102     return OK if $r->header_only;
103     $r->send_fd($fh);
104     return OK;
105 }
106 1;
```

Lines 84–85 call two functions imported from MP3::Info to recover information about the requested MP3 file. get_mp3tag returns the ID3 tag structure with information about the content of the audio file. It is a hash reference containing keys like TITLE, ARTIST, and so forth. get_mp3info returns low-level information about the audio file, such as its bitrate, length, and MPEG layer. get_mp3tag may return an undefined value if no ID3 information has been ever added to the audio file, but if get_mp3info returns undef, it's a good indication that the file isn't a valid MP3 file, in which case I bail out by returning DECLINED. Otherwise, I try to open the file for reading by calling Apache::File's new method (line 87). If, for whatever reason, this fails, I again bail by returning the DECLINED result code.

The next step is to generate a human-readable title string from the ID3 tag information. This title scrolls across the MP3 player's main screen and appears in its playlist window. After experimenting with various formats, I decided that I liked this one the best:

```
TITLE - ARTIST - ALBUM - YEAR - COMMENT
```

Lines 88–91 assemble this title from the ID3 tag information in such a way that undefined fields are simply ignored. If the TITLE field is undefined, I default to current URL.

Line 92 retrieves the ID3 genre tag, which is needed by the Shoutcast/Icecast headers. This information does not seem to be used by the clients that I've examined, and is probably used by the Shoutcast/Icecast system to create directory listings of available audio channels.

Lines 93 through 102 construct the Shoutcast/Icecast headers. Notice that these headers replace the normal HTTP headers—the usual call to send_http_header is absent. (This is one reason that it would be difficult to write this module in the form of a CGI script.) I print out the ICY status line, the title of the work, the genre, the URL, and the audio bitrate recovered earlier from the call to get_mp3info. I use carriage return/linefeed pairs (\r\n) at the end of each line rather than a simple newline because that's the way that Shoutcast/Icecast servers do it. The header is terminated by a blank line.

If the client sent a HEAD request, I stop here and return an OK status code (line 102). I doubt whether MP3 players ever make HEAD requests, but this was very useful during debugging when I only wanted to see the Shoutcast/Icecast headers. Otherwise, the subroutine calls the Apache request object's send_fd method to send the contents of the MP3 file to the client. This call suspends further processing until the entire file has been streamed to the client, or the client cancels. (Apache itself won't be suspended, just the one server process or thread that is handling the current request.) When send_fd returns, I return with a result code of OK.

Conclusion

With Apache::MP3 installed, I am able to load and play the entire contents of a directory with a single click of the mouse on a link like this one:

```
<a href="/samples/the_wheel.pls">The Wheel</a>
```

Xmms comes up (see Figure 51-1) and immediately begins to stream and play the first file. When done, Xmms moves on to the next. The playlist window is initially populated by the raw URLs of each selection, since the player hasn't yet received the title information. As each file begins to stream, the title provided by Apache::MP3 replaces the URL and scrolls across the player's main window. Neat!

To stream a single file, use a link like this one:

```
<a href="/samples/the_wheel/Imbolc.pls">Imbolc (Autumn)</a>
```

Finally, to download the entire MP3 file to disk in the conventional manner, use this link:

```
<a href="/samples/the_wheel/Imbolc.mp3">Download Imbolc (Autumn)</a>
```

Since this is neither a *.pls* nor a *.mps* URL, it is handled by Apache as a normal static file request.

I can think of several enhancements to this module. The first would be the ability to place an image of the album's cover art in the MP3 directory. If the module noticed the existence of this image file during streaming, it would use the image file's URL as the value of the icy-url: header rather than the home page of the server. The effect of this would be to make WinAmp's mini-browser display the album's cover art while streaming the file. Another useful capability would be specifying the order of files appended to the playlist, which currently come out in essentially random order. Finally, if you want to get really fancy, you could hook this module up to MySQL so that playlists could be constructed dynamically from relational database queries. Go wild!

## CHAPTER 52

A 74-Line IP Telephone

Lincoln D. Stein

Convergence! A buzzword of the dot-com era. Convergence is the magical integration of the desktop computer, the Internet, television, radio, and the telephone. In the words of the industry pundits, convergence will change everything, and the technology hailed as the forerunner of convergence is IP telephony, which allows you to make long distance calls with nothing more than an Internet connection and a high quality sound card.

I hate being left behind on the technology curve, so I decided to write my own IP telephone application in Perl. It isn't elegant, and it lacks most of the functions of real IP telephony applications, but it works. In this article, I'll show you the two versions of the application: a simple one which requires ISDN-speed connections to work well, and a somewhat more sophisticated version that uses the MP3 format to reduce the bitrate for slower connections.

Sound Cards and /dev/dsp

IP telephony requires three things:

1. Reading sound data from the microphone
2. Writing sound data to the system speaker
3. Moving sound data across the network

We know how to do item three with Berkeley sockets, but what about items one and two?

On Unix systems, the answer is simple. Audio-capable Unix systems have a special device file for communicating with the digital signal processor (DSP) driver. Common names include */dev/dsp*, */dev/audio*, and */dev/sound*. Just open the device like an ordinary file, read from it to capture sound data from the microphone, and write to it to send sound data to the speaker.

The programs in this article run on Linux systems, and assume the sound device is named */dev/dsp*. Linux sound drivers are available from a number of sources, including the kernel itself and an open source project called ALSA (for Advanced Linux Sound Architecture, available at *http://www.alsa-project.org*). A commercial vendor called 4Front Technologies sells an inexpensive package of sound drivers that work with a large number of sound cards on a variety of Unix operating systems, including FreeBSD, Solaris, HPUX, and AIX (*http://www.opensound.com*). Although I haven't tested it, the program should work fine on any system equipped with the 4Front drivers.

Only duplex-capable sound cards are suitable for telephony, because a telephone isn't much good if it can't send and receive at the same time. The sound driver must also support duplex operation, something that gave me a great deal of trouble on my Linux laptop until I discovered that the ALSA driver for my sound card lacked duplex support.

When you read from */dev/dsp* (or equivalent), the data is usually returned in PCM (pulse code modulation) format. Incoming sound is sampled at some number of times per second, and the amplitude of the sound is reported as a positive integer. Typical sampling rates range from 4,000 Hz (samples per second) to 44,100 Hz. Each sample may be 8 or 16 bits, and may be mono (1 channel) or stereo (2 channels). To send sound data from one sound card to another, the drivers for both cards have to be configured to accept data at the same sampling rate, sample size, and number of channels.

Unix provides a set of ioctl calls that let you adjust the sound card properties. More portably, you can use Seth Johnson's Audio::DSP module (available on CPAN) to change the sound settings for OSS and ALSA drivers. Unfortunately, Seth's module doesn't provide the direct filehandle access required for the more sophisticated telephony application, as you shall see later.

I don't know anything about working with audio with Perl on Win32 or Macintosh platforms. Please let me know if there's a way to do this.

The Simple Version

The simple version of the application is shown in Example 52-1 and Example 52-2. There are two programs: you run simple_send.pl to place a call, and simple_recv.pl to accept incoming connections. simple_recv.pl has to be running on the destination machine in order for simple_send.pl to work.

Here's what simple_send.pl looks like when running on my laptop (which is named pesto):

```
pesto> simple_send.pl prego.lsjs.org
Connected, go ahead...
```

And here's what simple_recv.pl looks like, running on my desktop machine, prego:

```
prego> simple_recv.pl
waiting for a connection...
accepting connection from 192.168.3.2
```

As soon as a connection is established, the two programs activate their audio systems, and I can conduct a telephone conversation across the network. It's particularly cool across my home wireless network—like a high-tech walkie-talkie!

Halting the conversation is very crude in my current version. One or the other of the parties must kill the application with the interrupt key.

Conceptually, the programs are simple. They first establish a network connection using the IO::Socket interface, then open up the DSP. Audio data read from the DSP is sent to the remote host via the socket, and data received from the socket is written to the DSP. The primary difference between the two programs is that simple_send.pl actively establishes the connection, while simple_recv.pl passively waits for incoming connections. The conversation itself is two way: both programs send and receive audio data.

simple_send.pl is the simpler of the two, so let's walk through it first. It's shown in Example 52-1.

Example 52-1. simple_send.pl: make a new outgoing connection

```
0    #!/usr/bin/perl

1    use strict;
2    use IO::File;
3    use IO::Socket;

4    use constant BUFSIZE => 4000;
5    use constant DSP      => '/dev/dsp';
6    $SIG{CHLD} = sub { exit 0 };

7    my $dest = shift || 'prego';
8    my $port = shift || 2007;
9    my $sock = IO::Socket::INET->new("$dest:$port") || die "Can't connect: $!";
10   warn "Connected, go ahead...\n";

11   my $dsp = IO::File->new(DSP, "r+") || die "Can't open DSP: $!";

12   my $child = fork();
13   die "Can't fork: $!" unless defined $child;

14   my $data;
15   if ($child) { # parent process
16      print $dsp $data while sysread($sock, $data, BUFSIZE);
17      kill TERM => $child;
18   } else {
19      print $sock $data while sysread($dsp, $data, BUFSIZE);
20   }
```

Let's walk through Example 52-1 line by line.

Load modules (lines 1–3)

Turn on strict type checking and load the IO::File and IO::Socket modules, providing an object-oriented interface to filehandles.

Define constants (lines 4–5)

Pick an arbitrary buffer size for buffering data passing between the network and the sound device. I also define a constant for the path to the DSP device.

sigCHLD *handler (line 6)*

Later you will see that when I establish a connection, I fork so that one process can read from the sound card while the other one writes to it. The CHLD handler helps ensure that when one process dies, the other dies with it.

Set up socket (lines 7–10)

Get the name and port of the destination machine from the command line, and call IO::Socket::INET's new method to establish a connection. If successful, this returns a socket object for communication with the remote host.

Open DSP (line 11)

Use IO::File to open the digital signal processor driver in read/write mode, using a file access mode of r+.

Fork (lines 12–13)

Call fork to separate the work among two processes. The parent process will read from the socket and write to the sound card, while the child performs the opposite task. In the parent process, the value returned by fork will be the process number of the child. In the child process, the value returned by fork is zero.

Parent process (lines 14–17)

The parent process is a tight loop, which reads BUFSIZE bytes of data from the socket and immediately sends it to the DSP using print. If the read from the socket returns 0, indicating that the remote end has hung up, I kill the child by sending it a TERM signal, and exit.

Child process (lines 18–20)

The child has the opposite task. It reads from the sound card and writes to the socket until either an error occurs while reading, or the parent kills it.

The receiver application, simple_recv.pl (Example 52-2), has a slightly more difficult job because it has to wait for an incoming connection, dispatch it, and then wait for another. Only one connection will be handled at a time because there's only one microphone and speaker system.

Example 52-2. simple_recv.pl: accept incoming connections

```
0    #!/usr/bin/perl

1    use strict;
2    use IO::Socket;
3    use IO::File;

4    use constant DSP     => '/dev/dsp';
5    use constant BUFSIZE => 4000;
6    $SIG{CHLD} = sub { wait };
```

Example 52-2. simple_recv.pl: accept incoming connections (continued)

```
7    my $port = shift || 2007;
8    my $listen = IO::Socket::INET->new(LocalPort => $port,
9                                       Listen => 5,
10                                      Reuse => 1)
                 || die "Can't listen: $!";

11   while (1) {
12       warn "waiting for a connection...\n";
13       my $sock = $listen->accept;
14       warn "accepting connection from ", $sock->peerhost, "\n";
15       unless (my $dsp = IO::File->new(DSP, "r+")) {
17           close $sock;
18       } else {
19           handle_connection($sock, $dsp);
20       }
21   }

22   sub handle_connection {
23       my ($sock, $dsp) = @_;
24       my $child = fork();
25       die "Can't fork: $!" unless defined $child;
26       my $data;
27       if ($child) { # parent process
28           eval {
29               local $SIG{INT} = sub {die};
30               print $dsp $data while sysread($sock, $data, BUFSIZE);
31           };
32           close $sock;
33           kill TERM => $child;
34       } else {
35           close $listen;
36           print $sock $data while sysread($dsp, $data, BUFSIZE);
37           exit;
38       }
39   }
```

Let's walk through Example 52-2.

Load modules (lines 1–3)

Turn on strict type checking and load the IO::Socket and IO::File modules as before.

Define constants and CHLD handler (lines 4–6)

I will also be forking when incoming connections come in, but in this case I don't want to terminate the parent process, but simply to wait on the child process in order to reap its status code (which I ignore). Otherwise, I will accumulate zombie processes; see the perlipc documentation bundled with Perl for more details.

Open listening socket (lines 7–10)

Get the port number from the command line, or assume a default. I will call IO::Socket::INET->new to create a listening socket, passing it values for the local port, the size of the listen queue, and the Reuse flag, which prevents problems reopening the socket when the server is killed and immediately relaunched.

Main accept loop (lines 11–20)

Enter an infinite loop. Each time through the loop I print a message and call the socket's accept method, which blocks until an incoming connection is received. When this happens, accept returns a connected socket. I print out an informational message containing the dotted IP address of the remote host, and open a filehandle on the DSP in the same manner as before. If the open is unsuccessful, I print a warning message and hang up. Otherwise, I call handle_connect to do the data transfer.

handle_connection *(lines 21–26)*

The handle_connection subroutine works like the main section of simple_send.pl. After forking, the parent process handles copying data from the socket to the DSP, while the child process handles the reverse operation.

Parent process (lines 27–33)

The part of the subroutine that handles the parent process is slightly different from the corresponding section of simple_send.pl. Instead of terminating when the user hits the interrupt key, I want to intercept at this point, gracefully close the connection, and go back to listening for a new connection.

In order to achieve this, I use an eval{} block as an exception handler. The eval{} creates a local sigINT interrupt handler, which simply calls die. This is followed by the tight read/write loop that you saw before. When the user hits the interrupt key, the eval{} block terminates with die, and execution resumes with the next statement following the block. I close the socket, send a TERM signal to the child, and return from handle_connection to resume the main accept loop.

Child process (lines 34–38)

The child process is identical to the one in simple_send.pl, except that I close the copy of the listening socket since I won't be needing it.

Adding an MP3 Encoder

This pair of programs works great across a LAN or a fast Internet connection. However, the conversation breaks up periodically on slower connections. The default sample rate for */dev/dsp* is 8 kHz at one byte per sample, monoaural, which means that the connection must support at least 8000 × 8 = 64,000 bits per second for one way communication and 128,000 bits per second for duplex communication. This can only be achieved with a really good dual-channel ISDN connection, or a DSL, cable, or leased line. Making matters worse, the connection must sustain this speed even if nobody's talking, because a second of silence generates just as much data as a second of conversation. Slower connections cannot keep up with these requirements.

There are several ways to reduce the bandwidth requirements. I could reduce the sampling rate and sacrifice the audio quality, but 8 kHz is already pretty low. I could apply a general compression utility, such as gzip, to the data stream. However, audio data is relatively uncompressible with text-oriented utilities like gzip due to the noisy, rapidly-varying nature of the data. Or I could redesign the application entirely, using discontinuous UDP packets rather than a continuous TCP stream and adjusting the UDP transmission rate dynamically to meet bandwidth availability. This is how it's done in the voice-over-IP (VoIP) protocol, which is popular in commercial IP telephony applications.

For fun, I tried a different approach. The popular MP3 audio compression format can achieve 10:1 or greater compression of audio streams. Furthermore, there are a number of Unix command-line tools for compressing and decompressing MP3s. My favorites are mpg123 (*http://www.sfs.nphil.uni-tuebingen.de/~hipp/mpg123.html*) for decompressing and playing MP3s, and lame (*http://www.sulaco.org/mp3*) for creating them. In principle, I can simply interpose lame between the DSP and the socket in order to compress the data, and uncompress it at the other end using mpg123. Although this will not work for reasons described below, conceptually I would want to open up two pipes:

```
open COMPRESS,   "lame - - </dev/dsp |";
open UNCOMPRESS, "| mpg123 -s >/dev/dsp";
```

The first pipe reads */dev/dsp* and passes it to lame for MP3 encoding. The encoded data is written to standard output where it is piped to my program. I would read from it like this:

```
print $socket $data while sysread(COMPRESS, $data, BUFSIZE);
```

The second pipe tells mpg123 to read MP3-encoded data from our program, uncompress it into PCM data, and write it to */dev/dsp*. I'd use it like this:

```
print UNCOMPRESS $data while sysread($sock, $data, BUFSIZE);
```

However, when I tried this, I found a couple of hitches. One is that lame will not accept 8-bit PCM data, requiring 16-bit data sampled at 16 kHz or higher. This problem was solved by calling the proper ioctls to put the DSP into the proper mode. The other hitch is that some sound drivers do not allow you to open the */dev/dsp* driver twice, so the straightforward strategy of opening two pipes does not work. I solved that one by opening */dev/dsp* once read/write, and then reopening STDIN and STDOUT on it, so that lame and mpg123 wouldn't try to open */dev/dsp* a second time. See Example 52-3.

Example 52-3. The DSP.pm module, which reads and writes MP3 data

```
0    package DSP;

1    use strict;
2    use IO::File;
3    use Carp 'croak';
4    use vars '%sizeof', '@ISA';
5    @ISA = 'IO::Handle';
```

```
6   BEGIN {
7     use Config;
8     %sizeof= ( int => $Config{intsize} );
9     require "sys/soundcard.ph";
10  }

11  use constant DSP        => '/dev/dsp';
12  use constant COMPRESS   => $Config{byteorder} eq '1234'
13                             ? "lame -r -x -m m -b32 -s16 - - |"
14                             : "lame -r    -m m -b32 -s16 - - |";
15  use constant UNCOMPRESS => "| mpg123 -s -m -";

16  sub new {
17      my $class = shift;
18      my $dsp = IO::File->new('/dev/dsp', 'r+')
                    or croak "Can't open /dev/dsp: $!";
19      croak "can't set samplesize: $!"
          unless ioctl $dsp, SNDCTL_DSP_SAMPLESIZE, pack("I", 16);
20      croak "can't set speed: $!"
          unless ioctl $dsp, SNDCTL_DSP_SPEED, pack("I", 16000);
21      croak "can't set mono: $!"
          unless ioctl $dsp, SNDCTL_DSP_STEREO, pack("I", 0);
22      return bless $dsp, $class;
23  }

24  # read from encode to get MP3 from microphone
25  sub compress {
26      my $self = shift;
27      open(S, "<&STDIN");
28      STDIN->fdopen($self, "r") or die "Can't reopen STDIN on DSP: $!";
29      my $encode = IO::File->new(COMPRESS) or croak "Can't open lame: $!";
30      open(STDIN, "<&S");
31      return $encode;
32  }

33  # write to decode to get sound from MP3
34  sub uncompress {
35      my $self = shift;
36      open(S, ">&STDOUT");
37      STDOUT->fdopen($self, "w") or die "Can't reopen STDOUT on DSP: $!";
38      my $uncompress = IO::File->new(UNCOMPRESS) or die "Can't open mpg123: $!";
39      $uncompress->autoflush(1);
40      open(STDOUT, ">&S");
41      return $uncompress
42  }

43  1;
```

To simplify matters, I put all the DSP-manipulating code in an object-oriented, self-contained module named DSP.pm, shown in Example 52-3. I create a new DSP handle by calling DSP->new. The object that is returned is a read/write IO handle attached to

/dev/dsp. It also has methods. The compress method returns a pipe that I can read from in order to retrieve MP3-compressed audio data. The uncompress method returns a second pipe that I can write MP3 data to. The data will be uncompressed and sent to the speakers. The following example reads MP3-compressed data from the microphone and immediately writes it back to the speaker, creating an awful racket:

```
my $dsp = DSP->new;
my $compress = $dsp->compress;
my $uncompress = $dsp->uncompress;
print $uncompress $data while sysread($compress, $data, 1024);
```

Walking through Example 52-3:

Module setup (lines 1–5)

The module begins by bringing in the modules I need. I inherit from IO::Handle to get all the available object-oriented filehandle methods.

Load ioctl definitions (lines 6–10)

I need to call a set of ioctls to configure the sound card driver. The constants for these ioctls are available in the file *sys/soundcard.ph*. If you don't already have this file in your Perl library directory, you'll need to run h2ph on your system's include files, as described in the documentation for h2ph bundled with Perl.

Many ioctl constants are calculated using a hash called %sizeof, which contains the sizes of various system-specific data types, such as integers. Although this is not well-documented, you have to create %sizeof before loading any *.ph* file that depends on it. A quick examination of *soundcard.ph* showed that it needs to know the size of int. Rather than code this in a nonportable way, I get the size of int from Perl's Config module and use it to initialize a global variable named %sizeof before loading the *.ph* file.

Constants (lines 11–15)

I declare a constant for the path to the DSP device special file, and constants containing the invocations of the lame MP3 encoder and the mpg123 MP3 decoder. The various command-line options passed to lame specify PCM-format input, monaural sound, a maximum bitrate of 32 kilobits, a sample rate of 16 kHz, and standard input and output for input and output. The only complication here is the -x flag, which must be set for little-endian architectures so that lame will byteswap the incoming PCM data. I determine the endian-ness of the architecture on the fly by looking at $Config{byteorder}.

The flags to mpg123 specify monaural sound and tell the program to send uncompressed PCM data to standard output.

new method (lines 16–23)

The new method opens the DSP for reading and writing. After successfully opening the device special file, I call ioctl three times. The first call sets the sample size to 16 bits (2 bytes). The second call sets the sampling rate to 16 kHz, and the third puts the DSP into monaural mode by setting the STEREO flag to false.

Notice that the second argument to each ioctl call is a constant defined in *sys/soundcard.ph*, while the third is a packed integer.

I return the handle, blessed into the DSP class.

compress method (lines 25–32)

The compress method returns a pipe suitable for reading MP3-compressed data. The trick here is to replace STDIN with the DSP handle, so that lame takes its input from */dev/dsp*, reading directly from the microphone. I save the current value of STDIN in a temporary filehandle, and then reopen STDIN onto the DSP filehandle, using the object-oriented fdopen method. I now call IO::File->new to open the lame pipe. I restore STDIN, and return the pipe to the caller.

uncompress method (lines 34–44)

The uncompress method returns a pipe suitable for writing MP3-compressed data. It uses the same trick as compress, except that now I operate on STDOUT rather than STDIN. After saving the current value of STDOUT in a temporary filehandle, I reopen it onto the DSP, and call IO::File->new to open the mpg123 pipe. I don't want data getting held up in standard IO buffering, so I activate the pipe's autoflush property. After restoring STDOUT, I return the pipe to the caller.

Example 52-4 and Example 52-5 show mp3_send.pl and mp3_recv.pl, versions of the earlier simple scripts modified to transmit MP3-encoded audio streams. Because they're nearly identical, we don't need to walk through them again. There are two important changes:

1. Instead of opening */dev/dsp* directly, the scripts load the DSP.pm module and create a new DSP object.

2. Instead of writing or reading to */dev/dsp* directly, the scripts invoke the DSP object's compress and uncompress methods to retrieve the filehandles for reading and writing.

Otherwise, the scripts are identical to the simple versions.

Example 52-4. mp3_send.pl initiates MP3-encoded telephone calls

```
0    #!/usr/bin/perl
1    # file mp3_send.pl

2    use strict;
3    use DSP;
4    use IO::Socket;

5    use constant BUFSIZE => 1024;
6    $SIG{CHLD} = sub { exit 0 };

7    my $dest = shift || 'prego';
8    my $port = shift || 2007;
9    my $sock = IO::Socket::INET->new("$dest:$port")
        || die "Can't connect: $!";
10   my $dsp = new DSP;
```

Example 52-4. mp3_send.pl initiates MP3-encoded telephone calls (continued)

```
11   my $child = fork();
12   die "Can't fork: $!" unless defined $child;

13   my $data;
14   if ($child) { # parent process
15       my $uncompress = $dsp->uncompress;
16       print $uncompress $data while sysread($sock, $data, BUFSIZE);
17       kill TERM=>$child;
18   } else {
19       my $compress = $dsp->compress;
20       print $sock $data while sysread($compress, $data, BUFSIZE);
21   }
```

Example 52-5. mp3_recv.pl accepts MP3-encoded telephone calls

```
0    #!/usr/bin/perl
1    # file: mp3_recv.pl

2    use strict;
3    use DSP;
4    use IO::Socket;

5    use constant BUFSIZE => 1024;
6    $SIG{CHLD} = sub { wait; };

7    my $dest = shift || 'prego';
8    my $port = shift || 2007;
9    my $listen = IO::Socket::INET->new(LocalPort => $port,
10                                      Listen => 5,
11                                      Reuse => 1) || die "Can't listen: $!";

12   while (1) {
13       warn "waiting for a connection...\n";
14       my $sock = $listen->accept;
15       warn "accepting connection from ", $sock->peerhost,"\n";
16       unless (my $dsp = new DSP) {
17           warn "DSP unavailable.  Hanging up.\n";
18           close $sock;
19       } else {
20           handle_connection($sock, $dsp);
21       }
22   }

23   sub handle_connection {
24       my ($sock, $dsp) = @_;
25       my $child = fork();
26       die "Can't fork: $!" unless defined $child;
27       my $data;
28       if ($child) { # parent process
29           eval {
30             local $SIG{INT} = sub {die};
31               my $uncompress = $dsp->uncompress;
```

Example 52-5. mp3_recv.pl accepts MP3-encoded telephone calls (continued)

```
32              print $uncompress $data while sysread($sock, $data, BUFSIZE);
33           };
34           close $sock;
35           kill TERM => $child;
36        } else {
37           close $listen;
38           my $compress = $dsp->compress;
39           print $sock $data while sysread($compress, $data, BUFSIZE);
40           exit;
41        }
42    }
```

Unfortunately, when I tested these scripts on my LAN, I discovered an annoying one-to-two second delay between speaking into the microphone at one end and hearing the sound at the other. Although the MP3 encoder and decoder can keep up with the data, there seems to be some latency. Perhaps the encoder needs to accumulate a certain amount of buffered sound data before it will encode it, or perhaps I just need faster computers. The main testing platform was a pair of 300 MHz Pentium II desktops. In any case, I couldn't eliminate this delay by playing with the script's transmission buffer, and the delay is long enough to make a normal conversation very difficult.

Nevertheless, the program does allow voice transmissions in realtime across slow network connections. Although the nominal MP3 bitstream rate is 32 kilobits, in practice less bandwidth is required because of the long pauses in speech. I expect it to work between two moderately well-connected sites on the Internet, and perhaps even between hosts connected by 56K modems. Although it doesn't make much of an IP telephone, you could use the system as an intercom, a baby monitor, or just surprise your work associates by suddenly speaking to them from an idle computer!

Summary

With a little ingenuity and a dab of Perl, you can turn your desktop into an IP telephony platform. Getting IP telephony to work across fast network connections is easy, but working with limited bandwidth is more of a challenge.

These scripts are the mere beginnings of a real application. They need all the bells and whistles, such as a built-in telephone directory, an auto-dial function, a way to screen calls, and cute little sound effects for the dial tone, the busy sound, and the ring. Feel free to take the source and start doing a little bit of your own convergence!

References

Perl modules
   The IO:: modules are available on CPAN, as is Audio::DSP.

ALSA
   http://www.alsa-project.org

Front Technologies

    http://www.opensound.com

mpg123

    http://www.sfs.nphil.uni-tuebingen.de/~hipp/mpg123.html

lame

    http://www.sulaco.org/mp3

## CHAPTER 53

Controlling Modems

Bill Birthisel

Serial ports are one of the oldest black boxes in computing: data goes in, data comes out, and few people understand how, even though serial ports have been around much longer than PCs and haven't changed much over the years. They're still a very common way to connect computers to their peripherals, or even computers to one another. This article describes how to use the Win32::SerialPort module to talk to devices like modems from your Win32 Perl programs. (If you're not using Windows, the Device::SerialPort module, also on CPAN, provides the same interface for Linux, AIX, Solaris, and other POSIX operating systems.)

Before communicating, serial ports have to agree about a few things. Sometimes the agreement is pre-arranged; for instance, operating systems typically know how to talk to many types of mice. But you probably have seen something like 9600,8N1 in a manual to describe a serial device configuration. Those are the serial characteristics: baud rate, data bits, parity, and stop bits.

Let's look at what that 9600,8N1 means. At all times, a serial line either has a voltage difference across it (an "on" bit) or no voltage difference (an "off" bit). The 9600 defines the time between bits: 1/9,600 second. The 8 tells you how many bits there are per character. ASCII requires only seven bits, but most connections these days find a use for that eighth bit. An additional bit, the *parity bit*, is sometimes used as a simplistic checksum for the others; here, the N means that there is no parity bit. Finally, the 1 is the *stop bit* used to separate the end of one character from the beginning of the next.

I'll assume you've installed at least Version 0.13 of the SerialPort module and the other prerequisite modules: Win32API::CommPort (currently bundled with SerialPort) and Aldo Calpini's Win32::API. SerialPort includes the high-level user interface, while CommPort provides low-level details, object creation, and other building blocks. For Device::SerialPort, the corresponding details are provided by POSIX.pm.

In this article, I'll show you eight examples that send data through a serial port. The first few will work on any serial device, but eventually they'll be modem-specific. The examples use the port COM2 (the second serial port).

```
#! perl -w

use strict;
use Win32::SerialPort;  ###
### use Device::SerialPort;

my $ob = Win32::SerialPort->new ('COM2') || die;  ###
### my $ob = Device::SerialPort->new ('/dev/modem') || die;

my $baud   = $ob->baudrate;
my $parity = $ob->parity;
my $data   = $ob->databits;
my $stop   = $ob->stopbits;
my $hshake = $ob->handshake;

print "B = $baud, D = $data, S = $stop, P = $parity, H = $hshake\n";

undef $ob;
```

This creates a SerialPort object and prints the five most common parameters. I don't set the parameters, and I don't send any data. These are the same five settings you see when you select File → Parameters → Configure in HyperTerminal. This example will work as long as your serial port was left in a sane state by whatever used it last; if you have a problem (occasionally a PC Card Modem will claim that the baud rate is 0), open and close the port with HyperTerminal.

For the modem port on Linux, substitute the equivalent "use" and "new" lines (the ### lines above).

Note that my examples turn on all of Perl's sanity checking (-w and use strict). This is strongly recommended for all SerialPort programs, because little bugs that would be mere irritations in other programs can confuse your hardware. Nothing will crash your system or cause any sort of permanent damage, but debugging will be tough, so it's best to take these precautions.

If you look at the Parameters display in HyperTerminal, you'll see that each setting has a menu of permitted values. You can get the same information in Perl by calling these methods in list context. The output below was generated by adding lines like these to the first example:

```
my @data_opt = $ob->databits;  # list context
print "\nData Bit Options:   ";
foreach $a (@data_opt) { print "  $a"; }
```

This complete example is a subset of the demo program *options.plx* included in the Win32::SerialPort and Device::SerialPort distributions. The resulting output will something look like this:

```
Data Bit Options:    8  5  6  7

Stop Bit Options:    1  2  1.5
```

```
Handshake Options:     none  rts  dtr  xoff

Parity Options:        none  mark  space  even  odd

Baudrate Options:      110  1200  300  2400  600  14400  56000  19200
                       4800  38400  9600

Current Settings:      B = 9600, D = 8, S = 1, P = none, H = rts <$>
```

Baud rates like 28,800 and 33,600 are actually synthesized by the modem hardware and don't appear in the list. SerialPort only supports speeds predefined by the operating system (the list varies by OS version).

Initializing Your Modem

Creating a SerialPort object opens the port, but doesn't initialize it for data transfer. You're ready to initialize it now.

SerialPort defers changes during initialization until the write_settings method is invoked. Then it validates your selections, and verifies that baudrate, databits, parity, and stopbits have been set. Setting the handshake is strongly recommended, but not required. Complete the initialization by adding the following:

```
$ob->baudrate($baud)     || die "fail setting baud";
$ob->parity($parity)     || die "fail setting parity";
$ob->databits($data)     || die "fail setting databits";
$ob->stopbits($stop)     || die "fail setting stopbits";
$ob->handshake($hshake)  || die "fail setting handshake";
$ob->write_settings      || die "no settings";
```

This complete example does even more checking than what you see above. Handily, you don't have to go through all this every time you want to initialize a serial port. Once you have a functioning setup, the save method generates a configuration file that specifies the parameters and their values. You can use this configuration file to duplicate the settings in a subsequent script. The next example creates the configuration for the rest of this article.

```
#! perl -w

use strict;
use Win32::SerialPort;  ###
### use Device::SerialPort;

my $ob = Win32::SerialPort->new ('COM2') || die;  ###
### my $ob = Device::SerialPort->new ('/dev/modem') || die;

$ob->user_msg(1);          # misc. warnings
$ob->error_msg(1);         # hardware and data errors

$ob->baudrate(38400);
$ob->parity("none");
## $ob->parity_enable(1);   # for any parity except "none"
```

```
$ob->databits(8);
$ob->stopbits(1);
$ob->handshake('rts');

$ob->write_settings;
$ob->save("tpj4.cfg");

print "wrote configuration file tpj4.cfg\n";

undef $ob;
```

The user_msg method enables messages intended for the user, such as "Waiting for CTS," and the error_msg method enables error messages like "Framing Error."

An error during write_settings closes the port but leaves your program alive; the module is designed so it could be used in tasks where error recovery is preferred over failure.

The save method checks whether write_settings succeeded, and then generates a file with a complete collection of settings—many more than the five parameters you see above.

Now that you have a configuration file, you can use it with a method called start that you call instead of the new in the examples above. start reads the file, validates the file format, sets all the parameters, and performs the write_settings for you. Bingo, instant port!

There is a similar restart method that reinitializes an already open port, a bit like stty sane in Unix. The next example requires a modem that understands the Hayes command set—most do. Try running it twice, using HyperTerminal to change the baud rate between trials. The start will change it back to 38,400.

```
#! perl -w

use strict;
use Win32::SerialPort;   ###
### use Device::SerialPort;

my $ob = Win32::SerialPort->start ("tpj4.cfg") || die;   ###
### my $ob = Device::SerialPort->start ("tpj4.cfg") || die;

my $baud = $ob->baudrate; print "baud from configuration: $baud\n";

$ob->write("ATE0X4\r");
sleep 1;
my $result = $ob->input;
print "result = $result\n";

$ob->write("AT&V\r");
sleep 2;
$result = $ob->input;
print "result = $result\n";

undef $ob;
```

The exact results will vary from modem to modem; this example is intended only to show data transfer. The `input` method gets all of the characters currently pending (which in real applications may be limited by the size of internal buffers—see the module documentation for details). The `write` method does just what you expect. I will revisit this example later at another speed.

Veteran Win32 Perl users will see the `sleep` statements and mumble about how the `alarm` function is unsupported on their platform. A pleasant surprise: SerialPort supports calls with time limits much like `alarm`. Although most Win32 user code offers no easy "abort-and-do-this-on-timeout" function, the serial driver supported by the Serial API runs as a *kernel service*, and can therefore interrupt system calls. It also supports both blocking and nonblocking I/O with *asynchronous* calls: background I/O based on a start/done_yet?/complete model that appears almost as though the operation is running in a separate thread.[*]

Now an example to clarify the usage. After you send an `ATE0X4` to your modem, you expect to see an `OK\r` in return, but you might get more than that if `E1` was previously set. So you ask for more characters than you need (20) and use `read_interval` to return 100 milliseconds after the final character. You don't want that timeout for the `AT&V` command, so issue a `read_interval(0)` to disable it. You'll read 40 characters, and then 4,000 more, having set a timeout of 5 seconds for both reads. The second read should fail—I haven't seen any modems *that* verbose. The `read_interval` method is not supported by Device::SerialPort, and does not appear to work on NT4 the same way it did on Win95, so the example provides a fallback plan.

```
#! perl -w

use strict;
use Win32::SerialPort;    ###
### use Device::SerialPort;

my $OS_win = ($^O =~ /win/i) ? 1 : 0;

my $ob = Win32::SerialPort->start ("tpj4.cfg");    ###
### my $ob = Device::SerialPort->start ("tpj4.cfg");
unless ($ob) {
  die "Can't open serial port from tpj4.cfg: $^E\n";
}

$ob->read_interval(100) if ($OS_win);
$ob->read_const_time(2000);
$ob->read_char_time(0);
```

---

[*] This mechanism is at the heart of Win32 multitasking. Since most applications are based on an "event loop" model, it was essential that a slow or failed call not disrupt the loop. The Windows 3.x serial driver had notorious defects and was commonly replaced wholesale by application vendors. This created additional bugs and incompatibilities. The Win32 serial drivers and API, by contrast, are full-featured, high-performance entities that permit application writers controlled access to a wider range of OS services than a "substitute" could easily provide.

```perl
$ob->write("ATE0X4\r");
my ($count, $result) = $ob->read(20);
print "count = $count,  result = $result\n";

$ob->read_interval(0) if ($OS_win);
$ob->read_const_time(5000);
$ob->write("AT&V\r");
($count, $result) = $ob->read(40);
print "count = $count,  result = $result\n";
($count, $result) = $ob->read(4000);
print "\ncount = $count,  result = $result\n";

undef $ob;
```

Getting Your Modem to Dial

Let's get the modem to dial a telephone number. There is no one telephone number that everyone can use; replace 555-1234 below with whatever number you like.

The next code example is long, so we'll just hit the high points. The important work is in the waitfor subroutine, which accepts a time (in seconds) and calls the built-in lookfor method. waitfor then returns all of the input through whatever string matched so you can see the results.

The are_match method lets you specify an array of strings that will satisfy lookfor. Here, you stuff it with all the responses you might receive from your modem: CONNECT, OK, and so on.

Run this example with the phone line disconnected, and if you can, try it again with a busy number. You could dial an actual number and CONNECT, but the example does not include any follow-up dialog.

```perl
#! perl -w

use strict;
use Win32::SerialPort 0.17;   ###
### use Device::SerialPort 0.07;

my $ob;
my $file = "tpj4.cfg";

sub waitfor {
  my $timeout=$ob->get_tick_count + (1000 * shift);
  $ob->lookclear;  # clear buffers
  my $gotit = "";

  for (;;) {
    return unless (defined ($gotit = $ob->lookfor));
    # characters before match
    if ($gotit ne "") {
      my ($found, $end) = $ob->lastlook;
      return $gotit.$found;
    }
```

```
    # match at beginning of buffer
    my $matchstart = $ob->matchclear;
    if ($matchstart ne "") {
      return $matchstart;
    }
    return if ($ob->reset_error);
    return if ($ob->get_tick_count > $timeout);
  }
}

# =============== execution begins here =======================

$ob = Win32::SerialPort->start ($file) or die "Can't start $file\n";   ###
### $ob = Device::SerialPort->start ($file) or die "Can't start $file\n";

$ob->error_msg(1);                  # use built-in error messages
$ob->user_msg(1);

$ob->are_match("BUSY","CONNECT","OK","NO DIALTONE","ERROR","RING",
               "NO CARRIER","NO ANSWER");

$ob->write("ATE0X4\r");
printf "%s\n", waitfor(1);  # 1 second

print "\nStarting Dial\n";
$ob->write("ATDT5555555\r");   # Use a different number!
printf "%s\n", waitfor(20);

print "\n5 seconds to failure..\n";
waitfor(5) || print "Timed Out\n";

undef $ob;
```

This example could be extended to handle any device—say, a pager—with well defined responses. But managing completely interactive dialogs is tough; don't expect to have your programs dial up your ISP and chat with your friends. However, if you're intrigued, consult the "nextline" example (demo5.plx) in the module distribution for some pointers. The module provides many of the functions of both stty and Expect, including echo control, line-ending conversion, backspace/backspace-echo, separate pre_match/match/post_match strings, and multiple match patterns.

To Block or Not to Block?

The examples so far are written as if the serial I/O operations were *blocking*—that is, as though you couldn't do anything else until the operation finished. Actually, input is nonblocking. It returns an empty string when nothing has been received. read and write are blocking, but each have nonblocking alternatives. These I/O operations are constructed from low-level primitive methods in Win32API::CommPort, which can be set to block or not. The operations and their corresponding primitive methods are shown in Table 53-1.

Table 53-1. Operations and their primitive methods

Function	Primitives
read($count)	read_bg($count), read_done($block)
write($out)	write_bg($out), write_done($block)
input	status, read_bg($waiting_count)
status	is_status

Unless you want to perform your own bitmask processing and error handling, use status instead of is_status. It handles user_msg and error_msg output, returning an array containing the number of characters in the input and output buffers of the serial driver. Hence, input only issues a read_bg when something is there to read. The next example is a slow version of the fifth example using nonblocking I/O. The response reported from status varies between Win95 and NT, although the nonblocking action is the same. This example is not relevant for Device::SerialPort, which does not support (or need) separate "background" methods to prevent blocking.

```perl
#! perl -w

use strict;
use Win32::SerialPort;

my $ob = Win32::SerialPort->start ("tpj4.cfg") || die;

my $baud = $ob->baudrate(1200);
print "baud for background demo: $baud\n";

$ob->read_interval(0);
$ob->read_const_time(1000);

$ob->write("ATE0X4\r");
sleep 1;
my $result = $ob->input;
print "result = $result\n";

print "Starting 500 character background read\n";
$ob->write("AT&V\r");
my $in = $ob->read_bg(500);
my $done = 0;
my $blk;
my $err;
my $out;

for (;;) {
  ($blk, $in, $out, $err) = $ob->status;
  print "got $in characters so far..\n";
  sleep 1;
  ($done, $in, $result) = $ob->read_done(0);
  last if $done;
}
```

```
print "got = $in\nresult = $result\n";

$baud = $ob->baudrate(38400);
sleep 2;
$result = $ob->input;
print "\n\n....And now the rest = \n$result\n";

undef $ob;
```

This example doesn't do much, but if you want to implement some serial protocol, you could prepare the next transmission at the same time as you send the current buffer. You can read and write at the same time, because read_done and write_done need not block; they can be used in a continuous loop construct such as those found in control systems (or in Perl/Tk).

What's Next?

Many modems include fax capabilities, and a basic fax capability could be built on top of a CommPort object. It might not use much of SerialPort, since fax characteristics are more rigidly defined. Win32 includes an extensive interface called TAPI for managing telephony issues such as incoming calls, line selection, voice interface, modem-specific extensions, and so on.

I haven't tested SerialPort on ports within an NT Service, but I don't foresee any problems. I also plan to add a simple file-transfer demo (xmodem) to the distribution. And the readline method will be expanded to allow a virtual login from the console but accessed as a limited command line from an external serial device. A mini-HyperTerminal (interactive dialout) with scripting capability is possible as well. Contributions of ideas, examples, and code are welcome. Any TAPI wizards out there?

With methods like read and write, SerialPort objects are similar to Perl filehandles. But they're not identical—you can't use <> or print, for instance. A tied filehandle interface is included in Versions 0.14 and later.

Afterword

I've left the "What's Next?" as originally published, but what actually happened was quite different. This article was written for Win95, and while adding NT Service support turned out to be easy, some serial API features act differently between Win95 and NT4 (and Win98, and ME, and Win2K, and XP, etc.). File transfer and interactive terminal emulation did not seem to interest most users, but an Expect-like function (including regular expressions and multiple match criteria) was a common request. That, and a complete tied filehandle implementation, were the important functional enhancements.

I received lots of code samples, including pager, fax, home automation, and Perl/Tk examples, which are available on my web site. The most interesting code contribution was from Joe Doss, who had cloned Win32::SerialPort 0.08 to run on Linux. This was developed further by myself, and later Kees Cook, into Device::SerialPort. While the development is essentially complete, the documentation, and parts of the test suite, still resemble "lab notes," and should be rewritten to make it easier for someone new to the module to learn to use it (and avoid traps such as known API differences).

References

Systems Programming for Windows 95, Walter Oney, Microsoft Press, 1996.

Communications Programming for Windows 95, Charles A. Mirho and Andre Terrisse, Microsoft Press, 1996.

## CHAPTER 54

Using Usenet from Perl

Graham Barr

The Internet is an ideal medium for disseminating information to masses of people. Email can be used to distribute information to the masses via mailing lists, but there's a drawback: every piece of mail is sent to every subscriber. If there are a thousand people on a mailing list, there will be a thousand separate copies of each message zipping around the Internet. Mailing list maintenance can be a hassle as well, as we all know from the occasional spasms of "subscribe" and "unsubscribe" messages on our favorite lists.

The most popular alternative to mailing lists is Usenet. By keeping articles in centralized repositories, Usenet avoids the traffic problems posed by large mailing lists. These repositories then exchange articles among themselves.

Users can read these articles and post new ones by connecting to a Usenet server using the *Network News Transfer Protocol* (NNTP).

The articles are categorized into newsgroups; each has a particular theme or subject. Articles can be associated with one or more newsgroups. There are hundreds of different newsgroups available. Four of the most important are devoted to Perl:

```
comp.lang.perl.misc
comp.lang.perl.announce
comp.lang.perl.modules
comp.lang.perl.tk
```

These groups are the ideal forum to ask questions and make Perl-related announcements. (comp.lang.perl.announce is moderated, which means that all articles must be approved by the group's moderator).

So what can we do with these newsgroups, or others, using Perl?

Finding Newsgroups

To start with, we can find a list of all the newsgroups on the nearest news server. The code below shows how to initiate a connection to the news server and retrieve the list of newsgroups.

```perl
#!/usr/bin/perl -w

use Net::NNTP;

# most systems provide the name 'news' as an
# alias for the news server. If yours
# doesn't, you'll need to change the following
# line to the name of your server.

$NNTPhost = 'news';
# Create the connection
$nntp = Net::NNTP->new($NNTPhost)
    or die "Cannot contact $NNTPhost: $!";

# The 'list' method returns a reference to a hash.  The keys are the
# group names; the values are short descriptions of the groups.
$groups = $nntp->list() or die "Cannot get group list";

print join("\n", keys %$groups), "\n";
# Always remember to quit the connection!
$nntp->quit;
```

If you're new to Usenet, you might be wondering which newsgroups to read. Help is at hand; most servers support a command that suggests newsgroups for new readers.

```perl
# Get a list of recommended subscriptions.  This might fail,
# since not all servers support this feature.

$subs = $nntp->subscriptions() or die "Cannot get subscription list";

# The 'subscriptions' method returns a reference to an array.
# Each element is the name of a recommended newsgroup.

print join("\n", @$subs), "\n";
```

Now we know what groups are available, and which are recommended for new readers. What else can we do? Besides write yet another newsreader, we can do something far more useful: filter out articles we don't want to see. If, like me, you don't have the time to read, or even browse, all the articles in your favorite newsgroups, you can use my News::NNTP module to write scripts that automatically extract articles matching criteria of your own design.

Retrieving Articles

Every article is assigned an article number by the news server. Your newsreader uses these numbers to keep track of which articles have been read. For example, if you use a newsreader on a Unix machine, you probably have a *.newsrc* file in your home directory, with lots of lines like:

```
comp.lang.perl.announce: 1-435
comp.lang.perl.misc: 1-42997
comp.lang.perl.modules: 1-1342
comp.lang.perl.tk! 1-2263,2512
```

This group information is available via a method aptly named group. When passed a group name, this method sets the *current group pointer* (CGP) and returns information about the group. If no group name is given, information about the current group is returned.

The CGP is one of two pieces of information that the NNTP server keeps: the other is the *current article pointer* (CAP). The CAP can be moved via three methods: last and next, which move the pointer backwards and forwards, and nntpstat, which takes a single argument and sets the CAP.

The content of an article can be retrieved with three methods as well: head, which retrieves the header of the article; body, which retrieves the body; and article, which retrieves both.

Luckily, you don't have to keep moving the CAP to retrieve each article. If you know the article number, you can pass it as an argument to head, article, or body and the required article will be returned. This also sets the CAP as a side effect.

The example below shows how to set the current group and retrieve parts of articles.

```
# Set the current group
($count,$first,$last,$group) = $nntp->group("comp.lang.perl.misc");

print join("\t", $count,$first, $last, $group), "\n";
print "-" x 60, "\n";

# Get the header of the last article
$arr = $nntp->head($last);
print @$arr if $arr;
print "-" x 60, "\n";

# Now get the previous article

$nntp->last;
$arr = $nntp->body;
print @$arr if $arr;

print "-" x 60, "\n";
# And finally the oldest article still available

$arr = $nntp->article($first);
print @$arr if $arr;
```

Besides setting the current group pointer and using article numbers, you can also retrieve articles via Message-ID strings. Just as with mail messages, each Usenet message is assigned a unique Message-ID, and this string can also be provided to the head, body, or article methods to retrieve articles. However, calling these methods with a Message-ID doesn't change the CAP.

If you don't care about article numbers and just want to find the articles that have been posted since yesterday, for instance, use the newnews method, which returns the Message-IDs of all articles posted to a group (or groups) since a specified date.

The example below shows how to retrieve all articles posted to comp.lang.perl.misc the previous day. It retrieves each article and places it into a file. But this could be extended further; for example, you could have the script mail these articles to you (see *Sending Mail Without sendmail*). Here, assume that you want to write each article to a separate file.

```
# Find all articles in comp.lang.perl.announce posted in the last 24 hours
$news = $nntp->newnews( time - 86400, 'comp.lang.perl.misc')
    or die "Cannot get newnews: $!";

foreach $msgid (@$news) {     # Get the text of the article
    $article = $nntp->article($msgid) or die "Cannot get '$msgid': $!";

    # Save the text in a file
    ($file = $msgid) =~ s/[\/\$]/_/g;

    open(ARTICLE, ">$file") or die "Cannot open $file: $!";

    print ARTICLE @$article;
    close(ARTICLE);
}
```

Now it's getting more useful. But you can take it a step further, scanning the headers of the articles and retrieving only those you might be interested in. I do this myself with the comp.lang.perl.misc newsgroup; personally, I find that there's too much traffic for me to browse every article. I run a script every hour that extracts articles satisfying particular criteria.

```
# Find all articles in 'comp.lang.perl.misc'
# that were posted in the last hour

$news = $nntp->newnews( time - 3600, 'comp.lang.perl.misc')
    or die "Cannot get newnews: $!";

foreach $msgid (@$news) {
    # Extract the subject line from the message
    $subj = $nntp->xhdr( 'Subject', $msgid ) or die "Cannot get subject: $!";

    next unless $subj =~ /CPAN/ios;

    # Get the text of the article
    $article = $nntp->article($msgid) or die "Cannot get '$msgid': $!";

    # Save the text in a file
    ($file = $msgid) =~ s/[<>\/\$]/_/g;

    open(ARTICLE, ">$file") or die "Cannot open $file: $!";

    print ARTICLE @$article;
    close(ARTICLE);
}
```

This code wastes a little too much network bandwidth, because it first requests subject lines, and only later requests the articles. Instead of retrieving the subject lines with xhdr, you could use the xpat method, which makes your news server perform the pattern matching. The only disadvantage is that, as you might expect, xpat's pattern matching is much simpler than Perl's.

The pattern matching scheme used by xpat is called *wildmat*, which you can think of as a stripped-down version of regular expressions. Here's a short description:

- All wildmat patterns are automatically anchored at beginning and end.
- An asterisk matches any sequence of zero or more characters.
- A question mark matches any single character.
- Square brackets delimit a range, just as with Perl. A leading caret negates the range.
- A backslash may be used to quote special characters.
- All patterns are case-sensitive.

The code below is similar to the previous example, but uses xpat to search for CPAN articles instead of a regular expression. Also, instead of using Message-IDs to reference the articles, we use article numbers just for kicks.

```
($count,$first,$last) = $nntp->group('comp.lang.perl.misc');

$subj = $nntp->xpat('Subject', '*[Cc][Pp][Aa][Nn]*', [$last - 20, $last])
  or die "Cannot get subject lines: $!";

foreach $msgnum (keys %$subj) {
    # Get the text of the article
    $article = $nntp->article($msgnum) or die "Cannot get '$msgnum': $!";

    open(ARTICLE, ">$msgnum") or die "Cannot open $file: $!";
    print ARTICLE @$article;
    close(ARTICLE);
}
```

Posting Articles

If your news server and newsgroup permit, you can post articles as well as read them. To do this with Net::NNTP, you'll need to create a series of lines similar to an email message, with a blank line separating the header from the body. In particular, you'll want these four fields:

Subject
> This line should always be present, and should contain a concise description of your article. Subject lines like "Help" and "Can any gurus answer this?" aren't very explanatory; see Dean Roehrich's periodic comp.lang.perl.misc posting about good Perl Usenet etiquette.

From
> This line should contain an email address for people who want to contact you directly instead of posting a followup for everyone to see.

Newsgroups

> This line must be present, containing a comma-separated list of groups to which this article is being posted. Do *not* put spaces after the commas!

References

> This line is an ordered list of Message-ID strings from previous articles in the thread. It is normally generated by the newsreader. If your article isn't a followup, you don't need it.

The following example reads an article from a file and posts it to the server.

```
# Open the file containing the new article
open(ART, "post.art") or die "Cannot read 'post.art'";

# Post the article
$nntp->post(<ART>) or die "Could not post article: $!";

# Close the file
close(ART);
```

The post method is great if your article is already formatted and ready for the world. But if you're constructing an article on the fly, you need a method that transmits your article line by line. That's what the datasend method does. Here's an example that uses datasend to post an article. It's functionally equivalent to the previous program, but has a little more flexibility: if you want, you can have the loop perform some transformation on certain article lines as they're read from the filehandle.

```
open(ART, "post.art") or die "Cannot read 'post.art'";

$nntp->post() or die "Could not post article: $!";

while (<ART>) {
    $nntp->datasend($_);
}

close(ART);
```

Those of you about to write scripts with Net::NNTP should know that it has a debug mode. The debug method, when called with a value greater than zero, echoes all communication between your program and your the news server to STDERR. If you ever have problems with your scripts, try it before you panic.

All examples in this article are written using my Net::NNTP module, which is bundled with Perl (and available on CPAN).

One final point: remember that Internet bandwidth is a finite resource. Don't abuse it.

In the next article, I'll discuss another Net module, Net::FTP, which lets you move programs from machine to machine via Perl.

## CHAPTER 55

Transferring Files with FTP

Graham Barr

This article shows how to create an FTP (File Transfer Protocol) client. You've probably used ftp, a program that is a user interface to the FTP protocol. The difference between the two is subtle but important, because the program I'll develop in this article is *also* an interface to FTP.

It might not surprise you to hear that most of the work has already been done: a module, Net::FTP, interprets the FTP protocol for you. So you don't have to mess with the nuts and bolts of FTP (defined in RFC 959) to have your program send and receive files all by itself.

FTP is a client-server protocol. That is, a server listens for client connections on an agreed-upon port address (FTP uses 21 by default). Once a connection is made, the server allocates a new port for communication with the client. This leaves port 21 free to accept the connection from the next client. The client and server communicate conversationally, with the client sending commands defined in the FTP protocol to the server, and the server sending responses back to the client. This is the architecture for many well known protocols on the Internet such as SMTP, NNTP, and HTTP.

Here's an example of a conversation between an FTP server and a client. It shows what communication is necessary to connect, log in, change directory, and retrieve a file. The commands sent from the client to the server are shown in bold.

```
220 ftphost FTP server (SunOS 4.1) ready.
> USER anonymous
331 Guest login ok, send ident as password.
> PASS perl-journal-staff@perl.com
230 Guest login ok, access restrictions apply.
> CWD pub
250 CWD command successful.
> PWD
257 "/pub" is current directory.
> PORT 127,0,0,1,16,110
200 PORT command successful.
> RETR testfile
150 ASCII data connection for testfile (127.0.0.1,4206) (0 bytes).
```

```
226 ASCII Transfer complete.
> QUIT
221 Goodbye.
```

The FTP protocol actually uses two connections: one for the commands just shown, and one for the actual data transfer. The PORT command tells the server which socket address the client is using. The server uses this information (four IP octets and a two-byte port address) to make the data connection.

You will see from the examples that Net::FTP simplifies this interface by keeping track of the status and providing methods for each of the commands.

A Simple Example

My first program contacts a CPAN site and retrieves all modules that have been uploaded within a given number of days. First, initialization:

```perl
#!/usr/bin/perl
# Load the Net::FTP package
use Net::FTP;
use File::Listing qw(parse_dir);

# Look for files under 7 days (in seconds),
$age = 7*24*60*60;

# Change this to the name of your nearest CPAN host
$CPANhost = 'CPAN';

# A likely path to the CPAN/modules directory
$CPANpath = '/mirrors/CPAN/modules';
```

Now I need to construct a Net::FTP object that talks to the remote server. The Net::FTP constructor expects the FTP hostname followed by some options:

Port
> The port number (or name) for the remote host.

Timeout
> The initial timeout value, in seconds, for responses (defaults to 120).

Debug
> The debug level.

Here, I use the Timeout option so that my program will die if a connection isn't made within a minute:

```perl
$ftp = Net::FTP->new($CPANhost, Timeout => 60) or die "Cannot contact $CPANhost: $!";
```

Once a connection has been made, the login method must be called before any other methods. login takes three optional arguments: login, password, and account.

If no arguments are supplied, Net::FTP searches the *.netrc* file in my home directory (on Unix machines). If no login information is found, the login defaults to anonymous.

When doing *.netrc* lookups, Net::FTP performs certain security checks, just like the ftp program. You must own the file, and nobody else should be able to read or write to it. If these checks fail, Net::FTP ignores your *.netrc*.

If no password is given and the login is anonymous, then Net::FTP guesses your email address and sends it as the password.

The third argument is account information that might be required by the FTP server. (It's unnecessary for anonymous FTP.)

```
# We'll login to the ftp server as anonymous;
# specifying a login id prevents a .netrc lookup.

$ftp->login('anonymous') or die "Can't login ($CPANhost):" . $ftp->message;
```

Now the server has accepted me. Little does it know that I'm not a mere surfer! First, I need to change directory to the root of the CPAN modules and retrieve a recursive directory listing. By changing directories first, I reduce the size of the listing and therefore the time required to transmit it.

```
# Change the working directory
$ftp->cwd($CPANpath)
    or die "Can't change directory ($CPANhost):" . $ftp->message;

# Retrieve a recursive directory listing
@ls = $ftp->ls('-lR');
```

Before I start to transfer the files, I need to tell the FTP server what type of file I'm expecting. FTP supports multiple transfer modes:

ASCII
> Data is transferred as 8-bit bytes with <CRLF> denoting end-of-line. This is the default mode.

EBCDIC
> This type is intended for transfer between the few hosts which still use EBCDIC instead of ASCII.

IMAGE
> The data are sent as contiguous bits that are packed into the 8-bit transfer bytes for transfer. The receiving site must store the data as contiguous bits. Also called BINARY.

LOCAL
> The data is transferred in logical bytes of a size chosen by the client.

However, only two of these modes are supported by Net::FTP: ASCII and IMAGE. In binary (IMAGE) mode the files are transferred as is, but in ASCII mode some translations, such as <CRLF> to <NL>, can be performed.

```
# We probably want binary, although some files may be ASCII
$ftp->binary();
```

Now I have a recursive directory listing in @ls and an FTP connection in $ftp. I use the parse_dir subroutine in the File::Listing module to split my directory listing into its components. (File::Listing is available in the LWP distribution on CPAN.)

From these components, I can access the filename, the last time the file was written, and its type, which can be one of l, d, or f, representing links, directories, and files.

```perl
foreach $file (parse_dir(\@ls)) {
    my($name, $type, $size, $mtime, $mode) = @$file;

    # We only want to process plain files
    next unless $type eq 'f';

    # Check age of file against $age.  $mtime is a UNIX time (seconds since
    # 1 Jan 1970), and $^T is the time this script started.
    if ($^T - $mtime < $age) {
        print "Retrieving ", $name, "\n";

        # Get the file from the ftp server
        $ftp->get($name) or warn "Couldn't get '$name', skipped: $!";
    }
}
# Close the connection to the FTP server.
$ftp->quit or die "Couldn't close the connection cleanly: $!";

# We're done!
exit;
```

Multiple FTP Connections

In this section, I'll show you how a client can manage several FTP data connections to the same server. Before I go into more detail, you'll need to know the four FTP commands for retrieving and storing files:

RETR
:   Retrieve (get) a file from the server.

STOR
:   Store (put) a file on the server, overwriting it if it's already there.

STOU
:   Store (put) a file on the server by generating a unique name.

APPE
:   Append to a file on the server.

If you want to be adventurous and speed up transfer, use multiple FTP connections managed either by multiple processes or by a select call. The latter is demonstrated below, with several Net::FTP objects, one per connection.

```perl
#!/usr/bin/perl

use Net::FTP;
use File::Listing qw(parse_dir);
```

```perl
# We'll need to open and write some files
use FileHandle;

# Look for files under 7 days (in seconds),
$age = 7*24*60*60;

# Change this to the name of your nearest CPAN host
$CPANhost = 'CPAN';

# The path to the CPAN/modules directory on most CPAN hosts
$CPANpath = '/mirrors/CPAN/modules';

# Create the initial connection
$ftp = connection();

# Retrieve a recursive directory listing
@ls = $ftp->ls('-lR');

# Set the transfer mode to binary
$ftp->binary or die "Cannot set binary mode: $!";

# Create a list of files we want to get
@files = ();
foreach $file (parse_dir(\@ls)) {
    my($name, $type, $size, $mtime, $mode) = @$file;

    # We only want to process plain files
    next unless $type eq 'f';

    # Compare the age of file to $age
    if ($^T - $mtime < $age) { push(@files, $name) }
}

# The maximum number of connections to make
$max_connection = 4;
$max_connection = @files if @files < $max_connection;

# Create a list of connections. We already have one: $ftp.
@ftp = ($ftp);

for ($i = 1; $i < $max_connection; $i++) {
    my $ftp = connection();
    $ftp->binary or die "Cannot set binary mode: $!";
    push(@ftp, $ftp);
}

print "Using ", scalar(@ftp), " connections,\n";
print " to download ",scalar(@files)," files.\n";

# Keep a list of data connections
@data = ();

# We'll start off with an empty file set.
$fdset = "";
```

```
# Prime the ftp servers with RETR commands
while (@ftp && @files) {
    my $ftp = shift @ftp;
    my $file = shift @files;
    my($data,$fh) = init_xfer($ftp, $file);
    push(@data, [$data, $fh]);
}

# Close any unused connections
while (@ftp) {
    my $ftp = shift @ftp;
    $ftp->close or warn "Can't close connection cleanly: $!";
}
```

I now have several FTP data connections to the same server, each in charge of one file. To service all of these connections simultaneously, I need select to tell me when there's data to be read. I loop for as long as there is data to read: on each iteration, up to 1,024 bytes are read from any descriptor with data available. If an EOF is found, the descriptor is closed. If there are still more files to be retrieved, a new file is requested on the corresponding command socket. This creates another descriptor. If there are no more files to transfer, the command socket is closed—when the list of data descriptors is empty, I'll know the transfer is complete.

```
# Loop while we have connections. They'll be closed and removed from @data when
# transfers finish and @files is empty.

while (@data) {
    $nfound = select($rout=$fdset, undef, undef, undef);
    next unless $nfound;
    die "select: $!" if ($nfound == -1);
    my @d = @data;

    # Empty @data, connections will be added back into @data
    # if they're still in use later.
    @data = ( );
    foreach $con (@d) {
        my ($data, $fh) = @$con;
        # Do we have data waiting on this connection?
        if (vec($rout, fileno($data), 1)) {
            my $buf = "";

            # Read some data. This may block if there's less than 1024 bytes ready
            # for reading. To reduce the blocking time, use a smaller number.
            my $l = $data->read($buf, 1024);
            die "Error reading data: $!" if $l < 0;

            if ($l) {
                # Write the data to the local file
                syswrite($fh, $buf, $l)
            } else {
                # The data transfer is complete, so we can close the data connection
                my $ftp = finish_xfer($data, $fh);
```

```
            # Reuse the FTP connection if there are files left to retrieve.
            if (@files) {
                my $file = shift @files;
                @$con = init_xfer($ftp, $file);
            } else {
                # Close the FTP connection and remove it from @data
                $ftp->close or warn "Can't close connection: $!";

                # The connection is no longer in use
                undef $con;
            }
        }
    }

    # If the connection is still in use, return it to @data
    push(@data, $con) if defined $con;
}
```

Finally, the three subroutines I've been using: connect, init_xfer, and finish_xfer.

```
# Create a new connection to the ftp server
sub connection {          # Create a new NET::FTP object
    $ftp = Net::FTP->new($CPANhost, Timeout => 60)
        or die "Can't contact $CPANhost: $!";
    # We shall login to the ftp server as anonymous;
    # specifying a login id stops any netrc lookup
    $ftp->login('anonymous')
        or die "Can't login ($CPANhost):" . $ftp->message;

    # Change the working directory
    $ftp->cwd($CPANpath)
        or die "Can't change directory ($CPANhost):". $ftp->message;
    return $ftp;
}

# Initialize a file transfer
sub init_xfer {
    my ($ftp,$file) = @_;

    # Send the retr command, and get a file descriptor for the socket
    my $data = $ftp->retr($file) or die "Can't retrieve file '$file': $!";

    # Store all files locally, in the current directory
    my ($path) = ($file =~ m!([^/]+)$!);

    # Open a filehandle to the local file
    my $fh = FileHandle->new($path, "w")
        or die "Cannot open file '$path': $!";
    print "Retrieving $file as $path ...\n";

    # Add data connection into fdset for select()
    vec($fdset, fileno($data), 1) = 1;
    return ($data, $fh);
}
```

```
# Cleanup after a file transfer has completed
sub finish_xfer {
    my($data, $fh) = @_;

    # Get the ftp command object
    my $ftp = $data->cmd;

    # Remove data connection from fdset for select( )
    vec($fdset, fileno($data), 1) = 0;

    # Close the data connection
    $data->close or warn "Cannot close data connection: $!";

    # Close the local file
    close($fh) or warn "Can't close filehandle: $!";

    return $ftp;
}
```

As you can see, the whole problem becomes a lot more complex, fun, or obscure, depending on how twisted you are.

Transferring Files Between Servers

So far I've looked at transferring files to and from one server. But what if you have two remote servers and want to transfer a file from one to the other? FTP contains a powerful facility for doing this, but first let's consider the obvious solution.

I could transfer the remote file to the local filesystem and then transfer it to the other remote server. A better method would be to connect to each of the servers simultaneously, and perform sequential reads and writes between them using the local machine as a waystation. The code for this is shown below.

```
#!/usr/bin/perl

use Net::FTP;

# Create connections to both remote servers...
$ftpf = Net::FTP->new('from') or die "Cannot connect to 'from': $!";
$ftpd = Net::FTP->new('dest') or die "Cannot connect to 'dest': $!";

# ...and login to them.
$ftpf->login('anonymous') or die "Can't login to 'from'";
$ftpd->login('anonymous') or die "Can't login to 'dest'";

# Place both servers into the correct transfer mode.
# In this case I'm using ASCII.
$ftpf->ascii() && $ftpd->ascii() or die "Can't set ASCII mode: $!";

# Send the RETR command to the source server
# and obtain a file descriptor
$ffile = '/pub/testfile';
$fdf = $ftpf->retr($ffile) or die "Can't retrieve '$ffile': $!";
```

```
# Send the STOR command to the destination server
# and obtain a file descriptor
$sfile = '/pub/outfile';
$fdd = $ftpd->stor($sfile) or die "Cannot store '$sfile': $!";

# Read and write the data between the two file descriptors
while ($fdf->read($buf,1024)) {
    $fdd->write($buf, length $buf);
}

$fdf->quit() && $fdd->quit() or die "Can't close connections: $!";
$ftpf->quit() && $ftpd->quit() or die "Can't quit ftp connections: $!";
```

While this is an improvement over reading the whole file to the local filesystem and re-sending it, the process is still not as good as it could be. Consider the situation when the file in question is rather large, say over 10 MB. It takes a long time to transfer just once, and here I'm actually transferring it *twice*, which could potentially double the transfer time. For those who pay by the minute, this could get expensive.

This is where the PASV ("passive") command comes in handy. Assuming that both of the remote servers can connect to one another, I can transfer the file directly:

```
#!/usr/bin/perl

use Net::FTP;

# Create connections to both remote servers...
$ftpf = Net::FTP->new('from') or die "Can't connect to 'from': $!";
$ftpd = Net::FTP->new('dest') or die "Can't connect to 'dest': $!";

# ...and log in to them.
$ftpf->login('anonymous') or die "Can't login to 'from'";
$ftpd->login('anonymous') or die "Can't login to 'dest'";

# Place both servers into the correct transfer mode.  In this case I'm using ASCII.
$ftpf->ascii() && $ftpd->ascii() or die "Can't set ASCII mode: $!";

# Send the PASV command to the destination server.  This returns a port address.
$port = $ftpd->pasv or die "Can't put FTP host in passive mode: $!";

# Send the port address to the source server so it
# knows where to send the data.
$ftpf->port($port) or die "Error sending port: $!";

# Send the RETR and STOU commands to the servers
$rfile = '/pub/testfile';
$ftpf->retr($rfile) or $ftpf->ok or die "Can't retrieve '$rfile': $!";
$sfile = '/pub/outfile';
$ftpd->stou($sfile) or die "Can't store '$sfile': $!";

# Wait for the transfer to complete
$ftpd->pasv_wait($ftpf) or die "Transfer failed: $!";
```

```
$fdf->close() && $fdd->close() or die "Can't close connections: $!";
$ftpf->quit() && $ftpd->quit() or die "Can't quit ftp connections: $!";
```

After creating the connections and placing them in the correct transfer mode, I send the destination server a PASV command. This tells the server that for the next command, it should listen on a port for a connection instead of making the connection itself. The PASV command returns the port at which it is listening. I then send this information to the source server with a PORT command, which tells the server where to make the data connection for the next command. Once this is done, I send the two commands, which start the transfer between the two servers, and wait for the transfer to complete.

All programs in this article are available on CPAN at *modules/by-author/id/GBARR/ftp_eg.tar.gz* and on the web page for this book. The next article demonstrates how to use Net::FTP to "spider" an entire FTP site.

## CHAPTER 56

Spidering an FTP Site

Gerard Lanois

This article is the result of my own personal adventures in maintaining a rapidly growing web site via FTP, without the benefit of a telnet shell on my server. If you have FTP access to your web server's file tree, there are four reasons why mirroring with FTP instead of HTTP might be a better choice:

1. Your ISP's web server munges links and image paths in your HTML pages, so you can't use HTTP to mirror the site.

2. There is a cache between your HTTP client and your web server, making you retrieve out-of-date pages.

3. Your web site contains dynamically generated content.

4. You have data besides HTML pages and images, such as Perl programs.

This article demonstrates how to recursively traverse an FTP site using the Net::FTP module bundled with Perl and available on CPAN. For the pedantically inclined, further background information regarding the FTP protocol is available in RFC 959 (*http://www.yahoo.com/Computers_and_Internet/Standards/RFCs/*).

Motivation

You may find yourself in the unenviable position of trying to maintain a remote file tree without shell access to the system where your file tree resides. Your file tree might contain a web site, an FTP site, or other data.

Many ISPs do not provide shell accounts, either for security reasons or because the host operating system has no concept of a remote login shell (such as Windows, or old versions of Mac OS). If you take the login shell out of the equation and wish to automate the process of moving data between file trees on your local machine and your server, a scriptable client becomes a necessity. Fortunately, the Net::FTP module provides an implementation of the FTP protocol so that you can write FTP scripts in your favorite scripting language.

Here are some off-the-shelf approaches to tackling this problem:

1. The classic command-line FTP client.

2. One of the larger, fully featured mirroring tools, such as Lee McLoughlin's mirror (*http://sunsite.org.uk/packages/mirror/*, written entirely in Perl), or Pavuk (*http://www.idata.sk/~ondrej/pavuk/*).

3. A graphical FTP client, such as gFTP (*http://gftp.seul.org/*), a fairly new but rapidly maturing graphical X Window FTP client, based on the gtk+ library), or WS_FTP (*http://www.ipswitch.com/*), a graphical Windows client.

Each of these tools has its own strengths and weaknesses, and a corresponding place in your toolbox. As my web site has grown over the last couple of years, I've found myself moving individual files and directories using either command-line FTP or one of the graphical clients mentioned above.

The cornerstone of the Perl philosophy is: "There's more than one way to do it." I propose the following corollary: "But it's always more fun to do it *your* way." This article will show you how. Here is an amusing anecdote illustrating why I think it's more fun to write your own software:

> An old friend of mine works for one of the big car companies, designing electric cars. One day he described the basic architecture of an electric car, saying "Well, you have some batteries, a motor, a transmission, some software..." I interrupted, "Hold it right there! I write software for a living, and believe me, I don't want ANY software in MY car—at least not any software that I haven't personally written and tested!"

When I stumbled across Net::FTP by accident one day, I began developing a small but effective mirroring program of my own. I had been avoiding the larger mirroring packages, since I find them to be too (how to say this delicately?) "feature-rich" for my taste.

If you have shell access, mirroring a file tree is trivial. Here are the steps.

1. Package up your file tree on your development machine:

```
% cd ~/filetree
% tar cvf - . | gzip > ../filetree.tar.gz
```

2. FTP your package over to the server:

```
% cd ..
% ftp someisp.net
Connected to someisp.net
220 someisp.net FTPServer (Version wu-2.4.2) ready.
Name (someisp.net:gerard): gerard
331 Password required for gerard.
Password:
230 User gerard logged in.
Remote system type is UNIX.
ftp> cd /home/html/users/gerard
250 CWD command successful.
ftp> bin
200 Type set to I.
```

```
ftp> put filetree.tar.gz
put filetree.tar.gz
local: filetree.tar.gz remote: filetree.tar.gz
200 PORT command successful.
150 Opening BINARY mode data connection for filetree.tar.gz.
226 Transfer complete.
333546 bytes sent in 0.0175 secs (1.9e+04 Kbytes/sec)
ftp> bye
221-You have transferred 333546 bytes in 1 files.
221-Total traffic for this session was 333977 bytes in 1 transfers.
221-Thank you for using the FTP service on lanois.
221 Goodbye.
```

3. Open a shell on the remote server:

```
% telnet someisp.net
Trying 127.0.0.1...
Connected to someisp.net.
Escape character is '^]'.

Red Hat Linux release 6.0 (Hedwig)
Kernel 2.2.5-15 on an i686
login: gerard
Password:
Last login: Mon Oct  4 21:53:57 on tty1
```

4. Change directory to the root of the remote file tree (and delete the old file tree, if necessary):

```
% cd /home/html/users/gerard
```

5. Unpack your new file tree:

```
% gunzip < filetree.tar.gz | tar xvf -
```

6. Close the shell on the remote server:

```
% exit
Connection closed by foreign host.
```

Here are the steps in the reverse direction.

1. Open a shell on the server:

```
% telnet someisp.net
```

2. Package it up:

```
% cd /home/html/users/gerard
% tar cvf - . | gzip > filetreemirror.tar.gz
```

3. Close the shell on the remote server:

```
% exit
Connection closed by foreign host.
%
```

4. FTP the tree onto your local machine:

```
% cd ~
% mkdir filetreemirror
% ftp someisp.net
...
```

```
ftp> get filetreemirror.tar.gz
...
ftp> bye
...
%
```

5. Unpack it on your local machine:

```
% gunzip < filetreemirror.tar.gz | tar xvf -
```

For these two simple cases, an automated Perl client is probably overkill. But if you take the shell account out of the equation, and you'll find yourself engaging in some *very* long conversations with your FTP server.

Net::FTP

Although the documentation for Net::FTP says that only a subset of RFC 959 is implemented, you will find that the implementation provided by Net::FTP is sufficiently robust for a wide variety of uses. The real power of Net::FTP stems from the power of the Perl programming language itself.

The Net::FTP module is contained in the libnet distribution, bundled with Perl and available from your favorite CPAN mirror in the directory *modules/by-module/Net*. (I also recommend the libnet FAQ at *http://www.pobox.com/~gbarr/libnet/*.) The filename will be of the form *libnet-X.YYYY.tar.gz*.

There is also a virtually identical FTP capability in the Win32::Internet extension module, although Net::FTP works well in the Unix and Windows environments.

Downloading a File (the Simple Case)

Here is a short example illustrating how to download a single file; I occasionally use this to download my web server's access log. It is a simple example, but demonstrates all the major steps involved in scripting an FTP session with Net::FTP.

1. Use the Net::FTP package:

```
use Net::FTP;
```

2. Instantiate an FTP object:

```
$ftp = NET::FTP->new("someisp.net") or die "ERROR: Net::FTP->new failed\n";
```

3. Start an FTP session by logging in to the remote FTP server:

```
$ftp->login("anonymous", "g_lanois@yahoo.com") or die "ERROR: login failed\n";
```

4. Navigate to the directory containing the file you wish to download:

```
$ftp->cwd("/pub/outgoing/logs") or die "ERROR: cwd failed\n";
```

5. Retrieve the file or files of interest:

```
$ftp->get("access_log") or die "ERROR: get failed\n";
```

6. End the FTP session:

```
$ftp->quit;
```

Recursion

Let's quickly review Perl's recursion capability, which barely gets a mention in the perlsub documentation: "Subroutines may be called recursively." This means that a subroutine can call itself.

Here is a short example that shows how useful this capability can be. The factorial of a number *n* is the product of all the integers between 1 and *n*. The factorial subroutine below is recursive: it computes the factorial of $n as $n multiplied by factorial($n - 1).

```
sub factorial {
    my $n = shift;
    return ($n == 1) ? 1 : $n * factorial($n - 1);
}
```

The conceptual model of a file tree is an example of what graph theoreticians call a *directed acyclic graph*. Recursion is the tool of choice for algorithms that traverse the nodes of a file tree.

Downloading a File Tree (the Recursive Case)

On the local machine, to crawl a file tree recursively, I would use the finddepth subroutine from the File::Find module. (See Recipes 9.7 and 9.8 in the *Perl Cookbook*). However, there is no way to perform a finddepth on a remote file tree via the FTP protocol.

Before I tackle the problem of mirroring a remote file tree, I'll first develop the technology to crawl the tree. My approach combines recursion with Net::FTP calls to perform a find-like recursive traversal of the remote tree. Here is a snippet of pseudocode:

```
sub crawl_tree {

    Get a list of all directories and files in the current directory.

    for (each item in the list) {
        if (item is a directory) {
            Save the current FTP remote working directory;
            Change into the directory called "item";
            crawl_tree();
            Restore the remote working directory to what it was before;
        }
    }
}
```

crawl_ftp is a Perl program that traverses a remote file tree, listing the directories and files it finds along the way. It's shown in Example 56-1.

I discovered several interesting issues when developing this script. Any script that uses Net::FTP needs to check for and handle these conditions:

1. $ftp->cwd will fail on a directory that has permission set to d---------.
2. $ftp->cwd will succeed on d--x--x--x, but $ftp->dir will fail on d--x--x--x.

3. Some (but not all) FTP servers include . and .. when you request a directory listing. Do not recurse on these directories. If you recurse on .., you'll crawl up the tree instead of down. If you recurse on . (the current directory), you'll cause a tear in the space-time continuum, and the computer the script is running on will turn into a Klein bottle.

4. RFC 959 does not dictate the format of a directory listing. The following assumptions are reasonable if you don't know the FTP server's listing format in advance:
    - The columns in the listing are separated by whitespace.
    - The last column contains the filename.
    - Directory items in the listing begin with d.

5. Handling filenames with spaces requires *a priori* knowledge of the listing format. (The unpack function is perfect for parsing out the columns of the directory listing.) The programs in this article do not handle filenames with spaces.

The crawl_ftp program shown in Example 56-1 produces a nicely-indented listing of the remote file tree.

Example 56-1. crawl_ftp

```perl
#!/usr/bin/perl -w
# Crawls remote FTP directory.
#      usage: crawl_ftp [-D] host remotedir name password
#            -D  Turn on Net::FTP debug messages

use Getopt::Std;
use Net::FTP;

getopts("D");
defined($opt_D) or $opt_D = 0;

my ($host, $dir, $name, $password) = @ARGV;

defined($host) and defined($dir) and defined($name) and defined($password)
   or die "usage: $0 [-D] host remotedir name password";

$ftp = Net::FTP->new($host, Debug => $opt_D ? 1 : 0);
$ftp->login($name, $password);
$ftp->cwd($dir);  # Go to the starting point in the remote tree.
print "DIRECTORY: ", $ftp->pwd, "\n";

crawl_tree(1);     # Crawl over the tree

$ftp->quit;

sub indent {   # A utility to indent our file tree listing.
    my $num_levels = shift;
    foreach (1..$num_levels) { print "    " }
}
```

Example 56-1. crawl_ftp (continued)

```perl
sub crawl_tree {
    my $level = shift;
    my @files = $ftp->dir;  # Make a listing of files and/or directories.

    foreach my $i (@files) {
        my @items = split(/\s/, $i);
        my $item = $items[$#items];
        my $parent = $ftp->pwd;

        if ($i =~ /^d(.*)/) {
            next if $item =~ /\.\.?$/;  # Skip . and .. if present
            indent($level);
            print "DIRECTORY: ",$parent,"/",$item,"\n";

            # Recursively crawl the subtree under this directory.
            $ftp->cwd($item);
            crawl_tree($level+1);

            $ftp->cwd($parent);  # Restore location in remote tree.
        } elsif ($i =~ /^-(.*)/) {      # It's a file
            indent($level);  print "FILE: ",$item,"\n";
        }
    }
}
```

It would be far more useful to generalize the crawl_tree subroutine, using the same subroutine reference callback mechanism employed by File::Find's find and finddepth. The perlref documentation brushes lightly over the concept of subroutine references, mentioning it in detail only in the context of anonymous subroutines. In this case, it allows me to package my tree-crawling technology into a Perl module.

Example 56-2 gives a modified version, with crawl_tree renamed to ftp_finddepth and generalized through the use of a subroutine reference.

Example 56-2. crawl_ftp2

```perl
#!/usr/bin/perl -w
# Crawls remote FTP directory.
#     usage: crawl_ftp [-D] host remotedir name password
#        -D  Turn on Net::FTP debug messages

use Getopt::Std;
use Net::FTP;

getopts("D");
defined($opt_D) or $opt_D = 0;

my ($host, $dir, $name, $password) = @ARGV;

defined($host) and defined($dir) and defined($name) and
  defined($password) or die "usage: $0 [-D] host remotedir name password";
```

Example 56-2. crawl_ftp2 (continued)

```perl
$ftp = Net::FTP->new($host, Debug => $opt_D ? 1 : 0);
$ftp->login($name, $password);
$ftp->cwd($dir);  # Go to the starting point in the remote tree.
print "DIRECTORY: ",$ftp->pwd,"\n";

ftp_finddepth(\&process_item, 1);    # Crawl over the tree

$ftp->quit;

sub indent {
    # A utility to indent our file tree listing.
    my $num_levels = shift;
    foreach (1..$num_levels) { print "    " }
}

sub process_item {
    my ($level, $isdir, $item, $parent) = @_;
    foreach (1..$level) { print "    " }
    if ($isdir) { print "DIRECTORY: ", $parent, "/", $item, "\n" }
    else        { print "FILE: ",$item,"\n" }
}

sub ftp_finddepth {
    my ($callback, $level) = @_;
    my @files = $ftp->dir;  # Make a listing of files and/or directories.

    foreach my $i (@files) {
        my @items = split(/\s/, $i);
        my $item = $items[$#items];
        my $parent = $ftp->pwd;

        if ($i =~ /^d(.*)/) {
            next if $item =~ /\.\.?$/; # Skip . and .. if present
            &$callback($level, 1, $item, $parent);  # Must be a directory

            # Recursively crawl the subtree under this directory.
            $ftp->cwd($item);
            ftp_finddepth($callback, $level+1);

            # Restore location in remote tree.
            $ftp->cwd($parent);
        } elsif ($i =~ /^-(.*)/) {                   # Must be a file
            &$callback($level, 0, $item, $parent);
        }
    }
}
```

The first step is to create a module for the general purpose ftp_finddepth technology I just developed: FTPFind, shown in Example 56-3. Then I can write a downloading application that uses the module to traverse the remote file tree's directory structure, transferring any files it finds along the way.

Example 56-3. FTPFind.pm

```perl
package FTPFind;
use strict;

use vars qw($VERSION @ISA @EXPORT);
use Exporter;
$VERSION = 1.00;
@ISA = qw (Exporter);
@EXPORT = qw(ftp_finddepth);

sub ftp_finddepth {
    my ($ftp, $callback, $level) = @_;

    # Make a listing of files and/or directories.
    my @files = $ftp->dir or die "ERROR: dir() failed\n";

    foreach my $i (@files) {
        my @items = split(/\s/, $i);
        my $item = $items[$#items];
        my $parent = $ftp->pwd;

        if ($i =~ /^d(.*)/) {
            next if $item =~ /\.\.?$/;          # Skip . and .. if present
            &$callback($level, 1, $item, $parent); # Must be a directory

            # Recursively crawl the subtree under this directory.
            $ftp->cwd($item) or die "ERROR: can't cwd() to $item\n";
            ftp_finddepth($ftp, $callback, $level+1);

            # Restore location in remote tree.
            $ftp->cwd($parent) or die "ERROR: can't cwd() to $parent\n";
        } elsif ($i =~ /^-(.*)/) {
            # It's a file - call the callback.
            &$callback($level, 0, $item, $parent);
        }
    }
}

1;
```

Writing an application to download a file tree is now just a simple matter of writing a process_item callback that mirrors the directory tree and retrieves files, depending on what ftp_finddepth passed it. Example 56-4 shows how to do that.

Example 56-4. mirror_get

```perl
#!/usr/bin/perl -w
# Transfers remote file tree to the local machine.
#     usage: mirror_get [-d -D] host remotedir name password
#         -d  Debug mode - don't actually transfer anything.
#         -D  Turn on Net::FTP debug messages
```

Example 56-4. mirror_get (continued)

```perl
use Getopt::Std;
use Net::FTP;
use FTPFind;
use Cwd;
use File::Path;

getopts("dD");
defined($opt_d) or $opt_d = 0;
defined($opt_D) or $opt_D = 0;

my ($host, $dir, $name, $password) = @ARGV;

defined($host) and defined($dir) and defined($name) and
defined($password) or die "usage: $0 [-D] host remotedir name password";

$ftp = Net::FTP->new($host, Debug => $opt_D ? 1 : 0)
    or die "ERROR: Net::FTP->new() failed\n";

$ftp->login($name, $password) or die "ERROR: login() failed\n";
$ftp->binary;   # Assume binary transfers.

# Go to the starting point in the remote tree.
$ftp->cwd($dir) or die "ERROR: can't cwd() on $dir\n";
my $root = cwd;   # Remember local root directory.
print "DIRECTORY: ", $ftp->pwd, "\n";

ftp_finddepth($ftp, \&process_item, 1);    # Crawl over the tree

$ftp->quit;

sub process_item {
    my ($level, $isdir, $item, $parent) = @_;

    foreach (1..$level) { print "    " }
    if ($isdir) {
        print "DIRECTORY: ",$parent,"/",$item,"\n";
        if (!$opt_d) {
            # Prepend the remote path with a . and hang it
            # off the directory where we started.
            my $path = ".".$parent."/".$item;
            chdir($root)  or die "ERROR: can't chdir() to $root\n";
            mkpath($path) or die "ERROR: can't mkpath() $path\n";
        }
    } else {
        print "FILE: ", $item, "\n";
        if (!$opt_d) {
            chdir($root) or die "ERROR: can't chdir() to $root\n";
            chdir("." . $parent) or die "ERROR: can't chdir() to .$parent\n";
            $ftp->get($item) or die "ERROR: get() failed on $item\n";
        }
    }
}
```

If process_item is called with a directory (as indicated by the $isdir parameter), I want to create a directory in the local filesystem. If process_item is called with a file, I issue an FTP get request to download the file.

Uploading a File (the Simple Case)

Uploading a file is exactly the same as downloading, except you call the Net::FTP get subroutine instead of put.

Uploading a File Tree (the Recursive Case)

You would think that using File::Find's find or finddepth would be the way to iterate over the local file tree. There is one small problem with this approach: find and finddepth report the *full* pathname of the local directories they find. I only want *relative* local pathnames of each directory, so that I can duplicate the relative file subtree on the remote system.

I can get by without a remote mkpath-like capability on the remote system, since I can mirror the local directory to the remote site on the fly as I descend the local tree. I will keep track of my relative location in the local file tree by pushing each directory I find onto the back of a Perl array.

So, leaving File::Find's find and finddepth behind, I'll develop my own finddepth. Longtime users of Perl might remember the old example program called down distributed with Perl 4. My version, called finddepth_gl (shown below), performs a similar function—but more portably, since it doesn't involve invoking a Unix command via the Perl system function. See Example 56-5.

Example 56-5. mirror_put

```
#!/usr/bin/perl -w
# Transfers local file tree to the remote machine.
#     usage: mirror_put [-d -D] host localdir remotedir name password
#          -d  Debug mode - don't actually transfer anything.
#          -D  Turn on Net::FTP debug messages
#
# NOTES
#     remotedir must already exist on the remote server

use Getopt::Std;
use Net::FTP;
use Cwd;

getopts("dD");
defined($opt_d) or $opt_d = 0;
defined($opt_D) or $opt_D = 0;

my ($host, $localdir, $remotedir, $name, $password) = @ARGV;
```

Example 56-5. mirror_put (continued)

```perl
defined($host) and defined($localdir) and defined($remotedir) and
defined($name) and defined($password)
    or die "usage: $0 [-D] host localdir remotedir name password";

$ftp = Net::FTP->new($host, Debug => $opt_D ? 1 : 0)
    or die "ERROR: Net::FTP->new( ) failed\n";

$ftp->login($name, $password) or die "ERROR: login( ) failed\n";

$ftp->binary;       # Assume binary transfers.

# Go to the starting point in the local tree.
chdir($localdir) or die "ERROR: can't cwd( ) to $localdir\n";

# Go to the starting point in the remote tree.
$ftp->cwd($remotedir) or die "ERROR: can't cwd( ) to $remotedir\n";

# Keep track of directory path as separate elements to
# facilitate mirroring of directory paths on remote system.
my @path;

finddepth_gl(\&process_item, 1);     # Crawl over the local tree

$ftp->quit;

sub process_item {
    my ($level, $isdir, $item, $parent) = @_;
    foreach (1..$level) { print "    " }
    if ($isdir) {
        print "DIRECTORY: ",$parent,$item,"\n";
        $ftp->mkdir($parent . $item)
            or die "ERROR: can't mkdir ", $parent, $item, "\n";
    } else {
        print "FILE: ",$item,"\n";
        my $save_remote = $ftp->pwd;
        $ftp->cwd($parent) or die "ERROR: can't cwd( ) to $parent\n";
        $ftp->put($item);
        $ftp->cwd($save_remote) or die "ERROR: can't cwd( ) to $save_remote\n";
    }
}

sub finddepth_gl {
    my ($callback, $level) = @_;

    # Make a listing of files and/or directories.
    my $cwd = cwd;
    opendir(DIR, $cwd) or die "ERROR: can't opendir( ) on $cwd: $!\n";

    my ($item, @list);
    while (defined($item = readdir(DIR))) { push(@list, $item) }
    closedir(DIR);
```

Example 56-5. mirror_put (continued)

```
    foreach $item (@list) {
        next if $item =~ /\.\.?$/;
        my $parent = "";
        foreach my $i (@path) { $parent .= $i . "/" }

        if ( -d $item) {   # It's a directory -- call the callback.
            &$callback($level, 1, $item, $parent);

            # Recursively crawl the subtree under this directory.
            push(@path, $item);

            my $save_local = cwd;
            chdir($item) or die "ERROR: can't chdir() to $item\n";
            finddepth_gl($callback, $level+1);

            # Restore location in local tree.
            chdir($save_local) or die "ERROR: can't chdir() to $save_local\n";
            pop(@path);
        } elsif ( -f $item) {   # It's a file - call the callback.
            &$callback($level, 0, $item, $parent);
        }
    }
}
```

Beware that Net::FTP's `mkdir` will fail if the directory already exists.

Applications

The ability to automate FTP operations relieves a great deal of the tedium of having to manually push and pull files to and from your remote file tree. This is particularly useful for periodic and repetitive tasks such as log file retrieval, or unattended updating of an otherwise static web site.

The mirroring applications provided here are a small sample of what is possible, given a generalized and recursive FTP site traversal mechanism. Such a mechanism allows you the ability to grind through your entire remote file tree. In the case of a web site, this ability is particularly helpful for rooting out missing or orphaned files. Another application is to automatically check and fix the permissions on all the files in your remote tree. Do you remember the last time you had to do *that* by hand?

## CHAPTER 57

DNS Updates with Perl

Jon Drukman

This article talks about the Net::DNS::Update module, and how you can use it to remotely update information on a DNS server. You might do this if you are a DNS administrator wanting to balance a load between a range of machines, or if you are the owner of a domain and want to programmatically update the information in that domain even though you don't have access to the DNS server's configuration files.

When this article was written, BIND 8 was the most recent version. BIND 9 is now available; the examples in this article will work with both versions.

DNS Basics

Whenever you send mail or visit a web site, your computer has to know how to reach a remote computer. In particular, it has to translate a name like "perl.com" to its Internet address, 199.45.135.9. Only when that address is known can your mail program send mail to *webmaster@perl.com* and your web browser display *http://www.perl.com/CPAN/*.

The act of translating hostnames to Internet addresses is called *name resolution*, and the infrastructure that supports it is the Domain Name System, or DNS. In this article, I'll demonstrate how to access some of the new features of the Berkeley Internet Name Daemon (BIND) Version 8 with the Net::DNS modules available on CPAN. In particular, I'll focus on Net::DNS::Update, which allows you to change the information stored in a nameserver on the fly. You could use this technique to take a crashed box in a server farm out of rotation, manage PPP or DHCP clients, or perform load balancing.

To get the most out of this article you should have a decent knowledge of the workings of DNS and BIND, a BIND Version 8 nameserver, and a zone to play around with. A *zone* is similar to a domain such as `perl.com`, but it could also refer to a subdomain such as `test.perl.com`.

A full description of DNS is beyond the scope of this article. For those who want the full story, I highly recommend Albitz & Liu's *DNS & Bind* (O'Reilly). While it is possible that the code examples will work with other RFC 2136-compliant nameservers, I haven't tested anything other than BIND 8 running on Unix.

DNS Servers

BIND, described at *http://www.isc.org/bind.html*, is the most popular nameserver. The current BIND implementation, BIND 8, is maintained by the Internet Software Consortium (ISC), and supports a feature called *dynamic update*; see *http://www.isi. edu/in-notes/rfc2136.txt* for the low-level description of the protocol. BIND 8 has been in production since May 1997, so you shouldn't fear upgrading.

One way to tell if your system is running BIND 8 is to look at how your named gets started. If it uses a file called *named.conf*, it is Version 8. The older model, Version 4, which is still quite common, uses *named.boot*. You could also look at the *named* log messages when it starts up. Mine looks like this:

```
Dec 16 11:41:09 hudsucker named[14993]: starting.  named 8.1.2 Thu
    Jan  8 12:47:42 PST 1998  jsd@hudsucker.gamespot.com:/usr/home/jsd/
                                        build/bind/src/bin/named
```

If your system uses Version 4, you should upgrade to version 8, since that's the only actively maintained and developed version. BIND 4 has been deprecated by the ISC.

Dynamic Update

In the old days, *zone files* (the files that map IP addresses to names and vice versa) were fairly static. You'd set up a machine, give it an address, and that was the end of the story. Most machines on the net were mainframes then, so there was no compelling need for a flexible, dynamic protocol.

In this day of dialup PPP, DHCP, and server farms, things are clearly different. We need a way to dynamically update entries in a zone file on the fly. Enter RFC 2136 and Net::DNS::Update.

Net::DNS is a collection of object-oriented modules designed to interface with nameservers. The author, Michael Fuhr, claims they're slow, but I've never encountered any debilitating speed problems. Usually there's more than enough latency in your network to offset any problems with script speed.

Setting Up Your Nameserver

Before you can start writing code, you must configure your nameserver to accept dynamic updates. I recommend creating a separate zone for dynamic updates, because BIND writes out the zone file when it changes, and it writes it out in a compact form without any formatting and comments you might have put in the original.

Say your zone is test.com and you want to create dyn.test.com to hold the dynamic updates. Put the following lines in your *named.conf* file:

```
zone "dyn.test.com" {
  type master;
  file "db.dyn.test.com";
  allow-update { 10.0.0.0/24; };
};
```

There are several salient features in this entry. First, the zone name, which is self-evident. The type can be either master or slave. In this case, you are authoritative for test.com and all its subdomains, so you are the master.

The filename can be whatever you want; it is created in the directory specified in the options section of your configuration file. The really important feature is the allow-update directive. Without this, the nameserver rejects all updates for the zone. I have specified the hosts in the IP/Netmask form. The number after the slash is the number of "one" bits in the netmask, counted from the left hand side. So, rendering the above in binary would give you:

```
00001010 00000000 00000000 00000000   host address
11111111 11111111 11111111 00000000   netmask
```

In English, this means that any IP address starting with 10.0.0 is allowed to update the zone.

If this discussion of host addresses and netmasks has you dizzy, don't worry. You aren't the first to be perplexed. However, I recommend that you spend some time learning about them, because if you deal with DNS or other Internet protocols on a regular basis, you will undoubtedly encounter them over and over again.

Delegating the Zone

Now that you have created a new zone, you need to tell your nameserver where to get information on it. In the test.com zone file, add the following line:

```
dyn IN NS nameserver.test.com
```

This assumes that test.com is already being served by nameserver.test.com and that you are creating dyn.test.com on the same machine. Now when people ask nameserver.test.com about dyn.test.com, it sends them a response that points right back at the same machine. Obviously, that's redundant in this case, but remember that one of the key features of DNS is its distributed nature—you could just have easily directed queries about dyn.test.com to a machine on the other side of the world. This process is known as *delegation*.

Incidentally, you can declare yourself authoritative for any zone, even if you actually aren't. What happens in this situation is that any clients using your nameserver for resolution will take whatever it says as gospel, whereas the rest of the net will get different information from the real authoritative nameservers. This could be extremely confusing, so if you are unsure whether you are authoritative for a zone, check with the appropriate registry, or use dig to find the answer. dig is invaluable for diagnosing DNS problems and is bundled with the BIND package.

```
$ dig test.com

; <<>> DiG 2.2 <<>> test.com
;; res options: init recurs defnam dnsrch
```

```
;; got answer:
;; ->> HEADER <<- opcode: QUERY, status: NOERROR, id: 6
;; flags: qr rd ra; Ques: 1, Ans: 1, Auth: 2, Addit: 2
;; QUESTIONS:
;;      test.com, type = A, class = IN

;; ANSWERS:
test.com.        3568     A      207.206.9.99

;; AUTHORITY RECORDS:
test.com.        3571     NS     mercury.xa.com.
test.com.        3571     NS     grail.BOOKS.com.
```

The real-world test.com is served by mercury.xa.com and grail.books.com. Replies coming from any other sources are *nonauthoritative*. The reverse of this situation, where a server is designated authoritative but is not responding authoritatively for a request, is called a *lame delegation*. If you run named with the default logging levels, you will see plenty of lame delegation warning messages!

You're still not done setting up. In the example below, you'll dynamically change the address of ftp.test.com. To avoid messing up the test.com zone, you're really going to change ftp.dyn.test.com, and to do that, you need to make an alias that maps ftp.dyn.test.com to ftp.test.com. In DNS jargon, such an alias is called a CNAME, which means "canonical name."

So put the following line in the test.com zone file:

```
ftp IN CNAME ftp.dyn.test.com.
```

It's time to restart the nameserver. I recommend using the ndc restart command. (See your BIND documentation for details.)

Now that you've configured a nameserver and delegated the zone, you can actually get down to writing some Perl code!

Using Net::DNS::Update

For this example, let's imagine that you have two FTP servers, ftp1.test.com and ftp2.test.com, both containing the same content. Their IP addresses are 10.0.0.1 and 10.0.0.2, respectively. You want users who come to ftp.test.com to end up on either of those machines, and you want the load distributed evenly between them. (Note that you don't need a script like this to achieve a round-robin distribution. That functionality is already built into BIND; this example is meant to be instructive rather than practical.)

Here's the Perl script:

```
1  use strict;
2  use Net::DNS;
3
```

```
 4  while (1) {
 5    set_dns('10.0.0.1');
 6    sleep 300;
 7    set_dns('10.0.0.2');
 8    sleep 300;
 9  }
10
11  sub set_dns {
12    my $new_ip=shift;
13    my $update = new Net::DNS::Update('dyn.test.com');
14        $update->push('update', rr_del('ftp.dyn.test.com'));
15        $update->push('update', rr_add("ftp.dyn.test.com 1800 A $new_ip"));
16
17    my $res = new Net::DNS::Resolver;
18        $res->nameservers('nameserver.test.com');
19    my $reply = $res->send($update);
20    if (defined $reply) {
21      if ($reply->header->rcode ne "NOERROR") {
22        print $reply->header->rcode,"\n";
23      } else {
24        print "Update to $new_ip succeeded!\n";
25      }
26    } else {
27      print 'Update failed: ', $res->errorstring, "\n";
28    }
29  }
```

In lines 4–8, an infinite loop changes the IP address and sleeps for five minutes. The interesting work occurs inside the *set_dns* subroutine. Line 12 grabs the IP address that you're going to associate with ftp.dyn.test.com, and creates a new Net::DNS:: Update object in line 13. Lines 14 and 15 push data into the update packet.

Update packets are processed atomically—once the nameserver determines that you are allowed to initiate your change, all of the requests in your packet are serviced in order, with no possibility of any other requestor changing data out from under you while your changes are being made. So, in this packet, you have a request to delete the current RR (resource record) set for ftp.dyn.test.com, followed by an immediate request to insert a new RR for ftp.dyn.test.com. The format of the string passed to rr_add is a little odd, but should be familiar to anyone who's worked with zone files. The first field is the hostname, of course. The second field is the *time-to-live* for the entry, expressed in seconds. This one says that this record is valid for 300 seconds (5 minutes), at which point any nameserver caching it should throw it out and request a new one from another nameserver. (Unfortunately the DNS resolver client in Windows is broken, and often ignores the timeouts. Sometimes it appears that your machine is fixated on a given IP address; the only way to get it to look up the new information is to reboot it.)

Now you have a nice packet of data. Net::DNS::Update doesn't actually do anything with the data, besides put it in a format that a nameserver recognizes. You have to bring in Net::DNS::Resolver. This is a somewhat misleading name, with roots in history. As I mentioned earlier, it used to be that nameservers were largely read-only. Clients that talked to DNS servers were known as *resolvers*, since resolving names to IP addresses was their exclusive function. Today, DNS clients are still called "resolvers," even though they can read and write.

In line 17, the resolver object is created, and line 18 tells it that the nameserver it will talk to is nameserver.test.com. Line 19 is where all the magic happens. The send method sends your carefully crafted update packet off to the nameserver specified in the resolver object.

At this point, you should check your nameserver log files to see if there are any messages about your action. A common mistake, such as not setting the permissions in named.conf properly, results in an error message like this:

```
Jan  7 10:29:38 ns1 named[12691]: unapproved update from
                            [205.216.163.199].3251 for dyn.test.com
```

If you don't see any errors, check the zone file directory for a file named *dyn.test.com. log*. This contains a log of your update requests, in a format like this:

```
[DYNAMIC_UPDATE] id 84 from [205.216.163.199].1541 at 985837961:
zone:   origin dyn.test.com class IN serial 199817937
update: {delete} ftp.dyn.test.com. IN
update: {add} ftp.dyn.test.com. 1800 IN A 10.0.0.1
```

Lines 20–28 do some error checking on the response. If the update fails because the nameserver is unavailable or some other network-related error occurred, $reply is undefined, and an error message is available in $res->errorstring. On the other hand, if the nameserver accepts the packet, it puts a cryptic shorthand message indicating the status of the request in $reply->header->rcode. For example, NOERROR means the update was accepted and performed. Some other common return codes are listed below in Table 57-1.

Table 57-1. Common nameserver return codes

Return code	Meaning
NOTAUTH	This nameserver is not authoritative for the zone you requested.
REFUSED	The nameserver refused your request for security reasons. (Your IP address is probably not listed in *named.conf*.)
NOTZONE	A name in the update packet does not exist in the target zone.

At this point, your IP change has taken effect. Remember that due to the distributed nature of DNS, your change may not be instantly visible everywhere. Any client that previously looked up ftp.test.com will hang on to the old response until it expires, at which point it will request a new one.

Paths for Futher Exploration

As I mentioned, the above script is merely an example, in that each IP address is active for only five minutes. Although round-robin is quite useful as a basic method of load balancing, what happens when ftp1 crashes, or is taken down for routine maintenance? When you put it back up, it has zero users, but even though ftp2 has many users, new connections are still assigned in a round-robin fashion. You need a way to intelligently know how many connections are active and reassign the IP address to the least-loaded machine. If you alter the while loop at the top of the example program to query each machine and determine its load, you can then intelligently decide whether to change the IP address to ftp1.

As you've seen, the basics of dynamic updates are easy to learn and implement. Using this framework, you could write an application that queries several machines to find out which one is best able to service new requests, or monitor a pool of machines and take a crashed box out of rotation. Some other ideas include having name.mydomain.com as your laptop no matter how it's connected, providing aliases for servers on a network with free resources (freedisk.domain.com, freecpu.domain.com, freeram.domain.com), or using mod_perl to configure Apache and the DNS server from one virtual host configuration file.

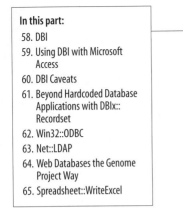

PART VII

Databases

In recent years, Perl has become an increasingly popular tool for database administrators—particularly those who can't afford to have their programs work with only one database system. The reason is Perl's Database Interface, or DBI. This section features three DBI articles, beginning with an article by DBI creator Tim Bunce and guru Alligator Descartes (both authors of O'Reilly's *Programming the Perl DBI*), who introduce DBI.

From there, Craig McElwee demonstrates how to use DBI with Microsoft Access, and Thomas Akin shows pitfalls that sometimes trip novices up when learning DBI. Next, Terrence Brannon stirs the pot with an article arguing that DBI isn't ideal for all database applications, expounding the virtues of his DBIx::Recordset alternative. Joe Casadonte then shows how to use the Win32::ODBC module to manipulate ODBC databases in *Win32::ODBC*; Tim Bunce pops in at the end of the article with a counterpoint comparing and contrasting Win32::ODBC to DBI.

Next, Joe Johnston shows how to use the Net::LDAP module to manipulate Lightweight Directory Access Protocol servers, which contain hierarchies of frequently-accessed but infrequently-updated information, such as address books. Lincoln Stein returns with an article on how the Human Genome Project uses web-enabled databases, and John McNamara closes out the section with an article showing how to create Excel files from Perl (and some tips for reading them, too).

## CHAPTER 58

DBI

Alligator Descartes and Tim Bunce

DBI, the Database Interface for Perl, is an ongoing effort to provide a robust interface for database connectivity that insulates the programmer from the variability of different database systems. With the explosion in popularity of Perl as the de rigeur language for web programming, a simple and standard interface to databases is imperative.

The Architecture of DBI

The architecture of DBI (pictured in Figure 58-1) is elegant. We are channelled toward the solution by the very concept of the interface that we are trying to define. As usual, Perl helps us along by providing powerful syntactic constructs and regular expressions that facilitate data processing on the scale required by large database applications.

The DBI *interface* is the term used to describe both the interface specification—the methods used to build programs—and the software modules that make this possible. We'll first take a look at why you should be using DBI, and then describe the modular structure of DBI and its interaction with Perl. Finally, we'll show you some sample DBI code.

Why DBI?

Database programming, as you will learn after you've programmed or administered a few different databases, is pretty much all the same. Hence DBI. The fundamental processes involved in doing anything with a database are pretty similar right across the board: connecting to and disconnecting from the database, storing and retrieving data, and opening and closing *cursors* (data structures identifying a particular set of rows in a database).

Here is the typical order in which this happens:

1. Load DBI
2. Connect to database, loading the required driver (DBD)

3. Open a cursor containing a SQL statement

4. Fetch the results

5. Close the cursor

6. Disconnect from the database

7. Exit

There are differences between each database engine, such as the data types of fields retrieved, precision, extra non-ANSI–compliant features and so on, but their basic operations are the same from system to system. DBI provides a unified layer so that people can write portable code while still having access to the nonstandard features as well.

Once we've fetched some data from the database, what next? In general, DBI simply provides your data as scalar variables, which you can then manipulate as you would any other scalar.

Another feature is the ability to connect to more than one database simultaneously from within the same Perl program—even (dare we say it?) to databases from different vendors. We can connect to an Oracle and a mSQL and an Informix database all at the same time. "What's the point in that?" you cry. Well, say we have a corporate Oracle database, and we want to display some of its data on the web. Oracle via CGI can be slow due to Oracle's internal login procedures, so we've decided to use mSQL as well.

Option one is to write a program that runs SQL scripts and dumps the data to a flat file, perhaps comma-separated, which another program then reads and loads into the mSQL database. This is hard work.

Option two is to write a single Perl script that connects simultaneously to both the Oracle and the mSQL databases, reads the data from Oracle, and puts it into mSQL transparently. Change Oracle to Informix and we won't need to alter a thing.

Think about that the next time you're writing two separate programs in C with different vendor precompilers on separate platforms. Then think about the paradise of cross-platform portability and cross-database connectivity. It makes sense.

DBI is a living organism and, coupled with Perl's current popularity for CGI scripting language and rapid development, will become a more important factor in decisions to use Perl as a "serious" programming language. Similarities have been drawn between DBI and ODBC that have led to questions of "Why do we need DBI?" (ODBC is discussed in the article *Win32::ODBC* later in this book.) For starters, DBI is simpler than ODBC, it runs on more platforms, and it supports more drivers—not just every ODBC driver, but also powerful, Perl-specific drivers like DBD::AnyData, DBD::Chart, and DBD::Proxy. And if that doesn't convince you, it's also faster.

Databases are engineered to store and retrieve data, whether they are Object Database Management Systems (ODBMS) or the more common Relational Database Management Systems (RDBMS). Unix was originally blessed with simple file-based "databases," namely the dbm system. dbm lets you store data in files, and retrieve that data quickly. However, it also has two notable drawbacks:

File locking
> Most dbm systems do not allow particularly robust file locking capabilities, nor any capability for correcting problems arising from simultaneous writes.

Arbitrary data structures
> Most dbm systems only allow a single fixed data structure: key-value pairs. That value could be a complex object, such as a struct, but the key had to be unique. This was a significant limitation of dbm systems.

However, most dbm systems still provide a useful function for users with simple datasets and limited resources, since they're fast, robust, and extremely well-tested. Perl modules to access dbm systems have now been integrated into the core Perl distribution via the AnyDBM_File module.

The Modules

Perl has a powerful mechanism to plug external modules into the Perl interpreter. This mechanism is realized by actually compiling and linking the module into the Perl interpreter, or by *dynaloading* (dynamically loading) the module into a running interpreter only when needed; see the article *Autoloading Perl Code* earlier in this book for details. This notion of separable modules is central to the philosophy of both Perl and DBI.

DBI essentially acts as a conduit for the DBD (Database Driver) modules. The DBDs all implement the methods defined in DBI (e.g., connect), but in a database-specific way. To clarify this somewhat: since you, the DBI user, wish to use a completely database-independent programming layer, *some* part of the system must know how to execute the database-dependent code. That's what the DBD does. Application programmers need never know the DBD is there! All they will be aware of is the database-independent methods defined by DBI. The DBD code is written and maintained by many volunteers and now covers all major database systems, including Oracle, MySQL, PostgreSQL, Informix, DB2, mSQL, Ingres, and Sybase. The web pages listed at the end of this article contain more detailed and up-to-date information about the state of the different DBDs and the DBI as a whole.

Before we even start looking at how to use DBI, you need to download and install the modules. You will *always* need the DBI module itself, as well as one of the DBD modules for whichever database you have installed. You can download DBI and the DBD modules from the CPAN.

Next, you need to inform the Perl interpreter that, hey, now would be a good time to load the DBI module in. This always happens before any other DBI work, such as loading one of the database vendor-specific libraries, or attempting to connect to a database. Now, this seems quite obvious, but if we had a dollar for each time...

```
#!/usr/bin/perl -w

use DBI;
```

That's it! Honest. If you don't believe us, try this (assuming you're running a Bourne-compatible shell):

```
$ PERL_DL_DEBUG=2 perl -e 'use DBI'
DynaLoader.pm loaded (/usr/local/lib/perl5/i486-linux/5.003
 /usr/local/lib/perl5 /usr/local/lib/perl5/site_perl/i486-linux
 /usr/local/lib/perl5/site_perl . /usr/local/lib /usr/local/lib /lib
 /usr/lib) DynaLoader::bootstrap for DBI (auto/DBI/DBI.so)
```

That simple statement dynamically loads the shared library containing the DBI code into the interpreter, and initializes the DBI interface, which means we can now start using DBI in anger.

If you refer to Figure 58-1, you can clearly see that all access to the databases are marshalled, or funnelled, through the DBI module. Therefore, we need to load the DBDs we want to use.

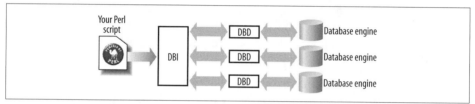

Figure 58-1. The DBI architecture

To simplify matters, DBI hides the details of loading the drivers. As you connect to a database with DBI->connect, DBI makes sure an appropriate driver is loaded and passes on the request to it. For example, this loads the DBI driver and then the mSQL driver (since it's not already loaded) and then attempts a connection to the specified database:

```
#!/usr/bin/perl -w

use DBI;

$dbh = DBI->connect( 'dbi:mSQL:connection_string', 'username', 'password' );

die "Can't connect to database: $DBI::errstr\n" unless $dbh;
```

This call returns a *database handle*, which we'll see more of later. To use this method for other DBDs, simply change the first argument to match your database engine. If not specified, the value of the DBI_DSN environment variable will be used instead.

The connect method will croak if the driver can't be installed. Otherwise, it'll return undef on any other error and $DBI::errstr will contain an error message. The available_drivers method returns a list of DBI drivers currently installed. Specific drivers can be loaded using the install_driver method.

Handles

Handles are Perl objects returned by various DBI methods which the programmer can use to access data at various abstracted layers. The handles used by DBI are listed below and can be seen in Figure 58-2.

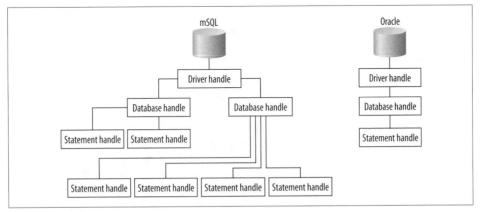

Figure 58-2. DBI handles

Driver handles
> A driver handle, or *drh*, encapsulates the database driver itself. The driver handle does *not* connect you to a database, nor does it let you perform any database operations. It merely acts as a conduit between the DBI and the low-level database API calls. Generally, you won't need to deal with driver handles, since DBI does that for you.

Database handles
> A database handle, or *dbh*, encapsulates a single connection to a given database via a driver handle. There can be any number of database handles per driver handle. For example, if you have a script that copies data from one database to another where both databases are mSQL, then you will have one driver handle but two database handles. In the earlier scenario with a mSQL database and an Oracle database, you would have two driver handles, each with a single database handle.

Statement handles
> A statement handle, or *sth*, encapsulates a command issued to a database via a database handle. As with database handles, there can be any number of statement handles per database handle—or at least as many as the vendor permits.

For example, if you have two tables in your database, one containing data and the other containing a stale copy of the data, and you have a program that refreshes the stale copy from the original, you could use two statement handles, one to SELECT the data from the first table, the second to UPDATE the data in the other table. The DBI provides methods to fetch and store data without having to prepare statement handles, but using statement handles is generally faster. Cursors are simply statement handles for SELECT statements.

Resources

Several resources dedicated to DBI are available in books, on the Web, on mailing lists, and via anonymous FTP.

Books

It's rather self serving, but we have to point out that there's an entire book dedicated to DBI: O'Reilly's *Programming the Perl DBI* by both of us.

Web

The DBI WWW pages are located at *http://dbi.perl.org/* and should be consulted at all opportunities. The FAQ, DBI specification and pointers to documentation sources including the mailing list archives are there, among other things. The modules are also available via the web pages through CPAN.

Mailing lists

There are three mailing lists related to DBI: dbi-users for general help and support, dbi-dev for developers to discuss ideas and ongoing development, and dbi-announce for announcements of new driver releases and so on. We strongly recommend that everyone subscribe to dbi-announce; it's moderated and has very little traffic. Most people should also subscribe to dbi-users, at least for a while. To join the lists, visit *http://lists.perl.org* or send email to *<listname>-help@perl.org*.

The dbi-users mailing list provides good support. The DBI and assorted drivers are in widespread use around the world, often in critical applications.

FTP

The DBI modules and drivers are available via anonymous FTP at *ftp://ftp.cpan.org/pub/CPAN/modules/by-category/07_Database_Interfaces/*.

Sample Code

We now present some sample code using the DBI interface. The parameters to the script, which are passed to the connect method, will vary depending on the database driver being used.

Example 58-1 shows how to connect to and disconnect from a database with DBI; Example 58-2 shows how to extract data from a database, and Example 58-3 shows how to execute immediate statements.

Example 58-1. Basic connection and disconnection

```perl
#!/usr/bin/perl -w
#
# (c)1996 Alligator Descartes <descarte@hermetica.com>
# inout.pl: Connects and disconnects from a database
use DBI;

die "Usage: inout.pl DSN DbUser DbPassword\n" unless @ARGV == 3;

# Create new database handle. If we can't connect, die().
$dbh = DBI->connect( @ARGV ) or die "Can't connect(@ARGV): $DBI::errstr\n";

$dbh->disconnect or die "Error disconnecting from database: $DBI::errstr\n";
exit;
```

Example 58-2. Selecting data from a database

```perl
#!/usr/bin/perl -w
#
# (c)1996 Alligator Descartes <descarte@hermetica.com>
#
# select.pl: Connects to a database called 'test' on
# a given database, then SELECTs some basic data out
# in array and list forms

use DBI;

die "Usage: select.pl DSN DbUser DbPassword\n" unless @ARGV == 3;

# Create new database handle. Use RaiseError to manage errors for us.
$dbh = DBI->connect( $ARGV[0], $ARGV[1], $ARGV[2], { RaiseError => 1 } );

# Prepare the statement for execution
$sth = $dbh->prepare(q{ SELECT id, name FROM table });

# Execute the statement at the database level
$sth->execute;

# Fetch the rows back from the SELECT statement
while ( @row = $sth->fetchrow_array ) {
    print "Row returned: @row\n";
}

# Re-execute the statement to bring the rows back again
$sth->execute;

# Fetch the data back into separate variables this time
while ( ( $id, $name ) = $sth->fetchrow ) {
    print "ID: $id\tName: $name\n";
}

# Disconnect from the database
$dbh->disconnect;
exit;
```

Example 58-3. Executing immediate statements

```perl
#!/usr/bin/perl -w
#
# (c)1996 Alligator Descartes <descarte@hermetica.com>
#
# execute.pl: Connects to a database called 'test' on a
# given database, then EXECUTEs an update # statement.
# This is non-cursorial, so do() is used.

use DBI;

die "Usage: execute.pl DSN DbUser DbPassword\n" unless @ARGV == 3;

# Create new database handle. Use RaiseError to manage errors for us.
$dbh = DBI->connect( $ARGV[0], $ARGV[1], $ARGV[2], { RaiseError => 1 } );

# Execute the statement immediately
$rows = $dbh->do(q{ UPDATE table
                    SET name = 'Alligator Descartes'
                    WHERE id = 1 });

print "Updated $rows rows.\n";

# Disconnect from the database
$dbh->disconnect;
exit;
```

## CHAPTER 59

Using DBI with Microsoft Access

Craig McElwee

The thing about magicians is that they do some rather amazing things and make it look easy. You *know* it's not really magic, but without a key secret or two, there is simply no way you can manage the same feat. The same can be said for putting together a little SQL-based web application on Windows; seeing the pros do it in a few paragraphs of documentation makes it look easy, then you try it yourself and it's no-go.

I once faced this situation. I considered myself a competent Perl programmer who simply hadn't had yet had the need for a SQL (Structured Query Language) database. I knew I eventually would, but I'd survived with tied hashes and CSV files until then.

CSV files

A CSV (Comma-Separated Values) file is simply a text file with lines containing data separated by commas, like this: `Johannes,Smythe,505 Oyster Street,555-1234`. This is a good method of saving data in "flat file" (that is, plain old text file) databases, since each line is a record that can be read by a Perl script, and the data extracted by splitting on the commas. Assuming the above line is in a file called *addresses.txt*, you could do something like this:

```
open(IN, "<addresses.txt");

while($line = <IN>) {
    ($first, $last, $address, $phone) = split /,/, $line;
    ...mangle data to heart's content...
}
```

If there are already commas in your data, this won't work; you'll have to either quote the items that have commas in the data, or use a different delimiter, such as the pipe symbol ("|"). There is even a DBI::DBD for CSV files, so you could start writing scripts with DBI now, and when you need a "real" database, migrating the scripts will be as easy as changing one line in your program.

The turning point came after I had put together a small web application at work: a customer address book with search capabilities. I had combined several databases of customer info into one CSV file (they were actually pipes and not commas, but no one seems comfortable with my calling it a PSV file), one record per line.

The application consisted of three HTML pages. One was a frameset, one was a "welcome to this app" page, and the last was a menu bar with several buttons to call CGI scripts that generated the content pages. One of the buttons, LIST ALL, called a CGI script that read through the CSV file one line at a time, pulling out each customer name and putting it into an array to be sorted. The user could then click on a customer name and be shown that customer's full contact information, formatted to resemble a Rolodex card.

There was also a text box with a search button activating a CGI script, which displayed the Rolodex cards matching the search keyword. On each card was a MODIFY button, which redisplayed the Rolodex card with each field in a text box so it could be edited and saved. Finally, there was a NEW button to add a new customer. Yes, it was a very sophisticated web application, now known as SupportNet (no patents pending).

My manager called me in one day and, as he was wont to do, discussed a few features he wanted my application to have. He wanted to add "a few more" functions to each card to help our support people be more productive. Click a button and an email window would pop open with the customer's email address already in the TO field. Click a different button and Microsoft Word would open up with a partially written letter. Click a button and a composition window would pop up to let you make notes about the customer's problem. A button that would autodial the phone. Oh, and each and every above action should be journaled, one journal per Rolodex card, with the action, date, time, and who did what. And the journals would have to be searchable, able to be sorted on different values, and each item listed would be hyperlinked to the actual item for perusal. I was given the standard in-house development budget: $0 and a gig of disk space on an NT server. He asked how long it would take; I said I'd get back to him and went off to sketch out the design.

I figured most of these tasks wouldn't be difficult at all. Cookies would keep track of what each support person did. Email and note composition would be achieved with a new browser window and an appropriately formatted form. I was pretty sure I had seen something about using Perl and OLE to manipulate Word and dial phones. The stumbling blocks I saw were intertwined: how to construct the journals, and that CSV file.

There were several schemes to keep all the client files centrally located and track who they belonged to. Most of these seemed like workarounds to cope with the CSV file, which also had inherent problems with record locking since the file had to be manipulated by multiple users simultaneously. It quickly became obvious that I should let a proper database do the work; the CSV file had to go.

Let me qualify "proper database." I had to use Microsoft Access—that's what was already installed and all my budget would allow. Before I added any new features, I wanted to convert the CSV file to Access and prove it still worked. Essentially my conversion task list looked like this:

- Put the data into the database: convert the CSV file to Access.
- Get the data out of the database: modify scripts to connect to database and then use SQL `SELECT` statements instead of `while(<INFILE>)` to retrieve data.

I would have to create a new database, but I had already discovered that CSV files— even my pipe-delimited ones—could be imported into Access with little difficulty. Here are the steps to take. Open Access, select File → New Database and from the resulting window, select Blank Database and click OK. After choosing a location for the database, feed it Select File → Get External Data → Import First, change the select box labeled "Files of type" to "Text Files." (If you only have Microsoft Access and ODBC Databases available as choices, then follow the message below ("Not all file types are installed by default") and run Office Setup to add all the data access options, which makes "Text Files" available. This is painless and takes less than a minute to do.

Now just change to the directory where your CSV file is and double-click it. You should be presented with an Import Text Wizard window, in the middle of which are the first several lines of your CSV file. If Fixed Width is selected (the default), click on the Delimited radio button and click Next. In "Choose the delimiter" click Other and fill in your delimiter. If your delimiter is a tab, semicolon, comma, or space, then by all means click that radio button. The first few lines of your CSV file should now be displayed with lines separating the data. Each column represents a field, and each row a record, in your database table. You're almost there—click Next.

Your next choice is to import this data as a new or existing table. This is rather self-evident, but if you are not sure, choose New and click Next. Now give names to all the fields; click in a column to highlight it, and fill in a field name at the top. Anything will do, but I recommend keeping field names short and without spaces—it will save headaches later when you are debugging Perl scripts with SQL statements inside. When you are done, click Next and on the next screen, let Access add a Primary Key field and click Next again. Enter a name for your table, and click Finish. You can quit now or double-click on the table icon to see a spreadsheet view of your database table. You can add, delete, or edit data as you will. When you are done, save your database and close Access.

Back to Perl: for getting the data out, I had read about DBI (Perl's Database Interface) in TPJ. It had an ODBC database driver, and Access was ODBC compliant (or so I hoped, since Microsoft developed ODBC and it stands for Open Database Connectivity). I figured the script conversion from flat-file to SQL would be a piece of cake: just toss in a few Perl modules and add a few lines of code and presto! I look like a genius.

I started looking closely at the articles and documentation. I managed to install DBI and DBD::ODBC without incident; so far so good. In my head, my test script went like this: open a connection to the database, for every record in the table print the record to screen, close the database. I started to write it.

I had a lot of documentation at hand: the Camel, Panther, and Ram books, Perl Journals with DBI articles, and pods and myriad other information from the Internet. While being chock full of useful information, most of these sources made the same assumptions. Specifically, people tended to say things like "enter the connection string" and "DSN" assuming I knew what these were. I didn't.

Eventually, I realized that I needed an Access ODBC driver installed. I couldn't believe it wasn't automatically installed in the standard Microsoft "ActiveBloat" installation methodology. After the standard exploration through the nether regions of Microsoft's site, I found the download: *http://www.microsoft.com/data/download/ mdacfull.exe*. Yes, there is other stuff in this installation, but there seems to be no way to get just the ODBC driver without a bunch of unneeded stuff.

Once I had it, installation was a snap. If you are following along, the procedure is:

1. Double-click on `mdacfull.exe`.
   If you forgot where you downloaded it, type `dir /s \mdacfull.exe` at a DOS prompt).

2. Click Yes to accept Microsoft's license statement.

3. Click Continue to go forward with the installation.

4. At this point Setup looks for installed components and asks whether you want a Complete or Custom installation. Complete is fine, automatically installing everything. If you would prefer a more discriminating install, choose Custom. To do what's mentioned in this article you only need three components: ODBC, OLE DB, and the ODBC driver for Microsoft Access. You can save yourself about two megabytes of disk space by unchecking the other components.

5. Setup checks for sufficient disk space, copies files to your system, and presents a dialog box informing you that setup was completed successfully. Click OK and you're done.

Still, my simple test script didn't work:

```
'Database connection not made: [Microsoft][ODBC Driver Manager]
 Data source name not found and no default driver specified
 (SQL-IM002)(DBD: db_login/SQLConnect err=-1) at test.pl line 14.'
```

Errors like this abounded. Luckily, I happened to decide that I didn't like the editor I was using and downloaded and installed a different one from the net. I went to the control panel to remove the old one. And there I saw the 32 bit ODBC applet, which I opened (Figure 59-1), and which had tabs saying User DSN, System DSN, and File DSN. Jackpot! (DSN stands for Data Source Name, and is akin to using a filehandle in your scripts to reference a file. Just think of it as a database handle.)

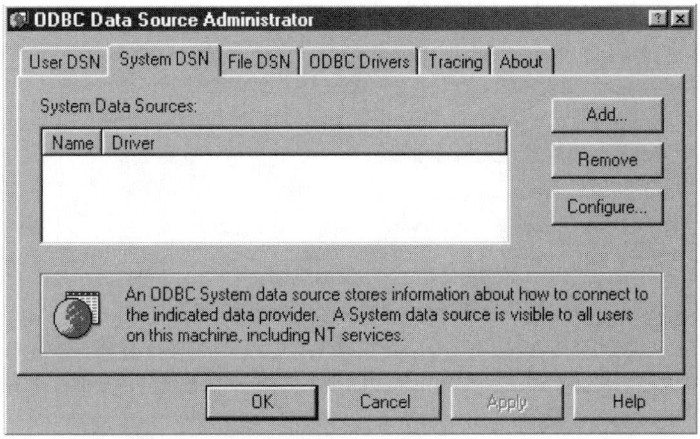

Figure 59-1. ODBC Access setup screen

You want to use System DSN since it allows access to your database by other users and system services. Click the Add button, select "Microsoft Access Driver (*.mdb)" from the displayed list, and click Finish. The "ODBC Microsoft Access 97 Setup" screen will be displayed (Figure 59-2). For DSN, put in anything you like, but keep it short and sweet since you will use this in every script. Fill in the Description field if you like. In the Database section, click Select and use the Explorer-like interface to find and select your database file. Then click OK. If you would like to add a user-name and password, click Advanced and enter it in the appropriate fields (Figure 59-3). Now click OK and you should see your database listed under the System DSN tab (Figure 59-4). Click OK to continue.

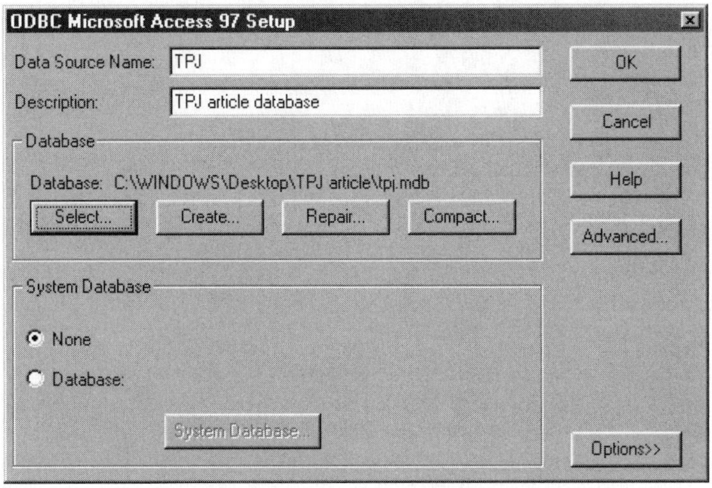

Figure 59-2. Advanced ODBC setup options

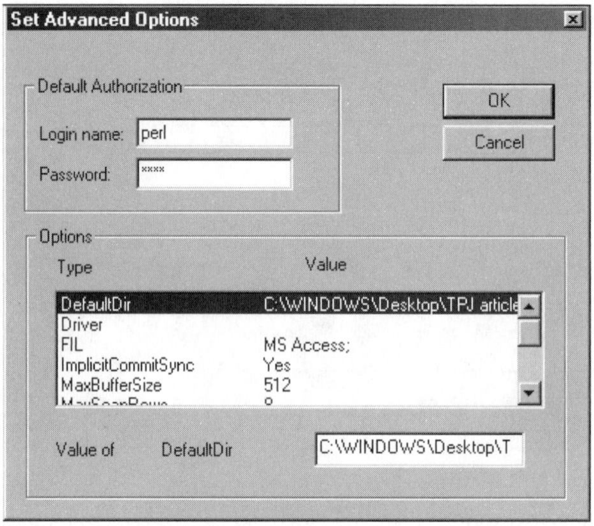

Figure 59-3. Adding a username and password

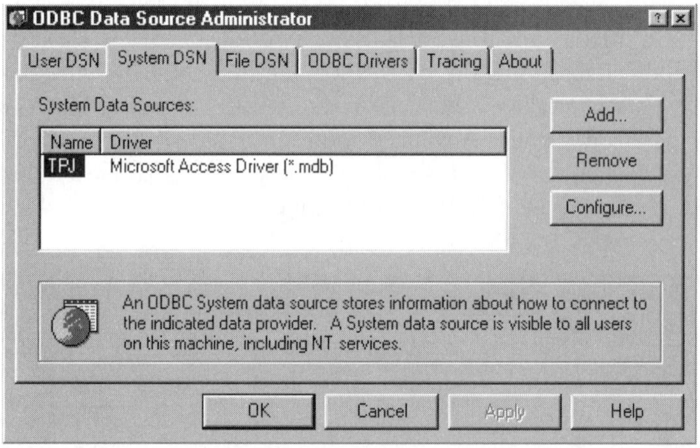

Figure 59-4. The System DSN tab

That mystery solved, it only took a minute to get a valid connection string, and presto—database output. The test script was simply this:

```perl
#!/usr/bin/perl

use DBI;

$dsn  = 'TPJ';        # Configure $dsn, $user, and $pass in...
$user = 'perl';       # ...Control Panel/32bit ODBC
$pass = 'lerp';
$dbd  = 'ODBC';       # A must if using ODBC.
```

```perl
# Connect to the database
$dbh = DBI->connect("dbi:$dbd:$dsn", $user, $pass, {RaiseError => 1});

# Prepare the statement for execution (the table is named "Rolodex")
$stmt = $dbh->prepare(" SELECT * FROM Rolodex " );

$stmt->execute;

# Print out first 5 records, each field on a line
for (1..5) {
    @record = $stmt->fetchrow_array( );
    print "\n\n\nRECORD:\n";
    foreach $field (@record) { print "$field\n" }
}

# Clean up and go home
$stmt->finish;              # Release the statement handle resources
$dbh->disconnect;           # Close database handle
```

When I incorporated the above into a CGI script complete with HTML statements, it became the LIST ALL script:

```perl
#!/usr/bin/perl

use DBI;

$dsn  = 'SupportNet';       # Configure $dsn, $user, and $pass
$user = 'perl';             # in Control Panel/32bit ODBC
$pass = 'lerp';
$dbd  = 'ODBC';             # A must if using ODBC.

# This is just a bunch of HTML to start the document
print <<END;
Content-type: text/html\n\n
<html><head><title>SupportNet</title>
<script language="javascript">
<!-- hide code from browsers that dislike embedded scripts
    function display(x) {
        document.forms[0].elements[0].value = x;
        document.forms[0].submit( );
    }
// -->
    </script></head><body background="../img/backgrnd.gif">
    <a href="../SupportNet/home.html">Home</a>
    <center><h1>Client List</h1>
    <form action="/cgi-bin/rolodex" method="POST" target="main"
    name="rolodexform">
    <input type="hidden" name="ID" value=" "></form>
    <table border="1" align="CENTER"><tr><td>
END

# Connect to the database
$dbh = DBI->connect("dbi:$dbd:$dsn", $user, $pass,
                    {RaiseError => 1, AutoCommit => 0 });
```

```
$stmt = $dbh->prepare( "SELECT ID, practice FROM Rolodex" );

$stmt->execute;      # Execute the statement at the database level

while (( $id, $prac ) = $stmt->fetchrow_array()) {  # Build hash from data
    $practices{$prac} = $id;
}

foreach $pract (sort keys %practices) {
    next if $pract =~ /^$/;                   # Skip blanks
    print "<a href='javascript:display(\"$practices{$pract}\")'
      onMouseOver=\"window.status=\'ROLODEX this\';return true\">$pract</a>
      <br>\n";
}

# Print HTML footers
print "</td></tr></table></center>\n\n<p></body></html>";

$dbh->disconnect;                        # Close database handle
```

The HTML snippet to call this script looks like this:

```
<form action="/cgi-bin/listall.pl" method="post">
    <input type="submit" value="List All">
</form>
```

Armed with this knowledge, converting my little CSV-based web application to a SQL-based one became the rather trivial task it was supposed to be. Here's to your first attempt being just as easy. Don't tell people how little time it took, and accept compliments graciously.

The Win32-Access-ODBC-DBI::DBD Checklist:

I'm assuming you have Perl and Access already installed, and have a comma-separated-values file ready to go.

1. Download and install MS Access ODBC drivers.

2. Import your CSV file into Access.

3. Define the Data Source Name and login/password for your database in Control Panel/32bit ODBC.

4. Run a test script to check connectivity.

References

SQL Tutorial: *http://www.sqlcourse.com/*.

The DBI home page: *http://dbi.perl.org*.

Win32 SQL databases. While not free, MS Access is usually available in most companies as part of the MS Office Suite, and MySQL is available for Win32 at *http://www.mysql.com/*.

## CHAPTER 60

DBI Caveats

Thomas Akin

Perl's DBI module allows you to use Perl with database engines. It's one of the most popular Perl utilities, and I have dozens of clients who make extensive use of DBI for their daily production needs. Some clients use DBI much more effectively than others, and in this article you'll see how.

DBI and Loops

DBI statements are often used within loops that store or fetch data from a database. You might insert the contents of a text file into a database line by line, or read and parse multiple lines of output from a database query. I often see code like the following from new DBI programmers:

```
foreach $line (<FILE>) {
    chomp $line;
    ($alpha, $beta, $charlie, $delta) = split(/,/,$line);
    $sql = qq{ insert into $table (col_a, col_b, col_c, col_d)
            values($alpha, $beta, $charlie, $delta) };
    $dbh = DBI->connect($dsn, 'login', 'password');
    $sth = $dbh->prepare($sql);
    $sth->execute;
    $dbh->disconnect;
}
```

This code works, but not very efficiently. With the above code it took an hour to insert 200,000 rows into a MySQL database—and MySQL is pretty fast! It might take half a day with Oracle.

There are lots of improvements we can make. The first is just common sense: never put anything in a loop that doesn't absolutely have to be there. For each of our 200,000 insertions, we connect to the database, prepare our SQL statement, execute it, and disconnect from the database. However, we only need to connect and disconnect once. We simply have to move our connect and disconnect outside the loop to drastically improve our performance:

```
$dbh = DBI->connect($dsn,'login','password');

foreach $line (<FILE>) {
    chomp $line;
    ($alpha, $beta, $charlie, $delta) = split(/,/,$line);
    $sql = qq{ insert into $table (col_a, col_b, col_c, col_d)
               values($alpha, $beta, $charlie, $delta) };
    $sth = $dbh->prepare($sql);
    $sth->execute;
}

$dbh->disconnect;
```

This reduces our runtime to half an hour, doubling our speed.

Placeholders

DBI allows us to further improve our code by using placeholders. We now connect and disconnect the database only once, but we still prepare and execute our SQL statement 200,000 times. The statement we prepare doesn't change much; all that changes is the insertion value. We can create a generic statement that we prepare only once, outside the loop. With this generic statement we can specify the insertion values at execution time. DBI uses a ? to define a placeholder, so our new SQL statement looks like this:

```
$sql = qq{ insert into $table (col_a, col_b, col_c, col_d) values(?, ?, ?, ?) };
```

The statement is prepared the same as before:

```
$sth = $dbh->prepare($sql);
```

Now we can fill in each ? at execution time. There are two ways to do this. First, we can use the bind_param subroutine to indicate what values to use:

```
$sql = qq{ insert into $table (col_a, col_b, col_c, col_d) values(?, ?, ?, ?) };

$sth = $dbh->prepare($sql);

foreach $line (<FILE>) {
    chomp $line;
    ($alpha, $beta, $charlie, $delta) = split(/,/, $line);
    $sth->bind_param(1, $alpha);
    $sth->bind_param(2, $beta);
    $sth->bind_param(3, $charlie);
    $sth->bind_param(4, $delta);

    $sth->execute;
}
```

The bind_param subroutine allows a data type as a third argument. Normally, this is used to tell the driver whether the placeholder is a number or a string:

```
$sth->bind_param(1, $alpha, SQL_INTEGER);
```

or:

```
$sth->bind_param(2, $beta, SQL_VARCHAR);
```

The second way to specify values at execution time is to pass them directly as arguments to the execute statement:

```
$sth->execute($alpha, $beta, $charlie, $delta);
```

Using this method our code simplifies to:

```
$dbh = DBI->connect($dsn,'login','password');

$sql = qq{ insert into $table (col_a, col_b, col_c, col_d) values(?, ?, ?, ?) };

$sth = $dbh->prepare($sql);

foreach $line (<FILE>) {
    chomp $line;
    ($alpha, $beta, $charlie, $delta) = split(/,/, $line);
    $sth->execute($alpha, $beta, $charlie, $delta);
}

$dbh->disconnect;
```

Our code now takes 20 minutes to run. We achieved this improvement despite the fact that the MySQL database driver only emulates placeholders. Had this been a database that *directly* supports placeholders, such as Oracle, the improvement would have been even more dramatic.

Placeholders are an easy way to improve your DBI coding, but there are a few gotchas that beginners need to avoid. First, notice that placeholders don't have quotes. This is correct:

```
$sql = qq{ insert into $table (col_a, col_b, col_c, col_d) values(?, ?, ?, ?) };
```

This is not correct:

```
$sql = qq{ insert into $table (col_a, col_b, col_c, col_d) values('?', '?', '?', '?') };
```

Placeholders cannot be used for column names or table names. This *won't* work:

```
$sql = qq{ select alpha, ? from table };
```

Nor will this:

```
$sql = qq{ select alpha, beta from ? };
```

Or even this:

```
$sql = qq{ select alpha, beta from table where ? > 200 };
```

However, you can use Perl variables for column and table names:

```
$sql = qq{ select alpha, beta from $table where $col > 200 };
```

You'll have to re-prepare this statement whenever you want to change the values of $table or $col.

Fetches

We've dealt mostly with inserting data into a database; now we'll look at the ways DBI provides to get data out. Most of those ways follow the same basic format:

```
$dbh = DBI->connect($dsn, 'login', 'passwd');

$sql = qq{ select * from $table };

$sth = $dbh->prepare($sql);
$sth->execute;

while (@row = $sth->fetchrow_array) { print "@row\n" }

$dbh->disconnect;
```

The most efficient of these is fetchrow_arrayref:

```
while ($row = $sth->fetchrow_arrayref) {
    print "@$row\n";
}
```

There's also fetchrow_hashref, which stores the keys and values of the database into a hash:

```
while ($ref = $sth->fetchrow_hashref) {
    foreach $key (keys %{$ref}) { print "$ref->{$key}, " }
    print "\n";
}
```

It's very handy, but much slower than the previous methods.

Bind Columns

Database fetches can be made even more efficient and elegant with the use of *bind columns*. Bind columns allow you to bind a variable to each column of a table, so that whenever a fetch is performed, the bound variables are automatically updated:

```
$sth->bind_columns(@list_of_references_to_variables_to_bind);
```

We can use it like this:

```
$sql = qq{ select alpha, beta, delta from table };

$sth->prepare($sql);
$sth->execute;

my ($alpha, $beta, $delta);
$sth->bind_columns(\$alpha, \$beta, \$delta);

while ($sth->fetch) { print "$alpha - $beta - $delta\n" }
```

Here, the fetch subroutine is synonymous with fetchrow_arrayref. This subroutine, combined with bind_columns, is *the* fastest way to fetch data with DBI.

Error Checking

There's a big problem with all the code snippets in this article: we never check the return values of DBI methods. We simply assume that every DBI call was successful. The obvious solution is to add an or die clause after every DBI method call:

```
$dbh = DBI->connect($dsn,'login','passwd') || die $DBI::errstr;
$sth = $dbh->prepare($sql)                 || die $dbh->errstr;
$sth->execute                              || die $sth->errstr;
```

However, there is a cleaner solution. Each DBI handle has a Boolean attribute called RaiseError. If we set this to true, any errors triggered by that handle cause the script to die with an appropriate error message, saving us from having to check every DBI call we make. RaiseError can be set via the connect statement:

```
$dbh = DBI->connect($dsn,'login','passwd', { RaiseError => 1 });
```

We can also call it after a connection is already made:

```
$dbh->{RaiseError} = 1;
```

Transactions

I've found that many administrators shy away from using *transactions* with DBI. For those who are unfamiliar with transactions, they provide a way to group multiple SQL statements together so that database changes are only made if *every* statement is successful. For example, a transaction for updating a customer order database might include statements to update inventory, accounts payable, and shipping manifests. All updates must succeed; otherwise, we don't want to perform any of them. If only some of the updates succeeded, we might bill a customer for an order not shipped, or ship an order to a customer without billing them.

By default, DBI commits each statement as it's performed. To use transactions, we need to disable this behavior with the AutoCommit variable:

```
$dbh = DBI->connect($dsn, 'login', 'passwd',
                    { RaiseError => 1,
                      AutoCommit => 0 });
```

We can also just say:

```
$dbh->{AutoCommit} = 0;
```

With AutoCommit off, changes are revocable until commit is called. Uncommitted statements can be undone with rollback.

Next, we need a way to group our statements that lets us test whether any failed. The easiest and most robust way to do this is to set RaiseError and wrap the statements in an eval block:

```
$dbh->{RaiseError} = 1;
eval { $sth_1->execute;      # Update Inventory
       $sth_2->execute;      # Update Accounts Payable
```

```
        $sth_3->execute;          # Update Shipping
        $dbh->commit;
    };

    if ($@) { $dbh->rollback }
```

If any statement in the eval block fails, $@ is set and we revoke all three statements.

Don't forget to commit your statements before you exit. If you do forget, what happens next depends on the database. Some databases automatically commit them; others roll them back.

References

The material for this article came from personal experience, a thousand or so readings of the DBI documentation and FAQ, and a generous review by DBI guru Tim Bunce. The DBI module and related documentation are at *http://dbi.perl.org*.

## CHAPTER 61

Beyond Hardcoded Database Applications with DBIx::Recordset

Terrence Brannon

Perl has been dubbed "The Duct Tape of the Internet," providing a comfortable interface to an ever-growing number of external technologies. In this article, I provide an introduction to one of the most convenient and powerful Perl interfaces to relational databases: DBIx::Recordset.

CRUD Without SQL

By and large, when using databases from a programming language, you are creating, reading, updating, or deleting data—CRUD, for short. If you use the DBI module directly, you have to write SQL for these operations. In contrast, DBIx::Recordset supports CRUD through the four simple functions Insert, Search, Update, and Delete.

Under the hood, DBIx::Recordset generates SQL and ensures that it is syntactically correct for whatever database you are using. There are large applications written using DBIx::Recordset that require no code changes to run on MySQL, Microsoft Access, or Oracle. This lets you ship database code off-site knowing that it will run with whichever database your users have. It also future-proofs internal applications against unforeseen changes in database systems.

Sample Usage

This article demonstrates how I used DBIx::Recordset to solve a real task I had during a contracting job. The company had a user registration table that contained basic information about a client: name, email address, phone number, and so on. However, a new table was developed to store demographic information about a client in addition to these fields. My task was to copy all the current information from the original table to the new table. The basic information would simply be copied over and the demographic information would be generated randomly.

Example 61-1 shows uregisternew, the destination table. The last four fields of uregisternew were the four demographic fields that the original table lacked. Each of these fields was to contain a non-negative integer.

Example 61-1. The uregisternew table

Field	Type
-----	----
firstname	varchar(50)
lastname	varchar(50)
userid	varchar(50)
password	varchar(50)
address1	varchar(50)
city	varchar(50)
state	char(2)
zippostal	varchar(20)
email	varchar(50)
phone	varchar(50)
fax	varchar(50)
dob	date
occupation	varchar(50)
gender	varchar(20)
income	varchar(25)
age	varchar(255)

For example, the user's gender might be Male, Female, or unspecified. Once a user indicates their gender, the integer is used to index into this anonymous array:

```
$Angryman::User::profile{gender} = [ 'n/a', 'Male', 'Female' ];
```

Thus, a user whose gender is Male will have a 1 for his gender field. There are similar anonymous arrays for age bracket, occupation, and income. Example 61-2 shows the program that copied the records from the original table to the new table.

Example 61-2. Copying user records from a source table (uregister) to a target table (uregisternew)

```
use Angryman::User;
use DBIx::Recordset;
use Math::Random;
use strict;
use vars qw(%table %connect %profile *uregister *uregisternew);

$table{in}  = 'uregister';
$table{out} = 'uregisternew';

%connect = ( '!DataSource' => 'DBI:mysql:test',
             '!Username'   => 'root' );

# Connect to database and SELECT * FROM uregister
*uregister = DBIx::Recordset->Search ({ %connect,
                                         '!Table' => $table{in} });

# Since we'll re-use the target table many times, we separate the
# connection and insertion steps with this recordset
*uregisternew = DBIx::Recordset->Setup({ %connect, '!Table' => $table{out} });

# Iterate through the recordsets from the old table
while (my $record = $uregister->Next) {
```

```
        &randomize_user_profile;
        # Insert the old table data into the new table along with
        # the computed hash of profile data
        $uregisternew->Insert({%$record, %profile});
}

# Angryman::User::Profile is a hash in which each key is a reference
# to an array of profile choices. For example:
#   $Angryman::User::Profile{gender} = [ 'male', 'female' ];
#   $Angryman::User::Profile{age} = ['under 14', '14-19', '20-25', ... ];
# Because we don't have the actual data for the people in uregister,
# we randomly assign user profile data when copying it to uregisternew.
sub randomize_user_profile {
    for (keys %Angryman::User::Profile) {
        my @tmp = @{$Angryman::User::Profile{$_}};
        $profile{$_} = random_uniform_integer(1, 0, $#tmp);
    }
    $profile{dob} = '1969-05-11';
}
```

Example 61-2 copies over the fields and generates a valid array index for the new profile fields. I'll go through the program step by step to see how DBIx::Recordset works.

First, I load modules. Angryman::User has all the company information (the demographic anonymous arrays) discussed above; DBIx::Recordset is the module I'm discussing in this article, and Math::Random is an excellent Perl module that allows you to create random numbers of all sorts. I want my code to be bulletproof, so I turn on strict and explicitly declare variables with the vars pragma:

```
use Angryman::User;
use DBIx::Recordset;
use Math::Random;
use strict;
use vars qw(%table %connect %profile *uregister *uregisternew);
```

Next, I define the original table with basic user information, and the target table that will hold demographic information as well.

```
$table{in}  = 'uregister';
$table{out} = 'uregisternew';
```

Then I define the information for connection to the database. (In the real script, this information was actually sequestered into a system configuration file; the code shown here is for illustration only.)

```
%connect = ( '!DataSource' => 'DBI:mysql:test',
             '!Username'   => 'root' );
```

This one line of DBIx::Recordset packs quite a punch: I connect to the database and retrieve all records from the original table. The %connect hash gives DBIx::Recordset

instructions on how to connect, and the !Table directive indicates which table I want
to retrieve records from.

```
# Connect to database and SELECT * FROM uregister
*uregister = DBIx::Recordset->Search ({ %connect,
                                        '!Table' => $table{in} });
```

Because I bind the results of the Search call to a typeglob, I actually have three things
I can use. A scalar ($::uregister) allows object-oriented access to the database. The
@::uregister array allows me to access all the records, and the %::uregister hash
allows me to access the fields of the current record.

```
*uregisternew = DBIx::Recordset->Setup({ %connect, '!Table' => $table{out} });
```

All of the DBIx::Recordset CRUD functions support connection and database processing in one line. However, since I'll be inserting many records into the target
table, I connect to the database and target table in the above lines and re-use the connection on each iteration of the loop. That way, I avoid having to connect and disconnect more than necessary.

When I connected to my original table, I set up the scalar, the array, and the hash. In
the next line, I make use of the scalar's Next method so that I can iterate across the
retrieved records. On databases that reliably return the number of rows retrieved, I
can make use of the array with for my $record (@::uregister).

```
# Iterate through the recordsets from the old table:
while (my $record = $::uregister->Next) {
```

I randomize the demographic fields and store the results in a hash named %profile:

```
&randomize_user_profile;
```

Finally, I take the data in both hashes and insert it into the database. Note that
Insert takes a hash reference as its argument, not a hash. DBIx::Recordset automatically takes the key-value pairs of the hash and creates the necessary SQL statements
to insert the data. This is a great time-saver. You needn't worry about getting your
data in order and you also don't have to manually quote your string fields.

```
# Insert the old table data into the new table,
# along with the computed hash of profile data
$uregisternew->Insert({%$record, %profile});
```

A DBI Version

One of the most important steps in Perl history was the creation of DBI. Previously,
you had to use a database-specific Perl extension such as oraperl and sybperl, and
code for one utility wouldn't work on another. With DBI, all basic database tasks
can execute on many databases with no changes in Perl code.

DBI has its place. When you really care about performance, DBI's fine-grained process lets you tweak the parts you need. When you need to prepare very complex SQL

queries, DBI lets you do it. And when you need to use database-specific features in queries or statements, DBI lets you do that too.

But the bulk of database work doesn't require the programmer to care about these details. This section will discuss Example 61-3, a DBI implementation of the same task, so you can see the benefits of DBIx::Recordset.

Example 61-3. Copying user records from a source table (uregister) to a target table (uregisternew)

```perl
use Angryman::User;
use DBI;
use Math::Random;
use strict;
use vars qw(%table $sql_field_term $insert_term %profile @ordered_fields);

$table{in}  = 'uregister';
$table{out} = 'uregisternew';

# Connect to database and SELECT * FROM uregister
my $dbh = DBI->connect('DBI:mysql:test', 'root') || die "$!\n";
my $sth = $dbh->prepare('SELECT * FROM uregister');
my $ret = $sth->execute;

&determine_target_database_field_order;

# We'll re-use the target table many times, so we separate the
# connection step and the insert step

# Iterate through the recordsets from the old table:
while (my $record = $sth->fetchrow_hashref) {
    &randomize_user_profile;
    &fiddle_with_my_data_to_get_it_to_work_with_the_DBI_API($record);

    # Insert the old table data into the new table along with
    # the computed hash of profile data
    my $sql = "INSERT into $table{out}($sql_field_term) values($insert_term)";
    $dbh->do($sql);
}

# Angryman::User::Profile is a hash in which each key is a reference
# to an array of profile choices. For example:
#   $Angryman::User::Profile{gender} = [ 'male', 'female' ];
#   $Angryman::User::Profile{age} = ['under 14', '14-19', '20-25', ... ];
# Because we don't have the actual data for the people in uregister,
# we randomly assign user profile data over a normal distribution.
# when copying it to uregisternew.
sub randomize_user_profile {
    for (keys %Angryman::User::Profile) {
        my @tmp = @{$Angryman::User::Profile{$_}};
        $profile{$_} = random_uniform_integer(1, 0, $#tmp);
    }
    $profile{dob} = '1969-05-11';
}
```

```
# Hmm, I can't just give DBI my data and have it figure out the order
# of the database fields.  We have to store it explicitly so that
# this code doesn't break with any switch of field position.
# In DBIx::Recordset, I would just say $handle->Names().

sub determine_target_database_field_order {
    my $order_sth = $dbh->prepare("SELECT * FROM $table{out} LIMIT 1");
    $order_sth->execute;
    @ordered_fields = @{$order_sth->{NAME}};
    $sql_field_term = join ',',  @{$order_sth->{NAME}};
}

# As ubiquitous as hashes are in Perl, the DBI API does not
# offer a way to directly commit hashes to databases.
sub fiddle_with_my_data_to_get_it_to_work_with_the_DBI_API {
    my ($record)=@_;
    my @output_data;
    for (@ordered_fields) {
        push @output_data, $dbh->quote( defined($record->{$_})
                                        ? $record->{$_}
                                        : $profile{$_}   );
    }
    $insert_term = join ',', @output_data;
}
```

As before, I'll go through this program step by step, skipping over the modules and starting with the DBI initialization.

```
# Connect to database and SELECT * FROM uregister
my $dbh = DBI->connect('DBI:mysql:test','root') || die "$!\n";
my $sth = $dbh->prepare('SELECT * FROM uregister');
my $ret = $sth->execute;
```

Here I connect to the database and retrieve all records from the original table. Notice that this takes three lines, and I still don't have my database data stored in Perl variables for automatic usage. It's possible to do this in two lines if I use DBI's selectall_arrayref function, but I'll never be able to shorten this to one line, because connection and statement execution occur in separate DBI calls.

```
&determine_target_database_field_order;
```

This line of code may seem rather innocuous, but it reveals the most about the difference between DBI and DBIx::Recordset. The whole idea of this program is to retrieve records from one table and put them in another, right? With DBI, you can retrieve data into an array, an array reference, or into a hash reference. If I wanted to assume that my target table would never change, I could extract my data into an array or array reference and then commit it to the target database.

I wanted my code to work regardless of whether the company moved around (or even deleted) a few fields in either database, so I chose hash references instead for this project. And since hashes are unordered, I needed an array with the key names in correct order. The function &determine_target_database_field_order does just that. With DBIx::Recordset, such a function is not necessary: it takes the hash references you give it and correctly quotes and orders it for writing to the database.

I fetch each row of the original table into a hash reference:

```
# iterate through the recordsets from the old table:
while (my $record = $sth->fetchrow_hashref) {
```

Creating a hash with the demographics data:

```
&randomize_user_profile;
```

Next, I manually order and quote the data to be inserted:

```
&fiddle_with_my_data_to_get_it_to_work_with_the_DBI_API($record);
```

This is unnecessary with DBIx::Recordset, since it handles these issues for you automatically. I finish by inserting the record into the target table:

```
# Insert the old table data into the new table along with
# the computed hash of profile data
my $sql = "INSERT into $table{out}($sql_field_term) values($insert_term)";
$dbh->do($sql);
```

Conclusion

DBIx::Recordset contains a wealth of functionality, allowing you to implement common tasks quickly and concisely. In addition to the features discussed in this article, DBIx::Recordset supports many other common tasks such as debugging, multi-table processing, and HTML-based navigation of tables. The next time you want your database code up and running quickly and portably, give DBIx::Recordset a try.

## CHAPTER 62

Win32::ODBC

Joe Casadonte

I was once told, "Look to your hobbies to start a business." About three years ago, I thought about starting a company that combined my hobbies: Perl and the Internet. I found a store in Delaware that sold thousands of hot sauces, another of my passions, and an idea came to me—I could sell the hot sauces for the store online. I would put the product data into a database and take orders over the Web, using Perl to generate the HTML and keep track of sales.

One part was missing. How would I connect to a database? Outside of work, I had access only to a Win95 machine. It ran Perl for Win32 from ActiveState. OraPerl and DBI hadn't yet been ported to the Win32 platform. For a long time I was stuck.

What I really wanted was an ODBC (Open Database Connectivity) solution. ODBC is Microsoft's attempt to standardize database access. If a program needs to connect to an Oracle database, an Informix database, and an Access database, it needs three different versions of the database code for each, because each of those databases has its own proprietary access scheme. With ODBC, you simply write your program to conform to the ODBC API and let the ODBC Manager and Driver take care of the database language specifics. Initially just a Windows solution, ODBC is now finding its way onto many Unix boxes.

Along came Dave Roth's Win32::ODBC module. Dave married the ODBC toolkit with Perl, giving me (and countless others) access to databases from Perl on Windows. I began to put together the pieces necessary to run a store, starting with the product database, data extraction routines, and the creation of on-the-fly HTML pages via Perl.

However, I found that the documentation was a little sparse. After talking to Dave about it, I set out to document the module more thoroughly. Since then, I've gotten many individual requests asking for help and examples. This article is an attempt to satisfy a lot of those questions at once.

Win32::ODBC Basics

This tutorial will walk you through the basics of Win32::ODBC programming. Some of the examples will use Lincoln Stein's CGI.pm module to make the applications more immediately useful. Because the purpose of this tutorial is to introduce you to Win32::ODBC, I'll assume a basic understanding of Perl, CGI, and HTML. I'll also assume that your web server, scripts, ODBC data sources, and everything else are already set up and working.

It's also important to know SQL—not just for Win32::ODBC, but for virtually any database application.

Demystifying SQL

SQL (Structured Query Language) is a standard for querying and manipulating databases. By standardizing commands, it provides a small measure of consistency when you switch from one database to another. Most modern commercial databases support SQL, and most of them also extend the language in useful but annoyingly different ways. You can usually accomplish what you need to with the standard SQL commands, but it's sometimes easier to perform the task with a database-specific command.

SQL commands are very basic, but they can be put together in complex ways. The commands are divided into two categories: DDL (Data Definition Language) for creating, modifying, and deleting tables; and DML (Data Manipulation Language), for creating, modifying, and deleting the data inside the tables. DML commands usually consist of an action (e.g., SELECT, DELETE, or UPDATE), a table identifier, and other modifiers. These modifiers include *conditionals*, used to act upon a subset of data rather than the whole set; *ordering directives*, to get the data back in a pre-determined order; and *aggregation directives*, to combine data in some way. By convention, SQL syntax is uppercase to help distinguish queries from data, even though SQL itself is case-insensitive.

To extract a list of names from a database, you use SELECT:

```
SELECT firstname, lastname FROM employees;
```

This extracts values for the FirstName and LastName fields in the Employees table. It iterates through all records in the table (in no guaranteed sequence) and returns the data in the two fields for each record. Here's how we might select the same fields only for Managers, and order them alphabetically:

```
SELECT firstname, lastname FROM employees WHERE is_manager = 1 ORDER BY
    lastname, firstname;
```

This uses a WHERE clause to limit the result set and an ORDER BY clause to give us the data in a predefined sequence. Similar commands exist for updating, adding and deleting data:

```
UPDATE employees SET lastname = 'Smith-Jones' WHERE firstname = 'Mary'
    AND lastname = 'Smith';
```

```
INSERT INTO employees (lastname, firstname) VALUES ('Brown', 'Mike');

DELETE FROM employees WHERE is_fired = 1;
```

More complex actions like *joins* and *subqueries* require complex SQL statements—but everything is constructed from these building blocks. This updates data from one table based on data in another table:

```
UPDATE employees SET hourly_wage = hourly_wage + 2 WHERE employee_number
    IN (SELECT employee_number FROM gets_a_raise);
```

For a more thorough introduction to SQL, see Jim Hoffman's excellent tutorial at *http://w3.one.net/~jhoffman/sqltut.htm.*

I'll use two tables in this application. Both the tables and the SQL are very simple, to keep the focus on the module. I'm importing these tables from an Access database running on my computer, but the joy of ODBC is that this could be any database running under any operating system. Table 62-1 shows the information in this database; the other table will be shown later.

Table 62-1. Sauces

Field name	Type	Length	Notes
ProductID	AutoNumber	N/A	Sequence/Primary key
ProductName	Text	25	
Quantity	Number	Double	In ounces
Price	Number	Double	
PepperType	Text	20	Main type of pepper in sauce
Scoville	Text	Long	Rating of heat content: Jalapeño pepper = 3–4,000 units; Scotch Bonnets (Habañero) = 2–300,000 units!

Installing Win32::ODBC

To install Win32::ODBC, you first need to determine the implementation of Perl you're running: type perl -v to find out. If you're running the core Perl distribution (that is, not from ActiveState), the module is included in the libwin32 bundle, available from the CPAN. You won't need a C compiler unless you're using a development release or built your own Perl using Visual C. If you have the ActiveState version, you'll need to locate the Perl installation directory is (referred to as $PERL below), and a temporary directory ($TEMP below). Then follow these installation steps:

1. Unzip the Win32::ODBC archive to *$TEMP*.

2. Copy the file *$TEMP\lib\win32\odbc.pm* to the directory *$PERL\lib\win32*.

3. Copy *odbc.pll* (you might have to dig to find it) into *$PERL\lib\auto\Win32\odbc*.

4. Copy the documentation from *$TEMP\docs* to *$PERL\docs*.

Getting Started

To get started, I'll write a simple script that extracts all the data from the database and writes it out to a table. The first thing to do, as with any Perl module, is to use it:

```
use Win32::ODBC;
```

Next, I create a new ODBC object:

```
my ($db) = new Win32::ODBC("Article");
```

This creates an object ($db) that connects to the data source named Article. If there were a username and password associated with Article, I could supply them in an ODBC connect string:

```
my ($db) = new Win32::ODBC("dsn=Article; uid=foo; pwd=bar");
```

where Article is the name of the data source, foo is the user ID, and bar is the password. Next, I use SQL to extract the data:

```
$db->Sql("SELECT * FROM Sauces");
```

and then loop to fetch the data, one row at a time:

```
while ($db->FetchRow()) { ... }
```

Programs using Win32::ODBC typically repeat two actions: first, a row of the database is fetched, and then the data from the row is extracted. There are two flavors of this second step: Data and DataHash. Data places the data in an array, in the order it was selected by the SQL statement. The latter places the data in a hash, in the form $hash{FieldName} = DataValue. If you select all fields using the * wildcard, then the field order of the returned data is undefined; it therefore makes more sense to use DataHash than Data. Finally, I close the ODBC handle. Putting everything together:

```
use Win32::ODBC;

my($db) = new Win32::ODBC('Article');

$db->Sql("SELECT * FROM Sauces");

while ($db->FetchRow()) {
    my(%data) = $db->DataHash();

    print HTML "<TR><TD>$data{'ProductName'}";
    print HTML " <TD>$data{'Quantity'} ounces";
    print HTML " <TD>\$$data{'Price'}";
    print HTML " <TD>$data{'PepperType'}";
    print HTML " <TD>$data{'Scoville'} Scoville Units";
}

$db->Close();
```

Debugging

Note the lack of error checking after calling the Win32::ODBC methods. That's poor programming practice, and I only do it here because space is limited. You should check for errors religiously.

When I called the Sql method, I "compiled" the SQL statement. Had I asked for a nonexistent column or table, an error would have been generated. If I do get an error, the error should be displayed and the program should die gracefully:

```
my ($stmt) = "SELECT HasGarlic FROM Sauces";

if ($db->Sql($stmt)) {
    my ($err) = $db->Error;
    warn "Sql() ERROR\n";
    warn "\t\$stmt: $stmt\n";
    warn "\t\$err: $err\n";
    exit;
}
```

In a scalar context, the Error method returns a string with the following format: *ErrorNumber ConnectionNumber ErrorText*.

The example above asked for a column that does not exist. On my system, this generated the following message:

```
Sql() ERROR
    $stmt: SELECT HasGarlic FROM Sauces
    $err: [-3010] [1] [0] "[Microsoft][ODBC Microsoft Access 97 Driver]
    Too few parameters. Expected 1."
```

The value of $err is generated by the ODBC Manager, not the Win32::ODBC module. As you see, the error messages can be a little cryptic.

Two other functions may help diagnose why you're not getting the data you expected: FieldNames and DumpData. FieldNames returns an array of field names in the current result set; if you're wondering why $data{'scoville'} is empty, FieldNames will tell you that you actually meant $data{'Scoville'}. DumpData dumps all field names and row data to the currently selected output filehandle—typically, STDOUT.

If you are convinced that you have found a bug, let me know. Include the Perl and Win32::ODBC versions. To determine your Win32::ODBC version, use this:

```
my ($pm, $pll) = $db->Version();
die "PM: $pm, PLL: $pll\n";
```

CRUD

The standard database functions are sometimes abbreviated as CRUD: create (insert), read (select), update, and delete. I'll show examples of each throughout the remainder of the article.

Suppose that instead of displaying all records in the Sauces database, I only want to display records whose last name contained a particular word. After all, the database might have millions of records. My previous SELECT statement would now look like this:

```
$db->Sql("SELECT * FROM Sauces WHERE PepperType LIKE '%chile%'");
```

Or, put into a program using CGI.pm:

```
# Extract the pattern submitted through the browser
$pattern = $query->param('pattern');

# Retrieve the data matching the pattern
$db->Sql("SELECT * FROM Sauces WHERE PepperType LIKE '$pattern'");
```

Both examples use the LIKE conditional, which takes a single-quoted string: a SQL wildcard, similar in spirit to a Perl regular expression. Perl has great pattern matching; SQL doesn't. The ANSI standard of SQL has two basic pattern matching operators: the percent sign ("%"), which matches zero or more of any character, and the underscore ("_"), which matches any single character. Some equivalencies are shown in Table 62-2.

Table 62-2. SQL wildcards versus Perl regular expressions

SQL wildcard	Perl regex
LIKE 'L%'	m/^L/
LIKE '%ing'	m/ing$/
LIKE '%foo%'	m/foo/
LIKE 'fo_'	m/^fo.$/

The WHERE clause just shown cuts down on the number of rows displayed. But assume that I have a lot of data to display (think of a Google search) and I only want to display ten rows per page. This is tricky with CGI because of its statelessness (although I could use mod_perl to maintain state if I needed to). I'll store the state in a State table, shown in Table 62-3, to keep the query results between accesses.

Table 62-3. State

Field name	Type	Length	Notes
PID	Number	Integer	Process ID—multi-key primary key
ProductID	Number	Long	Foreign key into Sauces table—multi-key primary key
Sequence	Number	Integer	Multi-key primary key

The first time I access the database, instead of displaying the results of the query, I'll store them in the State table. Inside the while loop, I could do one of two things: store the results in an array and then insert them later into the State table, or insert them into the State table as I fetch them. The former uses one ODBC object:

```
# SQL statement to fetch the data
$db->Sql("SELECT ProductID FROM Sauces WHERE Scoville > 10000 ".
         "ORDER BY Scoville, ProductName");

# Fetch each row
my ($cnt, $id, @ids) = 0;
while ($db->FetchRow) {
    # Store for later use
    push(@ids, $db->Data);
}

# Use stored IDs to populate State table
foreach $id (@ids) {
    $db->Sql("INSERT INTO State (PID, ProductID, Sequence) ".
             "VALUES ($$, $id, ". $cnt++ . ")");
}
```

The latter uses a second ODBC object (one for each SQL statement):

```
# New statement, same connection
my ($ins) = new Win32::ODBC($db);

# SQL statement to fetch the data
$db->Sql("SELECT ProductID FROM Sauces WHERE Scoville > 10000 ".
         "ORDER BY Scoville, ProductName");

# Fetch each row
my ($cnt, $id) = 0;
while ($db->FetchRow) {
    ($id) = $db->Data;
    # Immediately store in State table
    $ins->Sql("INSERT INTO State (PID, ProductID, Sequence) ".
              "VALUES ($$, $id, ". $cnt++ . ")");
}
```

The insert takes place as soon as $ins->Sql is called. It's immediately *committed* (a database term meaning unequivocally completed) unless you specify otherwise; see the "Transactions" section below.

After filling in the State table, I can pull rows out of it in sets of ten, using two ODBC objects:

```
# Get CGI parameters
$pid = $query->param('pid'};
$start = $query->param('start'};

# Fetch data out of State table
$dbstate->Sql("SELECT ProductID FROM State ".
              "WHERE PID = $pid AND Sequence >= $start ".
              "AND Sequence < ". ($start + 10) . " " .
              "ORDER BY Sequence");

# Fetch each row from State
my($id);
```

```
while ($dbstate->FetchRow) {
    ($id) = $dbstate->Data;

    # Fetch actual data from Sauces
    $dbsauce->Sql("SELECT * FROM Sauces WHERE ProductID = $id");

    # Output HTML
}
```

This works, but it's inefficient. I could accomplish it all in one SQL statement with a database join:

```
# Get CGI parameters
$pid = $query->param('pid'};
$start = $query->param('start'};

# Fetch Sauces data based on State table data
$db->Sql("SELECT sa.* FROM State st " .
        "INNER JOIN Sauces sa ON st.ProductID = sa.ProductID " .
        "WHERE st.PID = $pid AND st.Sequence >= $start " .
        "AND st.Sequence < ". ($start + 10) . " " .
        "ORDER BY st.Sequence");

# Fetch each row
while ($db->FetchRow) {
    my (%data) = $db->DataHash;

    # Output your HTML here
}
```

As you can see, the complexity is in the SQL, not the ODBC. I used calls to Sql and FetchRow, just like before.

Updating and deletion are similar to insertion. Given that I have this State table, I would need a process to clean it up. I could clean it up all at once:

```
$db->Sql("DELETE FROM State");
```

or only when a particular user is done with the data:

```
$pid = $query->param('pid');
$db->Sql("DELETE FROM State WHERE PID = $pid");
```

None of this is effective or efficient as CGI programs go. It's merely a convenient demonstration of basic Win32::ODBC concepts. For a more complete example, see PepperSearch.pl in Example 62-1.

Transactions

Some ODBC drivers support *transactions*, with commits and rollbacks. *Rollbacks* are another database term: retracting an action that hasn't yet been committed. (See the next section, "Data Sources," to find out how to determine if your driver supports them.) Sometime after connecting (usually immediately after, but it depends on your logic flow) you can set the AutoCommit option off, and then rollback or commit depending upon program flow:

```
$db->SetConnectOptions('SQL_AUTOCOMMIT', 'SQL_AUTOCOMMIT_OFF');
...
if ($fatal_error) {
    $db->Transact('SQL_ROLLBACK');
    die "Error - rolling back\n";
}
...
$db->Transact('SQL_COMMIT');
```

Data Sources

Sometimes you won't know beforehand which database you need to connect to. You can query the ODBC Manager and get a list:

```
print HTML "<SELECT NAME=\"DataSources\" SIZE=1>\n";
my (%dsn, $key) = Win32::ODBC::DataSources();
foreach $key (sort keys %dsn) {
    print HTML "<OPTION>$key\n";
}
print HTML "</SELECT>\n";
```

This produces an HTML selection box with all of the data sources listed. But suppose you know you only want Oracle databases. The value of the returned hash contains the name of the driver, so you could filter them:

```
my (%dsn, $key) = Win32::ODBC::DataSources();
foreach $key (sort keys %dsn) {
    print HTML "<OPTION>$key\n"
        if $dsn{$key} =~ /Oracle/;
}
```

Once you've connected to a driver, you can query to see if it can handle a specific ODBC API function, such as transactions:

```
my(%data) = $db->GetFunctions($db->SQL_API_SQLTRANSACT);
my($transOK) = $data{$db->SQL_API_SQLTRANSACT};
$db->SetConnectOptions('SQL_AUTOCOMMIT', 'SQL_AUTOCOMMIT_OFF') if $transOK;
```

You can query the connection for things like the database name and version:

```
my($db_ver) = $db->GetInfo($db->SQL_DBMS_VER);
my($db_name) = $db->GetInfo($db->SQL_DBMS_NAME);
```

You can also configure new data sources with ConfigDSN:

```
$db->ConfigDSN($db->ODBC_ADD_DSN, "Microsoft Access Driver (*.mdb)",
               "DSN=foo", "DBQ=c:\\temp\\foo.mdb");
```

The second argument is the driver name and has to be specified exactly right. The subsequent arguments are all driver-specific. One way to determine the name and the arguments is to set up a dummy data source of the correct type, connect to it, and then use GetDSN to find out what it expects when configuring it:

```
my (%data, $key) = $db->GetDSN();
foreach $key (keys %data) {
    print "$key: <$data{$key}>\n";
}
```

Then, specify these same elements when adding a new data source, like I did above.

Data Dictionary

After connecting to a data source, you can find out what tables are in it:

```
my(@tables) = $db->TableList;
```

This will return all tables regardless of who owns them. You can use the more versatile Catalog if you wish to find only specific tables or table types:

```
# Table-type is VIEW
my(@views) = $db->Catalog("", "", "", 'VIEW');

# Owner is UBER, type is SYSTEM TABLE
my(@uber) = $db->Catalog("", 'UBER', "", 'SYSTEM TABLE');
```

You can't determine which fields are in a particular table, because the corresponding function for fields, SQLColumns, wasn't implemented in Win32::ODBC. You can, however, find out what fields or columns are in a specific result set and get their column attributes:

```
$db->Sql("SELECT * FROM State");
my (@fields) = $db->FieldNames;

my (%type) = $db->ColAttributes($db->SQL_COLUMN_TYPE);
my (%len)  = $db->ColAttributes($db->SQL_COLUMN_LENGTH);
my (%null) = $db->ColAttributes($db->SQL_COLUMN_NULLABLE);

foreach $field (sort @fields) {
    print HTML "<TR><TD>$field<TD>$type{$field}",
            "<TD>$len{$field}<TD>",
            $null{$field}==$db->SQL_NO_NULLS ? "NOT NULL" : "","<BR>";
}
```

For my State table, this would produce:

```
<TR><TD>PITD4<TD>4<TD><BR>
<TR><TD>ProductITD4<TD>4<TD><BR>
<TR><TD>Sequence<TD>5<TD>2<TD><BR>
```

Conclusion

I never did start that hot sauce business. Once I had all the pieces together and working, I found that solving the problem was much more interesting than running a company. I now use Perl and Win32::ODBC to help with my web site, generating hundreds of pages from several different databases.

Check out the Win32::ODBC FAQ at *http://www.roth.net/odbc/odbcfaq.htm*. The PepperSearch.pl program demonstrating the issues in this article appears in its entirety in Example 62-1.

Example 62-1. PepperSearch.pl

```perl
#!/usr/bin/perl -w

use strict;
use Win32::ODBC;
use CGI qw(:standard);

# Open database connection
my ($DSN) = "Article";
my ($db) = new Win32::ODBC($DSN) ||
    die qq{Cannot open ODBC connection to "$DSN":}, Win32::ODBC::Error, "\n";

# Get incoming CGI parameters
my ($query) = new CGI;
my ($submit, $pid, $heat, $start, $maxrows);
$submit  = $query->param('submit');
$pid     = $query->param('pid');
$heat    = $query->param('heat');
$start   = $query->param('start');
$maxrows = $query->param('maxrows');

$pid = $$ unless $pid;

# Globally used
my ($rc, $stmt, $num_rows, $end);
$num_rows = 10;

# Determine Scoville limits
my ($max, $min);
if ($heat eq 'MILD') {          # Just a hint of pepper
    $min = 0;
    $max = 500;
} elsif ($heat eq 'MEDIUM') {   # Where most people like it
    $min = 500;
    $max = 2500;
} elsif ($heat eq 'HOT') {      # Finally, some flavor!
    $min = 2500;
    $max = 10000;
} elsif ($heat eq 'SCORCHER') { # Now we're talking
    $min = 10000;
    $max = 100000;
} else {                        # Implied: $heat eq 'INSANE'
    $heat = 'INSANE';
    $min = 100000;
    $max = 0;                   # No limit.
}
```

Example 62-1. PepperSearch.pl (continued)

```perl
    # What button was used?
    if ($submit eq 'new') {          # Delete old search results from State table
        $stmt = "DELETE FROM State WHERE PID = $pid";
        $rc = $db->Sql($stmt);
        die "SQL failed \"$stmt\":", $db->Error(), "\n" if $rc;

        # Fill State table
        # Get second DB connection
        my ($ins) = new Win32::ODBC($db);

        # Perform new search
        # Build SQL statement
        $stmt = "SELECT ProductID FROM Sauces WHERE Scoville >= $min ";

        # Add in maximum value (if there is one)
        $stmt .= "AND Scoville < $max " if $max;

        # Add sequence request
        $stmt .= "ORDER BY Scoville, ProductName";

        # Compile the SQL statement
        $rc = $db->Sql($stmt);
        die qq{SQL failed "$stmt": }, $db->Error(), "\n" if $rc;

        # Loop through all rows
        my ($cnt, $id) = 0;
        while ($db->FetchRow) {
            ($id) = $db->Data;       # Get Product ID

            # Immediately insert into State table
            $stmt = "INSERT INTO State (PID, ProductID, Sequence) " .
                    "VALUES ($$, $id, " . $cnt++ . ")";
            $rc = $ins->Sql($stmt);
            die qq{SQL failed "$stmt": }, $ins->Error(), "\n" if $rc;
        }

        # Set start, maxrows and pid
        $start = 0;
        $pid = $$;
        $maxrows = $cnt;
    } elsif ($submit eq 'next') { $start += $num_rows }
    else { $start -= $num_rows }

    # Check min and max
    $start = $maxrows - $num_rows if $start > $maxrows;
    $start = 0 if $start < 0;
    $end = ($start + $num_rows > $maxrows ? $maxrows : $start + $num_rows);

    # Print HTML headers
    print qq(<!DOCTYPE HTML PUBLIC "-//W3C//DTD HTML 3.2//EN">\n\n);
    print qq(<HTML><HEAD>\n);
    print qq(<TITLE>Peppers, Inc. Search Results</TITLE>\n);
    print qq(</HEAD>\n);
```

Example 62-1. PepperSearch.pl (continued)

```perl
print qq(<BODY>\n);
print qq(<H1 ALIGN=center>Peppers, Inc. Search Results</H1>\n);

# Print search results
$max -= 1 if $max;
print qq(Search: $heat [$min], ($max ? " - $max" : "+"),
     qq( units Scoville]<BR>\n);
print qq(Search results: ), $start + 1, qq( - $end of $maxrows<BR>\n);

# Start form, table
print qq(<FORM METHOD=POST ACTION="http://foobar.com/cgi-bin/PepperSearch.pl">\n);
print qq(<TABLE BORDER=1>\n);
print qq(<TR><TH>Scoville<TH>Name<TH>Pepper<TH>Quantity<TH>Price\n);

# Fetch Sauces data based on State table data
$stmt = "SELECT sa.* FROM State st " .
        "INNER JOIN Sauces sa ON st.ProductID = sa.ProductID " .
        "WHERE st.PID = $pid AND st.Sequence >= $start " .
        "AND st.Sequence < $end ORDER BY st.Sequence";

# Compile the SQL statement
$rc = $db->Sql($stmt);
die qq{SQL failed "$stmt": }, $db->Error(), "\n" if $rc;

# Fetch each row
while ($db->FetchRow) {
    my(%data) = $db->DataHash;
    print qq(<TR><TD>$data{'Scoville'}<TD>$data{'ProductName'}),
       qq(<TD>$data{'PepperType'}<TD>$data{'Quantity'}<TD>$data{'Price'}\n);
}

# End table, and print hidden form elements
print qq(</TABLE>\n);
print qq(<P>\n);
print qq(<INPUT TYPE=HIDDEN NAME="pid" VALUE="$$">\n);
print qq(<INPUT TYPE=HIDDEN NAME="heat" VALUE="$heat">\n);
print qq(<INPUT TYPE=HIDDEN NAME="start" VALUE="$start">\n);
print qq(<INPUT TYPE=HIDDEN NAME="maxrows" VALUE="$maxrows">\n);

# Print buttons (next, prev, new) and we're done!
print qq(<INPUT TYPE=SUBMIT VALUE="Prev $num_rows" NAME="prev">\n)
  if $start > 0;
print qq(<INPUT TYPE=SUBMIT VALUE="Next $num_rows" NAME="next">\n)
  if $end < $maxrows;
print qq(<P>\n) if ($start > 0) || ($end < $maxrows);
print qq(<INPUT TYPE=SUBMIT VALUE="New Search" NAME="new">\n);
print qq(<INPUT TYPE=RADIO VALUE="MILD" NAME="heat"> Mild\n);
print qq(<INPUT TYPE=RADIO VALUE="MEDIUM" NAME="heat"> Medium\n);
print qq(<INPUT TYPE=RADIO VALUE="HOT" NAME="heat"> Hot\n);
print qq(<INPUT TYPE=RADIO VALUE="SCORCHER" NAME="heat"> Scorcher\n);
print qq(<INPUT TYPE=RADIO VALUE="INSANE" NAME="heat" CHECKED> Insane\n);
print qq(</FORM></BODY></HTML>\n);
```

Counterpoint: The DBI Alternative to Win32::ODBC

The DBI is Perl's standard, portable, and database-independent interface. It's similar to an ODBC "Driver Manager" in that it requires *driver modules* to communicate with different types of databases. DBI drivers (known as DBDs) are available for many database types, including Oracle, Informix, Sybase, DB2, Ingres, mSQL, Solid, Postgres, Illustra, Empress, and, of course, ODBC!

The DBI has a different philosophy than Win32::ODBC. The Win32::ODBC module is a "thin" layer over the low-level ODBC API; the DBI defines a simpler, higher level interface.

The Win32::ODBC module gives you access to more of the ODBC API. The DBI and DBD::ODBC give you access to everything most applications need. However, unlike Win32::ODBC, the DBI and DBD::ODBC do support *parameter binding* and *multiple prepared statements*, both of which can dramatically increase performance.

The Win32::ODBC module only works on Win32 systems. The DBI and DBD::ODBC are very portable and work on Win32 and Unix. The DBI and DBD::ODBC modules are supplied as a standard part of Perl for Win32. Scripts written with the DBI and DBD::ODBC are faster than Win32::ODBC on Win32 and are trivially portable to other supported database types.

The DBI offers optional automatic printing or dieing on errors, which makes applications simpler and more robust.

In summary, Win32::ODBC is your best choice if you need access to more of the ODBC API than the DBI gives you. Otherwise, the DBI and DBD::ODBC combination may be your best bet.

## CHAPTER 63

Net::LDAP

Joe Johnston

Your little black book has become threadbare over the years from frenetic discothe-queing, tardy nocturnal appeals to friends for bail money, and other shady Saturday night activities best left to the godless Carter years of double digit inflation and oil embargos. These days, you're on the go. You're mobile. You're wireless. You can't be tied down to one workstation, but you need your address book to follow you. After all, these are the days of robot maids and personal jet packs, right?

Perhaps you're the type of person who realizes it's not all about you. You might be an administrator for a workgroup whose members all need access to the same set of email addresses and aliases. Maybe your workgroup users have an eclectic set of email clients, like Eudora, Outlook, and Netscape. Do you want to maintain three separate address books for each client and then replicate the changes to each work-station? Only if you relish pain.

Centralized network address books, which can be used by client email programs like Outlook or Netscape Mail, are just one example of the kinds of programs that can be built with LDAP (Lightweight Directory Access Protocol, defined at *http://www.faqs. org/rfcs/rfc2251.html*). In this article, we'll look at what goes into building just such a program with Perl.

What Is LDAP?

LDAP is a protocol for directory services (database systems designed to allow fast searching against records all in a similiar format). LDAP is optimized to serve infor-mation that is frequently requested but rarely changed. Address books are the most common type of LDAP application.

Because modifications to the data are supposed to be infrequent, transactional data-base logic is not implemented by most LDAP servers. LDAP's emphasis is on speed, not robustness.

LDAP servers store data in a *Directory Information Tree* (or DIT), which is a hierarchical grouping of related data. LDAP clients (such as web browsers, or your Perl programs) access this data for the user.

To make this more concrete, let's build a directory of national restaurants using an LDAP system. By using an LDAP client, we'll be able to get a list of restaurants given a city or state.

Each restaurant's information would be stored in the LDAP's DIT structure called an *entry*. Each entry has several fields, like "name," "telephone," "city," or "state." Here's an example of a skeletal restaurant entry in LDAP Data Interchange Format (LDIF), which is commonly used to move text data into and out of LDAP servers:

```
dn:          o=Canestaro, l=Boston, st=MA
o:           Canestaro
l:           Boston
st:          MA
description: Fine eatery in the heart of the Fens
telephone:   999 555 1234
objectclass: top
objectclass: organization
```

In order to be found in the DIT, an entry must have a unique *distinguishing name*, or DN for short. In database speak, the DN is record's key. The distinguishing name field found in every entry will be made up of one or more *relative distinguishing names*, or RDNs. An entry's RDN is a set of the entry's fields that uniquely identify it from the rest of its siblings. In the restaurant example, the RDN is the organizational name, o=Canestaro. This restaurant is in the city of Boston, in the state of Massachusetts, and should be grouped with the rest of Beantown's bistros. To represent the city and state groupings, we need to add cities and states to our DIT. Here are the two entries needed to describe Boston, MA:

```
dn: st=MA
st: MA
objectclass: top
objectclass: name

dn: l=Boston
l: Boston
st: MA
objectclass: top
objectclass: name
```

We have nearly all the components necessary to describe the DN of our example restaurant. The order in which attributes are listed in the DN are from the most entry-specific to the least. Our example DN describes the name of the restaurant in its home city, which is located in some state.

The rest of our restaurant's entry description is a series of hash-like name-value pairs called *attributes*. Unlike the DN, which contains data of use only to the LDAP server, attributes are the information that users care about. Attribute names are usually terse, case-insensitive, and no more than two letters. You can find full descriptions of these in RFC 2256, but here o means "organization name," l stands for "locality" or city, and st is short for "state." The description field provides human-readable text about the entry.

The final attribute is objectclass: it tells the LDAP server which fields are allowable and which aren't. Again, RFC 2256 is a good resource for learning about all the objectclass options. Like Perl's OO object, LDAP object classes are hierarchical. Unlike Perl's objects (whose parentage can be found in the @ISA array), LDAP entries must explicitly list all of their parent classes. All object classes are descended from top (the equivalent of Perl's UNIVERSAL).

Two popular LDAP implementations are OpenLDAP and Netscape's LDAP. Both come with a command-line utility called ldapsearch that allows us to examine our DIT. The basic arguments to ldapsearch are a search filter, which contains our search criteria, and an option list of fields to display. We will discuss how to build LDAP search filters in the section "A Searchable Web Interface to Manage Your Directory." To find all our Boston restaurant options, we could type:

```
% ldapsearch "(&(l=Boston)(st=MA)(o=*)" o telephone
```

This would give us output like this:

```
o=Canestaro, l=Boston, st=MA
o=Canestaro
telephone=999 555 1234

o=Boston BeerWorks, l=Boston, st=MA
o=Boston BeerWorks
telephone=999 555 1235
```

Obviously, this list has been shortened a bit, since there is at least one more good Boston restaurant.

Now that we know what information our LDAP server will contain, let's examine the server itself.

Setting Up an OpenLDAP Server

I recommend the open source LDAP server from the OpenLDAP Project, at *http://www.openldap.org*. Follow the supplied directions for compiling (./configure and make) to install it (for more detailed instructions, see *http://metalab.unc.edu/Linux/HOWTO/LDAP-HOWTO-1.html*).

As mentioned above, OpenLDAP comes with a variety of command-line tools, which all start with the word ldap, to manipulate our DIT. We've already seen ldapsearch. We could put our data into LDIF format and use ldapadd to populate our DIT. Check your local documentation for usage options.

The standalone LDAP daemon (slapd) is what provides access to our DIT. The most important item required by slapd is a definition of the *suffix* field, which is used for the backend storage system used by LDAP. There must be at least one suffix field defined in the configuration file. The suffix is the topmost RDN, containing the rest of the DIT. All our entries will need to have this RDN tacked on to their DN. We'll use our hostname, daisypark.net, as our suffix:

```
suffix "dc=daisypark, dc=net"
```

No authorization is required by our LDAP server to read the DIT. It's considered a public resource, much like a web server. But in order to make changes to the DIT, we need an administrative account. Like everything else, this account will be stored in our DIT as an entry. This account is normally called Manager (the cn below stands for canonical name) and ought to have a decent password:

```
rootdn "cn=Manager, dc=daisypark, dc=net"
rootpw s3cr3t
```

The password is stored in clear text in the configuration file. Worse, it's passed to the server unencrypted. The specification for LDAP 3 details two authentication schemes. The first, called "simple," transmits passwords in clear text. The other, Simple Authentication and Security Layer, is a protocol for plugging in our choice of authentication schemes. If our DIT will be updated over a public network, that's what we'll want to use.

One last detail is to create an entry corresponding to the suffix that slapd requires. Recall that the suffix is tacked on to each and every entry as an RDN, and all RDNs have a entry. Here is the entry for our example DIT:

```
dn:   dc=daisypark, dc=net
dc:   daisypark
dc:   net
o:    Testing, Inc
objectclass: top
objectclass: organization
objectclass: dcobject
```

Now that the configuration file is tailored to our system, let's start the server and populate it with our sample address data. Directions for starting the LDAP server vary from system to system, so consult your server's documentation for more detail.

Loading Data into the Directory

Graham Barr wrote an excellent object-oriented interface to client LDAP operations: the Net::LDAP module, which should work with all standard LDAP servers. We'll use it to build an LDAP client that populates a DIT.

Our sample data is in tab-separated format, with the field names occupying the first line of the file. We'll assume that our field values won't have any embedded tabs, so parsing the file will be easy.

The interesting fields in this text file are FirstName, LastName, EmailAddress, HomePhone, Address, PostalCode, and StateOrProvince. We could use all of this information for each entry, but we will only be looking at names, email addresses, and phone numbers.

In our client that loads the addresses into the server (Example 63-1), we'll focus on the code responsible for using the LDAP protocol. If you've worked with DBI, you may find similiarities in the way Net::LDAP operates: connect to a server, do something, and then disconnect.

Example 63-1. A data-loading LDAP client

```
 1   #!/usr/bin/perl --
 2   # Script to transform tab delimited address data into LDAP.
 3
 4
 5
 6   use Net::LDAP;
 7   use strict;
 8
 9   my $infile = $ARGV[0] || "addresses.txt";
10
11   my $conn = Net::LDAP->new("ldap.daisypark.net") or # Replace with your LDAP server
12     die "ERROR: Can't connect: $@";
13
14   # make a authenticated connection
15   $conn->bind( dn => 'cn=Manager, dc=daisypark, dc=net',
16               password => 'secret',
17             );
18
19   my $progress = 1;
20   $|++;
21   while ( my $rec = get_next_record($infile) ) {
22
23       next unless "$rec->{FirstName}$rec->{LastName}";
24
25       my $result = $conn->add(
26         dn => "cn=$rec->{FirstName} $rec->{LastName}, dc=daisypark, dc=net",
27
28         attr => [
29             cn               => "$rec->{FirstName} $rec->{LastName}",
30
31             sn               => $rec->{LastName},
32             mail             => $rec->{EmailAddress},
33             telephoneNumber  => $rec->{HomePhone},
34             street           => $rec->{Address},
35             postalCode       => $rec->{PostalCode},
36             st               => $rec->{StateOrProvince},
37             l                => $rec->{StateOrProvince},
38             c                => 'US',
39             objectclass      => [ 'top', 'person',
40                                   'organizationalPerson', 'inetOrgPerson',
41                                 ],
```

Example 63-1. A data-loading LDAP client (continued)

```
42                ],
43        );
44
45        if ( $result->code ) {
46            warn "WARN: Failed to add entry: $rec->{FirstName}, $rec->{LastName}: ",
47            sprintf "%x", $result->code;
48        }
49
50        printf "seen: %d\r", $progress++;
51    }
52
53    print "\nClosing LDAP connection\n";
54    $conn->unbind;
55    print "done\n";
56
57    #------
58    # Subroutines
59    #------
60    # get_next_record() opens the tab-delimited file, returning successive
61    # hashref records, one per entry.
62    {
63      my ($seen, @headers); # persistent variables
64      sub get_next_record {
65          my $file = shift || return;
66
67          unless ( $seen ) {
68              open F, $file or die "ERROR: Can't open $file: $!";
69              @headers   = split "\t", scalar ;
70              $seen = 1;
71          }
72
73          my $line;
74          unless ( defined ($line = ) ) {
75              close F;
76              return;
77          }
78
79          until ( $line ) {
80              chomp $line;
81              $line =~ s/\s*$//;
82          }
83
84          my $record = {};
85
86          @$record{ @headers } = (split "\t", $line);
87
88          return $record;
89      }
90    }
```

After connecting to our LDAP server as Manager, we read in our tab-delimited data one line at a time. Each line is a record that will be transformed into a hash, and each hash will become an entry in the DIT.

Line 11 instantiates a new Net::LDAP object that expects to find an LDAP server on a machine named daisypark.net. Recall that we can make changes to the DIT only if we are the authorized user, Manager. We use the Net::LDAP bind method to "log in" to the LDAP server as this account. We pass the password and the full DN of the Manager account, cn=Manager, dc=daisypark, dc=net, to the bind method to prove that we are who we say we are.

As we fetch more records from our text file, we add new entries to the DIT with the add method. Line 25 does this with the dn and attr parameters. We put the entry attributes in an anonymous array of name-value pairs, beginning on line 28. To determine whether the add fails, we examine the object returned by this method. This Net::LDAP::Message object, labeled in our script as $results, has a method called code. If this method returns a nonzero value, we know that an error occurred during the add call; the check is on line 45.

Once we've read through the source text file, we perform a little object cleanup on line 54 by closing down the connection to the LDAP object with the unbind method.

After running Example 63-1 against our flat text address file, we should vet the data in the DIT for errors. There are a couple of ways to do this. LDAP servers typically come with tools to examine the DIT, like the previously mentioned ldapsearch. We can also use the Netscape 4.x Mail address book—itself an LDAP client—to look at our LDAP server. Either way, we can perform various searches until we are satisfied that all went well with our upload.

If we only needed to setup a company-wide Rolodex to which existing user email clients (and their accompanying LDAP address books) could connect, we'd be done. This may be all you ever want to do with LDAP. However, we can do more with the Net::LDAP module. Let's build a searchable, editable web client interface to this DIT.

A Searchable Web Interface to Manage Your Directory

Our CGI LDAP client (Example 63-2) is long but straightforward; you can tailor this code for your needs. Example 63-2 creates a form in which the user can enter a search term; it then displays all the matches found as an HTML table. Each row of the table can be edited and saved back into the DIT.

Example 63-2. A CGI interface to an LDAP server

```
1   #!/usr/bin/perl --
2   # jjohn 6/2000
3   # A CGI interface to a LDAP server.
4
5   use strict;
6   use CGI          qw/:all *table/;
7   use CGI::Carp    qw/fatalsToBrowser/;
8   use CGI::Pretty  qw/:all/;
9   use Net::LDAP;
10
```

Example 63-2. A CGI interface to an LDAP server (continued)

```
11   # first, set up the main objects
12   my $cgi     = CGI->new( );
13
14   my $base_dn = 'dc=daisypark, dc=net';
15   my $conn     = Net::LDAP->new("ldap.daisypark.net") or
16     die "ERROR: Can't connect: $@";
17
18   # Make a authenticated connection with the s3cr3t password
19   $conn->bind( dn       => "cn=Manager, $base_dn",
20               password => 's3cr3t',
21            );
22
23   # Have we been asked to do anything?
24   my $action = $cgi->param('action');
25
26   for ($action){
27       my $message = '';
28       /search/ && do {
29         $message = search(
30                           ldap   => $conn,
31                           base_dn => $base_dn,
32                           cgi    => $cgi,
33                         );
34       };
35
36       /modify/ && do {
37         $message = modify(
38                           ldap    => $conn,
39                           base_dn => $base_dn,
40                           cgi    => $cgi,
41                         );
42       };
43
44       paint( ldap    => $conn,
45             base_dn => $base_dn,
46             cgi     => $cgi,
47             message => $message,
48          );
49   }
50
51   $conn->unbind;
52   exit;
53
54   #-------
55   # Subroutines
56   #-------
57   sub paint{
58       my %params = @_;
59
60       print
61         header,
62         start_html( -bgcolor => "#FFFFFF",
63                     -title   => ($params{title} ||
```

Example 63-2. A CGI interface to an LDAP server (continued)

```
64                              'View LDAP for Daisypark'),
65                  ),
66          h2( ($params{title} || 'View LDAP for Daisypark') ),
67          hr,
68          ($params{message} || 'Please perform a search');
69
70      print
71          hr,
72          start_form,
73          '<INPUT TYPE="HIDDEN" NAME="action" VALUE="search">',
74          'Search: ',
75          textfield( -name => 'search'),
76          submit,
77          end_form,
78          end_html;
79  }
80
81  # ldap_lookup( ) returns an LDAP entry object
82  # for the provided search term.
83  sub ldap_lookup {
84      my %params = @_;
85
86      my $criteria = $params{search};
87      my $filter;
88
89      # hack, I want to search for everything
90      # if I have an empty string
91      undef $criteria if $criteria eq '';
92
93      for (qw/c mail sn cn telephonenumber/) {
94          # todo: $params{search} needs to escape meta-chars!
95          if ( defined $criteria ) {
96              $filter .= "($_=*".$criteria."*) ";
97          } else {
98              $filter .= "($_=*) ";
99          }
100     }
101     $filter = "(| $filter)";
102
103     my $mesg = $params{ldap}->search(
104                                 base   => $params{base_dn},
105                                 filter => $filter,
106                                 );
107     if ( $mesg->code ) {
108         die "Oops ($filter): ", $mesg->error;
109     }
110
111     return $mesg;
112 }
113
114 # search( ) performs a lookup in the LDAP for a given string,
115 # returning a nice HTML table.
116
```

Example 63-2. A CGI interface to an LDAP server (continued)

```perl
117  sub search {
118      my %params = @_;
119
120      my $mesg = ldap_lookup( @_,
121                              search => ( $params{search} ||
122                                          $params{cgi}->param('search')
123                                        ),
124                            );
125
126      if ( $mesg->count == 0 ) {
127          return "No matches found for '$params{search}'";
128      }
129      my $results;
130      $results .= p(small('Matches: ' .
131                          b($mesg->count) .
132                          ' for term ' .
133                          b( $params{cgi}->param('search') )
134                  ));
135      $results .= start_table( -cellspacing => 0,
136                               -cellpadding => 0,
137                             );
138      $results .= Tr(
139                      th({-bgcolor=>'pink'},
140                        [qw/Name E-Mail Phone Change/])
141                    );
142      # add some pretty color every third row
143      my $row = 0;
144      for my $entry ( $mesg->all_entries ) {
145
146          my $cn = $entry->get('cn')->[0];
147
148          $results .= Tr(
149                          {-bgcolor => (!($row%3) ? "#CCCCCC" :"#FFFFFF") },
150                          start_form,
151                          '<INPUT TYPE="HIDDEN" NAME="action" VALUE="modify">',
152                          qq/<INPUT TYPE="HIDDEN" NAME="old_cn" VALUE="$cn">/,
153                          td(textfield( {   -name => 'cn',
154                                            -default => $entry->get('cn')
155                                          })),
156                          td(textfield( {-name    => 'mail',
157                                         -default => $entry->get('mail')
158                                       })),
159                          td(textfield( {-name    => 'telephonenumber',
160                                         -default => $entry->get('telephonenumber')
161                                       })),
162                          td( submit ),
163                          end_form,
164                        );
165
166          $row++;
167      }
168
```

Example 63-2. A CGI interface to an LDAP server (continued)

```
169         return $results .= end_table;
170   }
171
172   sub modify {
173     my %params = @_;
174
175     my $old_cn = $params{cgi}->param('old_cn');
176     my $mesg = ldap_lookup( @_,
177                            search => $old_cn );
178
179     if ( $mesg->count == 0 ) {
180         return "Oops: Can't find $old_cn";
181     }
182
183     my $cgi = $params{cgi};
184     my $entry = $mesg->entry(0); # really need to iterate over results
185
186     # Delete if 'cn' is empty, else modify
187     my $report = '';
188     if ( $cgi->param('cn') =~ /^\s*$/ ) {
189         $entry->delete();
190         $report = "Deleted";
191     } else {
192         $entry->replace(
193                        cn              => $cgi->param('cn'),
194                        mail            => $cgi->param('mail'),
195                        telephoneNumber => $cgi->param('telephonenumber'),
196                        );
197         $report = "Updated";
198     }
199
200     $entry->update( $params{ldap} );
201     return $report . " " . $cgi->param('cn');
202   }
```

Perl has a wealth of modules to make a programmer's life easier, and Lines 5–9 demonstrate some familiar standbys: CGI, CGI::Carp (for error reporting), CGI::Pretty (for aesthetically displaying CGI output), and Net::LDAP. Efficiency wonks will note that CGI::Pretty is both slow and unneccessary, but it sure is nice being able to look at human-readable HTML during development. Also helpful for debugging is the fatalsToBrowser option of CGI::Carp.

As before, we need to make an authenticated connection to the LDAP server (lines 19 through 21) in order to make changes to the DIT.

The script has three functions. It renders a blank HTML form (shown in Figure 63-1) prompting for a search term if none is given. (I call this "painting.") If a search term is given, the script looks through our DIT and returns the results to the generic paint function. If a entry is edited, it makes the requested change and repaints the screen.

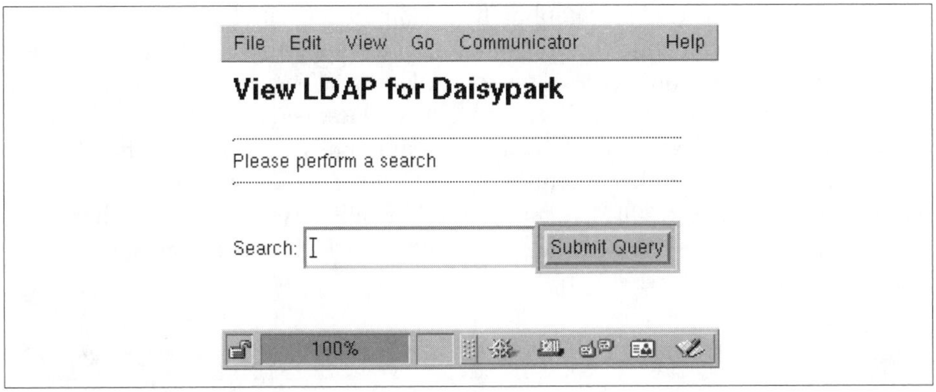

Figure 63-1. A web client awaiting a search term

Lines 26 to 49 contain an odd for loop. This is simply a switch statement that enumerates the three functions of the program. The script looks for the CGI variable `action` to determine which function to execute. The default function is painting a blank form. The first interesting function begins on line 83. `ldap_lookup` queries the LDAP server for the given terms and returns the results as an LDAP message object.

RFC 2254 describes the many ways that LDAP can compare data. In Example 63-2, we use only one of those ways: the partial case-insensitive match. If the search term matches any part of the country, email, full name, or telephone fields, the search is considered successful. More refined search functions can be created easily.

LDAP requires a somewhat odd syntax for describing search filters. Like anything that deals with a set of data, LDAP defines a group of Boolean operators (e.g., "or" and "and"). These must *precede* the terms that they join. Fortunately, the operators should look familiar to Perl programmers:

```
(| (c=US)(cn=joe*) )
```

```
(& (c=US)(cn=joe*) )
```

In the first example, we're looking for entries in the DIT that have a country field of US or ("|") have canonical names that begin with joe. In the second, we have the same terms "and"ed together ("&"), which selects only entries fulfilling both of those criteria.

The Net::LDAP search method returns a message object. We can check for error conditions by looking at the numeric code returned from the code method; any non-zero value indicates an error. The specific error message can be retrieved with a call to the error method. On line 120, the search terms are passed to `ldap_lookup`. Assuming no fatal errors occurred, we then look at the message object's count method, which returns the number of matched entries for our terms. Provided at least one entry matches, we can use a simple foreach loop to iterate over all the entry objects returned by the message object's `all_entries` method.

This Entry object is our interface to an individual DIT entry. Because all fields in an entry can be multivalued, the get method returns an anonymous list of values.

The spreadsheet is a useful metaphor for manipulating tabular data such as this address book. Implementing this metaphor calls for some tricky HTML code. Lines 148 to 164 create one row, representing one DIT entry. This row is an editable form that can update the entry if the user changes any values. Figure 63-2 shows the result of searching for an empty string, which in our program is a special case that displays the whole DIT. The number of entries in this address book was trimmed for this screenshot, but I specifically left my mother's name in the list to give her some reward for reading this article. She's not really into Perl, and doesn't quite know what I do. (Mom, this is what I do.)

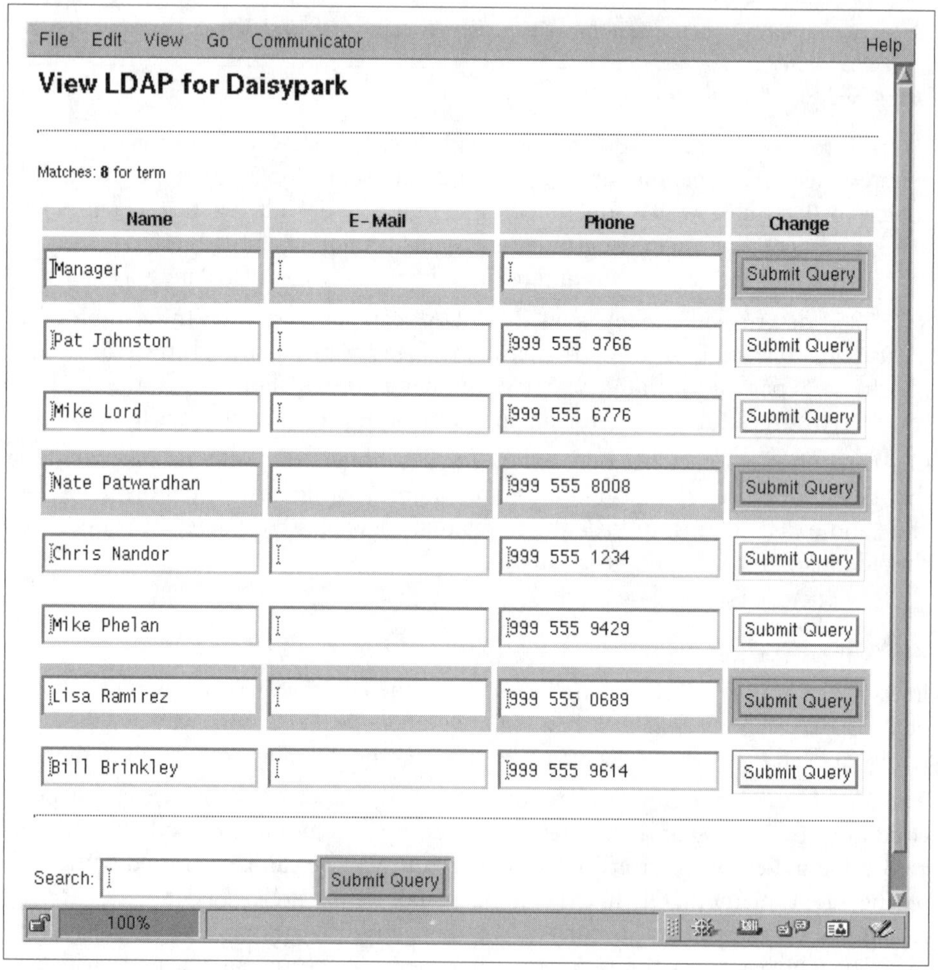

Figure 63-2. A web client displaying the whole DIT

Before we modify an existing DIT node, we have to locate the desired entry. This code locates entries by searching for the right cn field, which our CGI program stores in a hidden field. Here, I'll admit to a fudge: the search *could* return more than one entry. After all, the CN, unlike the DN, isn't guaranteed to be unique. It would have been better to use the DN of the desired entry. That's what it's there for, after all.

If the user cleared out the CN field in the form, we will erase that entry. Otherwise, the script will call the Entry object's replace method to change the relevant fields. The Entry does not get updated on the LDAP server until the update method is called on line 200. Figure 63-3 shows the result of looking for bill. After I add his email address and press the submit button, Figure 63-4 depicts the dramatic results.

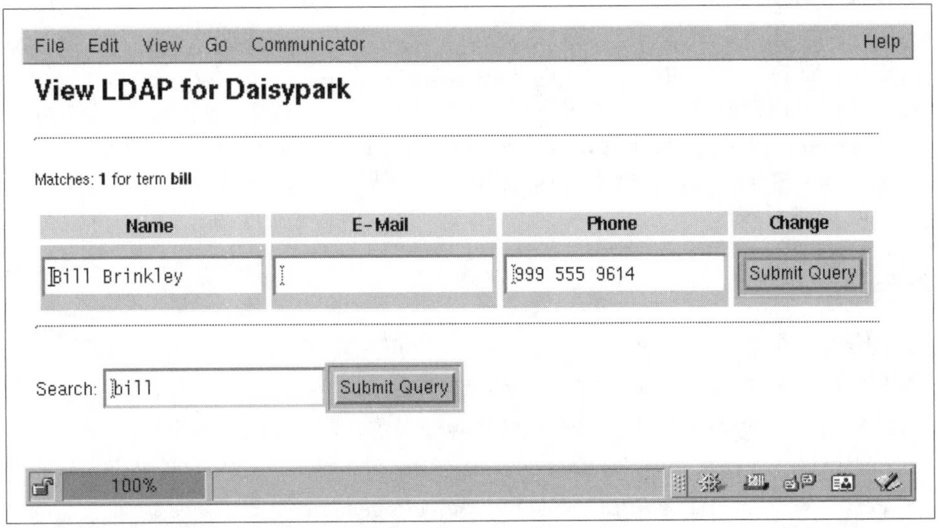

Figure 63-3. An entry before modification

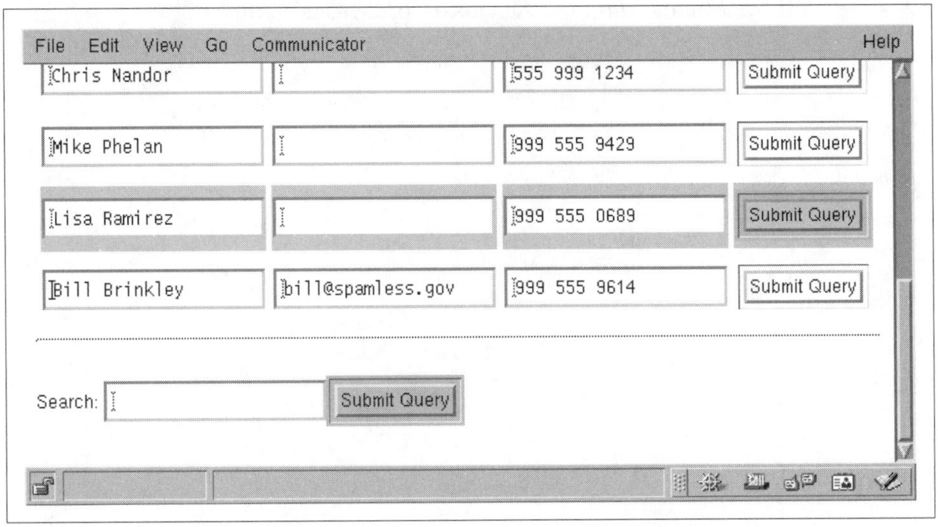

Figure 63-4. An entry after modification

So there we have it. In about two hundred lines of code, we have a platform-independent address book. You can easily adapt the concept shown here to make a fabulous Perl/Tk version. One important note: this code does not ensure data integrity on updates. That is, if multiple users attempt to update the DIT at the same time, LDAP will make no attempt to lock its data. This sort of "Atomic Consistency Isolation and Durability" (ACID) support is well beyond LDAP's capabilities. If you find yourself needing it, use a real relational database management system.

Where LDAP Is Going

LDAP is becoming pervasive. It forms the backbone of both Microsoft's Active Directory system as well as Novell's Network Directory Services. Netscape has also been very active in developing their own LDAP server implementation, and even Sendmail, Inc. is supporting LDAP address systems. You'll likely see directory services mature and grow, eventually eclipsing such old network standards like NIS and possibly even DNS.

References

- LDAP 3: *http://www.faqs.org/rfcs/rfc2251.html*
- OpenLDAP project: *http://www.openldap.org/*
- PerLDAP home page: *http://perl-ldap.sourceforge.net/*
- Set up OpenLDAP: *http://metalab.unc.edu/Linux/HOWTO/LDAP-HOWTO-1.html*
- PerLDAP home page: *http://perl-ldap.sourceforge.net/*
- inetOrgPerson LDAP objects: *http://www.faqs.org/rfcs/rfc2798.html*
- LDAP Object Schemas: *http://www.faqs.org/rfcs/rfc2256.html*

## CHAPTER 64

Web Databases the Genome Project Way

Lincoln D. Stein

This article is going to be a bit different. Instead of describing a neat trick or technique for Perl web programming, I'm going to talk a bit about my own work in the Human Genome Project.

The data generated by the Genome Project is more complex than the type of data one usually sees in business applications. Instead of a few simple relationships between objects, biological objects are woven into a rich web of interconnections. For example, a DNA sequence will contain a number of genes, each of which encodes one or more proteins, each of which has a confirmed or predicted function. The protein functions, in turn, are related to diseases, which are related to disease mapping information, which are related to genes, which are related back to DNA sequences. You can describe biological information in the familiar terms of a relational database schema, but you might not like the results. Inevitably you "fracture" the original biological objects into many small tables. Some Oracle-based genome databases use relational schemas of over 600 tables and require a database guru just to formulate and execute useful queries!

A more natural solution for storing biological data is to use an object-oriented system. In such a system, real-world objects like genes and DNA sequences are mapped directly onto database objects. This makes it easier for the end users (the biologists), to understand the database, and facilitates communication between the users and the database designers.

The ACEDB Database

There are a variety of object-oriented databases in use in the Genome Project. The most widely used one, and the one I talk about in this article is called ACEDB. ACEDB was originally written to support the sequencing of a small soil-living worm called *C. elegans*, a fact reflected in its name (ACEDB stands for "A *C. elegans* dataBase"). However, it's now used by groups sequencing everything from barley to swine, and is the primary database used by several of the larger labs in the human sequencing project as well.

The primary authors of ACEDB are Richard Durbin and Jean Thierry-Mieg, aided and abetted over the years by a large number of volunteers and collaborators. It consists of some 250,000 lines of C code, and is available for unrestricted use and distribution under open source terms. My role in the ACEDB project has been to develop Java and Perl client APIs, as well as to develop web interfaces to a variety of ACEDB databases. These APIs and web interfaces are also available on an open source basis.

ACEDB can operate in single-user mode on Unix or Windows NT systems, in which case it interacts directly with end users via a graphical frontend, or can operate as a faceless server, providing read/write or read-only access to network clients. As a database engine, the system compares favorably to MySQL and even to some commercial database engines; server reliability is excellent, even when working with databases containing millions of objects.

Although there are many features of ACEDB that betray its origins as a biological database (what other database has a primitive data type called "DNA"?), there's nothing preventing it from being used for other purposes. For instance, ACEDB has been used by the quality control division of Intel corporation to store test results on chip components. For the purposes of illustration, this column uses a small database of movie films called *moviedb* that was generously provided by Fred Wobus of the Sanger Centre in Cambridge, England.

You can browse *moviedb* at the *http://stein.cshl.org/perl/ace/search/moviedb*, but be aware that this database is intended as a demo only. It only contains a few entries, and none of its contents are to be taken too seriously. To see a real biological database in action, have a look at the *C. elegans* genome database, a copy of which is located at *http://stein.cshl.org/elegans.html*.

ACEDB Objects and Classes

Figure 64-1 shows you an ACEDB data object from *moviedb* in the form displayed by one of the CGI scripts that I'll describe. Every ACEDB object has a *class*, which describes its data type, and an identifier called its *name*. In the case of the object shown in the figure, the class is Person, and the name is scorsese. Together the name and class uniquely identify an object in the database.

Every ACEDB object is a hierarchical tree consisting of tags and values. A few of the tags defined by the Person class are Full_name, Address, Stars_in, and Directed. To the right of each tag is either a data value, or more tags. Tags give the tree structure and serve to name portions of the subtree. For example, the subtree to the right of the Full_name tag is the single data value Martin Scorsese, while the subtree to the right of Address is a complex data type organized by the subtags Mail and Email. In ACEDB data objects, any part of the tree is potentially multivalued. The tree anchored at the Directed tag, for example, consists of a list of five entries corresponding to the Movie objects that Martin Scorsese has directed. ACEDB data types can be more complex than this, allowing the database designer to specify a wide variety of constructed types, lists, and sets.

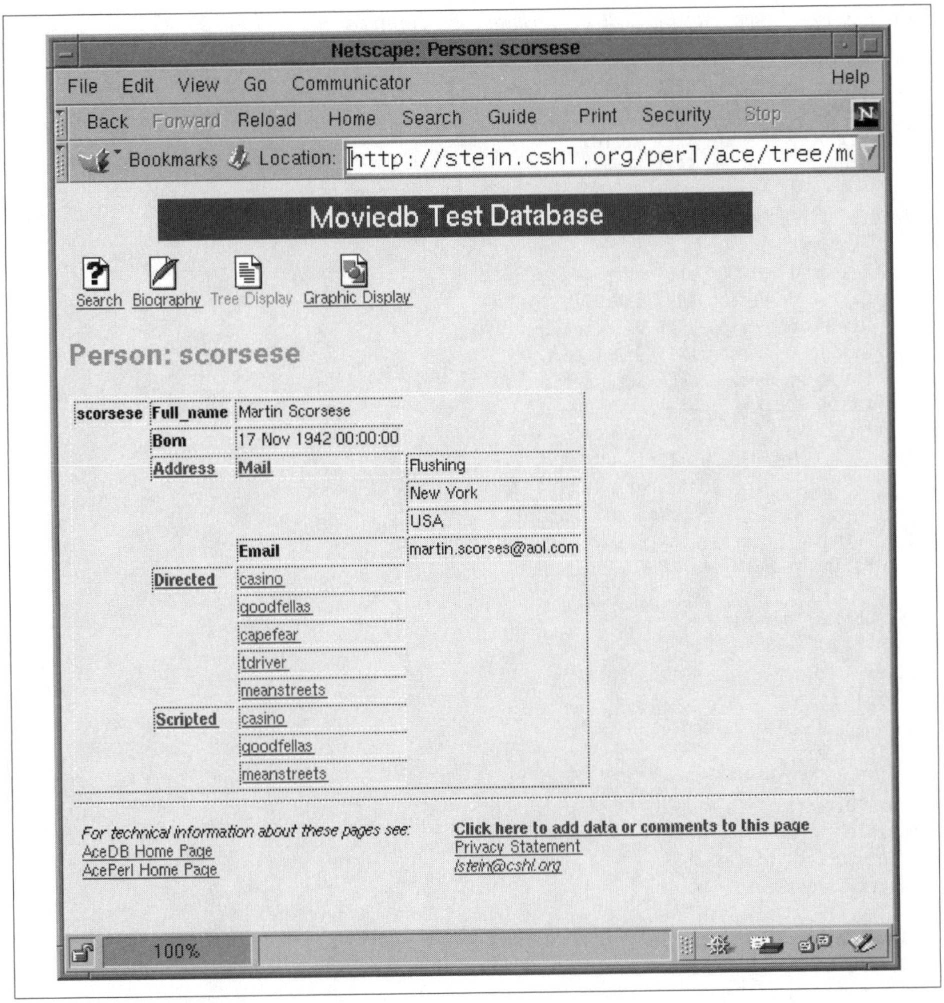

Figure 64-1. An ACEDB data object

Example 64-1 shows the complete schema for *moviedb* (known as the "model file" in ACEDB parlance). The schema definition language looks a lot like a set of ACEDB objects, and in fact is represented as such in the database. Classes are denoted using the notation ?Classname, tags are short string identifiers containing no whitespace, and data values are indicated using a series of reserved data type names like Text.

Example 64-1. Schema for moviedb demo database

```
// moviedb schema

?Person Full_name UNIQUE Text
    Born UNIQUE DateType
    Address  Mail Text
            Email Text
            Phone Text
```

Example 64-1. Schema for moviedb demo database (continued)

```
            Height UNIQUE Int
            Stars_in  ?Movie XREF Cast
            Directed  ?Movie XREF Director
            Scripted  ?Movie XREF Writer
            Wrote     ?Book  XREF Author

    ?Movie  Title UNIQUE Text
            Aka Text
            Released UNIQUE DateType
            Cast      ?Person XREF Stars_in
            Director ?Person XREF Directed
            Writer   ?Person XREF Scripted
            Based_on ?Book   XREF Script_for
            Rating UNIQUE Float

    ?Book      Reference     Title UNIQUE ?Text
                            Publisher UNIQUE Text
                                Year UNIQUE Int
            Author     ?Person XREF Wrote
            Script_for ?Movie  XREF Based_on

    // subclass definitions

    Class Actor
    Visible
    Is_a_subclass_of Person
    Filter Stars_in

    Class Director
    Visible
    Is_a_subclass_of Person
    Filter Directed

    Class ScriptWriter
    Visible
    Is_a_subclass_of Person
    Filter Scripted

    Class Author
    Visible
    Is_a_subclass_of Person
    Filter Wrote
```

Capitalized directives specify attributes for certain parts of the tree. For example, in the Person class, the subtree to the right of the Full_name tag has the attribute UNIQUE followed by the data type Text. This ensures that the Full_name subtree will never have more than a single data value, and that it will be of the Text, or string, type. The tree anchored at Height is a unique integer; however, the tree to the right of Phone is not tagged as unique, indicating that a Person can have multiple phone numbers (most of these Hollywood stars do, although they're all unlisted).

Still focusing on the definition of the Person class, examine the subtrees anchored at the Stars_in, Directed, Scripted, and Wrote tags. Instead of pointing to a primitive data type, these four tags all point to other constructed classes. For instance, the Stars_in tag points to one or more Movie objects, signifying the movies that the Person has starred in. Further, the XREF attribute establishes a cross-reference relationship between two classes. For example, the Stars_in tag of the Person class is cross-referenced with the Cast tag of the Movie class. This means whenever a new Movie is added to the Stars_in list, the Movie object's Cast list will be updated as well. A similar XREF in the Movie definition establishes the reverse relationship. The ACEDB data definition language provides a number of other features for controlling indexing and constraints.

At the bottom of the schema file is a set of subclass definitions (ordinarily these belong in a separate file, but I've added them to this listing for simplicity). Unlike most other object-oriented databases, ACEDB's subclassing system is entirely data driven. An object is subclassed based on its contents. The definitions given here subclass the generic Person class into Actor, Director, ScriptWriter, and Author subclasses based on a Filter directive. In the *moviedb* database, the Actor subclass is defined as any Person who has a Stars_in tag. Similarly, the Director subclass is any Person who has the tag Directed. These are all simple examples of the Filter directive, but interestingly, a filter can be any arbitrary ACEDB query. For example, you could define a SuperStar as a Person who has starred in more than 20 movies. Another consequence of this type of subclassing is that multiple inheritance is easy and natural.

Setting up a new ACEDB database is as simple as editing the schema file with a text editor, and launching the database application from the command line. The system will ask whether it should initialize itself, and, if you confirm, it will set up an empty database. You'll then load some data as described below. At any later point, you can edit the schema file and update the database by issuing the read models command. ACEDB will modify the data in-place to match the new schema, adding or removing tags as needed. This is in contrast to some other object-oriented systems, where schema evolution is tricky at best.

Data can be added to an ACEDB database in several ways. One way is to use the standalone application or a remote client to load a flat file in the format shown in Example 64-2. This format, which is easily generated by a Perl script, consists of each object flattened in such a way that each row of the object occupies a separate line. The entire hierarchy of tags doesn't have to be given, just the rightmost subtag. The ACEDB system knows how to rehydrate the tree based on the schema. A blank line separates objects. ACEDB databases are commonly exported and dumped in this format, which makes it easy to transfer data from one database to another or to rebuild a corrupted database (although this is an extremely uncommon occurrence).

Example 64-2. Flat file import/export representation of ACEDB data (excerpt)

```
// Class Person

Person : "brando"
Full_name    "Marlon Brando"
Born         1924-04-03
Mail         "Omaha"
Mail         "Nebraska"
Mail         "USA"
Stars_in     "godf1"
Stars_in     "apclypnow"

Person : "scorsese"
Full_name    "Martin Scorsese"
Born         1942-11-17
Mail         "Flushing"
Mail         "New York"
Mail         "USA"
Email        "martin.scorses@aol.com"
Directed     "casino"
Directed     "goodfellas"
Directed     "capefear"
Directed     "tdriver"
Directed     "meanstreets"
Scripted     "casino"
Scripted     "goodfellas"
Scripted     "meanstreets"

Person : "coppola"
Full_name    "Francis Ford Coppola"
Born         1939-04-07
Mail         "Detroit"
Mail         "Michigan"
Mail         "USA"
Directed     "godf1"
Directed     "godf2"
Directed     "apclypnow"
Scripted     "godf1"
Scripted     "godf2"
Scripted     "apclypnow"
```

Another way to load data into ACEDB is to enter data graphically using various editors that come with the graphical version of ACEDB. A third option is to use the Perl API described in the next section to create objects programatically.

Accessing ACEDB from Perl

The Perl interface to ACEDB makes good use of Perl's object-oriented features to accomplish a transparent mapping from ACEDB objects to Perl objects.

Example 64-3 is a simple AcePerl script that fetches an object from a networked ACEDB server, reads a data value, then updates it.

Example 64-3. Updating the "scorsese" Person object in a networked ACEDB database

```
#!/usr/local/bin/perl

use Ace;

my $db = Ace->connect(-port=>200008, -host=>'stein.cshl.org')
          || die "Can't connect ", Ace->error;

my $scorsese = $db->fetch(Person => 'scorsese')
        || die "Can't get scorsese object ", Ace->error;

my (@phone) = $scorsese->Phone;

unless (@phone) {
    $scorsese->add(Phone => '555-1212');
    $scorsese->commit || die "Can't commit ", Ace->error;
}
```

We'll walk through it a chunk at a time.

```
#!/usr/local/bin/perl

use Ace;

my $db = Ace->connect(-port=>200008, -host=>'stein.cshl.org')
            || die "Can't connect ", Ace->error;
```

The script begins by loading the Ace.pm module. It then calls the Ace class's connect method to connect to an ACEDB server at the indicated host and port. If connection fails, the script dies with an error message, calling the Ace::error method to obtain a description of the problem. If the connection succeeds, it returns a database accessor object, which we store into a local variable, $db. It is possible to establish connections with multiple databases simultaneously, and to open up both remote and local (non-networked) databases.

```
my $scorsese = $db->fetch(Person => 'scorsese')
            || die "Can't get scorsese object ", Ace->error;
```

The script now attempts to fetch the Person object with the name scorsese. If it succeeds, it returns a Perl object blessed into the Ace::Object class. Otherwise the script dies with an error. This is the simplest way to fetch an object. Other ways include wildcard matches, or ACEDB query language statements, either of which can return multiple objects at once. It is also possible to create a cursor over the database in order to fetch objects one at a time in a memory-efficient manner.

```
my @phone = $scorsese->Phone;
```

The script now attempts to find Martin Scorsese's phone number by calling the object's Phone method. Ace.pm dynamically generates Phone and other data access methods by consulting the schema of the connected database. The returned phone number, if any, is stored into a local variable, @phone. Notice that since the Phone tag is potentially multivalued, the script uses an array to store the data. Because ACEDB objects can be quite large (some of the DNA Sequence objects are many megabytes in size), data access is done in a bandwidth- and memory-conserving manner. Unless we specify otherwise, only those parts of an object that we need are ever moved from the database into Perl.

```
unless (@phone) {
    $scorsese->add(Phone => '501 555-1212');
    $scorsese->commit || die "Can't commit ", Ace->error;
}
```

If the list of phone numbers is empty, the script updates the Phone tag by adding a new value. It then attempts to commit the change to the server.

Although the host and port given here are real ones, this script won't work in your hands because the host is behind a firewall. If you wish to experiment with ACEDB, however, you can connect to some of the publicly-accessible read-only servers for DNA sequencing data that I give at the end of this article. A variety of demo scripts comes with the AcePerl package.

The Perl representation of ACEDB objects has many more methods than the few shown in this sample script. Among other things, it is possible to navigate through objects without advance knowledge of the database schema. For example, you could obtain the list of top-level tags in the $scorsese object in this way:

```
@tags = $scorsese->tags;
```

Then you could fetch and print the contents of these tags one by one:

```
foreach (@tags) {
    print $scorsese->get($_);
}
```

Other methods allow you to determine the type of each node of the object tree. In this way you could detect which nodes of the tree were subtags, and recurse on them. In fact, built-in methods do just this to transform ACEDB objects into various text and HTML representations.

Some ACEDB subtrees are in fact pointers to other database objects. When you retrieve such subtrees, you obtain lists of Ace::Objects that will perform further database accesses when necessary. For example, here's how to find the titles of all the movies that Martin Scorsese has starred in:

```
my @movies = $scorsese->Starred_in;
for my $movie (@movies) {
    print $movie->Title;
}
```

And here's a way to find all Scorsese's co-authors for screenplays:

```
my %coauthors;
for my $movie ($scorsese->Scripted) {
```

```
    foreach my $author ($movie->Writer) {
        $coauthors{$author}++ unless $author eq 'scorsese';
    }
}
```

If you are looking carefully, you'll notice an interesting bit of magic in the fourth line. The Perl string operators are overloaded in the Ace::Object class, allowing you to compare ACEDB objects to strings in a natural way. You can also print out objects and incorporate them into strings. During string interpolation, the object reference is replaced with its ACEDB object name.

Because ACEDB keeps its objects intact, it's very easy to move objects from one database to another. Provided that their schemas are compatible, you can move an object from database A to database B as easily as this:

```
my $object = $databaseA->fetch(...);
$databaseB->put($object);
```

ACEDB Meets the Web

Recently, I've been writing Perl modules for making ACEDB databases available for web browsing. These modules, collectively called AceBrowser, sit on top of AcePerl and consist of several parts. There's a utility module called AceSubs.pm that exports a variety of useful functions for displaying ACEDB objects on HTML pages, and handles such things as making the ACEDB client/server connection persistent. There's a series of CGI scripts that display objects in different ways. There are both schema-independent displays, such as the generic tree browser shown in Figure 64-1, and schema-dependent displays, such as those that display DNA Sequence and Protein objects. Then there are several types of search pages, which again come in schema-dependent and schema-independent groups. Finally, there's a configuration file that contains site-specific definitions for what databases should be made available to the Web and how to connect to them. This configuration file also implements a simple object registration system that associates ACEDB object classes with the CGI scripts that display them.

Out of the box, AceBrowser supports two different generic views on ACEDB objects. There's the tree browser, tree, which produced Figure 64-1. It is smart enough to collapse subtrees that are too long to display on a single page, and turn their tags into links that expand and collapse the subtree like the outliners of word processor programs. It is also capable of recognizing ACEDB object references and turning them into links to the appropriate CGI script.

Then there's a graphical browser named pic. The pic display asks the ACEDB server to return the graphical representation of the object. Several ACEDB classes have special display methods on the server side that allow biological objects like sequence maps and clones to be graphed. The pic script takes advantage of this ability by turning server-generated graphics into clickable image maps. The pic script isn't particularly useful for the *moviedb* database since the server doesn't have any special graphical representations for the classes defined in *moviedb*. However, I've kept this script associated with the *moviedb* database in case someone decides to add pictures of the cast or MPEG trailers to the database; ACEDB knows what to do with images and other types of multimedia.

The tree display is useful for debugging and development, but isn't particularly attractive. For that, you need schema-dependent views that reformat data objects into nice HTML pages. Example 64-4 shows a CGI script named person, which displays a Person object.

Example 64-4. The person script

```perl
#!/usr/local/bin/perl
# -*- Mode: perl -*-
# file: person
# Moviedb "person" display

use strict;
use vars '$DB';
use Ace 1.51;
use AceSubs;

use CGI 2.42 qw/:standard :html3 escape/;

# print HTTP header & open the database
AceInit();
$DB = OpenDatabase() || AceError("Couldn't open database.");
AceHeader();

my $person_name  = param('name');
my ($person)     = $DB->fetch(-class =>'Person',
                              -name  => $person_name,
                              -fill  => 1) if $person_name;

print_top($person);
print_warning($person_name)    if $person_name && !$person;
print_prompt();
print_report($person) if $person;
print_bottom();

exit 0;

sub print_top {
  my $person = shift;
  my $title = $person ? "Bio for $person" : 'Moviedb Person Report';
  print start_html ('-Title'   => $title, '-style'   => Style() ),
        HEADER, TypeSelector($person,'Person'),  h1($title);
}

sub print_bottom {
    print FOOTER;
}
```

Example 64-4. The person script (continued)

```perl
sub print_warning {
  my $name = shift;
  print p(font({-color => 'red'},
        "The person named \"$name\" is not found in the database."));
}

sub print_prompt {
    print start_form({-name=>'form1',-action=>Url(url(-relative=>1))}),
          p("Database ID", textfield(-name=>'name')),
          end_form;
}

sub print_report {
    my $person = shift;

    print h2($person->Full_name);

    if (my @address = $person->Address(2)) {
        print h3('Contact Information'),
              blockquote(address(join(br,@address)));
        print a({-href=>'mailto:' . $person->Email(1)},
              "Send e-mail to this person") if $person->Email;
    } else {
        print p(font({-color=>'red'},'No contact information in database'));
    }

    if ($person->Born || $person->Height) {
        print h3('Fun Facts'), table({-border=>undef},
              TR({-align=>'LEFT'}, th('Height'),
              td($person->Height(1) || '?')),
              TR({-align=>'LEFT'}, th('Birthdate'),
              td($person->Born(1)|| '?')));
    }

    if (my @directed = $person->Directed) {
        print h3('Movies Directed');
        my @full_names = map { a({-href=>Object2URL($_)},$_->Title) } @directed;
        print ol(li \@full_names);
    }

    if (my @scripted = $person->Scripted) {
        print h3('Movies Scripted');
        my @full_names = map { a({-href=>Object2URL($_)},$_->Title) } @scripted;
        print ol(li \@full_names);
    }

    if (my @stars_in = $person->Stars_in) {
        print h3('Starring Roles In');
        my @full_names = map { a({-href=>Object2URL($_)},$_->Title) } @stars_in;
        print ol(li \@full_names);
    }

}
```

We'll walk through Example 64-4 now, a screenshot from which is shown in Figure 64-2.

```
use strict;
use vars '$DB';
use Ace 1.51;
use AceSubs;
use CGI 2.42 qw/:standard :html3 escape/;
```

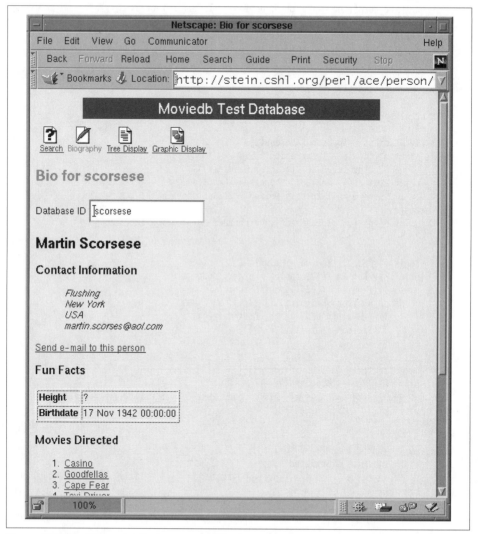

Figure 64-2. The Biography display generated by Example 63-4

The script begins by turning on strict syntax checking and importing routines from Ace.pm. It also loads up handy subroutines defined by the AceSubs.pm module of the AceBrowser system, and imports various symbols from the CGI.pm module. A variable named $DB is declared global for use as the database handle.

```
AceInit();
$DB = OpenDatabase() || AceError("Couldn't open database.");
AceHeader();
```

AceInit is defined by the AceBrowser subsystem, and does some internal variable initialization. OpenDatabase is another AceBrowser call; it consults the configuration file to determine which database to open and attempts to open it; the returned handle is stored in $DB. The name of the database is actually derived from the additional path information of the script URL. If this script were installed as */cgi-bin/ace/person*, then calling it as *http://your.site/cgi-bin/ace/person/moviedb* would tell the system to open the "moviedb" database. The generation of these URLs is ordinarily done internally by AceSubs—you don't have to worry about it.

AceHeader prints out the HTTP header and the top HTML boilerplate defined in the configuration file.

```
my $person_name  = param('name');
my ($person)     = $DB->fetch(-class =>'Person',
                              -name  => $person_name,
                              -fill  => 1) if $person_name;
```

The script looks for a CGI parameter named name. If present, it calls the Ace fetch method to retrieve the named Person object. This is a slightly longer version of the fetch method than we saw previously. The motivation for this is to use the -fill argument, which indicates that the entire Person object should be fetched in a single operation. Since the Person class is a relatively small one, it is more efficient to do the fetch in a single operation rather than a bit at a time as per default.

```
print_top($person);
print_warning($person_name)     if $person_name && !$person;
print_prompt();
print_report($person) if $person;
print_bottom();

exit 0;
```

The script now prints out the top of the HTML page and a warning if the requested Person does not exist in the database. It then prints out a textfield that allows the user to directly request another Person object without returning to the AceBrowser search pages. The print_report function prints out a short report on the requested Person object, and print_bottom prints out some bottom boilerplate. The script exits at this point.

```
sub print_top {
    my $person = shift;
    my $title = $person ? "Bio for $person" : 'Moviedb Person Report';
    print start_html ('-Title'  => $title, '-style'  => Style()),
          HEADER, TypeSelector($person,'Person'), h1($title);
}
```

```
sub print_bottom {
    print FOOTER;
}
```

The print_top and print_bottom functions are responsible for the top and bottom boilerplate of the HTML page. Most of this is self explanatory, except for a few calls into the AceBrowser system. Style, defined in AceSubs.pm, returns a stylesheet for the page, based on settings in the configuration file. HEADER and FOOTER are constants derived from other definitions in the configuration file; they are responsible for the banner at the top of the page and the various links and attributions at the bottom.

TypeSelector, defined in AceSubs.pm, produces a navigation bar for the object. It creates a row of icons at the top of the page that allow the user to navigate to the search pages, or to various alternative displays for the object. In Figure 64-2, I show the Biography display generated by the current script. Alternative displays include Tree Display generated by tree, and Graphic Display generated by pic. Some of the more complex biological objects have half a dozen alternate displays available.

```
sub print_warning {
    my $name = shift;
    print p(font({-color => 'red'},
        "The person named \"$name\" is not found in the database."));
}

sub print_prompt {
    print start_form({-name=>'form1',-action=>Url(url(-relative=>1))}),
        p("Database ID", textfield(-name=>'name')),
        end_form;
}
```

The print_warning and print_prompt functions use CGI.pm methods to create HTML fragments. print_warning is called when the requested Person object is not found in the database and produces a nice red error message. print_prompt produces a tiny fill-out form containing a single textfield named "name". The user can type in the name of a new Person object in order to display a new database object.

```
sub print_report {
    my $person = shift;

    print h2($person->Full_name);
```

The print_report function is where the object is actually displayed. The function begins by shifting the Person object off the subroutine stack and storing it in a local variable. It then calls the object's Full_name method, and incorporates it into a level 2 header.

```
if (my @address = $person->Address(2)) {
    print h3('Contact Information'),
        blockquote(address(join(br,@address)));
    print a({-href=>'mailto:' . $person->Email(1)},
        "Send e-mail to this person") if $person->Email;
} else {
    print p(font({-color=>'red'},'No contact information in database'));
}
```

The next step is to print out the Person's address. This section uses a new and useful feature of the ACEDB API. Subtrees are often structured so that higher-level tags indicate generic attributes, while subtags indicate more specific ones. In the Person object, the Address tag anchors a subtree of address attributes, and the subtags Mail, Phone, and EMail indicate specific types of addresses. We could generate the address by calling Mail, Phone, and EMail explicitly, but what would happen if the schema later evolved to contain a new subtag named Fax? In many cases, what we want to do is jump two steps to the right of the generic tag and retrieve all the lines in the column we find there. The data access methods allow this to be done easily by accepting an optional numeric argument, which specifies an offset from the tag into the data. Address(2) retrieves all the data two steps to the right of the Address tag. We incorporate these lines into a <BLOCKQUOTE> section and print it out.

If the Person has an email address, we turn it into a mailto: link. Note that we call Email(1) here, explicitly stepping one data element to the right of the Email tag. This is because the data access methods have slightly different behaviors in scalar and array contexts. In an array context, data access methods return the column of data to the right of the tag (unless modified by a numeric value). This is the form we've previously seen. In a scalar context, data access methods return a reference to the tag itself. This allows constructions like $person->Address->Email to work the way you'd expect. When in doubt, it's safest to give an explicit offset.

```
if ($person->Born || $person->Height) {
    print h3('Fun Facts'), table({-border=>undef},
        TR({-align=>'LEFT'}, th('Height'),
        td($person->Height(1) || '?')),
        TR({-align=>'LEFT'}, th('Birthdate'),
        td($person->Born(1)|| '?')));
}
```

If either the Born or Height fields is defined, the script prints out a table titled "Fun Facts" and prints the information. If one of these fields is missing, a question mark is printed instead (*moviedb* has a notable shortage of fun facts).

```
if (my @directed = $person->Directed) {
    print h3('Movies Directed');
    my @full_names = map { a({-href=>Object2URL($_)},$_->Title) } @directed;
    print ol(li \@full_names);
}
```

This section prints out a list of the movies that the Person has directed, if any. It calls the Directed method to recover a list of Movie objects. If not empty, the code turns them into a series of links by calling the Object2URL function defined in AceSubs.pm. Object2URL consults the object registry given in the configuration file, and turns it into a URL that links to the appropriate display script. We could use the Movie object's name as the link, but it is more elegant to dereference the object and recover the movie's full title for use in the link text. If using the raw database name in the

link text were appropriate, we could shorten the code a bit by using the AceSubs.pm
ObjectLink method:

```
my @full_names = ObjectLink(@directed);
```

The movie links are then incorporated into an ordered list.

```
if (my @scripted = $person->Scripted) {
    print h3('Movies Scripted');
    my @full_names = map { a({-href=>Object2URL($_)},$_->Title) } @scripted;
    print ol(li \@full_names);
}

if (my @stars_in = $person->Stars_in) {
    print h3('Starring Roles In');
    my @full_names = map { a({-href=>Object2URL($_)},$_->Title) } @stars_in;
    print ol(li \@full_names);
}
```

We do the same thing for movies that the Person has scripted, and for movies that
the Person has starred in. It's left as an exercise to the reader to turn this bit of
repeated code into a common subroutine.

Registering ACEDB Displays

The last thing that remains to do is to register "person" and "movie" with the Ace-
Browser object registration system. This allows the system to automatically generate
the right object reference URL when Object2URL is called, and provides a navigation
bar containing a list of alternative object displays when TypeSelector is called. Unfortunately, unlike the rest of the system, the object registration code is in an incomplete state of evolution. Although functional, it is unsightly and will be replaced by a
more elegant object-oriented approach in the near future.

All object registration information is contained in a site-wide file called SiteDefs.pm.
In addition to registration information, it contains a variety of defaults and user pref-
erences. An excerpt of the relevant sections of my site's SiteDefs.pm file is given in
Example 64-5.

Example 64-5. SiteDefs.pm for moviedb (excerpt)

```
package SiteDefs;

# ... deleted stuff ...

my %movie_displays;

# This constant maps symbolic database names to host/port pairs.
%DATABASES = (
  # .... deleted stuff ....
  'moviedb'    => {
      host        => 'localhost',
      port        => 200008,
```

Example 64-5. SiteDefs.pm for moviedb (excerpt) (continued)

```
        stylesheet => '/stylesheets/moviedb.css',
        searches   => [qw(search grep query)],
        url_mapper => \&movie_mapper,
        displays   => \%movie_displays,
        title      => '<span class=banner>Moviedb Test Database</span>',
    },
);


############################################################
# These are displays for the test "movie" database
############################################################

# Mapping objects to displays for the movies
sub movie_mapper {
    my ($display,$name,$class) = @_;
    my $n = escape($name);
    return ('person' => "name=$n") if $class eq 'Person';
    return ('movie' => "name=$n")  if $class eq 'Movie';

    # fall through
    return basic_mapper($display, $name, $class);
}

%movie_displays =
    (
    # In the movie database, there are special pages for
    # people and movies.
    Person     => [
                    {'url'   => 'person',
                     'label' => 'Biography',
                     'icon'  => '/icons/quill.gif'},
                  ],
    Movie      => [
                    {'url'   => 'movie',
                     'label' => 'Movie Report',
                     'icon'  => '/icons/movie.gif'},
                  ],
    );

# ... deleted stuff ...

1;
```

We'll walk through Example 64-5 beginning with the %DATABASES hash:

```
%DATABASES = (
# Deleted stuff...
    'moviedb'     => {
        host       => 'localhost',
        port       => 200008,
        stylesheet => '/stylesheets/moviedb.css',
        searches   => [qw(search grep query)],
        url_mapper => \&movie_mapper,
```

```
        displays   => \%movie_displays,
        title      => '<span class=banner>Moviedb Test Database</span>',
      },
    );
```

The %DATABASES hash contains a list of all the databases that should be made visible to the web interface. Each database has a symbolic name, used as the hash key, and an anonymous hash containing attributes of the database, which is used as the hash value. In this example, we only show a single database entry, the *moviedb* database. The anonymous hash contains keys that describe the host that the database lives on, its port number, a stylesheet to use for displaying pages from this database, a list of search scripts to be made available for this database, and a title to display at the top of each of the pages from this database. There are also two keys named url_mapper and displays that tell the system what CGI scripts are to be made available for displaying objects fetched from the database.

```
sub movie_mapper {
    my ($display,$name,$class) = @_;
    my $n = escape($name);
    return ('person' => "name=$n") if $class eq 'Person';
    return ('movie'  => "name=$n")  if $class eq 'Movie';

    # Fall through

    return basic_mapper($display, $name, $class);
}
```

The movie_mapper subroutine, referred to by the %DATABASES hash, defines how object links are turned into URLs for the *moviedb* database. The subroutine takes three arguments: the name of the current script (e.g., tree), the name of the object, and the class of the object. It returns two arguments: the URL of the CGI script to use to display the object (e.g., movie), and the URL-escaped arguments to pass to the script. In this case, the logic is to turn references to Person objects into links to a CGI script named person, and similarly to turn references to Movie objects into links to the movie script. Other classes, for example the Book class, will fall through to the basic_mapper routine, which defines the default behavior of using tree and pic as the generic displays.

```
%movie_displays =
    (
    # In the movie database, there are special pages for
    # people and movies.
    Person    => [
                    {'url'   => 'person',
                     'label' => 'Biography',
                     'icon'  => '/icons/quill.gif'},
                 ],
    Movie     => [
                    {'url'   => 'movie',
                     'label' => 'Movie Report',
                     'icon'  => '/icons/movie.gif'},
                 ],
    );
```

The last bit of *SiteDefs.pm* defines the alternative representations for each object that will be displayed in the TypeSelector-generated navigation bar. %movie_displays is a hash with keys that are object class names, and with values that are anonymous arrays containing lists of alternative representations. In the simple *moviedb* database, Person and Movie each have one representation; in a more complex application, multiple representations can be defined.

Information about each display is given as a hash in which the key url indicates the URL to call to display the object, label indicates a short descriptive string to print on the navigation bar, and icon gives the URL of the icon to display above the label.

Conclusions

Working with ACEDB is fun and easy because you're dealing with whole objects at a time, not bits and pieces of them. AceBrowser allows you to take any ACEDB database and make it browsable without writing a line of code, or to create customized data reports quickly and easily. The next time you're using DBI to fetch one row one at a time from a relational database, pause for a moment to reflect. Wouldn't you rather be doing this job the genome way?

References

- ACEDB: *ftp://ftp.ncbi.nlm.nih.gov/repository/acedb*
- ACEDB Documentation and FAQs: *http://probe.nalusda.gov:8000/*
- AcePerl code and documentation: *http://stein.cshl.org/AcePerl*
- AceBrowser code and documentation: *http://stein.cshl.org/AcePerl/AceBrowser*
- AcePerl access to the *C. elegans* data (read only):

```
server: wormsrv1.sanger.ac.uk
port:   210201

server: beta.crbm.cnrs-mop.fr
port:   20000100
```

## CHAPTER 65

Spreadsheet::WriteExcel

John McNamara

 Since this article was published, several new features have been added to Spreadsheet::WriteExcel. The module now supports formatting of cells, rows, and columns; page set-up for printing; formulas and functions; hyperlinks; bitmap images; and it can now be used with mod_perl. Development work continues and the module has been adopted by a large number of institutions and companies, including several international banks and investment companies. And at least one user has employed it to placate his mother-in-law. Takanori Kawai has also written the Spreadsheet::ParseExcel module that provides a cross-platform means of reading Excel files. As such, Perl is currently the only language to have open source support for reading and writing Excel files.

One of Perl's great strengths is the ability to filter data from one format into another. Data goes in one end of a Perl program and miraculously comes out the other end as something more useful. Your Sybase file goes into Perl counseling and after a few short sessions comes out feeling like a brand new Oracle file.

However, not all file formats are readily accessible. Certain proprietary file formats, and in particular binary files, can be difficult to handle. One such format is the Microsoft Excel spreadsheet file.

Excel is the spreadsheet application at the heart of the Microsoft Office suite. It is a popular tool for data analysis and reporting, and even though it is only available on Windows and Macintosh platforms, Excel-compatible files are often required on Unix platforms.

This article describes Spreadsheet::WriteExcel, a cross-platform Perl module designed to write data in the Microsoft Excel binary format. It highlights the fact that although Perl is most often associated with text files, it can readily handle binary files as well. This article also looks at alternative methods for producing Excel files and suggests some methods for reading them.

Using Spreadsheet::WriteExcel

A single Excel file is generally referred to as a *workbook*. A workbook is composed of one or more *worksheets*, which are pages of data in rows and columns. Each row and column position within a workbook is referred to as a *cell*.

Spreadsheet::WriteExcel creates a new workbook to which you can add worksheets. You can then write text and numbers to the cells of these worksheets. The following Perl program is a simple example:

```perl
#!/usr/bin/perl -w

use strict;
use Spreadsheet::WriteExcel;

# Create a new Excel workbook called perl.xls
my $workbook  = Spreadsheet::WriteExcel->new("perl.xls");
my $worksheet = $workbook->addworksheet();

# Write some text and some numbers
# Row and column are zero indexed
$worksheet->write(0, 0, "The Perl Journal");
$worksheet->write(1, 0, "One"              );
$worksheet->write(2, 0, "Two"              );
$worksheet->write(3, 0,  3                 );
$worksheet->write(4, 0,  4.0000001         );
```

Here, I'm using the Spreadsheet::WriteExcel module to create a variable that acts like an Excel workbook. I add a single worksheet to this workbook and then write some text and numbers. Figure 65-1 shows how the resulting file looks when opened in Excel.

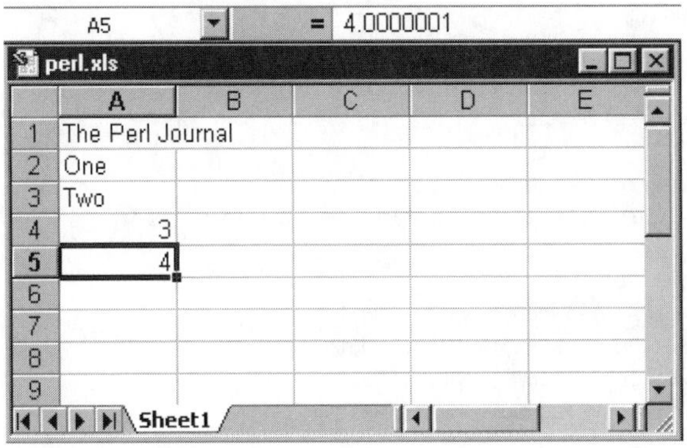

Figure 65-1. Example file written with Spreadsheet::WriteExcel

The Spreadsheet::WriteExcel module provides an object-oriented interface to a new Excel workbook. This workbook is an object (a variable) that acts as a container for worksheet objects (more variables), which themselves provide methods (functions) for writing to their cells.

The primary method of the module is the new constructor, which takes a filename as its argument and creates a new Excel workbook:

```
$workbook = Spreadsheet::WriteExcel->new($filename);
```

Then the workbook is used to create new worksheets using the addworksheet method:

```
$worksheet = $workbook->addworksheet($sheetname);
```

If no $sheetname is specified, the general Excel convention for worksheet naming will be followed: Sheet1, Sheet2, and so on. The worksheets are stored in an array called @worksheets which can be accessed through the workbook object.

In a multisheet workbook, you can select which worksheet is initially visible with the activate method.

The worksheet objects provide the following methods for writing to cells:

```
write($row, $column, $token)
write_number($row, $column, $number)
write_string($row, $column, $string)
```

The write method is an alias for one of the other two write methods. It calls write_number if $token looks like a number according to the following regex:

```
$token =~ /^([+-]?)(?=\d|\.\d)\d*(\.\d*)?([Ee]([+-]?\d+))?$/
```

Otherwise, it calls write_string. If you know in advance what type of data needs to be written, you can call the specific method, and otherwise you can just use write.

Here is another example that demonstrates some of these features:

```perl
#!/usr/bin/perl -w

use strict;
use Spreadsheet::WriteExcel;

# Create a new Excel workbook
my $workbook = Spreadsheet::WriteExcel->new("regions.xls");

# Add some worksheets
my $north = $workbook->addworksheet("North");
my $south = $workbook->addworksheet("South");
my $east  = $workbook->addworksheet("East");
my $west  = $workbook->addworksheet("West");

# Add a caption to each worksheet
foreach my $worksheet (@{$workbook->{worksheets}}) {
    $worksheet->write(0, 0, "Sales");
}

# Write some data
$north->write(0, 1, 200000);
$south->write(0, 1, 100000);
```

```
$east->write (0, 1, 150000);
$west->write (0, 1, 100000);

# Set the active worksheet
$south->activate( );
```

The output from this program is shown in Figure 65-2.

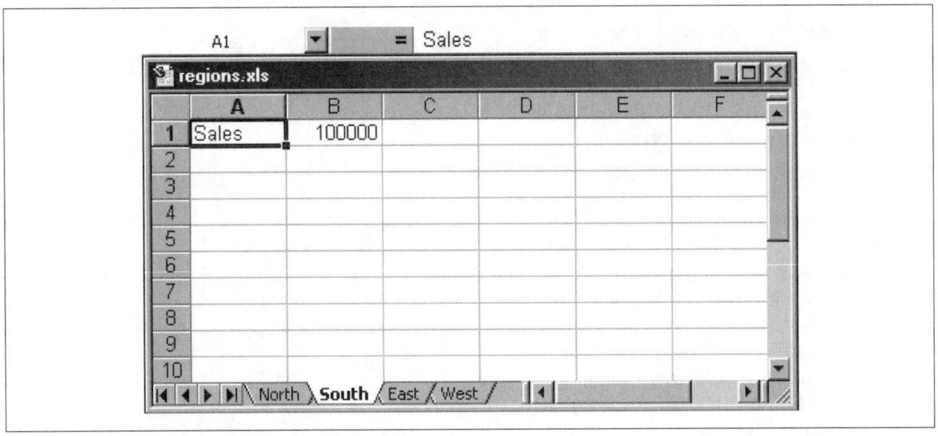

Figure 65-2. A multiple worksheet example

You can also create a new Excel file using the special Perl filehandle -, which redirects the output to STDOUT. This is useful for CGI programs generating data with a content-type of `application/vnd.ms-excel`.

```
#!/usr/bin/perl -w

use strict;
use Spreadsheet::WriteExcel;

# Send the content type
print "Content-type: application/vnd.ms-excel\n\n";

# Redirect the output to STDOUT
my $workbook  = Spreadsheet::WriteExcel->new("-");
my $worksheet = $workbook->addworksheet( );

$worksheet->write(0, 0, "The Perl Journal");
```

The Spreadsheet::WriteExcel module also provides a close method that can be used to explicitly close the Excel file. As usual, the file will be closed automatically when the object reference goes out of scope or when the program ends.

Finally, the following is a slightly more useful example of a Perl program that converts a tab-delimited file into an Excel file:

```
#!/usr/bin/perl -w

use strict;
use Spreadsheet::WriteExcel;
```

```
# Check for valid number of arguments
if (($#ARGV < 1) || ($#ARGV > 2)) {
    die("Usage: tab2xls tabfile.txt newfile.xls\n");
};

# Open the tab-delimited file
open (TABFILE, $ARGV[0]) or die "$ARGV[0]: $!";

# Create a new Excel workbook
my $workbook  = Spreadsheet::WriteExcel->new($ARGV[1]);
my $worksheet = $workbook->addworksheet();

# Row and column are zero indexed
my $row = 0;

while (<TABFILE>) {
    chomp;
    # Split on single tab
    my @Fld = split('\t', $_);

    my $col = 0;
    foreach my $token (@Fld) {
        $worksheet->write($row, $col, $token);
        $col++;
    }
    $row++;
}
```

How the Spreadsheet::WriteExcel Module Works

Now that you have seen how the module is used, I will turn to the structure of the module, a discussion of the Excel format, a history of the module's development, and the glory of Perl's pack function.

The Excel Binary Interchange File Format

Excel data is stored in the *Binary Interchange File Format*, also known as BIFF. Details of this format are given in the Excel SDK, the "Excel Developer's Kit" from Microsoft Press. It is also included in the MSDN CD library, but is no longer available on the MSDN web site. Issues relating to the Excel SDK are discussed, occasionally, at *news://microsoft.public.excel.sdk*.

The BIFF portion of the Excel file is composed of contiguous binary records that have different functions and hold different types of data. Each BIFF record is composed of the following three parts:

Record name
> A hexadecimal identifier (two bytes)

Record length
> The length of following data (two bytes)

Record data
> The data, which can be of variable length

The BIFF data is stored along with other data in an OLE Compound File. This is a structured storage format that acts like a filesystem within a file. A Compound File is composed of *storages* and *streams* which, to follow the filesystem analogy, are like directories and files. The Compound File is shown schematically in Figure 65-3.

Figure 65-3. The Compound Filesystem used to store Excel data

One effect of the filesystem structure is that the BIFF data within the Compound Files is often fragmented, and the files occasionally contain lost blocks of data. The location of the data within a Compound File is controlled by a file allocation table.

The documentation for the OLE::Storage module contains one of the few descriptions of the OLE Compound File in the public domain, at *http://user.cs.tu-berlin.de/~schwartz/pmh/guide.html*. The source code for Gnumeric spreadsheet Excel plugin also contains information relevant to the Excel BIFF format and the OLE container at *http://www.gnome.org/projects/gnumeric/*.

A Brief History of Time Wasted

Spreadsheet::WriteExcel started life as a C program written to convert the numerical output of a Fortran Finite Element Analysis program into an Excel spreadsheet. The prototype version produced a tab-delimited file that Excel digested without problem. However, I thought a native binary file would be nicer. Therein lies a true tale of human vanity.

The SDK documentation for Excel 5 lists 127 binary records that can be included in a file, but doesn't say which records are required. By a painful process of trial and error, I removed binary records from a standard Excel file until I reached a minimum configuration that would load without crashing the application. This process has a nice name: reverse engineering. The memory of this drudgery was brought home to me two years later when I came across the following article in MSDN: "Records needed to make a BIFF5 file Microsoft Excel can use, Q147732", at *http://support.microsoft.com/support/kb/articles/Q147/7/32.asp*.

Everything went fine until Excel 97.

Excel 4 files are pure BIFF files. Excel 5 files aren't. They're Compound Files with BIFF files embedded inside. However, Excel 5 will also accept a pure BIFF file for backward compatibility. Excel 97 will not. The Fortran-to-Excel filter that had worked so successfully with Excel 5 caused Excel 97 to choke and die.

The solution was to open a Compound Document stream using a C++ interface and write the BIFF records into it. In C++ on Windows this is relatively easy; for a brief example, see "How to Create a BIFF5 File, Q150447", at *http://support.microsoft.com/support/kb/articles/Q150/4/47.ASP*.

In Perl, or in C for that matter, this approach is more difficult, since the OLE interface is closely tied to C++. The only cross-platform resource available for use with Perl is the OLE::Storage module, which is an interface to OLE documents. However, it doesn't provide any facility for writing into a document stream.

The first version of Spreadsheet::WriteExcel exploited a backward-compatibility feature in Excel to avoid using the OLE container. However, this limited the file to a single worksheet and the addition of features such as formatting wasn't possible.

So it was back to the hex editor, although this time I was also armed with the OLE::Storage documentation and the Gnumeric source code. The current version of Spreadsheet::WriteExcel supports the OLE container, paving the way for the addition of other Excel features.

The addition of the OLE container meant the files produced by this module are also compatible with the Linux/Unix spreadsheet applications Gnumeric and OpenOffice.

The pack Programming Language

Perl contains several mini-languages each with its own syntax: format, pod, regex, sprintf, and pack. The pack function is described in perlfunc as follows: "pack(template, list) takes an array or list of values and packs it into a binary structure, returning the string containing the structure". This function is ideal for writing the BIFF records contained in an Excel file. For example, consider how pack is used to write the BOF binary record in the following subroutine from Spreadsheet::WriteExcel:

```perl
sub _store_bof {

    my $self    = shift;
    my $name    = 0x0809;        # Record identifier
    my $length  = 0x0008;        # Number of bytes to follow

    my $version = $BIFF_version; # 0x0500 for Excel 5
    my $type    = $_[0];         # 0x05 = workbook, 0x10 = worksheet

    my $build   = 0x096C;
    my $year    = 0x07C9;
```

```
        my $header  = pack("vv",   $name, $length);
        my $data    = pack("vvvv", $version, $type, $build, $year);

        $self->_prepend($header, $data);
    }
```

The string written to the Excel file looks like this in hexadecimal:

```
09 08 08 00 00 00 10 00 00 00 00 00
```

The v template produces a two-byte integer in little-endian order, regardless of the native byte order of the underlying hardware. Since the majority of the BIFF and OLE data in an Excel file is composed of little-endian integers, it's possible to write a cross-platform binary file with very little effort. The complementary function for reading fixed format structures is unpack. Perl's reputation originates from text processing, but it's equally versatile at handling binary data.

One problem I encountered was with the binary representation of a floating-point number, since Excel requires a 64-bit IEEE float. pack provides the d template for a double precision float, but its format depends on the native hardware. If Spreadsheet::WriteExcel cannot generate the required number format, it will croak with an error message. During installation, make test will also catch this. Nobody has reported a problem yet, probably because the owners of PDPs or Crays are involved in real computing and aren't interested in such fripperies as Microsoft Excel.

There is one feature of writing binary files that traps everyone at least once. Consider the following example, which writes the Excel end-of-file record identifier, 0x000A. What file size is printed out?

```
#!/usr/bin/perl -w

use strict;

open (TMP, "+> testfile.tmp") or die "testfile.tmp: $!";
print TMP pack("v", 0x000A);
seek (TMP,0,1);
my $filesize = -s TMP;

print "Filesize is $filesize bytes.\n";
```

The answer depends on your operating system. On Unix the answer is 2, and on Windows the answer is 3. This is because 0x0A is the newline character, \n, which your Windows's I/O libraries will translate to 0x0D 0x0A or \r\n. This is a "feature" of Windows, not Perl. To write a binary file with exactly the data you want and nothing else, you need to use the binmode function on the filehandle.

The Structure of the Module

Spreadsheet::WriteExcel was designed with a object-oriented interface so that it most closely represents Excel's own interface. The fact that Excel relies heavily on an object-oriented model can be seen from the Excel object hierarchy, and from its interaction with Visual Basic for Applications (VBA). The Excel object hierarchy is shown in the help file that comes with Excel VBA under the entry "Microsoft Excel Objects". The main strand of the hierarchy of interest is:

```
Application->Workbook->Worksheet
```

Here, "Application" means Excel. In other contexts it might mean Word or PowerPoint.

Spreadsheet::WriteExcel mimics this hierarchy with five classes, each split into its own packages. For ease of development, these packages are each contained in a separate module:

WriteExcel
    The main module

Workbook
    A container for worksheets

Worksheet
    Provides the write methods

BIFFwriter
    Writes data in BIFF format

OLEwriter
    Write data into an OLE storage

From the user's point of view, these are seen as follows:

```
WriteExcel->Workbook->Worksheet
```

The interaction of these packages is shown as low-tech UML in Figure 65-4. Only the documented public methods are included.

The relationships can be described as follows: WriteExcel is a Workbook. Workbook is a container for Worksheets and it uses the OLEwriter class. Workbook and Worksheet are both derived from the abstract base class BIFFwriter.

Alternative Ways of Writing to Excel

Depending on your requirements, background, and general sensibilities, you may prefer one of the following methods for storing data in Excel:

CSV, comma separated variables, or text
    If the file extension is csv, Excel will open and convert this format automatically.

HTML tables
    This is an easy way to add formatting.

DBI or ODBC
    Connect to an Excel file as a database.

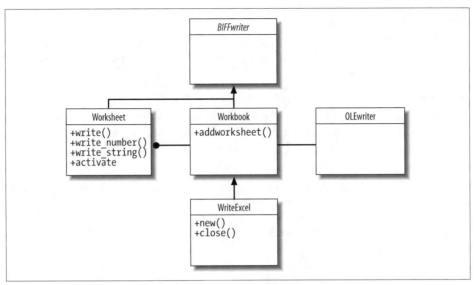

Figure 65-4. The structure of the Spreadsheet::WriteExcel module

Win32:OLE module and automating Microsoft Office
This is discussed in more detail in a later section.

XML and HTML
There are XML and HTML specifications available for Excel Workbooks. The HTML specification goes beyond single tables and allows you access to all of Excel's features. However, there are no modules currently available to write Excel files in these formats. (If you're interested, see *http://msdn.microsoft.com/library/officedev/ofxml2k/ofxml2k.htm.*)

Other sources of information are the source code for Gnumeric and OpenOffice.

Reading from Excel

Despite the title of the Spreadsheet::WriteExcel module, the most commonly asked questions I receive are about reading Excel files. The following are some suggestions:

Spreadsheet::ParseExcel
Takanori Kawai's module is a cross-platform module for extracting data from an Excel file; it's located at *http://search.cpan.org/search?dist=Spreadsheet-ParseExcel.*

HTML tables
If the files are saved from Excel as a HTML table the data can be accessed using HTML::TableExtract, which can be found at *http://search.cpan.org/search?dist=HTML-TableExtract.*

DBI or ODBC
Win32::OLE module and office automation.

Win32::OLE

As is often quoted, only perl can parse Perl. Similarly, only Excel can grok and spew Excel. Tackling the binary file head on is fine up to a certain point. After that it's best to leave the dirty work to Excel.

By far the most powerful method of accessing an Excel file for either reading or writing is through OLE and OLE Automation. Automation is the process by which OLE objects, such as Excel, act as servers and allow other applications to control their functionality. When applied to the Microsoft Office suite of applications, this process is known as Office Automation.

The following is a textual description of how you might use Automation with Excel:

1. Request Excel to start.
2. Request Excel to write some cells.
3. Request Excel to save the file.
4. Request Excel to close.

To do this in Perl requires a Windows platform, the Win32::OLE module, and an installed copy of Excel. An example:

```perl
#!/usr/bin/perl -w

use strict;
use Cwd;
use Win32::OLE;

my $application = Win32::OLE->new("Excel.Application");
my $workbook    = $application->Workbooks->Add;
my $worksheet   = $workbook->Worksheets(1);

$worksheet->Cells(1,1)->{Value} = "The Perl Journal";
$worksheet->Cells(2,1)->{Value} = "One";
$worksheet->Cells(3,1)->{Value} = "Two";
$worksheet->Cells(4,1)->{Value} =  3;
$worksheet->Cells(5,1)->{Value} =  4.0000001;

# Add some formatting
$worksheet->Cells(1,1)->Font->{Bold}       = "True";
$worksheet->Cells(1,1)->Font->{Size}       = 16;
$worksheet->Cells(1,1)->Font->{ColorIndex} = 3;
$worksheet->Columns("A:A")->{ColumnWidth}  = 25;

# Get current directory using Cwd.pm
my $dir = cwd();

$workbook->SaveAs($dir . '/perl_ole.xls');
$workbook->Close;
```

The result is shown in Figure 65-5. Without the formatting code, this program produces an Excel file that is almost identical to the one shown in Figure 65-1.

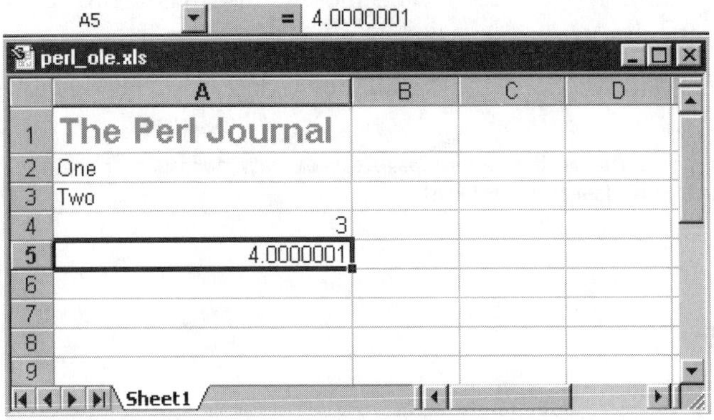

Figure 65-5. An example file written with Win32::OLE and Excel

I've skirted some issues, particularly in relation to starting and stopping an OLE server. Further examples and documentation can be found on ActiveState's web site at *http:// www.activestate.com*.

As a brief diversion, the following program uses Win32::OLE to expose the flight simulator Easter Egg in Excel 97 SR2:

```perl
#!/usr/bin/perl -w

use strict;
use Win32::OLE;

my $application = Win32::OLE->new("Excel.Application");
my $workbook    = $application->Workbooks->Add;
my $worksheet   = $workbook->Worksheets(1);

$application->{Visible} = 1;

$worksheet->Range("L97:X97")->Select;
$worksheet->Range("M97")->Activate;

my $message =   "Hold down Shift and Ctrl and click the ".
                "Chart Wizard icon on the toolbar.\n\n".
                "Use the mouse motion and buttons to control ".
                "movement. Try to find the monolith. ".
                "Close this dialog first.";

$application->InputBox($message);
```

Obtaining Spreadsheet::WriteExcel

The latest version of the module is always available at CPAN, at *http://search.cpan.org/ search?dist=Spreadsheet-WriteExcel*. The module also has a project page at Fresh-Meat (*http://freshmeat.net/projects/writeexcel/*).

ActivePerl users can download and install the module using PPM as follows:

```
C:\> ppm
PPM> set repository tmp http://homepage.eircom.net/~jmcnamara/perl
PPM> install Spreadsheet-WriteExcel
PPM> quit
C:\>
```

References

Perl modules
Spreadsheet::WriteExcel, Spreadsheet::ParseExcel, OLE::Storage, Win32::OLE, and HTML::TableExtract are all available on CPAN.

XML specs for Excel
http://msdn.microsoft.com/library/officedev/ofxml2k/ofxml2k.htm

Gnumeric
http://www.gnome.org/projects/gnumeric/

OpenOffice
http://www.openoffice.org/

Excel SDK newsgroup
news://microsoft.public.excel.sdk

OLE Compound File
http://user.cs.tu-berlin.de/~schwartz/pmh/guide.html

Filters
http://atena.com/libole2.php

xlHtml
http://www.xlhtml.org/

PART VIII

Internals

When I created the `comp.lang.perl.modules` and `comp.lang.perl.tk` newsgroups, I was on a roll. After some brainstorming on the perl5-porters mailing list, we decided to create a newsgroup dedicated to Perl internals called `comp.lang.perl.guts`. Normally, when you submit a proposal to create a newsgroup, there are two phases: the RFD (request for discussion) and the CFV (call for votes). But a Lord of Usenet denied even my request for discussion, claiming that the name wasn't formal enough for Usenet.

To this day, there is no newsgroup dedicated to Perl internals. You'll have to settle for the perl5-porters and perl6-porters lists—and this section, which has six articles about the guts of Perl. We begin with Nathan Torkington's article on *How to Improve Perl* (originally titled "Hacking the Perl Core" in TPJ #16). Nathan tells you what to do if you want to contribute to the Perl development process, identifying some timeless principles that work just as well for Perl 6 as Perl 5.

Perl guru Chip Salzenberg follows with four of the articles from his *Guts* column. *Components of the Perl Distribution* provides a very brief overview of the components of a Perl distribution, followed by an explanation of how Perl interprets your programs in *Basic Perl Anatomy*. Next, he explains how Perl breaks apart your programs into tokens in *Lexical Analysis*, and then shows you the utility of the -D command-line switch in *Debugging Perl Programs with -D*. All Perl programmers should use -d occasionally to run interactive Perl sessions (`perl -de 0`), but the -D flag is for serious detective work only.

The section, and the book, end with Simon Cozens' article on *Microperl*, a stripped-down version of Perl that is either a wonderful step toward portable bootstrapping of our favorite language, or a bizarre frivolity exuded from a dangerous and fearsome mind. No one, including Simon, knows which.

## CHAPTER 66

How to Improve Perl

Nathan Torkington

This article explains how Perl development takes place, ending with some suggestions for people wishing to become bona fide porters. Perl 6 is on the distant horizon as this book goes to press, and when it becomes reality you can expect that most of the URLs and mailing lists I mention here will change. Nevertheless, the broader concepts underlying internals hacking—the principles and procedures behind improving Perl—will still apply.

The perl5-porters mailing list is where the Perl standard distribution is maintained and developed. The list gets anywhere from 10 to 150 messages a day, depending on the heatedness of the debate. Most days there are two or three patches, extensions, features, or bugs being discussed at a time. A searchable archive of the list is at *http://www.xray.mpe.mpg.de/mailing-lists/perl5-porters/*.

List subscribers (the porters themselves) come in several flavors. Some are quiet, curious lurkers, who rarely pitch in and instead watch the ongoing development to ensure they're forewarned of new changes or features in Perl. Some subscribers represent vendors, and are there to make sure that Perl continues to compile and work on the vendors' platforms. Some subscribers patch any reported bug that they know how to fix, some are actively patching their pet area (threads, Win32, the regex engine), and others seem to do nothing but complain. In other words, it's your usual mix of technical people.

Over this group of porters presides Larry Wall. He has the final word in what does and does not change in the Perl language. Various releases of Perl are shepherded by a *pumpking*, a porter responsible for gathering patches and deciding on a patch-by-patch and feature-by-feature basis what goes into the release. For instance, Hugo van der Sanden is the pumpking for the 5.9 release of Perl. In addition, various people are pumpkings for different areas, such as maintaining Perl's *Configure* process, and ensuring that all of Perl's documentation is up to date.

Larry sees Perl development as emulating the U.S. government: there's the legislative branch (the porters), the executive branch (the pumpkings), and the Supreme Court

(Larry). The legislature can discuss and submit patches to the executive branch all they like, but the executive branch is free to veto them. Rarely, the Supreme Court will side with the executive branch over the legislature, or the legislature over the executive branch. Mostly, the legislature and the executive branch are supposed to get along and work out their differences without impeachments or lawsuits.

You might sometimes see people talk about Rule 1 or Rule 2. Larry's power as Supreme Court is expressed in The Rules:

Rule 1
> Larry is always by definition right about how Perl should behave. This means he has final veto power on the core functionality.

Rule 2
> Larry is allowed to change his mind about any matter at a later date, regardless of whether he previously invoked Rule 1.

Got that? Larry is always right, even when he was wrong. It's rare to see either Rule exercised, but they are often alluded to.

New features and extensions to the language are contentious, because the criteria used by the pumpkings, Larry, and other porters are not codified in a few small design goals, as with some other languages. Instead, the heuristics are flexible and often difficult to fathom. Here is one person's list, roughly in decreasing order of importance, of heuristics that new features have to be weighed against:

Does the concept match the general goals of Perl?
> These haven't been written anywhere in stone, but one approximation is:
> - Keep it fast, simple, and useful.
> - Keep features/concepts as orthogonal as possible.
> - No arbitrary limits (platforms, data sizes, cultures).
> - Keep it open and exciting to use/patch/advocate Perl everywhere.
> - Either assimilate new technologies, or build bridges to them.

Where is the implementation?
> All the talk in the world is useless without an implementation. In almost every case, someone who argues for a new feature will be expected to implement it. Porters capable of coding new features have their own responsibilities, and won't necessarily be available to implement your idea, no matter how good.

Backwards compatibility
> It's a cardinal sin to break existing Perl programs. New warnings are contentious—some say that a program that emits warnings is broken, and others say the opposite. Adding keywords has the potential to break programs, and changing the meaning of existing token sequences or functions might break programs.

Could it be a module instead?

Perl 5 has extension mechanisms—modules and XS—specifically to avoid the need to keep changing the Perl interpreter. You can write modules that export functions, you can give those functions prototypes so they can be called like built-in functions, you can even write XS code to mess with the runtime data structures of the Perl interpreter if you want to implement really complicated things. If it can be done in a module instead of in the core, it's highly unlikely to be added.

Is the feature generic enough?

Is the feature something that only the submitter wants added to the language, or would it be broadly useful? Sometimes, instead of adding a feature with a tight focus, the porters might decide to wait until someone implements a more generalized feature. For instance, instead of implementing a "delayed evaluation" feature, the porters wait for a macro system that would permit delayed evaluation and much more.

Does it potentially introduce new bugs?

Radical rewrites of large chunks of the Perl interpreter have the potential to introduce new bugs. The smaller and more localized the change, the better.

Does it preclude other desirable features?

A patch is likely to be rejected if it closes future avenues of development. For instance, a patch that places a true and final interpretation on prototypes is likely to be rejected because there are still options for future prototypes that haven't been addressed.

Is the implementation robust?

Good patches (tight, complete, correct code) stand more chance of going in. Sloppy or incorrect patches might be placed on the back burner until the pumpking has time to fix them, or might be discarded altogether without further notice.

Is the implementation generic enough to be portable?

The worst patches make use of a system-specific feature. It's highly unlikely that nonportable additions to the Perl language will be accepted.

Is there enough documentation?

Patches without documentation are probably ill-thought out or incomplete. Nothing can be added without documentation, so submitting a patch for the appropriate manpages as well as the source code is always a good idea. If appropriate, patches should add to Perl's test suite as well.

Is there another way to do it?

Larry has said "Although the Perl Slogan is *There's More Than One Way to Do It*, I hesitate to make 10 ways to do something." This is a tricky heuristic to navigate, though—one man's essential addition is another man's pointless cruft.

Does it create too much work?

This might mean work for the pumpking, work for Perl programmers, or work for module authors. Perl is supposed to be easy.

Patches speak louder than words.

Working code is always preferred to pie-in-the-sky ideas. A patch to add a feature stands a much higher chance of making it to the language than a random feature request, no matter how fervently argued the request might be. This ties into "Will it be useful?", as the fact that someone took the time to make the patch demonstrates a strong desire for the feature.

If you're on the perl5-porters list, you might hear the word "core" bandied around. It refers to the standard distribution. "Hacking on the core" means you're changing the C source code to the Perl interpreter. "A core module" is one that ships with Perl.

The source code to the Perl interpreter, in its different versions, is kept in a repository managed by the CVS revision control system and available at *http://cvs.perl.org*. Read-only access is available to all; only the pumpkings and a few others have access to the repository to check in changes. Periodically the pumpking for the development version of Perl releases a new version, so the rest of the porters can see what's changed.

Always submit patches to `perl5-porters@perl.org`. This lets other porters review your patch, which catches a surprising number of errors in patches. Either use the `diff` program (available in source code form from *ftp://ftp.gnu.org/pub/gnu/*), or use Johan Vromans' makepatch utility. Unified diffs are preferred, but context diffs are accepted; don't send RCS-style diffs or diffs without context lines. More information is given in the *Porting/patching.pod* file in the Perl source distribution. Please patch against the latest *development* version (e.g., if you're fixing a bug in the 5.005 track, patch against the latest 5.005_5x version). Only patches that survive the heat of the development branch get applied to maintenance versions. Your patch should also update the documentation and test suite.

To report a bug in Perl, use the `perlbug` program bundled with Perl (if you can't get Perl to work, send mail to the address `perlbug@perl.com` or `perlbug@perl.org`). Reporting bugs through `perlbug` feeds into the automated bug-tracking system, with access provided at *http://bugs.perl.org/*. It often pays to check the archives of the perl5-porters mailing list to see if the bug you're reporting has been reported before, and if so, whether it was considered a bug.

The CPAN testers (*http://testers.cpan.org/*) are a group of volunteers who test CPAN modules on a variety of platforms. Perl Labs (*http://labs.perl.org/*) automatically tests Perl source releases on platforms and gives feedback to the CPAN testers mailing list. Both efforts welcome volunteers.

To become an active and patching Perl porter, you'll need to learn how Perl works on the inside. Chip Salzenberg's articles in this section are a good place to start. The `perlguts` documentation explains the internal data structures, which are also illustrated at *http://gisle.aas.no/perl/illguts/*. And, of course, the C source code (sometimes sparsely commented, sometimes commented well) is a great place to start (begin with *perl.c* and take it from there). A lot of the style of the Perl source is explained in the *Porting/pumpkin.pod* file in the source distribution.

It is essential to be comfortable using a good debugger (such as gdb or dbx) before you can patch perl. Stepping through Perl as it executes a script is perhaps the best (if sometimes tedious) way to gain a precise understanding of the overall architecture of the language.

If you build a version of the Perl interpreter with -DDEBUGGING, Perl's -D command line flag emits copious debugging information (as described in the perlrun manpage). If you build a version of Perl with compiler debugging information (typically with your C compiler's -g option instead of -O), you can step through the execution of the interpreter with your favorite C symbolic debugger, setting breakpoints on particular functions.

It's a good idea to read and lurk for a while before chipping in. That way you'll get to see the dynamic of the conversations, learn the personalities of the players, and hopefully be better prepared to make a useful contribution when do you speak up.

If after all this you still think you want to join the perl5-porters mailing list, send mail to perl5-porters-subscribe@perl.org. To unsubscribe, you can send mail to perl5-porters-unsubscribe@perl.org.

## CHAPTER 67

Components of the Perl Distribution

Chip Salzenberg

My first exploration of Perl's internals was more of a toe-dip than a high gainer. Back in 1988, I wanted to use Perl 2.0 on a Xenix/286 system, so I ported it. Over the next few years I contributed some minor patches, and one major patch: support for System V interprocess communication (the msg*, sem*, and shm* operators).

Cut to October 1996. Occupied with other matters, Larry Wall left active development to other interested people. Perl 5.003 was the current version. Andy Dougherty released seven development "subversions" (5.003_01 through 5.003_07), but was unable to continue. Patches started piling up, with no one to collect and order them. Finally, seeing an opportunity to help Perl development move forward, I volunteered to collect patches, issue a few more subversions, and slap a "Perl 5.004" label on the result. I figured it would be a quick (if not easy) job.

7 months and 45 subversions later, I finally put Perl 5.004 to bed. It wasn't quick, and it certainly wasn't easy, but it was educational. I learned about Perl's internals the hard way, going backwards and forwards through the code, discovering how it worked so that my patches would actually fix bugs instead of making new ones.

The Components of Perl

Perl is a complex programming system. Just as humans are single individuals, but can be analyzed usefully in parts, so Perl can be dissected for analysis. What follows is a description of Perl's major organs.

The Core

The Perl core is the minimum portion of the Perl distribution that must be compiled and installed to run any Perl program. The Perl core is written almost entirely in C.

The Standard Library

The standard library consists of the standard modules, the standard extensions, and pragmas. There are also a few vestigial files left over from Perls of yesteryear:

Standard Modules

Perl modules are simply packages defined in library files of the same name, and are designed to be reusable. The Perl distribution includes many modules of general utility; Perl 5.004 includes 104 module files. See the `perlmodlib` documentation for descriptions.

Standard Extensions

Extensions are modules that include portions written in a language other than Perl (usually C) and linked directly into your Perl process as it runs. That linking can be delayed until runtime, if your operating system supports dynamic loading of shared libraries. Otherwise, the extensions can be included in the Perl binary through static linking, which occurs when Perl is installed at your site.

Perl 5.004 includes 11 standard extensions. Among them are DynaLoader, which performs dynamic loading if your operating system supports it; IO, the recommended interface for file and socket input and output in Perl 5.004; and POSIX, which provides direct access to POSIX system calls. (POSIX is a set of standards for operating systems.)

Pragmas

Pragmas let you change fundamental aspects of the Perl language, such as whether arithmetic is floating-point or integer-only. By convention, pragma names consist entirely of lowercase letters, which is why it's a good idea to capitalize the names of your personal modules.

Configuration and Installation

Perl is an amazingly portable system. It runs on virtually all Unix and Windows variants, as well as VMS, OS/2, Plan 9, AmigaOS, and a few others that you've probably never heard of. A significant portion of the Perl distribution is devoted to adapting to the environment in which Perl is built and installed.

Test Suite

The Perl distribution includes an extensive test suite. It exercises a large fraction of the language and pragmas, a fair fraction of the standard extensions, and a few of the standard modules. (If you know Perl fairly well and you have some free time, the Perl development team would love to have your help extending the test suite to cover more of the Perl distribution.)

Utilities

Perl comes with some auxiliary utility programs that help people make more effective use of Perl. Here is a partial listing:

- a2p and s2p convert awk and sed programs to Perl.
- h2ph attempts to convert C header files to Perl.

- h2xs takes some of the work out of creating Perl extensions.
- perlbug mails a Perl bug report to perlbug@perl.com.
- perldoc searches for and displays Perl documentation.
- splain provides verbose explanations for Perl error messages.

In general, Perl utilities are useful for developing Perl code, but are never required simply to run Perl programs.

Summary

There's more in the Perl distribution, but most of it is documentation of one kind or another. Nevertheless, for the good of my readers, I must mention the Frequently Asked Questions (FAQ) document, written and maintained by Tom Christiansen and Nathan Torkington. If you read it, I promise you will learn something. (I know I did.) To take a look at it, run perldoc perlfaq.

Now that you know what goes into a Perl distribution, you're ready to look at the files in a distribution and understand their basic roles, and this is illustrated in Table 67-1. (The wildcard ** is taken from the zsh shell; it means to search all subdirectories, in the style of the Unix find program.)

Table 67-1. Files in the Perl distribution

Files	Description
*.h, *.c, *.y, *.pl	Core (but not lib/*.pl)
os2/*, plan9/*, vms/*, cygwin32/*, win32/*	Core support for special environments
Configure, hints/*, **/*.SH, installperl	Configuration and installation
ext/**/*	Standard extensions
lib/**/*	Remainder of standard library
utils/*, x2p/*, h2pl/*	Utilities
t/**/*	Test suite
INSTALL, README*, pod/*	Documentation

Perl is more than just a language; it's a programming system. What we may think of as "the real Perl" is only a part. It is important to remember that the standard library—especially the set of pragmas—is just as much a standard part of Perl as the print operator.

In the next article, I'll delve into the organization of the core and some of the fundamental data structures that lay at the, um, core of Perl. Share and enjoy!

## CHAPTER 68

Basic Perl Anatomy

Chip Salzenberg

In *Components of the Perl Distribution*, I described the overall content and layout of the perl distribution. Now that the stage has been set, I'll show how perl implements the Perl language, with occasional excursions into the standard library.

We'll survey the major portions of perl and their functions. You'll notice that the word "perl" isn't always capitalized in this column. That's because Larry Wall draws a distinction between "Perl" the language and perl the program—in theory, there could be other programs besides perl that implement Perl. Thus, this article is not about "the guts of Perl" but rather "the guts of perl."

How Perl Works

Here's a bird's-eye view of how perl executes your Perl programs:

Lexical analysis
    perl reads your program and breaks it down into basic syntactic elements, called *tokens*.

Parsing
    perl figures out the meaning of those tokens in that specific sequence.

Compilation
    perl builds an internal structure representing operations that, when executed, will perform the actions specified by your program.

Execution
    perl steps through those operations and performs them, one by one.

Note that perl distinguishes Step 3 from Step 4. The line is blurred by BEGIN {} blocks, which specify Perl code to be executed during the compilation phase—before your program runs.

Step 3 settles one of the frequently asked questions about Perl: perl is a compiler, not an interpreter. Specifically, it's a "load-and-go compiler." Incidentally, current plans for perl 5.005 include a module to produce C code directly from a Perl program—

something that would have been nearly impossible were perl not a compiler. I'll examine these four steps in detail.

Lexical Analysis

This subsystem takes the input stream (your Perl program) and interprets it as a sequence of *tokens*. Tokens are the basic elements of program syntax in any language. Perl's tokenizer is in the file *toke.c*.

For example, consider this program:

```
print "Hello, world\n";
```

Lexical analysis produces tokens that represent the operator print, the string "Hello, world\n", and the final semicolon.

Tokens vary from computer language to computer language, and even from implementation to implementation for a given language. What constitutes a token varies depending on how much complexity or regularity should be visible in the grammar. For example, given a Perl scalar $i, should the dollar sign and the letter be two tokens, or just one? The former makes the grammar more complicated and the lexical analysis simpler; the latter does the opposite. Neither is really wrong in itself—it depends on other factors, including history and consistency with existing code.

As you might imagine if you have any experience with writing compilers, lexical analysis of Perl is a complex and exacting task, full of special cases and best guesses.

Consider the expression new Foo. If the new subroutine has been defined or declared when new Foo is encountered, this is interpreted as a function call, as if it had been spelled new(Foo). If the subroutine hasn't been defined or declared, and if a package Foo has been defined through use, then the expression is taken as a method call, as if it had been spelled Foo->new. But if there is no package Foo, then the expression is taken as a function call after all. This is just a small example of how Perl's lexical analysis is aware of, well, just about everything.

There's enough interesting complexity in Perl's lexical analysis to fill several columns, so I won't go into detail here about how it works. Perhaps it will be enough for now to explain that the main entry point for perl's lexical analysis is a function called yylex. If you're familiar with the lex or flex utilities, you might assume yylex is automatically generated by one of them. It's not. yylex is handcrafted specifically for the special cases and best guesses that make Perl so useful.

The responsibility of yylex is, whenever it's called, to return the next token from the script currently being compiled. Also, because each token is represented internally as a single integer, there's often additional data associated with it; yylex puts this additional data into a global structure named yylval before returning the token number.

Parsing

The tokens produced by lexical analysis don't themselves constitute a program. Even if perl can enumerate the tokens in your program, it can't tell what your program means until it understands those tokens in a valid order and context. Perl's *grammar* is a description of all valid arrangements of tokens, and what those arrangements mean.

It is possible to implement a grammar in a general-purpose language like C. But that's unnecessarily difficult and error-prone. Specialized tools for writing grammars and translating them to executable code have existed for decades; one such tool is yacc. The name is an acronym for "Yet Another Compiler Compiler."

yacc grammars contain a set of grammatical rules, and actions (C code) to be taken when a rule is triggered. It generates C code that, when executed, "accepts" that grammar and performs the specified actions. This may seem a bit vague and magical, but it's really simple in concept: yacc writes C code for a function named yyparse. When called, yyparse repeatedly calls yylex and does whatever the tokens demand.

The grammar of perl is designed for input to yacc.[*] It is distributed in the file *perly.y*. You might expect that the perl build procedure includes running yacc on this file. However, to save Perl builders the trouble, and because yacc isn't available everywhere, the distribution of perl includes *perly.c* and *perly.h*, created from *perly.y* by the creator of the perl distribution.

Compilation

The purpose of the yacc grammar is to build trees of structures called OPs. Each OP represents a low-level operation to be performed at runtime. Its primary field is

---

[*] That's not quite true. The files *perly.c* and *perly.h* are not actually created with yacc, but rather with byacc (also known as "Berkeley yacc"), a clone of yacc. To be precise, perl uses byacc 1.8.

op_code, an integer that represents the action to be performed when execution reaches the given OP. Valid opcodes are enumerated in *opcodes.h*, which is automatically generated from *opcode.pl* before distribution. One OP, alone and afraid, isn't much good to anyone. So OPs are built into trees, which are then either stored for later use (as subroutines) or executed immediately.

There is a lot of low-level manipulation of OP structures that occurs during compilation. Not much of it would make sense if I described it out of context. Suffice it to say there's a fair amount of code, particularly in *op.h* and *op.c*, to define OPs, create them, and build and optimize trees of them.

Execution

With this subsystem, we cross the Rubicon from preparing to doing. Until now we've been getting ready to run. Now we run.

The execution stage is the part of perl that users can imagine most easily. For each opcode OP_FOO, there is a function pp_foo that is called to execute the given OP. For example, pp_add adds two numbers; pp_chdir changes the current directory, and so on.

Many opcodes are relatively simple to execute. Some, however, are quite complex, or have significant portability issues, or both. So there is a lot of code in this subsystem, more than you might expect from a surface examination of perl's list of opcodes.

Perl Subsystems

There's more to perl than these four stages. It's a large program, and as such has many widely used services that aren't tied firmly to any particular stage. For example, exception handling involves all four stages.

To save space and time, code that implements such idioms or provides such services is typically collected into what would be a library if it were compiled and installed separately. When it's not installed separately, it's sometimes called a *subsystem*. I'll look at some of those subsystems now.

Internal flow control and exception handling

Perl's semantics include exception handling. As perl runs, it may at almost any time interrupt the flow of execution and unwind the call stack back to a previously established checkpoint. This behavior is visible from Perl in the form of the eval and die operators, but it can also be triggered by perl's internals, such as by the detection of internal errors or a user's attempts to perform illegal operations.

This subsystem implements Perl's exception-handling semantics. Nonlocal transfer of control is the (relatively) easy part of exception handling: perl uses the standard C functions setjmp and longjmp for that purpose. The (relatively) hard part is freeing allocated memory and performing other cleanup operations, which perl monitors with a stack of actions to be performed when leaving each dynamic scope. If that doesn't make a lot of sense to you, relax. Or breathe deeply and dive into *scope.h* and *scope.c*. Or both.

User-visible data structures

Perl's user-visible data structures are scalars (including references and type globs), arrays, hashes, and subroutines. This subsystem implements them. It's fairly straightforward, as perl goes. Its major complication is "magic", a catch-all feature used to implement tied variables, special variables (like $!, $., and $1), operator overloading, and a few other miscellaneous features.

Regular expressions

Perl's use of regular expressions is one of its cardinal features. The subsystem that implements them for perl is deep magic. I mean *deep* magic. Here there be dragons.

That's not to say that perl's regex code is impossible to understand. However, it is written for speed, not clarity. There are so many special cases that the general flow is difficult to untangle, which makes grasping the fullness of the regex code a real challenge.

Input/output

Perl's input/output model is quite simple in concept. Most of the complication arises from variations in configuration. While perl has historically used C's stdio interface directly, recent versions of perl have been designed to use the sfio library ("Simple Fast I/O," an optional extension) instead.

An intermediate layer, the "PerlIO" abstraction, lives in between perl and whatever I/O library you're using. It provides the point of control for perl's configuration procedure. In theory, PerlIO should allow you to host perl on any adequately rich I/O library.

Standard classes

In present releases of perl, this subsystem is tiny, consisting entirely of just one class: UNIVERSAL. Run the command perldoc UNIVERSAL for details of its services.

Support for extensions

This subsystem consists of support for user-written extensions—modules that include not only Perl code but also executable binary code, typically written in C for speed. This subsystem is also tiny; it consists entirely of a single header file with some convenient macros. The majority of perl's support for extensions isn't in the core, but in the build process, library, and external utilities.

Portability and configuration

Since perl is one of the world's most portable large programs, there is a lot of bulk to its configuration mechanism. It's so extensive that Larry Wall created a tool, called dist, just to automate some of the more tedious work of maintaining and extending it.

From the point of view of a user installing perl in a reasonably Unix-like environment, configuration starts with the execution of a massive shell script named

Configure. (Configuration procedures in non-Unix environments will vary widely; see the appropriate README for information.)

Configure has two primary jobs: examining the system to figure out what facilities are available for perl to use, and asking the person building perl to specify his preferences for building and runtime options. The primary product of Configure is a configuration file named *config.sh* that has the form of a Bourne shell script. Here are selected lines from perl 5.004_04, configured for my Linux machine:

```
archlib='/usr/lib/perl5/i486-linux/5.004'
bin='/usr/bin'
byteorder='1234'
cc='gcc'
ccflags='-g -pipe -Dbool=char -DHAS_BOOL -DFIXNEGATIVEZERO -DDEBUGGING'
cf_email='chip@pobox.com'
d_sigaction='define'
extensions='Fcntl GDBM_File IO Opcode POSIX SDBM_File Socket'
lddlflags='-shared -L/usr/local/lib'
ldflags='-g -L/usr/local/lib'
libs='-lm -lgdbm -ldl'
privlib='/usr/lib/perl5'
```

As you can see, config.sh contains a mixture of information about hardware ($byteorder), operating system, compiler, and library ($cc, $d_sigaction), and user preferences ($bin, $privlib).

After Configure creates config.sh, it calls the shell scripts in the perl source tree that have the suffix *.SH*. Each *.SH* script creates a configured output file based on the information in config.sh: *Makefile.SH* creates Makefile, config_h.SH creates config.h, and so on. Also, during the build process, the Perl module Config.pm is created to provide a simple Perl interface to config.sh. All these files, based on config.sh, are how perl configures its build process and behavior.

For Further Reading

PerlGuts Illustrated, a visual tutorial of Perl's internal data structures, is available online at *http://gisle.aas.no/perl/illguts/*.

In the next article, I'll describe how Perl reads your source code and converts it into something it can execute.

## CHAPTER 69

Lexical Analysis

Chip Salzenberg

It's been said that "the only program that can parse Perl is `perl`." If you've ever tried to get a smart editor like Emacs to properly indent your Perl program, you'll probably agree. And while Ilya Zakharevich has made great strides with `cperl-mode.el`, Perl's syntax is still more complex and exception-ridden than most.

Now, ask yourself: given that Perl's syntax is riddled with oddities, exceptions, and attempts to do what you mean instead of what you say, what bizarre twists and turns must a program take to *understand* it? You're about to find out.

Tokenizing

Lexical analysis consists of turning a source file—a single unbroken stream of characters—into discrete units, called *tokens*. (That's why lexical analysis is often called *tokenizing*.) Tokens are the fundamental units of a programming language. Typical tokens are identifiers like `foo`, literal strings like `"bar"`, and operator names or symbols like `print` or `+`.

The next stage after lexical analysis, called *parsing*, takes those tokens and, based on their context, figures out what they mean. After all, `foo` might be a subroutine name, a filehandle, or even a variable name if it follows a dollar sign. The full glory of parsing is a discussed in Chapter 21.

Lexical analysis of Perl is a seriously hairy job, and *toke.c* contains some seriously hairy code. (Like the rest of Perl, the tokenizer is written in C.) You'd probably find an exhaustive treatment of its ins and outs to be, well, exhausting. I certainly would. Instead, we'll be hitting some of the high points—specific features that are representative or revealing. Follow along at home if you have the strength. Otherwise, just remember that when you're done reading this article, *toke.c* is there.

Perl's Lexer

The details of lexical analysis vary from language to language, but one constant endures: its job is to turn text into tokens for feeding into the parser. But how does the lexing code communicate those tokens to the parser? The answer may surprise you, because it's so simple.

The primary interface to the lexer is the function yylex. The parser calls yylex when it wants another token, and yylex obligingly returns the next token from the current Perl program. Eventually, yylex serves your entire Perl program up to the parser, one token at a time.

yylex doesn't accept any parameters, so we must keep state information about the current Perl program in global variables. Now, this may seem like a strange and restrictive interface. Why not allow parameters, which would eliminate the need for nasty globals? And, for that matter, why use the odd name "yylex"? Becuase Perl's parser just has to have its way. The parser is mechanically generated from the grammar in *perly.y*. Perl's build process uses a program called byacc (a variant of yacc—Yet Another Compiler Compiler) to generate a program that can parse that grammar. (You can find the generated parser in the files *perly.h* and *perly.c* bundled with the Perl distribution, but don't expect much; they're not intended for human consumption.)

Now, yacc is a wonderful tool and saves everyone a lot of grunt work—everyone, that is, except for the person writing the lexer. That's because the lexer's author has to put up with yacc's quirks, one of them being that yacc-generated parsers must get their tokens by calling a function called yylex with no parameters. (This is what we engineers call a "tradeoff.")

Another quirk of yacc-generated parsers is that they require tokens to be represented as unique small integers. Zero represents end of input. Integers between 1 and 255 usually represent an ASCII character; for instance, the token for an A is 65, the ASCII code for "A". Larger integers (256 and up) represent more complex tokens, which needn't be single characters.

The complete list of tokens supported by the lexer is rather long and would be fairly confusing at this point. When you're ready, see *perly.h* or the top of *perly.y*. In the meantime, here's a taste:

WHILE
> Loop control keyword: while or until

LSTOP
> List operator: print, sort, and others

DOTDOT
> Range or list constructor: ".." or "..."

MULOP
> An operator with the same precedence as *: /, %, x, or *.

You may have noticed by now that something is missing from the interface to yylex. It's all well and good for yylex to return the token WHILE when it sees the keyword while or until—it does this because the syntax for both is identical, even though the meanings differ. But when it's time to build the OP tree for a loop, it's vitally important for the parser to know the difference between them. How does the parser know *which* of those keywords triggered the WHILE token?

The answer is a second and key part of the interface between yylex and the parser: the global variable yylval. When tokens require additional information to fully describe them, yylex is required to put that information into the global variable yylval before returning. The type of the additional information varies from token to token: it may be as simple as a line number, or as complex as a large tree of Perl OPs. Therefore, yylval is a *union* of various data types, as specified with the %union directive in *perly.y*. The grammar in *perly.y* has %type directives that tell yacc which tokens are accompanied by additional data in yylval, and the types of those data.

So the job of yylex each time it's called is to figure out what the next token is, set yylval with any additional data appropriate for the token, and return the token.

Incidentally, Perl has a catch-all token: THING. The lexer returns THING whenever it would prefer to just build an OP tree and hand it to the lexer instead of returning tokens and letting the parser build the OP tree. If it weren't for yylval's ability to hold any data type (including an OP pointer), this convenient shortcut would not be possible.

Lexer Variables

As we've already seen, the lexer has to keep state in global variables (seeing as how yacc requires yylex to take no parameters). You may be wondering just what kind of state it has to keep, and what variables are used to keep it. Well, I'm glad you're wondering that, because right here is an (incomplete) list of the global variables that the lexer uses to tokenize your Perl programs.

SV *linestr
> The linestr variable holds the current input line from the script being compiled. The SV data type is the single most important data structures in the implementation of Perl. It holds a Scalar Value. Therefore, anything that is legal to put in a scalar variable in Perl can be stored in an SV. Here, however, the full power of the SV is not needed; linestr is never anything fancier than a simple string. Still, using an SV saves us the trouble of tracking memory allocation as the buffer grows and shrinks. (Perl's good at string manipulation, as you may have noticed.)

char *bufptr; char *bufend
> The bufptr and bufend variables point into the buffer held by linestr—specifically, the current position and the next byte beyond the end of the current line. These are two of the most commonly used variables in the lexer.

`FILE *rsfp`

The file that the current Perl program is in. When the source code in `linestr` has been completely tokenized, it's refilled by reading more source code from this file.

`line_t copline`

The current input line number, incremented each time a newline is encountered.

`enum expectation expect`

The `expect` variable records the lexer's idea of what it is likely to see next. `expect` can be any of `XOPERATOR`, `XTERM`, `XREF`, `XSTATE`, `XBLOCK`, or `XTERMBLOCK`. This variable is critical to many of Perl's context-dependent syntax rules.

For example, curly braces might represent a naked block or an anonymous hash constructor. How does the lexer know the difference? By checking `expect`. When `expect` is `XSTATE`, the lexer is eXpecting a STATEment; thus, a left brace is taken as the start of a naked block. But when `expect` is `XTERM`, the lexer is eXpecting a TERMinal (part of an expression); thus, a left brace is interpreted as the beginning of an anonymous hash constructor. Likewise, an asterisk may be a multiplication symbol or the first character of a typeglob. With `expect`, the lexer sorts them all out correctly.

Computer science purists will decry the cooperation between parser and lexer required to maintain a correct value for `expect`. The computer science ideal is for the lexer to be able to work without getting a cheat sheet from the parser. Well, all we can say is that Perl would be nigh impossible to parse without this parser-lexer love-in, because it's not a traditionally pure language (i.e., written by a professor with an axe to grind).

`U32 lex_state`

You might expect that when the lexer sees a double-quoted string, it limits its efforts to finding the end of the string. (That's how most languages' lexers work.) And, in fact, the lexer includes a subroutine called `scan_str` that does just that.

But if that were all the lexer did with strings, then the parser would have to figure out all those tricky behaviors related to case shifting and variable interpolation. In particular, consider the interpolation of array and hash elements: their subscripts are full Perl expressions. It would be a Bad Idea to duplicate all of the lexer's logic in the parser just because the lexer didn't want to dig into a double-quoted string.

Fortunately, Larry did things another way. When the lexer encounters a double-quoted string, it digs in. It goes so far as to return fabricated tokens to the parser, making the parser think any fancy double-quoted string behaviors were spelled out the long way using Perl operators. For example, `\Q$x\E$y` is returned to the parser as if the programmer had written `join('', quotemeta($x), $y)`. (That's why the operation of `\Q` is affected when you import a customized `quotemeta` function.)

The changing value of `lex_state` helps the lexer keep track of the different parts of fancy double-quoted strings and the different rules that apply to their various parts.

`lex_inwhat`

Perl plays the same games with regular expressions as it does with strings, creating the illusion of Perl operators to implement case modifiers and interpolation. For example, the lexer still calls `scan_str` (via `scan_pat`) to grab the regex text.

However, there are some differences between the interpolation rules of regexes and strings. For example, the regex `/(a$)/` doesn't interpolate the $), whereas the string `"(a$)"` does. The variable `lex_inwhat` keeps track of the current interpolation rules, so that the lexer can adapt for the differences between regexes and strings.

`I32 lex_casemods; char *lex_casestack`

The lexer uses `lex_casemods` and `lex_casestack` to keep track of how case modifiers are nested. (In this context, the phrase "case modifiers" includes \Q, even though it doesn't actually work with letter cases.) For example, `"\Qhi.\Ubye."` evaluates to `'hi\.BYE\.'`. Without a stack like `lex_casestack`, if the lexer saw the \U it would be unable to remember the \Q still in progress, so the effect of the \Q would stop, and the second dot wouldn't get backslashed.

`I32 nexttoke; I32 nexttype[]; YYSTYPE nextval[]; lex_defer`

Sometimes the lexer decides that it knows not only what the next token is, but also what the token after *that* is, and sometimes even the token after *that*. For example, when it sees `foo Bar`, it may decide that `foo` is a method name and `Bar` is a package name. However, `yylex` can't return more than one token at a time.

To simulate returning multiple tokens, the lexer keeps pending tokens in these variables. It then sets `lex_state` (discussed above) to `LEX_KNOWNEXT` to remind itself that it already knows what the next token is supposed to be, and `lex_defer` to the value that `lex_state` would otherwise have had. Subsequent calls to `yylex` return the saved tokens, one at a time, until they are all used up, at which time `lex_state` is reset to the value of `lex_defer` and normal lexing resumes.

As you can see, lexical state is a complicated assortment of various data. This is a reflection of the lexical complexity of Perl itself. Remember, Larry wrote Perl to be like a natural language, and if you think Perl is lexically complex, just think about the translation quality of your last VCR manual.

Tokenizing Considerations

There are many little choices that were made when Perl's tokenization was designed. In this section, I'll describe a few of those decisions.

- To support consistent behavior across various systems, a ^D or ^Z (ASCII code 4 or 26) is considered just as good as a real end of file.

- NUL bytes (ASCII code zero) are ignored outside of string constants. However, `yylex` keeps the current line in `linestr`, which is an SV; and all SVs keep a NUL byte after the end of the strings they hold. So Perl's lexer takes advantage of that:

it uses the NUL after the end of linestr to trigger behavior that should happen when the line buffer is empty.

One such behavior is the introduction of fake source code. Now, don't panic—it's perfectly normal. Consider the -n command-line flag, which effectively wraps your entire Perl program in a while (<>) loop. You might expect that what really happens is a lot more complex than that, but it's not. It turns out that the code for the while (<>) is introduced in the first call to yylex, by the code that notices a NUL and figures out that the line buffer is empty. It's doing its job by providing more code to tokenize—not necessarily code from your program, but code none-theless. So the -n flag literally *does* wrap your program in a while loop.

Barring such tricks, though, the code that handles NUL refills the line buffer by reading a line from rsfp, which is open on the current Perl program during its compilation. (Perl saves and restores rsfp, and most of the other variables we discussed here, when processing require or use statements.)

And if perchance the line that is read is the first line of a Perl program, then here in yylex is the code that interprets the "shebang" line (the line starting with #!). If you've ever wondered why Perl is able to read multiple options from a she-bang line (e.g. #!perl -w -l) even when your operating system supports only one option on a shebang line, the answer lies here in yylex.

And now you know why Perl has the warning Too late for -T option. Taint mode isn't effective unless it's done from the very start, i.e., from the real com-mand line. By the time yylex is called, a lot of taint-related things should already have happened, so Perl can't guarantee that your data is safe. To avoid this prob-lem, always make -T the first option on the shebang line.

- All whitespace is ignored outside of string constants (although it can separate tokens that might otherwise run together). But yylex keeps aware of newlines so it can maintain copline.

- A dash can be either a unary or a binary operator. Of course, that's not unusual in Perl (nor in other languages, for that matter). But there is something unusual about the dash in Perl: it's the first character of a file test operator.

  Perl's lexer makes a special case for a dash followed by a single letter: it returns it as the token UNIOP—that is, a unary operator. (A code indicating *which* unary opera-tor is returned in yylval.) So, despite its odd appearance, a file test operator like -f follows the same grammatical rules as other unary operators like chr and int.

- An equal sign can be the first character of ==, =~, or =>. But if it immediately fol-lows a newline (i.e., it's at the left margin), then it may also be the introduction to a piece of Plain Old Documentation (pod) embedded in the program. The job of yylex includes skipping over embedded documentation and getting on with tokenizing the rest of the program.

Further Information

If you want to delve deeper into Perl's lexical analysis, here are three resources:

toke.c
> The source of all evil—er, tokens. There is a lot more evil lurking here in the heart of Perl. Feel free to browse, but also feel free to skip the parts that are completely incomprehensible; there are a few.

perly.y
> Perl's grammar. This is the definition of the larger structure of the Perl language. Here is where you find out just how those tokens returned by yylex are allowed to be arranged in a valid Perl program. (And it's also where you find out just what's done with the additional information that the lexer puts in yylval.)

-Dp
> If you want to see the various tokens returned by the lexer in real time, compile your Perl binary with -DDEBUGGING and then run Perl with the -Dp option. It will show you debugging output from the parser, including a description of the tokens it's working with and the grammatical rules that those tokens are triggering.
>
> Be warned, this generates a *lot* of output. But it can reveal to you where things are going wrong when you thought you had valid Perl code but your Perl binary disagrees with you.

In my final article, I'll discuss how to use knowledge of Perl's internals to debug your programs when conventional methods fail.

## CHAPTER 70

Debugging Perl Programs with -D

Chip Salzenberg

Easy debugging of Perl programs has been a standard feature of Perl for a very long time. There's the -w flag which warns you about potential errors, and for more serious bug hunting, there's the Perl debugger. Perl's debugger—written in Perl!—is invoked with the -d flag.

This article is not about the -d flag.

This article is about something much more wizardly: the -D flag. This flag is your gateway to a set of debugging behaviors inside Perl's guts. If you're up against a tough bug and you can't figure out where it's coming from, -D may be just what the sergeant ordered.

Not all Perl binaries let you use the -D flag. The code to support it makes the Perl binary a bit larger and slows down execution just a hair. Since Larry is loathe to enlarge or slow Perl, the binary includes support for -D only if it was explicitly compiled with the -DDEBUGGING option, which is turned off by default.

You can tell whether your Perl was compiled with -DDEBUGGING by examining the output of perl -V. The last section of perl -V output is "Characteristics of this binary". If you have a fairly recent version of Perl, then the first line in that section will be "Compile-time options"; if that line includes the word DEBUGGING, then your Perl supports -D.

What -D Does for You

Perl is too complex and juggles too many eggs to have just one debugging flag. And in fact -D isn't really just one flag. Rather, it's a prefix that lets you turn on multiple debugging flags. The flags you use depend on what aspect of Perl you're trying to debug (or understand).

Below is a list of debugging flags accessible via -D, as listed in the perlrun documentation. Each flag has a letter that you can put after the -D to turn on a particular type of debugging. You can combine them by listing multiple letters. Each flag also has a number, so if you prefer setting debugging flags by number instead of by letter (but why?) follow -D with the sum of the numbers you want. The flags are listed in Table 70-1.

Table 70-1. Debugging flags

Letter	Number	Meaning
p	1	Tokenizing and parsing
s	2	Stack snapshots
l	4	Context (loop) stack processing
t	8	Execution trace
o	16	Method and overloading resolution
c	32	String/numeric conversions
P	64	Print preprocessor command for -P
m	128	Memory allocation
f	256	Format processing
r	512	Regular expression parsing and execution
x	1024	Syntax tree dump
u	2048	Tainting checks
L	4096	Memory leaks (not supported anymore)
H	8192	Hash dump—usurps values( )
X	16384	Scratchpad allocation
D	32768	Cleaning up

We'll now examine these flags, starting with the most useful.

Trace Execution with -Dt

Perl is a compiled language; every Perl program is fully compiled before its execution begins.

The output of the Perl compiler isn't machine code, but an intermediate form designed for execution at reasonable (though not machine-code) speed. This scheme is rather like Java's, except that Perl doesn't save its intermediate form after compilation; it just executes it.

When the -Dt option is used, Perl prints (to STDERR) the opcode name, line number, and source file for each opcode it executes.

For example, if the file *foo* contains this Perl program:

```
$a = 1;
print $a + 1;
```

We can see the opcodes executed by Perl with -Dt:

```
$ perl -Dt foo
EXECUTING...
(foo:0)      enter
(foo:0)      nextstate
(foo:1)      const(IV(1))
```

```
(foo:1)        gvsv(main::a)
(foo:1)        sassign
(foo:1)        nextstate
(foo:2)        pushmark
(foo:2)        gvsv(main::a)
(foo:2)        const(IV(1))
(foo:2)        add
(foo:2)        print
(foo:2)        leave
```

Some of these opcodes will be described in the next section.

The -Dt option is helpful if your Perl binary is dumping core or otherwise misbehaving, and you want to find out what part of your program is triggering the problem.

Stack Snapshots with -Ds

Perl is not a stack-based language like, say, Forth. (For any Forth aficionados reading this column, I offer my idea of the ideal Forth bumper sticker: YOU FORTH LOVE IF HONK THEN.) But under the hood, the Perl runtime *is* a stack machine: each Perl opcode takes operands from a stack of values and leaves its results on that same stack of values. (There are a few exceptions for efficiency reasons.)

When run with -Ds, Perl prints a snapshot of the values on the stack before the execution of each opcode. This is difficult to read without -Dt, so we'll combine them:

```
$ perl -Dts -le '$a = 1; print $a'
    =>
(-e:0)        enter
    =>
```

This opcode comes before the sample code—there's an enter at the start of every program. (Or of any scope that requires cleanup on departure, for that matter.)

```
(-e:0)        nextstate
    =>
(-e:1)        const(IV(1))
    => IV(1)
(-e:1)        gvsv(main::a)
    => IV(1)  UNDEF
(-e:1)        sassign
    => IV(1)
```

This is the first statement: nextstate clears the already empty stack; const pushes a constant (the integer 1) onto the stack; gvsv pushes $a (which has no value yet); and sassign performs the scalar assignment to $a, leaving the value assigned on the stack. Now for the print $a:

```
(-e:1)        nextstate
    =>
(-e:1)        pushmark
    => *
(-e:1)        gvsv(main::a)
    => *  IV(1)
```

```
(-e:1)          print
1
        =>  SV_YES
```

nextstate clears the stack; pushmark pushes a *mark*, which shows up as an asterisk—list operators like print use marks to keep track of the number of arguments they're passed. Next, gvsv pushes $a (which now has the value 1); and finally print prints everything to the right of the mark, pushing a true value onto the stack to indicate success.

In this case, the true value is the internal constant SV_YES. The named constants you'll see in stack snapshots are SV_YES ('1'), SV_NO (the empty string), and SV_UNDEF (for undef).

```
(-e:1)          leave
```

There's always a leave at the end of the program. (Or of any scope that requires cleanup on departure.)

Syntax Tree Dump with -Dx

The -Dt and -Ds options, discussed above, reveal the runtime execution of Perl's opcodes. Sometimes, watching the sequence of execution is less revealing than an examination of the tree of OP structures created by the compiler.

When the -Dx option is specified, Perl prints (to standard error) the entire OP tree just before it's executed. The format of -Dx output is:

```
{
    ##  TYPE = optype  ===> next_index
        FLAGS = (flags)
        kids
}
```

Here, *optype* is the OP's type—enter, const, sassign, and so on. The ## placeholder marks the location of the OP index, which is a small integer. To the right of the arrow is *next_index*, the index of the next OP to be executed at runtime after the current OP. (The OP tree is singly-linked in order of execution: each OP structure has an OP *op_next pointer.)

If the OP has parameters or other subsidiary OPs, they are listed where the word *kids* appears. They're indented to show the nested structure of kids of kids.

The FLAGS line lists various OP flags by name. Most OP flags are specific to particular *optype*s, but a few are common to all OPs:

VOID, SCALAR, LIST
> These flags indicate how many values the OP may produce: either nothing or one value (which will be ignored); one value; or any number of values, respectively.

KIDS
> The OP has kids.

REF

The OP should return a reference to the things it accesses, instead of their contents.

MOD

The OP should modify (or prepare to modify) the things it accesses.

Here's a real-life example of the output of -Dx:

```
$ perl -Dx -le '$a = 1'
{
6   TYPE = leave   ===> DONE
    FLAGS = (VOID,KIDS,PARENS)
```

This is typical: since kids are almost always executed before their parents, the first OP you see is usually the last one executed. That's why the first OP in most -Dx outputs is leave. (Note that the leave has no *next_index* because after the leave executes, there's nowhere else to go—your program is finished.)

```
    {
    1           TYPE = enter   ===> 2
    }
```

And as the first kid of the top OP, this enter is the first OP executed.

```
    {
    2           TYPE = nextstate   ===> 3
    FLAGS = (VOID)
    LINE = 1
    }
    {
    5           TYPE = sassign   ===> 6
    FLAGS = (VOID,KIDS,STACKED)
    {
    3               TYPE = const   ===> 4
        FLAGS = (SCALAR)
        SV = IV(1)
    }
    {
    TYPE = null   ===> (5)
      (was rv2sv)
    FLAGS = (SCALAR,KIDS,REF,MOD,SPECIAL)
    {
    4                 TYPE = gvsv   ===> 5
        FLAGS = (SCALAR)
        GV = main::a
    }
    }
    }
    }
```

Note that the sassign (scalar assignment) operator has the VOID flag, because the value of the assignment statement as a whole is thrown away. That wouldn't be true if the assignment were part of a larger expression, like $b = $a = 1.

Note also that Perl's optimizer pass eliminated an rv2sv OP and left a null in its place. That has no effect on runtime efficiency, since the execution order is nextstate, const, gvsv, sassign—none of the OPs has that null as its *next_index*.

A full interpretation of -Dx output requires detailed understanding of the OP tree structure. But even without that level of detail, -Dx is still useful in figuring out why Perl isn't executing your code the way you think it should.

Regular Expression Parsing and Execution with -Dr

Regular expressions are indispensable parts of Perl programming. They can also be hard to write, harder to read, and impossible to debug.

The /x regex modifier has reduced this problem somewhat by allowing programmers to put whitespace inside patterns for clarity. However, it's sometimes still difficult to figure out just what a regular expression means and how it works (or doesn't work).

Enter -Dr, which has Perl print a description of each regular expression it compiles, and a running commentary on each regular expression it executes.

Before you get your hopes *too* high, I should warn you that -Dr is nowhere near the pretty animated pictures of regular expressions in action (available via a regex visualizer on CPAN). But it's a way to see every detail of your regular expressions, and to pinpoint exactly where a regular expression might have gone wrong.

Let's suppose you are scanning a bunch of old Usenet articles, looking for old-style UUCP bang paths, like seismo!gatech!usfvax2!ateng!chip (one of my old email addresses). You might start with a pattern like this:

```
/ ( \w+ (?: !\w+ )+ ) /x
```

Which means "a hostname, followed by one or more repetitions of an exclamation point followed by a hostname," where "hostname" here means "one or more alphanumerics or underscores." And this works for many cases. But it doesn't match Larry Wall's old address, which always ends with ...!jpl-devvax!lwall. That's no good. But how can we fix this bug if we don't understand it?

This is where -Dr comes in. However, before actually using -Dr to debug a regex problem, you should create a *small* test program to exercise it. The output of -Dr can be astoundingly verbose; separating the wheat from the chaff is hard enough without irrelevant regexes cluttering things further.

A reasonable test program for our situation might be:

```
$_ = 'seismo!jpl-devvax!lwall';
print $1, "\n" if / ( \w+ (?: !\w+ )+ ) /x
```

This program, when run, outputs only devvax!lwall. But why did the pattern match only part of the target string? This is the kind of question -Dr was designed to answer.

When run with -Dr, Perl generates some debugging output before execution, and more during execution. The pre-execution output is a listing of the *compiled* representations of all of the program's regular expressions—at least, all of them that can be compiled ahead of time. Perl always compiles regexes down to compact *bytecodes* so they can be executed faster. (Of course, patterns constructed at runtime can't be compiled until they're used.)

With -Dr and our test program, we'll see this interpretation of the test regex:

```
1:  OPEN1(3)
3:    PLUS(5)
4:      ALNUM(0)
5:    CURLYX {1,32767}(12)
7:      EXACT <!>(9)
9:      PLUS(11)
10:       ALNUM(0)
11:     WHILEM(0)
12:    NOTHING(13)
13: CLOSE1(15)
15: END(0)
```

This is a listing of the bytecodes in the compiled regex. Each bytecode is a fundamental unit of regex execution. This listing shows each bytecode with its byte position on the left, then its name, then its parameters (if applicable), then the position of any related bytecode in parentheses. (A 0 means there is no related bytecode.)

The outermost construct is an OPEN1/CLOSE1 pair; these specify the beginning and ending of the first set of memory parentheses, which you may think of as \1 or $1. (In this pattern, the first set is also the only set.)

Inside the OPEN1/CLOSE1, the first item is a PLUS (one or more repetitions) controlling an ALNUM (single alphanumeric character). This combination means "one or more alphanumerics," i.e., the leading hostname in the bang path.

After the leading hostname is CURLYX{1,32767}(12), which specifies no less than one and no more than 32767 repetitions of all bytecodes up to but not including #12. (As it happens, #12 is a NOTHING put there as a placeholder.)

This bytecode is named CURLYX because the general notation for repeat counts uses curly braces: X{N,M} means "no more than N and no more than M X's."

Within the CURLYX loop is an EXACT<!>, which matches the exact string !; then another PLUS/ALNUM pair, which matches another sequence of one or more alphanumerics. Together, these match a bang followed by a name (hostname or username).

Because the EXACT, PLUS, and ALNUM are inside the CURLYX loop, they may be applied many times in a successful match—which is just fine, since we want the regex to match both long and short bang paths.

Further down in the output, we see Perl start executing the test program. Soon thereafter, we see the regular expression engine applying the test regex to the test string:

```
EXECUTING...
Matching ' ( \w+ (?: ! \w+ )+ ) ' against 'seismo!jpl-devvax!lwall'
   Setting an EVAL scope, savestack=3
   0 <> <seismo!jpl-d>    |  1:  OPEN1
```

This line illustrates the general format of the trace that -Dr generates. First is the current offset in the target string, which usually starts out at zero. Next are small portions of the target string found just to the left and to the right of the current position, printed inside angle brackets. Finally, the bytecode position and bytecode name about to be executed.

The job of regex debugging largely consists of keeping clear in your mind two things: the position in the target string where the regex engine is attempting to match, and the bytecodes that the regex engine is executing.

Now some more of the output:

```
0 <> <seismo!jpl-d>     |  3:  PLUS
                            ALNUM can match 6 times out of 32767...
```

The first \w+ matches six characters: seismo. So far, so good.

```
Setting an EVAL scope, savestack=3
  6 <eismo> <!jpl-de>   |  5:    CURLYX {1,32767}
  6 <eismo> <!jpl-de>   | 11:    WHILEM
                               0 out of 1..32767  cc=bffff8e8
```

We begin the !\w+ loop:

```
  6 <eismo> <!jpl-de>   |  7:      EXACT <!>
  7 <ismo!> <jpl-dev>   |  9:      PLUS
                            ALNUM can match 3 times out of 32767...
```

Whoa! Only three? We expected ALNUM to match ten characters: jpl-devvax. Yet it only matched three: jpl. It stopped at the dash. The test pattern expects \w+ to match hostnames, but \w doesn't match dashes. There's the bug.

Sure enough, when we change the test program to this, it prints the entire path:

```
$_ = 'seismo!jpl-devvax!lwall';
print $1,"\n" if / ( [-\w]+ (?: ! [-\w]+ )+ ) /x
```

Using -Dr to its fullest requires an understanding of all regex bytecodes. Such understanding is, to say the least, rare; *Mastering Regular Expressions* is a thick book for a reason.

However, even a minimal knowledge of the internals of Perl's regexes—such as you now have from reading this section—can be enough to make some use of -Dr. And there's no better way to get started learning the ins and outs of regexes than to play around a little.

Method and Overloading Resolution with -Do

Object-oriented Perl programming is fairly easy to learn. However, debugging object-oriented Perl presents unique challenges. Sometimes the prounounced modularity of object-oriented code results in failures that are hard to track down.

The -Do flag assists with such difficulties by reporting whenever a class or object lookup occurs.

For example, this code produces a runtime failure:

```
sub Base::foo {
    print "hi";
}

@Derived::ISA = qw/Bake/;   # bug here -- typo!

Derived->foo;
```

Due to the typo in @Derived::ISA, the foo method is not found.

In a small program this bug is trivial to find; in a large program it isn't. However, with -Do, the nature of the problem becomes much clearer. Let's call the program otest:

```
(otest:7)     Looking for method foo in package Derived
(otest:7)     Looking for method foo in package UNIVERSAL
(otest:7)     Looking for method AUTOLOAD in package Derived
(otest:7)     Looking for method AUTOLOAD in package UNIVERSAL
Can't locate object method "foo" via package "Derived"
        at /u/home/chip/c5 line 7.
```

The first thing you'll notice is that package Base isn't mentioned at all. Perl doesn't realize that Derived is derived from Base. This points the finger at the variable that specifies derivation, namely, @Derived::ISA. And there's the bug.

Context (Loop) Stack Processing with -Dl

Perl uses two kinds of scoping. When -Dl is specified, Perl prints a record of the dynamic scopes. The stack of pending scopes is vital to the runtime behavior of Perl control structures like subroutines and loops.

Here's an example of -Dl output:

```
$ perl -Dl -le 'if (@ARGV) { print @ARGV }' Hello
EXECUTING...
Entering block 0, type BLOCK
Hello
Leaving block 0, type BLOCK
```

Every Perl program is surrounded by an implicit block, so what you see here appears in every -Dl output. Now that you know this, you might be surprised not to see *two* BLOCK messages, since the print statement is in an if block. However, Perl elided the second BLOCK as an optimization; it does this whenever the block's contents don't require runtime tracking for cleanup. To force a BLOCK scope, we need only put something in the block that would require cleanup—say, a my declaration:

```
$ perl -Dl -le 'if (@ARGV) { my @a = @ARGV; print @a }' Hello
EXECUTING...
Entering block 0, type BLOCK
```

```
Entering block 1, type BLOCK
Hello
Leaving block 1, type BLOCK
Leaving block 0, type BLOCK
```

The output of -Dl may include these scope types:

BLOCK

A code block, usually surrounded with { }, but not a naked block.

LOOP

A loop: whileuntil, for, foreach, or a naked block. Naked blocks are blocks of code surrounded by bare curly braces. Perl does not consider them to be BLOCKs, but LOOPs, because naked blocks are degenerate loops that by default execute exactly once. This fact allows you to use redo and last in a naked block to restart and exit it, respectively.

SUB

A subroutine call.

EVAL

Code executed via the eval operator, either eval BLOCK or eval STRING.

SUBST

The replacement expression in the substitution operator s///. If the replacement string is complex enough to require calculation at runtime—perhaps because it interpolates match variables like $1 or because it's a full expression invoked via s///e—Perl uses the special SUBST context to keep track of the replacement and clean up if it dies.

Tokenizing and Parsing with -Dp

As we discussed in Chapter 69, *tokenizing* is the process of taking the textual input of a Perl program and figuring out what it means—i.e., figuring out that print $a+$b is really print, $a, +, and $b, in that order.

The next step is *parsing*: figuring out the meaning of those tokens according to the language grammar. The code that does this job is called, unsurprisingly, the *parser*.

To avoid a lot of grunt work, Larry originally used a derivative of the yacc program to generate Perl's parser. All yacc-generated parsers include optional debugging code. That debugging code is compiled only if the YYDEBUG macro is defined, which happens automatically when Perl is compiled with -DDEBUGGING. And even then, it generates debugging output at runtime only if the variable yydebug has a nonzero value. That's one of the things that happens when you use -Dp.

When compiled and enabled, yacc debugging code prints each token returned by the tokenizer as well as any meaning that the parser gives it. Since Perl's tokenizer is so closely tied to the grammar, it also generates occasional -Dp debugging messages.

The advantage of -Dp is that it helps track down obscure syntax errors by showing what Perl saw, token by token. Some parsing errors are difficult to track down without it. The disadvantage of -Dp is that its output is quite voluminous. Be sure to redirect STDERR to a file when you use -Dp. Here's sample output, with interspersed commentary:

```
$ perl -Dp -le 'print $INC[0], "\n"'
yydebug: after reduction, shifting from state 0 to state 2
yydebug: state 2, reducing by rule 7 (lineseq :)
yydebug: after reduction, shifting from state 2 to state 3
```

In order to make sense of these first three lines of the output—particularly the state numbers—you need to run byacc (the yacc derivative used by Perl) with its -d option, which creates a file called *y.output*. Then you need to use that file's list of state numbers as a cross-reference. Assuming you don't go to that much trouble, the "shifting" messages will make no sense to you, so I'll omit them from the rest of this section.

For yacc-generated parsers, the term "reduce" roughly means "decide the meaning of what's been seen." From the bit of output quoted above, it's apparent that Perl's grammar has decided—without having seen anything yet—that the Perl program starts with a sequence of lines ("lineseq") and has decided that it's looking for zero or more such lines. This always happens. More debugging output:

```
### Tokener expecting STATE at
```

This message comes from the lexer. Perl's lexical analysis is heavily dependent on context, so the lexer has to be primed to know what to look for. This message tells us that detail. In this case, the lexer is looking for the beginning of a new statement.

```
yydebug: state 3, reading 286 (LSTOP)
```

Here the parser has read its first token from the lexer: the integer 286, which has the name LSTOP. A LSTOP is a LiST OPerator. This one happens to be the print in our sample code.

```
yydebug: state 3, reducing by rule 44 (label :)
```

This reduction is the parser's decision that there must not be a label on this statement. (A label is a WORD and a colon, and since print isn't a WORD, there isn't a label on this statement.)

```
### Tokener expecting REF at  $INC[0], "\n"
```

Expecting a REF is usual after a list operator; it's how the tokener grabs, say, the optional filehandle name after print or the optional sort subroutine name after sort.

```
yydebug: state 43, reading 36 ('$')
yydebug: state 62, reading 257 (WORD)
yydebug: state 87, reducing by rule 173 (indirob : WORD)
yydebug: state 136, reducing by rule 168 (scalar : '$' indirob)
### Tokener expecting OPERATOR at [0], "\n"
```

At this point, Perl has seen print $INC and figured out that it's a LSTOP followed by what looks like a scalar. However, there are still several possible interpretations, depending on what comes next. If the next token is a semicolon, then it's a print of the scalar variable $INC. If the next token is an operator—which as you can see is what the lexer is primed to find—then it's a print of whatever comes next to the file-handle named in $INC (e.g. print $INC @stuff). But as it happens, the next token is neither of those:

```
yydebug: state 111, reading 91 ('[')
### Tokener expecting TERM at 0], "\n"
```

Having found the left square bracket, Perl knows that it's looking for an array element expression, which implies that there is no explicit filehandle. Therefore, the lexer is expecting a TERM—that is, an array subscript expression.

```
yydebug: state 170, reading 260 (THING)
```

Yes, THING. To simplify its interface, Perl's lexer returns strings, numbers, and other miscellaneous values under the catch-all name THING. Each THING token carries with it an OP tree—a sequence of fundamental Perl operations. This particular THING carries an OP of type OP_CONST (constant value), attached to an SV (scalar value) of zero.

Well, there's more; lots of work goes into parsing even short Perl expressions. But what we've discussed so far should be enough to help you figure out what Perl thinks it's seeing when you and Perl disagree.

Other -D Debugging Flags

There are more debugging flags available via -D, but space and sanity prevent their full description. In brief, they are:

String/numeric conversions with -Dc
> This prints a diagnostic whenever a string is automatically converted to a number, or vice versa.

Cleaning up with -DD
> This reports cleanup of objects at program termination.
>
> When a Perl program terminates in an orderly fashion—no signals or core dumps—Perl does its best to find all objects that haven't yet been DESTROYed, and DESTROY them. This lets Perl programs use object destruction to trigger important cleanup.

Format processing with -Df
> This shows details of format field processing and pagination.
>
> If you use Perl formats, this flag may help you understand how Perl executes them. However, the diagnostics it generates are designed for debugging Perl, not for debugging users' Perl code, so it probably won't help much.

Taint checks with -Du

This prints a (minimal) diagnostic whenever a potentially dangerous operation finds its inputs *tainted* (untrustworthy). See the *perlsec* documentation for a discussion of tainting and its uses.

Show the -P *preprocessor command with* -DP

This shows the command line executed for the -P flag, which runs your program through the C preprocessor. You probably don't use -P, but if you do you'll understand why you might need this.

Hash internals with -DH

This reports on hash internals when the values operator is used. Unless you want to understand and/or debug Perl's implementation of hashes, you won't need this.

Scratchpad allocation with -DX

This flag shows the allocation and use of scratchpad slots. Unless you want to track down bugs in Perl's use of my variables and temporary values, you won't need this.

Memory allocation with -Dm

This reports on every low-level memory activity: allocation, resizing, and freeing. Perl does a *lot* of this. Expect a lot of output. You might find this flag useful if you think Perl (or a loaded extension) is committing memory allocation violations, but you'll need to write a program to digest the diagnostics, if only for their sheer volume.

Memory leaks with -DL

This identifies any memory allocated but not freed when Perl exits. It doesn't work with all versions of Perl, and there may be a few false positives in the report. However, large numbers of leaked memory blocks usually indicate a serious problem.

## CHAPTER 71

Microperl

Simon Cozens

Perl 5.7.0 shipped with an obscure and barely announced new feature—microperl. microperl is something I've worked on for quite a few months now and, while I expect it to be useful to only a tiny fraction of Perl users, I'd like to explain why it's included and what's so cool about it.

First, though, what is it? Well, when you compile a version of Perl, the first thing that gets built is a program called miniperl. miniperl is more or less just like ordinary perl, except that it doesn't have the Dynaloader XS module linked in. An XS module is a C extension module, allowing Perl to run C code, and it's usually written in a special glue language, XS, rather than in C.

What makes Dynaloader special is that it's the module that allows Perl to load other XS modules dynamically—without that, you can't use modules like IO::File, your DBM database library (DB_File, SDBM_File or equivalent), or any of the modules on CPAN with XS components.

miniperl, however, has just enough brains to run a program which translates the XS language in which Dynaloader is written into a C program; once we've done that, we can compile Dynaloader and link it into perl. In effect, we're building perl in stages: first without XS support, and then using that first effort to help build the next stage with XS support.

Bootstrapping

This process—starting small and using the result to build up to the next stage—is called "bootstrapping," since you've started from the ground and are pulling yourself up by your own bootstraps. In fact, it's exactly what happens when you turn up your computer and it "boots up;" the raw circuitry knows enough to activate the BIOS, and the BIOS knows enough to find and run the first block on the disk, which is a program which in turn knows enough to find the boot loader, which finds and runs the operating system.

The idea behind microperl is to take the bootstrapping nature of miniperl and perl to its logical conclusion. microperl is a very, very simple build of perl which will hopefully one day be used to build miniperl.

At the moment, before miniperl can be built, a program called Configure must be run. To make sure that perl builds properly on the plethora of different computers it supports, Configure performs hundreds of tests to work out the characteristics of the current system—which character set is being used, how large the various C datatypes are on the machine, what libraries are available, how to use the C compiler, and so on.

The problem with Configure is that you need to make a few assumptions about the system in order to run it. Configure is written in Bourne shell, so you need a copy of sh around. It also uses grep, awk, sed, and a bunch of other Unix utilities to probe the system. Of course, this will only work on something that smells like Unix. It would be a lot better if Configure was written in something portable (something like Perl, for instance). Of course, you'd need a Perl interpreter to be able to run it, and since the purpose of the exercise is to build a Perl interpreter, we've hit a chicken-and-egg problem.

This is where microperl comes in. The aim of microperl is to be a Perl interpreter that can be built on as many machines as possible, even small operating systems like WinCE and PalmOS, before any probing of the system occurs. Simply unpack your Perl distribution, compile it, and go. In fact, let's do that.

Building Microperl

Unpack Perl 5.7.0, and change to the directory perl5.7.0/. Now issue this command:

```
%make -f Makefile.micro
```

If all goes well, you should see something like this happen:

```
cc -c -o uav.o -DPERL_CORE -DPERL_MICRO av.c
cc -c -o udeb.o -DPERL_CORE -DPERL_MICRO deb.c
cc -c -o udoio.o -DPERL_CORE -DPERL_MICRO doio.c
cc -c -o udoop.o -DPERL_CORE -DPERL_MICRO doop.c
[... time passes ...]
cc -c -o uutil.o -DPERL_CORE -DPERL_MICRO util.c
cc -c -o uperlapi.o -DPERL_CORE -DPERL_MICRO perlapi.c
cc -o microperl uav.o udeb.o udoio.o udoop.o udump.o uglobals.o ugv.o
uhv.o umg.o uperlmain.o uop.o uperl.o uperlio.o uperly.o upp.o upp_ctl.o
upp_hot.o upp_sys.o uregcomp.o uregexec.o urun.o uscope.o usv.o utaint.o
utoke.o uuniversal.o uutf8.o uutil.o uperlapi.o -lm
```

You might see a few warnings, which are probably harmless. If you don't get past the first file, check that your C compiler is available and replace the line CC = cc in Makefile.micro with CC = /path/to/your/cc. If you use a separate linker, alter the line LD = $(CC) to LD = ld, for example. Eventually, you should end up with an executable file called microperl. (If you get stuck between the first file and the big statement at the end, then you probably have a bug.)

microperl is a real, honest-to-goodness Perl interpreter; no core elements of the Perl language have been removed. The regular expression engine is exactly the same, the language is exactly the same, it has the same Unicode support, and so on. The only things that have been removed from it are functions that are completely system specific, like crypt and readdir.

```
% ./microperl -le 'print q/Hello world/'
Hello world
% ./microperl t/base/cond.t
1..4
ok 1
ok 2
ok 3
ok 4
```

How Microperl Works

The idea for microperl came from Ilya Zakharevich, who produced a package called crazyperl along the same lines. What I've done, together with a lot of help from Jarkko Hietaniemi, is to make it easy to build, extend the number of systems it can work on, and keep up it to date with the changes as Perl develops.

To understand how it works, however, we've got to go back to looking at how perl is built. Once Configure has tested the system and found everything it needs to know, it writes out its results to a shell file, *config.sh*. This file is then rearranged into a C header file, *config.h*, and the rest of the Perl source files use the values from that as they are compiled.

You can examine the *config.sh* file that was used to build your version of Perl through the Config module:

```
#!/usr/bin/perl
use warnings;
use strict;
use Config qw(config_sh);
print config_sh();
```

This should print out something like the following:

```
archlibexp='/usr/local/lib/perl5/5.7.0/cygwin'
archname='cygwin'
cc='gcc'
ccflags='-fno-strict-aliasing -I/usr/local/include'
cppflags='-fno-strict-aliasing -I/usr/local/include'
...
```

This result tells us that this Perl will store its machine-specific modules in the directory /usr/local/lib/perl5/5.7.0/cygwin, that the architecture we're running on is cygwin, and the flags passed to the C compiler and C preprocessor respectively; you can find documentation on what the rest of the options mean with perldoc Config. You can use this to determine characteristics about the current Perl build:

```
#!/usr/bin/perl
use warnings;
use strict;
use Config;
...
if ($Config{use5005threads}) {
    # OK, we have threads:
    require Threads; import Threads;
    threading_child();
} else {
    # Make do with fork:
    forking_child();
}
```

microperl provides a *config.sh* which specifies the lowest common denominator: almost all optional items are turned off, all tests are set to have failed, and so on. We then build a version of Perl with this minimal configuration—since Perl is able to cope with pretty much every combination that can be thrown at it, it does its best to work around everything that we claim is lacking.

Practical Uses for Microperl

What's the point? Is microperl anything more than a cool hack?

Well, it certainly is a cool hack, and I quite like it just for that, but here are three real, practical uses for microperl.

Hacking

When you're working on the Perl core, you'll naturally end up doing a load of tweaking, testing ideas, and so on. This means a lot of recompiling, and recompiling a full perl—or even just miniperl—takes a lot of time. microperl builds fast. Furthermore, it's simple and uncluttered, and therefore useful for debugging and making patches; the microperl kit, if placed in a separate directory, would be a core of 71 files (29 C program files) rather than the 1,700-or-so files in a full Perl distribution.

It's also great for checking out a fresh Perl distribution without having to take the time to plod through Configure; Configure is pretty slow, taking between 10 and 20 minutes on my old machine.

On top of this, because microperl assumes the absolute minimum permissible, it can help root out edge cases in the configure process—if a function is used on the assumption that everyone has it, for instance. microperl has already found a few assumptions in the Perl source, and will hopefully guard against any more.

Porting

Because microperl is a lowest common denominator, it's very, very easy to port to new systems: you don't need to know anything about the characteristics of the system you're compiling on. Replace CC in Makefile.micro with a cross-compiler, and you can instantly port a version of Perl to another operating system.

(In fact, this is what I'm doing to put Perl onto the Palm Pilot port of Linux, but there are a few wrinkles left to be smoothed.)

Further, since you can build `microperl` with nothing other than a C compiler and make, it's useful for porting to systems that don't have `sh`, `awk`, `grep`, and all the other things `Configure` demands. Once you have experience of how *config.sh* works, you can build up a version of Perl by steadily adding features to `microperl`.

Bootstrapping

As mentioned before, we can theoretically use `microperl` to bootstrap a Perl build; the "steadily adding features" part mentioned above can be automated and run by the machine itself. Ideally, you'd unpack your Perl kit, type make, and a `microperl` would be built, which would run a Perl version of `Configure` and then build a full `perl`.

Now, when someone says "theoretically," they usually mean "not really," but let's have a look at a simple proof of concept. One of the tests we need to do is to examine the size of C integer storage:

```
$ ./microperl.exe fixbytes.pl
Checking to see how big your integers are...
ints are 4, longs are 4, shorts are 2
Fixing uconfig.sh
Reprocessing uconfig.sh
Extracting uconfig.h (with variable substitutions)
Making myself!
cc -c -o uav.o -DPERL_CORE -DPERL_MICRO av.c
...
cc -o microperl uav.o udeb.o udoio.o udoop.o udump.o uglobals.o ugv.o
uhv.o umg.o uperlmain.o uop.o uperl.o uperlio.o uperly.o upp.o upp_ctl.o
upp_hot.o upp_sys.o uregcomp.o uregexec.o urun.o uscope.o usv.o utaint.o
utoke.o uuniversal.o uutf8.o uutil.o uperlapi.o -lm
I'm still here.
```

Now we've built a new version of `microperl` using the information we've discovered. Here's the code that did that:

```
require "bootstrap.pl";
print "Checking to see how big your integers are...\n";
open (OUT, ">intsize.c") or die $!;
print OUT <<'EOF';
#include <stdio.h>
int main()
{
    printf("$intsize=%d;\n",   (int)sizeof(int)  );
    printf("$longsize=%d;\n",  (int)sizeof(long) );
    printf("$shortsize=%d;\n", (int)sizeof(short));
    exit(0);
}
EOF
close OUT;
system("cc -o intsize intsize.c");
if (!-x "./intsize") { die "Didn't compile" }
$sizes = `./intsize`;
```

```
unlink "intsize", "intsize.c";
eval $sizes;
print "ints are $intsize, longs are $longsize, shorts are $shortsize\n";
changeit ( intsize   => $intsize,
           longsize  => $longsize,
           shortsize => $shortsize
);
rebuild( );
```

Of course, it'll take a lot of work before we can bootstrap Perl to the same degree as an ordinary Configure run. But I'll get there!

Problems

The major problem I've had developing microperl is that the definitions that *config.sh* needs to provide to *config.h* constantly change, and so I've had to add new entries to microperl's *config.sh*.

To avoid doing this manually, I wrote a little Perl program that checks for undefined symbols during the make process and attempts to divine what they should be for microperl, adds in the relevant entries to *config.sh* and tries again. It's a crude future-proofing, but it saves me a lot of work.

Apart from that, it's been a question of rearranging things in the Perl core to make them more friendly to completely impotent configurations like microperl's: signal handling, for instance, had to be excised, and file modes such as O_CREAT generated for systems without the relevant system header files.

Future Work

Where do I see microperl going? Hopefully, it'll one day be more than just a toy for me. It's certainly useful for anyone working on the Perl core to quickly check out their changes or Perl's operation; it's good for people learning the internals of Perl because it strips away everything but the essentials. I'd like to see it building itself and even making an attack on the current Configure system.

But no matter what happens to it, it's still a neat hack.

Index

Symbols

(?!) negative lookahead operator, 40
<–> comparator, 42
+ in regular expressions, 100
+? in regular expressions, 100
.* in regular expressions
    .* comparison, 107
    .*? comparison, 107
    .*? in regular expressions, 105
->, methods and, 57
!~ operator, 38
=~ operator, 38
(?:...)?, regular expression matches and, 111
$&, regular expressions and, 105
/".*"/ regular expression, 93, 95
/\b/, whitespace and, 116
/\G/ regular expression, 119
/.*/ in regular expressions, 92
    greed and, 112
    regex paths, 95

Numbers

2-3 trees, 228

A

accessors, 58, 349
AceBrowser, ACEDB objects, 645
ACEDB database, Genome Project, 637
    accessing, 642
    display registering, 652
    web accessibility, 645

activate method,
    Spreadsheet::WriteExcel, 658
addition, precedence and, 25
address labels, 2
aggregation directives, SQL commands, 609
Akin, Thomas (DBI Caveats), 595–600
Alak, game tree, 209–220
algorithms
    minimax, trees and, 209
    streams and, 140
aliases
    glob and, 297
    local, 297
    option words, 306
ALSA (Advanced Linux Sound
    Architecture), 519
alternation, regex, 100
ambiguous codes, compression, 153
    Huffman coding and, 154
angle brackets, context and, 72
anonymous arrays, 79
ANSI C generator, random numbers, 262
Apache::MP3, playlists, generating, 510–516
applications, truth and, 52
arbitrary data structures, databases, 581
arcs, trees, 201
argument passing, Parse::RecDescent, 194
arguments, caching and, 163
arrays
    anonymous, 79
    attribute collisions, 351
    foreach loops, 11

We'd like to hear your suggestions for improving our indexes. Send email to *index@oreilly.com*.

wrappers, 404
  C functions, 405
write method, Spreadsheet::WriteExcel, 658
writing source filters, 331–334

X

XS, 264
  datatypes and, 265
  Inline and, 401
  Makefile.PL and, 268
  Math::TT800 and, 269
  modules, miniperl and, 705
  overview, 264
  SWIG utility, 264

xsubpp program, 264
XSUBs, 264

Y

yacc, 681
  lexical analysis and, 686
yacc program, parsing and, 181
Yahoo! links example of regexes, 115
yylex, 686

Z

Zakharevich, Ilya, microperl and, 707
zombie processes, 500
zone files, 571

About the Authors

Thomas Akin (Chapter 60, *DBI Caveats*) is a Certified Information Systems Security Professional (CISSP) who has worked in Information Security for almost a decade, and Perl has been the best tool in his security toolkit the entire time. He is director of the Southeast Cybercrime Institute and an active member of the Georgia Cybercrime Task Force. Thomas also works with Atlanta's ISSA, InfraGard, and HTCIA professional organizations. He spends his spare time teaching, writing, and using Perl for fun things like intrusion analysis and penetration testing. Thomas can be reached at *takin@crossrealm.com*.

Greg Bacon (Chapter 35, *Building Objects Out of Arrays*) develops software tools for Marshall Space Flight Center's verification and validation effort on the Space Shuttle Main Engine Controller software at the Rocketdyne Propulsion and Power Division of The Boeing Company. He enjoys playing with his young son Cal, hunting, fishing, scuba diving, playing ultimate, and tinkering in graph theory. He can be reached at *gbacon@cs.uah.edu*.

Graham Barr (Chapter 54, *Using Usenet from Perl*, Chapter 55, *Transferring Files with FTP*) is a senior programmer for ValueClick. He is the author of many modules on CPAN, the most popular probably being Net::FTP and Net::LDAP. He was also the pumpking for perl5.005_03. He lives in Guildford, England and can be reached at *gbarr@pobox.com*.

Hildo Biersma (Chapter 34, *Overloading*) works for a New York financial firm and is the maintainer of the MQSeries Perl module on CPAN. He is also co-moderator of the comp.lang.perl.moderated newsgroup. He lives in New York and can be reached at *hpp@guest.lunatech.com*.

Bill Birthisel (Chapter 53, *Controlling Modems*) is self employed, and developed the Win32::SerialPort and Device::SerialPort modules for talking to serial ports. He is a co-author of the ControlX10::CM11 and ControlX10::CM17 modules, which use serial ports to talk to home automation devices, and the MARC and MARC::XML modules for library automation. He has also done projects in e-commerce, machine control, and code maintenance and testing. He splits time between Clinton, Wisconsin and Portland, Maine. He is a father—and sometimes gets a chance to sing. He can be reached at *wcbirthisel@alum.mit.edu*.

Scott Bolte (Chapter 39, *SWIG*) worked for GE Medical Systems in Milwaukee as a Lead Software Architect for the Unix Foundation Group. He can be reached at *bolte@niss.com*.

Terrence Brannon (Chapter 61, *Beyond Hardcoded Database Applications with DBIx: :Recordset*) is a wandering mongering Perl consultant in search of complex assignments. His CPAN modules SQL::Catalog and SQL::Secretary form the basis for a robust approach to developing portable, succinct database application layers. His hobbies are chess, gardening, and meditation. He can be reached at *tbone@cpan.org*.

Tim Bunce (Chapter 58, *DBI*) has been an active perl5-porter since 1994, contributing to the development of the Perl language and many of its core modules such as DynaLoader, MakeMaker, and Exporter. He is also the author and maintainer of the DBI, DBD::Oracle, and Oraperl modules, and author and co-maintainer of the Perl Module List. He is currently responsible for building and releasing maintenance versions of Perl 5.004. Tim was recently recognized by British Telecom for his role in the launch of their Call Management Information service, a system implemented in Perl. He is co-author, along with Alligator Descartes, of *Programming the Perl DBI*, published by O'Reilly & Associates in February 2000.

Sean M. Burke (Chapter 8, *Using Object-Oriented Modules*, Chapter 22, *Trees and Game Trees*) is a columnist for *The Perl Journal*, a language technologist for Native American language preservation projects, and an all-around freelance roustabout and jackanapes. He is also the author of O'Reilly's *Perl and LWP*. His professional interests include markup languages and computational linguistics. He is one of the most prolific CPAN authors; among his best-known modules are MIDI-Perl, for composing and processing MIDI music files; the current generation of HTML::TreeBuilder, for building parse trees of HTML documents; and Class::Classless, a framework for classless OOP. He lives in Albuquerque, New Mexico; and in his spare time, he sleeps, reads the *Guardian*, and obeys his feline overlord, Fang Dynasty. He can be reached at *sburke@cpan.org*.

Joe Casadonte (Chapter 62, *Win32::ODBC*) is an Engineering Manager for Manugistics, Inc. In his spare time, he advocates the use of Perl to anyone who will listen, especially on Win32 systems, which he dislikes intensely but is forced to use. He also delights in writing Perl scripts to do the most trivial tasks.

Nigel Chapman (Chapter 36, *Hiding Objects with Closures*) is a well-known author of books on new media technologies and programming languages, whose books include *Perl: The Programmer's Companion* and (with Jenny Chapman) *Digital Multimedia*. He lectured in computer science at University College London until he left to become a freelance writer, researcher, consultant, and occasional visiting lecturer on web animation technologies at the Edinburgh College of Art. He lives in a remote part of the Western Highlands of Scotland, and in his spare time he stands in the sea. He can be reached at *nigel@macavon.demon.co.uk*.

Damian Conway (Chapter 21, *Parsing*, Chapter 37, *Multiple Dispatch in Perl*) is a Senior Research Fellow at Monash University, Melbourne, Australia. He works full time for the international Perl community and is supported by donations from individuals and corporations around the world, through the Perl Foundation (*www.perl-foundation.org*). He is a member of the core team designing Perl 6 and is the author of over two dozen CPAN modules, as well as the book *Object Oriented Perl* (Manning, 2000). When not designing, coding, or writing, he travels the world, speaking and teaching on a wide range of topics related to Perl. He lives in rural Australia with his beautiful wife, and in his spare time enjoys reading, cycling, and lifting weights.

Simon Cozens (Chapter 71, *Microperl*) is an open source programmer and author; he is a columnist for *The Perl Journal*, the author of *Beginning Perl* by Wrox Press, and co-author of *Using Perl and C*. He is the release manager for Perl 6, and the author of a wide range of Perl modules.

Alligator Descartes (Chapter 58, *DBI*) has been an itinerant fiddler with computers from a very early age, which was ruined only by obtaining a BSc in computer science from the University of Strathclyde, Glasgow. His computing credits include several years of Oracle DBA work, multi-user Virtual Reality servers, high-performance 3D graphics programming, and several Perl modules. He spends his spare time trudging around Scotland looking for stone circles and Pictish symbol stones to photograph. Alligator Descartes is not his real name.

Richard Dice (Chapter 24, *Making Life and Death Decisions with Perl*) is a freelance sysadmin, Perl programmer, author, conference speaker, and corporate trainer. He has helped out with a few CPAN modules (most significantly, "Chart"), and has co-authored several books, including *Applied Perl*. He is also the author of Webmonkey's *Choosing the Right Database System* tutorial series. He lives in Toronto and in his spare time, he swims, runs, reads, and shoots pool. He can be reached at *rdice@pobox.com*.

Mark Jason Dominus (Chapter 4, *Precedence*, Chapter 11, *References*, Chapter 17, *How Regexes Work*, Chapter 18, *Infinite Lists*, Chapter 19, *Compression*, Chapter 20, *Memoization*, Chapter 23, *B-Trees*, Chapter 28, *Suffering from Buffering*, Chapter 29, *Scoping*, Chapter 30, *Seven Useful Uses of local*) is an itinerant freelance Perl trainer. He is the author of the Text::Template, Algorithm::Diff, Interpolation, and Memoize modules, and his work on the Rx regular expression debugger won the 2001 Larry Wall Award for Practical utility. He was for a time the managing editor of *www.perl.com*, is the author of the perlreftut manpage, and is a moderator of the comp.lang.perl. moderated newsgroup. His book, tentatively titled *Perl Advanced Techniques*

Handbook, will be published in 2003 by Morgan Kaufmann, unless he dies of it first. When he is not teaching Perl, he lives in Philadelphia with his wife and a large number of toy octopuses.

Jon Drukman (Chapter 12, *Perl Heresies*) is a system administrator and techno artist (*http:///www.cyborganic.com/bass-kittens/*). He lives in San Francisco with his wife and cat.

Frossie Economou (Chapter 6, *Comparators, Sorting, and Hashes*) manages software projects for the Joint Astronomy Centre. She co-authored a mission-critical application in Perl that has now grown to 100,000 lines of code (including pod!). She lives in Hawaii with the writer of File::Temp, two house rabbits, and way too many books. Her address is *frossie@jach.hawaii.edu*.

brian d foy (Chapter 40, *Benchmarking*) is the president of the Perl Mongers.

Jeffrey Friedl (Chapter 13, *Understanding Regular Expressions, Part I*, Chapter 14, *Understanding Regular Expressions, Part II*, Chapter 15, *Understanding Regular Expressions, Part III*, Chapter 16, *Nibbling Strings*) folds, spindles, and mutilates financial news and data for Yahoo! Finance (*http://finance.yahoo.com*). He is the author of O'Reilly's *Mastering Regular Expressions*, and as this book goes to press slaves over the second edition. In his free time he.... oops, no, he doesn't have free time. He lives in Silicon Valley, and can be reached at *jfriedl@yahoo.com*.

Brian Ingerson (Chapter 38, *Using Other Languages from Perl*) is the author of Inline.pm.

Joe Johnston (Chapter 63, *Net::LDAP*) is an independent contractor, co-author of O'Reilly's *Programming Web Services with XML-RPC*, and a contributor to IBM's developerWorks web site. For contact information, please see *http://taskboy.com*.

Gerard Lanois (Chapter 56, *Spidering an FTP Site*) is the author of ubh—the Usenet Binary Harvester, a Net::NNTP-based Perl application that automatically discovers, downloads, and decodes single-part and multi-part Usenet binaries. He is also the author of several other useful Perl applications, including a Perl implementation of metamail and a Net::POP3 mailbox filtering program called rifle. His main areas of interest are the libnet family of modules, libxml-perl, and the Template Toolkit. He can be reached at *gerard@lanois.com*.

Otmar Lendl (Chapter 27, *Random Number Generators and XS*) has left academia and is now responsible for the servers of KPNQwest Austria. Recent projects used Perl (and rrdtool) to build a network statistics portal and a netflow accounting system. He lives in Vienna, Austria, and in his spare time teaches mathematics and helps local civil liberties groups. He can be reached at *otmar@lendl.priv.at*.

Paul Marquess (Chapter 33, *Source Filters*) works in the telecommunications industry. He has been a perl5-porter on and off since the initial development of Perl5 and has developed a number of Perl modules including: DB_File, an interface to Berkeley

DB; Compress::Zlib, an interface to the zlib compression library. He lives in Belfast and can be reached at *pmqs@cpan.org*.

Craig McElwee (Chapter 59, *Using DBI with Microsoft Access*) designs and builds applications for a small financial firm in Philadelphia. He can be reached at cmcelwee@mindspring.com, or if you're passing by his neighborhood, he's the one playing hockey in the street with his children.

John McNamara (Chapter 65, *Spreadsheet::WriteExcel*) is a Software Engineer for Tecnomen Ltd. In his spare time he develops and supports Spreadsheet::WriteExcel, Inline::Awk and to a lesser extent Acme::Inline::PERL. He lives in Limerick, Ireland, the home of rain and rugby. He can be reached at *jmcnamara@cpan.org*.

Tim Meadowcroft (Chapter 49, *Microsoft Office*) is a software consultant based in London in the UK, designing and advising on innovative data visualisation and how to develop world class software as if people really mattered. In addition to his commercial products and services, he also produces free tools such as HttpSniffer.pl and ProfileStartup.pm—available from his web site at *www.schmerg.com*.

Jon Orwant (Chapter 26, *Randomness*) founded *The Perl Journal* and served all editorial and production roles through TPJ #13, and remained editor-in-chief until TPJ #20. He is a co-author of *Programming Perl* and *Mastering Algorithms with Perl*, was CTO of O'Reilly, and now creates AI-laced communication systems for French Telecom and teaches game design at MIT. He can be reached at *orwant@media.mit.edu*.

Ulrich Pfeifer (Chapter 25, *Information Retrieval*) was supposed to do research in IR in a former life. Instead he wrote a bunch of Perl modules—some related to the topic like WAIT, and some quite unrelated like Math::Mathematica. Now he has a serious day job and codes only in his spare time. He can be reached at *pfeifer@wait.de*.

Tom Phoenix (Chapter 9, *Unreal Numbers*) is frequently found in a city near you, working as a Perl instructor or consultant. When he's not teaching or traveling or hacking or posting to comp.lang.perl.misc or writing about himself in the third person, you may find him speaking Esperanto to his cat, Timmy, who resides in Portland, Oregon. At least one of them will be glad to get email from you, if you write to *rootbeer@redcat.com*.

Arthur Ramos, Jr. (Chapter 5, *The Birth of a One-Liner*) is a Senior Systems Analyst, Systems Administrator, and Adjunct Instructor at Orange County Community College (*http://www.sunyorange.edu*) in Middletown, New York. He is also the owner of Winning Web Design (*http://www.winningweb.com*). He lives in Middletown, New York, with his wife, Katie, and his daughters, Jessica and Allison. In his spare time, he wishes he had more spare time. He can be reached at *aramos@sunyorange.edu*.

Randy J. Ray (Chapter 42, *MakeMaker*, Chapter 43, *Autoloading Perl Code*, Chapter 44, *Debugging and Devel::*) is a Web Applications Engineer for Red Hat, Inc., and occasional writer on subjects such as Perl, XML, and Web Services. He is an active contributor to CPAN with modules such as Perl-RPM, RPC::XML, and Image::Size. He has also done work in, and written papers on, Software Configuration Management. His other software interests include applying software engineering ideas to Perl projects, and component-based programming. He lives outside of San Jose, CA, and spends his spare time on crafts and reading about military history. He can be reached at *rjray@blackperl.com*.

Jay Rogers (Chapter 48, *Net::Telnet*) works as a software consultant in the Boston area. He developed the Net::Telnet Perl module to make it easy to interact with a TCP server. He lives in Wayland, Massachusetts, and in his spare time enjoys reading and being a dad. He can be reached at *jay@rgrs.com*.

Chip Salzenberg (Chapter 67, *Components of the Perl Distribution*, Chapter 68, *Basic Perl Anatomy*, Chapter 69, *Lexical Analysis*, Chapter 70, *Debugging Perl Programs with -D*) was coordinator and primary programmer for Perl 5.004. His major solo project was Deliver, the free email local delivery agent that allows flexible, safe, and reliable message handling. His hobbies include patching Perl, tending to his six parrots, and memorizing Mystery Science Theater 3000 episodes.

Dan Schmidt (Chapter 32, *Building a Better Hash with tie*) has been using Perl for various tasks since 1991, back when Perl didn't have any of those fancy-schmancy features like objects, references, and ties. He can be reached at *dfan@dfan.org*.

Bob Sidebotham (Chapter 41, *Building Software with Cons*) is currently trying to figure out what to do with the rest of his life. In the meantime, he has developed yet another collaborative web site which he calls the "Community Notebook," soon to be available as the "conotebook" project on SourceForge. He developed this for use at the Windsong Cohousing community, *http://www.cohousing.ca/cohsng4/windsong/*, near Vancouver, BC, where he makes his home. Bob believes firmly in small business, and helped a small organic home delivery business get started by building a software system for them. He's now working on extending that concept to empower similar businesses. He can be reached by email at *bob_sidebotham@yahoo.com*.

Lincoln D. Stein (Chapter 50, *Client-Server Applications*, Chapter 51, *Managing Streaming Audio*, Chapter 52, *A 74-Line IP Telephone*) is a researcher at the Cold Spring Harbor Laboratory and is the author of *Writing Apache Modules with Perl and C* (O'Reilly), *Network Programming with Perl* and *How to Set Up and Maintain a Web Site* (Addison-Wesley), and *Official Guide to Programming with CGI.pm* (Wiley). He is the author of the Perl CGI module and the World Wide Web Security FAQ.

Dan Sugalski (Chapter 45, *Email with Attachments*, Chapter 46, *Sending Mail Without sendmail*) is the chair of the Perl 6 internals group, and tasked with herding whatever cats are necessary to make Perl 6 a reality. He's worked on, and written about, Perl 5's threading implementation, and worked on the VMS port of Perl.

Nathan Torkington (Chapter 2, *All About Arrays*, Chapter 3, *Perfect Programming*, Chapter 7, *What Is Truth?*, Chapter 10, *CryptoContext*, Chapter 66, *How to Improve Perl*) is a miserable husk of a man. Although most people don't know about his intellectual shortcomings and speech impediment, most have noticed the ravages caused by his desperate search for a miracle cure to his ongoing weight problem. With so many personal issues, it's no wonder the poor guy said "Author bio? Can't you write it, Jon?"

Johan Vromans (Chapter 31, *Parsing Command-Line Options*) has engaged in software engineering research since 1975. Convinced of the importance of a good programming environment, he became an expert in using GNU Emacs and the Perl programming language. He was also instrumental in bringing the Internet to the Netherlands as a commercial activity. He is the author of the *Perl 5 Pocket Reference* (O'Reilly), the Perl core module Getopt::Long, as well as several other modules available on CPAN. He owns the Squirrel Consultancy, providing Perl training and Open Source consultancy. He loves music and can be reached at *jvromans@squirrel.nl*.

Colophon

Our look is the result of reader comments, our own experimentation, and feedback from distribution channels. Distinctive covers complement our distinctive approach to technical topics, breathing personality and life into potentially dry subjects.

The animal on the cover of *Computer Science and Perl Programming: Best of the Perl Journal* is a camel (one-hump dromedary). Camels are large ruminant mammals, weighing between 1,000 and 1,600 pounds and standing six to seven feet tall at the shoulders. They are well known for their use as draft and saddle animals in the desert regions, especially of Africa and Asia. Camels can go for days without water. If food is scarce, they will eat anything, even their owner's tent. Camels live up to 50 years.

Colleen Gorman was the production editor and the copyeditor for *Computer Science and Perl Programming: Best of the Perl Journal*. Emily Quill and Jane Ellin provided quality control. Johnna VanHoose Dinse wrote the index.

Hanna Dyer and Ellie Volckhausen designed the cover of this book, based on a series design by Edie Freedman. The cover image is a 19th-century engraving from the Dover Pictorial Archive. Emma Colby produced the cover layout with QuarkXPress 4.1 using Adobe's ITC Garamond font.

David Futato designed the interior layout. Erik Ray, Mike Sierra, and Neil Walls converted the files from pod to FrameMaker 5.5.6. The text font is Linotype Birka; the heading font is Adobe Myriad Condensed; and the code font is LucasFont's TheSans Mono Condensed. The illustrations that appear in the book were produced by Robert Romano and Jessamyn Read using Macromedia FreeHand 9 and Adobe Photoshop 6. The tip and warning icons were drawn by Christopher Bing. This colophon was written by Colleen Gorman.

Other Titles Available from O'Reilly

Perl

Learning Perl, 3rd Edition

By Randal Schwartz & Tom Phoenix
3rd Edition July 2001
330 pages, ISBN 0-596-00132-0

Learning Perl is the quintessential tutorial for the Perl programming language. The third edition has not only been updated to Perl Version 5.6, but has also been rewritten from the ground up to reflect the needs of programmers learning Perl today. Other books may teach you to program in Perl, but this book will turn you into a Perl programmer.

Mastering Regular Expressions, 2nd Edition

By Jeffrey E. F. Friedl
2nd Edition July 2002 (est.)
456 pages (est.), ISBN 0-596-00289-0

Written by an expert in the topic, this book shows programmers not only how to use regular expressions, but how to think in regular expressions. Updated with a wealth of new material, the second edition explains how to use regular expressions to code complex and subtle text processing that you never imagined could be automated. Included are such key topics as avoiding common errors and optimizing expressions. The book covers many new features added to Perl—a language well endowed with regular expressions—as well as other languages such as Java, Python, and Visual Basic that include support for this powerful tool.

Embedded Perl in HTML with Mason

By Dave Rolsky & Ken Williams
1st Edition October 2002
304 pages, ISBN 0-596-00225-4

Mason, a Perl-based templating system, is becoming more and more popular as a tool for building websites and managing other dynamic collections. While using Mason is not difficult, creating Mason-based sites can be tricky, and this concise book helps you navigate around the obstacles. The book covers the most recent release of Mason, 1.10, which has many new features including line number reporting based on source files, sub-requests, and simplified use as a CGII. It also explores using Mason for dynamic generation of XML documents.

Perl & XML

By Erik T. Ray & Jason McIntosh
1st Edition April 2002
224 pages, ISBN 0-596-00205-X

Perl & XML is aimed at Perl programmers who need to work with XML documents and data. This book gives a complete, comprehensive tour of the landscape of Perl and XML, making sense of the myriad of modules, terminology, and techniques. The last two chapters of Perl and XML give complete examples of XML applications, pulling together all the tools at your disposal.

Mastering Perl/Tk

By Steve Lidie & Nancy Walsh
1st Edition January 2002
768 pages, ISBN 1-56592-716-8

Beginners and seasoned Perl/Tk programmers alike will find *Mastering Perl/Tk* to be the definitive book on creating graphical user interfaces with Perl/Tk. After a fast-moving tutorial, the book goes into detail on creating custom widgets, working with bindings and callbacks, IPC techniques, and examples using many of the non-standard add-on widgets for Perl/Tk (including Tix widgets). Every Perl/Tk programmer will need this book.

Perl Cookbook

By Tom Christiansen &
Nathan Torkington
1st Edition August 1998
794 pages, ISBN 1-56592-243-3

The *Perl Cookbook* is a comprehensive collection of problems, solutions, and practical examples for anyone programming in Perl. You'll find hundreds of rigorously reviewed Perl "recipes" for manipulating strings, numbers, dates, arrays, and hashes; pattern matching and text substitutions; references, data structures, objects, and classes; signals and exceptions; and much more.

O'REILLY®

To order: *800-998-9938* • *order@oreilly.com* • *www.oreilly.com*
Online editions of most O'Reilly titles are available by subscription at *safari.oreilly.com*
Also available at most retail and online bookstores.

Perl

Perl & LWP

By Sean M. Burke
1st Edition, June 2002
464 pages, 0-596-00178-9

This comprehensive guide to LWP and its applications comes with many practical examples. Topics include programmatically fetching web pages, submitting forms, using various techniques for HTML parsing, handling cookies, and authentication. With the knowledge in Perl & LWP, you can automate any task on the Web, from checking the prices of items at online stores to bidding at auctions automatically.

Mastering Algorithms with Perl

By Jon Orwant, Jarkko Hietaniemi &
John Macdonald
1st Edition August 1999
704 pages, ISBN 1-56592-398-7

There have been dozens of books on programming algorithms, but never before has there been one that uses Perl. Whether you are an amateur programmer or know a wide range of algorithms in other languages, this book will teach you how to carry out traditional programming tasks in a high-powered, efficient, easy-to-maintain manner with Perl. Topics range in complexity from sorting and searching to statistical algorithms, numerical analysis, and encryption.

Practical mod_perl

By Stas Bekman & Eric Cholet
1st Edition December 2002 (est.)
700 pages (est.), ISBN 0-596-00227-0

This is the only book that gives detailed instructions on how to use, optimize, and troubleshoot mod_perl. An excellent place for new mod_perl users to start, Practical mod_perl shows how to get this Apache module running quickly and easily. However, the bulk of this insightful volume shows how to take full advantage of the power of mod_perl through discussions on the Perl programming language, Apache's Perl API, and scripts that run under Apache::Registry. The authors provide tips and advice from their experience, as well as those from the mod_perl community at large.

Perl Graphics Programming

By Shawn Wallace
1st Edition, December 2002 (est.)
504 pages (est.), 0-596-00219-X

This insightful volume focuses on scripting programs that enable programmers to manipulate graphics for the Web. The book also helps demystify the manipulation of graphics formats for web newcomers with a practical, resource-like approach. While most of the examples use Perl as a scripting language, the concepts are applicable to any programming language. The book documents ways to use several powerful Perl modules for generating graphics, including GD, PerlMagick, and GIMP.

Programming Web Services with Perl

By Randy J. Ray & Scott Guelich
1st Edition December 2002 (est.)
280 pages (est.), ISBN 0-596-00206-8

O'Reilly presents another Perl first: Programming Web Services with Perl. Like most O'Reilly books, it cuts through the hype on web services and concentrates on the useful and practical. It shows how to use Perl to create web services, introducing the major web service standards (XML-RPC, SOAP, WSDL, UDDI) and how to implement Perl servers and clients using these standards. Moving beyond the basics, the book offers solutions to the problems of security, authentication, and scalability.

Programming the Perl DBI

By Alligator Descartes & Tim Bunce
1st Edition February 2000
362 pages, ISBN 1-56592-699-4

The primary interface for database programming in Perl is DBI. Programming the Perl DBI is coauthored by Alligator Descartes, one of the most active members of the DBI community, and by Tim Bunce, the inventor of DBI. The book explains the architecture of DBI, shows you how to write DBI-based programs and explains both DBI's nuances and the peculiarities of each individual DBD. This is the definitive book for database programming in Perl.

O'REILLY®

To order: 800-998-9938 • order@oreilly.com • www.oreilly.com
Online editions of most O'Reilly titles are available by subscription at safari.oreilly.com
Also available at most retail and online bookstores.

Perl

Programming Perl, 3rd Edition

*Larry Wall, Tom Christiansen &
Jon Orwant*
3rd Edition July 2000
1104 pages, Features ISBN 0-596-00027-8

Programming Perl is not just a book
about Perl; it is also a unique introduction to the language and its culture,
as one might expect only from its authors. This third
edition has been expanded to cover Version 5.6 of Perl.
New topics include threading, the compiler, Unicode,
and other features that have been added or improved
since the previous edition.

The Perl CD Bookshelf, Version 3.0

By O'Reilly & Associates, Inc.
Version 3.0 September 2002 (est.)
768 pages, Features CD-ROM
ISBN 0-596-00164-9

Version 3.0 of O'Reilly's *The Perl CD
Bookshelf* gives programmers convenient online access to their favorite
Perl books, all from their CD-ROM
drive. We've updated this best-selling product with electronic versions of 7 popular books. Included are the second edition of *Perl in a Nutshell*, the third editions of
Learning Perl and *Programming Perl*, the *Perl Cookbook*,
and 3 new titles: *Perl & XML*, *Perl & LWP*, and *Mastering Perl/Tk*. A paperback version of *Perl in a Nutshell*
rounds out this incredible package.

Perl Pocket Reference, 4th Edition

By Johan Vromans
4th Edition July 2002
96 pages, ISBN 0-596-00374-9

The fourth edition of our popular *Perl
Pocket Reference* now covers the latest
release—Perl 5.8—with a summary of
Perl syntax rules, a complete list of
operators, built-in functions, and standard library modules. All with brief,
easy-to-find descriptions. You'll find the newest Perl features, such as enhanced regular expressions, multithreading, the Perl compiler, and Unicode support. *Perl Pocket
Reference* provides a complete overview of Perl, packed
into a convenient pocket-sized guide that's easy to take
anywhere.

CGI Programming with Perl, 2nd Edition

By Shishir Gundavaram
2nd Edition July 2000
470 pages, ISBN 1-56592-419-3

Completely rewritten, this comprehensive explanation of CGI for those who
want to provide their own Web servers
features Perl 5 techniques and shows
how to use two popular Perl modules, CGI.pm and
CGI_lite. It also covers speed-up techniques, such as
FastCGI and mod_perl, and new material on searching
and indexing, security, generating graphics through
ImageMagick, database access through DBI, Apache configuration, and combining CGI with JavaScript.

Advanced Perl Programming

By Sriram Srinivasan
1st Edition August 1997
434 pages, ISBN 1-56592-220-4

This book covers complex techniques
for managing production-ready Perl
programs and explains methods for
manipulating data and objects that
may have looked like magic before. It gives you necessary
background for dealing with networks, databases, and
GUIs, and includes a discussion of internals to help you
program more efficiently and embed Perl within C or C
within Perl.

Perl

Perl for System Administration

By David N. Blank-Edelman
1st Edition July 2000
444 pages, ISBN 1-56592-609-9

Perl for System Administration is aimed at all levels of administrators on the Unix, Windows NT, or Mac OS platforms. Assuming only a little familiarity with Perl, it explores the pockets of administration where Perl can be most useful, including filesystem management, user administration, directory services, database administration, log files, and security and network monitoring. *Perl for System Administration* is for anyone who needs to use Perl for administrative tasks and needs to hit the ground running.

Perl in a Nutshell, 2nd Edition

By Ellen Siever, Stephen Spainhour &
Nate Patwardhan
2nd Edition May 2002
768 pages, ISBN 0-59600-241-6

This complete guide to Perl includes the basics of the programming language itself, plus CGI programming, XML processing, network programming, database interaction, and graphical user interfaces. The expanded second edition features the latest version of Perl, and covers modules for recent technologies such as XML and SOAP. This book is for experienced and beginning programmers alike who want a single reference for all their needs.

O'REILLY®

To order: *800-998-9938* • *order@oreilly.com* • *www.oreilly.com*
Online editions of most O'Reilly titles are available by subscription at *safari.oreilly.com*
Also available at most retail and online bookstores.

How to stay in touch with O'Reilly

1. Visit our award-winning web site

http://www.oreilly.com/

★ "Top 100 Sites on the Web"—PC Magazine
★ CIO Magazine's Web Business 50 Awards

Our web site contains a library of comprehensive product information (including book excerpts and tables of contents), downloadable software, background articles, interviews with technology leaders, links to relevant sites, book cover art, and more. File us in your bookmarks or favorites!

2. Join our email mailing lists

Sign up to get email announcements of new books and conferences, special offers, and O'Reilly Network technology newsletters at:

http://www.elists.oreilly.com

It's easy to customize your free elists subscription so you'll get exactly the O'Reilly news you want.

3. Get examples from our books

To find example files for a book, go to:

http://www.oreilly.com/catalog

select the book, and follow the "Examples" link.

4. Work with us

Check out our web site for current employment opportunities:

http://jobs.oreilly.com/

5. Register your book

Register your book at:

http://register.oreilly.com

6. Contact us

O'Reilly & Associates, Inc.
1005 Gravenstein Hwy North
Sebastopol, CA 95472 USA
TEL: 707-827-7000 or 800-998-9938
      (6am to 5pm PST)
FAX: 707-829-0104

order@oreilly.com
For answers to problems regarding your order or our products. To place a book order online visit:

http://www.oreilly.com/order_new/

catalog@oreilly.com
To request a copy of our latest catalog.

booktech@oreilly.com
For book content technical questions or corrections.

corporate@oreilly.com
For educational, library, and corporate sales.

proposals@oreilly.com
To submit new book proposals to our editors and product managers.

international@oreilly.com
For information about our international distributors or translation queries. For a list of our distributors outside of North America check out:

http://international.oreilly.com/distributors.html

O'REILLY®

To order: *800-998-9938* • *order@oreilly.com* • *www.oreilly.com*
Online editions of most O'Reilly titles are available by subscription at *safari.oreilly.com*
Also available at most retail and online bookstores.